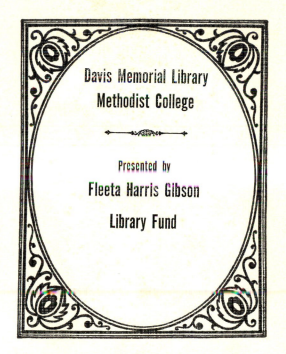

BRITISH
LITERARY
MAGAZINES

HISTORICAL GUIDES TO THE WORLD'S PERIODICALS AND NEWSPAPERS

This series provides historically focused narrative and analytical profiles of periodicals and newspapers with accompanying bibliographical data.

Black Journals of the United States
Walter C. Daniel

Mystery, Detective, and Espionage Magazines
Michael L. Cook

American Indian and Alaska Native Newspapers and Periodicals
Daniel F. Littlefield, Jr., and James W. Parins

British Literary Magazines: The Augustan Age and the Age of Johnson, 1698–1788
Alvin Sullivan, Editor

BRITISH LITERARY MAGAZINES

The Romantic Age, 1789–1836

Edited by
Alvin Sullivan

Historical Guides to the World's Periodicals and Newspapers

Greenwood Press
Westport, Connecticut · London, England

Library of Congress Cataloging in Publication Data

Main entry under title:

British literary magazines.

(Historical guides to the world's periodicals and
newspapers)
    Includes bibliographies and indexes.
    Contents: [1] The Augustan age and the age of John-
son, 1698–1788—[2] The romantic age, 1789–1836.
    1. English periodicals—History. 2. Literature—
Periodicals—History. 3. English literature—Periodicals
—History. I. Sullivan, Alvin. II. Series.
PN5124.L6B74   1983   820'.8   82-21136
ISBN 0-313-22871-X (v. 1 : lib. bdg.)
ISBN 0-313-22872-8 (v. 2 : lib. bdg.)

Library of Congress Catalog Card Number: 82-21136
ISBN: 0-313-22872-8

First published in 1983

Greenwood Press
A division of Congressional Information Service, Inc.
88 Post Road West
Westport, Connecticut 06881

Printed in the United States of America

10 9 8 7 6 5 4 3 2 1

Contents

Preface

British Literary Magazines: The Romantic Age, 1789–1836, continues the four-part reference guide begun with *British Literary Magazines: The Augustan Age and the Age of Johnson, 1698–1788.* Additional volumes will cover the Victorian and Edwardian Age (1837–1913) and the Modern Age (1914–   ). Each of the first three parts profiles eighty to ninety titles, and appendixes in the works covering the Augustan Age and the Age of Johnson and the Victorian and Edwardian Age treat another eighty-three and one hundred and ninety-seven titles, respectively.

Of the four periods, the Romantic Age is the shortest and in many ways the most "self-contained." Of the eighty-four titles treated in this part, only a quarter of them, or twenty-one, survived beyond 1836. Of these twenty-one, eight began late in the period (1830 or after), and one might argue that they belong more properly to the Victorian period: the *British and Foreign Review* (1835), *Chambers's Edinburgh Journal* (1832), the *Dublin Review* (1836), the *Dublin University Magazine* (1833), *Fraser's Magazine* (1830), *Leigh Hunt's London Journal* (1834), the *Metropolitan Magazine* (1831), and *Tait's Edinburgh Magazine* (1832). In order for this reference guide to be useful, however, conventional arbitrary dates had to be assigned and adhered to, and these eight magazines are, therefore, included in this part on the basis of the year in which they began publication. Six of the great periodicals might be classified as Romantic, Victorian, or Modern: the *Athenaeum, Blackwood's Edinburgh Magazine,* the *Edinburgh Review,* the *Quarterly Review,* the *Spectator,* and the *Westminster Review.* They also began in the Romantic period, and so appear in this part. (Two, *Blackwood's* and the *Quarterly Review,* are also discussed separately in *The Modern Age.*) At the other extreme, some of the magazines in this part belong in spirit if not in date to the age of the *Tatler* (1709) and the *Spectator* (1711), covered in the preceding part of this reference guide: the *Literary Speculum* (1821), the *Loiterer* (1789), and the *Cabinet, or Literary*

Olio (1807). They carry on the periodical essay tradition, while the *Gossip* (1821) looks back longingly on "those feelings which arise in humble, calm and rural life . . . the milder and gentler emotions of the soul."

Even the *Gossip,* though, became caught up in the new century it was stuck in; it printed a letter from Laurence Sterne in Elysium criticizing Keats's harsher critics. And most of the magazines belong more firmly to the Romantic Age: from the 1789 publication of Blake's *Songs of Innocence,* to the apogee year of 1798 when *Lyrical Ballads* appeared, to 1821, 1822, and 1824, the last years respectively of Keats, Shelley, and Byron. Indeed, thirty-eight of the titles began publication after 1798 and ended by or in 1825; they belong completely to the most revisionary years of the single most important movement in English literary history. Not all of the journals were organs of Romanticism. Some, like the *Literary Panorama,* never reviewed Shelley, Keats, or Coleridge; some found "genius" in Robert Bloomfield and George Colman instead of in Hazlitt and Wordsworth (the *Literary Speculum*). Others echoed the sentiments of the *Prospective Review* in its review of *The Prelude:* "A poet could surely tell the story of his mental growth more clearly and effectively in prose." The *British Review and London Critical Journal* reflected the dilemma of readers accustomed to authorial intrusion and control; it wanted Byron to write a commentary condemning the sentiments of his character Harold.

Every artistic movement has some advocate in print, but the Romantic movement was embraced by more journals, reviews, and miscellanies than any other. The Romantics early became a rallying point for literary magazines' quarrels. The *Edinburgh Review* opposed the *Quarterly; Scourge* supported the *Edinburgh* in its conservative view of Romanticism, and excoriated the *Quarterly* and *Examiner.* John Scott (of the *London Magazine*) lost his life over a quarrel with *Blackwood's.* David Douglas wrote a satirical pamphlet in 1820, *Visions of Taste,* parodying the *London Chronicle and Weekly Review,* the *Literary Gazette,* and the *London Magazine* as three feuding cocks on a dunghill. (The *London Chronicle* couldn't decide: it published *Adonais* and then said the Romantics would be "entirely forgotten.") When John Wilson Croker took apart Keats's *Endymion* in the *Quarterly,* the poet's fortunes declined drastically. *Honeycomb* came to his defense and attributed the motives of the *Quarterly* to a need to "gratify a vitiated appetite for libel, and increase their monthly sales." (There may have been truth in *Honeycomb*'s accusation, for the circulation of another major review, the *Edinburgh,* was never larger than when Francis Jeffrey reviewed the Romantics.) Leigh Hunt started a journal, the *Examiner,* to counter John Scott's criticism in the *Champion.* And at least one small journal, the *Literary Guardian,* became famous in its time for publishing letters from Byron that explained his role in another Romantic journal by Hunt, the *Liberal.*

Even magazines that did not enter the fray became beneficiaries of the ideas and spirit that the Romantic movement fostered. *Fraser's Magazine* picked up on the German transcendentalist strain in Coleridge (and Carlyle), and that became an aesthetic underlying all its reviews. Small magazines caught the revisionary breeze. The *Album* looked back to the eighteenth century, but decided that it had to reject it. The Augustan masters must be replaced—it didn't matter whether by Elizabethans or Romantics—but by someone.

Causes have always been magazines' passions. When the Romantics did not fill the pages of the magazines, other issues of the day dominated. Many, especially the *London Magazine* and the *Annals of the Fine Arts*, advocated the purchase of the Elgin Marbles. Others—the *Literary Journal*, the *Imperial Magazine*, the *Examiner*, and *Dublin University Magazine*—argued long and hard over Catholic Emancipation. Leigh Hunt began his *Examiner* as a reflection of his public self (the *Inquirer* was one of his private self), attacked the King's behavior, and found himself in prison. The *Literary Panorama* was a panorama of issues rather than of literature: it had a combined social security and unemployment scheme as well as a society to improve the working conditions of chimney sweeps. And the *British and Foreign Review* strikes a startlingly familiar note when one reads its argument for the active containment of Russia and the restoration of Polish independence.

The Romantic Age fostered a number of innovations—the first international review (the *Foreign Quarterly Review*); the prototype of *Reader's Digest* (the *Mirror*); the widespread use of illustrations (notably Cruikshank's in *Scourge*); the practice of identifying reviewers (the *London Review*); the serialization of fiction (the *Metropolitan*); the tremendous growth of book reviews (typical is the *London Chronicle*); the great decline in satirical journals; and the anticipation of the popular cheap magazines (*Nic Nac*) and popular but literary ones (*Chambers's*) that would flower in the next age. As in the first part, the aim of *British Literary Magazines: The Romantic Age* is to reflect the variety of the age as it found expression in its literary magazines. We include, therefore, the important reviews, representative minor magazines, and the prodigious efforts of the Hunt brothers, John and Leigh, in the cause of the Romantic movement. In their discussions of magazines, some authors correct inaccurate impressions or provide new information. Helen B. Ellis notes that James Mill's commentary in the *Literary Journal* disproves his critics' contention that he conveniently ignored the Industrial Revolution and its attendant problems. John O. Hayden changes the impression that some hold of *La Belle Assemblée* as an intellectually shallow ladies' magazine. And Keith Wilson has located a unique editor's copy of the *Inquirer* that identifies contributors and provides evidence for membership of the Zetosophian Society. Other contributors, notably Douglas Morris in this book, have communicated with literary agents and others to correct or obtain information. These are the ancillary rewards for researchers of literary magazines and for the users of this volume of their research.

Each profile in this book concludes with sections in which data on Information Sources and Publication History are provided in tabular form. The section on Information Sources gives bibliographic information, index sources, reprint sources, and location sources. The section on Publication History lists title changes and alternative titles, volume and issue data, publisher and place of publication, and editors.

The Information Sources have been supplied by the authors of essays and verified in the *National Union Catalog* and the *British Museum Catalogue of Printed Books* (vols. 184–86), the catalogues of microform reprints by University Microfilms International, Ward's *Finding List of Serials*, the *Wellesley Index to Victorian Periodicals*, Poole's *Index to Periodical Literature*, the *British Union Catalogue of Periodicals*, and the *Union List of Serials*. The last three are frequently unreliable, and where additional information (from Ward's *Finding List* or authors' sources) is given, we have relied on that. If, for example, authors advise that only a partial run may be found at "Xy" though the *ULS* lists a complete run there, we have indicated a partial run. In most cases, however, for locations we have had to rely on the *BUCOP* and the *ULS* listings. We have also relied extensively on the *BUCOP* to list reprint editions. For reprint microforms, we have also searched the 1982 *Guide to Reprints* and the *Guide to Microforms in Print;* the latter lacks many titles that we found in reprint house catalogues, notably that of University Microfilms International, and should not be regarded as an authoritative source. We have tried to list all the index sources and reprints available, but given the vagaries of publishing history over the centuries, others undoubtedly remain to be discovered. For a more accurate listing of location sources than Ward's, the *BUCOP* and the *ULS,* Richard Fulton is presently preparing a findings list for literary periodicals. For earlier titles readers may consult *The Graphical Directory of English Newspapers and Periodicals, 1702–1714*, by two *British Literary Magazines* contributors, W. R. and V. B. McLeod. It graphically correlates volumes and dates, and gives publication details for all extant newspapers and periodicals.

Indexes are listed only if the magazine is completely indexed by author, title, and/or subject, either internally or in a separate publication. Items from some magazines have been included in special indexes. For example, Donald Reiman's *The Romantics Reviewed* includes all reviews of Romantic works published in magazines. Such specialized or partial indexes are not listed, since they usually cover a narrow part of the magazines' contents.

Reprints are listed by date only when the title remains unchanged; the city is London if no other is given. If publishers have given editions, we have listed them with dates. Many editions may be facsimiles, but not described as such.

Most microform editions are by University Microfilms International, and are catalogued in one of two series, Early British Periodicals or English Literary Periodicals. We have identified series and reel numbers from catalogues. When other sources report UMI reprints that we have not found in catalogues, we list only UMI.

Location sources are listed by complete and partial runs and by reprints, when that information is available. If a title is held by ten or more libraries, we report it as "widely available," and users should consult the *Union List of*

Serials and *National Union Catalog* for American holdings, the *British Union Catalogue of Periodicals* for holdings in the United Kingdom, and Ward's *Finding List of Serials* for additional locations.

The following information is also helpful for users of this work:

When the magazine being discussed is cited, the citation is given in the text in parentheses by volume and page or by number and page, unless a note specifies another system of citation. When another source is cited, the citation is given in a numbered note at the end of the profile.

When magazines spanned two or more eras, they are assigned to parts of *British Literary Magazines* according to the year in which they began publication:

1698–1788	*The Augustan Age and the Age of Johnson (AAAJ)*
1789–1836	*The Romantic Age (RA)*
1837–1913	*The Victorian and Edwardian Age (VEA)*
1914–1982	*The Modern Age (MA)*

There is only one entry for magazines spanning two or more ages, with the exception of five titles. The longevity of these five and their literary importance call for entries in both the age in which they began publication and the *Modern Age: Blackwood's Edinburgh Magazine (RA, MA)*, *Contemporary Review (VEA, MA)*, *Cornhill Magazine (VEA, MA)*, *Fortnightly Review (VEA, MA)*, and *Quarterly Review (RA, MA)*. Appendixes A, B, and C, which list the titles included in *The Augustan Age and the Age of Johnson*, in *The Romantic Age*, and in *The Victorian and Edwardian Age*, will help those who are not certain when a magazine began publication to locate specific profiles.

The inclusion of cross-references within the text provides further access to the profiles. An asterisk following a periodical title mentioned in the text indicates that the periodical has been profiled in *British Literary Magazines*. In some cases a *see* reference to another part of *British Literary Magazines* appears after the asterisk, for example, *"Cornhill Magazine* (see VEA)."* An asterisk not followed by a *see* reference indicates that the profile appears in this part of *British Literary Magazines*. When a magazine began publication close to the end of an age or is more in spirit with the preceding or the following age, thus making it likely that a reader might look under the wrong age for a profile, there is an entry providing a cross-reference to the proper part of *British Literary Magazines;* for example:

ANALYTICAL REVIEW, THE. See AAAJ

Finally, when a magazine underwent title changes, cross-references are provided to the title under which the magazine is discussed.

The editor welcomes additions and corrections.

Alvin Sullivan

Acknowledgments

I am indebted to the forty-two scholars who have contributed essays to this part of *British Literary Magazines,* especially to John O. Hayden, who introduces this volume and profiles eleven of its eighty-four titles.

Introduction

The year 1798 rings down the halls of literary history. As the date of William Wordsworth's *Lyrical Ballads* with its prototype of the famous Preface, it is often taken to mark the beginning of the English Romantic period. But the date has another significance for literature and especially for literary magazines, for in 1798 two events occurred that transformed printing from what was essentially an industry of hand production to a mechanized industry such as we know today.

In 1798 Lord Stanhope invented the iron printing press, the first major advance since the printing press itself was invented.[1] It more than doubled production and made possible the further inventions and the application of power that so quickly followed. In the same year, when a Frenchman, Nicholas-Louis Robert, took out a patent for a paper-making machine, the second essential step in mechanizing the printing process was made—essential because with the hand production of paper even more time was required to make a sheet of paper than to imprint it.[2] Within twenty-five years half of all paper made in England was machine-produced. These inventions were to revolutionize printing and the literature that depended on it.

The new technology was matched by a rapidly expanding reading public, which indeed had very likely made that technology inevitable. Using the old hand methods of printing, an edition of 10,000 copies of a book of 320 pages would take one press three-quarters of a year to produce, and the tying up of capital entailed would add to the price of each volume.[3] Even though books consequently tended to be shorter, few would reach an imprint of 10,000 copies; most would run to little more than 600 copies; but this was not from lack of buyers.[4]

Britain was already experiencing a population explosion. The population of

England, Scotland, and Wales, estimated at 6 million by the mid-eighteenth century, totalled 10.5 million in the first census taken in 1801, and increased after that at approximately 15 percent each decade.[5] The book-buying public, however, was still limited by illiteracy and high prices; thus the expansion of the reading public took place mainly in the newly educated and affluent commercial and industrial middle class. The increase in the production of books caused by that expansion is dramatic: from 1700 to 1750 an average of 93 books were published each year in England; by 1790–1800 that number had more than quadrupled to an average of 372 books; from 1800 to 1827 the average increased to 588; and by 1853 the number of books published was more than triple that in 1827.[6]

Not only the volume, but the price of books rose sharply in the same period. The cost of the average octavo volume in 1700, for example, was five to six shillings; in 1800 the price had risen to ten shillings; and by 1827, the same book would have cost twelve to fourteen shillings.[7] This rise in prices seems to have been greater than the rise for other commodities, partly perhaps because of the large profits enjoyed by some of the booksellers.[8] But the largest part of the increased prices was no doubt caused by rises in the cost of labor and paper, which began to show the effects of the new technological advances only after 1827, when the price of books began to decline rapidly.[9]

The process of mechanization affecting prices was apparently slowed early in the century by the conservatism of publishers, who could not, or at least did not see that larger editions would naturally bring down prices at the same time that they would raise profits.[10] Consequently book prices continued their upward spiral despite the new technology that was born in that *annus mirabilis*, 1798.

Not so the price of periodicals, however; for by their nature they would, if even reasonably successful, enjoy a larger demand, and thus produce large editions and consequently lower prices; and of course periodicals were published unbound and would be still cheaper as a result.[11] In 1797 the circulation of the major monthly reviews and magazines was between 3,250 and 5,000, which, compared to the average run for a book, was quite large.[12] The prices for these periodicals were given in the *Literary Panorama* * a few years later; they averaged between one shilling, sixpence, and two shillings, sixpence, considerably below the price of a book printed on the same quality paper and with contents of similar (or inferior) quality.[13] The *Edinburgh Review*,* as high in quality as anything published at the time, sold for five shillings, half the price of a comparable book.

Given the demand of an expanding reading public and magazine prices well below those of books, it is no wonder that the early nineteenth century experienced an explosion of periodicals. For by 1811 a contemporary witness observed: "It must be obvious to every attentive observer, that the number and character of critical Reviews is a striking peculiarity of the age."[14] Within a few years he might have replaced "critical Reviews" with "literary periodicals,'' for magazines were on the verge of a similar revolution, which would be led by *Blackwood's Edinburgh Magazine;* * even at the time the statement was made, moreover, there was a profusion of all kinds of periodicals.

In 1800 the rising demand for literary entertainment, information, and critical guidance was met by magazines and reviews already long in existence: the *Monthly Review* * (see *AAAJ*) and the *Critical Review* * (see *AAAJ*), and the *British Critic,* * the *Monthly Magazine,* * the *European Magazine,* * and the *Gentleman's Magazine* * (see *AAAJ*). The magazines were typically old-fashioned miscellanies, with short articles, correspondence, and a monthly chronicle; the reviews were similarly dated in their simple, straightforward critiques of newly published books. Both kinds of periodicals clearly showed their age; and although those that were founded in the last decade of the eighteenth century were more attuned to the times, they all seem comfortable, self-assured, and unexciting, perhaps even a bit predictable. Only a few years later, contemporary accounts of the reviews even seem to exaggerate their inferiority.[15]

Comparison with the state of affairs several years later probably led to such immoderate judgments. For late in 1802 the Whiggish *Edinburgh Review* was founded, and all of the old ways began to change. A small group of un- and under-employed young men in Edinburgh decided it was time for something new in periodicals: intellectual vigor, good pay, independence from booksellers, and freedom to depart from a strict critique of books to a wider discussion of a subject. The formula worked beyond everyone's expectations; because of the extent of its success within six short years, the *Quarterly Review* [1] was founded in 1809 by men in London of the opposite political persuasion; and the two reviews became the most powerful critical organs for a long time to come. In the process, Edinburgh and London were firmly established as the two centers of literary periodicals for the early nineteenth century.

Following long-standing traditions, most editors and contributors to the reviews were anonymous, but many have been identified from sets of marked staff copies and from remarks in letters and autobiographies.[16] And one thing is clear: the editors and contributors were not hired hacks, not mercenaries set loose to savage the writers of the period. Quite the contrary; most were critics of considerable reputation in their respective fields or soon would enjoy such a reputation. Some, it is true, had already written for reviews in the 1790s—Samuel Taylor Coleridge, Francis Jeffrey, Robert Southey, and William Taylor of Norwich; these were joined by writers such as William Hazlitt and Sir Walter Scott, and by eminent lawyers, doctors, professors, and members of Parliament. The days of Grub Street were past; it was now an honor to be discovered as a reviewer hiding behind the often flimsy veil of anonymity.

The great fertility of reviewing periodicals, moreover, is evidenced by the profusion of kinds. Besides the great quarterlies and those of lesser note such as the *British Review* * (1811–1825), there was the *Annual Review* (1802–1808), intended for readers stranded in the Colonies, as well as both the older month-lies, and the newer ones such as the *Eclectic Review* * (1805–1868). The annual and monthly reviews offered straightforward descriptions and evaluations of books; even so, they often produced arguably better criticism than the giants. They were probably most influential in the first decade of the century before the *Edinburgh Review* and the *Quarterly Review* overtook them. Then there were the earlier weeklies, Leigh Hunt's *Examiner* * (1808–1881) and the *Champion* * (1813–1822), which probably did not have much critical impact until the early 1820s since they contained other features besides reviews and presented more extreme political views that may have turned away readers; in any case, they were generally of high quality; for example, both printed new poems by John Keats. The later weeklies, the *Literary Gazette* * (1817–1863) and its many imitators, brought with them more critical influence, for they were totally devoted to literature.

The critical values of all these reviewing periodicals are worth considering, if only briefly. R. G. Cox in his overview of the criticism in question mentioned on the one hand the eighteenth-century point of view and approach often found in the reviews and, on the other, the anticipation in them of such critics as Matthew Arnold and T. S. Eliot.[17] There is a reason for this seemingly contradictory backward-looking, forward-tending appearance of so many of the reviewers, and the reason can be rendered in one word—tradition. It was no accident, either, that much of what Coleridge had to say about Wordsworth's poetry had been said before by the reviewers, and again the explanation involves a concept of tradition.[18]

Samuel Johnson, the reviewers, Matthew Arnold, Coleridge, and Words-worth, for that matter—all of them worked in the same critical tradition, one that had been initiated by Aristotle and refined by Horace, and later by Sidney and Dryden as it passed down through the English line of critical thought.[19] They all shared a belief in mimesis, a close relationship between literature and human experience, as well as in the moral effect of that literature. In their central literary principles the reviewers, in short, were not throwbacks to some nebulous "neoclassical" way of looking at literature, but rather part of a living tradition of literary thought.

In their practice, they did not, of course, always live up to their theories. There are several notorious instances of critical short-circuiting, especially Francis Jeffrey's review of Wordsworth's *Poems in Two Volumes* in the *Edin-burgh Review* and John Gibson Lockhart's review of Keats's *Poems* (1817) in *Blackwood's*. And there are other critiques that are simply wrong-headed or uninspired. But on the whole these critics performed their functions as review-ers (that is, as critics of contemporary literature) with distinction.

Wordsworth, for example, occasioned the following short defense, which I believe has never been surpassed as a brief summary judgment of his poetic career:

Wordsworth demands from his reader, not only the sacrifice of many prejudices, and the conquest of some reasonable dispositions to laughter, or mortification, but also an open heart, and a patient exercise of his intellect. People may doubt, whether a poet has a right to demand all these, but of this we are certain, that he who can, and will grant them, will derive from Wordsworth nearly as high gratification as any poet is capable of bestowing.[20]

And has anyone surpassed the following attack by John Scott on the reviewers' abuse of Keats?

> The author [Keats] provokes opposition . . . . : not unfrequently he even suggests angry censure. We cannot help applying the word insolent, in a literary sense, to some instances of his neglectfulness, to the random swagger of occasional expressions, to the bravado style of many of his sentiments. But coupling these great faults with his still greater poetical merits, what a fine, what an interesting subject did he offer for perspicacious, honourable criticism![21]

Critical appreciations of Keats are easy to come by today—open almost any book on the poet—but how seldom are his shortcomings considered alongside his merits.

In short, if you are looking for rule-ridden critics bent on forcing a return to heroic couplets and circumlocutions, you will be a long time at the task and will never find any critic who will completely satisfy your preconceptions, although there were a few who were less flexible than they might have been. For on the whole the reviewers in the period welcomed the new literary outburst, sometimes openly preferring it to what came before. By way of example we could take the words of Francis Jeffrey, who is often supposed to be an epitome of critical reaction: "We are of opinion, then, that the writers who adorned the beginning of the last century have been eclipsed by those of our own time; and that they have no chance of ever regaining the supremacy in which they have thus been supplanted."[22] The reviewers are often rigorous in their critical judgments and expect writers to live up to their high calling, but this characteristic should not be confused with inflexibility.

Almost every magazine of the period carried reviews in order "to give it a chance of taking," according to one contemporary,[23] but of course these magazines also had many other features, such as articles, correspondence, verse and fiction, and various kinds of news material. Despite their different contents, moreover, they were all finally of a kind, at least in terms of how seriously they saw their function. There was certainly none of the radical division, found in magazines later in the century, between those that merely entertained and "those concerned, like the reviews, with the formation of opinion."[24] Almost all the earlier magazines would have seen themselves as performing a higher role than mere entertainment.

Even the distinction sometimes made between standard magazines like the *Gentleman's* and fashionable magazines like *La Belle Assemblée* * relies more on the question of size and appeal to a female readership than on quality or aims. Magazines such as the *Lady's Magazine* * (see *AAAJ*), *Le Beau Monde*,* and the *Lady's Monthly Museum* were not the vapid, undemanding periodicals we have come to expect women's magazines to be. Cynthia White, who wrote a study on the subject, concluded that

> during the first decade of the nineteenth century, women's magazines continued to be frank, vigorous and mentally stimulating, representing a cross-section of feminine (and often masculine) opinion, and reflecting a broad spectrum of interests and activities. Editors saw as their prime function the cultivation of women's minds. . . . In consequence, space devoted to beautifying the female person was kept to a minimum, an interesting reversal of the priorities which obtain in women's periodicals today.[25]

At times these fashionable magazines are quite unpredictable in their public concern and intellectual independence: *Le Beau Monde* endorsed both the abolition of the slave trade and Catholic Emancipation, while the *New Bon Ton* * advocated divorce. In many such magazines, moreover, there were regular mathematical and scientific departments, as well as many articles on current affairs and serious reviews of literature; by 1825, however, these features were beginning silently to disappear from those fashionable magazines that survived.[26]

One look at other magazines earlier in the period, such as the *Monthly Magazine* and the *European*, should relieve any doubts about the image of self-importance shared by all of them; they also offered more than the escapist entertainment we have come to associate with the word *magazine*. The poets of the first generation—Wordsworth, Coleridge, Southey, and Scott—had no problem, in any case, contributing articles of verse and prose or reviewing for these magazines.

One of the first reviews of Keats's *Poems* (1817) appeared in the venerable *European Magazine*, arguing for the persistence of some quality in that journal, but the second generation of Romantic writers—Byron, Keats, Shelley, Hazlitt, and Hunt—had more exciting magazines to contribute to and be reviewed by. For in the same year that saw the beginning of Keats's short career, Edinburgh once again witnessed a major event in the history of literary periodicals, this time in the field of magazines. *Blackwood's Magazine* (1817–1980) changed the by now conventional layout of the magazines by dropping all the formal departments and mixing together articles, reviews, and correspondence, and it threw in the extra ingredient of vitality.

The *New Monthly Magazine** (1814–1884), already in circulation, soon changed its format to resemble *Blackwood's,* and the *London Magazine** (1820–1829) under John Scott began with *Blackwood's* as a model. These three constituted the most important of the later magazines in the period. Along with Leigh Hunt's *Liberal,** they published most of the important literature that made its way into periodicals.

These influential reviews and magazines, however, by no means exhaust the matter of the variety and fecundity of literary periodicals in the early nineteenth century. There was also a lush undergrowth, a profusion of periodicals that sprang up and flourished for a year or two and then withered away in the shade of the giants.

Many seem to have deserved a better fate, at least inasmuch as they were daring enough to introduce interesting innovations. The *Literary Journal and General Miscellany** (1818–1819), for example, set its price at sixpence, well below its competitors, in a deliberate populist attempt to bring together a readership of all classes for its higher-pitched material.[27] *Le Beau Monde* (1806–1810) contained an interesting attempt to produce a fashionable magazine with a unisex appeal; it even offered a sporting section. And the *New Review** (1813–1814) was new in offering very structured reviews that included a replica of the title page of the book under review and a list of the author's other works; in its encyclopaedic fervor, it likewise provided elaborate indexes by author, title, subject, and category of publication, as well as a list of every author treated in all reviewing periodicals. But, alas! as the date-spans indicate, these, like so many journals, simply could not compete adequately for readers even in an expanded market.

One enormous subject usually addressed early on in a discussion of Romantic periodicals is one that I have not forgotten but deliberately postponed: politics. One recent scholar has remarked "how impossible it is to overestimate the importance of politics in periodical criticism of the early nineteenth century," but I would disagree.[28] Not only can the subject be exaggerated; it almost always is.

Thomas De Quincey deals at some length with the general question of politics in the period, and since he claims that the influence of partisan politics as a whole has been exaggerated, he provides a fitting place to begin the discussion as well as an antidote to more extreme views. De Quincey sets up the major divisions: "Whig, Tory, or Radical" or "under a new classification, ... Conservative or Reforming."[29] But almost immediately he moves to qualify the distinctions, or at least the adherence to them by most citizens, who, he claims, "are of no party whatsoever, own no party designation, care for no party interest, but carry their good wishes by turns to men of every party, according to the momentary purpose they are pursuing."[30] The only two groups that care much about party loyalties, he adds, are politicians and retainers. The Radicals or Reformers present a similar case; while Tories and Whigs "express only two modes of aristocratic partisanship,"[31] all good citizens of an enlightened country care about the reform of their institutions, but again they do so in a general way and do not subscribe to the peculiar partisan views of the Radicals.

The one issue that divided the Tories from the Whigs (and the Radicals) was their attitude toward the war with Napoleon. According to De Quincey, the Whigs, who were the "outs" or opposition party, made the grave error of going beyond being merely anti-ministerial to being anti-national in their opposition to the war, even denigrating victories that awoke popular enthusiasm. But again this attitude was largely found in "official" Whigs, especially those in Parliament, and was not shared by the Whig-on-the-street. Even with the Tories, support for the war was not a matter of principle, but rather an accident of their being in office at the time.[32]

Perhaps De Quincey's generalizations need some qualification, but they at least are the views of a contemporary who lived through those turbulent times; and like Dr. Johnson's pronouncement that most citizens are not really concerned with the type of government they live under provided it leave them alone, De Quincey's remarks have the ring of truth to them. Many of the periodicals had at least some partisan affiliations, but these are not likely to have prevented any but the most partisan readers from the enjoyment of reading them. More partisan journals, such as *John Bull** or the *Examiner*, would of course have presented more difficulties along political lines. But journals like the *Edinburgh Review* with a less extreme partisan bias would have found a readership across party lines and only have experienced serious reactions from more partisan articles. One of these, the famous "Don Cevallos on the French Usurpation of Spain" (1808), which disparaged a favorable event in the war with France, caused the Earl of Buchan to kick the volume in question "out to the centre of the Street, where he left it to be trodden into the mud."[33] But then he was a Tory in Parliament and so would have reacted more strongly than most, at least if De Quincey is right.

It is, moreover, also worth repeating that if he is right, more or less disinterested citizens comprised the bulk of the readers of Romantic periodicals, and so the politics of the reviews and magazines would have been a matter of less concern than might otherwise be supposed. There is also evidence of considerable independence even in periodicals of opposing political persuasions, and in the reviews it is not rare to find a crossing of party lines, with a Tory writer receiving a favorable review in a Whig journal and vice versa. If partisan politics was introduced in a work, a partisan political response in a review should surprise no one; if no politics appeared in the work under review, on the other hand, there was often exemplary objectivity in the criticism. The few contrary examples in the *Quarterly Review* and *Blackwood's* should not be allowed to misrepresent the situation.

One thing De Quincey failed to mention, however, was the sort of politics that transcends party and even issues like parliamentary reform—dangerous political ideologies, such as Jacobinism or Republicanism. Against these, the Romantic periodicals were more or less aligned, even if in the more conservative Tory journals the reaction became especially shrill. The years following the French Revolution were dangerous, fearful times, and politics presented burning contemporary issues. The political volatility of the age, both partisan and ideological, therefore should not be ignored, but, I would argue, should be put into perspective.

If political interference of one kind or another did not overwhelm the general reader, still less would the religious involvement of the periodicals that manifested itself in articles and especially in reviews. It is more likely to disturb the reader today, for from a vantage in a secular society it is difficult to comprehend another in which the culture is permeated with Christian thinking. With the major exceptions of the *Edinburgh* and *Quarterly* and the later weeklies, almost all the reviewing periodicals—including all the major monthlies, the quarterly *British Review*, and the *Annual Review*—and some of the magazines were connected either officially or informally with religious groups. But with few exceptions all the periodicals were Christian in general outlook.

The periodicals concerned themselves with religious issues when pertinent; the officially affiliated were naturally more involved; but there was in all the periodicals an unembarrassed readiness to deal with such matters that we would find awkward. There was some sectarian backbiting; it was especially popular to ridicule Methodists and Evangelicals for what Byron called "entoosymoosy." Just as the extreme and ideological political views, however, had occasioned far more difficulties with the reviewers, so the radical religious views—scepticism, polemical atheism, and religious trifling—riled the reviewers more than sectarianism.

An example from a religiously nonaligned review will perhaps convey the sort of involvement at issue. Francis Jeffrey, in his review of Byron's *Cain*, notes that two-thirds of the play is taken up with discussion of the problem of the origin of evil, and then he objects, not to the topic, but to the handling of the topic:

> But we do not think it fair, thus to argue it partially and *con amore,* in the name of Lucifer and Cain; without the responsibility or the liability to answer that would attach to a philosophical disputant—and in a form which both doubles the danger, if the sentiments are pernicious, and almost precludes his opponents from the possibility of a reply.[34]

What is disturbing to the modern reader is not so much, I believe, that such issues are raised, nor even that terms like *danger* are used, but that Jeffrey cared to raise these issues at all.

The vast bulk of the reviewers did care about religious matters, but usually raised them only when they first occurred in the works under review. A modern reader may consider such religious reactions in the reviews to be either fussy or fanatical, but it makes more sense to think of them as exhibiting what must have been a natural concern of a society more or less in agreement in its general beliefs.

It is truly remarkable that so many people in the early nineteenth century read serious literature and patronized so many reviews. And then, too, there were the large numbers of critics who felt capable of judging contemporary literature immediately, thus manifesting a well-read and articulate class. Likewise astonishing is the active body of contributors of verse and prose to the numerous magazines and again, of course, the large public that supported them. It is difficult in fact not to make comparisons with our own times. Progress, we know, is our most important product, and yet belief in cultural progress does not come without effort. Having considered the same evidence, R. G. Cox has concluded, that "if we compare their work with the [present] scene . . . , it is . . . certain which is the healthier state of culture."[35]

Notes

1. Louis Dudek, *Literature and the Press* (Toronto, 1960), pp. 20, 37.

2. Dudek, pp. 58–59.

3. Charles Knight, *The Old Printer and the Modern Press* (London, 1854), pp. 253–54.

4. Dudek, p. 28. In Theodore Besterman's edition of *The Publishing Firm of Cadell and Davis: Select Correspondence and Accounts 1783–1836* (London, 1938) there is evidence that during the years 1788–1815 "750 copies was evidently the standard figure for a serious book of some general interest, the sort of book of which 1500 copies are printed nowadays" (p. xxxi).

5. Dudek, p. 39. For the 15 percent growth statistic, see Nathaniel Teich, "Decorum and Taste in Romantic Periodical Criticism: Reviews of Wordsworth, 1793–1822" (Ph.D. dissertation, University of California at Riverside, 1970), pp. 33n–34n.

6. Dudek, p. 27; Knight, pp. 238, 260–61. Marjorie Plant, in *The English Book Trade* (London, 1974), finds it "doubtful whether the total number of volumes had risen in the same proportions" as the new titles (p. 462).

7. Knight, p. 238. Comparable figures are given for quarto and duodecimo volumes.

8. Dudek, pp. 28–29.

9. Plant (p. 462) claims that wages from 1780 to 1851 rose 50–100 percent. For the rise and drop in prices, see Knight, pp. 238, 261.

10. Knight, pp. 238–39.

11. Ibid.

12. C. H. Timperly, *Encyclopedia of Literary and Topographical Anecdotes*, 2d ed. (London, 1842), p. 795.

13. *Literary Panorama* 2 (1807):65.

14. Josiah Conder [J. C. O'Reed], *Reviewers Reviewed* (Oxford, 1811), p. 2.

15. John Hayden, *The Romantic Reviewers 1802–1824* (Chicago, 1969), p. 8. See also R. P. Gillies, *Memoirs of a Literary Veteran* (London, 1851), 1:304.

16. See Hayden, Appendix 2, for attributions.

17. R. G. Cox, "Nineteenth Century Periodical Criticism: 1800–1860" (Ph.D. dissertation, Cambridge University, 1939), pp. 84, 88.

18. John Hayden, "Coleridge, the Reviewers, and Wordsworth," *Studies in Philology* 68 (1971):105–19.

19. See John Hayden, "Wordsworth and Coleridge: Shattered Mirrors, Shining Lamps?" *Wordsworth Circle* 12 (1981):71–81.

20. *British Critic*, 2d ser., 11 (1819):603.

21. *London Magazine* 2 (1820):320–21.

22. *Edinburgh Review* 27 (1816):2.

23. Conder, p. 44.

24. Walter E. Houghton, "Victorian Periodical Literature and the Articulate Classes," *Victorian Studies* 22 (1979):407.

25. Cynthia White, *Women's Magazines 1693–1968* (London, 1970), p. 38.

26. White, pp. 38–39.

27. *Literary Journal and General Miscellany* 1 (19 April 1818):63.

28. Alan Lang Strout, ed., *John Bull's Letter to Lord Byron* (Norman, Okla., 1947), p. 6.

29. David Masson, ed., *The Collected Writings of Thomas De Quincey,* 2d ed. (Edinburgh, 1889), 2:215.

30. Masson, 2:216.

31. Ibid.

32. Masson, 2:218–22.

33. Lord Henry Cockburn, *Life of Lord Jeffrey,* 2d ed. (Edinburgh, 1852) 1:190n.

34. *Edinburgh Review* 36 (1822):438.

35. Cox, p. 369.

Bibliography of Principal Reference Works on British Romantic Periodicals

Hayden, John. *The Romantic Reviewers 1802–1824*. Chicago, 1969.

Houghton, Walter E., ed. *The Wellesley Index to Victorian Periodicals 1824–1900*. Toronto, 1966.

Madden, Lionel, and Diana Dixon. *The Nineteenth-Century Periodical Press in Britain: A Bibliography of Modern Studies 1901–1971*. New York, 1976.

Reiman, Donald H., ed. *The Romantics Reviewed: Contemporary Reviews of British Romantic Writers*. 8 vols. New York, 1972.

Ward, William S. *British Periodicals and Newspapers, 1789–1832*. Lexington, Ky., n.d. [1974?].

——. *Index and Finding List of Serials Published in the British Isles 1789–1832*. Lexington, Ky., 1953.

——. *Literary Reviews in British Periodicals 1798–1820: A Bibliography*. 2 vols. New York, 1972.

——. *Literary Reviews in British Periodicals 1821–1826: A Bibliography*. New York, 1977.

John O. Hayden

PROFILES OF BRITISH LITERARY MAGAZINES, 1789–1836

A

ALBUM, THE

The first essay in the *Album* for April 1822, "On Albums," traces this genre of publications back to the temple of Aesculapius, where the ancient walls bore inscriptions written by the sick. Hippocrates collected their descriptions of maladies and cures into the first album. The ruins of the recently discovered Herculaneum provided more examples of ancient collections of random commentaries on life. Lovers of Rousseau, who make a pilgrimage to Montmorency, leave their comments in written form, as do those brave souls who climb to the top of the steep Strasbourg steeple. On these occasions sentiment and danger provide the incentives for the album entries just as the sublime sight of the Alps once inspired entries in the album in which St. Bruno recorded the comments of travellers. Modern albums, the essayist claims, are usually kept by women, and are often curious collections of poetry, music, prose, wit, and sentiment interspersed with original contributions from friends and people of eminence.

Evoking both ancient tradition and modern practice, the *Album* promises to "embrace original papers on all literary subjects." There will also be reviews and "Scraps" or brief literary fragments and anecdotes. Comments on the fine arts will be welcomed, but politics will be "scrupulously avoided." Politics, the editor confesses, pervades everything and "infects and poisons our enjoyments of all kinds." It causes arguments and is "the very apple of discord of this age" (1, no. 1:6, 7).

Although the *Album* contains contributions in various forms, including essays, stories, poems, letters, and reviews, its scope and point of view are less varied, and more homogeneous. The mood and general attitude of the periodical was set by its editor, the minor Irish novelist Francis Barry Boyle Saint-Leger. His point of view, beyond that of his aversion to politics, might be characterized as that of a man of liberal sentiment with a streak of liking for the Gothic. Part of his best known novel, *Some Account of the Life of the Late Gilbert Earle, Esq,* was first printed in the *Album.* A melancholy tale of over-wrought love and its pathetic aftermath, it illustrates well the author's intention to "display the effects of strong passion, both in action and in its general influence upon character, and the progress of the narrative."[1]

Several other stories in the *Album* display a similar pattern. In one of these, women—although evoking great sympathy from the author because of their plight—suffer extended and morbid punishments for their sexual transgressions. Another tale, which tells of the unfortunate predicament of a beautiful woman forced by a father into an inappropriate marriage, concentrates in lavish detail on the ravages of remorse, self-denial, and eventual madness that follow her attempt to escape from her marriage. Essays on melancholy and Lethe, or forgetfulness, further extol the sentiments suggested in the fiction. Stories and essays about the suffering poor, abused animals, the destruction of old trees, and exploited womankind provide objects to elicit the readers' sympathy and sentiment.

In the essay "Intellectual Women," the author discusses the many legal, social, and moral injustices by which women are oppressed. While declaring he is no "Mary Wollstonecraft in breeches" and has an "utter abhorrence" of the "fopperies—the affectations—the shallowness—of the blues" he argues fervently for giving women the opportunity and encouragement to pursue a good education. Citing Madame de Staël as a model, he argues that intellectual women would make better citizens, companions, and mothers (2, no. 2:6, 12, 13).

The *Album* reflects a sentimental attitude reminiscent of Laurence Sterne and Henry Mackenzie, an intensity that is Byronic, and a morbid streak in keeping with Ann Radcliffe. In its critical attitudes, as well as in its fiction, the *Album* both looks back to and rejects the eighteenth century. In the most important critical article, "The Augustan Age in England," the author declares that the time has come for reevaluation of the poets of the last century. For too long, he argues, they have been considered infallible. In truth other ages in English literary history would cast the Augustan Age "into the most humiliating shade." Pope is not the greatest of poets, Addison no poet at all, and Swift as gross as he is humorous. The subjects selected by Pope, explains the critic, exclude him from being a great poet, since they allow him no opportunity to paint the "working of human passions," the true calling of poetical genius. Addison when serious is "cold, stale, and feeble," and, at his best, in the stories of Sir Roger de Coverley, he has taken his ideas from Steele. If Pope and Addison deserve to have their reputations deflated, Swift, in the author's view, deserves outright condemnation as "one of the worst men that ever lived." The passages referring to Stella and Vanessa make the author's heart rise with indignation. Verses to Stella on her birthday are "the most revolting specimens of heartless falsity we ever remember to have seen." His writings "breathe an almost fiendish spirit of rancour and revenge'' and are as ''contemptible in poetry as they are odious in feeling'' (1, no. 2:183–89).

Of the second rank of poets of the Augustan Age—Sir James Prior, Thomas Parnell, John Gay, Richard Steele, and Sir Samuel Garth among them—he places Arbuthnot as deserving the most praise. They all have considerable talent, but none can be considered a man of genius. The Augustan Age may have produced political, moral, and literary disquisitions and satirical, reasoning poetry, but, the author asks, can one name a single production that ''excites or softens our hearts,'' kindles our imagination, or ''speaks to the responsive feelings of nature within us?'' (1, no. 2:190–93).

These ''cold productions of rigid judgment,'' these ''compositions of elegant and fanciful frivolity'' seem pale indeed when compared with Shakespeare and the poets of the Elizabethan age. In Shakespeare we are certain of finding feelings in accord with our own, either as ''enjoyment of the healthy mind or medicine for the wounded one.'' Although Shakespeare among his contemporaries is ''as Mont Blanc among the Alps,'' one can easily appreciate the ''exquisite imagination'' of Spenser, the ''full, deep, engrossing voluptuousness'' of Marlowe, the ''flowing and gentlemanly wit'' of Beaumont and Fletcher, and the ''severe and lofty gravity'' of Jonson (1, no. 2:194–203).

In English literature, the author of ''The Augustan Age in England'' asserts, there have been great ''single stars of the first magnitude''—Milton, Dryden, Young, Thomson, Bolingbroke, Hume, Gray, Collins, Johnson, Goldsmith, and Cowper—but only the ages of Elizabeth and Anne, and the present age, have seen constellations of literary genius. Never, the author asserts, have there been so many distinguished living authors at one time as in the present day. He lists Lord Byron first among living poets, the very ''personification of Genius.'' His poetry exerts unusual power over the minds of his readers. ''Our memories are peopled with images of his poetry,'' the admiring critic declares, ''our hearts commune with the beings of his creation.'' The second living poet who, the author predicts, will retain the ''foremost rank'' is the Rev. George Crabbe. His ''peculiar power'' to give pain by the ''terrible reality in his pictures of suffering'' impresses the critic. Thomas Campbell's poetry forms a link between the past and the present. Written with ''the meter and manner'' of the eighteenth century, it nevertheless has ''the glow, animation and energy'' of the present school of poetry. His qualities of ''exquisite sweetness and mildness, and pathos'' seem to flow ''uncontrolledly'' from the poet's heart and consequently, the critic asserts, ''irresistibly win their way to ours.'' Of contemporary poets, the critic also appreciates Thomas Moore for his ''boundless imagination,'' profuse voluptuousness, brilliant wit, and ''unrivalled touch of melancholy feeling.'' In contrast to Moore, Henry Hart Milman pleases by his ''grace, severity and order.'' The critic compares reading Milman's poetry with gazing at a Greek temple. The author also admires Barry Cornwall for his ''pure and peaceful feelings'' and Samuel Rogers for his ''true tenderness'' (1, no. 2:204–14, 219–24).

A number of contemporary poets, many of whose names are better known in the twentieth century than are those of Crabbe, Milman, or Moore, are acknowledged by the critic as men of talent, even genius, but he has severe criticisms of their poetry. Wordsworth, he complains, "has lost the world for a hypothesis." Some of his poems are a "tissue of infantine absurdity" which only he and his "confraternity" can understand. Coleridge, less a poet than a metaphysician, also earns the critic's contempt. He dismisses *Christabel* as a "miserable absurdity." Robert Southey is condemned by the critic as well. Southey's "contemptible impertinence" and "most disgusting system of self-praise" show, he asserts, that "bathos is totally bottomless." The critic reserves his most negative criticism for the Lake poets, but he also is worried by Shelley's "offensive philosophy," and "occasional obscurity," Hunt's affectation, and Maturin's extravagance. Keats he fails to mention at all (1, no. 2:215–19).

Like many other critics of the 1820s the author of "The Augustan Age in England" wished to turn his back on the past, but was yet unable to accept a radical new aesthetic. Willing to accept the more romantic subject matter of Byron, he could not condone the new verse patterns of the Lake poets. Another article, "On the Character of the Dark Ages," also breaks with the attitudes of the past. The author declares the Greek and Roman periods much overpraised and looks instead to the Dark Ages as the period from which modern social organization and love of liberty derive (2, no. 4:273–309).

One other theme runs through the pages of the *Album*: arts are encouraged, not by the lavish expenditure of money, but by public pride in works of art and the public's appreciation of the work of the artist. If we know how property is distributed in a society, the author of "On the Patronage of the Arts" declares, we will know the character of that society and its disposition toward art and literature. The artist must learn to work for glory, not for profit. Our own age, declares the reviewer of *The Memoirs of Benvenuto Cellini,* is "cold and calculating," preferring the merely pretty to the grand, and placing private enjoyment before public greatness (3, no. 6:264–92; 2, no. 3:163–77).

When the *Album* ceased publication after eight numbers, *Blackwood's Edinburgh Magazine* * regretted its demise, calling it a "clever and gentlemanlike periodical" possessing "some capital contributors." Most of these contributors, the reviewer noted, were taken over by "Christopher North" (John Wilson). Saint-Leger, the reviewer added, was too much of a Whig for *Blackwood's*.[2] Instead Saint-Leger began another short-lived periodical, the *Brazen Head*.

The *Album,* though a minor periodical, is interesting because it represents a definite and consistent point of view. Poised between a dislike for politics and a despair over injustice, between rejection of the cold rational values of the past and caution about the Romantic formal upheavals of the present, it held to a core of humane sentiment and warm feeling.

Notes

1. Francis Barry Boyle Saint-Leger, *Tales of Passion* (London, 1829), n.p.
2. *Blackwood's Edinburgh Magazine* 15 (June 1824):720.

Information Sources

INDEXES
> None.

REPRINT EDITIONS
> None.

LOCATION SOURCES
> *American*
>> Complete runs: Columbia University Library; Hamilton College Library; Princeton University Library; State Historical Society of Wisconsin; U.S. Library of Congress; University of Minnesota Library; Yale University Library.
>> Partial runs: Buffalo and Erie County Public Library; California State Library, Sutro Branch; Newberry Library; New York Psychiatric Institute; New York Public Library; University of California, Berkeley, Library; University of Illinois Library; University of Michigan Library.
> *British*
>> Complete runs: Birmingham Public Library; Bodleian Library; British Museum; Cambridge University Library; Edinburgh University Library.
>> Partial runs: Glasgow University Library; St. Andrews University Library.

Publication History

MAGAZINE TITLE AND TITLE CHANGES
> *The Album.*

VOLUME AND ISSUE DATA
> Volumes 1–4, numbers 1–8, April 1822–April 1825.

FREQUENCY OF PUBLICATION
> Quarterly.

PUBLISHER
> J. Andrews, London.

EDITOR
> Francis Barry Boyle Saint-Leger (St. Leger).

Helene E. Roberts

ANALYTICAL REVIEW, THE. See AAAJ

ANNALS OF THE FINE ARTS

Although it lasted only four years (1816–1820), the *Annals of the Fine Arts* was a lively and informative journal, and it is still dearly regarded by students of John Keats, who first published four of his poems in its pages. Its editor, the architect James Elmes, was, like Keats, a good friend and admirer of the fiery young "historical" painter Benjamin Robert Haydon. Elmes championed Haydon and his causes, and gave him full voice in every issue of his journal. Since Haydon was volatile, supremely egotistical, and a great lover of verbal battle, this guaranteed that the journal would be continuously supercharged with controversy on most of the artistic issues of its day.

From the very beginning, Elmes and Haydon sallied forth with at least two major missions: to praise and promote the Elgin Marbles, which were at that time a subject of debate among academicians, art lovers, and even politicians; and to chastise the Royal Academy of London. The first mission becomes obvious immediately, for the first volume, in July 1816, is "respectfully and gratefully inscribed" to "the Select Committee of the honourable the House of Commons, who by duly estimating the value and recommending the purchase of the Elgin Marbles to the British Legislature, have created an epoch in the history of their country." The third volume is dedicated to Lord Elgin himself, in gratitude for his "rescuing the Splendid Remains of Grecian Genius from the Hands of the Barbarians." It may seem strange to us today to realize that these great works needed defending, but the fact is that, from their first purchase in 1803 and subsequent shipment to England until Elgin offered to sell them to the country in 1811, the authenticity and quality of the Marbles, and Elgin's right to have them, had been a constant subject of controversy. Most of these questions were settled by 1815, when the Marbles were judged authentic by the architect Visconti and the sculptor Canova, but many doubts remained, and Parliament was still debating the issue by the time the *Annals* began in July 1816. This was all the encouragement Haydon needed to sound repeated calls in the journal. He had been enraptured with the Marbles since he was first allowed to see them in 1808. For years he had badgered everyone to get Parliament to purchase them, and when the Select Committee recommended the sale, he and Elmes and their circle poured their considerable energies into swaying public and parliamentary opinion. Thus virtually every issue of the *Annals* has something in it concerning the Elgin Marbles. Volume 1, for instance (p. 97), contains a laudatory review of Haydon's book on *The Judgement of Connoisseurs . . . on the Elgin Marbles,* followed soon by an anonymous poem in praise of Haydon's defense of the treasures.

Especially fascinating to modern readers is a section in volume 1 containing an "Abstract of a Report from the Select Committee" which gives the testimony of many witnesses, including Elgin himself, John Flaxman, Sir Thomas Lawrence, and Benjamin West. All of them thought that the Marbles were in the "first class" of art. Richard Payne Knight, a director of the British Institution whom Haydon had attacked in an earlier article, stated that the Marbles were merely second rank art from the time of Hadrian, and were furthermore in a bad state of preservation. The *Annals* reports, "[He] thinks the Elgin Marbles only valuable as a school of art, and would not sell as *furniture,"* leaving the reader to shake his head in wonder (pp. 225–42). When, later in 1816, Parliament voted to buy the Marbles, Haydon "was convinced—and convinced his friends—that his article had won the case, and extravagant tributes to his victory, including sonnets from Wordsworth and Hunt, poured in from all sides." [1] Even after the parliamentary purchase, the theme of the Elgin Marbles continued throughout the *Annals* as a boost to Haydon's ego and an instruction to the public. Perhaps the major literary value of the issue is that two sonnets by Wordsworth, addressed to Haydon, and two sonnets by Keats on the Elgin Marbles, also addressed to Haydon, appeared in the second volume of the *Annals* in 1817. The real fruit of the controversy, however, would emerge in two of Keats's greatest poems, published in issues after 1817.

The second mission of the *Annals*—the reformation of the Royal Academy—was an even more preponderant concern of the journal. Elmes and Haydon's opinion is clearly stated in the preface to the third volume: "We conceive the Royal Academy to be a perverted institution. . . . We conceive historical painting ought to be the great object of the nation, the government and the sovereign" (p. vii). It was no accident, of course, that Haydon was a historical painter, having already exhibited his "Judgment of Solomon." Haydon already felt that he had been slighted by the Royal Academy in its previous treatment of him, and his animosity shows up in nearly every issue of the *Annals*. There is, for instance, a series of letters in defense of the painter James Barry—who was purportedly expelled from the Academy in earlier years for proposing certain coloring techniques—which runs throughout the first volume, and is characterized by remarks of Haydon's to the effect that the Royal Academy "is become a vast organ of bad taste and corruption" (1:274). The attack is continued throughout volume 2 by use of a series of letters "from the ghost of James Barry" (letters which Haydon protests disarmingly as not being by himself) which accuse the Academy of having become a "laughing stock" (p. 133) and of harboring a "cabal" that preys on its vitals (p. 142); and by the end of volume 3 Elmes himself joins in the fun with a long list of complaints, finishing with a synthesizing accusation that the Academy failed to defend the Elgin Marbles.

Aside from these missions and hobbyhorses, editor Elmes felt that his journal should respond to "the numerous and anxious inquiries" concerning the fine arts, and accordingly the *Annals* tries to be useful and informative, and often succeeds. Nearly every issue contains a section of "Biography of Eminent Artists, Lately Deceased," reporting the achievements of both major and minor artists of the time. "Biographical Sketches of Living Artists" appears occasionally, and most issues contain catalogues of private collections of works of art, reports on the transactions of fine arts academies and societies, and a section entitled "Announcement of works in hand: intelligence relative to the Fine Arts, etc." The final issue for each year gives the names and residences of the principal artists in the London area. The list includes the names of engravers—an innovation prompted by Elmes's belief that the academicians had neglected that valuable group of artists.

Elmes devotes extensive space to art and architecture. Various architectural styles are discussed, and a student of Ruskin or Pugin gains insight into the taste of the 1810s. Most revealing, for instance, is an article by "Philotecton-Londinensis" entitled "An Enquiry into the Claims of Gothic Architecture over other Styles for Religious Edifices," in issue 5 for 1817. The author disparages the Gothic style, claiming that it lacks "harmony of the parts" (p. 175), and that "sensual pleasure or gratification is the only recompense it promises its votaries" (p. 172). Elmes and Haydon encourage native English artists. The new widespread appreciation of the fine arts in England should allow native artists equally extensive public appreciation; academicians are attacked for their neglect of English artists. Many short articles, catalogues, and notices tell the locations and virtues of contemporary British art, and there is frequent praise for those who advance the home cause—especially the British Institution. A very useful article by Sir Richard Colt Hoare, for instance, can be found in the beginning of volume 2 (1817), entitled "On the Conduct of the Directors of the British Institution, in Regard to Their Patronage of British Artists." Hoare draws a large list of fine artists who have emerged in England since the days when Reynolds and Gainsborough alone were the major names in order to show the general increase of talent in England: West, Sir Thomas Lawrence, Flax-man, Westmacott, and Turner. Hoare goes on to praise the British Institution for exhibiting "the old masters from foreign countries" and "allowing the student to have unceremonious intercourse with them" (2:16). As part of their encouragement of native art, the editor of the *Annals* and his circle constantly urged that there be frequent and accessible showings of foreign art in order to help young English artists develop ideas and form their taste and technique.

Tucked away in the back page or two of most issues of the journal is a section of "Original Poetry on the Fine Arts." This section was obviously considered a minor part of the journal, and it is often filled with odd poems by strange or anonymous poets of no consequence. Built into its title, though, is a view which has its significance for literature. As Ian Jack has pointed out, a most important feature of the *Annals* is "the emphasis laid by its contributors on the close affinity between the visual arts and literature."[2] Jack has Keats especially in mind here, but anyone familiar with subsequent British literature will recognize the significance of the thought, particularly the aspect of it which includes "the insistance on the relationship between poetry and painting throughout the *Annals*."[3] One need only think of Tennyson and Browning, Morris and Rossetti, or Yeats and Pound, to realize the validity of the *Annals'* perception, however ineffectually it may have been actualized through the journal's publication of even such poems as Charles Lamb's "Lines on the Celebrated Picture by Leonardo da Vinci . . . ." (5:163–64), Robert Southey's "The

Painter of Florence'' (4:497–99), or Wordsworth's sonnet "Upon the Sight of a Beautiful Picture'' (1:561).

At this point the final irony emerges. The reader of the *Annals,* after making his way through such poetry issue after issue, turns yet another page and is suddenly presented with a poem at the back of issue 13 for 1819, entitled "Ode to a Nightingale,'' and signed only with Keats's dagger symbol (4:345–56). Some pages later, at the end of issue 15 (4:638–39), the reader receives a further, unexpected sense of climax by discovering the same familiar Keatsian dagger, this time placed under a poem called "Ode on a Grecian Urn,'' in its first published version which ends by stating, without quotation marks, that

> Beauty is Truth, Truth Beauty. —That is all
> Ye know on Earth, and all ye need to know.

With this rather inadvertent production of greatness the *Annals of the Fine Arts* nears its end. After the "Grecian Urn" ode there were to be only two more issues of the journal before it ceased publication in the middle of 1820. At the end, in a somewhat forced way, the reader is given a sense of catharsis and aims achieved: the Elgin Marbles have been purchased and appropriately praised; the British Academy has been properly reformed; and Haydon is reported to have progressed to the end of his "Christ's Triumphant Entrance Into Jerusalem." But ultimately larger ends have been achieved for the modern reader. One can see not only the flowering at last of Keats's genius, but also the artistic context out of which his poems grew. And beyond its value to students of Keats, the *Annals* is ultimately valuable as a window through which we can see the specific issues and conditions that characterized the state of the fine arts in the early nineteenth century and pointed directly toward the literature that was to follow—Browning, for instance, or Ruskin, or the Pre-Raphaelites—and the emergence of the peculiarly "eclectic" Victorian styles and tastes.

Notes

1. Aileen Ward, *John Keats: The Making of a Poet* (New York, 1963), p. 85.
2. Ian Jack, *Keats and the Mirror of Art* (Oxford, 1967), p. 53.
3. Ibid., p. 54.

Information Sources

BIBLIOGRAPHY
Jack, Ian. *Keats and the Mirror of Art*. Oxford, 1967.
Ward, Aileen. *John Keats: The Making of a Poet*. New York, 1963.
INDEXES
None.
REPRINT EDITIONS
None.

LOCATION SOURCES
British
> Complete runs: Bodleian Library; British Museum; Cambridge University Library; Victoria and Albert Museum Library.
> Partial runs: Aberdeen University Library; Ashmolean Museum (Oxford); Edinburgh University Library; Glasgow University Library; Manchester Public Library.

Publication History

MAGAZINE TITLE AND TITLE CHANGES
> *Annals of the Fine Arts.*

VOLUME AND ISSUE DATA
> Volumes 1–5, numbers 1–17, July 1816–April 1820. (Volume 1 has issues 1–3; volume 5 has issues 16 and 17; volumes 2–4 have four issues each.)

FREQUENCY OF PUBLICATION
> Quarterly.

PUBLISHERS
> Sherwood, Neely, and Jones, Paternoster Row, London. Boydell and Co., Cheapside, London. Carpenter and Son, Old Bond Street, London. Arch, Cornhill, London. T. and G. Underwood, Fleet Street, London. A. Black, South Bridge Street, Edinburgh.

EDITOR
> James Elmes.

George Allan Cate

ANTI-JACOBIN REVIEW, THE

In late 1797 three talented young men, George Canning, John Hookham Frere, and George Ellis, published a prospectus for the *Anti-Jacobin; or, Weekly Examiner,* dedicating it to a close examination of the daily and weekly press, "detecting falsehood,—and rectifying error,—by correcting misrepresentation, and exposing and chastising malignity." [1] Edited by William Gifford, who was later to edit the *Quarterly Review,** the *Anti-Jacobin Weekly* only lasted for thirty-six issues, from 20 November 1797 through 9 July 1798, but it still merits attention for its brilliantly witty and savage parodies of contemporary poets. [2] And although unconnected with the *Anti-Jacobin Weekly,* when the *Anti-Jacobin Review and Magazine; or, Monthly Political and Literary Censor* began publication in July 1798, it announced in its prospectus its intention to continue the activities of its namesake: "we shall frequently *review* the *Monthly* [*], *criticise* the *Critical* [*], and *analyse* the *Analytical Review* [*] [for all, see *AAAJ*], on the principle already adopted by the WEEKLY EXAMINER, in its comments on the daily prints" (1:3). The editor of the new journal—which inherited the savagery but not the wit of its predecessor—was "John Gifford," a pseudonym for John Richards Greene. [3] The *Anti-Jacobin* lasted for twenty-three years, until 1821, surviving its original editor by three years.[4] In 1810, in its thirty-sixth volume, it changed its name to the *Antijacobin Review, and True Churchman's Magazine; or, Monthly, Political, and Literary Censor,* and thereafter an even larger proportion of its attention was focused on religious affairs. Shortly before this it had abandoned its regular section, "Reviewers Reviewed," but continued to attack other reviews, although the list had greatly expanded from its original three targets.

When the weekly and monthly Anti-Jacobin magazines were founded, the threat of "Jacobin" ideas seemed very real.[5] Both the success and the excesses of the French Revolution were feared, and the ideas that spawned and supported the Revolution were anathema. In June 1819 the *Anti-Jacobin* cast a retrospective eye on its founding and the source of its name:

> The Antijacobin Review was first instituted for the express purpose of opposing the Atheistical tenets of a cabal who met at Paris in a Monastery belonging to an Order called Jacobines, or followers of St. James. These tenets were alike opposed to all settled opinions in religion, politics, and morals. In the first, their motto was *Ecrasez l'infame;* in politics, assassination and plunder were their aim; and in morals, they justified alike adultery and sodomy. [56:313]

And according to the *Anti-Jacobin,* the Jacobins' actions followed their principles: "Have we to remind our readers that these philosophers, these wise men, free from prejudice and bigotry, amused their leisure hours by nailing to the cross on Good Friday, young and delicate females ALIVE and NAKED?" (56:314). The palpable falsehoods of these accusations are not atypical. Continually appealing to the grosser prejudices of its readers, the *Anti-Jacobin* throughout its twenty-three years used invective, innuendo, distortion, misrepresentation, and vicious personal abuse. On occasion, however, the review went too far for even its readers—it admitted in December 1798 that some of Gillray's cartoons had been misunderstood (1:739), and very few more appeared.

The two most opprobrious terms that the *Anti-Jacobin* could apply to those it thought needed scourging were *Jacobin* and *licentious.* Licentious had its modern signification of sexually loose or promiscuous, but it also carried other connotations. The *Anti-Jacobin* was against popery (18:530), Catholics (20:426), the Irish (20:16), Irish Catholics (18:318), Catholic Emancipation (20:284), Quakers (30:329–30), Dissenters (59:86), and Scots, who received less disapproval than the Irish because they were at least Protestant (8:387). It attacked the *Monthly* (18:415), *Critical* (9:87), and *Analytical* (1:75–76) reviews. The *Edinburgh Review** was too savage, and, besides, it was Scottish (20:88). Arthur Aikin's *Annual Review* was opposed because it espoused Unitarian and other schismatic doctrines (18:512); Unitarians because they did not believe in the Trinity (35:121–23); Methodists because they did not respect property and class distinctions (8:157–59); the Toleration Act because it allowed unlicensed and uneducated Dissenters to preach on the Sabbath (18:102–3). Similarly, the anti-slavery movement was bad: the slaves were better off in the West Indies than they were in Africa (26:26). It believed that newspapers should not disseminate political information to the laboring poor (43:152); that Sunday schools should not teach the laboring poor to read and write (26:36–37); and that the Lancastrian system of education did not teach Christianity according to the Church of England (29:292). The British and Foreign Bible Society was censured because priests of the Church of England sat in the same room as Dissenting ministers (21:53).

Literature did not escape: Byron questioned God and impugned the fair sex (42:345); Mary Wollstonecraft was a "concubine" and prostitute who disgraced the fair sex (1:97); Walter Scott insisted on using Scottish themes and dialect in his poems (36:310–12); and it was impossible to decide whether Maria Edgeworth's morality was pagan or Christian: moreover, she was Irish and the *Edinburgh Review* praised her (34:416–17).[6] Landor's *Gebirus* was attacked not only because Landor praised Napoleon but because the *Critical Review* liked it (17:179–82); the reviewer insisted that the *Monthly Review* praised Mrs. Barbauld's *Eighteen Hundred and Eleven: A Poem* only because she was a Dissenter (42:203–9); Samuel Rogers, described by the *Monthly Review* as an original genius, was really a plagiarist (5:71–73). "Original Criticism" and "Reviewers Reviewed" were not distinct compartments—if a previous journal had commented on a work being reviewed, the *Anti-Jacobin* carried out its self-imposed task of reviewing both.

Not all of the reviews were denigratory. A brief review of the 1798 *Lyrical Ballads* praised "The ancyent Marinere," "The Foster Mother's Tale," "Simon Lee," "The Idiot Boy," and "Goody Blake and Harry Gill" (5:334 [434]).[7] Since this review did not appear until April 1800, and said that "the author possesses a mind at once classic and accomplished," one wonders just how good the literary information was. The reviewer obviously thought the entire volume by one person,[8] and did not suspect the hand of either Wordsworth or Coleridge. Both poets had been attacked as Jacobins in a long poem that appeared in the final issue of the *Anti-Jacobin Weekly* for 9 July 1798, and that was in part reprinted in the *Anti-Jacobin Review*'s own first issue as an explanation of Gillray's cartoon. In this particular section, the Jacobin sect is chanting:

> "*Couriers* and *Stars,* Sedition's evening host,
> "Thou *Morning Chronicle,* and *Morning Post,*
> "Whether ye make the rights of man your theme,
> "Your country libel, and your GOD blaspheme,
> "Or dirt on private worth and virtue throw,
> "Still, blasphemous or blackguard, praise LEPAUX!
> "And ye, five other wandering bards that move
> "In sweet accord of harmony and love,

"C———DGE and S——TH—Y, L——D, and L——BE and Co,
"Tune all your mystic harps to praise LEPAUX!"[9]

[1:115]

In the editor's "Farewell Address to the Public" of 1821, he repeats with pride that the *Anti-Jacobin* attacked the "Jacobinical Poets of that day," "Coleridge and Southey, Lloyd and Lamb, and Co" (61:356).

On occasion, however, the criticism of the *Anti-Jacobin* could be relatively sensible and even perceptive. Its review of Mrs. Radcliffe's *The Italian* questions whether Schedoni is not the true hero, and makes sensible comments on problems with the plot (7:27–29). When it says of the second stanza of Thomas Campbell's highly popular *Gertrude of Wyoming*—

> It was beneath thy skies that, but to prune
> His autumn fruits, or skim the light canoe,
> Perchance, along thy river calm at noon
> The happy shepherd swain had nought to do.
> From morn till evening's sweeter pastime grew,
> Their timbrel, in the dance of forests brown,
> When lovely maidens prank't in flow'ret new;
> And aye, those sunny mountains half way down,
> Would echo flagelet from some romantic town,

that "this stanza . . . is most inelegant, perplexed, and obscure" (34:3), one must agree with the reviewer.

On an occasion where one expects the opposite, the *Anti-Jacobin* can be amazingly fair. Southey's *Joan of Arc* is deplored because of its choice of subject, a choice "directed by Jacobin principles." On this occasion, however, the quotations bear out the charge that the poem has anti-English sentiments. The "Mission'd Maid," Joan, exhorts her followers to

> ———Avenge their fall
> On England's ruffian hordes. In vain her chiefs
> Madly will drain her wealth, and waste her blood
> To conquer this vast realm———
> To force the yoke of slavery upon men
> Determin'd to be free!

[3:126]

Despite many passages such as this, the magazine praises Southey's descriptive talents and his characterization.

Among the few positive principles of the *Anti-Jacobin* is a strong regard for morality, a regard that at times forces it to attack the institution of the monarchy. When the House of Commons decided that the Duke of York, then Commander-in-Chief of the Army, was ignorant of the fact that his mistress was selling commissions, the *Anti-Jacobin* said that unfortunately its examination of the evidence led them to believe that the Duke must have known what was going on (32:318). It also attacked the Duke of Clarence, saying that "while he has held the rank and received the pay of an admiral, he has remained at home, passing his time in the arms of a pr******te, and left others to fight his country's battles" (30:166). A journal that felt it was its sacred duty to reveal hypocrisy and vice, even in the royal family, did not need a sudden perception of Byron's liberal politics to attack *Childe Harold*, which it characterized as irreligious and immoral. Nor, since one of its justifications for attacking Quakers was that they did not recognize that some wars—such as the present one against France—were just, could it accept Byron's attack on war, or his description of papal and Protestant religions as rival superstitions (42:343–60).

Perhaps the most interesting and significant review in the *Anti-Jacobin,* however, is that of Blake's designs for Blair's *The Grave* in November 1808 (31:225–34).[10] Although highly critical, the reviewer does not condemn the designs out of hand, and his comment on "Christ Descending into the Grave" is just: it is "deficient in dignity. . . . There is in fact, a prettiness about the face, which were it not for the beard would better consort with the graceful character of a young female, than with the majesty of the 'ETERNAL KING whose *potent arm* sustains / The Keys of Hell and Death.' " "Death's Door" is praised, as is "The Death of the Strong Wicked Man": "The extremities convulsed with agony, the expanded chest heaving with inexpressible pain, the swelling muscle, and the breadth of limb, are well adapted to the idea of strength laid low." The reviewer objects, however, in this and in the "Death of the Good Old Man," to the "corporeal" representation of non-material beings: "The beings of another world, when depicted on the same canvas as earthly bodies, should be sufficiently immaterial to be veiled by the gossamer, and not, as they are here designed, with all the fullness and rotundity of mortal flesh." It is obvious that the reviewer's dislike of these details is as much religious as aesthetic, and as such must be accepted as legitimate disagreement over the proper way to depict the soul in art. Even this criticism, however, the reviewer tempers:

> They are executed with much spirit and truth, yet we doubt whether Mr. Schiavonetti has done complete justice to the original drawings. A considerable time has elapsed since we had an opportunity of seeing them, but if our memory fails not, the defect of giving strong corporeal semblance to spiritual forms was much less glaring in them, than in the prints. The figures were more shadowy and insubstantial; and consequently, the effect of the whole was greatly improved.

It is only in the very last paragraph that the reviewer reverts to the bludgeoning tactics of the typical *Anti-Jacobin* review, in a comment on Blake's poetical dedication to Queen Charlotte: "Should he again essay to climb the Parnassian heights, his friends would do well to restrain his wandering by the strait waist-coat. Whatever license we may allow him as a painter, to tolerate him as a poet would be insufferable.'' This comment, however, in the context of the entire essay, hardly earns the description of it as a "slashing review" which "excoriates Blake's designs."[11] Moreover, it does not equal Robert Hunt's accusation in the *Examiner* * of 7 August 1808 that the designs contain "inde-cent attitudes," bear "an appearance of libidinousness," and "have more for their object the benefit of the licentious than the amusement of the virtuous."[12]

Few *Anti-Jacobin* reviews are as interesting as this one, and in its later years the magazine seems to go out of the way to avoid reviewing works that one would expect it to tear apart. Leigh Hunt's *Juvenilia* and Shelley's pseudony-mous *Original Poetry, By Victor and Cazire* are reviewed (10:313–17; 37:206), but their later works are ignored. For a journal dedicated to exposing and erad-icating Jacobin ideas one would have thought Shelley a godsend. But, despite a violent attack on Coleridge's *Christabel* volume (50:632–36) and Hazlitt's *Political Essays* (57:312–24), the magazine only occasionally reverts to its campaign against Jacobin poets, and even then it simply repeats epithets coined by others. In its lead article of November 1819 it praises *Thoughts of Happi-ness, A Poem,* by Rev. Francis Homfray:

> Deluged, as the literary world has been, with infidelity and indecency, disguised with all the allurements of poetry, and disgusted with the child-ish simplicity of the Lake School, and the bombastic sublime of the Cockney, we hail with pleasure the publication of a christian poet; a publication which we may read to our wives, and put into the hands of our sons and daughters. [57:209]

Perhaps the review thought that if Jacobin poets were ignored they would sim-ply fade away; it says of Jeremy Bentham that if his works were not noticed they would not do any mischief: "Impressed with this idea, we left these wretched ravings of an unconfined maniac to be forgotten" (57:5).

It is difficult to be objective about the *Anti-Jacobin.* Journals that make no pretense of objectivity arouse a similar response in the reader. And its reviews swing widely from the occasional balanced and sensible comment to the foulest accusations. The controversy over Bowles's edition of Pope engendered many bitter attacks, but surely none more unjustifiably malignant than the *Anti-Ja-cobin* attack on the *Quarterly* critic:

> We trust our readers shudder at the cold-blooded atrocity now before them. And yet, alas! in the concerns of domestic life we could give par-allel instances of calumny more malignant, and of misrepresentation more atrocious. How the mind can overlook the recollection of that all-seeing Judge unto whom all hearts are open, and from whom no secrets are hid, is to us most mysterious. Does it arise from latent insanity, or is it pro-

duced by the constant use of pernicious drugs, which first intoxicate, and then irritate the mental powers? [60:266]

Such personal attacks were not uncommon in the period, however, and could be even more direct and blunt, like the notorious and repeated attacks on Leigh Hunt in *Blackwood's Edinburgh Magazine,** but calumny and personal abuse are never justifiable critical tools, whatever the provocation, and they are tools used all too often by the *Anti-Jacobin.*

Still, however, there were obviously readers for this kind of attack: *Blackwood's* throve, and the *Anti-Jacobin* lasted for twenty-three years. Its social and political opinions must have been shared by some part of the British population. J. Conder thought it on the point of dying in 1811, but the review survived for ten more years.[13] And since those writers whose work we still read from the Romantic period did not share its extreme conservatism, the magazine can be a valuable aid in understanding the period. Twentieth-century readers who know of the "Peterloo Massacre" only from footnotes to Shelley's "The Mask of Anarchy" will find in the *Anti-Jacobin* a defense of the Manchester magistrates and a violent attack on Henry Hunt and the radicals who caused the outrage (59:66–68). Reading a journal, too, that disapproves of the distribution of Bibles without adequate annotation because this can lead to violent sectarian strife (46:520–33), and that asserts that the purpose of such distribution is to destroy the Church of England (46:27–31), can demonstrate to the twentieth-century reader that Blake's comment—"To defend the Bible in this year 1798 would cost a man his life"—is not paranoia, but, rather, a perception of the violently repressive attitudes of that portion of the British population for which the *Anti-Jacobin* had elected itself spokesman.[14]

Notes

1. Prospectus of the *Anti-Jacobin; or, Weekly Examiner* (1797–1798; reprint ed., New York, 1968), p. i.

2. For identification of authors and explanatory notes, see *Poetry of the "Anti-Jacobin,"* ed. Charles Edmonds (London, 1852), and *Poetry of the "Anti-Jacobin,"* ed. L. Rice-Oxley (Oxford, 1924). See also Owen E. Holloway, "George Ellis, the *Anti-Jacobin* and the *Quarterly Review,*" *Review of English Studies* 10 (1934):55–66.

3. See *Dictionary of National Biography,* s.v. "Greene, John Richards."

4. The identity of the second editor is not known.

5. There is a sympathetic account of the reality of these fears in Rice-Oxley's introduction to *Poetry of the "Anti-Jacobin,"* pp. xvii–xxii. William S. Ward, on the other hand, is much less sympathetic, emphasizing the repressiveness of the government. See "Some Aspects of the Conservative Attitude toward Poetry in English Criticism, 1798–1820," *Publications of the Modern Language Association* 60 (1945):386–98.

6. For an excellent summary of some of these vicious personal attacks, see Ford K. Brown, *The Life of William Godwin* (London, 1926), pp. 154–64.

7. John O. Hayden identifies the author of this review as W. Heath, and evidently made this identification from the copy of the first six volumes (1798–1800) in the Brit-

ish Museum that has names of contributors. I have not seen this copy. See *The Romantic Reviewers 1802–1824* (Chicago, 1969), pp. 46, 296.

8. In the second edition of 1800 the preface had clearly indicated that the poems were by two different poets. It is questionable that the reviewer had read *Lyrical Ballads,* since the poems he singles out were those commonly praised. Also, when the *Anti-Jacobin* praises Leigh Hunt's *Essays on . . . the London Theatres* and Donald Reiman expresses surprise at such commendation—"the timing of this notice is strange, coming after Hunt had begun to make himself obnoxious to the government by his *Examiner* articles"—I would suggest that the magazine was not "trying to encourage him to give up politics and return to theatrical criticism," but, rather, that it did not know the two Hunts were identical. Reiman, *The Romantics Reviewed,* part C (New York, 1972), 1:30.

9. Dorothy Marshall, *The Rise of George Canning* (London, 1938), p. 183. Lepaux was "striving to introduce a new revolutionary religion based on a love of Humanity."

10. This article is reprinted in *William Blake: The Critical Heritage,* ed. G. E. Bentley, Jr. (London, 1975), pp. 122–31.

11. G. E. Bentley, Jr., *Blake Books* (Oxford, 1977), p. 723.

12. This review by Robert Hunt is also reprinted in *Blake: The Critical Heritage,* pp. 119–21; the quotations are from p. 121.

13. Jno. Chas. O'Reid [Conder's pseudonym], *Reviewers Reviewed* (Oxford, 1811), p. 43.

14. Annotations to *An Apology for the Bible,* by R. Watson, in *The Poetry and Prose of William Blake,* ed. David V. Erdman, with commentary by Harold Bloom (Garden City, N.Y., 1970), p. 601.

No one has unearthed evidence that the *Anti-Jacobin* received any direct subsidy from the government, but John Gifford was made a police magistrate. In *Politics and the Press c. 1780–1850* (1949; reprint ed., Brighton, 1973), p. 176n., A. Aspinall cites this as one of a series of such posts given to journalists as rewards for supporting the government's position. The last editor of the *Anti-Jacobin,* however, thought this totally inadequate compensation. "The original Editor, J. Gifford, Esq., has long ago paid the debt of nature. All the reward which he received from Government for planning and executing a work so advantageous to the nation was,—The appointment of Police Magistrate at Worship-Street! Magnificent boon! By which he was so enriched that his widow and orphans were rescued from actual want by private bounty" (61:358). As usual, the truth of the matter probably lies somewhere between, especially since the *DNB* records that he was also made a police commissioner at Great Marlborough Street, and that these two positions were rewards for his six volume *Political Life* of Pitt of 1809, rather than the editorship of the *Anti-Jacobin.*

Information Sources

BIBLIOGRAPHY

Aspinall, A. *Politics and the Press c. 1780–1850.* 1949. Reprint. Brighton, 1973.
Bentley, G. E., Jr. *Blake Books.* Oxford, 1977.
———, ed. *William Blake: The Critical Heritage.* London, 1975.
Brown, Ford K. *The Life of William Godwin.* London, 1926.
Conder, J. [Jno. Chas. O'Reid]. *Reviewers Reviewed.* Oxford, 1811.
Edmonds, Charles, ed. *Poetry of the "Anti-Jacobin."* London, 1852.
Hayden, John O. *The Romantic Reviewers 1802–1824.* Chicago, 1868.

Holloway, Owen E. "George Ellis, the *Anti-Jacobin* and the *Quarterly Review.*" *Review of English Studies* 10 (1934):55–56.

Marshall, Dorothy. *The Rise of George Canning*. London, 1938.

[Pontey, William]. *The Rotten Reviewers; or, a Dressing for the Morbid Branches of the "Anti-Jacobin" and "Critical" Reviews.* Huddersfield, England [1810].

Reiman, Donald. *The Romantics Reviewed.* 9 vols. New York, 1972.

Rice-Oxley, L. *Poetry of the "Anti-Jacobin."* Oxford, 1924.

Ward, William S. "Some Aspects of the Conservative Attitude Toward Poetry in English Criticism, 1798–1820." *Publications of the Modern Language Association* 60 (1945):386–98.

INDEXES

Each volume indexed.

REPRINT EDITIONS

AMS Press, New York, 1968.

Microform: English Literary Periodicals (UMI), reels 652–667.

LOCATION SOURCES

American

Complete runs: Widely available.

British

Complete runs: Birmingham Public Library; British Museum; Edinburgh Public Library; Manchester Public Library.

Partial runs: Widely available.

Publication History

MAGAZINE TITLE AND TITLE CHANGES

The Anti-Jacobin Review and Magazine, volumes 1–35, July 1798–April 1810. *The Antijacobin Review, and True Churchman's Magazine*, volumes 36–50, May 1810–August 1816. *The Antijacobin Review; True Churchman's Magazine; and Protestant Advocate*, volumes 51–55, September 1816–February 1819. *The Antijacobin Review; and Protestant Advocate*, volumes 56–61, March 1819–December 1821. (Subtitle throughout: *or, Monthly, Political, and Literary Censor.*)

VOLUME AND ISSUE DATA

Volumes 1–35, July 1798–April 1810; volumes 36–50, May 1810–August 1816; volumes 51–55, September 1816–February, 1819; volumes 56–61, March 1819–December 1821.

FREQUENCY OF PUBLICATION

Monthly.

PUBLISHERS

Volumes 1–27: J. Whittle, at the *Anti-Jacobin* Office, Petersborough Court, Fleet Street, London (volumes 1–8); 3 Southampton, Strand, London (volumes 9–16); 22 Old Boswell-Court, Strand, London (volumes 17–24); 20 Wych-Street, Drury-lane, London (volumes 25–27). Other publishers irregularly assisted; for example: C. Chapple, 66 Pall Mall, London; Bell and Bradfute, Edinburgh; Reid and Best, Glasgow; J. Milliken, Dublin; W. Cobbett, Philadelphia; T. Pierson, Birmingham; E. Harding, Pall Mall, London.

Volumes 28–48: C. Cradock and W. Joy, 3 Maria Lane, London (volumes 28–30); 32 Paternoster-Row, London (volumes 31–34); 52 Paternoster-Row,

London (volumes 35–46); 47 Paternoster-Row, London (volumes 47–48).
Volumes 49–61: Sherwood, Neely and James, Paternoster Row, London.

EDITORS

"John Gifford" (John Richards Greene), 1798–1818(?). Unknown, (?) 1818–1821.

Helen B. Ellis

ATHENAEUM, THE

After a precarious first three or four years, from 1828 to 1831 or 1832, the *Athenaeum* rapidly outgrew all other weeklies in circulation and maintained its lead through the end of the century, reaching a peak circulation of approximately eighteen thousand in the late 1830s and returning its editor and owner, Charles Dilke, an estimated annual profit of 5,000 pounds during the 1850s.[1] The *Athenaeum*'s advantages during the 1830s and 1840s over its chief competitors, among them the *Literary Gazette** and the *London Weekly,* derived from the strength, good judgment, and business sense of editor Charles Dilke. He avoided religious and political controversy, and was careful about questions of influence on reviewers by authors and publishers; he was more successful than his competition in enlisting contributors who were well read in their subject areas; and his review provided more extensive extracts than did the competition's. In July 1831 Dilke cut the price of an issue in half, greatly increasing both circulation and the demand for advertising space. In 1835 he went to a larger sheet, allowing for an increase of 15 percent in print, but he did not increase the price. In 1835 he issued nineteen double numbers, reaching twenty-six annually by 1841.[2] The next editors, T. K. Hervey (1846–1853) and Hepworth Dixon (1853–1869), allowed the quality of the magazine to decline; at the same time, the *Spectator** and the *Saturday Review** (see *VEA*) offered serious competition. Still, circulation and profits held up fairly well. Hervey and Dixon departed from the policy of avoiding political controversy. After the brief editorship of John Doran (1869–1871), Norman MacColl became editor and remained through the end of the century. He restored the quality of the magazine and attempted to make it more appealing to readers by adopting larger type and broader columns.

The *Athenaeum* continued to dominate other weeklies during most of the century because it offered a broader range of subject-matter than did any of its competitors. In the second number, for 9 January 1828, the *Athenaeum* named its subjects: literature, art, and science. Specifically, it promised to cover a broad range of books, including news of works in progress; poetry; fiction; drama, including opera; literary gossip; proceedings of learned societies; foreign literature; theater and items of cultural interest; and architecture, sculpture, painting, and engraving (p. 30). The *Athenaeum* provided lists of scientific publications, reviews of the more important books, and, especially valuable, detailed and at times lengthy records of the meetings of the Royal Society, the Royal College of Physicians, the British Association for the Advancement of Science, and the Geographical, Botanical, Horticultural, and Ornithological societies. Often the records of meetings were published in special numbers. In the controversy over Darwin's theories, the *Athenaeum* first argued for their acceptance. After the arrival of MacColl as editor, it opposed Darwinism. After Dilke's editorship ended in 1846, the *Athenaeum* gave less attention to scientific subjects, although a number of the most respected scientists of the times were contributors during the later years of the magazine. The *Athenaeum*, especially under Dilke, provided lengthy essays on music. Henry Chorley, the main contributor of music criticism, wrote on Rossini, Mendelssohn, Meyerbeer, Paganini, Liszt, Ernst, Chopin, Jenny Lind, and Berlioz. Beginning with the number for 4 April 1828, the magazine frequently published essays on foreign literature, particularly French and Spanish; and by the middle of the century, the magazine was rivaled in its attention to foreign publications only by the *Foreign Quarterly Review* * and the *Westminster Review.* * Among the many correspondents were Sainte-Beuve, Janin, and Heine. The magazine enjoyed an excellent reputation abroad. The *Athenaeum*'s contributions on folklore, begun in 1846, attracted so much interest that William Thoms, in charge of the column, established *Notes and Queries* * (see *VEA*) in 1849 for their publication and for the publication of related matter. The obituaries in the *Athenaeum* were a main source of information for the *Dictionary of National Biography,* and the names proposed for that project were published regularly in the *Athenaeum* for reader comment.

The typical range of the magazine's content is apparent in number 499 for Saturday, 20 May 1837. The issue contains approximately eight pages of general reviews, on Carlyle's history of the French Revolution; *Venetia,* a novel; an account of a voyage to Africa; an account of a voyage to the Black Sea; and Moxon's edition of Wordsworth. Two pages contain a list of new books and a table of meteorological observations made at the Cape of Good Hope on 20–22 December 1836. There are a five-page serial review of nineteenth-century French literature; three pages of short reviews of scientific publications; four pages of advertisements; and two pages on music, drama, art, literary gossip, and "Miscellanea." Though the range is still relatively broad, there are significant differences three decades later in number 2195 for Saturday, 20 November 1869. There are only approximately thirteen pages of general reviews: on a biography of Mary Russell Mitford; an account of life on the pampas; two biographies of Durer; a book on Somersetshire birds; William Cullen Bryant's *Letters from the East;* a European tour book; a history of India; two novels and a collection of stories; new poetry by Andrew Wallace, William J. Courthope, Frederick G. Lee, T. Clifford O'Connor, Joseph Allis, and "M." These reviews appear under the headings "Novels and Novelettes," "Gift Books," "New Poetry," "Our Library Table," "Educational Books," "List of New Books," and "Literary Gossip." Absent is the emphasis that Dilke placed on science and foreign literature, and the advertisements have shrunk to two-thirds of one page.

During most of the century the *Athenaeum* followed a moderate path in literary criticism. It praised the poetry of the Brownings, Tennyson, and Morris, but it did not care for Clough, Patmore, Meredith, or Christina Rossetti. It ranked Dickens highest among the novelists. It favored Thackeray, Eliot, Trollope, Gaskell, and Kingsley, but not Reade, Meredith, Hugo, or Samuel Butler. It found admirable things in Carlyle and Ruskin, but not in Arnold. It mixed praise and blame in its reviews of Swinburne. During the 1850s and 1860s the quality of the literary criticism in the *Athenaeum* was below that of its rivals, the *Spectator* and the *Saturday Review*. But during the 1870s and 1880s MacColl restored the magazine to the position it held under Dilke, chiefly by attracting outstanding writers such as Dante Gabriel Rossetti, Edmund Gosse, Andrew Lang, W. E. Henley, and Richard Garnett, among others; and in scholarly matters, Skeat, Furnivall, Sweet, and Trevelyan. In the twentieth century the *Athenaeum,* especially under John Middleton Murry, began the publication of important fiction and poetry, by Katherine Mansfield, Max Beerbohm, Virginia Woolf, Edwin Arlington Robinson, Edith Sitwell, Robert Graves, T. S. Eliot, and Wilfred Owen, among others, until it merged in 1921 with the *Nation**
(see *MA*).

Notes

1. Leslie A. Marchand, *"The Athenaeum": A Mirror of Victorian Culture* (1941; reprint ed., New York, 1971), pp. 44–45, 81. I am indebted to this study for much of the information below.

2. Marchand, pp. 25, 42–45, 74; J. D. Jump, "Weekly Reviewing in the Eighteen-Sixties," *Review of English Studies,* n.s. 3 (1952):245.

Information Sources

BIBLIOGRAPHY

"Address" (new year). *Athenaeum,* 5 January 1833, p. 1.

"The *Athenaeum* Centenary." *Nation and Athenaeum,* 14 January 1928, p. 559.

Dilke, Charles W. *The Papers of a Critic.* 2 vols. London, 1875.

Fahnestock, Jeanne. "Authors of Book Reviews in *The Athenaeum,* 1830–1900." *Victorian Periodicals Newsletter* 5, no. 15 (1972):47–52.

Francis, John. *John Francis, Publisher of the "Athenaeum": A Literary Chronicle of Half a Century.* Compiled by John C. Francis. 2 vols. London, 1888.

Graham, Walter. *English Literary Periodicals.* New York, 1930.

Houghton, Walter E., ed. *Wellesley Index to Victorian Periodicals.* 3 vols. Toronto, 1966.

Jump, J. D. "Weekly Reviewing in the Eighteen-Fifties." *Review of English Studies* 24 (1948):42–57; "Weekly Reviewing in the Eighteen-Sixties." *Review of English Studies,* n.s. 3 (1952):244–62.

Keith, Sara. *"The Athenaeum* as a Bibliographical Aid." *Victorian Periodicals Newsletter* 8 (1975):25–28.

Marchand, Leslie A. *"The Athenaeum": A Mirror of Victorian Culture.* 1941. Reprint. New York, 1971.

"Prospectus for the New Series." *Athenaeum,* 16 January 1830, p. 17.
Stebbing, Henry. "The *Athenaeum* in 1828–30." *Athenaeum,* 19 January 1878, pp. 88–89.

INDEXES

Each volume indexed.

REPRINT EDITIONS

Microform: Early British Periodicals (UMI), reels 526–567. Microcard Editions, Washington, D.C.

LOCATION SOURCES

American

Widely available.

British

Widely available.

Publication History

MAGAZINE TITLE AND TITLE CHANGES

The Athenaeum, 2 January 1828. *The Athenaeum and London Literary Chronicle,* 30 July 1828. *The Athenaeum and Literary Chronicle,* 6 August 1828.
The Athenaeum and Weekly Review of English and Foreign Literature, Fine Arts and Works of Embellishment, 1830–11 February 1921. (Incorporated in the *Nation,* 11 February 1921, thereafter *Nation and Athenaeum* until 21 February 1921; thereafter the *New Statesman and Nation* with separate note "Incorporating the *Athenaeum,*" until 13 January 1934.)

VOLUME AND ISSUE DATA

Numbers 1–4737, 2 January 1828–11 February 1921.

FREQUENCY OF PUBLICATION

Weekly (Saturdays), 2 January 1828–29 January 1829; weekly (Tuesdays) and twice weekly (Tuesdays and Fridays), February 1828–15 April 1828; weekly (Wednesdays for a short time, then Saturdays), 23 April 1828–December 1915; monthly, January 1916–March 1919; weekly, 4 April 1919–4 February 1921.

PUBLISHERS

1828: William Lewer, 147 Strand, London. 1829–1838: F. C. Westley, 65 Strand, London. 1838–1918: John Francis, at various addresses but chiefly Took's Court and Bream's Buildings in Chancery Lane, London. 1920–1921: British Periodicals, 70 Fleet Street, London.

EDITORS

James Silk Buckingham, 2 January–30 July 1828. Frederick Denison Maurice, 30 July 1828–May 1829. John Sterling, May 1829–5 June 1830. Charles Wentworth Dilke, 5 June 1830–23 May 1846. T. K. Hervey, 23 May 1846–December 1852. Hepworth Dixon, January 1853–August 1869. John Doran, August 1869–1871. Norman MacColl, 1871–1900. Vernon Rendall, 1901–1916. Arthur Greenwood, 1916–1919. John Middleton Murry, 1920–1921.

Dickie A. Spurgeon

AUGUSTAN REVIEW, THE

The *Augustan Review* was first published in 1815 as a monthly, and ran for only twenty issues before it ended, with little comment from its editors, in 1816. During its brief span it published articles that were, for the most part, excellent and instructive. It set out to rival the doctrinaire tone of both the *Edinburgh Review** and the *Quarterly Review,** with an expressed aim to provide "a far more miscellaneous" survey of contemporary life and letters. The editors professed that they belonged to "no party," that is, Whig or Tory, and that their comments would be free from political considerations. The preface to the first issue stated that policy of moderation: "Should the writers of the Augustan Review succeed in blending, in literary matters, pertinent observations free from asperity, with occasional instruction, void of dogmatism; and, in political affairs, the first delineation of important measures and events, with the censure proscribed by faction, or the reverence due to patriotism, they will consider themselves sufficiently fortunate" (1:iii). That moderate approach to politics, religion, and literature was to be the guiding principle of the journal, and perhaps its downfall. The times were not ripe for any sort of moderation, as the success of the partisan *Edinburgh* and *Quarterly* illustrated. At a much later time, Matthew Arnold complained about the blending of politics and religion with literary criticism, but that aspect of literary criticism in the nineteenth century did not readily come to an end.[1]

But if 1815 was not a good time for moderation in politics or literature— Europe was "threatened with a convulsion," said the editors (1:iii)—it was an especially good year for English literature. The new poetry was slowly making its way to a general acceptance. Scott's *Guy Mannering* was published in that year, as was his friendly rival Jane Austen's *Emma* (2:484). Plays were being written in abundance, and a minor genre, the Napoleonic epic, was also receiving an enormous amount of attention from writers and critics. The stimulus for these epics was the war with France, and, judging from the *Augustan*'s reviews of them, they were popular by reason of the intense patriotism that was manifested in them (cf. 1:89ff.).

The most interesting aspect of the *Augustan*'s literary policy (if it had one) was its response to the emerging challenge to the eighteenth century's view of the poet and his place in society. The *Augustan* was quite severe with what it regarded as the posturing of Wordsworth's second volume of poetry, *The White Doe*. In his "Supplementary Essay" Wordsworth had put forward a new idea about the poet and had argued at length that the very neglect of his own poetry was a proof of its intrinsic merit. The *Augustan* responded: "Civilization creates taste and discernment of worth; and literary merit will always find admirers in an enlightened nation" (1:346). In its view, Wordsworth's problem was not an ill-informed audience. He was simply not a good poet and should turn his talents to the writing of literary essays, for his "poetry" was in fact "the very commonest of prose": "If he would but consent to abandon slovenly meter, and addict himself to good plain prose, his increasing benevolence and his lines of thought always so moral and religious, might render him a highly respectable Essayist" (1:356). In spite of this criticism, the reader will notice a certain moderation in the *Augustan*'s comments on Wordsworth's poetry. Even John Keble's review in the *Quarterly* was more hostile in its comments on both the poetry and Wordsworth's theory of the poet's elevated sensibility.[2]

The above comments are distinctive, moreover, for they represent the only essay in the twenty issues of the *Augustan* that was not enthusiastic about Romantic literature. Byron, Scott, and Coleridge all received favorable reviews of their poetry. Scott's *Lord of the Isles* was praised for the "wild and sublime natural scenery" in the poetry, and Byron's *Hebrew Melodies* received an especially complimentary treatment because of its skillful rendering of a sacred theme (1:479, 209). In the third volume of the *Augustan* (almost the final issue), Coleridge's *Christabel* received one of its very strongest and most positive early reviews (3:310). What is relevant about these critical essays on Romantic poetry is the challenge they present to the recurrent image of the Romantic poet's struggle for acceptance in the early nineteenth century. The *Augustan,* at least, was more than sympathetic to the new poetry.

Some of the other reviews of poetry published in 1815 and 1816 are notable. Southey's *Roderick,* Hogg's *Pilgrim of the Sun,* and Hunt's *The Story of Rimini* were reviewed at length and with general approval, though Hunt's poem was faulted for the "incorrectness" of its verses. In addition, there are numerous reviews of far more obscure poetry.

Yet the literary tastes of the *Augustan* were not confined to the new poetry. An 1815 edition of Cowper's poetry was enthusiastically praised, and the reviewer took particular pains to acquit Cowper of the charge of egotism, a failing that had been attributed to Wordsworth. New editions of Claudian's *Poems* and Juvenal's *Satires* in translation were elaborately praised. Another review essay endorsed John Morrell's work on classical studies that argued the traditional view of using the poets of Greek and Latin antiquity as the basis of education (2:479).

The *Augustan* has a sizeable number of reviews of fiction published or reedited during its tenure. Fanny Burney's *Tales of Fancy* and Scott's *Guy Mannering* were both praised, though the reviews of both were, more exactly, largely summaries of the plot. But the *Augustan*'s most significant failure was occasioned by Jane Austen's *Emma.* That novel was condemned for its similarity to the other novels of Jane Austen. As in the case of the reviews of poetry, there are many reviews on novelists who have fallen into hopeless obscurity (1:32, 325, 496, 698; 2:484; 3:219).

Not much attention was given to literary theory or works of literary criticism, but Schlegel's *Lectures on Dramatic Poetry* was reviewed (2:297), and in the second volume of the *Augustan* there is a long and interesting review of the "state of modern tragedy" in which it is argued that "Venice Preserved is one of the noblest tragedies, if not the best, in the English Language" (2:522). The plays of Shakespeare do not receive any extensive commentary, but even the brief notices of his work suggest that the *Augustan,* like its contemporaries, accorded to the Bard a quasi-religious veneration.[3] On a lower level, tragedies and comedies written at the time were discussed (reviewed) with interest and approval (for example, Barrett, Wilmot, and Milman). The preferences of the reviewer were in the direction of eighteenth-century comedies and tragedies.

No consistently held theory of literature is evident in the many essays on novels, plays, and poetry. A critical position emerges only in the frequent quarrels with the *Edinburgh, Quarterly,* and *British Review.** The *Augustan* frequently challenged these rival journals for their "partizanship" in literary, political, and religious matters. According to the *Augustan,* Southey had received a notorious, biased review of his *Roderick* from the *Quarterly* because of his politics (2:80, 222). On a different matter, the *Edinburgh*'s reviews of contemporary religious books and issues were condemned for the "sceptical" approach to religion, the *British* sounded as if it were written by "evangelical lawyers," and the *Quarterly* as if Christianity were no more than a "nationalistic" concern (2:309).[4]

For those interested in non-literary matters, the *Augustan Review* is especially valuable. There are numerous essays on the Church of England and on non-Anglican religions. The lengthy commentaries on the war with France and its aftermath are especially informative, though many of the problems and scandals discussed are fairly arcane. Despite the range of its interests and the quality of its reviews, the *Augustan* had little if any impact on the literature or politics of its time. In an "Advertisement" in the last issue the editors reported that "to alter its size, the periods of its publications . . . No. XXI will not appear next month" (3:359). The efforts to regroup and continue were apparently futile; the twenty-first issue never appeared.

Notes

The author wishes to thank the Faculty Research Committee and Dr. Louise Allen of the University of Southern Colorado for a grant-in-aid which supported this work, and the staff of the Newberry Library, Chicago, where the research for this essay was conducted.

1. "The Function of Criticism at the Present Time," in *Works of Matthew Arnold* (London, 1888), 3:21. John Clive, *Scotch Reviewers* (Cambridge, Mass., 1957), p. 66.

2. Cf. John Griffin, "Keble and the *Quarterly Review," Review of English Studies* 28 (1978):454–58.

3. For a survey of early nineteenth century dramatic criticism, see C. Maliakail, *Textual and Dramatic Criticism of Shakespeare's Plays in the London Dramatic Periodicals, 1800–1825* (Combiatore, India, 1966); Maliakail does not include the *Augustan* in his survey.

4. For the validity of the *Augustan* comments, see *Letters and Correspondence of John Henry Newman* (London 1891), 2:14 *passim;* see also John Griffin, *The Oxford Movement: A Revision* (Front Royal, Va., 1980), chap. 3.

Information Sources

BIBLIOGRAPHY

Arnold, Matthew. "The Function of Criticism at the Present Time." *National Review* 19 (1864):230–51.

Clive, John. *English Bards and Scottish Reviewers.* Cambridge, Mass., 1957.

Griffin, John. "John Keble and the *Quarterly Review.*" *Review of English Studies* 28 (1978):454–58.

———. *The Oxford Movement: A Revision.* Front Royal, Va., 1980.

Maliakail, C. *Textual and Dramatic Criticism of Shakespeare's Plays in the London Dramatic Periodicals, 1800–1825.* Combiatore, India, 1966.

INDEXES

Each volume indexed.

REPRINT EDITIONS

Microform: English Literary Periodicals (UMI), reel 752.

LOCATION SOURCES

American

Complete run: Newberry Library.

British

Complete runs: Aberdeen University Library; Bodleian Library; British Museum; Cambridge University Library; Edinburgh University Library; St. Andrews University Library.

Partial run: Glasgow University Library.

Publication History

MAGAZINE TITLE AND TITLE CHANGES

The Augustan Review; a monthly production.

VOLUME AND ISSUE DATA

Volumes 1–3, numbers 1–20, May 1815–December 1816.

FREQUENCY OF PUBLICATION

Monthly.

PUBLISHER

A. J. Valpy, London.

EDITORS

Unknown.

John R. Griffin

B

BEAU MONDE, LE

Seeking "the patronage of an enlightened and polished public,"[1] John Browne Bell (son of John Bell, the publisher of *La Belle Assemblée* *)[2] began *Le Beau Monde* in 1806, the same year in which *La Belle Assemblée* was first published. It was like his father's magazine in both content and lay-out. In fact, *La Belle Assemblée* had a section entitled "Le Beau Monde."

The son's periodical has been said to have been in direct competition with *La Belle Assemblée,* but it seems more likely to have been founded with his father's blessing, for *Le Beau Monde* is an interesting experiment in reaching beyond the female public of the father's journal to appeal to a mixed audience.[3] The "Biographical Sketches of Illustrious Ladies" had their counterpart in *Le Beau Monde* in the same sort of sketches of "Illustrious Men," and there was a new section, "Sporting Varieties," that dealt with such male diversions as hunting, boxing, and horse racing. None of this masculine appeal, however, is suggested in the motto found on every contents page, *"Non praeter solitum leves"* (Horace, *Odes,* 1. 6. 20: "[I sing] lightly as is my custom").

The question of lightness, on the other hand, seems absent from the stated aims of the magazine—to "become a LIBRARY BY ITSELF, and an indispensible requisite to every admirer of Literature" and to "tend more to disseminate information and useful reading, than any Book of the kind hitherto published" (1 [January 1807]). To accomplish these aims, in any event, there were regular departments: the Biographical Sketches already mentioned, History, State of Society and Manners (of foreign nations), Retrospect of Politics (for the previous month), Public Amusements (reviews of the opera and theater), Fine Arts, Poetry, Original Communications (prose tales and essays), and Le Beau Monde (women's and men's fashions).

There were also literary reviews, usually one or two of considerable length.

There was a policy of selection: "To the *Review of Literary Productions* a particular care has been directed: and as the plan of *Le Beau Monde* is not so much to notice every thing, as to describe what is generally interesting, we have been able to devote to works of importance more room than can be bestowed by other Reviews" (3:385). Works by Scott, Moore, Byron, and Wordsworth received critical attention in serious reviews, for despite the "fashionable" quality of the magazine there was never any attempt to popularize or to write down to the readership. The quality of the reviewing is perhaps partly owing to the promise in the issue for September 1807 that all reviews would be *"liberally paid for."*

Another feature of which the proprietors could be proud—and of which they were in fact vain—was the "embellishments" or engravings that appeared in every issue. Contemporary artists like Sir William Beechey allowed engravings to be made of portraits they had painted of "Illustrious Men." These portraits were said to form a valuable group if collected over two years (1 [January 1807]). There were also two or three colored plates usually of fashions (both for men and women) but sometimes of furniture or monuments.

An engraving also accompanied a semi-annual supplement of about forty pages (priced at sixpence). In April 1808, moreover, a series of "Dramatic Memoirs and Criticism of Eminent Performers" began, of five to seven pages (separately numbered). These memoirs included portraits engraved by a "Mr. Scriben, from the Drawings of Mr. De Wilde and Miss Emma Smith" (3:385).

What are most surprising in a fashionable magazine, however, despite its attempt to appeal to men as well as women, are the enlightened political views of *Le Beau Monde*. At the end of the "Index to Volume 1" (unnumbered page), the proprietors claimed that they were "not attached to any party" and received no favors from any. Their stated adherence to "the principles of the British Constitution" does not prepare one for their stand favoring Catholic Emancipation (1:383–84) and the abolition of the slave trade (1:319–25). Considering the clearly "fashionable" readership to which *Le Beau Monde* was largely directed, the pronouncement of such views is extraordinary.

In notices "To the Public" appearing on the reverse of contents pages, the proprietors were constantly promising more and better features, as if there were indications of a falling-off in subscriptions. And advertisements appeared at the end of issues (especially noticeable are large ads for "mineral teeth") beginning as early as the second volume. After the fourth volume the magazine underwent a reconstruction, perhaps indicating some difficulties inherent in the unisex appeal, and the issues were labeled "Novel Series," even though the volumes and issues continued the original numbering.

This new organization lasted three months, and then something unusual happened. The last issue in April was repeated in the new *Le Beau Monde, and Monthly Register;* that is, there were two separate April numbers. The new title heralded another reorganization to something more like the original magazine before the "Novel Series" began. One major difference, however, was that the longer reviews were replaced by a section entitled "Catalogue Raisonné," which attempted to give a short critical notice to all new publications. Another difference was a new emphasis on music. There was a large monthly "Critical Catalogue of Music," mainly reviews of newly published songs, and songs were printed in each issue with both words and music. Under the list of new publishers in the two volumes, in fact, was the following phrase: "And by All Other Book and Music Sellers throughout the United Kingdom." But apparently there were still problems, for the number of pages dropped from ninety in volume 1 to seventy in volume 2 before the magazine stopped after three issues in April 1810.

Notes

1. *Le Beau Monde* 2 (July 1807), reverse of contents page. Hereafter cited in the text; each citation will refer to the unnumbered page on the reverse of the contents page of the issue in question unless a page number is given.

2. *The Satirist* 1 (1808):304.

3. Stanley Morrison, *A Memoir of John Bell* (London, 1930), p. 65.

Information Sources

BIBLIOGRAPHY
Morrison, Stanley. *A Memoir of John Bell*. London, 1930.
INDEXES
    Each volume indexed.
REPRINT EDITIONS
    Microform. English Literary Periodicals (UMI), reel 853.
LOCATION SOURCES
American
    Complete run: Brooklyn Public Library.
    Partial runs: California State Library, Sutro Branch; Connecticut College; Easton Public Library; U.S. Library of Congress.
British
    Complete run: British Museum.
    Partial runs: Birmingham Public Library; London Library; National Library of Ireland; Victoria and Albert Museum.

Publication History

MAGAZINE TITLE AND TITLE CHANGES
    Le Beau Monde; or, Literary & Fashionable Magazine, November 1806–April 1809. *Le Beau Monde, and Monthly Register,* April 1809–April 1810.
VOLUME AND ISSUE DATA
    Volumes 1–5, November 1806–April 1809 (volume 5, February 1809–April 1809, entitled "Novel Series").
    New series, volumes 1–2, April 1809–April 1810.
FREQUENCY OF PUBLICATION
    Monthly.

PUBLISHERS
    Volumes 1–2: John Browne Bell & Co., 11 Catherine Street, Strand, London.
    Volumes 3–5: John Browne Bell, V. J. Decamp, The Office of the National
    Register, 11 Catherine Street, Strand, London.
    New series, volumes 1–2, April 1809–April 1810: Neely and Jones, and J.
    Walker, Paternoster Row, London. Black, Parry, and Kingsbury, Leadenhall
    Street, London. J. Richardson, Cornhill, Taylor and Hessey, Fleet Street, Lon-
    don. Goulding and Co., New Bond Street, London. Wilkinson and Co., Hay-
    market, London. Button and Whitaker, St. Paul's Churchyard, London. Consta-
    ble and Co., Edinburgh/Ludgate Hill, London.
EDITOR
    Unknown.

John O. Hayden

BEE, THE

In December 1790 a prominent citizen of Edinburgh, James Anderson,
launched an ambitious new project: a weekly miscellany magazine called the
Bee. It was designed for a class of readers hitherto neglected by the literary
and intellectual world: men of business—those engaged in agriculture, manu-
facturing, and commerce; as well as clergymen and others in remote parts of
the country, whose isolation cut them off from the new ideas and inventions of
the metropolis. The new magazine would disseminate knowledge, encourage
the reading and writing of literature, and extirpate error.

> Nor does the editor confine his views to Britain alone. The world *at*
> *large* he considers as the proper theatre for literary improvements. . . .
> he hopes to be able to establish a mutual interchange of knowledge, and
> to effect a friendly literary intercourse among all nations. . . . the editor
> warmly solicits communications from ingenious men of all nations. . . .
> [In addition] he hopes for communications on interesting subjects, as they
> occasionally occur, from literary characters in Britain who are entire
> strangers to him.[1]

Two features distinguished the *Bee* from other contemporary periodicals. First,
the magazine printed many illustrations—of men, animals, plants, buildings,
machinery—some occupying a full page, some a half page; thereby leading
directly to the illustrated magazine of the nineteenth century.[2] Second, the editor offered awards or "premiums" for the best original writing submitted in
certain specified categories, thereby encouraging the writing and study of such
compositions.
Five premiums and the rules governing them were announced in the Prospectus:

First. For the best written, and the most characteristic sketch of the life
of any of the great men or philosophers . . . who appeared in Europe
between the revival of letters, and the beginning of the present century:
A GOLD MEDAL, or FIVE GUINEAS.
Second. For the best and most striking characteristical sketch of any eminent statesman, philosopher, or artist now living, or who has died within
the present century: A GOLD MEDAL, or FIVE GUINEAS.
Third. For the best original miscellaneous essay, story, apologue, or tale,
illustrative of life and manners; or effusion or disquisition on any subject
that tends to interest the heart, and amuse the imagination, in prose: A
GOLD MEDAL, or FIVE GUINEAS.
Fourth. For the best original essay, in verse; ode, tale, epistle, sonnet, or
short poetic effusion of any kind: A SILVER MEDAL, or TWO GUIN-
EAS.
Fifth. For the most spirited translation, or elegant imitation of any select
poem in foreign languages, whether ancient or modern: A SILVER
MEDAL, or TWO GUINEAS.[3]

The editor retained the option of continuing or discontinuing the premiums
after the first year. Prize-winning pieces would be published in the *Bee*. Worthy
entries that did not win prizes would also be considered for inclusion in the
magazine. The premiums had the desired effect. Entries poured in and judges
were sometimes hard put to choose among contending pieces. On at least one
occasion, when the judges could not agree, duplicate prizes were awarded
(15:80).

For help in fleshing out the *Bee,* Anderson recruited a group of correspondents and contributors, both abroad and at home: Dr. Matthew Guthrie in St.
Petersburg; Dr. James Anderson, physician-general of the East India Company
in Madras; the merchant William Knox in Gothenburg; Col. Thomas Johnes
(or Johns) and the lawyer Thomas Christie in London. There were others, not
yet identified, in America (probably at Philadelphia), in France, and in Germany.

Closer to home were a host of fellow Scotsmen, including two noblemen:
David Steuart Erskine, eleventh earl of Buchan, and Francis Garden, Lord Gardenstone. Buchan was a founder of the Society of Scottish Antiquaries and a
frequent contributor to the *Gentleman's Magazine** (see *AAAJ*) and other periodicals. To the *Bee* he sent sketches, brief satires, light verse, and didactic
essays on varied topics, signed "Albanicus," "A.B.," "Ascanius Trimon-
tanus," "Biographicus," etc. Lord Gardenstone, described by Anderson as
"an old, shrewd, sagacious, witty judge on the Scotch bench," was a wealthy
and eccentric old bachelor, who possessed considerable knowledge of classical
and other elegant literature. Besides his "Remarks on Some English Plays"
and "Travelling Memorandums," he contributed "Remarks on Dr. Young's
Night Thoughts," selections from *Miscellanies in Prose and Verse* (Edinburgh,
1791) and several other short pieces.

Other notable contributors included Dr. Thomas Blacklock, a blind poet and one of Anderson's original supporters in the venture; James Thomson Callander, an acerbic essayist and poet; and George Dempster, veteran M.P., and, like Anderson, a great agriculturist and improver of land.[4] A number of other correspondents sent in occasional pieces.[5]

Anderson himself was well prepared for his function as editor. A student of agriculture and chemistry at Edinburgh, he had come under the tutelage of the famous Dr. William Cullen, who had introduced him to many famous persons. Returning to farming, Anderson made several innovations, including the small two-horse "Scottish plough" without wheels. He began his writing career with a series of "Essays on Planting" (1771), followed by important articles on the Corn Laws (1777) and the Scottish fisheries (1783). He had contributed to the *Monthly Review**" (see *AAAJ*) and to the first edition of the *Encyclopedia Britannica*. When at age fifty-one he began to edit the *Bee* he already held an honorary LL.D. from Aberdeen, an F.R.S., and membership in learned societies in Bath, Manchester, London, Paris, Dijon, and St. Petersburg.

With a wide circle of acquaintance, Anderson numbered among his correspondents Jeremy Bentham and George Washington. With Bentham he maintained a flow of friendly letters asking and giving advice, despite a sharp disagreement over Anderson's pamphlet on the Scottish fisheries, which Bentham severely criticized. Anderson sent a stern reply, questioning Bentham's understanding of it and his judgment. It is creditable to both men that their friendly intercourse survived for another decade.[6] In 1793, however, another difference of opinion caused a permanent estrangement.

Anderson described his friendship with George Washington as beginning when a few copies of the prospectus of the *Bee*

were, by the obliging intervention of the earl of Buchan, transmitted to General WASHINGTON, who received them with a kind partiality, that nothing but the most genuine benignity on his part could inspire. The PRESIDENT of the UNITED STATES of AMERICA became from that moment a warm and disinterested patroniser of the intended work. He caused it to be advertised in the American newspapers at his own expense; and at his recommendation the author had the honour of being admitted a member of that very respectable body of men who constitute the philosophical society of Philadelphia; the news of which honour Mr. WASHINGTON communicated with his own hand, accompanied by the most obliging expressions of kindness. . . . The correspondence thus begun suffered no interruption at any future period

until Washington's death in 1799.[7]

Anderson's wide reading and varied interests are reflected in the *Bee,* which embraced articles on agriculture, economics, history, biography, science and invention, morals and manners, travel, grammar, architecture, and especially, literature. Poetry, tales, satire, criticism, and miscellaneous essays dot its pages.

The poetry is of two kinds: original and reprinted. One of Anderson's aims as editor was to encourage the writing of original literature, including works by obscure or unknown writers. The bulk of this original verse is brief, conventional, superficial. Themes most frequently treated include love and marriage, friendship, death, the beauty of nature in a particular locale, and pious musings on human life. Though much of this verse is mediocre, some few pieces possess touches—sincerity of feeling, understanding of human nature, freshness of concept or of description—that raise them above the commonplace. Among the love lyrics, "The Fair Thief" (2:71) pays graceful tribute to a maiden's charms, and "The Siege of a Heart" (16:24) describes the various unsatisfactory suitors whom Belinda rejects before finding her ideal mate. "The Death Song of a Cherokee Indian" (2:109) captures well the pride, courage, and defiance of a noble captive facing death. "Anacreontic" (4:338) gives a light, clever comment on sleep—when rejected, when welcomed. "The Country Parson. In Imitation of Horace's Country Mouse" (12:215) draws ludicrous parallels in witty couplets. "View of the Last General Judgment" (5:249), a contender for the premium, describes a dramatic and vivid scene in competent iambic tetrameter couplets, ending with a prayer. Not to be overlooked are several rollicking drinking songs: "Do you sigh for the frowns of the fair?" (6:115) and an "Original Ode" on freedom (7:217) as well as some authentic folksongs in Scots dialect (7:27, 9:28).

Reprinted poetry ranged from Elizabethan to contemporary times and included the collection "Gleanings of Ancient Poetry" with selections from Southwell, Quarles, Carew, Drummond of Hawthornden, etc. There were also modern reprintings from Thomson, Burns, et al., and a few poems by the latter two marked "never before published." An unusual version of Collins's "Ode on the Popular Superstitions of the Highlands of Scotland" has the missing parts supplied by a "Mr. MacKenzie"—probably Henry MacKenzie, author of *The Mirror* and *The Lounger*.

Short tales, published in installments, appear in almost every volume of the *Bee*. Some of the titles are indicative: "Elmina, or the Flower That Never Fades"—the flower is virtue; "Hospitality and Gratitude, An Allegoric Tale"; "Indian Magnanimity"; "The Temple of the Sun, an Oriental Tale"; "Alladin the Persian." Most of the tales are romantic, sentimental, escapist. The protagonists are mainly upper-class and wealthy, or poor but honest lads on their way to becoming upper-class and wealthy. The heroines are all beautiful, magnanimous, and helpless. There is little analysis of character or motives. The settings, for the most part, are faraway exotic places. Some of the tales are allegorical; all are didactic. Most have happy endings. (In their fantasy adventures and sentiments the tales resemble the modern "soap-operas" of television and radio, and probably appealed to their readers for many of the same reasons.)

One of the most attractive features of the *Bee* is the short original satires of almost every volume; an example is "The Rights of Women," a parody of Paine, or perhaps of Wollstonecraft. Women's rights include scolding, crying, falling into fits, visiting watering places, and running up bills. "Thoughts on the Great Benefit to be derived from Want of Health (in High Life)" demonstrates that poor health (real or imaginary) is an excuse for all occasions. "The Matrimonial Creed," a parody of the Athanasian, attacks petticoat rule. "The Necessity of Roguery Exemplified" shows that rigid honesty would ruin most trades and professions, to say nothing of politics.

Literary criticism is one of the prominent features of the *Bee,* ranging from reviews of recent books to detailed discussions of individual authors or works. The reviews include books in many categories, among them literature, economics, history, travel, and education. The reviews give genuine evaluations, not merely summaries. Although the works examined became obsolete long ago, the reviews hold interest since they reveal contemporary attitudes and the criteria for excellence in the 1790s. All of the criticism is of the "common-sense" variety, expressed in layman's language for the general reader. Criticism of literature includes genres, authors, works, and critical theory.

Of the genres, drama receives most attention, and Shakespeare is the author most often discussed. There is a perceptive essay on *Othello* (1:56, 87, 132, 175); an appreciation of *The Merchant of Venice* (3:310); a spirited defense of *Coriolanus* (2:57); and a discussion of Shakespeare's "low" characters (4:290). In "Remarks on Some English Plays" Lord Gardenstone compares many of the eighteenth-century comedies and farces to those of Shakespeare with devastating results, though he acknowledges whatever merits the later plays possess. His "Travelling Memorandums" also contain brief references to Shakespeare.

Critical essays on individual authors are frequent. Horace, George Buchanan, Will Drummond of Hawthornden, Edward Young, Allan Ramsay, and Laurence Sterne are subjects of separate articles. Anderson himself contributed a series of "Critical Remarks on Some Celebrated English Authors"—detached comments on Hume, Robertson, Johnson, Gibbon, Gilbert Stuart, Dr. John Gregory, Shakespeare, Milton, and Sterne. By the 1790s Pope and Johnson had become controversial figures, and articles both attacking and defending them appeared in the *Bee.* There are tributes in verse to Jean Froissart and to Henry MacKenzie.

Among the best critical essays are those dealing with some aspect of critical theory. "On Imagination and the Abuses of It" (1:252) points out that imagination is allied with both feeling and judgment. "Its sphere is among what is magnificent and beautiful in matter or what is heroic and amiable in mind; its business is to seize upon whatever is astonishing, or melt with whatever is amiable." It is not confined to poets, but may appear in Euclid or Locke as well. It is not necessarily extravagant: "A poet must never lose sight of Nature. He may deal with what does not exist, but it must be possible." The essay in its broad outlines follows Addison and Akenside, while anticipating the exaltation of the imagination by Coleridge, Shelley, and Keats.

"On the Essential Qualities of Poetic Genius" expands upon Horace's dictum that a poet must have three qualities: invention, a diviner mind (than a non-poet), and talents of powerful expression. "On Wit" describes the types of modern wit: that of the scholar, which depends upon nature and natural sympathy; that of the man of fashion, which consists of puns, double entendres, jingling verses, and swearing; and that of the country squire, which comprises a round of merry stories, brought forth as occasion warrants. The essay closes with ironic advice on how to attain wit.

Miscellaneous essays deal with manners and morals in the light, didactic vein of the *Tatler** and *Spectator** (for both, see *AAAJ*). Others describe pastoral poetry and old Scotch folk songs. One contrasts the novels of Fielding and Richardson (8:132); another discusses the novels of Smollett (7:130). Separate series of articles trace the history of professional authorship, and delineate the advantages of periodical publications. The life of James Thomson the poet is sketched (6:281). Several pieces entitled "Hints to the Learned" suggest new projects for scholarship and for the recovery and preservation of ancient manuscripts. A number of essays treat the topic of education, and include a systematic plan for an improved educational regime for the young.

Disciplines related to or peripheral to literature, such as history and biography, and other arts such as painting and architecture, also received their share of attention in the *Bee*. A strong interest in history is reflected in the *Bee*'s many articles on life in the past, not only in Scotland but throughout the world. Antiquities of Scotland—dhunes and towers, old vitrified fortifications, ruins of castles and abbeys—are portrayed both in words and in sketches. Customs and traditions are reported: the uncouth manners of Europeans in early times, the preparation of a youth for knighthood in the age of chivalry, the Moorish ceremony of succession to the throne, and, in more recent times, slavery in Jamaica, and Brahmin widows immolating themselves on their husbands' funeral pyres. There are articles on the character of the Arabs; on the interment of Charles I (with the detail that his head was sewn back onto his body before burial); and on the varieties of men, differentiated by merely accidental variations of color, language, or habits. Readers of the *Bee* were thus not only furnished with brief interesting glimpses of particular aspects of the past, but were frequently reminded of the larger world outside Scotland, and the essential brotherhood of all men.

Biography was another concern of the *Bee,* which printed items ranging from short anecdotes to detailed biographical sketches, and from the Roman poet Horace to the contemporary Prince of Denmark. Most of the biographees are English or Scotch, with a few Frenchmen (Jean Froissart; Abbé Blanchet; Cardinal Dubois; Jean de la Fontaine); a few Germans (Frederick II of Prussia, counts Hertberg and Lalippe); a few Russians (Peter the Great, Chancellor Andrei Ostermann, Grigori Potemkin); an occasional Swede or Swiss or Dutchman. Among biographies of natives of Great Britain are those of Will Drummond of Hawthornden; Sir James Stewart Denham; George Buchanan, the poet; George Heriot, goldsmith and philanthropist; Andrew Fletcher, Lord Milton;

and several Scots who won fame and fortune abroad: John Law of Laurieston; John Stewart, Constable of France; and Marshal General James Keith, who held commands in both Russia and Germany. Almost all leading British politicians of the eighteenth century are included: Walpole, Carteret, Chatham, Pelham, the Duke of Newcastle, the Earl of Bute, William Grenville, Lord North, George III, the Marquis of Rockingham, and others. The clergy are well represented, from John Knox to John Wesley and George Whitefield.

Series of articles deal with categories: "A Biographical Catalogue of Eminent Scottish Artists," "British Officers Who Fell in the Russian Naval Service," "Obituary of the Learned." Adam Smith is the subject of several accounts, as is the poet James Thomson. Other men of letters chronicled include Dr. Thomas Blacklock, Sir James Foulis, and Henry Home, Lord Kames. Of more than seventy biographical items published in the *Bee,* only four deal with women: Joan of Arc; Madame de Maintenon; a Miss Linsey, locally famous for her charities to the poor; and Mrs. Sheridan, the singer.

Anderson's failing health, and a financial collapse brought on by the failure of subscribers to keep up their payments, halted publication of the *Bee* in January 1794. One of the most informative and wide-ranging periodicals of its age, it amply fulfilled the purposes for which it had been founded. Nor has its usefulness ended. *"The Bee* can today still entertain and improve readers," write two modern critics, "almost two centuries after its last number was published."[8] It is a magazine that deserves to be better known.

Notes

1. From the prospectus, pp. ii and iv.

2. George S. Marr believes that these illustrations are the most important contribution of the *Bee* to the history and development of magazines. See *The Periodical Essayists of the Eighteenth Century* (New York, 1924), pp. 253–55.

3. Prospectus, p. iv.

4. Most articles in the *Bee* are signed with a pen name; some are unsigned. An original run of the magazine reproduced on microfilm in the Early British Periodicals series and bearing the name "B. B. Wisner" contains handwritten identifications of many of the authors of the articles. Where possible, these have been verified from other sources and have been found to be correct. Where it has not been possible to verify them, Wisner's ascriptions have been tentatively accepted.

Dr. Blacklock sent in a few short poems over the name "Adam Eard-Apple." James Thomson Callander wrote the article on *The Merchant of Venice,* and many of the essays, including the series "On the Political Progress of Britain." This series was so radical that, despite some commentary by way of rebuttal, Anderson was hauled before the authorities and asked to reveal the author—which he refused to do. When the investigation into authorship persisted, Callander hinted that the articles were the work of Lord Gardenstone, whose secretary he had been. Upon this false accusation, Anderson disclosed that Callander was the real author. Callander shortly thereafter fled to America. His articles in the *Bee* are signed "Timothy Thunderproof," "Bombardinion," "Popocurante," "J.T.C.," "B.B.," etc.

Dempster wrote an account of a voyage to the Hebrides by the British Fisheries

Society, essays on the cotton and woolen manufactures of Scotland, a "political Bible," and other pieces. He signed himself "Alphabet," and "An Old Correspondent."

5. They were mostly local Scots: James Haig and R. Strong of Leith; A. Hector McNeil; W. MacNab; "Mr. Ramsey of Auchertype"; William Druthin; P. Felmat; D. Hopkins; J. C. Lettsom; Dr. Thomas Anderson, a surgeon of Leith; and a number of clergymen, both Scotch and English.

"Matthew Bramble" [Andrew McDonald] and Mrs. Charlotte Smith are quoted, as are many other authors and works, but it is not always clear whether the works were originally written for the *Bee,* or had been published earlier elsewhere. The editor's son, James Anderson, Jr., also contributed articles on economic and political subjects, signed "Trader" or "Trader Political."

6. See *The Works of Jeremy Bentham,* ed. John Bowring (1833–1838; reprint ed., New York, 1962), 10:127–29, 254–58, 288.

7. From Anderson's pamphlet, "Correspondence Between General Washington and James Anderson," p. 10.

8. Daniel Fader and George Bornstein, *British Periodicals of the 18th and 19th Centuries* (Ann Arbor, 1972), p. 12.

Information Sources

BIBLIOGRAPHY
Cook, Davidson. "The Editor of 'The Bee.' " *Times Literary Supplement,* 27 August 1920, pp. 552–53.

Currie, A. W. "Literary Views of Adam Smith." *Notes and Queries* 207 (1962):296.

Dictionary of National Biography. S.v. "Anderson, James (1739–1808)."

Fader, Daniel, and Bornstein, George. *British Periodicals of the 18th and 19th Centuries.* Ann Arbor, 1972.

Graham, Walter. *English Literary Periodicals.* New York, 1930.

Marr, George S. *The Periodical Essayists of the Eighteenth Century.* New York, 1924.

Mullett, Charles F. "*The Bee* (1790–1794): A Tour of Crotchet Castle." *South Atlantic Quarterly* 66 (1967):70–86.

Sinclair, George A. "Periodical Literature of the Eighteenth Century." *Scottish Historical Review* 2 (1905):136–49.

"Sketch of the Life of Dr. James Anderson." In *The Gentleman's Magazine* for December 1808. Vol. 78, pt. 2, pp. 1051–54. (Obituary notice—unsigned.)

INDEXES
Each volume indexed.

REPRINT EDITIONS
Microform: Early British Periodicals (UMI), reels 55–56.

LOCATION SOURCES
American
Widely available.
British
Widely available.

Publication History

MAGAZINE TITLE AND TITLE CHANGES
The Bee, or Literary Weekly Intelligencer.

VOLUME AND ISSUE DATA
>Volumes 1–18, numbers 1–162, 22 December 1790–1 January 1794. (Number 163, "Appendix to *The Bee, or Literary Weekly Intelligencer,* vol. XVIII, Wednesday, 21 January 1794.")

FREQUENCY OF PUBLICATION
>Weekly.

PUBLISHERS
>Volumes 1–3: Mundell and Son, Parliament Stairs, Edinburgh. Volumes 4–6: James Anderson, Edinburgh. Volumes 7–17: Printed for the Editor (James Anderson), Edinburgh. Volume 18: Printed *By* the Editor (James Anderson): Edinburgh.

EDITOR
>James Anderson.

Daniel L. McCue, Jr.

BELLE ASSEMBLÉE, LA

When confronted on the title page with the announcement, "Addressed Particularly to the Ladies," one can easily enough dismiss *La Belle Assemblée,* first published in February 1806, as an early nineteenth-century light-weight forerunner of *Ladies Home Journal.* One scholar has in fact described *La Belle Assemblée* as "a magazine without intellectual pretensions,"[1] but even considering the murky dimensions of the term *intellectual,* this scholarly dismissal was made with insufficient evidence and deliberation.

Does the dismissal, for example, consider the frequent mathematical and scientific articles, and the serious reviews of contemporary literature? And how many modern magazines worthy to be called "intellectual" would publish in supplementary issues the whole of *Paradise Lost,* Thomson's *Seasons,* and Young's *Night Thoughts?* According to a study of women's magazines, *La Belle Assemblée* and several survivors of the eighteenth century remained "frank, vigorous and mentally stimulating" until at least 1825.[2]

Little of the contents of the magazine could in fact be described as lightweight. Each issue contained a portrait and "Biographical Sketch[es] of Illustrious Ladies" (later changed to "Illustrious Characters" to include an occasional male). There were also sections entitled "State of Society and Manners" and "Retrospect of Politics." And there were a number of departments dealing with the fine arts, music, poetry, and drama. Only in the second division of the work, "La Belle Assemblée," is there any relenting; here fashions are illustrated and discussed.[3] Most of these features continued throughout the history of the journal in one guise or another.

With the scope of coverage involved, the proprietors quite legitimately puffed their magazine—"the comprehensiveness of its instruction, the variety of its amusements, and the elegance of its embellishments."[4] But the proprietors seemed at first undecided about the tone the magazine would assume. They rejected one contribution as "too dry and serious for a work that chiefly aspires to light instruction and elegant amusement" (1 [May 1806]). Two months before, however, they had offered their magazine as a vehicle for conveying "some precept or admonition [under cover of fiction] to friends or relations," as they claimed happened in the *Spectator** (see *AAAJ*) and other periodicals early in the previous century (1 [March 1806]). Two years later the moral tone was again an issue; there was an apology for having printed "certain expressions, too unguarded and indelicate."[5] The pages concerned were cancelled, reprinted, and redistributed, and "a Lady of great distinction in the literary world" would in the future supervise each issue.

Considerable attention was directed toward literature in the initial series of *La Belle Assemblée*. Some reviews were scattered in issues, but most appeared in semi-annual supplementary numbers. These reviews were modeled on those in the *Edinburgh Review**: they were "to confine their criticism chiefly to ORIGINAL DISCUSSION, and to trespass as little as possible upon the ordinary functions of a Review" (1 [July 1806]). The poetry, when not extracted from publications of established poets, would be the work of readers, but it was to be superior work in either case: "To our poetical correspondents we . . . beg leave to observe, that no poetry, but of a very high quality indeed, can obtain admission into this work" (1 [September 1806]).

John Bell, the publisher of *La Belle Assemblée,* began a new series of the magazine in January 1810, but it remained very much the same.[6] There was an additional signature (sixteen pages) and some new features were announced on the title page: "A New System of Botany and a Series of Original Music. By Mr. Hook." Reviews of new publications and dramatic productions appeared under a new section, "Monthly Miscellany"; light news under "Incidents near London" and "Provincials." Requests were quickly made for "Original Communications" on all subjects, "written in a chaste and classical manner" (2d ser., 1:170). "Whenever pecuniary recompense is required," the editor added, "it shall be liberally granted."

In the third volume of the second series, songs (with both words and music) appeared by "Mr. Dibdin," presumably either Charles Dibdin or one of his sons. Anonymous serialized novels, such as "Oakwood House" and "Hymenaea in Search of a Husband," began about this time, as well as illustrated patterns for needlework. More weighty matter likewise continued; in May 1812 (pp. 271–80) appeared "A Circumstantial Account of the Assassination of Mr. Perceval by John Bellingham," and in the supplement to volume 8 of the second series the whole of *The Book (or Proceedings of Inquiry into the Conduct of the Princess of Wales in 1806)* was printed. But, generally, public affairs were already beginning to be slighted by the magazine.

Literary reviews in the second series appeared in both the monthly sections (noted above) and in the semi-annual supplements—"Containing a Critical Review, and Abridgment of the Most Distinguished Works of Literature." By 1819 some reviews also appeared under "Literary Intelligence"—reviews of works "of light nature, and novels" (2d ser., 20 [August 1819]). Heavier items continued to be reviewed in the supplements.

In 1815 the drama reviews expanded to include Parisian theaters, and in the following year French fashions and literature were also reported upon by correspondents in Paris. This new French interest stayed with *La Belle Assemblée* until the very end.

Two shifts in formats occurred during the second series, both of them slight: in volume 9 (1814) of series 2 the titles of departments changed and a chronicle was added; in volume 24 (1821) of that series even less of the magazine was affected. By that time, however, the articles on science, especially those on botany, had all but stopped, and a new "Universal Advertising Sheet" (sixteen pages) appeared in February 1820, celebrating patent medicines and other such products and services. Despite these changes, however, the contents remained more or less intact.[7]

Volume 24 of the second series carried the same address of John Bell's establishment as the preceding volume, but his name had been silently removed as publisher and replaced by the phrase "The Proprietors." This situation continued for several volumes until G. and W. B. Whittaker (and Oliver and Boyd, Edinburgh) assumed publication. Several announcements of improvements were made; finally in January 1825 a third series was announced by the same publishers.

The contents of the third series were described as "chaste and correct, elegant and tasteful in their character, . . . contributed by some of the most accomplished writers of the age, . . . [and] *entirely original.*" In short, more of the same, for the few differences in format were slight. Literary reviews became a section of the "Monthly View," which was a single, long, critical monthly report; this review was reinforced by a "Sketch of the Progress and State of Literature for the Last Six Months," appearing in the semi-annual supplements along with summaries of fashions for the same period. And for some reason the table of contents for each issue disappeared by volume 7 of the third series.

In volume 9 of the third series the editor listed the new "literary talent" at the service of *La Belle Assemblée:* "*Don Telesforo de Trueba y Cosio, author of 'Gomez Arias,' and 'The Castilian'; Derwent Conway, Esq., author of 'Tales of Ardennes,' &c.; Edward Southey, Esq., the brother of the Laureate; Thomas Pringle, Esq., author of 'Ephemerides, or Occasional Poems written in Scotland and South Africa'* " (p. i). Mrs. Hofland and Misses Porter, Browne, and Webb completed the list, but the next volume reminds the reader of the "many others whose names we have not received permission to announce" (3d ser., 10 [December 1829]).

In the same issue the editor bemoans the demise of both Ackerman's *Repository of Arts* and Sharpe's *London Magazine* * but exults that *La Belle Assemblée* is now "the *only* embellished periodical devoted to the *Fine Arts and Poetic Literature,* to all that can interest and charm the cultivated mind; in fact, the only Magazine that is received in the first circles of fashion—the only Magazine that is honored and sustained by the ennobling sanction of the highest orders of the State.''

The last part of the description introduces the question of the politics of the magazine, and in fact the political position of *La Belle Assemblée* is hard to describe inasmuch as it is rarely, if ever, noticeable. In volume 8 of the third series, the readers are told that, on the eve of the passage of the Great Reform Bill, while all the campaigning is going on, with little written ''but reform and anti-reform tirades,'' the magazine ''has kept on 'the even tenor of its way,' '' as is not surprising in a periodical aimed at ''the first circles of fashion.''

Meanwhile the magazine had been changing hands frequently. Edward Bull became publisher in January 1832; nothing else changed except that verse was printed in single-column for the first time. And for the first time we are told the name of an editor, ''The Honorable Mrs. Norton'' (1808–1877), a poet and granddaughter of Richard Brinsley Sheridan, the dramatist.[8]

The single-column verse continued into the *Court Magazine and Belle Assemblée,* which was a new magazine established by Edward Bull in June 1832 as a continuation of *La Belle Assemblée.* The verse itself was scattered through each issue even though the rest of the format remained more or less the same. Mrs. Norton may have continued as editor for a while; volume 4 (1834) contained a ''Genealogical Memoir'' of her in one issue and some of her verse in another.

When Edward Churton became sole publisher in June 1834, a new section appeared reflecting the new title of the magazine, ''The Court,'' described as a ''chronicle of the movement of the Court.'' But the *Court Magazine and Belle Assemblée* was to last only a few more volumes and was to end in a haze of confusion. Volume 9 (1836) announced on the title page that it was also volume 2 of a new series even though there is no indication of a new series in the previous volume. Then volume 10 (1837) carried a new title on the title page for the volume, the *Court Magazine and Monthly Critic,* even though the titles for each issue continued as the *Court Magazine and Belle Assemblée.* By volume 11, however, every vestige of the title *La Belle Assemblée* had disappeared from the magazine.

Notes

1. Donald H. Reiman, ed., *The Romantics Reviewed* (New York and London, 1972), Part B, 1:81.

2. Cynthia White, *Women's Magazines* (London, 1970), p. 38.

3. Only in the first two volumes is this section shown in the table of contents to be clearly a second main division of each issue, but this effort seems to have been aimed at keeping the more frivolous material separate.

4. *La Belle Asemblée* 1 (February 1806), reverse of the contents page. Hereafter cited in the text; each citation will refer to the unnumbered page on the reverse of the contents page of the issue in question unless a page number is given.

5. *La Belle Assemblée* 5 (September 1808), reverse of the contents page. In the next

number the offending article is identified as a translation of an essay from the French on personal beauty, one "too literally translated."

6. In 1806 John Bell's son, John Browne Bell, began a complementary periodical, *Le Beau Monde*,* which was clearly modeled on *La Belle Assemblée* but attempted to appeal to both sexes. See Stanley Morrison, *A Memoir of John Bell* (London, 1930), p. 65.

7. One poetical contributor for the years 1820–1824 has been identified—Mary Leman Rede, sister of William Leman Rede, the dramatist. See *Notes and Queries,* 6th ser. 10 (1884):408.

8. Laman Blanchard (1804–1845) has been identified as an editor during the 1820s; see Felix Sper, *The Periodical Press of London* (Boston, 1937), p. 19. No authority is given for this identification.

Information Sources

BIBLIOGRAPHY
Morrison, Stanley. *A Memoir of John Bell*. London, 1930.
Notes and Queries, 6th ser. 10 (1884):408.
Sper, Felix. *The Periodical Press of London*. Boston, 1937.
White, Cynthia L. *Women's Magazines 1693–1968*. London, 1970.
INDEXES
Each volume indexed.
REPRINT EDITIONS
Microform: Early British Periodicals (UMI), reels 749–754. EP Group, Wakefield, England.
LOCATION SOURCES
American
Complete run: Boston Public Library.
Partial runs: Widely available.
British
Complete run: National Library of Ireland.
Partial runs: Widely available.

Publication History

MAGAZINE TITLE AND TITLE CHANGES
La Belle Assemblée, or Bell's Court and Fashionable Magazine, February 1806–May 1832. *The Court Magazine and Belle Assemblée,* June 1832–June 1837. (Continued as the *Court Magazine and Monthly Critic* * [see *VEA*].)
VOLUME AND ISSUE DATA
Volumes 1–7, February 1806–December 1809 (volume 1 has two parts covering all of 1806).
New series, volumes 1–30, January 1810–December 1824.
Third series, volumes 1–15, January 1825–June 1832.
FREQUENCY OF PUBLICATION
Monthly.
PUBLISHERS
Volume 1–new series, volume 23: John Bell, at various addresses: Southhampton Street, Strand, London (volumes 1–7–new series, volume 6); Clare Court,

Drury Lane, London (volumes 7–17); 104 Drury Lane, London (volume 18); 4 Brydges Street, Covent Garden, London (volumes 19–23).

Volumes 24–27: "Published for the Proprietors," 4 Brydges Street, Covent Garden, London (address of John Bell's establishment but his name has been removed as publisher). Volumes 28–30–third series, volumes 1–5: G. and W. B. Whittaker, Ave Maria Lane, London; Oliver and Boyd, Edinburgh. Volumes 6–8: George B. Whittaker, London. Volumes 9–14: Whittaker, Treacher, and Co., Ave Maria Lane, London. Volume 15: Edward Bull, 26 Holles Street, Cavendish Square, London.

EDITORS

Unknown, February 1806–1832 (third series, volume 15). Laman Blanchard, possibly editor during the 1820s. The Honourable Mrs. (Caroline) Norton, 1832 (volume 15, third series—length of her editorship unknown).

John O. Hayden

BLACKWOOD'S EDINBURGH MAGAZINE

In the second decade of the nineteenth century, the Whig *Edinburgh Review** and its publisher, Archibald Constable, ruled the publishing world of Edinburgh. The Tory response was John Murray's plodding, London-based *Quarterly Review*.* William Blackwood, head of the moderately successful Edinburgh publishing firm bearing his name, seized what he viewed as his chance to publish a Tory periodical to offset the *Edinburgh*'s growing influence and, probably just as important, Constable's increasing local success. In addition, Blackwood wanted his periodical to be a magazine rather than a review, that is, to offer humor, a variety of articles, and original creative works.

Eventually, Blackwood succeeded. *Blackwood's Edinburgh Magazine,* always conservative in its political discussions, also published poetry by several important authors and articles by major essayists: Thomas De Quincey, for example, found a comfortable home in *"Maga,"* as it was affectionately called, for "On Murder Considered as One of the Fine Arts," the four installments of "Suspira De Profundis," "The English Mail Coach," and "The Vision of Sudden Death," in addition to many shorter pieces.

Maga's most important contribution to English literature, however, was its publication of original fiction, often serialized. The tales it included in its pages and reprinted in several series of collections helped make magazines "the cradle of Victorian fiction."[1] In addition to novels by authors best forgotten, *Blackwood's* became the medium for John Galt's first literary success, "The Ayrshire Legatees," in 1820, followed the next year by "Annals of the Parish"; for frequent appearances of Edward Bulwer-Lytton's work, including "The Caxtons" from April 1848 to October 1849 and "What Will He Do With It" a decade later; for George Eliot's first published fiction, "Scenes of Clerical Life," in eleven installments in 1857; for five novels by Anthony Trollope, published between 1866 and 1882; and by the end of the century for Joseph

Conrad's "Karain," "Youth," "Heart of Darkness," and "Lord Jim."

In its literary criticism, *Blackwood's* made little attempt to present a consistent point of view. Often, especially in its early years, the politics of the authors being reviewed seemed as significant as the works being discussed. In addition, critics writing for *Blackwood's* used pseudonyms or wrote anonymously, and thus were able to damn an author in one article and praise him in another. Such a practice guaranteed controversy and, as it turned out, success.

However, the *Edinburgh Monthly Magazine,* William Blackwood's original title, was phenomenally dull. From April through September 1817 the editors, James Pringle and Thomas Cleghorn, offered dry compilations of contemporary events in England, the rest of Europe, and America; commercial and agricultural reports; and births, marriages, and deaths. They also offered unimaginative articles about new developments and publications in literature and science.

Realizing that his project's success was threatened, Blackwood stepped in, changed the name and, until his death in 1834, controlled editorial policy. At times, however, his writers seemed to be running the publication. Certainly, the policy of anonymous authorship kept offended parties off guard and enabled Blackwood as publisher and as anonymous editor to shift blame between writers and editor without ever clearly admitting his own responsibility.

Many readers were offended by the biting satire and heavy-handed humor of the articles and reviews in *Blackwood's.* Some attacks on perceived enemies, both political and literary, in fact were nearly libelous. In the infamous October 1817 issue, the first of the renamed and revamped magazine, Blackwood's three major contributors—John Gibson Lockhart, John Wilson, and James Hogg—collaborated on a "Translation from an Ancient Chaldee Manuscript," actually a thinly veiled allegorical attack on Edinburgh literary and publishing society. The mock-scriptural language, pretending to transcribe a recently discovered manuscript, attacked Whigs and Whig organs, including Constable and his *Edinburgh Review.* While Walter Scott enjoyed the jests, he persuaded Blackwood to withdraw the article from subsequent printings: Scott had promised to contribute to *Blackwood's,* and wanted a vehicle more acceptable to local publishers. Blackwood agreed, and the "Chaldee Manuscript" became a collector's item. It also caused *Blackwood's* to be an instant success. William Blackwood happily paid off those people threatening suit, though he disclaimed any role in the article.[2]

In the same issue Lockhart published the first of a series of articles, "On the Cockney School of Poetry," accusing Leigh Hunt of moral depravity and of being "an underbred person" (2:30). Subsequent articles contained further *ad hominem* attacks as well as attacks on the quality of literature written by the subjects. In November Lockhart compared Hunt and Byron, obviously favoring the latter but warning that Byron should not—at peril of his art and character—associate with Hunt. Throughout the series Lockhart maintained his anonymity by hiding behind the signature "Z," despite public pressure from Hunt and William Hazlitt (a regular contributor to Hunt's weekly *Examiner* *), to whom he referred in his August 1818 essay as "pimpled." William Blackwood paid damages and expenses to prevent the threatened lawsuits.[3]

Blackwood's Edinburgh Magazine for October 1817 also contained a major attack by John Wilson on Samuel Taylor Coleridge in general, and on the *Biographia Literaria* in particular, which Wilson dismissed as rambling, disorganized, and obscure. Coleridge considered suing, but chose not to.[4]

Based on the "Chaldee Manuscript," the "Cockney School," and the attack on Coleridge, we may too easily view the early *Blackwood's* as entirely negative. However, subsequent articles on Coleridge were positive, Lockhart viewing "The Rime of the Ancient Mariner" as "original," "touching," and a clear indication of Coleridge's "poetical genius" (6:3–12). In fact, Blackwood even asked Coleridge to contribute; in November 1819 he published a sonnet in *Maga*. Earlier, John Wilson had attacked William Wordsworth in the June 1817 *Edinburgh Monthly Magazine:* while calling Wordsworth a "lyrical ballad-monger," he nonetheless maintained that Wordsworth's "poetry is less absurd than his criticism" (1:265–66). In an anonymous letter published in October, Wilson defended Wordsworth against his own criticisms, but in November attacked again. Over the next four years, however, Wilson and Lockhart praised his poetry, and Wordsworth published several sonnets in the magazine.

Keats and Shelley also received abuse, though for different reasons. Lockhart first attacked Keats in his fourth "Cockney School" article, when he called *Endymion* "drivelling idiocy" (3:519). Shelley's political and moral stances were anathema to Lockhart and to George Croly but, while Croly called *Adonais* "this unintelligible stuff," Lockhart genuinely appreciated Shelley's abilities: "Under due discipline and self-management," he maintained, Shelley "will be a great poet" (10:697). During Shelley's lifetime, *Blackwood's* reviewed every publication known to be his, and included lengthy quotations. In fact, the magazine contained passages from all the poets it discussed, and thus was an important medium through which the reading public became acquainted with the English Romantics.

Blackwood's also played a significant role in introducing German literature to an English audience. The twenty-seven numbers of "Horae Germanicae," for example, appearing between November 1819 and August 1828, included both discussions and translations of Schiller, Goethe, Lessing, and other German Romantics. In addition, Thomas De Quincey contributed several articles on German prose fiction. But it was apparently John Gibson Lockhart, having visited Germany and heard Fichte lecture, who was particularly influential in creating an audience for German Romanticism. He and Robert Pearse Gillies wrote most *Blackwood's* articles on German literature during this time.[5] *Blackwood's* legitimately claimed credit for being the first periodical in Great Britain to do "justice" to German literature (31:693). But the magazine also contained articles on other Continental literature, with particular emphasis later on Spanish, French, Scandinavian, and Italian literature.

Throughout the nineteenth century *Blackwood's Edinburgh Magazine* developed strong loyalties in its authors: John Wilson contributed 500 articles over a thirty-five year period; in 1831 Archibald Alison began an association of nearly a quarter of a century, and in 1844 his son began over fifty years of contributions; in 1839 W. E. Aytoun started his twenty-five years of publications in the magazine; from 1839 to 1871 William Henry Smith published over 125 essays; John Galt, Caroline Bowles, George Croly, G. R. Gleig, D. M. Moir, and J. H. Burton also contributed over long periods of time. *Maga's* policy of anonymity allowed its authors to write with relative impunity; when signatures did appear, they were a means of obscuring authorship rather than clarifying it. "Z" was generally Lockhart, "Christopher North" was Wilson, and "The Ettrick Shepherd" was James Hogg. But some evidence exists that William Blackwood's writers may have occasionally exchanged signatures to confuse readers. "Timothy Tickler" most often was Lockhart, but was sometimes William Maginn, who helped found *Fraser's* * in 1830.

Often articles were collaborative creations, as the *Noctes Ambrosianae* initially were, though John Wilson ultimately assumed the responsibility of writing them. These imaginary conversations at a neighborhood pub were published from March 1822 through February 1835, and covered a broad range of topics political, literary, and social. *Bentley's Miscellany* * (see *VEA*) called the series "one of the greatest *coups* ever achieved by Blackwood," especially because for a long while much of the reading public believed that the conversations had actually taken place.[6] William Blackwood III attempted unsuccessfully to revive the *Noctes Ambrosianae* in 1899.

At the beginning of the 1826 volume, Blackwood printed an "Apologia" praising Scott, Byron, Wordsworth, Southey, and Coleridge. More important, this preface represented a change in *Maga's* approach to criticism from the early vicious, often *ad hominem,* attacks to a more responsible form. Lockhart had just left to edit the *Quarterly Review;* Maginn was being phased out by Blackwood himself; Wilson had become less vehement. Over the next quarter of a century Walter Savage Landor occasionally contributed, and often argued over editorial changes; Alfred Mallalieu contributed major papers on politics and political economy; Samuel Warren, whose reputation as a fiction writer briefly rivaled Dickens's, was active for *Blackwood's;* John Sterling published poetry and sketches until his death; and George Henry Lewes published essays on science and literature into the early 1860s. In July 1852 Margaret Oliphant's short story, "Katie Stewart," appeared in *Blackwood's,* the first of nearly a half century of her fiction and criticism in its pages.

John Blackwood became editor in May 1845, after Alexander Blackwood's death. In September Archibald Alison expressed the class-conscious view of *Blackwood's,* prevalent in all areas, here specifically in literature: the contemporary novel has concentrated on "the very lowest stages of society"; as a result, current fiction does not "elevate and purify the minds" of its readers (58:341–42). These ideas—that the upper classes are the proper subjects of all literature, which must itself provide a moral lesson—pervade the literary criticism during much of John Blackwood's tenure. The Rev. John Eagles, a frequent contributor around the middle of the century, especially of a series of "Letters to Eusebius," returned often to these premises. In October 1848, for example, he attacked Dickens's "purpose . . . [as] a very mischievous one . . . [intended] to decry, and bring into contempt as unfeeling, the higher classes." But for Eagles, another test for literature was the extent to which it presented life realistically: Dickens gave "a very false view of life as it is" (64:468). A decade later George Henry Lewes maintained that the novelist must "represent" human life; but those descriptions that disgust while serving no other purpose should be omitted (86:99–113).

Eagles and Lewes reflected the moral view of literature taken by *Blackwood's* at this period, but the magazine's truly reactionary nature was perhaps best exemplified in an article by Margaret Oliphant. One cannot improve upon the existing literature of the masses, she wrote in August 1858, without "taking into full account all the class-characteristics which have helped it into being." Mrs. Oliphant admitted that "it is not with a very lofty opinion of the multitude" that she has discussed the literature that has emanated from the lower classes; in fact, they are no more heroic, honest, or sincere than are members of the other classes: "Their limited opportunities of observation . . . confer upon them all a certain class in consequence and want of logic, . . . a propensity to blame somebody for every grievance or hardship they experience" (84:214–15).

The seriousness of Mrs. Oliphant's attack on the literature of the lower orders—and on the lower orders themselves—should not blind us to the continued existence of satirical humor in *Blackwood's* throughout the century. Probably the most famous satire of mid-century *Blackwood's* was W. E. Aytoun's May 1854 review of the allegedly soon-to-be-published *Firmilian*. The poem, quoted at length, was actually Aytoun's own creation and was intended to lay to rest the "Spasmodic School" of poetry. Aytoun succeeded, and his review has become a minor classic of justifiable literary homicide (75:533–51).

In the last third of the nineteenth century, *Blackwood's* settled into middle age. It renewed its readers' acquaintance with authors it had discussed, not always favorably, earlier in the century; Mrs. Oliphant's series, "A Century of Great Poets, From 1750 Downwards," which appeared from June 1871 through December 1872, emphasized biographical information on Cowper, Scott, Wordsworth, Burns, Shelley, Byron, and Goethe, but also attempted to provide historical continuity among them. Replacing the diatribes of some of Wilson's and Lockhart's early reviews was the moderation that comes with historical perspective.

Perhaps best exemplifying both this moderation and the resulting loss of fire in its articles was the view of the magazine taken by a more radical periodical, the *Examiner*. Writers in that weekly paper acknowledged in 1867 that *Blackwood's* "maintains its vigour as a leading representative of Tory thought . . . although it is hardly as fresh in spirit as when the 'Noctes Ambrosianae' perfumed its pages."[7]

Some things, of course, never changed. Even after Charles Dickens's death,

Blackwood's had little good to say about him. "Dickens has scarcely left us one character which is above ridicule," Mrs. Oliphant wrote in 1871, "or of which we can think with a smile and a tear mingled, as it is the highest boast of your true humorist to mingle smiles and tears." Because he never attained a "fine sense of moral excellence," he was limited in what he could achieve artistically (109:675, 694). Although Mrs. Oliphant lacked the venom of a "North" or a "Scorpion," she reflected a characteristic of *Blackwood's* throughout the century: always opinionated, often wrong, but never in doubt.

So it was to the end of the century with *Maga*'s view of Thomas Hardy. As early as 1879 he was labeled "an original thinker and writer, although less original than he appears at first sight," and *The Return of the Native* was described as "labouring after originality which has rather the air of affectation" (125:322, 344). Those were the nicest comments about Hardy to appear in *Blackwood's* and they were not by Margaret Oliphant. When she turned her attention to his novels, she found them "immoral," "shameful," and "coarsely indecent" (151:464–74). Long after he ceased writing novels, and long after Mrs. Oliphant had died, Thomas Hardy refused to forgive her criticism.

In the last decade of the century, the amount of both literature and literary criticism in *Blackwood's* declined slightly in favor of more articles on politics, on the background to and information about the Boer War, on sporting activities, and on foreign travel. But William Blackwood III, who had become editor in November 1879, did not turn his back on the poetry and especially the fiction of which *Maga* had always been justifiably proud. By 1900, with Joseph Conrad's second major serialized work, "Lord Jim," appearing in its pages, *Blackwood's Edinburgh Magazine* was building on its past successes as it looked ahead to a new century.

Notes

1. *Contemporary Reviews of Romantic Poetry*, ed. John Wain (London, 1953), p. 25.

2. For more discussion of the "Chaldee Manuscript," see Josephine Bauer, *"The London Magazine, 1820–29," Anglistica* (Copenhagen, 1953), 1:53–54; Edgar Johnson, *Sir Walter Scott* (London, 1970), 1:613–15; Mrs. M(argaret) O. Oliphant, *Annals of a Publishing House: William Blackwood and His Sons. Their Magazine and Friends* (Edinburgh, 1897), 1:130–31.

3. Edmund Blunden, *Leigh Hunt and His Circle* (New York, 1930), pp. 130–32. Wain, pp. 179–80, maintains that the series of articles, like the "Chaldee Manuscript," was a group undertaking; Lockhart nonetheless has been given responsibility for authorship. A. L. Strout, *A Bibliography of Articles in "Blackwood's Magazine," Volumes I Through XVIII, 1817–1825*, Library Bulletin no. 5 (Lubbock, Tex., 1959), p. 7, estimates that in the early years of the magazine Blackwood paid well over 800 pounds for libel and legal expenses.

4. "Some Observations on the 'Biographia Literaria' of S. T. Coleridge, Esq.," *Blackwood's* 2 (1817):3–18. A. L. Strout, "Samuel Taylor Coleridge and John Wilson

of *Blackwood's Magazine," Publications of the Modern Language Association* 48 (1933):100–128, maintains that Wilson's reviews were based more on his personal relationship with the author at the particular time than on the merits of the work.

5. *German Literature in British Magazines, 1750–1860,* ed. Bayard Quincy Morgan and A. R. Hohfeld (Madison, Wis., 1949), pp. 51–57.

6. "Of the Late Professor Wilson," *Bentley's Miscellany* 53 (1854):583.

7. *The Examiner,* 5 January 1867, p. 7; 7 December 1867, p. 776.

Information Sources

BIBLIOGRAPHY

Alison, Archibald. *Some Account of My Life and Writings.* . . . Edited by Lady Alison. 2 vols. Edinburgh, 1883.

Douglas, Sir G(eorge) B(risbane) S(cott). *The Blackwood Group.* Edinburgh, 1897.

Eagles, John. *Essays Contributed to "Blackwood's Magazine."* Edinburgh and London, 1857.

Gifford, Douglas. *James Hogg.* Edinburgh, 1976.

Gordon, Martha H. *Christopher North: A Memoir of John Wilson.* 2 vols. Edinburgh, 1862.

Graham, Walter. *English Literary Periodicals.* 1930. Reprint. New York, 1966.

Johnson, Edgar. *Sir Walter Scott.* Vol. 1. London, 1970.

Lang, Andrew. *The Life and Letters of J. G. Lockhart.* 2 vols. London, 1897.

Lockhart, John Gibson. *Memoirs of the Life of Sir Walter Scott.* Vol. 3. Boston, 1901.

Neal, John ["Holmes, Carter"]. *American Writers, a Series of Papers Contributed to "Blackwood's Magazine," 1824–1825.* Edited by Fred Lewis Pattee. Durham, N.C., 1937.

Noctes Ambrosianae. 4 vols. Philadelphia, 1843. ("New" and "revised" editions were published throughout the rest of the century.)

Oliphant, M(argaret) O. *Annals of a Publishing House: William Blackwood and His Sons. Their Magazine and Friends.* 3 vols. Edinburgh, 1897–1898. (Volume 3 is written by Mrs. Gerald Porter.)

Roberts, David. "The Social Conscience of Tory Periodicals." *Victorian Periodicals Newsletter* 10 (1977):154–69.

Stories from "Blackwood." New York, 1852.

Strout, A(lan) L(ang). *A Bibliography of Articles in "Blackwood's Magazine," Volumes I Through XVIII, 1817–1825.* Library Bulletin no. 5. Lubbock, Tex., 1959.

Strout, Alan Lang. "John Wilson, 'Champion of Wordsworth.' " *Modern Philology* 31 (1934):383–94.

Strout, A(lan) L(ang). "Samuel Taylor Coleridge and John Wilson of *Blackwood's Magazine." Publications of the Modern Language Association* 48 (1933):100–128.

Tales from "Blackwood." 12 vols. Edinburgh, 1858–1861; New Series. 12 vols. Edinburgh, 1878–1880; Third series. 6 vols. Edinburgh, 1889–1891.

Travel, Adventure and Sport. From "Blackwood's Magazine." 6 vols. Edinburgh, 1889–1891.

The Wellesley Index to Victorian Periodicals, 1824–1900. Edited by Walter E. Houghton. Vol. 1. Toronto, 1966.

INDEXES

Each volume indexed. 1817–1881 in *Poole's Index*. 1824–1900 in *Wellesley Index* 1. Index to volumes 1–50, separately published, 1855 (rpt. ed., Carrollton Press).

REPRINT EDITIONS

Microform: Microcard Editions, Washington, D.C.; Princeton Microfilm Corp., Princeton, N.J.; UMI.

LOCATION SOURCES

American

Widely available.

British

Widely available.

Publication History

MAGAZINE TITLE AND TITLE CHANGES

The Edinburgh Monthly Magazine, April–September 1817. *Blackwood's Edinburgh Magazine,* October 1817–December 1980.

VOLUME AND ISSUE DATA

Volume 1, number 1–volume 328, number 1982, April 1817–December 1980. (Volumes consisted of six monthly issues, and contained April through September issues or October through March issues through volume 8. Volume 9 contained April through August (part 1) 1821; volume 10 contained August (part 2) through December 1821. Thereafter, volumes contained January though June issues or July through December issues. The second printing of number 7 (October 1817) omitted the "Chaldee Manuscript" and contained a revised version of "On the Cockney School of Poetry.")

FREQUENCY OF PUBLICATION

Monthly.

PUBLISHERS

Volume 1, number 1–volume 1, number 6, April–September 1817: William Blackwood, 17 Prince's Street, Edinburgh/Baldwin, Cradock, and Joy, Paternoster Row, London. Volume 2, number 7, October 1817: William Blackwood, 17 Prince's Street, Edinburgh/John Murray, Albemarle Street, London. Volume 2, number 8, November 1817: William Blackwood, 1 Prince's Street, Edinburgh/T. Cadell and W. Davies, Strand, London. Volume 2, number 9–volume 3, number 15 or 16, December 1817–June or July 1818: William Blackwood, 17 Prince's Street, Edinburgh/Baldwin, Cradock, and Joy, Paternoster Row, London. Volume 3, number 6 or 7–volume 4, number 22, July or August 1818–January 1819: William Blackwood, 17 Prince's Street, Edinburgh/John Murray, Albemarle Street, London. Volume 4, number 23, February 1819: William Blackwood, 17 Prince's Street, Edinburgh. Volume 4, number 24–volume 10, number 55, March 1819–September 1821: William Blackwood, 17 Prince's Street, Edinburgh/T. Cadell and W. Davies, Strand, London. Volume 10, number 56–volume 27, number 166, October 1821–May 1830: William Blackwood, 17 Prince's Street, Edinburgh/T. Cadell, Strand, London. Volume 27, number 167–volume 36, number 227, June 1830–October 1834: William Blackwood, 45 George Street, Edinburgh/T. Cadell, Strand, London. Volume 36, number 228–

volume 48, number 302, November 1834–December 1840: William Blackwood and Sons, 45 George Street, Edinburgh/T. Cadell, Strand, London. Volume 49, number 303–volume 57, number 356, January 1841–June 1845: William Blackwood and Sons, 45 George Street, Edinburgh/22 Pall Mall, London. Volume 58, number 357, July 1845–: William Blackwood and Sons, 45 George Street, Edinburgh/37 Paternoster Row, London. (American edition: Leonard Scott & Co., begins with volume 1 in 1833 and is double-numbered with the Edinburgh edition.)

EDITORS

James Pringle and Thomas Cleghorn, April–September 1817. William Blackwood, October 1817–September 1834. Alexander Blackwood, October 1834–April 1845. John Blackwood, May 1845–October 1879. William Blackwood III, November 1879–.

Roger P. Wallins

BRITISH AND FOREIGN REVIEW, THE

From its establishment in 1835 until its demise nine years later, the *British and Foreign Review; or, European Quarterly Journal* was less a literary than a political organ. Its wealthy owner, Thomas Wentworth Beaumont, was a member of Parliament for Northumberland and president of the Literary Association of the Friends of Poland; and the journal's prospectus, which was probably written by Beaumont, laid out a political program in no uncertain terms. The *British and Foreign* aimed to disturb English complacency over the plight of less fortunate nations and to emphasize the close relation between social and intellectual progress at home and abroad. In particular, the review pledged to campaign for the active containment of Russian imperialism and the restoration of Polish independence. Only by strong measures, the prospectus argued, could the liberty of England and western Europe be secured (1:1–4). At first these narrow goals were pursued so stringently that the *Athenaeum*** commented on the new journal's "Russo-phobia," but the Polish question assumed less prominence over the years.[1] Throughout its existence, however, the review sustained its disillusionment with existing parties and advocated moderate constitutional reform.[2]

The *British and Foreign*'s first five numbers appeared under the rapid succession of three different editors: William Wallace, Gilbert Ainslie Young, and Beaumont. Each gave relatively little space to artistic and literary subjects. The condition of English letters was presented as lamentable. While the prospectus found literature "at a low ebb" (1:2) despite the vital importance of current topics deserving exploration, the review's introduction suggested, surprisingly, that the sterility of literature came from the public's exclusive interest in politics. Poetry was "almost extinct," Sir Walter Scott was overrated and vulgar, and even Lord Byron fell victim by courting the public taste (1:13–15).

During the journal's first three years the most frequent contributor on literature seems to have been Wallace, a critic of mechanically neoclassical tastes. Finding present literature "humble, perishable, profuse, and non-descript" (1:190), Wallace looked back to better times and condemned the Lake and Cockney schools of poetry as "excrescences" whose day was nearly past (1:216). His distaste for fashionable novels and light literature made favorite targets of Edward Bulwer-Lytton and Frances Trollope. In the former, Wallace detected some talent; nonetheless, Bulwer became the regular example of prurient vanity and effeminate puffery who shamelessly corrupted popular taste. For Mrs. Trollope's "political obscenities" Wallace had even less patience (6:232). Unable to forgive her for trivializing Metternich in *Vienna and the Austrians,* Wallace recommended that her next tour be to St. Petersburg, where her qualities would be fully appreciated (6:679).

In the fall of 1836 the editorship of the *British and Foreign* passed to John Mitchell Kemble, the Anglo-Saxon scholar and archeologist. A man of strong opinions, Kemble changed the review's profile considerably—and helped to bring on its collapse. "[A]ll reform is misplaced," Kemble told William Bodham Donne, who had become the chief literary contributor, "which does not begin by reforming our system of *education.*" [3] That conviction remained visible in the subsequent thirty numbers, which featured a dozen extensive treatments of the subject: Russian and Indian education, popular and religious instruction, the Oxford movement (a dim view), and suggestions for reforms at Oxford and Cambridge (the latter, by Kemble himself, a splendid example of his wit and common sense). The heading of these last articles, "British and Foreign Universities," suggests that the editor had hopes for a continuing series. But a new emphasis on educational reform was not the only, or even the most significant, alteration made by Kemble. He was determined to bring down "the old tattered rag of *Classicism* in English poetry" that Wallace had helped unfurl. [4] Sympathetic articles appeared on Wordsworth, Coleridge, and Shelley. Politics and social issues continued to be discussed, but greater space than before was given to art and literature.

If Wallace had been harshly pessimistic in his assessments of current letters, Donne noticed those works that permitted him to remain charitably hopeful. A tolerant critic, he was most provoked by unsound scholarship and doctrinal poetry. Even Bulwer's *Athens* was complimented for its unusual accuracy (7:36), while Walter Savage Landor's imaginary conversations were faulted mainly for their author's misguided approval of "crafty and encroaching" Russia and his fanciful conceptions of Plato and Dante (5:43, 7:521). Donne warmly welcomed Henry Hallam's *Introduction to the Literature of Europe* as well as current editions of verse drama and pre-Romantic, Romantic, and contemporary poets. Several of his individual judgments may be pointed out as typical. In light of the continuing growth of knowledge, Donne believed that Shelley's intellectualism had destined him to influence future poets more than any writer of his age (10:125). Yet "the desire of Beauty," not the expression of truth, remained "the artist's one and indivisible aim" (12:183). Thus Keats belonged to "that laureate fraternity which time does not antiquate nor fashion supersede" (10:126).

During the last three years of the *British and Foreign,* George Henry Lewes contributed eight essays that further marked how far the review had moved from its original literary orientation—and, indeed, from the explicitly Romantic standards that Donne had more recently applied. In search of firm aesthetic principles, Lewes propounded a theory of art that spurned older ideas of poetic composition. The poet did not imitate nature or reflect eternal truth; he symbolized relative truths through emotive images. For Lewes, the intellectual role of poetry (which Donne had touched upon) deserved greater emphasis, since the best verse elevated its reader *"into a higher sphere of thought"* (13:18). Lewes's long and influential article on Goethe (14:78–135) again stressed the cognitive value of poetry: the objectivity of poets like Dante, Shakespeare, and Goethe far excelled the egocentrism of a Wordsworth, Byron, or Shelley. Further, Lewes's three balanced essays on current French thought helped offset the review's prejudice against life and literature just across the Channel, one instance of which may be found in "The Works of George Sand" (8:360–90), probably by H. F. Chorley.

Kemble's stable of contributors was large, and under his editorship the *British and Foreign* attained a wide scope. For example, the 718 pages of volume 9, which represented half the year 1839, contained articles on English painting, the rural police, free grain trade with Hungary, international law, Lamartine's poems, the Turkish commerce treaty, general domestic reform, the Russian church, the life of Joseph Brant Thayendenegea (a Mohawk Indian), Maurice and Gladstone on church-state relations, the African slave trade, Neapolitan farming, Meadows Taylor's *Confessions of a Thug,* the Dutch-Belgian conflict, England under Edward VI, the Irish question, and the problem of authorship in Homer.

Kemble thus was able to pursue the liberal aims outlined in the review's first number, if not exactly to establish "a common standard of taste and public opinion among the enlightened and polished nations of Europe" (1:10). Although the restoration of Polish independence seemed increasingly unlikely, other early goals remained intact, and under Kemble the *British and Foreign* presented sensible essays on domestic reform as well as articles geared to diminish England's intellectual insularity (some of them, like Lewes's, of impressive breadth). The contributions may have "want[ed] lightness," as Thackeray told the editor,[5] but their humanitarianism was always evident and their information was generally solid.

The last number of the *British and Foreign Review* appeared in December 1844; the journal was "finally doomed by a combination of financial difficulties, administrative incompetence, and disagreements between editor and proprietor."[6] After a time its circulation shrank; at least from 1837 on, Beaumont annually sustained a considerable financial loss. There were also problems in keeping up regular publication. Occasionally a long time elapsed between an article's acceptance and its appearance, so that it became outdated. Perhaps more important, Kemble and Beaumont had lasting differences of opinion, chiefly on foreign policy and, ultimately, on who was to run the review. Before circumstances became intolerable, however, Kemble was able to transform a rather narrow, ideological journal into "a periodical of the highest class," as the *Times* noted in its obituary, "which exercised considerable political and literary influence."[7]

Notes

1. *Athenaeum* no. 472 (1836):801.

2. See [H. B. deGroot], *"British and Foreign Review:* Introduction," *The Wellesley Index to Victorian Periodicals 1824–1900,* ed. Walter E. Houghton (Toronto, 1979) 3:63–64. On political and technical matters, the present discussion closely follows de Groot's scrupulous account, and the *Index* has also been the source for attributions of articles in the review.

3. Quoted by Peter Allen, *The Cambridge Apostles: The Early Years* (Cambridge, England, 1978), p. 164.

4. Quoted by de Groot, 3:67.

5. *The Letters and Private Papers of William Makepeace Thackeray,* ed. Gordon N. Ray (Cambridge, Mass., 1946), 1:325. Thackeray's one probable article, "Manners and Morals in St. Petersburg" (8:33–63), was glibly anecdotal, but Kemble was not persuaded on the point; finally Thackeray gave up: "I am not going to write for the B & F. Jacky Kemble gives himself such airs that he may go to the deuce his own way" (*Letters,* 1:420).

6. de Groot, 3:72.

7. "Death of Mr. John M. Kemble," [London] *Times,* 31 March 1857, p. 11.

Information Sources

BIBLIOGRAPHY

Block, Maurice. *"The British and Foreign Review; or European Quarterly Journal":* Ein Beitrag zur Geschichte der Aufnahme deutscher Literatur in England. Göttingen, 1921.

Groot, Hans Bart de. *"The British and Foreign Review* (1835–1844): An Account of Its Publishing History, Its Political Attitudes and Its Contributions to Literary Criticism." Ph.D. dissertation, University of London, 1969.

———. *"British and Foreign Review:* Introduction." *The Wellesley Index to Victorian Periodicals 1824–1900.* Vol. 3. Edited by Walter E. Houghton. Toronto, 1979.

———. "Lord Brougham and the Founding of the *British and Foreign Review."* *Victorian Periodicals Newsletter* no. 8 (April 1970):22–32.

Winegarner, Lela. "Thackeray's Contributions to the *British and Foreign Review."* *Journal of English and Germanic Philology* 47 (1948):237–45.

INDEXES

Each volume indexed; *Poole's Index; Wellesley Index* 3.

REPRINT EDITIONS

Microform: Early British Periodicals (UMI), reels 41–44.

LOCATION SOURCES
American
    Widely available.
British
    Complete runs: Birmingham Public Library; Birmingham University Library; British Museum; Cambridge University Library; Edinburgh University Library; Glasgow University Library; Guildhall Library; St. Andrews University Library.
    Partial runs: Bedford Public Library; Bodleian Library; Royal Institute; Sheffield Public Library.

Publication History

MAGAZINE TITLE AND TITLE CHANGES
    The British and Foreign Review; or, European Quarterly Journal.
VOLUME AND ISSUE DATA
    Volumes 1–18, numbers 1–35, July 1835–December 1844.
FREQUENCY OF PUBLICATION
    Quarterly, but after April 1840 issue becoming irregular.
PUBLISHERS
    Volumes 1–5, July 1835–October 1837: James Ridgway and Sons, Piccadilly, London. Volumes 6–18, January 1838–December 1844: Richard and John Edward Taylor, Fleet Street, London.
EDITORS
    William Wallace, volume 1, July 1835. Gilbert Ainslie Young, volumes 1–2, October 1835–January 1836. Thomas Wentworth Beaumont, volumes 2–3, April–July 1836. John Mitchell Kemble, volumes 3–18, December 1836–December 1844.

                                                        K. K. Collins

BRITISH CRITIC, THE

The *British Critic,* throughout its fifty-year existence, maintained its fidelity to "British principles in Church and State." In its third and fourth series (from 1825), it became primarily a theological journal in content and perspective, but it began in 1793, in the late eighteenth-century tradition, to provide complete coverage of all worthwhile publications in all fields of knowledge. In prefaces to the semi-annual volumes of the first series (to 1813), the editors enunciated and then more stridently defended this "old plan" of reviewing against the new one of the *Edinburgh Review,** in which fewer works were treated in longer, livelier articles.

With a change of editors in 1814, the *British Critic* compromised somewhat the principle of complete coverage for longer reviews of fewer works. Short notices of books and a monthly list of publications were retained; however, the encyclopedic organization of reviews by subject area was lost with the termination of the synthetic prefaces to each volume. The magazine retained some popular appeal and financial success, although the butt of remarks such as those in the satiric monthly, *Scourge,** which referred to the magazine in 1811 as "totally destitute of elegance and spirit" and "only read by a few clergymen of the old school." [1]

In 1791 some Tory churchmen proposed a new review be set up to oppose the primarily liberal bent of the four major reviews (the *Monthly,** the *Critical,** the *English,** and the *Analytical** [for all, see *AAAJ*]) which supported reformers and Dissenters. For its entire first series the *British Critic* was edited by Rev. Robert Nares, assisted by Rev. William Below, a classicist. The review was owned jointly by them and the publishers, the Rivingtons. Initially they were aided financially by a hundred pounds of William Pitt's Secret Service money. [2] Although the magazine remained absolutely anti-revolutionary, at one point asserting the need "to preserve our rights, liberty, and property from the attacks of Republicans and Levellers" (34:iv), there is no evidence of direct government interference or financial help beyond the first year. The religious influence, however, was pronounced. Initially, according to Derek Roper, it was "middle-of-the-road Anglicanism"; later, in the third and fourth series, under editors of High Church persuasions, it became "an organ of the Oxford Movement." [3]

The goal of comprehensiveness is evident from the first number, in which the editors proposed "to give a fair and satisfactory account of every publication," thus making the *British Critic* "a repository of the most accurate knowledge this distinguished country can produce" (1:ii). Throughout the first series, after editorial commentary varying from a paragraph to three pages, the prefaces contained a lengthy summary digest (later called the "retrospect") of the best works that were reviewed in the six numbers of that semi-annual volume. The editors stated that "literary history essentially demands selection. To tell the reader what deserves his notice is the highest service we can render" (3:iv, 4:iii).

These highlights were always short (at most a sentence or two) and positive, since they represented those works reviewed favorably. While the "retrospect" (ranging from ten to twenty pages per volume) has little critical or analytical value, it serves an important function of collecting and cross-referencing reviews under topic headings. The "convenient arrangement" always began with the topic of divinity ("the first in . . . dignity and value") and included the following in roughly the same order throughout the first series: divinity, history, biography, antiquities, travels, topography, politics, law, philosophy, poetry, English classics republished, translations of classical authors, mathematics, medicine, chemistry, natural history, botany, miscellaneous.

Following the preface was an alphabetical "Table to the Books Reviewed" in the volume. At the end of each volume was "An Index to the Remarkable Passages in the Criticisms and Extracts." End matter in each number included a "British Catalogue" and a "Foreign Catalogue," which contained one- or two-paragraph notices arranged by subject, a "Monthly List of Publications" by subject, "Literary Intelligence," and notes to correspondents. The catalogues contained up to fifty short notices in about twenty-five pages, after fifteen to twenty works were featured in the major reviews. Each number contained about 120 pages.

With the retirement of the original editors and the start of a new series in 1814, the prefaces and retrospective summaries were dropped. Since there was no table of contents, but only the alphabetical list of books reviewed, the *British Critic* lost the helpful feature that provided a ready reference by subject to the books reviewed. Reviews were longer; however, the emphasis was shifting. Although major literary figures like Byron and Wordsworth continued to be covered, in the first volume of the new series twelve books of sermons were reviewed, an average maintained throughout the series. By 1816 the short review catalogues had disappeared.

In 1825 a third series shifted to quarterly publication and an explicit emphasis on "criticism, theology, classical learning, and science" (1:v). There were about fifteen long articles per number, which averaged about 260 pages. With series 4 (1827) the title was expanded to include the *Quarterly Theological Review and Ecclesiastical Record*. Subject matter focused on sermons, essays and letters, church-related history and philosophy, with end matter including "State of the Dioceses in England and Wales," "Proceedings of the Universities" (Oxford, Cambridge, Dublin), and "List of Foreign Theological Publications." In 1834 there was a change in the end matter to expand the "Ecclesiastical Record" from a list of preferments to "a general survey of the times . . . as they affect the cause of the Church." Also added was a catalogue of short reviews organized by subject area (3d ser., 15:227). Few works of general literature were reviewed in this last phase. Exceptions were a sixty-seven page review, generally hostile and moralistic, of Byron's *Letters and Journals* by Thomas Moore and the *Life* by John Galt (9:257–324). Lyell's *Principles of Geology* was treated respectfully but ultimately rejected as "unscriptural" (15:334–63).

Earlier the *British Critic* reviewed the first edition of Malthus's *On the Principle of Population* and, while ridiculing some of his arguments and evidence, gladly supported the implications that undermined Godwinian philosophy. Malthus "sets himself seriously to refute this doctrine of perfectability" (17:279). The magazine maintained a conservative attitude toward the poor and lower classes. In reviewing a five-volume "Report of the Society for Bettering the Conditions of the Poor," the reviewer concluded "that every kind of assistance that is injudiciously given to another induces a habit of helplessness; and that all relief which is not so given as to be a spur to industry has a tendency to promote idleness" (35:617).

For over twenty years the *British Critic* reviewed Wordsworth favorably, supporting him consistently in the major publications of his career. *Lyrical*

Ballads (1798) was praised for "that judicious degree of simplicity" that corrects excessive refinement and even leads to "the sublime." The editors added in their preface: "Nor does the author so often descend to the flat ground of mere conversation in rhyme, as he seems to threaten" (14:364–65, xv). In a deviation from the policy of periodicals not to review subsequent editions, the *British Critic* carried a detailed analysis of *Lyrical Ballads* (1800) by John Stoddard, who was known to the Wordsworth circle.[4] He argued that Wordsworth's sentiments and subject matter were appropriate and his "natural style" and "simple language" expressed genuine human passion (17:125–31). In long, laudatory, and analytical reviews of *The Excursion* (1814), *Peter Bell* (1819), and *The Waggoner* (1819), the *British Critic* described Wordsworth, in effect, as a meditative or devotional poet who could "spiritualize all sensible objects," thus evaluating his common subjects and leading his readers to sympathy and moral instruction (2d ser., 3:452–53; 2d ser., 11:584–603).

The magazine defended poets, like Wordsworth and Montgomery, whose work sustained a spiritual interpretation. Regarding the latter, the editors commented: "When we speak with delight of the elegant and touching compositions of Montgomery, we are not . . . supported by fashion; we rather take under our protection a poet who, by some critics, has been harshly and unjustly treated" (36:xvii).

In their prefaces to the first series, the editors expressed not only a sense of duty to retain the reviewing principle of complete coverage, but also a ministerial goodness in limiting the retrospective summaries in their prefaces to the best and most useful works, "books that *are* worth buying" (32:iv). In the prefaces there was no trace of "the books and authors we have been obliged to censure" (40:iii). A major objection to the "new plan" of the *Edinburgh Review,* popularized by other periodicals, was the spreading tone of "ridicule," as reviewers indulged their wit to amuse readers at the expense of authors. The *British Critic* asked for justice rather than "sneer, sarcasm, and severity." The editors in 1809 pledged to "persevere" in following the "old plan" (34:v–vi). But the coverage often contained puffs for works published by the Rivingtons, the publisher, such as *The Christian Minister's Affectionate Advice to a Newly-Married Couple,* and the eighteen-page review of the editor Nares's *Essays* (1:220, 37:154–71).

In 1811 the editors attacked the *Edinburgh Review* and its imitators directly. While expressing no surprise at their popularity, the editors in "self-defence" argued that "they are not in fact Reviews, as to their principle design and plan." The editors asserted that "Reviews ought to be, so far as is practicable, complete histories of contemporary literature." In addition, the editors plugged their "half-yearly prefaces, in which we briefly recapitulate the works which best deserve attention." In comparison, the editors calculated that the *British Critic* treated about thirty-five works per month (over four hundred each year), while the *Edinburgh Review* covered no more than ten in one quarterly number.

Moreover, the long essay format of the *Edinburgh,* rather than being a balanced critique, took "the title of a book (or even several together) . . . as a mere introduction to an original dissertation" on the subject. As a result, this was not a review "but a new pamphlet on the same subject and requiring to be reviewed as much as that or those which gave occasion to it." The editors insisted that their aim was not "to diminish the sale of works reviewed," but to contribute to the "progress" of knowledge. Thus only those periodicals following the "old plan" should rightly be called reviews. "The Preface, which we are now about to begin, will contain more literary facts than several volumes of quarterly essays, however ingenious, able, or amusing" (37:iii–vi). However, trends in the reviews and the popular appeal of periodicals swept beyond the old principles of the early *British Critic,* accounting for its permutations through several series and its shifting focus to theological subjects more appropriate for its lofty critical ideals.

Notes

1. *Scourge* 1 (1811):419.
2. Derek Roper, *Reviewing Before the "Edinburgh," 1788–1802* (Newark, Del., 1978), p. 23 n. 50; p. 36 n. 147; p. 180 n. 36.
3. Roper, pp. 27, 202–3.
4. Identified by Shaver in *The Letters of William and Dorothy Wordsworth: The Early Years, 1737–1805,* ed. E. de Selincourt; 2d ed., rev. C. L. Shaver (Oxford, 1967), pp. 319–20; cf. Roper, p. 99.

Information Sources

BIBLIOGRAPHY
Hayden, John O. *The Romantic Reviewers: 1802–1824.* Chicago, 1969.
Roper, Derek, *Reviewing Before the "Edinburgh," 1788–1802.* Newark, Del., 1978.
INDEXES
    Volumes 1–20, separately published in 1804; volumes 21–42 separately published in 1815. *Wellesley Index* 4 (projected).
REPRINT EDITIONS
    Microform: English Literary Periodicals (UMI), reels 85–109.
LOCATION SOURCES
American
    Widely available.
British
    Complete runs: Bristol Public Library; British Museum; Chetham's Library (Manchester); Gloucester Public Library; Harris Public Library (Preston); Leeds University Library; London Library.
    Partial runs: Widely available.

Publication History

MAGAZINE TITLE AND TITLE CHANGES
    The British Critic, a new review, May 1793–December 1798. *The British Critic,* January 1799–December 1826. *The British Critic, Quarterly Theological Re-*

view, and Ecclesiastical Record, January 1827–December 1837. *The British Critic, and Quarterly Theological Review,* January 1838–October 1843.

VOLUME AND ISSUE DATA

Volumes 1–42, May 1793–December 1813; new series, volumes 1–23, January 1814–June 1825; series 3, volumes 1–3, October 1825–October 1826; series 4, volumes 1–24, January 1827–October 1843.

FREQUENCY OF PUBLICATION

Monthly until June 1825, then quarterly.

PUBLISHERS

Volumes 1–22, 1793–1803: F. and C. Rivington, 62 St. Paul's Church Yard, London. Volumes 23–n.s. 22, 1804–1824: F. C. and J. Rivington, London. New series 23–series 3, number 3, 1825–1826: J. Mawman, 39 Ludgate Street, London. Series 4, numbers 1–2, 1827: C. and J. Rivington and J. Mawman, London. Series 4, numbers 3–34, 1828–1843: C. and J., C. J. G. and F., J. G. and F., J. G. F. and J. Rivington (consecutively), London.

EDITORS

Robert Nares, assisted by William Below, May 1793–December 1813. Thomas F. Middleton, W. R. Lyall, Thomas Rennell, William Van Mildert, 1814–1825. Edward Smedley, J. S. Boone, J. H. Newman, and others, 1827–1843.

Nathaniel Teich

BRITISH LADY'S MAGAZINE, THE

The *British Lady's Magazine* was a monthly periodical, of eighty double-column pages, issued in two series from 1 January 1815 to 31 December 1819; the second series, from June 1817 to December 1819, was renamed the *New British Lady's Magazine, or Monthly Mirror of Literature and Fashion.* The Miltonic epigram—"Greatness of mind, and nobleness their seat / In *her* build loveliest"—which heads the first number and appears on the first page of all subsequent numbers of the first series aptly encapsulates the spirit of the magazine. The preface to volume 2 purports "to offer the female sex a work worthy of it, that should be entertaining without frivolity and instructive without dullness."

Written during the heyday of the Romantic movement with its belief in the expansive powers of the self and the extraordinary abilities of imaginative humankind, the *British Lady's Magazine* shares the predominant Romantic notions concerning mankind's educative capabilities, most especially as applied to the female sex. If Romantic poets could preach a gospel of the almost godlike creative powers of man based on the operative use of his imagination, it is little wonder that the editor of the *British Lady's Magazine* claimed similar creative, expansive powers for the "second sex." As he observes in his "Introductory Address" to volume 1, "the Principal inducement to the dedication of a new Journal to the sex exclusively, originates in a firm conviction, that the female is partaking, to an unprecedented extent, in that taste for intellectual acquirment, so perceptible in every department of civilized life." Women are to be given access to the latest news and observations in "the progressive march of science, literature, policy, morals, manners, religion, and, in short, to whatever may reasonably be expected to please or inform."

In order to understand and appreciate the special quality of its content and the general tone and mood adopted by the first editor, it is important to recognize the general instructional purpose of the *British Lady's Magazine*. Unlike the numerous reviews that were popular during this revolutionary 1798–1832 period, the *British Lady's Magazine* did not preach one opinion, harp on one political platform, or sanction insurrection and rebellion. Instead, it is marked by an open and non-partisan view of life. It presents a "liberality bounded only by decorum, good sense, and the salutary influence of a superintending spirit" and ultimately hopes to educate its female readers so that they will be able to judge and form appropriate, well-balanced, and well-reasoned opinions.

From the first, the *British Lady's Magazine* did not cater specifically to "female" concerns to the exclusion of more masculine subjects. The "departments" or standard sections that make up the first series of the *British Lady's Magazine* are wide-ranging and reflect the eccentric if not eclectic philosophy of its editor. There are sections on "The Fine Arts," "The Drama," the "Opera," and "Poetry." To satisfy the curiosity—a quality supposedly strong in the make-up of the female—the *British Lady's Magazine* included a monthly chronicle of "Occurrences, Births, Marriages, and Obituaries." Initially it covered both the metropolitan and provincial areas, but after the second number it was shortened to include just the gossip for London proper.

The *British Lady's Magazine* further offered its readers a monthly cultural calendar. Not only could feminine curiosity be satiated with frivolous society gossip like the following: "With much regret we record an action brought by Lord Roseberry against Sir Harry Mildmay, for adultery with Lady Roseberry, in which damages were laid at 30,000 pounds" (1, no. 1:79), or "Lord Byron has presented a silver vase to Mr. Walter Scott, which is estimated at the value of 300 pounds" (1, no. 6:159); but their appetite could further be whetted (and their minds expanded) by acquaintance with reviews of recent publications, works of art, and public buildings. Public exhibitions are critiqued, hours of visiting listed, and, in some cases, entrance fees quoted. For example, in the first number such diverse announcements as an upcoming lecture on the "History of the Rise and Progress of Chemical Philosophy, and its Application to Agriculture and the Arts" by W. T. Brande is found alongside a lecture by the Rev. Edward Forster "On the Poetry of Milton." One of the strongest and, perhaps, most surprising features is the magazine's solid reviews of the musical scene. With the new series this interest is even expanded to include copies of current favorite scores, for example the "Albion Country Dance" by Mr. Wilson or "The Royal Waltz" by Mr. Skarret. Throughout, the editor meticulously avoids discussions of fashion and dress and the "conventional language and *persiflage* of modern gallantry" (1, no. 1:6).

Interested in creating this "renaissance" woman, in the first series the editor, John Souter, devotes a large amount of space to political matters, "Retrospect of Foreign and Domestic Politics," in order to breed the insularity and "femininity" out of his readers. Volume 1, number 2 reports on the Congress of Vienna, while succeeding numbers in the first series closely follow Bonaparte's political stratagems and counter-stratagems. However, like the tone that is present throughout the periodical, here "a spirit of calm impartiality" (1, no. 5) reigns. "Without sacrificing the right of private judgment, [the *British Lady's Magazine*] will aim at *statement* in preference to *decision;* and, avoiding the tone dictatorial, seek rather to supply premises than to anticipate conclusion" (1:5, emphasis added).

One of the best sections in the magazine is the "Memoirs of Eminent Women" included in the first three volumes. Covering both contemporary and historical figures (for example, Lady Jane Gray; Mrs. Lucy Hutchinson; Mrs. Susanna Centlivre, the dramatist; Lady Grace Gethin, who wrote *Reliquae Gethinianiae;* Mary Beale, the painter; Margaret Roper; Margaret Cavendish, the Duchess of Newcastle; and Mrs. Hannah Cowley, the dramatist), these vignettes are offered as role models for the numerous readers. As the editor writes about Madame de Staël, one of the early figures considered:

> Yet far more beneficial has this extraordinary woman been, in giving an example to her own sex not so much of mingling or interfering in the labyrinths and ill-temper of political feeling, as in shewing them that, by a just cultivation of their mental powers, they may afford council as well as endearment to those on whom their solicitude is placed." [1, no. 1:22]

Since several of the women featured in the memorable profiles are authors, one would expect to find a preponderance of women writers and their work reviewed and presented in the literature and fine arts sections of the *British Lady's Magazine*. But most contributions were unsigned in the first series, and it is difficult to determine exactly the proportion of male and female contributors; however, signed articles and letters in the second series do indicate a majority of women—Mary Lamb was one of these. In the literary review sections, mention is made of women who publish, but there is no distinction made between good and not-so-good writers. For example, Mrs. West's *Alicia de Lacy, an Historical Romance* keeps company with *Christabelle, the Maid of Rouen; a Novel Founded on Facts,* by Mrs. Hanway, while Anna Laetitia Barbauld's "Eighteen Hundred and Eleven; a Poem" can be found next to Byron's "Lara." Lord Byron is a favorite of the *British Lady's Magazine* audience, for "the novel softness of their subjects, and the peculiarities of their language . . . have captivated ladies' hearts with a success far above all other productions of the present day" (1, no. 1:175). Leigh Hunt and William Wordsworth are also singled out and praised for their style.

With the 1 November 1815 issue a new note suddenly appears in the magazine: learning becomes a more serious business. The "Lady's Cabinet of Literature" is introduced and becomes a standard feature. "The Mirror of the Metropolis," with its critiques of new buildings, theater schedules, and the like, continues the chatty society gossip, but a more refined tone has entered into the observations. Similarly, there is now a new "Foreign Influence" section which provides monthly commentaries on France, Spain, India, and other countries. "Fashions of London and Paris" becomes a regular feature together with "Domestic Hints" such as how to make currant wine. The primary object remains "that of illustrating principles connected with the improvement of the intellectual qualities of the fair Sex" (2, no. 1:12), yet, paradoxically, there is a definite shift with this number and in the entire second series toward more typically "feminine" concerns. After the November issue there is a marked increase in female contributors both in the superficial letters to the editor and in the more substantial literary contributions.

The new series, or *New British Lady's Magazine, or Monthly Mirror of Fashion,* which began on 1 June 1817, more informally known as McKay's *New British Lady's Magazine,* continues the earlier editorial policy of feminine instruction: "The Editors . . . would countenance the erection of a judicious and elegant Academy for the maturer Mind—a College, wherein advanced Juvenility can be instructed in Moral Obligation and Personal Accomplishment; and where its Professors can establish their seat, and interchange classical inquiry. . . . In short, this Miscellany shall hold intellectual requisites, so as to raise up and support the Female, and induce her not to remain second in mental acquirement" (n.s. 1, no. 1:iii–iv). However, there is more focus on "her happiness" and "relaxation" and on "pieces tending to amuse" in the new pages. New features like the introductory "Embellishments" which in the first number include "The Parisian Lady's Walking Dress," "The British Lady's Walking Dress," and "Patterns for Needlework" indicate the changed, more frivolous mood. Further, the inclusion of advertisements, such as "Ladies Superb Leghorn Hats," "The Durability of Irish Linen," and the like together with dance instruction, directions for "Bellows for Fumigating Bees," or an article on "Whitely's Self-Acting Kitchen Range" clearly indicate the more feminine approach of the second series. The political section is greatly reduced, while sections on the drama are expanded to include a critique of "Foreign Drama." "Memoirs of Eminent Women" shrinks to "Biographical Sketches of Celebrated Women" together with vignettes of prominent males (Byron, Scott, the Prince Regent). Longer, non-edifying fiction is reprinted as well.

The *New British Lady's Magazine* had changed significantly. At the end of its publication, it mirrored the frivolousness of the Regency period with its focus on feminine, trivial concerns. Considered as a whole, though, the magazine reflects the turbulent and exciting years of the early nineteenth century.

Information Sources

BIBLIOGRAPHY

Altick, R. D. *The English Common Reader*. Chicago, 1957.
Graham, Walter. *English Literary Periodicals*. New York, 1930.
Hayden, J. O. *The Romantic Reviewers, 1802–1824*. Chicago, 1969.
Madden, Lionel, and Diana Dixon. *The Nineteenth-Century Periodical Press in Britain. A Bibliography of Modern Studies, 1901–1971*. New York, 1976.
Ward, William S. *British Periodicals and Newspapers, 1789–1832. A Bibliography of Secondary Sources*. Lexington, Ky., 1972.
White, Cynthia L. *Women's Magazines, 1693–1968*. London, 1970.

INDEXES

Each volume indexed.

REPRINT EDITIONS

Microform: English Literary Periodicals (UMI), reels 759–760.

LOCATION SOURCES

American

Partial runs: Boston Public Library; Peabody Institute Library.

British

Complete run: British Museum.

Partial runs: Aberdeen University Library; Birmingham Public Library; British Museum; Cambridge University Library; Edinburgh University Library; Glasgow University Library; St. Andrews University Library.

Publication History

MAGAZINE TITLE AND TITLE CHANGES

The British Lady's Magazine and Monthly Miscellany, 1 January 1815–1 May 1817. *New British Lady's Magazine, or Monthly Mirror of Literature and Fashion*, 1 June 1817–31 December 1819. (Also known as *McKay's New British Lady's Magazine*.)

VOLUME AND ISSUE DATA

Volumes 1–5, 1 January 1815–1 June 1817. New series, volumes 1–2, 1 July 1817–1 June 1818. 3d series, volumes 1–3, 1 July 1818–31 December 1819.

FREQUENCY OF PUBLICATION

Monthly.

PUBLISHERS

1 January 1815–1 May 1817: J. Adlard. 1 June 1817–31 December 1819: J. Robins and Company.

EDITORS

John Souter, 1 January 1815–1 May 1817. D. MacKay, 1 June 1817–31 December 1819.

Mary Anne Schofield

BRITISH MAGAZINE, THE

The *British Magazine* (1830) and its immediate predecessor, *Spirit and Manners of the Age* (1826–1829), provided the ubiquitous editor S. C. Hall with one of his first assignments—to provide (as the subtitle indicates) "a monthly journal of literature, science, and art."[1] In its year of publication, from January to December 1830, the *British Magazine* published sketches and tales by several popular nineteenth-century authors now largely forgotten. An example of these narratives is "Jack the Shrimp" (1:14–20) by Anna Maria Fielding Hall, the editor's wife, in which an apparently meek old shrimp-gatherer shocks the village by avenging himself on an evil police captain who had murdered his son and seduced his daughter. This brief tale, like the other works of fiction in the magazine, concludes with a specific moral—here, a plea for all classes to obey the law. Other similar sentimental and didactic works were contributed by Maria Jane Jewsbury ("My Last Night's Dream," 1:89–92) and Mrs. Amelia Opie ("Tale of Pere La Chaise," 1:99–102). Among the numerous poems appeared works by the then-popular "L. E. L." (Letitia Elizabeth Landon). The only writer still remembered who appeared in the *British Magazine* was John Clare, whose first publications in 1820 had brought him a measure of fame. However, neither of Clare's two contributions exemplify his distinctive style of nature poetry. "Mary Lee" (1:168) imitates but hardly equals Wordsworth's "Lucy" poems in describing rustic love, while "The Summons" (2:285–88) provides an account of Death (here personified as a rude old man) as social leveler.

Nonfictional works predominated in the magazine. It proffered such fare as accounts of faraway romantic lands and people (such as reports on the North American Indian and Thomas Pringle's serialized *South African Sketches*). Several articles recounted the legends of the Welsh, Scots, and Jews. Other accounts surveyed contemporary and historic events, and the "Modern Improvements in Science" provided a lengthy illustrated narrative of the historic competition between four rival steam engines on the Liverpool and Manchester railroad (1:121–29). Book reviews examined new works in religion and theology, history, literature, travel, science, medicine, and the arts. Overall, the *British Magazine* provides a good example of the periodical directed toward the genteel reader, fond of informative articles on improvements in the arts and science, of a regular diet of theological and inspirational discourse, and of an occasional sentimental tale or poem.

Note

1. S. C. Hall, *Retrospective of a Long Life: From 1815 to 1883* (New York, 1883), p. 181.

Information Sources

BIBLIOGRAPHY
Hall, S. C. *Retrospective of a Long Life: From 1815 to 1883.* New York, 1883.
INDEXES
    Each volume indexed.
REPRINT EDITIONS
    None.

LOCATION SOURCES
American
Complete run: University of Minnesota Library.
British
Complete runs: British Museum; Cambridge University Library; Edinburgh University Library; St. Andrews University Library.
Partial runs: Bodleian Library; Glasgow University Library; Manchester Public Library.

Publication History
MAGAZINE TITLE AND TITLE CHANGES
The British Magazine; a monthly journal of literature, science, and art.
VOLUME AND ISSUE DATA
Volume 1, numbers 1–6, January–June 1830; volume 2, numbers 7–12, July–December 1830.
FREQUENCY OF PUBLICATION
Monthly.
PUBLISHER
Frederick Westley and A. H. Davis, 10 Stationers' Court, and Ave Maria Lane, London.
EDITOR
S.(amuel) C.(arter) Hall.

Lance Schacterle

BRITISH REVIEW AND LONDON CRITICAL JOURNAL, THE

From the inception of the *British Review* in 1811, its conductors regarded their work as unique among the periodicals of the day. Among those periodicals they found no examination of contemporary society that was satisfactory to the evangelical party of the Church of England, or to "that part of the public, who view religion as a vital principle."[1] More specifically, the *British Review* viewed itself as fulfilling roles neglected by the *Edinburgh Review** and the *Quarterly Review** and by the patently religious journals, such as the *Christian Observer*. This unique middle position was set forth in an advertisement which appeared four years after the magazine's founding: "No writers have come forward to maintain in any general periodical work, the principles to which the British Review has shown itself so steadily attached; and to pursue that sober and yet warm and spirited line of thought and feeling on the great subjects of Religion, Politics, and Morals, by which this Journal has been distinguished." The advertisement further pledged the *Review* to a continuation of "sincere, steady, and consistent" advocacy of "those public maxims which constitute public strength, those vigorous and efficacious principles of social morality, which sustain the dignity and purity of private life, and that essential religion without which forms are only the trappings of imbecility." Although ultimate religious and moral ideals were in view, "the foreground in the land-scape" from which "all parts of the intellectual scene" were to be observed was an analysis of publications in a variety of disciplines.[2]

From first to last the *British Review* zealously reached toward a realization of these objectives. Through 1822 the editors apparently attempted to publish a general review of new books, frequently discussing issues from an evangelical perspective. The degree of diversity they achieved can be seen in the portioning of some 75 percent of the articles of these years among their principal interests of belles lettres, theology, politics, accounts of travel, and biography.[3] The remaining 25 percent considered publications in such fields as mathematics, history, economics, agriculture, and the sciences. A change of editors in 1823 drastically diminished this variety, with approximately 63 percent of the articles treating religious books. This change was, however, more a matter of degree than of kind, and produced an intensification of the positions held all along. The *Review* early asserted its independence from the government and political parties, abjured any association with the "disorderly fanaticism" of Methodism, and spoke of running "a great risk of being set down for methodists and saints" (1:215, 314, 361). It insisted rather that "nothing but the CHURCH OF ENGLAND as by law established will content us" (1:215). Similarly, a review in the last year took offense at the association of evangelical Anglicans with Methodists and Calvinists, but at the same time condemned "a debased and secularized Christianity" (22:465). This included what the *Review* regarded as the worldly element within the Established Church.[4]

It is hardly surprising to discover that a review that charted its course through such narrow ideological straits experienced periods of crisis. Twice it came close to extinction. The reputed founder, John Weyland, "resolved upon the bold enterprize" out of dissatisfaction "with the tone and spirit of the two popular reviews," but before the first year was completed he had resigned the editorship to one of his principal contributors, a fellow barrister and a university man with some editorial experience, William Roberts.[5] The first six numbers appeared with quarterly precision from March 1811 to June 1812; but numbers 7 through 10, directed by the apparently harried but energetic Roberts, came out at four- to six-month intervals, from October 1812 to February 1814. Then, for almost a year and a half, no *British Review* was published. It was resumed in August 1815 and brought out quarterly to the end of 1822, when Roberts abandoned his position. After a lapse of seven months a thin number 41 for July 1823 appeared, announcing the continuation of the journal under "new Conductors" but on its old principles, and suggesting, in fact, an even stronger emphasis upon religious reviewing (21:i). The remaining nine numbers were published with quarterly regularity to November 1825, when the *Review* concluded without explanation. For these last two years, however, the anonymous editor(s) made very little room in its pages for criticism of belles lettres; the *British* was virtually a theological review during its last brief phase.

In an overview of the entire span of the magazine, the brevity of the first editorship and the anonymity of the last single out for prominence William Roberts. Despite the periodical's occasional faltering under his guidance, he stamped it with the character for which it is still known. The quantity of his contributions to the first twenty volumes must have been enormous. John O. Hayden, in his study of reviewers of this period, correctly observes that "the *British* probably more than any other journal of the period was the work of one man—William Roberts, the editor."[6] Not only did he usually write the lead article, but he also extensively revised contributors' articles and often prepared about half of the reviews in an issue.[7] Increasing commitments from 1812 to 1822 sorely cramped Roberts's editorial activities so that one wonders that he could have conducted the *Review* at all. Hannah More called him "an able but over-laboured man," and Wilberforce, in his journal for 1814, wondered at Roberts's getting "through the labour he undergoes, . . . writing nearly all [of the *Review*] sometimes."[8]

How many of the more than 530 articles of the *Review* came entirely from the pen of Roberts is not now known, but his son confidently attributed some twenty-five, including all of the Byron reviews.[9] A study of these attributed essays evokes a generally consistent profile of Roberts's interests, habits of thought, critical standards, and stylistic traits that can, moreover, be seen in most of the other seventy-odd reviews of works of belles lettres. Writing much of a number and having editorial control over the remainder, he effected a remarkable consistency of viewpoint and of tone in a periodical whose struggles were more conducive to confusion. Assurance of Roberts's authorship is usually unimportant, then, since in the literary reviews under consideration here the criticism identified as his is repeatedly echoed in the unattributed articles. The result is an almost uniform critical approach, perhaps most succinctly expressed in the 1821 review of *Don Juan*, cantos 3–5. Roberts observed, "We can only review the work as Englishmen and Christians" (21:246). Patriotic and/or religious commentary accordingly found a place in almost every article.

Although the *Review* insisted on its freedom from political parties and government connections, its conservative sympathies were too strong to be long concealed (4:314). Something like an admission of this bias appeared in an 1819 examination of Lockhart's *Peter's Letters:* "We do not find fault with [the author's] toryism,—for we ourselves, compared with certain partizans, may pass for tories" (14:439). And where the cause of Mother England could be pleaded, the *Review* became blatantly patriotic, even chauvinistic. It lamented the spread of the "provokingly offensive . . . cant of cosmopolitanism" (9:8) and, in Roberts's last issue, "the misfortune of the British Review . . . that it is growing more and more British every day" (20:407). Occasional disdainful glances at foreign cultures discovered "Italian debauchery" (11:239), "unintelligible" German philosophers (15:242), and "nasty" Turks and Greeks (18:250). Ever impatient with the taste for orientalism in poetry, Roberts could say that "an English hospital is sweeter far than any Mahometan haram" (18:250). But it was for the French that the *Review* reserved its most malicious tone. They were said to be a people that "cherish a sottish lethargy on all points of intellectual or moral inquiry" (10:441) and that pamper themselves "with one or other false notion of the refined, the splendid, and the elegant" (10:447). Educated and pious women like Hannah More and Elizabeth Carter were placed in contrast to the women of the Parisian salons, those "coteries of dissipated old countesses, French flattery, French perfidy, and French intrigue" (2:288). One article ended with a warning about "the dangerous tendencies of the contagious intercourse" with France (12:70), and another speculated, "Had [Horace Walpole] never visited France, or known a single savant or savante, he might have been . . . an useful, well-mannered, well-instructed English gentleman" (13:280).

Closely related to these patriotic asides is the *Review*'s sense of high calling to be the guardian of the moral, religious, and social well-being of its readers. "The candid critic . . . will not be deterred from performing his duty, as a watchman for the moral weal of the community," and having analyzed "morbid symptoms of mind," he will "communicate the result of his inquiry to those around him, for their instruction and safety" (22:346). Seven years before, the reviewer had intoned, *"We* cannot,—we dare not,—be inconsistent; we *must* always raise our voice against all writings, in poetry or prose, in which we perceive a tendency to emasculate the British mind" (10:54). Of cardinal importance in the journal's social perspective was the moral responsibility of the upper classes, for "the people are what their superiors make them," and "a degraded peasantry always implies a degraded yeomanry and gentry" (1:412). Not a little of Roberts's distress over the works of Byron grew out of this conviction. Most significantly, the editors' moral imperative tended to determine the shape and substance of many articles. It sometimes appears that a literary work was selected for review because it lent itself to digressive commentary on a topic of religion or morality (cf. 4:453–60, 2:451).

The evangelical sensibility is widely evident, moreover, in the phraseology of the *Review*'s criticisms and in its literary preferences. Shortly after suggesting that Byron might "have interwoven a running commentary" condemning the sentiments of his Harold, Roberts exclaimed, "Perish poetry, live the moral principle—the virtuous constitution of the soul! May genius rather be dumb than endanger the hopes of an hereafter, or even disturb the righteous dispositions of our present existence!" (12:3). Furthermore, the *Review* often protested against any feature of a work that ran counter to its sense of decorum. Commenting on an edition of Anna Seward's poems, an early review complained of the "disgusting indelicacy in the allusions of this maiden lady" (2:181), and there would be numerous subsequent lecturings on unbecoming exclamations, oaths, irreverence, and causal references to the Deity. In a review of the drama *Bertram* in 1816, the author, the Rev. Charles Maturin, was thus rebuked: "On the stage there should be no tampering with the Majesty of Heaven. Neither appeals, nor addresses, nor prayers . . . can be decorously or safely introduced on the stage, or adopted for the purposes of mere poetical effect, or pretended situations'' (8:80). Sensuous poetry or fiction was eyed with suspicion. The oriental exoticism of Byron or Moore (10:31), the ''pruri- ence'' of Richardson (11:40–41), and Jane Porter's tendency to dwell too much ''on the thewes and sinews of a man'' (11:54) all brought a frown to the brow of the reviewers for the *British*. Of the major writers of the period, it was Wordsworth who received the most consistently favorable notice, for in his poetry the *Review* recognized and approved the ''meditative disposition, inno- cent tastes, calm affections, [and] reverential feelings'' (6:51). Among others making up the short list of morally inoffensive authors were Joanna Baillie, Henry Milman, William Cowper, Bernard Barton, and (above all) the sainted Hannah More, to whom the *British* usually referred with reverence or praise.[10] A longer list of generally reprehensible men of letters included Rousseau, Vol- taire, Hazlitt, and Thomas Moore.

Chief among the latter group was Lord Byron, whose rise to fame in his final decade was almost exactly contemporaneous with the fourteen-year span of the *British Review,* which devoted more than 225 of its pages in criticisms of his works.[11] Roberts, it seems, was obsessed with the poet's career and its influence on British readers and therefore wrote perhaps fifteen reviews of his works between 1812 and 1822. After Byron's death there was a final ''moral inquest'' in true Roberts style, although he was by that time no longer editor (22:345–56). He often repeated an admiration for Lord Byron's talents and stated a belief that the poet was ''no intentional enemy'' to ''the cause of virtue'' (5:511). Most of the criticism is adverse, however, especially Roberts's passionate and verbose condemnations of the moral implications of Byron's works. The critic once registered his displeasure with Byron's performances ''because we have sons and daughters: but this is but a partial reason; let us add—because Britannia has sons and daughters, and in the duration of their characteristic virtue and modesty we behold . . . the continuance of our hap- piness and greatness'' (7:456). Out of patience with the tedious sameness of a succession of Byronic heroes, he objected even more to the moral qualities of ''these sturdy sentimentalists, these elegant outlaws, these stately despisers of form'' (5:393). He summed up his repugnance well in the critique of the char- acter Manfred: ''The mischief that lurks in all Lord Byron's productions is this—they are lying representations of human nature; they bring qualities of a most contradictory kind into close alliance . . . a man of crime and blood . . . and yet a certain air of native nobleness. . . . These representations involve . . . a confusion of principle'' (10:86–87).

Byron's response to these criticisms and its consequences for Roberts and the *British Review* now make up one of the interesting and well-documented chapters of the literary history of the period.[12] Indeed, that facetious accusation of bribery in *Don Juan* (1:209–10) has done more to draw attention to the *British* than its own twenty-three volumes: ''For fear some prudish readers should grow skittish / I've bribed my Grandmother's Review—the British.'' Roberts responded obtusely to the jest in his review of *Don Juan* (August 1819) and became a literary laughingstock, a humiliation which seems to have had a part in bringing him to give up the editorship.[13]

A few of the literary reviews in the *British* are conspicuous for their lack of the features of a Roberts article. The work of some other hand is suggested by an absence of top-heavy introductions only obliquely related to the book under consideration, of moralistic digressions, of animadversions on non-British cultures, and of lordly tone. The reviews of Sismondi's *De la Littérature du Midi de l'Europe* (7:155–90), of Duppa's edition of Dr. Johnson's *Diary of a Journey into North Wales* (9:205–12), and of Gifford's edition of *Works of Ben Jonson* (10:135–55) are such articles; yet only the first can definitely be attributed to someone other than the editor. The Sismondi article is by Dr. John Mason Good, who is also credited with the authorship of four other reviews in the *British*.[14] In fact, only two other contributors, both of reviews, have been identified: John Bowdler and John Henry Newman.[15] It is probable, of course, that Weyland contributed, especially during his close association with the *Review* in its early issues, but evidence for an attribution has yet to appear.

The demise of the *British Review* is hidden in more mystery than its beginning, but the discontinuation seems to have been the result of lack of support from those quarters most likely to aid the journal. Roberts, apparently weary of editing it, humiliated by the Byron incident, and pessimistic for the future of the *Review*, dropped it at the end of 1822. A letter he wrote on 2 January 1823 to an anonymous literary associate discouraged any attempt to continue publishing under the old title a new publication which he believed would inevitably "proceed in a different spirit" from that which he had personally breathed into it. He refused, moreover, to contribute to any "new" *British Review*, not willing to "be involved in the character of a work over which I should have no control." He further suggested that the most helpful contribution he could make would be an announcement that he had no concern in the publication, thereby removing the "connection with 'my Grandmother' " which had lingered since 1819.[16] In a final analysis, however, it might be seen that the *Review* perished because it attempted to infuse literary criticism with an austere evangelicalism. The *Christian Observer,* a sympathetic sister journal, noted in 1829 that the *British* had "deserved a larger measure of patronage than it received" and that its failure "proved either that the religious world were too little literary, or the literary too little religious to tolerate the union of their respective topics."[17]

Notes

1. Arthur Roberts, *The Life, Letters, and Opinions of William Roberts* (London, 1850), pp. 37–38.

2. *The Monthly Literary Advertiser,* 10 August 1815, p. 58.

3. In the approximately 450 articles published in the *British Review* from 1811 through 1822, roughly 21 percent of the works reviewed were belletristic, 18 percent religious, 11 percent political, 16 percent travel, and 11 percent biographical.

4. See "Periodical Literature, no. III," in *The Monthly Repository* 15 (1820):673–74, where in a brief notice the *British Review* is described as "perhaps the most zealous and seemingly honest Tory Journal which is published."

5. Arthur Roberts, *Life, Letters, and Opinions,* p. 37. Another source suggests that Weyland may have had assistance in founding the *Review:* "He had a principal concern in the establishment of the *British Review* of which he was for some time the reputed editor." *A Biographical Dictionary of the Living Authors of Great Britain and Ireland* (London, 1816), p. 381. See also *Dictionary of National Biography,* s.v. "Roberts, William."

6. John O. Hayden, *The Romantic Reviewers, 1802–1824* (London, 1969), p. 51.

7. Arthur Roberts, *Life, Letters, and Opinions,* p. 40.

8. Quoted by Arthur Roberts, ibid., p. 64.

9. Ibid., pp. 44–45. For references to the various articles attributed to William Roberts by his son, see the *Life, Letters, and Opinions,* pp. 41–42, 44–45, 50–51, 53, 58, 61–62, 80, and 98. Another article, the 1811 review of Hannah More's *Practical Piety,* is attributed to William Roberts in *Letters of Hannah More to Zachary Macaulay,* ed. Arthur Roberts (London, 1860), p. 39n.

10. Hannah More (1745–1833) was once characterized in the *Review* as the " 'wisest, virtuousest, discreetest, best' woman which this age has to boast" (8:193). Although Roberts wrote the four-volume *Memoirs of the Life and Correspondence of Mrs. Hannah More* (London, 1834), he was apparently only slightly acquainted with her. His sisters, however, were her intimate friends, and through one of them he had access to her letters. More was an appreciative reader of the *British Review* (*Memoirs,* 4:6). See also Mary A. Hopkins, *Hannah More and Her Circle* (New York, 1947), p. 254.

11. All of these reviews are reprinted in Donald H. Reiman's *The Romantics Reviewed,* Part B (New York, 1972), 1:394–510.

12. For the most detailed account, see W. S. Ward, "Lord Byron and 'My Grandmother's Review,' " *Modern Language Notes* 64 (1949):25–29. See also William H. Marshall, *Byron, Shelley, Hunt, and "The Liberal"* (Philadelphia, 1960), pp. 56–57 n. 33; 86–88.

13. It is probably significant that Roberts resigned within two months of John Hunt's publication of Byron's "Letter to the Editor of 'My Grandmother's Review' " in the first issue of the *Liberal,* * for October 1822, a devastating satire written in response to Roberts's foolish review of the offensive stanzas of *Don Juan.* A year later the interlocutors of *Noctes Ambrosianae* number 12 took up the jest in a reference to "Mrs. Roberts (who) edits the British Review. It was a whim of the proprietors to try a female; so they bought Mother Roberts a pair of spectacles, a black sarsnet gown, and an armchair. . . . She delivers the contributors, and swathes their bantlings." *Blackwood's Edinburgh Magazine* 14 (1823):495.

14. Olinthus Gregory, *Memoirs of the Life, Writings, and Character, Literary, Professional and Religious, of the Late John Mason Good, M. D.* (London, 1828), p. 108.

15. Cf. *British Review* 5:273–329; 22:144–67. Excerpts are reprinted in John Bowdler's *Select Pieces in Verse and Prose,* 2d ed. (London, 1817). For Newman, see Sir William Cope, comp., *List of Works Written and Edited by His Eminence Cardinal Newman, in the Library of Sir William H. Cope, Bart., at Bramshill* (Portsmouth, England, 1885), p. 4.

16. Quoted in Arthur Roberts, *Life, Letters, and Opinions,* pp. 73–74.

17. Anonymous review of *The Portrait of a Christian Gentleman, Christian Observer* 29 (1829):432.

Information Sources

BIBLIOGRAPHY
Dictionary of National Biography. S. v. "Roberts, William."
Gregory, Olinthus. *Memoirs of the Life, Writings, and Character, Literary, Professional, and Religious, of the Late John Mason Good, M. D.* London, 1828.
Hayden, John O. *The Romantic Reviewers, 1802–1824.* London, 1969.
Hopkins, Mary Alden. *Hannah More and Her Circle.* New York, 1947.
Marshall, William H. *Byron, Shelley, Hunt, and "The Liberal."* Philadelphia, 1960.
Roberts, Arthur. *The Life, Letters, and Opinions of William Roberts, Esq.* London, 1850.
———, ed. *Letters of Hannah More to Zachary Macaulay, Esq., Containing Notices of Lord Macaulay's Youth.* London, 1860.
Roberts, William. *Memoirs of the Life and Correspondence of Mrs. Hannah More.* 3d ed. 4 vols. London, 1835.
Ward, W. S. "Lord Byron and 'My Grandmother's Review.' " *Modern Language Notes* 64 (1949):25–29.

INDEXES
   Each volume indexed.
REPRINT EDITIONS
   Microform: English Literary Periodicals (UMI), reels 184–187.
LOCATION SOURCES
   American
      Complete runs: Harvard University Library; Newberry Library; New York Public Library; U. S. Library of Congress; Williams College Library; Yale University Library.
      Partial runs: American Philosophical Society; Boston Athenaeum; Drew University; Library Company of Philadelphia; Princeton University Library; Trinity College, Watkinson Library; Union Theological Seminary Library; University of Illinois Library; Western Reserve University Library.
   British
      Complete runs: Birmingham Public Library; Bodleian Library; British Museum; Worcester Public Library.
      Partial runs: Edinburgh University Library; Glasgow University Library; Leeds University Library; Literary Philosophical Society Library; London Library; New College (Edinburgh) Library; St. Andrews University Library.

Publication History

MAGAZINE TITLE AND TITLE CHANGES
   The British Review and London Critical Journal.
VOLUME AND ISSUE DATA
   Numbers 1–50, volumes 1–23, March 1811–November 1825. (Issued quarterly during most of this period but irregularly from October 1812 to November 1815, no issues being published from March 1814 through July 1815 and in the first seven months of 1823.)

FREQUENCY OF PUBLICATION

Quarterly, with some irregularity.

PUBLISHERS

Numbers 1–6, March 1811–June 1812: Longman, Hurst, Rees, Orme, and Brown, Paternoster Row, London. Numbers 7–10, October 1812–February 1814: John Hatchard, Piccadilly, London. Numbers 11–40, August 1815–December 1822: John Hatchard, Piccadilly, London/Baldwin, Cradock, and Joy, Paternoster Row, London. Numbers 41–50, August 1823–November 1825: L. B. Seeley and Son, Fleet Street, London.

EDITORS

John Weyland (reputed editor of the first one or two numbers), 1811. William Roberts, late (?) 1811–December 1822 (through number 40). Edited by unknown person(s) supportive of the principles of the *Review* under Weyland and Roberts, 1823–1825.

Douglas K. Morris

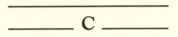

C

CABINET, THE

According to the *Satirist,** John Litchfield started the *Cabinet* in February 1807 in order to defend the professional reputation of his wife, the actress Mrs. Harriet Litchfield, to the London theater managers who had refused her services for the winter season.[1] While Litchfield denied this charge, it is true that Mrs. Litchfield's performances always received favorable reviews, including one of an amateur charity benefit in Gloucester that featured a special prologue quoted in the *Cabinet*

> We sought a well-known public fav'rites aid [Mrs. Litchfield],
> Whose talent, as we found, neglected laid.
> Nor sought in vain; she comes; and you will find
> *The London Managers have both been blind.*
>   [February 1808, p. 143]

Litchfield's association with the theater, as is evident in the focus of the *Cabinet,* was not only through his wife. He retained a boyhood friendship with Charles Mathews, the comedian (and the son of his publisher), and wrote drama criticism for the *Oracle* (probably under the pseudonym ''Chorides'') and the *World* (under ''Pollio'').[2] While his style was described as ''rhapsodical,'' his criticism has been called some of the best of the day.[3] Before beginning the *Cabinet,* Litchfield was a privy councillor and drama critic for the *Monthly Mirror,**[4] and he has been identified as the author of dramatic prologues and epilogues, ''Remarks on Mr. Coleman's Preface to the *Iron Chest,*'' and as the dramatic character for *The Life of Mr. William Parsons, Comedian.*[5]

The absorption with drama and the theatrical scene is evident in the prospectus:

> The affairs of the drama will be discussed minutely and with spirit. To effect the improvement of the English Stage, considering it as a NATIONAL INSTITUTION, highly important to the morals, and to the literary character of the country; and to advance the credit and respectability of the *members* of that profession, is the desire and shall be the strenuous effort of the conductor of the *Cabinet*. [March 1807, p. iii]

The articles on drama include readings of dramatic literature, especially Shakespeare, comments on the acting profession, reviews of current productions, and news of theatrical interest. Biographies of actors, singers, and playwrights were conspicuously featured as were historical accounts of acting and performances. The reviews, although brief, were stringent and addressed both the merit of play and performance. The gesture, delivery, movement, and suitability of an actor were especially noted. John Kemble received pointed criticism for his mispronunciation and misreadings. Listings of performances for the month were given for London, country, and occasionally foreign theaters. Reviews followed the listings. "Theatrical Intelligence" listed personal news of marriages, births, and benefits.

Throughout the biographies of famous actors, reviews of current productions, and articles on theater subjects, both in the original and in the new series, there was an underlying concern with promoting the reputation of the acting profession. Actresses were admonished to avoid roles of promiscuous women and actors were warned to live moral private lives; those actors who had elevated themselves in rank and riches or by association with eminent people were also duly noted. The concern with morality underpinned many of the miscellany articles as well.

A special feature of the magazine was the *Cabinet Edition of the English Theatre*. Popular plays printed from authoritative editions, they were accompanied by annotations, biographies, and engravings making up a volume separate from the magazine itself. Four plays, *Macbeth, Comus, The Provok'd Husband,* and *Isabella* were published. The new series discontinued this feature as unnecessarily complicated to assemble and unlikely to establish a drama library.

Other departments of the *Cabinet* featured music and art reviews, improving essays, and moral fiction. General articles presented brief historical accounts, scientific findings, exotic descriptions, and unusual anecdotes. While most of the contributions were unsigned, some previously published material was identified by author although not by source. These authors included Richard Cumberland, James Mackintosh, Tony Aston, Sydney Smith, Edward Hickey Seymour, Edmund Malone, and others. Two unsigned and original articles have been identified as written by Mrs. John Taylor and Mrs. Amelia Opie (December 1807, p. 324).[6]

The book reviews in the first four volumes focused on belles lettres and discussed a number of books briefly. The criticism frequently commented on the appropriateness and interest of the subject, the elegance and tastefulness of the language, and the forcefulness and novelty of the writing. In addition, illustrative excerpts, plot summary, and character study were provided. Besides many books of travel, history, poetry, and popular literature, the *Cabinet* reviewed Wordsworth's *Poems in Two Volumes,* Coleridge's *Prefaces and Sonnets,* Southey's *The Remains of Henry Kirke White* and *Letters from England,* Scott's *Marmion,* and Abbe Prevost's *Manon Lescaut* in the first four volumes. While there is no unifying critical theory behind these reviews, they are similar to the general critical reaction.

The review in the *Cabinet* of *Poems in Two Volumes* is noteworthy (although this work generally received unfavorable reviews) as being "perhaps the most virulent review of the lot."[7] The language of the review is unequivocal in berating Wordsworth's misuse of his poetic abilities. The reviewer deplored the fact "that a man of genius should disgrace himself by such contemptible effusions" (April 1808, p. 249). Despite Wordsworth's imagination, originality, and inspiration, his lack of taste and self-criticism were said to undercut his abilities. However, "To Sleep" and part of "Resolution and Independence" received praise. Wordsworth was also criticized by W. M. T., who wrote many of the literary articles in both series, for "juvenalities and wretched absurdities" while being admired for his originality (December 1807, pp. 258–59).

Of the other literary reviews, Coleridge's *Prefaces and Sonnets* were quickly dismissed, the former as pedantic and unoriginal and the latter as a genre in which he had never succeeded (March 1808, pp. 164–65). Of Southey's two volumes, *The Remains of Henry Kirke White* did not impress the reviewer, despite the reputation of the author, as having an especial merit; while *Letters from England* was found to be clever, informative, and lively. The comments on *Marmion* are typical of the review format in the *Cabinet:* plot and character summary, brief evaluative comments (in this case very favorable except for the sketchy characterization), and excerpts illustrating the beauties of the work (May 1808, pp. 321–32; December 1808, pp. 33–36). Another approach to reviewing is exemplified by the moral essay on the dangers of an early and uncontrollable passion which follows a plot summary of *Manon Lescaut.*

After four volumes Litchfield left the *Cabinet* to a new editor who, by the changes he announced in the prospectus, underscored the weaknesses in the original volumes. Besides abandoning the *Cabinet Editions,* the new editor, perhaps in response to criticism in the *Satirist,* pledged to use original material or, if reprints were used, to identify the source (January 1809, pp. iii–v).[8] Submissions of poetry were screened to eliminate the magazine verse that filled pages of the earlier volumes. Drama articles, criticism, and reviews remained the focus of the *Cabinet* while the new management promised objectivity unmarred by personal relationship. The editor noted the new interest in Old English literature and other literature previous to the eighteenth century. This interest is seen in a series of articles on Chaucer's poetry and in selections from Herrick and Lovelace. In addition, contemporary authors such as Monk Lewis and Coleridge were treated in essays.

The article on Coleridge is also indicative of the popular-mind orientation to criticism found in the *Cabinet*. Mostly biographical, the article views poetry as an extension of biographical data (February 1809, pp. 99–104). Coleridge's poetry is approved of for being manly in comparison to contemporary "love-ditties." The foremost feature of Coleridge's poetry is described as a "strong and ardent love of domesticity" (February 1809, p. 101). The article ends by noting the melancholy strain throughout the poetry, the splenetic political thoughts, and the misconceived religious ideas. It proposes as a curative a six-hour daily bout of regular employment; though it may deprive the poet of bursts of genius, it will make him a much happier man.

The moral value of literature continued to be a criterion for evaluating its worth in the new series. A four-part series, "Antidote to Little's Poems," attempted to diminish the pernicious effect of the poetry (which is correctly assumed to be Thomas Moore's) by analyzing its plagiarisms and pointing out its sophistry. Passages are cited and voluptuous language analyzed to demonstrate the danger of prurient yet subtly sensuous language on the young and untrained. In comparison, Maria Edgeworth's *Tales of Fashionable Life* is praised as being both captivating and useful in entertaining the reader while providing a moral lesson. She is applauded for her ability to depict minor vices and the reviewer feels assured that this book will be read by all the *Cabinet*'s readers (July 1809, pp. 64–65).

The review section in the new series was, according to the prospectus, to be greatly enlarged, with fewer works being reviewed in greater depth. This was only selectively true; the choice of books that received greater coverage reveals the standards that governed the magazine. Byron's *English Bards and Scotch Reviewers* received brief attention. The reviewer argued that the satire showed too much talent to be Byron's; and if that was not conclusive, Byron as a nobleman was not likely to make the mistaken references to Italian opera which appear in the poem. Finally the reviewer chided Byron for making his satire as severe as that he was criticizing in the *Edinburgh Review** (June 1809, pp. 527–29).

Receiving more attention is Leigh Hunt's *Critical Essay on Performers of the London Theatres,* which the *Cabinet* reviewed as a valuable record of actors and actresses, while not agreeing with specific assessments (February 1809, pp. 141–48). Given the distinctive focus of this magazine, interest in Hunt's volume is not surprising. The book is criticized for a style that is "disfigured by quaintness" and for wit that "degenerates into flippancy" (February 1809, p. 147). However, the reviewer believes the book is worthy of a second edition because of the thoughtful and ingenious manner in which it treats theater criticism. In this case the long review is merited by the pre-eminent interest in the subject.

The significant contribution of the *Cabinet* is as a theatrical magazine. With its wealth of drama and theater articles it educated the public and stimulated new interest. Through the innovation of the *Cabinet Editions,* it attempted to introduce drama into home libraries in carefully prepared editions. Most important, the *Cabinet* revealed the multiplicity and excitement of the theater scene from 1807 to 1809. In criticism the magazine neither established a new critical perspective nor stringently applied an existing one; rather, the popularly written articles were intended to improve, entertain, and educate.

Notes

1. *The Satirist,* December 1807, pp. 323–24.
2. Charles Harold Gray, *Theatrical Criticism in London to 1795* (New York, 1931), pp. 289–91.
3. Anne Mathews, *Memoirs of Charles Mathews, Comedian* (London, 1938), 1:58.
4. Mathews, p. 232. *Dictionary of National Biography,* s.v. "Mathews, Charles."
5. Robert W. Lowe, *A Bibliographical Account of English Theatrical Literature* (New York, 1888), pp. 63, 258.
6. Gertrude Townshend Mayer, *Women of Letters* (1894; reprint ed., Freeport, N.Y., 1973), 2:75–76.
7. John O. Hayden, *The Romantic Reviewers: 1802–1824.* (Chicago, 1969), p. 31.
8. *The Satirist,* December 1807, p. 324.

Information Sources

BIBLIOGRAPHY
Graham, Walter. *English Literary Periodicals.* 1930. Reprint. New York, 1966.
Gray, Charles Harold. *Theatrical Criticism in London to 1795.* New York, 1931.
Hayden, John O. *The Romantic Reviewers 1802–1824.* Chicago, 1969.
Lowe, Robert W. *A Bibliographical Account of English Theatrical Literature.* New York, 1888.
Mathews, Mrs. Anne. *Memoirs of Charles Mathews, Comedian.* London, 1838.
Mayer, Gertrude Townshend. *Women of Letters.* Vol. 2. 1894. Reprint. Freeport, N.Y., 1973.
Rees, Thomas. *Reminiscences of Literary London from 1779 to 1853.* With additions by John Button. 1890. Reprint. Detroit, 1969.
Reiman, Donald H., ed. *The Romantics Reviewed.* New York, 1972.
Sper, Felix. *The Periodical Press of London 1800–1830.* Boston, 1937.
Wain, John. *Contemporary Reviews of Romantic Poetry.* London, 1953.
INDEXES
Each volume indexed.
REPRINT EDITIONS
Microform: English Literary Periodicals, (UMI), reels 750–751.
LOCATION SOURCES
American
Complete run: U. S. Library of Congress.
Partial runs: Boston Public Library; Connecticut College Library; New York Public

Library; Peabody Institute; State University of Iowa Library; University of Illinois Library; University of Minnesota Library; Wesleyan University Library; Yale University Library.

British

Complete runs: Mitchell Library (Glasgow); Sheffield Public Library.

Partial runs: Birmingham Public Library; Bodleian Library; British Museum; Manchester Public Library.

Publication History

MAGAZINE TITLE AND TITLE CHANGES
   The Cabinet; or, monthly report of polite literature.

VOLUME AND ISSUE DATA
   Volumes 1–4, March 1807–December 1808; new series, volumes 1–2, January–August 1809.

FREQUENCY OF PUBLICATION
   Monthly.

PUBLISHERS
   Volumes 1–4, March 1807–December 1808; new series, volume 1, January–June 1809, July 1809: Mathews and Leigh, 18 The Strand, London. New series, August 1809: Gale and Curtis, Paternoster Row, London.

EDITORS
   John Litchfield, volumes 1–4, March 1807–December 1808. Unknown, new series, volumes 1–2, January–August 1809.

Phyllis F. Harnick

CABINET MAGAZINE

The *Cabinet Magazine, or Literary Olio* was a literary monthly published in London in 1796–1797 by a group of young people, most of whom were associated with the theater.[1] It featured regular columns of poetry and satire, a drama column which reviewed the offerings of the London theaters, and articles with by-lines identifying the writers. Each number included a full-page illustration that accompanied one of the articles or tales.

The principal movers were two Dibdin brothers: Charles Isaac Mungo Dibdin, generally called "Charles Dibdin the Younger" to distinguish him from his famous father; and his younger brother, Thomas John Dibdin. Charles acted as proprietor and joint editor.[2] (A second joint editor, mentioned but not named, was probably Thomas.) Both were actors and managers of minor theaters, especially Sadler's Wells; in later life both won fame as dramatists and songwriters.

The Dibdin brothers wrote many of the songs, tales, and essays published in the *Cabinet*. Other major contributors included their half-brother, Cecil I. Pitt, a theater musician; Mark Lonsdale, an actor-manager; and Francis Godolphin Waldron, an actor. Some contributors were not connected with the theater:

George Walker, novelist and poet, later a prominent bookseller; Anna Maria Porter, a precocious young novelist who published her first article in the *Cabinet* at age seventeen; Anna Seward, "the Swan of Lichfield"; and a few minor writers of whom little more is known than their names, including James Bacon, Messrs. M. Herder, N. Cansick, J. Cobbin, Sansom, and Davenport. Some items were signed only with initials; others were unsigned.

Since the *Cabinet* was primarily a literary journal, its contents fall into well-defined literary categories.

A column of poetry, "The Cabinet of Apollo," appeared in every number. It consisted of selected short poems of many types: songs and sonnets, odes, elegies, ballads, epigrams, and miscellaneous lyrics. There were a few works by older poets such as Ben Jonson and Robert Southwell, but most of the poems came from contemporary authors. Apparently the purpose of the column was to introduce readers to new poems, and to good but unfamiliar poems of the past. Chaucer, Shakespeare, Milton, Pope, and similar favorites are not included, but there are many pieces by minor poets such as the Dibdin brothers, Anna Maria Porter, and George Walker. Coleridge, Southey, and Henry Pye, the Poet Laureate, are each represented by one poem.[3]

Though many of the poems are conventional and sentimental, some few are worth preserving. Waldron's "The Holy Vengeance, or Death of Cardinal Beaton," a swift-moving dramatic ballad, contains some perceptive characterization and realistic Scots dialogue. The first of Southey's *Botany Bay Eclogues*, "Elinor," is reprinted in an expanded version as "The Female Convict."[4] W. Walsh contributes a brief philosophic poem on "The Mind." Though political issues are generally avoided, a supposed "Prophecy: Translated from an Old Welsh Manuscript" by George Walker turns out to be a thinly veiled satire on the French Revolution.

Especially delightful are the half-dozen comic songs, most in Irish dialect, by the Dibdin brothers, including "The Ventriloquist," "The Telegraph," and "Irish Comic Song." Humor shines also in some of the narrative verse, including "The Challenge," "The Elephant—a Comic Tale," "A New Way to Pay Old Debts," and others.

A column on the drama was a regular feature of each monthly number except the issue for March 1797. The anonymous critic reviewed the offerings of the London theaters one by one, commenting randomly on the acting, the plots, the music, and sometimes on the theater itself. He allotted more praise than censure, but condemned the disorganized spectacles at Astley's Amphitheatre, and gave mixed reviews to many mediocre new plays on their way to deserved oblivion.

He held a low opinion of contemporary comedy and wrote:

Of a modern comedy it is difficult, and perhaps scarcely necessary, to attempt a description of the plot. The writers of the present day, little sedulous of fame, aim only to amuse for the moment; and, on quitting

the theatre, it is not to be determined whether we have laughed more at
the whim of the piece, or at its paucity of more rational amusement.
[April 1797, p. 355]

The critic mainly focused his comments on acting, using the work of the late
David Garrick as the standard of excellence:

To those who have not seen the paragon, Garrick, Kemble must appear
the *ne plus ultra,* in Hamlet; to those who have, he must certainly, of all
other performers, in or since Mr. Garrick's time, appear the nearest him
in excellence: if anything human may be called perfection, Garrick's
Hamlet might. [December 1796, pp. 113–14]

The popular actor Elliston was hailed as the "alter-Garrick." James Bannister
Jr. shone in the title role of Cumberland's *The Jew.* Lesser actors received their
due: Dowton in tragedy, Dighton for singing, Laurent as clown. Leading ladies
of the day were likewise praised: Miss Farren (then retiring) for her first-rate
acting; Mrs. Siddons for both her acting and her private worth; Mrs. Jordan for
her influence in promoting a new comedy. An obituary notice of the veteran
Mrs. Pope praised both her acting and her private character. Criticism of drama
is neither profound nor complete, but it conveys the opinions of a person well
acquainted with the theater of his day.

The drama column contained much other interesting information. It revealed,
for example, current taste for opera, both serious and comic; for ballet, pantomime, and burlettas; and the interest in specific types of stage characters, including the Jew, the Quaker, and the Negro. It showed that Shakespeare still
held the stage: *Othello, Hamlet, The Merchant of Venice,* and *Cymbeline* were
all presented within a seven-month period. And it exposed the contrivances of
some theater managers for holding down expenses. The manager at Covent
Garden, for example, each year dismissed his experienced actors, who could
command higher wages, and hired young novices at a pittance.

The column also revealed that several of the current stage presentations were
revivals or adaptations of earlier works. The reviewer hailed the revival of
Lillo's *The London Merchant; or, The History of George Barnwell,* "too long
the scoff of witlings," with Mrs. Siddons exhibiting her "exquisite talents" as
the meretricious Millwood. At Covent Garden, Chaucer's "Knight's Tale" was
transposed into a comedy called *Fortune's Fool;* and Lewis's novel *The Monk*
furnished the basis for a serious ballet, *Raymond and Agnes; or, the Castle of
Lindenbergh.* At the Opera House Antonio Sacchini's *Arvire et Evelina,* translated from the French by DuPonte, was staged in an English version called
"Evelina."[5]

At times the drama column discussed more substantial concerns—for example, the troubles of the struggling Royalty Theatre, and its need for better management and governmental subsidy.

Tales constitute a large portion of the items published in the *Cabinet*. They range from didactic and occasionally satiric to sensational and Gothic. In some, the moralizing is obvious and heavy-handed ("The Danger of Unsteadiness; Exemplified in the History of Jacobus"; "Eliza Worvel, or, the Victim of Indolence"; "I Wish I Had: A Tale for the Ladies"; etc.). In others it is more subtly conveyed, but the plots are sentimental and improbable. Among these are: "Civil War: A Tale," the story of two brothers on opposite sides; "Matilda," in which the heroine dies of a broken heart when her fiancé, who had been impressed into the navy, is lost at sea; and "The Pauper," the story of a well-to-do gentleman who conceals from his bride that the source of his income is begging; upon her tragic discovery of this fact he deserts her. "The Recluse" is a tale with a thesis, refuting Pope's dictum that retirement, health, and a competent income constitute happiness.[6]

Some tales are both didactic and satiric. "The Adventures of Ability and Inclination" represents these two allegorical figures as young men embarked on parallel careers. Their experiences are at once amusing and instructive. Voltaire's satirical tale *The Adventures of Scarmentado*—reprinted in installments—exposes the cruelty and irrationality of the religions and governments of many nations.[7]

In the later numbers Gothic and sensational tales predominate. Among these tales are: "Rodolph. A Fragment," chilling experiences in a charnel house; "Raymond Castle," a deserted ruin with specters and a plot borrowed from *Hamlet;* "Ethelind," a tale of Druids and evil spirits.

In general, the tales are romantic and sentimental, and are set in distant countries, such as Russia, Persia, and Indostan. Most have little reference to contemporary life, though one—"More Meant Than Said," translated from the French by George Walker—is a thinly disguised satire on the political conditions in France that produced the revolution. The *Cabinet* published many short essays, on both literary and non-literary subjects. Of the former, "On Biography" emphasizes the advantages of biography in teaching virtue and piety. A later sketch of Charles XII of Sweden illustrates the point. "On Novel Reading" warns that novels do not aim to inculcate virtue, hence should be screened by parents and guardians before young people are allowed to read them. The essence of many of the essays is conveyed in their titles: "Resolution: A Necessary Quality in the Pursuit of Study"; "Of the Ill Effects of Reading Without Digesting" and of reading light popular novels ("Fielding, Richardson and Smollett") instead of solid philosophy ("Plato, Aristotle, and Epictetus").

Several of the critical essays deserve mention. "A Comparison Between Apollonius and Homer, Jonson and Shakespeare," though promising more than it fulfills, attacks the "Rules" revered by the neoclassical writers: "It may be questioned whether rules have so frequently served to correct the disorders of a bold, luxuriant genius, as to cause others to write without any spirit at all." Homer and Shakespeare, though they transgressed the "rules," were considered greater authors than Apollonius and Jonson, who did not (December

1796, pp. 90–92). Dr. Vicesimus Knox's "On the Moral Tendency of the Writings of Sterne" (February 1797, pp. 193–96) asserts that though Sterne has caused the milk of human kindness to flow "all cheerily," in general his influence is bad. His wit is mere allusive blasphemy. His humor is but quaintness. His sermons are admittedly pathetic, but that is their chief virtue. *Tristram Shandy* and *A Sentimental Journey* promote adultery and other illicit commerce between the sexes.

A satiric column, "The Projector," by Plume Aircastle, Esq., appeared in every issue. Each column criticized a particular far-fetched scheme or proposal. These included a general reformation of manners; a plan for bringing water from Lethe to Apothecaries' Hall to make doctors forget to issue prescriptions or send bills; a scheme to replace the hide on horses by sheepskin, so that the horses would furnish both transportation and wool; a meter to detect deceit and hypocrisy; and similar proposals. A few other satiric essays are scattered through the magazine.

Essays on non-literary topics deal chiefly with manners and morals. Most are pious and didactic: "Advantages of a Prudent Marriage," "On the Evil Consequences of Gaming," "On the Pleasures of Reflection," "On Perseverance," and others. An essay "On Private Education" for January 1797 (pp. 140–42) favors public schooling over private, quoting Samuel Johnson and Oliver Goldsmith in support. It resembles the debate on this subject between Parson Adams and Joseph Andrews in Fielding's novel.[8] "On Madness" (March 1797, pp. 287–89) reflects the contemporary interest in abnormal states of mind concurrently being exploited by Blake and Wordsworth. "Strictures on the Female Sex" by Anna Maria Porter attacks certain kinds of female conduct then regarded as fashionable: pretending indifference to love and the opposite sex; delighting in arousing competition and jealousy among suitors before marriage; making a fuss over the smallest slight, and tyrannizing over one's spouse. Woman's proper weapons, Miss Porter asserts, are tenderness, good example, and forgiveness.

Only a handful of the essays discuss current events. Among events covered are Elphinstone's capture of the Dutch fleet at Saldanha Bay, Lord Malmesbury's embassy to Paris, and the dispersion of the French fleet at Bantry Bay. Another handful of essays describes natural phenomena, chiefly uncommon birds and animals. Several essays take a stand on contemporary social issues, among them, that punishment of criminals should be proportionate to their crimes, and that Negro slaves should be treated with more humanity. Like the *Tatler** (see *AAAJ*) and *Spectator** (see *AAAJ*) of Addison and Steele, upon which it seems to have been modeled, the *Cabinet* encouraged sound morals, good manners, and proper education of the young. It tried to instruct its readers in drama and poetry. With its feature columns—The Drama, The Cabinet of Apollo, The Projector—its romantic tales, and its didacticism enlivened with occasional humor, it furnished instruction and entertainment throughout its brief existence.

Notes

1. Copies of all numbers from the inception of the magazine through May 1797 have been examined, with the exception of the last two numbers (for June and July 1797), which were unobtainable and therefore excluded from this discussion.

2. *Professional and Literary Memoirs of Charles Dibdin the Younger* ed. George Speaight (London, 1956), p. 8.

3. Coleridge's poem, "On Kisses"—a tribute to his new bride, Sara Fricker—was first published in 1796, though written earlier. A note by the poet's son, Rev. Derwent Coleridge, in the London edition of 1852 says that the poem was originally addressed to Miss F. Nesbitt of Plymouth circa 1791; "Nesbitt" was later altered to "Sara."

4. It is not clear who wrote the expanded version, or on what authority. In Southey's own collection of his *Poetical Works* (London, 1837) he reprints the shorter, original version from the Oxford edition of 1794.

5. Sacchini died before it was completed, and the third act was added by J. B. Rey, orchestra conductor at the Paris Opera, where the work was first staged on 29 April 1788. Popular in France, *Arvire et Evelina* was presented intermittently until 1827.

6. Alexander Pope, *An Essay on Man,* epistle 4, lines 77ff.

7. Originally published in 1756 as *Histoire des Voyages de Scarmentado, Écrité par Lui-Meme.*

8. Henry Fielding, *Joseph Andrews,* bk. 3, chap. 5.

Information Sources

BIBLIOGRAPHY

Dibdin, Thomas John. *Reminiscences of Thomas Dibdin, of the Theatres Royal Covent Garden, Drury Lane, Haymarket, &c, and Author of The Cabinet, &c,* 2 vols. London, 1827.

Dictionary of National Biography. S.v. "Dibdin, Charles."

————. S.v. "Dibdin, Thomas John (1771–1841)."

Graham, Walter. *English Literary Periodicals.* New York, 1930.

Speaight, George, ed. *Professional and Literary Memoirs of Charles Dibdin the Younger.* London, 1956.

INDEXES
  Unknown. Last numbers are missing.

REPRINT EDITIONS
  None.

LOCATION SOURCES
  American
    Partial run: Yale University Library.
  British
    Partial run: Bodleian Library.

Publication History

MAGAZINE TITLE AND TITLE CHANGES
  Cabinet Magazine or Literary Olio.

VOLUME AND ISSUE DATA
  Volume 1, numbers 1–9, November 1796–July 1797.

FREQUENCY OF PUBLICATION
   Monthly.
PUBLISHER
   J. S. Jordan, 166 Fleet Street, London.
EDITOR
   Charles Isaac Mungo Dibdin (generally called "Charles Dibdin the Younger").

                                                    Daniel L. McCue, Jr.

CAMBRIAN AND CALEDONIAN QUARTERLY MAGAZINE, THE. See CAMBRIAN QUARTERLY MAGAZINE, AND CELTIC REPERTORY, THE

CAMBRIAN QUARTERLY MAGAZINE, THE. See CAMBRIAN QUARTERLY MAGAZINE, AND CELTIC REPERTORY, THE

CAMBRIAN QUARTERLY MAGAZINE, AND CELTIC REPERTORY, THE

Although its "proprietors" chose in 1829 to have the *Cambrian Quarterly* published at St. Martin's-le-Grand near Saint Paul's Cathedral in the city of London, they were motivated by "love strong as death" for their native principality of Wales (1, no. 1:1). Perhaps the London location was indeed suitable because the *Cambrian* aimed to combat the "general neglect" of Welsh literature, and to make it known outside of Wales as well as to those anglicized members of the Welsh gentry who could neither write nor speak Welsh. Despite the literary emphasis professed in the first editorial, the *Cambrian Quarterly* from its inception covered most aspects of Welsh life and history, including topography, geography, music, philology, the legal system, and rural conditions. Translations of ancient Welsh poetry were naturally frequent, but equally prominent were new poems recounting ancient and contemporary themes in both Welsh and English. Almost every contribution to the *Cambrian* was anonymous or pseudonymous, including most of the poetry. Such anonymity conformed with the journalistic practice of the time, and reinforced the "long established and still prevalent custom whereby almost all Welsh poets and prose writers adopted pseudonyms or bardic names."[1] Because early Welsh poetry was based on Welsh history, its publication could not help but foster Welsh nationalism. Arthur, Merlin, and Owen Glyndwyer were popular subjects for nineteenth century poets also.

The "proprietors" of the *Cambrian Quarterly* were Anthony Ashley Cooper, the future seventh Earl of Shaftesbury, and Rice Pryce Buckley Williams.[2] Lord Ashley had not yet entered the career of social reform which established his fame. He visited Shropshire in September 1827, travelled into Wales, and there made a companion of a Welsh clergyman whose enthusiasm for his native literature and for the Welsh language resulted in Ashley's spending two months in Aberystwyth. His biographer asserts that this period of intensive study resulted in his gaining reading proficiency in Welsh.[3] A year later Ashley's "sympathy and assistance" were enlisted in starting the *Cambrian Quarterly*. By this time he had been appointed by Wellington's government as a commissioner of the India Board of Control, a post he retained until the government went out of office in 1830. Lord Ashley wrote the prospectus for the new magazine in the voice of a Welshman. He used the editorial "we" to state that one object of the new magazine would be "to save our poets from night, our manuscripts from the flames and our venerable tongue from contempt." It was undoubtably no coincidence that Williames, the co-proprietor and editor, was a Welshman from Montgomeryshire and also attached to the India Board. The first number of January 1829 is dedicated to Ashley. It pays tribute to his Welsh scholarship and suggests resentment at the cultural domination imposed by centuries of British rule: "You have turned to the humble treasures of long-neglected and almost forgotten Wales" (p. 1).

Two other principals should be mentioned.[4] Peter Bailey Williams had been a student at Jesus and Christ Church colleges, Oxford. After having taken orders, he spent most of his life as curate at Llanberis in Carnarvonshire. Williams collected old manuscripts and published extracts and translations from them, including several in the *Cambrian Quarterly*. John Jenkins or "Ifor Ceri" (1770–1829) was also a Welsh clergyman who studied at Jesus and Merton colleges. He had a strong interest in Welsh music and established the first provincial *eisteddfod* (assembly of Welsh bards and minstrels) in 1819. Jenkins's home in Kerry, Montgomeryshire, was a center for Welsh singers, composers, and harpists. He was probably responsible for the publication of "A Bridal Song by a Modern Welsh Harper" in the April 1829 issue, among other pieces. The "Sexagenarian Friend" who wrote Jenkins's obituary for the fifth number (January 1830) praised him as a "cherisher of native talent." His death was a severe loss to the *Quarterly*.

The *Cambrian Quarterly*, far from being merely an outlet for nostalgia and retrospection, was greatly aware of contemporary problems. The very first issue contained a long (and unsigned) article on Welsh jurisprudence, and this was followed up in the third number (July 1829) by a correspondent who found the criticism far too vituperative, noting that the author did not distinguish between the jurisdiction of a court and how well it was administered.

Nonetheless, in an era when vituperation was a common mode of journalistic argument, the *Cambrian* was basically non-combative in tone. Aside from the piece attacking the British administration of courts in Wales, the magazine lashed out on only one other occasion. Using the *nom de plume* "Lucius O'Trigger," Sheridan's fire-eating Irishman in *The Rivals*, a "contributor" in the sixth number (April 1831) attacked the Scots for their continuous vilification of all other nations and their boastful claims of intellectual pre-eminence. If contemporary readers had any doubt as to who was meant by "Scots" they were quickly enlightened by an article which followed, berating a piece on national characteristics. Alaric Alexander Watts in the November 1829 issue of *Blackwood's Monthly Magazine* * had advanced the fantastic argument that the only "good" English were to be found residing in Lancashire and Yorkshire; their qualities derived solely from Pictish forebears.[5] To a modern reader the *Blackwood's* article might appear to be a satire on extreme xenophobia; but given the often vicious attacks on persons and ethnic groups in the periodicals of the time, it was quite probably intended seriously, although *Blackwood's* writers enjoyed presenting extreme cases in order to gain notoriety. The *Cambrian Quarterly* recognized in the article a spirit not of legitimate national pride but of divisiveness and slander.

The age of coaching, which reached its peak of efficiency in the early years of the nineteenth century, had made the beauties of North Wales an objective of the well-to-do British tourist in search of the "picturesque" and the "sublime." The *Cambrian Quarterly,* which aimed to teach readers of non-Welsh as well as Welsh background, offered a series on "Summer Rambles in Wales" with special emphasis on such sublime sights as Mount Snowdon. This series was illustrated with woodcuts, as were some of the articles on geology. The printing of previously unpublished historical material, such as the series of documents on the Siege of Chester in 1645 during the time of the Civil War, advanced Welsh scholarship (1, no. 2).

In the last two years of its brief existence the *Cambrian* took a more direct interest in political questions than it had first shown. Its initial assumption that Welsh readers would be uninterested in political questions because they "are remarkable the rather for more secluded studies than for paying any great attention to the common run of passing events" (4, no. 13:68) proved unfounded. Therefore, "the proprietors" discussed the impending Reform Bill of 1832 in the July 1831 and January 1832 issues. In the latter issue the *Cambrian* asserted that it did not wish to "throw down all distinctions" but did favor greater representation for Wales in Parliament. It looked with horror upon "misrule." In short, it took a middle-of-the-road position which could offend few. The same issue contained a scathing indictment of rampant alcoholism as the source of the "squalid semi-barbarism and poverty" that was gripping the lower orders in Wales. No mention was made of the dislocations caused by the rapid industrialization that was overtaking parts of Wales, especially the Rhondda Valley of Glamorganshire and Swansea in southeastern Wales, or of the accompanying brutish living conditions that characterized the earlier years of industrialization in nineteenth-century Britain. The April 1832 issue continued to point up social problems in a long "Letter to the Lord Chancellor . . . on State Insurance to Provide for a Rural Police" which dwelt on the "alarming increase in pauperism, vagrancy and crime," but did not assign causes. The London Metropolitan Police Force (the "Bobbies" named after Sir Robert Peel) had only been established in 1829 after bitter opposition from those who felt that such a force would inhibit the liberty of Englishmen. Clearly the idea of a kingdom-wide national police force was an idea far in advance of its era.

The *Cambrian Quarterly* published several short stories, all in the guise of first-person narratives and set in frame stories. They are rhetorical and artificial in the worst sense of those terms. The one that merits some mention here is "A Welsh Shepherd's Story," alleged to be "from the journal of a Welsh medical student," found in the April 1832 issue. Its central incident, of a young countryman coming to London and finding that his fiancée has become a prostitute, is the subject of Dante Gabriel Rossetti's picture, "Found." As it is most doubtful that Rossetti ever saw the *Cambrian,* the story may have been a well known one.

The *Cambrian Quarterly*'s book reviews naturally favored Welsh subjects. Two novels of Thomas Love Peacock which include Welsh scenes and legends, *The Misfortunes of Elphin* (1829) and *Crochet Castle* (1831), received favorable notices, although the reviewers did not seem as enchanted with Peacock's wit as they were taken with him as a booster of Welsh history and ancient literature (1, no. 2:240; 4, no. 10:225). *Elphin* contains the memorable character Seithengn, "the Welsh Falstaff." Peacock had long admired Welsh scenery. In 1820 he married a Welsh woman and undertook the study of Welsh archaeology and bardic writing. The reviewer of *Elphin* called it "the most entertaining if not the best that has yet been published on the ancient customs and traditions of Wales," but appeared oblivious of the author's satire on the love of antiquity for its own sake. Contemporary subjects, such as William Provis's account of John Telford's engineering feat, the Menai Suspension Bridge of 1820, were also reviewed along with numerous historical works (1, no. 2:211). The concluding pages of each issue, following the reviews, were devoted to "London and Provincial News" and included a register of births, deaths, and marriages among the gentry as well as such news of Welsh interest as the transactions of the Royal Cambrian Institute and the founding of the Saint David's Club in November 1831 to promote the study of Welsh literature.

Samuel Rush Meyrick, the well-known antiquarian whose home at Ross-on-Wye contained a large collection of medieval arms and armour, was a frequent "correspondent" in his own name. Among his most interesting contributions is the translation of portions of a manuscript from the Harleian Library (British Museum manuscript 3859) which had claim to be the oldest extant document in Welsh. Dating from the tenth century, it is mainly a list of Welsh heroes (4, no. 13:16). A long article on Irish mythology demonstrated Meyrick's interest in comparative study of Celtic legends (4, no. 14:144).

The reason for the sudden demise of the *Cambrian* is not clear. It had the interest of Lord Ashley and writers of substance and even repute. However, its subscription list probably did not number over a few hundred at any one time. With number 19 for July 1833 the name was changed to *Cambrian and Caledonian Quarterly Magazine and Celtic Repertory* and it took on a distinctly

Scottish emphasis. Without a word of warning this first of the Welsh "little magazines"—to use an anachronistic term—ended with the next issue, for October 1833.

Notes

1. John Edward Lloyd et al., *Dictionary of Welsh Biography Down to 1940* (London, 1959), p. xx.

2. For these identifications and the following reference I am indebted to Mr. Huw Walters of the College of Librarianship, University of Wales, and Ms. Marian B. Hughes, Assistant Librarian in the Department of Printed Books at the National Library of Wales. For Williames see E. H. Rowland, *Biographical Dictionary of Eminent Welshmen, 1700–1900* (Wrexham, Denbighshire, 1907), p. 278.

3. Edward Hodder, *Life and Work of the Seventh Earl of Shaftesbury, K. G.* (London, 1888), 1:74–75.

4. Readers of Welsh may consult G. T. Roberts, *Bywyd a gwaith Peter Bailey Williams* (Bangor, 1935), the bibliography of which contains (pp. 310–16) a list of his contributions to the *Cambrian Quarterly*. See also Rowland, p. 1027. For Jenkins, see Richard Williams, *Montgomeryshire Worthies* (London, 1875–1891), pp. 137–40; Bedwyr Lewis Jones, *Yr Hen Bersoniaid Llengar* (Penarth, 1963), pp. 32–36.

5. See "Characters of the English, Scots and Irish," *Blackwood's Monthly Magazine* 26, no. 159 (1829):818–29. Watts's purpose was to determine the "manner in which national character is formed." He is full of observations such as, "The mental faculties of the Englishman are not absolutely of the highest order." For identification of Watts as author of this piece see Walter Houghton et al., *Wellesley Index to Victorian Periodicals, 1824–1900* (Toronto, 1966), 1:37.

Information Sources

BIBLIOGRAPHY

The following references provide information about the principal contributors.

Dictionary of National Biography. S.v. "Meyrick, Samuel Rush."

Hoddern, Edward. *Life and Work of the Seventh Earl of Shaftesbury, K.G.* 3 vols. London, 1888.

Lloyd, John Edward, et al. *Dictionary of Welsh Biography Down to 1940*. London, 1959.

Rees, T. Mardy. *Notable Welshmen*. Carnarvon, 1908. [The contributions of Sir Samuel Rush Meyrick are discussed.]

Roberts, G. T. *Bywyed a gwaith Peter Bailey Williams*. M.A. thesis, University of Wales, 1935. [The bibliography contains a list of P. B. Williams's contributions to the *Cambrian Quarterly*.]

Rowland, E. H. *Biographical Dictionary of Eminent Welshmen, 1700–1900*. Wrexham, Denbighshire, 1907.

Williams, Richard. *Montgomeryshire Worthies*. London, 1875–1891. [See pp. 137–40 for discussion of John Jenkins's contributions.]

INDEXES

Each volume indexed.

REPRINT EDITIONS

Microform: English Literary Periodicals (UMI), reel 295.

LOCATION SOURCES

American

Complete runs: Columbia University Library; Harvard University Library; Historical Society of Pennsylvania; Lloyd Library and Museum; Newberry Library; University of Chicago Library; University of Minnesota Library; U.S. Library of Congress.

Partial runs: Colorado College Library; State Historical Society of Wisconsin; Yale University Library.

British

Widely available.

Publication History

MAGAZINE TITLE AND TITLE CHANGES

The Cambrian Quarterly Magazine, and Celtic Repertory, January 1829–June 1833. *The Cambrian and Caledonian Quarterly Magazine, and Celtic Repertory,* July 1833–October 1833 (merged with the *Caledonian Quarterly Magazine* with volume 5, number 19, July 1833.)

VOLUME AND ISSUE DATA

Volumes 1–5, January 1829–October 1833. (Numbers are consecutive, beginning with volume 1, number 1, January 1829–volume 5, number 20, October 1833.)

FREQUENCY OF PUBLICATION

Quarterly.

PUBLISHER

H. Hughes, St. Martin's-le-Grand, London.

EDITOR

Rice Pryce Buckley Williams.

Barbara J. Dunlap

CHAMBERS'S EDINBURGH JOURNAL. See CHAMBERS'S JOURNAL

CHAMBERS'S JOURNAL

About 1830 Britain embarked upon a vigorous program of political reform, while in the literary sphere a cheap-literature craze swept over the island. The two most prolific and practical publishers who carried education and wholesome entertainment to humble homes were Charles Knight and the Chambers brothers, Robert and William. *Chambers's Edinburgh Journal* appeared almost simultaneously with Knight's *Penny Magazine* in the spring of 1832.

The Chambers brothers, sons of a once prosperous muslin weaver ruined by the introduction of mechanized looms, had a decent education and at an early age established themselves first as booksellers and then as publishers in Edinburgh. Robert, already respected as the author of the *Traditions of Edinburgh* (1823), was highly intelligent and broad in his outlook. William was somewhat narrower, and didactic, but together they made an excellent publishing team.

The motives that guided the founders of *Chambers's Journal* are set forth in "The Editor's Address to his Readers" which is the leader of the first issue:

> The great leading principle of this paper is to take advantage of the universal appetite for instruction which at present exists; to supply to that appetite food of the best kind, and in such form and at such a price, as must suit the convenience of every man in the British dominions. . . .
>
> I shall present, but not too hurriedly, papers on Literary and Scientific subjects, articles on the Formation and Arrangements of Society, observations on Education and our Scholastic Institutions, sketches on Agriculture, Gardening, Sheep-farming, the making of Roads, the increase of Population, the Uses of Machinery—indicative of the vast improvements effected and of what remains to be accomplished. For the express use of the poor man, I shall open a flow of information for his guidance, should he be disposed to emigrate. For the benefit of those who live among the hills, and who cannot come to church, I shall give pithy passages from the great British moralists. For the recreation of those who reflect, I shall present passages from the works of Newton and Bacon, from the Encyclopedists, and other English luminaries.
>
> To the ladies and gentlemen of the "old school" I shall relate innumerable amusing anecdotes, not one of which probably they heard before. With the ladies of the "new school," and all my fair young countrywomen in their teens, I hope to be on agreeable terms. I will tell them what I intend to do for them: I shall make a point of giving them every week, if I can find room, a nice amusing tale, either original or selected from the best modern authors—no trash about Italian coaches and daggers, and ghosts in the blue chamber, but something really good. I will also inform them of a thousand useful little receipts of housewifery, calculated to make them capital wives: and perhaps I may give them new insight into sewing, painting in water-colours, drawing with pencils or chalk, or singing and improving their taste in music.

This cheap weekly periodical carried out its program from the beginning and its success was instantaneous. At one and one-half pence it promptly reached a circulation of 50,000, and this rose to 90,000 by the 1840s with its Scottish, English, and Irish editions. The articles were varied and instructive—a description of the scene of Burns's *Jolly Beggars;* a series on the origin and progress of printing; reports of travellers in Spain, Africa, and Siam; a regular feature by William Chambers, his "Column for the Boys"; and dozens of "Familiar Sketches and Moral Essays." Wood-engravings occasionally illustrated a piece.

At first the Chambers brothers believed that their audience was a very democratic one, as they intended it to be. In Scotland, shortly after its debut, *Chambers's* was read by factory hands, shepherds, even milk-boys, as well as in the drawing rooms of the exalted. However, after the initial euphoria had passed the brothers were forced to admit that their paper did not reach as far down on the social scale as they had at first believed. The paper was read, they declared in 1840, by "the elite of the laboring community; those who think, conduct themselves respectably, and are anxious to improve their circumstances by judicious means. But below this worthy order of men, our work, except in a few particular cases, does not go." However much one may debate the character of the readership of *Chambers's* and the *Penny Magazine,* no one would disagree that the popularity of these two periodicals resulted in an unprecedented growth in the field of cheap journalism.

Unquestionably *Chambers's Journal* owed its success among periodicals not only to the diligence of the Chambers brothers but also to other writers who were famous or were to become so. To the third number Mary Russell Mitford, the talented author of *Our Village,* contributed a pleasant sketch. James Hogg, the Ettrick Shepherd, contributed an article on emigration to an issue of May 1833 and, in the following month, a sketch entitled "The Watchmaker." Hugh Miller contributed some legendary Scottish tales and George Thomson, the friend and correspondent of Burns, a relative of Charles Dickens, and an authority on Scottish music, wrote an article advocating the study of music by the working classes. The journal was the medium through which George Combe circulated his views on phrenology. Robert Gilfillan, the once popular writer of that plaintive emigrant song, "Why Left I My Home," was also a prolific contributor.

Several lady novelists of the Victorian scene wrote for this magazine, which paid its contributors quite handsomely. In 1847 Maria Edgeworth wrote a tale for children, in order that she might "honestly earn twenty guineas for the poor." Mrs. Gaskell charmed not only Robert Chambers but the readers of the journal with a series of sketches. Dinah Maria Murlock, later Mrs. Craik, also contributed a series of sketches, and Mrs. Caroline E.S. Norton's efforts, favorites of periodical readers, also found a warm reception here.

Not a few of the foremost writers of the Victorian period owed to *Chambers's* their introduction to a wide audience. In the *Journal* for July 1849 appeared George Meredith's early poem, "Chillianwallah." Like so many other twenty-one-year-old men Meredith was also attracted to the heroic exploits of the fiery Hungarian nationalist, Louis Kossuth. The future novelist wrote an article on the leader of the Hungarian revolution, which was forwarded to the *Journal,* but it was deemed too controversial. Thomas Hardy was another eminent Victorian writer who first came before the public in the pages of this journal. Hardy had first sought to become an architect and at the age of twenty-five he had forwarded to the *Journal,* not a piece of fiction, but an essay on modern design. This contribution, "How I Build Myself a House," appeared in March 1865, six years before the appearance of his first novel, *Desperate Remedies.* Many years later when he had become a leading man of letters, the editor of the *Journal* attempted to pry forth another contribution, but Hardy, who was then in his seventieth year, was reluctant to descend from Olympus. "The fact is," he explained, "that what I now write, though it interests some, does not interest the general reader." [1]

If Hardy proved standoffish in that instance, he came forward in the issue for January 1925 with a hitherto unpublished poem, entitled "A Bird-Scene at a Rural Dwelling." The contribution was notable on two counts. Not only was it the work of a great master, but it marked the sixtieth anniversary of the writer's first appearance in print, the essay on modern architecture having been printed in *Chambers's* in 1865.

Sir Arthur Conan Doyle was another young author who was given encouragement in the *Journal*. While a medical student at Edinburgh University he forwarded his first effort, "The Mystery of Sassasa Valley," which was published in 1879, some dozen years before he emerged with his celebrated creations, Holmes and Watson. Other writers whose early work appeared in the *Journal* included Sir Walter Besant, the social critic; David Christie Murray, who in 1879 published his first novel, *A Life's Atonement,* in serial form in *Chambers's;* S. Baring Gould, best known for his compilation of medieval legends; W. W. Jacobs, the delightful teller of sea stories; and Stanley Weyman, with his talent for historical novels. In the early twentieth century John Buchan, the novelist, biographer, and historian, was still another writer who found a warm reception from editors and readers.

For over a hundred years *Chambers's Journal* was a source of instruction and delight to millions of readers, dispensing literary and scientific articles, good quality fiction, and essays on subjects of general interest. "I don't think the name of Chambers will ever be mentioned without a sentiment of gratitude," said Disraeli, when he received from William Chambers's hands the freedom of the city of Edinburgh in 1867. Of course, the Victorian statesman was referring to the achievement of the brothers in the widest sense. Their journal, however, was one of the most prominent elements in what Professor Saintsbury has called the most distinctive feature of the literary history of nineteenth-century England—the development of periodical literature.

In their *Memoir* William and Robert Chambers generously praise Thomas Smibert, W. H. Wills, Leitch Ritchie, and James Payn, all professional men of letters, for their assistance in the publication of the *Journal.* [2] At first Robert Chambers was the chief editor of the enterprise, but as the publishing business developed he was no longer able to give his undivided attention to the weekly. Thomas Smibert, in 1837, became the first of his editorial assistants and in the course of five years wrote some six hundred literary articles, tales, and biographical essays. Upon his premature death in 1854, William Henry Wills, the friend and colleague of Dickens, came on the scene and vigorously discharged the duties of co-editorship for two years. However, when Dickens invited him to return to London and become his secretary as well as assistant editor of *Household Words* * (see *VEA*), Wills resigned and resumed his London life.

The successor of Wills was Leitch Ritchie, already the author of a history of France and the companion and collaborator of Turner on a series of travel books. A shrewd judge of literary talent, he was an ideal editor in the 1850s. Upon his retirement James Payn, long a contributor to *Household Words* and to *Chambers's* and co-editor with Ritchie, became sole editor in 1859. He held the position successfully for fifteen years, picking and choosing with a shrewd eye as well as writing a great deal for the *Journal*. One of his many novels, *Lost Sir Massingberd,* ran serially in the magazine, and increased its circulation by 20,000 copies.

Payn was succeeded in the editorship by Robert Chambers Jr., who guided the publication until his death in 1888. Then the direction of the *Journal* passed to his son, E.E.S. Chambers, who eventually was aided by his son, Reginald J. Chambers, and J. Liddell Geddie. For some sixty years members of the second, third, and fourth generations of the Chambers family worked to maintain the standards set by the founding brothers.

Notes

1. Quoted in W. Forbes Gray, "A Hundred Years Old Chambers's Journal 1832–1932," *Chamber's Journal,* 8th ser. 1 (1932):95.
2. William Chambers, *Memoir of Robert Chambers with Autobiographical Reminiscences of William Chambers* (London, 1872).

Information Sources

BIBLIOGRAPHY

Cooney, S. M. *Publishers for the People: W. & R. Chambers: The Early Years 1832–1850.* Ph.D. dissertation, Ohio State University, 1971.
Dalziel, M. *Popular Fiction 100 Years Ago.* London, 1957.
"End of Chambers's Journal." [London] *Times,* 7 December 1956, p. 7.
Feldberg, M. "Knight's *Penny Magazine* and *Chambers's Edinburgh Journal:* A Problem in Writing Cultural History." *Victorian Periodicals Newsletter* no. 3 (1968).13–16.
Gray, W. Forbes. "A Hundred Years Old Chambers's Journal 1832–1932." *Chambers's Journal,* 8th. ser. 1 (1932):81–96.
Lehmann, J. *Ancestors and Friends.* London, 1962.

INDEXES
Volumes 1–12, in volume 12. New series volumes 1–20 in volume 20. Afterwards, indexes at end of volumes. 1844–1881 in *Poole's Index.*

REPRINT EDITIONS
Microform: Bell and Howell, Wooster, Ohio. Brook Haven Press (Northern Micrographics), La Crosse, Wis. Early British Periodicals (UMI), reels 579–583.

LOCATION SOURCES
American
Partial runs: Widely available.
British
Partial runs: Widely available.

Publication History

MAGAZINE TITLE AND TITLE CHANGES

Chambers's Edinburgh Journal, 1832–1853. *Chambers's Journal of Popular Literature, Science, and Arts,* 1854–November 1897. *Chambers's Journal,* December 1897–December 1956.

VOLUME AND ISSUE DATA

Volumes 1–12, 4 February 1832–December 1843; new series, volumes 1–20, 1844–1853. *Chambers's Journal of Popular Literature,* third series, volumes 1–20, 1854–1863; fourth series, volumes 1–20, 1864–1883; fifth series, volumes 1–14, 1884–November 1897. *Chambers's Journal,* volume 1–9th series, volume 10, December 1897–December 1956.

FREQUENCY OF PUBLICATION

Weekly until 1854; then monthly.

PUBLISHERS

1832–1956: W. and R. Chambers, London and Edinburgh.

EDITORS

William Chambers, numbers 1–14, 1832–1833. Robert Chambers and William Chambers, jointly, 1833–1837. Robert Chambers, 1837–1858 (assisted by Thomas Smibert, 1837–1842; William Harry Willis, 1842–1844; and Leitch Ritchie, 1845–1858). Leitch Ritchie, co-editor, 1858–1862. James Payn, co-editor, 1858–1862. James Payn, 1862–1873. Robert Chambers, Jr., 1873–1888. C.E.S. Chambers, 1888–, assisted by J. Liddell Geddie, joint-editor, 1920–.

Cornelius P. Darcy

CHAMPION, THE

The *Champion* was the first important editorial venture of the remarkable John Scott. He was born in Aberdeen in 1784, and was educated at its grammar school, where he met the young Byron.[1] He later attended Marischal College of the University of Aberdeen, but never took a degree. Scott entered journalism and became the editor of Drakard's *Stamford News* in Lincolnshire. He then edited the new *Drakard's Paper* in London throughout 1813, a periodical that he took over in January 1814 and renamed the *Champion.* The weekly represents Scott's longest editorial endeavor.

In format the *Champion* followed the pattern of its fellow weeklies. It began with a long leading article, usually by the editor, on national and international events, and included an editorial on a center page surrounded by local news, detailed reporting on crucial issues in Parliament, foreign intelligence, reports on the law courts, market prices, bankruptcies, crimes, and accidents, as well as obituaries and other social news. Advertising was at first restricted to notice of a few books on the back page. Both a Saturday edition (for rural subscribers) and a Sunday edition were published. In 1817–1818 a Monday edition was regularly announced.

The *Champion*'s chief rivals were Leigh Hunt's *Examiner,** which in Scott's day was politically further left than the *Champion* and the *Edinburgh Review.**

In 1814 the *Examiner* quarreled with the *Champion* over the sharp criticism of Byron begun by Barnes and continued by Scott. Byron received Barnes's criticism mildly, but was deeply indignant when the *Champion,* without permission, published his "Condolatory Address" to Lady Jersey in 1814, and his "Fare thee well, and if for ever" and "A Sketch from Private Life" in 1816, the time of his marital separation.[2] The *Edinburgh Review,* the great Whig quarterly, was more substantial as a liberal organ than either the *Champion* or the *Examiner*—which were, strictly speaking, newspapers—but, as time has proved, it was inferior to both in literary perception.

The period was stormy and culturally lively. The Prince Regent (later George IV), an extravagant, profligate, and unpopular man, was a frequent target of the *Champion,* although the attacks were not sufficient to incur government prosecution. In 1813 the *Champion* sympathized with the Hunt brothers when they received a two-year sentence for the *Examiner*'s attacks on the Prince Regent. In 1817, as reflected in the *Champion,* the death of the popular Princess Charlotte, the daughter and heir of the Prince Regent, was viewed as a national disaster. Napoleon returned from Elba and met decisive defeat at Waterloo. Luddite riots brought a one-year government suspension of habeas corpus, an act that the *Champion* protested. In 1819, in the "Peterloo Massacre," eleven were killed when the military at Manchester fired into a gathering of reformists. In 1820 George III died, and the new king tried to divorce his wife, Queen Caroline. The *Champion* took her side. For its views on all these matters, the *Champion* was allegedly read by cabinet ministers. Scott was unusual in that he maintained a non-partisan stance. He believed in the ultimate sanity of England and in the soundness of its constitution, but deplored ministerial folly and injustice.[3]

Enlisting able writers was Scott's great strength. In addition to Scott, the *Champion*'s chief contributors were Horace Smith, Thomas Barnes, and later John Hamilton Reynolds. Others included the historical painter Benjamin Robert Haydon, William Hazlitt, Lord Byron, William Wordsworth, Thomas Noon Talfourd, Charles Lamb, John Thelwall, and John Keats. In addition, Charles Wentworth Dilke, a friend of Keats and later the editor of the *Athenaeum,** made contributions, as did Benjamin Bailey and Charles Brown, also friends of Keats.[4]

In the spring of 1814 Hazlitt contributed his first articles, and continued to enliven the *Champion* for a year. He also wrote on drama, signing himself "W.H." or "H.," and sometimes replaced Scott on politics. Hazlitt moved to the *Examiner* beginning in March 1815, probably because he and Scott disagreed on Napoleon, whom Hazlitt admired. Charles Lamb's contributions, apart from "On the Melancholy of Tailors" in December, are impossible to identify with certainty, although "A Challenge," which appeared on 23 January 1814, could very well be his.[5] The piece was an amusing letter on the actress Frances Maria Kelly from a talking dog. (Lamb later proposed to her unsuccessfully.) In September Hazlitt's "Fine Arts: Whether They Are Promoted by Academies and Public Institutions'' aroused wide interest. Lamb wrote in December that he was ready to contribute regularly, but a few days later his sister Mary fell ill, and apparently he was forced to retract.[6] His contributions do not reappear until 1820.

Barnes continued his profiles for a few issues in 1815, but ceased them after early spring because of poor health and other commitments. In June Haydon introduced Scott to Wordsworth and on 25 June Scott called Wordsworth the greatest poet of the age in the *Champion*.[7] A cordial correspondence ensued between the two. Passionately interested in France, Scott managed to visit Paris each summer; excerpts from his two fine travel books, *Paris Visited in 1814* and *Paris Revisited in 1815*, were printed in the *Champion*. Scott himself gradually faded from the *Champion*. At the end of 1815 J. H. Reynolds joined the staff and remained for two years. He probably contributed in all departments and certainly wrote on cultural affairs. His first signed work, which appeared on 9 December, praised Wordsworth's poetry.

On 4 February 1816 the *Champion* published three Wordsworth sonnets, "Inscription for a National Monument, in Commemoration of the Battle of Waterloo," "Occasioned by the Same Battle," and "The Siege of Vienna Raised by John Sobieski." In the same month Scott twice discussed the Elgin Marbles and in March provided an article on "The Political Importance of the Fine Arts." In April Byron's "Fare Thee Well" and "Sketch," which Scott had contrived to obtain from Henry Brougham,[8] caused a sensation, although in general, as Scott had written in the issue of 9 January 1814, the *Champion* avoided "scandal." His long accompanying note to Byron's poems read, in part:

> Lord Byron will not pretend that these poems were not designed as an appeal to the public to throw the blame of his early separation from Lady Byron on the weak and defenceless party. . . . Lord Byron takes advantage of his ground as a popular Poet to attempt to turn the whole current of public reproach and displeasure against his wife, and of its sympathy and admiration towards his injuries and his tender sorrow.[9]

Scott later indicated that he had been misled by others against Byron.[10]

A letter of Wordsworth's dated 11 June 1816 shows that Scott now wished to sell the *Champion* and go abroad. On 27 July 1817 Scott's name was dropped as publisher for that of R. D. Richards. Horace Smith notes that the *Champion* had not proven "a very thriving concern," a statement confirmed by Scott's unpublished letters, and that

> in 1816, the whole was sold to Mr. J. Clayton Jennings (Jennyns), who had been Fiscal at Demerara and Essequibo, in which capacity he considered himself to have been aggrieved by the tyrants of Downing-street; and wanting some weapon wherewith he might blow the foreign secretary

to atoms, he purchased *The Champion* for the accomplishment of his benevolent purpose. His long and heavy charges eventually caused the instrument to explode, dismally shattering its owner's purse, and leaving the foreign secretary undemolished![11]

This account may not be wholly accurate, but Wordsworth's letter of 20 January 1817—"I am glad that Scott has got rid of his *Champion*, I hope he has sold it well"—provides evidence that Scott did indeed sell late in 1816 or soon after, allowing his name to be listed as publisher for another seven months.[12] Jennyns possibly remained the owner until Thelwall bought the *Champion* late in 1818, in which case Reynolds acted only as a manager. Headlines such as "Tyrant Kings and Rebel Subjects," which appeared on 22 June 1817 over what purports to be an abstract discussion, suggest why circulation soon fell off, although the new radical tone was not usually so sharp.

On 17 August 1817 Keats's "On the Sea" appeared. For the first time Keats was contributing to a periodical other than the *Examiner*—perhaps, as Amy Lowell thought, to show independence from Hunt or perhaps merely to show gratitude to Reynolds.[13] Hazlitt reappeared in 1817 with three political articles.[14] His *Characters of Shakespeare's Plays* had been reviewed warmly by Reynolds in July, and presumably Hazlitt found the new *Champion* climate congenial. When the liberty of the press again came under attack by the government, the *Champion* in its December issue extolled the writer and publisher, William Hone, for his vigorous self-defense against government charges of seditious blasphemy and rejoiced in his three acquittals. In December, when Reynolds was about to leave the *Champion*'s staff, he enlisted Keats as a temporary drama critic. On 21 December Keats's "Mr. Kean" ecstatically praised the actor for his Shakespearean roles and for his portrayal of Luke in *Riches*, adapted from Massinger by Sir James Burges. On 4 January 1818 the *Champion*, by then a quarto, carried Keats's reviews of John Dillon's *Retribution, or the Chieftain's Daughter*, a tragedy playing at the Covent Garden, and *Harlequin's Vision* at the Drury Lane.[15] Keats liked neither, and if his reviews show signs of haste, due no doubt to impatience at inferior productions, they are lively and forgiving.

In late 1818 and 1819 the best days of the *Champion* appeared to have passed. On 3 January 1819 Thelwall announced himself as editor and proprietor. He had been acquitted in the State Treason Trials of 1794 and was notorious as a rabble-rouser against the "Gagging Acts" of 1795, although his danger to the nation was much exaggerated. A practicing poet and crusader, he had published his research on inhuman factory conditions and defended the poor against the rich. After government persecution had forced him into political retirement, he taught elocution—and once tried to cure Lamb's stammer. He had been close to Coleridge, Wordsworth, and Southey when all were young, and maintained a tenuous friendship even though they disapproved of his politics.

Under Thelwall circulation of the *Champion* declined from 1,200 in 1817 to a low of 500 in 1819. Contributors became hard to identify except for a few, including Thelwall, Thomas Noon Talfourd, and Charles Lamb. Talfourd was Lamb's first biographer, and as "T. N. T." he reviewed Lamb's 1818 *Works* in two issues for May 1819 with unadulterated enthusiasm. Lamb contributed his poem, in Latin, to Haydon in the issue for 7 May 1820, and the following week published a translation of it. "A Lady's Sapphic" in the issue for 5 November 1820 may be Mary Lamb's.[16] In 1822 Thelwall published, at the Champion Press, *The Poetical Recreations of The Champion,* and revealed that most of the unmemorable verse was his own, published under various signatures. By 1822 the magazine clearly had failed in its wish to become again what it had been under Scott, in part because of Scott's new *London Magazine,** which had attracted some of the old writers as well as many fine new ones.

Notes

1. D. A. Low has established 1784 as Scott's birthdate from Aberdeen records. "A Biographical and Critical Study of John Scott," Ph.D. dissertation, Cambridge University, 1968, p. 7.

2. E. L. Brooks, "Byron and the *London Magazine,*" *Keats-Shelley Journal* 5 (1956):49–67; on Bailey and Brown, see L. M. Jones, "Reynolds and Keats," *Keats-Shelley Journal* 7 (1958):49n.

3. See Jacob Zeitlin, "The Editor of the *London Magazine,*" *Journal of English and Germanic Philology* 20 (1921):328–54; Benjamin R. Haydon, *Autobiography and Memoirs* (New York, 1929), p. 206.

4. Horace Smith, "A Graybeard's Gossip about his Literary Acquaintance," *New Monthly Magazine and Humorist* 81 (1847):415.

5. Low and Josephine Bauer, the latter in "John Scott's Weekly *Champion,* 1813–1817," (Ph.D. dissertation, Birbeck College, 1954), have both identified this article and two others as Lamb's on internal evidence alone.

6. *The Letters of Charles and Mary Lamb,* ed. E. W. Marrs, Jr. (Ithaca, 1978), p. 123.

7. Benjamin R. Haydon, *Diary* (Cambridge, Mass., 1960), 1:450; Zeitlin, p. 340.

8. Haydon, 2:482.

9. T. Rowland Hughes, "John Scott: Editor, Author, and Critic," *London Mercury* 21 (1930):518–28.

10. *Byron: Selected Prose,* ed. Peter Gunn (Harmondsworth, England, 1972), p. 417.

11. Smith, p. 416. I am informed by Prof. Leonidas M. Jones that Smith was wrong to call the buyer Jennings; it was Jennyns, who so signed certain articles in the *Champion.*

12. *The Letters of William and Dorothy Wordsworth,* ed. E. de Selincourt, rev. Mary Moorman and Alan G. Hill, 2d ed. (Oxford, 1969), 2:361–62.

13. Amy Lowell, *John Keats* (Boston, 1925), 1:483.

14. See Herschel Baker, *William Hazlitt* (Cambridge, Mass., 1962), p. 203n.

15. Keats did not mistake the pantomime title, as has been suggested. See, for example, the wrong title given at the head of his review in the Hampstead edition of his *Works,* ed. Forman, 5:252. A glance at the *Champion* shows that he simply failed to

give it. The review title is "Drury Lane Theatre" and Keats's mention of Mozart's title in his first sentence merely indicates the theme, in a discussion of its popular uses. See Robert Gittings, *John Keats* (Boston, 1968), p. 173n.

16. See Charles and Mary Lamb, *Works,* ed. E. V. Lucas (New York, 1903–5), 5:324–25, 335–38.

Information Sources

BIBLIOGRAPHY
Bauer, Josephine. "John Scott's Weekly *Champion,* 1813–1817." Ph.D. dissertation, Birkbeck College, 1954.
Brooks, E. L. "Byron and the *London Magazine.*" *Keats-Shelley Journal* 5 (1956):49–67.
Cestre, Charles. *John Thelwall: A Pioneer of Democracy and Social Reform in England During the French Revolution.* London, 1906.
Hayden, John O. *The Romantic Reviewers, 1802–1824.* Chicago, 1969.
Haydon, B. R. *Diary.* Edited by W. B. Pope. 2 vols. Cambridge, Mass., 1960.
Hudson, Derek. *Thomas Barnes of the "Times."* 1943. Reprint. Westport, Conn., 1973.
———, and Parker, W. M. "Thomas Barnes and 'The Champion.' " *Times Literary Supplement,* 1 and 15 January 1944.
Hughes, T. Rowland. "John Scott: Editor, Author, and Critic." *London Mercury* 20 (1930):518–28.
Jones, L. M. "Keats's Theatrical Review in the *Champion.*" *Keats-Shelley Journal* 3 (1954):55–65.
Low, D. A. "A Biographical and Critical Study of John Scott, 1784–1821." Ph.D. dissertation, Cambridge University, 1968.
O'Leary, Patrick. *Regency Editor: A Life of John Scott.* Aberdeen, 1983.
The Poetical Recreations of the Champion, and His Literary Correspondents; with a Selection of Essays, Literary and Critical, which have appeared in the Champion Newspaper. Edited by John Thelwall. London, 1822.
Scott, John. Unpublished letters from and to him: Houghton Library (Harvard), the National Library of Scotland, and Dove Cottage Library, Grasmere.
(Smith, Horace). "A Graybeard's Gossip about his Literary Acquaintance." *New Monthly Magazine and Humorist* 81 (1847):415–20.
Turnbull, John M. "Keats, Reynolds, and *The Champion.*" *London Mercury* 19 (1929):384–94.
Zeitlin, Jacob. "The Editor of the *London Magazine.*" *Journal of English and Germanic Philology* 20 (1921):328–54.
INDEXES
Bound volumes have indexes.
REPRINT EDITIONS
Microform: British Museum Newspaper Library, London. World Microfilms Publications, London.
LOCATION SOURCES
American
Partial runs: California State Library, Sutro Branch; State Historical Society of Wisconsin; U. S. Library of Congress; University of Illinois Library; University of Texas Library; Yale University Library; New York Public Library.

British
    Complete run: British Museum (London Copy has prospectus).
    Partial runs: Bodleian Library; Guildhall Library; London University Library.

Publication History

MAGAZINE TITLE AND TITLE CHANGES (Dates are of Sunday edition)
    Drakard's Paper: A London Saturday and Sunday Journal, 10 January–4 April 1813
    (folio, eight-page format). *Drakard's Paper: A London Weekly Journal*, 11 April–
    26 December 1813. *The Champion: A London Weekly Journal*, 2 January 1814–
    15 June 1817. *The Champion and Sunday Review of Politics, Literature, and the
    Arts*, 4 January–29 March 1818 (changes to sixteen-page quarto). *The Champion
    and Sunday Review of Weekly News, Literature, and the Arts*, 5 April 1818–23
    January 1820. *The Champion*, 30 January 1820–9 June 1822. *The Investigator*,
    16 June–7 July 1822.
VOLUME AND ISSUE DATA
    Numbers 1–496, 10 January 1813–7 July 1822.
FREQUENCY OF PUBLICATION
    Weekly.
PUBLISHERS
    10 January 1813–20 July 1817: John Scott, 177 Fleet Street, London/1 Catherine
    Street, Strand, London. 27 July 1817–13 September 1818: R. D. Richards(?) or
    J. Clayton Jennyns(?), 1 Catherine Street, Strand, London. 20 September 1818–
    27 December 1818: (no publisher listed) 1 Catherine Street, Strand, London. 3
    January 1819–30 December 1821: John Thelwall, 1 Catherine Street, Strand,
    London/271 Strand, London. 6 January 1822–24 February 1822; Thomas Wood,
    393 Strand, London/276 Strand, London/271 Strand, London. 3 March–2 June
    1822: C. H. Cowdroy, 271 Strand/49 Wyck St., Picket St., Strand, London. 9
    June–7 July 1822: D. Deans, 49 Wyck St., Picket St., Strand.
EDITORS
    John Scott, 10 January 1813–20 July 1817. Unknown (part Thelwall?), 27 July
    1817–27 December 1818. John Thelwall, 3 January 1819–30 December 1821.
    Unknown, 6 January–7 July 1822.

Winifred F. Courtney

COMPANION, THE

Leigh Hunt was quite specific, in the first number, about his purposes and
principles in his new 1828 weekly *Companion:* in "occasionally" reviewing
new books, "we shall obey, in all cases, the impulse of the moment, answering
only for sincerity and good intention"; "our politics will be addressed to those,
who caring little for them in detail, are desirous of becoming acquainted with
anything that concerns mankind at large"; "we hope to have a criticism on
some play or performer every week" and "say to the performers:—'If you do
not give way to your impulses and animal spirits, and act as if you cared no
more for a critic than an old crust, we shall have no respect for you'" (no.
1:5–8).[1] Hunt began the paper on Wednesday, 9 January 1828, as an eight-

page, three-pence weekly, but expanded it after the fourth number to sixteen pages, at four pence.[2]

"Chatting comfortably in good faith with our companion the reader," no matter what his topic, Hunt continues in the *Companion* the casual, pleasant, desultory, associative writing that had characterized his essays in the *Indicator*.* But the *Companion* differs from the *Indicator* in its attention to theatrical criticism and in its more direct statement of the philosophy underlying Hunt's topical observations.

Hunt's theatrical criticism contains its share of chatter: comments on the goings-on around him, digressions only barely relevant to the play before him—remarks that lead even Hunt at one point to realize, "but we are forgetting the play" (no. 3:19). The one subject that again and again propels Hunt above rather predictable notices of routine performances is the acting of Madame Pasta. Hunt was clearly enamoured of "the soul in her voice," "the sincerity in her face." Her genius lay in her "truth," her ability to produce effects without any evidence of theatrical effort: "She never pretended that she had taken herself for the character she represented; but she had sympathized with it so strongly, that it became the next thing to reality." With the exception of two later articles on Madame Pasta, the theatrical notices ended with the ninth number, as Hunt was forced by ill health to give up late nights at the theaters (no. 4:30–31; no. 7:75. Cf. no. 5:34–39; no. 9:112; no. 15:194).

Sincerity, whether in things theatrical, personal, or political, lay at the heart of Hunt's belief that man "can philosophize, and reform, and cast off old customs, and take steps for laying the whole globe nearer to the sum of wisdom and happiness" (no. 28:412). Hunt openly proclaimed "the advancement of the glorious progress of society"—a "moral as well as mechanical advancement"—perhaps divinely directed and certainly aided by a free press which helps "to render the stream of public opinion irresistible (no. 19:258; no. 29:429; no. 1:6). Hunt's philosophy was as casual as his style; only rarely in the *Companion* did he specifically discuss the political or religious aspects of this advancement (cf. 16:209–13, 221–23; no. 17:232–39; no. 18:241–43; no. 19:257–61), and at times it led him into strange apologies:

> But how, it may be said, are we to enjoy ourselves with reflection, when our very reflection will teach us the quantity of suffering that exists? How are we to be happy with breakfasting and warming our hands, when so many of our fellow-creatures are, at that instant, cold and hungry?—It is no paradox to answer, that the fact of our remembering them, gives us a right to forget them:—we mean, that "there is a time for all things," and that having done our duty at other times in sympathising with pain, we have not only a right, but it becomes our duty, to shew the happy privileges of virtue by sympathising with pleasure. [no. 2:11]

Hunt's easy faith is the more remarkable considering his own difficult life, though he feels it was in fact this faith that made that life bearable. He writes in the "Introduction" to the collected edition of *The Indicator, and The Companion* that both works "were written during times of great trouble with him, and both helped him to see much of that fair play between his own anxieties and his natural cheerfulness, of which an indestructible belief in the good and the beautiful has rendered him perhaps not undeserving.[3]

The "illness and other circumstances"—perhaps the distraction of the controversy surrounding the publication at this time of his *Lord Byron and Some of His Contemporaries*—that forced Hunt to abandon his theatrical reviews soon forced him to give up the *Companion* altogether (no. 15:193). Even as early as numbers 8 and 9, issues were filled up with long extracts; number 10 and half of number 11 were devoted to a review of Hazlitt's *Plain Speaker,* a work published in 1826.[4] Hunt seems to have recovered from mid-March to early May, but with number 19 (14 May 1828) reprinted material again becomes predominant. The end came with the twenty-ninth number on 23 July 1828.

Louis Landré has called the *Companion* "hardly viable," its author "appeased and a little tired."[5] Yet it seems typically Hunt, in its manner and its matter, and no less in its demise. In bidding farewell to his readers, Hunt says: "I could neither pay attention enough, nor afford to wait time enough, to get it up to a sale that should indemnify all parties concerned, without more help than the speculation was thought to warrant. I therefore take leave of my readers; shaking them by the hand all round" (no. 29:428).[6]

Notes

1. The essay, "Books, Politics, and Theatricals," is reprinted in *Leigh Hunt's Literary Criticism,* ed. Lawrence Huston Houtchens and Carolyn Washburn Houtchens (New York, 1956), pp. 239–42.

2. In number 4 (30 January 1828) Hunt noted that some had objected that the paper was too short for its price; but having before published the *Indicator* "at a price below what it ought to have been; we recollected under what circumstances of trouble and ill-health we wrote them," and so in the *Companion* "we allowed ourselves to go to something of the other extreme" (p. 32).

3. (London, 1834), 1:x. See also the *Companion,* no. 29 (23 July 1828):428.

4. No. 10 (12 March 1828):113–28; no. 11 (19 March 1828):129–36; reprinted in *Leigh Hunt's Literary Criticism,* pp. 243–67.

5. *Leigh Hunt (1784–1859): Contribution à l'histoire du Romantisme Anglais,* Société d'Édition "Les Belles-Lettres," (Paris 1936), 1:183 (my translation).

6. See also *The Autobiography of Leigh Hunt,* new ed., rev. by the Author, with a further revision and an introduction, by his Eldest Son (London, 1860), p. 408. "The Companion's Farewell to His Readers" is reprinted in *Leigh Hunt's Literary Criticism,* pp. 268–74.

Information Sources

BIBLIOGRAPHY

Hunt, Leigh. *The Indicator, and The Companion; A Miscellany for the Fields and the Fire-side.* 2 vols. London, 1834. [Reprints, with revisions, fourteen of the essays from the *Companion.*]

————. *Leigh Hunt's Literary Criticism*. Edited by Lawrence Huston Houtchens and Carolyn Washburn Houtchens. New York, 1956.

Landré, Louis. *Leigh Hunt (1784–1859): Contribution à l'histoire du Romantisme Anglais*. 2 vols. Paris, 1936.

INDEXES
> None.

REPRINT EDITIONS
> *The Indicator, and The Companion,* 2 vols., 1834. AMS Press Inc., New York, 1967.
>
> Microform: English Literary Periodicals (UMI), reel 714.

LOCATION SOURCES

American
> Widely available.

British
> Complete runs: Birmingham Public Library; Bristol University Library; British Museum; Chetham's Library (Manchester); Greenock (Scotland) Library; Manchester Public Library.
>
> Partial run: Cambridge University Library.

Publication History

MAGAZINE TITLE AND TITLE CHANGES
> *The Companion.*

VOLUME AND ISSUE DATA
> Numbers 1–29, 9 January–23 July 1828.

FREQUENCY OF PUBLICATION
> Weekly.

PUBLISHER
> Hunt and Clarke, York Street, Covent Garden, London.

EDITOR
> Leigh Hunt.

N. S. Bauer

COUNTRY LITERARY CHRONICLE, THE. See LITERARY CHRONICLE AND WEEKLY REVIEW, THE

COURT MAGAZINE AND BELLE ASSEMBLÉE, THE. See BELLE ASSEMBLÉE, LA

CRITICAL REVIEW, THE. See AAAJ

——— D ———

DIRECTOR, THE

When the first issue of the *Director* appeared on Saturday, 24 January 1807, its founder, the Rev. Mr. Thomas Frognall Dibdin, announced his resolution "that my countrymen shall be indebted to me, for the *chivalrous attempt* to promote, improve, and refine, the arts and sciences in the British empire." The title for this weekly publication was chosen because of Dibdin's offer of himself "to the public as a mere *guide post, to direct* the course of others to moral and intellectual excellence." His direction takes the form of essays on literature, the fine arts, and manners; of accounts of rare books and the book sales in England beginning at the end of the seventeenth century; of summaries of the lectures of the Royal Society and the Royal Academy; and of minutes of the proceedings of the societies of Antiquaries and of Arts, and of the Royal, London, and British institutions.[1]

When he summarizes a lecture, Dibdin does mention the name of the speaker; but when, in keeping with his usual plan, he begins each issue with an essay, he variously ascribes that effort to "Y," who is "a learned and valuable friend" (no. 2), "A Friend to English Artists" (no. 4), "Rusticus" (no. 16), or "A.Z." (no. 19 and elsewhere). It may be that Dibdin himself is responsible for such essays, although the *Dictionary of National Biography* estimates that Dibdin himself "wrote, perhaps, two-thirds, [of] the 'Bibliographiana' and 'British Gallery.' "[2] Although there is some question concerning authorship of particular items, there is none concerning the moral intention or pietistic tone of the magazine. In the second of his lectures on drama, the Rev. Mr. Crowe labels the Restoration as the period of profligacy, and the present age as the period of correctness (no. 10). In his sixth lecture, dealing with "that part of tragedy, by which the characters are made known, viz. the sentiments," Crowe advises that morally bad sentiments "should be sparingly introduced," and informs readers that sentiments are rendered faulty when the writer "ascribes mean or low sentiments to characters of dignity" (no. 12). In the tragedies of early English writers, dignity was also diminished by the inclusion of a "sanguinary catastrophe" and scenes that were "indecorus, and savage, and horrid" (no. 10). Describing pictures in the British Gallery illustrating the effect of good and bad conduct, Dibdin rates J. Northcote's "The good girl in her chamber, at her devotions," as perhaps the best picture of the series:

> When the pencil is employed on such subjects, the connoisseur readily assents to the sacrifice of the higher departments of the art, in consideration of the extensive good which such representations seldom fail to produce. One immoral character converted, is worth a thousand rapturous exclamations of the knowing. [No. 8]

The sketches of modern characters, although written in a lighter vein and slightly reminiscent of Addison and Steele, are equally didactic. There are beaus engaged in all manner of trivia. There are the superficial "dashing Beaus," who skim, "like summer swallows, along life's surface"; and the theatrical beau, "who can just endure to hear Kemble deliver a soliloquy or Cooke utter a sarcasm, but to sit a whole play through, is an effort beyond the strength of his faculties to bear" (no. 8). These sketches are followed, in later issues, by delineations of the modern belle. Equally mindless are the sprightly belle and the funny belle. The features of the sprightly belle "are never saddened with melancholy: the funeral of a statesman, or the concert of a duchess, equally witness the smiling complacency of her countenance." With the coming of age and the habit of reflection, such women discover "that a few hours devoted in their former days to reading and meditation, would have made them much more sprightly at sixty then [sic] does a retrospect of their gaieties and amusements" (no. 10). With no sense of decorum, the funny belle is alike prone to titter during the "impressive warbling of Catalini" or the efforts of Mrs. Siddons to wring the hearts of her audience.

A similar approach is made to the correction of taste. Henry Rusticus, retired from London to the country for some years, writes to Mr. Director what his family have seen during a visit to London, where the shops frequently offend against good taste. Noticeable in the upholstery and furniture shops are exteriors so grand as to suggest temples. This grand effect is heightened by the use of marble in exterior decoration, and by affixing to the fronts of shops ornaments more appropriate to the bow of a ship than to places of business. Nor does Henry, whose tastes were formed from a study of such men as Vitrivius and Inigo Jones, approve of the Gothic decoration of furniture with satyrs, fauns, and animals of all kinds (no. 16).

Despite his enthusiasm for bibliography, Dibdin's ability in that field has been questioned. Luard cites Dyce, who describes Dibdin as "an ignorant pretender, without the learning of a schoolboy, who published a quantity of books swarming with errors of every description.'' In particular Luard criticizes Dibdin's catalogue of the major rarities of Lord Spencer's library. Unable to read Greek, Dibdin composed descriptions ''so full of errors that it may be doubted if a single one is really accurate.''[3] There is, however, no doubting the zeal of the author of ''Bibliographiana,'' for whom rare books are the ''blazing stars and comets in the bibliographical region'' (no. 3). His regret seems genuine when he recalls that the part of the Harleian Library which was disposed of to Thomas Osborne for 10,000 pounds cost Lord Oxford 18,000 pounds for the binding alone.

Dibdin also touches upon the book sales of two men mentioned in Pope's poetry, Dr. Mead and Mr. John (Orator) Henley.[4] A generous man, Dr. Mead treated without charge all clergy and needy laymen (no. 10). Remarkable for its ''whimsical publications,'' Henley's collection befitted a man unfortunate enough to be berated three times in Pope's *Dunciad*. Item 170 was, according to Dibdin, ''Speech upon Speech. A Telescope for Tournay. No Battle, but worse, and the true Meaning of it. An Army Beaten and interred'' (no. 15). But for anyone reading the *Director* almost two centuries after its publication, the magazine's assessment of problems in the theater with the proscenium and the use of scenery and properties will be undoubtedly more interesting than information about book sales.

An unidentified critic reasons that, as a picture requires a frame, so the stage needs to be set apart by the proscenium, as is done on the Continent but not in England. Here boxes fill more space on the stage than does scenery. To that considerable portion of the audience seated in boxes by or over the stage, scenery must lose some of its effectiveness, and actors must likewise lose some of their effectiveness because they are viewed from behind. Although abroad the proscenium is solid, in England it contains doors through which actors enter and exit, and because of the proximity of boxes to the proscenium, the laughter of an audience blends with the speeches of actors, and voices on stage are swallowed by the doors.

In the Continental theater, every change of scenery is accomplished by the use of machinery. Unfortunately, such is not true of the English theater where, when scenery is to be shifted, ''out pop a parcel of fellows in ragged laced liveries, to announce the event, and to bring it about by mere manual labour'' (no. 23). Their talking distracts the actors, and the random nature of their movements disturbs the audience: ''Here a wing comes rolling on the stage before its time, there another lags behind until perhaps the time for a new removal is arrived'' (no. 23). Nor, in violation of the laws of perspective, do wings, drops, and flats unite to form a single theme. On the French stage, a scene representing a room always contains, in the very center of the flat or closing part, a door, through which the actors may enter and exit. When the text of the play calls for them, doors are also placed in the side wings. In England, however, actors must either use the proscenium doors or weave their way ''in and out, between the intervals of the wings, which are generally intended to represent a solid cohering wall'' (no. 23). Whereas the French stage is always appropriately furnished, the English stage is supplied with furniture only when needed. As if they are endowed with second sight, liveried servants appear, dragging onto an otherwise unfurnished stage two cumbersome arm chairs. Such are the faults of English theater.

Whatever faults the *Director* may have, excessive length is not among them. In the twenty-third issue of the magazine Dibdin announces his intent to cease publication for the season after the next number. Although he says ''adieu till the year 1808,'' he did not resume publication.

Notes

1. The Society of Antiquaries had been founded by Bishop Matthew Parker about 1572 and lasted until 1604, when James I, suspecting the political intentions of the Society, abolished it. The Society of Arts, founded in 1754, met at the Adelphi to hear lectures on art. The Royal Institution was founded in 1799, largely through the efforts of Count Rumford, to spread the knowledge of scientific discoveries and to apply that knowledge to the improvement of arts and industry. The London Institution was founded in 1805 principally to develop the economical means of supplying heat and food to the poor. The Society's lectures were extended to include talks on art and literature by men like Coleridge and Landseer.

The British Institution was founded in 1805 to foster the development of the fine arts. Its founders were aristocrats and wealthy businessmen who thought that the government was not doing enough to encourage the arts. The British Gallery was an adjunct of the British Institution and held a biannual exhibition in competition with the Royal Academy.

2. *Dictionary of National Biography,* s.v. ''Dibdin, Thomas Frognall.''

3. Ibid.

4. Mead is mentioned in *Moral Essay* 4, 1. 10; Henley in *The Dunciad* 2, 11. 2, 425; 3, 1. 29.

Information Sources

BIBLIOGRAPHY

Halévy, Elie. *A History of the French People in 1815*. Translated by E. I. Watkin and D. A. Barker. New York, 1924.

Jones, Spence. *The Royal Institution: Its Founders and Its First Professors*. 1871. Reprint New York, 1975.

INDEXES

Indexed at end of volume 2.

REPRINT EDITIONS

Microform: Early British Periodicals (UMI), reel 235.

LOCATION SOURCES

American

Widely available.

British

Widely available.

Publication History

MAGAZINE TITLE AND TITLE CHANGES
The Director: a weekly literary journal.
VOLUME AND ISSUE DATA
Volumes 1–2, numbers 1–24, 24 January–4 July 1807.
FREQUENCY OF PUBLICATION
Weekly.
PUBLISHER
William Savage, Bedford Bury, London.
EDITOR
Thomas Frognall Dibdin.

Jay H. Hartman

DRAKARD'S PAPER. See CHAMPION, THE

DUBLIN LITERARY GAZETTE, THE

A number of periodical publications made their appearance in Dublin in the 1830s. Nearly all of them were ephemeral; they flourished for a brief season, then wilted and died in a literary climate where only the rhetoric of debate could survive. Most of them were so obscure and short-lived that they sank without a trace, so that even their titles are forgotten and they can no longer be traced.

One of the better known, however, was the *Dublin Literary Gazette*. It appeared weekly from 2 January to 26 June 1830. From July 1830 until the end of the year it was issued monthly as the *National Magazine,* and in January 1831 it appeared as the *National Magazine and Dublin Literary Gazette.* Another number appeared in April of that year, after which it ceased publication.

Except for the last two numbers, it was edited by a novelist, song-writer, and portrait painter, Samuel Lover, who later achieved fame with his novels *Rory O'More* (1837) and *Handy Andy* (1842). The last two numbers were edited by Philip Dixon Hardy, journalist and minor writer on religious controversy. The editorial introducing the first number explained the object in publishing a thing "so novel in Ireland as a periodical devoted to the interests of Literature, and the pursuits of Science and the Arts."

The want of such a journal . . . has long been a reproach to the Capital of Ireland, and throws a damp over every effort to raise her to her national rank in the publishing and literary world. In genius, talent and learning, Dublin yields to no Metropolis in Europe, of similar extent; but these . . . are consigned to silence and oblivion because they want a popular record. Men whose exertions have been already stamped with the seal of public approbation in the literature of Great Britain, have now united for the purpose of taking away this reproach from their native City.

The editor, however, did not underestimate the difficulties facing such a venture and realized that in Ireland a double task awaited him. He had, in some measure, to create the taste he sought to satisfy. A weekly number consisted of an average of fifteen pages, and the contents were normally made up as follows: a main article; book reviews (followed by shorter notices); a second article or sketch; notices of foreign literature; reviews of contemporary journals; correspondence; reports of the stage, music, and art exhibitions; and "original poetry." Many of the main articles appeared in serial form, and all except the first were anonymous. The first article was a sketch of Irish life entitled "Kate Connor," and was specially written for the journal by the novelist Anna Maria Hall (Mrs. S. C. Hall), author of *Sketches of Irish Character* (1829) and various other works. Perhaps the most interesting of the main articles that appeared serially were the "Notes from the Log-book of a Rambler." These autobiographical accounts of the author's travels were contributed anonymously by a medical student, Charles James Lever, future author of *Harry Lorrequer* (1837) and *Charles O'Malley*. Other features include a series of "Personal Sketches"—of Wellington, Edward Pennefalter (an Irish barrister), Brougham, Sir James Scarlet (attorney-general), Whitley Stokes (the physician), Joseph Hume, and Denman (a lawyer)—articles on the fine arts in Ireland, "the Irish in London," "Reveries and Recollections in Dublin," "Highways and Byways in Ireland," and Sir Walter Scott's "Autobiography."

Information Sources

INDEXES
List of contents for each volume.

REPRINT EDITIONS
None.

LOCATION SOURCES
American
Complete runs: Louisiana State University Library; New York Public Library; St. Mary of the Lake Seminary Library; University of Chicago Library; University of Illinois Library; Yale University Library.

British
Complete runs: British Museum; London Library; National Library of Ireland; Victoria and Albert Museum.
Partial runs: Cambridge University Library; Edinburgh University Library; Linen Hall Library (Belfast).

Publication History

MAGAZINE TITLE AND TITLE CHANGES
The Dublin Literary Gazette, or Weekly Chronicle of Criticism, Belle Lettres, and Fine Arts, 2 January–26 June 1830. *The Dublin Literary Gazette and Na-*

tional Magazine, July–December 1830. *The National Magazine and Dublin Literary Gazette*, January–April 1831.

VOLUME AND ISSUE DATA

Volume 1, numbers 1–26, 2 January–26 June 1830; Volume 1, numbers 1–6 (27–32), July–December 1830; Volume 2, numbers 7–10, January–April 1831.

FREQUENCY OF PUBLICATION

Weekly, 2 January–26 June 1830; monthly thereafter.

PUBLISHERS

W. F. Wakeman, 9 D'Olier Street, Dublin. Hurst Chance and Co., 65 St. Paul's Churchyard, London. Oliver and Boyd, Edinburgh.

EDITORS

Samuel Lover, January–October 1830. Philip Dixon Hardy, November 1830–April 1831.

Austin Seckersen

DUBLIN REVIEW, THE

The *Dublin Review,* founded in London in 1836, quickly became a major voice of the Catholic revival in England, appealing to an educated readership on a variety of topics: history and politics, theology and church affairs, philosophy and ethics, education and the position of women, natural history, travel, and the arts.

Michael Joseph Quin, an Irish lawyer and journalist in London, interested the scholarly young churchman Nicholas Wiseman in starting a Catholic review. Daniel O'Connell, already something of an elder statesman, was the third co-founder; he was listed as a proprietor and financial contributor until 1843.[1] Wiseman welcomed the proposal provided "that no extreme political views" should intrude.[2]

Quin's experience as editor of the *Monthly Review** (see *AAAJ*) from 1825 to 1832 made him the obvious first editor, although, since he drew no salary, he could handle only numbers 1 and 2. His association with the *Dublin* as a writer, however, was lifelong. Over two dozen articles from his versatile pen over the first seven years reveal him as an earnest and well-informed ecologist,[3] seasoned traveller, critic and historian of music and poetry, and commentator on current affairs at home and abroad. About one-fourth of Quin's articles dealt with Irish problems.

The title of the new journal and its green cover with "Eire go brath" certainly suggested concern with, but did not mean to imply exclusive or even primary attention to, Irish affairs. The *Dublin Review,* it was hoped, would be a Catholic counterweight to the powerful *Edinburgh Review.** The word *Catholic* was avoided in the title as suggesting militancy, sectarianism, or an ineffective predecessor (198:284–310).

Although in 1836 he was still rector of the English College in Rome, Wiseman proved to be the most enthusiastic and persevering co-founder of the *Dub-*

lin Review. He contributed substantial articles—some were lectures delivered during his 1835–1836 visit to England—and with that "Christian gentleman . . . scholar," Charles William Russell of Maynooth,[4] shaped editorial policy during the crucial decades of the Tractarian Movement, Newman's submission to Rome (1844), and the influx of Oxford converts.

Fragile finances and tensions between liberal and conservative elements within the Catholic body, the newcomers and the old Catholics, made Wiseman's task a delicate one (198:199–200). In fact, his second editor, Mark Aloysius Tierney, a distinguished antiquarian and chaplain to the Duke of Norfolk, was by 1847 an opponent of Wiseman, the new Vicar Apostolic of the London district, preferring "a bishop of the less Roman School."[5] Tierney edited only the third number of the *Dublin Review* for December 1836. The next two issues for April and July 1837 were edited by James Smith, a Scottish lawyer, convert from Presbyterianism, and defender of Roman Catholicism, who had founded the *Edinburgh Catholic Magazine* in 1832 and, after interim service on the *Dublin,* inaugurated the annual *Catholic Directory* in 1838. Stability came with the sixth number for October 1837, when Henry Ridgard Bagshawe became executive editor, with Wiseman and Russell largely controlling the selection of articles. Stability remained until William George Ward, succeeding Bagshawe in July 1863, began a new series and a new era, actively combating the liberal Catholicism of the *Rambler* * (see *VEA*), the *Home and Foreign Review,* and the *North British Review* * (see *VEA*).[6]

It speaks much for the vigor and tenacity of the first men that the *Dublin Review* weathered its beginnings; in the incredible hexameters of Shane Leslie's "Centennial Ode," "Few were the Quarterly-calibred writers and few the subscribers. . . . Keeping the flag at the masthead once Russell wrote five of his papers" (198:187–88). With reason Wiseman worried in an 1853 letter about "getting into too few hands" (198:203). After the restoration of the English hierarchy in 1850 and the storm of prejudice such "papal aggression" unleashed it required all Wiseman's urbanity to sustain his position as newly created cardinal without appearing embattled.

The proprietorship of the *Dublin* was given to and remained officially with the archbishops of Westminster.[7] From Wiseman the editorship passed in 1862 to Henry Edward Manning. Herbert Alfred Vaughan bought it in 1878 and willed it to his successors.[8] The two editors immediately after W. G. Ward were bishops—the learned Benedictine John Cuthbert Hedley, and Vaughan himself.[9] When the latter became the archbishop in 1892 he transferred the *Dublin* editorship (while retaining a measure of control) to Monsignor James Moyse, after whom it returned in 1906 to lay editors, including Ward's son, Wilfrid, under whom the quarterly "became a focus for the whole of Catholic opinion" (198:241). Ward was assisted in his last two issues by Monsignor Arthur Stapylton Barnes, Shane Leslie (with Wilfrid Meynell as able deputy),[10] and Algar Thorold, whose editorship regretfully terminated in 1934 because of financial stress. Burns and Oates (and, at this time, Washbourne), who had printed the *Dublin* for years, could manage editorial matters without the luxury of "an official appointed editor."[11] But Denis Gwynn was called in to edit the centenary number in 1936 and continued as associate editor with Lord Clonmore until Christopher Dawson began the 1940s, followed by T. S. Gregory and T. F. Burns before the decade was out.[12]

During Michael Derrick's editorship Cardinal Godfrey changed the title to the *Wiseman Review* as a tribute to the quarterly's chief founder and to dispel lingering misapprehensions of its Irishness.[13] After just four years the old title was restored (Spring 1965) by the editor Norman St. John-Stevas, "with the consent and approval of the proprietor, Cardinal Heenan" (239:3). But the *Dublin*'s days were numbered. An "Important Notice to All Subscribers" at the beginning of the Winter 1968–1969 issue of the *Dublin Review* announced the end of the journal's independent existence and its incorporation into the *Month* * (see *VEA*) from the latter's July/August 1969 issue. Thomas Corbishley (one of the editors of the *Month*), greeted this "Marriage of Two Minds" as a "logical step" in an "increasingly competitive situation."[14]

Over its 134 years of continuous publication, a remarkably high standard of intellectual content and literary quality prevailed. The beginning and end of the founders' period saw Wiseman's article on *Tracts for the Times* (August 1839), which triggered Newman's capitulation to Rome (7:139–80), and C. W. Russell's "Critical History of the Sonnet" in the numbers for October 1876 and January 1877 (79:400–430; 80:141–80).

Even when it was a "theological battering ram" under W. G. Ward, especially on the subject of papal infallibility, the *Dublin* maintained a balance of interests. Ward wisely left to his sub-editors Edward Healy Thompson and Cashel Hoey all matters literary, historical, and political. Frances Hoey, Cashel's wife, did several articles on novelists—Trollope, Charles Lever, Dickens, Thackeray, Jane Austen. Frances Mary Ward, W. G.'s wife, was an occasional reviewer. Bishop Hedley reduced the polemical ingredient, broadened the cultural coverage, brought in more foreign and non-Catholic contributors, and published more signed articles, book notices, and science notes.[15]

The *Dublin Review* did not remain the single Catholic voice of theology, culture, and current comment. The *Month* (Jesuit, from 1865), *Downside Review* (Benedictine, 1880), *Blackfriars* (Dominican, 1920, declaring itself the *Catholic Review* "revived and renamed"), and the *Clergy Review* (1931, "seminary priests writing for seminary priests") came to share the responsibility and to some extent the same pool of contributors. The competition was healthy, and the *Dublin Review,* particularly during Wilfrid Ward's ten-year editorship, "its most distinguished" period, demonstrated with new vigor and fresh content the very "stability of . . . outlook" and "continuity of thought" that made it still, in 1948, "the 'high-brow' quarterly of the Church."[16]

Notes

Original volume numbers of the *Dublin Review* are cited in the text and in the notes.

1. Denis Gwynn says O'Connell "repudiated all connection . . . at an early stage, because he disagreed with the politics of its editors." "The *Dublin Review* and the Catholic Press," *Dublin Review* 198 (1936):312.

2. Nicholas Wiseman, "Preface to Essays on Various Subjects" (London, 1853), reprinted after Wiseman's death in Henry Edward Manning, "Memorial," *Dublin Review* 56 (1865):268–70.

3. "Economy of the Earth," 1 (1836):1–27; "Economy of the Atmosphere," 9 (1840):289–316.

4. S. Austin Allibone, in *A Critical Dictionary of English Literature and British and American Authors Living and Deceased* (London, 1872), so characterizes Russell, quoting the *Athenaeum* (1858). Dr. Russell continued his active cooperation up to the beginning of 1877. See P. J. McLaughlin, "Dr. Russell and the *Dublin Review*," *English Studies* 41 (1952):175–88. McLaughlin's five-page list of some 160 articles by Russell is appropriately confirmed, corrected, and supplemented by the *Wellesley Index*. See also Matthew Russell in the *Irish Monthly* of the early 1890s: 20 (1892) and 21 (1893) *passim;* 22 (1894):632–42; 23 (1895):51–56.

5. Wilfrid Ward, *Life and Times of Cardinal Wiseman* (London, 1897), 1:515.

6. The *Rambler* began in 1848 and was replaced by the *Home and Foreign Review* (1862–1864). The *North British Review* had existed since 1844 but became a liberal Catholic organ under Lord Acton only in 1869 (until 1871).

7. See Denis Gwynn, "The Centenary of the *Dublin Review*," *Clergy Review* 11 (1936):372–80.

8. Francis Alphonsus Bourne, 1903–1935; Arthur Hinsley, 1935–1943; Bernard Griffin, 1943–1956; William Godfrey, 1957–1963; John Carmel Heenan, 1963–1975.

9. See the tribute by Wilfrid Ward, "Bishop Hedley," 158 (1916):1–12: "We have lost in Bishop Hedley almost the last link with the memorable past that immediately succeeded the Oxford Movement." A born Catholic and a monk, he was nonetheless strongly influenced by Newman and known for great openness of mind.

10. Viola Meynell, *Francis Thompson and Wilfrid Meynell: A Memoir* (London, 1952), pp. 83, 141, 199.

11. Gwynn, p. 374.

12. William Cecil James Howard became the eighth earl of Wicklow. After taking Anglican Orders in 1929 he was received into the Catholic Church in 1931. His *Pius IX and World Peace* attracted critical notice in 1937, in which year he became a director of Burns, Oates and Washbourne and, plausibly enough, began his three years of associate editorship of the *Dublin*.

Theophilus Stephen Gregory, born 1897, became a Methodist minister in 1921 and a Roman Catholic in 1935. He is remembered for his *Unfinished Universe,* 1936.

Thomas Ferrier Burns, born 1906, was experienced in the publishing world—with Sheed and Ward, 1928–1934, then with Longmans. He became a director of the *Tablet* in 1936, and gave the *Dublin Review* a new lease on life in 1947.

13. *Wiseman Review (Dublin Review)* 235 (1961):(3). During Godfrey's proprietorship the journal for the first time carried an *Imprimatur* and *Nihil Obstat*. This ecclesiastical permission had been implicit before 1961 and was evidently so considered again after 1965.

14. *Month* 42 (1969):4–7.

15. See Hedley's "Catholicism and Culture," 84 (1879):3–26, for his attitude at the beginning of his editorship. His failure to mention Newman in this article was construed by some as hostility, but this charge was belied by Hedley's sincere praise of the newly made cardinal in July 1879 (85:187–203). Newman contributed only one article to the *Dublin*, on Keble's *Lyra Innocentium* (20 [1846]:434–61). His aversion to Daniel O'Connell had originally put him off, and the ultramontanism of Manning and W. G. Ward was a deterrent later. See Henry Tristram, "Cardinal Newman and the *Dublin Review*," 198 (1936):22–34.

16. Thomas Corbishley, "Marriage of Two Minds," *Month* 42 (1969):6; Barbara Wall, "London Letter," *America* 79 (1948):409.

Information Sources

BIBLIOGRAPHY
Corbishley, Thomas. "Marriage of Two Minds." *Month* 42 (1969):4–7.
Dublin Review 198 (April 1936). (Centenary number.)
Houghton, Walter. *The Wellesley Index to Victorian Periodicals*. Vol. 2. Toronto, 1972.
Wall, Barbara. "London Letter." *America* 79 (August 1948):409.
Walsh, Leo J. "William Ward and the Dublin Review." Ph.D. dissertation, Columbia University, 1962.
Ward, Wilfrid. *Life and Times of Cardinal Wiseman*. 2d ed. 2 vols. London, 1897.
———. *William George Ward and the Catholic Revival*. London, 1893.

INDEXES
Indexes for each volume, May 1836–October 1910. Volumes 1–52 in *"Dublin Review": Complete List of Articles*. London, 1936. Volumes 1–118, list of contents by volume, in volume 118. Indexes to volumes 1–197, reprinted separately (Carrollton Press). 1836–1881 in *Poole's Index*. 1836–1900 in *Wellesley Index* 2.

REPRINT EDITIONS
Microform: Early British Periodicals (UMI), reels 320–344.

LOCATION SOURCES
American
Widely available.
British
Widely available.

Publication History

MAGAZINE TITLE AND TITLE CHANGES
The Dublin Review, 1836–1960. *The Wiseman Review*, Spring 1961–Winter 1964. *The Dublin Review*, 1964–1969.

VOLUME AND ISSUE DATA
Numbers 1–518, volumes 1–242, May 1836–Winter 1968–1969. (These volumes were issued as follows: old series, volumes 1–51, May 1836–April 1863; new series, volumes 1–31, July 1863–October 1878; 3d series, volume 32 [sic]–24, January 1879–October 1891; 4th series, volume [110] numbers 1–56 [no volume designation given internally], January 1892–October 1905. Another

"new" series [old series numbering], volumes 138–219, January 1906–July 1946. Another "new" series, Spring 1947 [this issue is marked "volume 1" but the next resumes old numbering as volume 220] with no further numbering changes despite changes of editor and new policy statements until the end, Winter 1968–1969, volume 242, number 518.)

FREQUENCY OF PUBLICATION

Quarterly. (During World War II and the recovery there were only two "double issues" a year.)

PUBLISHERS

1836–1837: William Spooner, 377 Strand, London. 1838: Booker & Dolman, 61 New Bond Street, London. 1839–1844: C. Dolman, 61 New Bond Street, London. 1844–1863: Thomas Richardson & Son, 172 Fleet Street, London/26 Paternoster Row, London (1862). 1863–1864: Burns & Lambert, 17 & 18 Portman Street, London. 1864–1867: Burns, Lambert & Oates, 17 Portman Street, London/63 Paternoster Row, London. 1867–1919: Burns & Oates, 28 Orchard Street W., London. 1920–1946: Burns, Oates & Washbourne, 28 Ashley Place, S. W. 1, London. 1947–1952: Burns, Oates (same as above). 1953–1957: Burns & Oates (same as above). 1958–1969: The Tablet Publishing Co., 128 Sloan Street, S. W. 1, London/14 Howick Place, S. W. 1, London (1960)/48 Great Peter Street, S. W. 1, London (Summer 1968).

EDITORS

Michael Joseph Quin, May–July 1836. Mark Aloysius Tierney, December 1836. James Smith, April–July 1837. Henry Ridgard Bagshawe, October 1837–April 1863. William George Ward, July 1863–October 1878. John Cuthbert Hedley, January 1879–October 1884. Herbert Alfred Vaughan, January 1885–October 1891. James Moyes, January 1892–October 1905. Wilfrid Ward, 1906–1915. "Wilfrid Ward & Monsignor Barnes," January–April 1916. Shane Leslie (with Wilfrid Meynell), 1916–1925. Algar Thorold, 1926–Summer 1934. (Publisher) Denis Gwynn, 1936. Denis Gwynn with Lord Clonmore, 1937–1939. Christopher Dawson, 1940–1944. T. S. Gregory, 1945–1946. T. F. Burns, 1947–1956. Michael Derrick, 1956–1961. Norman St. John-Stevas, 1961–Spring 1968. Unknown, Winter 1968–1969.

Mary Anthony Weinig

DUBLIN UNIVERSITY MAGAZINE, THE

The *Dublin University Magazine* first appeared on 5 January 1833, founded by a group of young Tory dons and students at Trinity College, Dublin. The mood of these men was bitter and the avowed purpose of the magazine reactionary: the first Reform Bill had passed the year before, in effect enfranchising the British middle classes; in Ireland, the threat of Catholic Emancipation loomed large; and Trinity, their own staunchly Protestant enclave of classical learning and privilege, had become a center for liberal thought.[1] Moreover, from a more pragmatic point of view, the recent successes of conservative political literary journals—particularly *Blackwood's* * in Edinburgh and *Fraser's* * in London—

presented an irresistible invitation to an Irish imitator. The essential tone, as well as content, of *Dublin University Magazine* in its early years is effectively conveyed in the first piece of the first number:

> Never will England again retain the rank which she has so insanely relinquished. Our parliament will henceforth resemble dogs with kettles tied to their tails. If the members are not mad, they must seem to be mad, or they will not be trusted. No; our day has gone by; we have taken a plunge from a height of glory and prosperity unrivalled in the history of the world, and will not find our level until we reach the opposite point of misery and humiliation. It is maddening to think of this. In the case of France, the madness of the people forced revolution upon the King; in our case the contrary has taken place, and revolution has been forced, by those high in authority, upon an astonished and reluctant people. [1:7–8]

And so the magazine goes on for the better part of its first decade, assailing Whigs and Radicals while detecting Popish conspiracies at every turn. It was a journal that mixed, in Michael Sadleir's words, "labored facetiousness and tiresome verbosity," with a "fine careless rapture" and the "engaging naivete of its mutual backscratching." These talents were applied to "praising the *Quarterly*[*] or slanging the *Edinburgh*[*]; sneering at Bulwer and insulting Harriet Martineau; belauding Southey and acclaiming Scott or Croker or the Duke of Wellington."[2]

Nevertheless, *Dublin University Magazine* should not chiefly be remembered for its religion or politics or derivative editorial practices. Rather, its importance lies in its determination from the first to be a truly Irish magazine. At the end of the first number, the editor faces the challenge directly: "Thus it is, that while the English and Scotch periodicals number among their most talented contributors many of our countrymen, there rests upon our metropolis the stigma of never having supported a good general Magazine; and Irish talent, like Irish valour, is valued and distinguished everywhere but at home" (1:88). Indeed, *Dublin University Magazine* did become Dublin's first successful literary periodical. From the beginning the magazine not only devoted many of its pages to Irish culture, but pioneered in publishing such diverse native writers as Charles Lever, Samuel Lover, James Mangan, William Carleton, and J. S. LeFanu.

The paradoxes inherent in such a Tory nationalism are never invisible, but the magazine grew and matured in spite of them. By 1835 it had shed its close identification with Trinity College, and by 1839 there was a distinct muting of the shrillness of its political and religious antagonisms. In 1842 Charles Lever, the popular novelist whose serialized fiction had contributed heavily to the success of the magazine, became editor. He immediately set about giving the magazine a greater variety of subject matter, more reviews, a more international outlook (with special attention given to France) and, most important, heavy doses of his own picaresque romances. By the time he stepped down as editor, in 1845, he had managed to raise the circulation of *Dublin University Magazine* from 2,500 to 4,000; but he had also, in Sadleir's opinion, "largely destroyed its individual character by his abstention from (or indifference to) the internal dissentions of Ireland, of Dublin City, and of Trinity College."[3]

Following Lever's departure the magazine returned to the hands of one of the original founders, John Francis Waller, whose pen name was Jonathan Freke Slingsby. Waller managed to steer a safe course between the excesses of the 1830s and Lever's cosmopolitanism. The internal affairs of Trinity College were given attention, as were biographical portraits of well-known Irishmen which had been borrowed in the early years from the "Fraser Gallery." Twenty years after the founding of the magazine, Waller was able to assert that he was at the helm of a "NATIVE PERIODICAL" dedicated to latitudinarianism in literature while faithfully adhering to one political and religious faith (41:1).

Unfortunately, both the quality and Irishness of the magazine soon fell off. The magazine was purchased in 1856 by the London publishers, Hurst and Blackett, and floundered without direction until 1861, when it was taken over by Joseph Sheridan LeFanu. LeFanu, who had already established a reputation as an author of historical romances in both verse and prose, was just entering the period of his best work, that for which he is remembered today, sensational crime fiction with supernatural overtones. As editor-in-chief and proprietor, he not only provided serializations of his best thrillers—*The House by the Churchyard*, *Wylder's Hand*, and *Uncle Silas*—but infused its pages with his own exotic tastes for the supernatural, abnormal psychology, Irish folklore, and crime. The result often lies somewhere between a Celtic Twilight and the Newgate Calendar, with an interest in faraway places mixed in. In 1862, for example, there appeared not only chapters from *The House by the Churchyard* and profiles of murderers, but articles on Carlyle, Goethe, spiritualism, a walking tour of Nagasaki, haunted houses, medieval mysticism, Leinster folklore, the Irish wake, and the Irish wedding. In one particular respect does LeFanu carry on the tradition of the little magazine founded within the walls of Trinity in 1833. "Although as editor," says S. M. Ellis, "he advocated High Tory doctrine, at heart . . . his sympathies were ever with the Nationalists."[4]

When LeFanu sold the magazine after about a decade, Waller took over again. By this time the founding Young Turk was a man in his sixties and his attempt to restore the original spirit of the magazine failed. When he in turn sold it in 1877, *Dublin University Magazine* quickly deteriorated into the amorphous internationalism of the late 1850s. The only notable items to be found in these last years are the first published pieces of poetry and prose by one Oscar O'F. Wills Wilde.

The *Dublin University Magazine*'s place in the history of literary magazines, then, is at once derivative and original. Its style and politics were borrowed from *Blackwood's* and *Fraser's,* but its devotion to Irish matters and to the publication of native Irish writers established for it a sure place in the history of not only Irish literature, but the literature of the English-speaking world.

If these juxtapositions are contradictory—the derivative with the original; English Tory principles with a kind of Irish nationalism (and an authentic one, however mitigated by condescension and religious prejudice)—such paradox constitutes the essence of the forty-five years of the magazine's existence. Its history is one of vacillation from the parochial to the cosmopolitan, from obsessive internecine political squabbles to writings tailored to the international literary marketplace.

The ultimate irony is that *Dublin University Magazine* was most popular under the guidance of Lever (a middle-brow purveyor of melodrama) and most distinguished under LeFanu (a visionary arcanist). During these high points the magazine reflected not only the Irishness of its editor and contributors but, to an equal degree, the larger literary world in London. Lever left the magazine under the accusation that he had turned it into an Irish *Bentley's** (see *VEA*), and the shocking stories that LeFanu had been producing at home found a ready market during his last years (1869–1873) in *Temple Bar,** Dickens's *All The Year Round,** and Miss Braddon's *Belgravia* (see, for all three, *VEA*).* The most interesting work in the "Native Periodical" was also very much in the English literary mainstream of the times in which it appeared.

Notes

1. From this same background, in the same year, emerged the *Dublin University Review* (the title soon emended to the *Dublin Review**), which under the direction of Joseph Cardinal Wiseman became the voice of opposition to all for which the *Dublin University Magazine* stood.

2. Michael Sadleir, *"Dublin University Magazine," Its History, Contents, and Bibliography* (Dublin, 1938), pp. 62–64.

3. Sadleir, p. 73.

4. S. M. Ellis, *Wilkie Collins, LeFanu and Others.* (London, 1931), p. 155.

Information Sources

BIBLIOGRAPHY

Browne, Nelson. *Sheridan LeFanu.* London, 1951.

Ellis, S. M. *Wilkie Collins, LeFanu and Others.*

Sadleir, Michael. *"Dublin University Magazine," Its History, Contents, and Bibliography.* Dublin, 1938.

INDEXES

Each volume indexed. *Poole's Index.* In Sadleir, Michael, *"Dublin University Magazine," Its History, Contents, and Bibliography,* Dublin, 1938. *Wellesley Index* 4 (projected).

REPRINT EDITIONS

Microform: Bell and Howell, Wooster, Ohio.

LOCATION SOURCES

American

Widely available.

British
> Complete runs: British Museum; Cambridge University Library.
> Partial runs: Widely available.

Publication History

MAGAZINE TITLE AND TITLE CHANGES

> *The Dublin University Magazine.* (Subtitle varies, for example, "A literary and political journal"; "a literary and philosophical review.") A month after the *Dublin University Magazine* stopped publication, another magazine appeared featuring not only its cover design but also many of its contributors. The *University Magazine,* as it was called, ran from January 1878–June 1880. It was then followed by a quarterly series of which one number only—Christmas 1880—appeared. Although it seems clear that this was a different journal and was intended as such, many libraries and *The Union List of Serials* list the two publications together as "*University Magazine* (Dublin)" crediting the monthly issues from 1878 to 1880 as volumes 91–95 or "new series volumes 1–5." The quarterly series is then listed as volume 96 or as "quarterly series volume one, numbers 1–2." Sadleir is emphatic in his belief that the *University Magazine* should be considered as a different bibliographical entity from the *Dublin University Magazine.*

VOLUME AND ISSUE DATA

> Volumes 1–90, numbers 1–540, January 1833–December 1877.

FREQUENCY OF PUBLICATION

> Monthly, January 1833–June 1880 (see above).

PUBLISHERS (All in Dublin)

> 1833–1842: William Curry, Jr. 1842–1856: James McGlashan, 21 D'Olier Street. 1856–1861: William Robertson, 23 Upper Sackville Street. 1861–1876: George Herbert, 117 Grafton Street. 1877: W. Ridings, 117 Grafton Street.

EDITORS

> Reverend Charles Stuart Sanford, January 1833–August 1834. Isaac Butt, August 1834–1838. James Wills, 1838–1839. (According to Michael Sadleir, Wills remained official editor until 1842, but someone whose name is now lost acted for him after 1839.) Charles Lever, April 1842–Summer 1845. John Francis Waller(?), Summer 1845–1853. (It is not known when Waller resigned, nor are any specifics known about his successors before 1856.) Cheyne Brady, 1856–1861. J. S. LeFanu, 1861–1869 or 1872 (depending on whether S. M. Ellis or J. S. Crone is followed. Internal evidence supports 1869 as the year in which LeFanu severed his ties with the magazine). John Francis Waller, 1869–1877. Keningale Cook, 1877.

Thomas F. Boyle

 E

ECLECTIC REVIEW, THE

For more than six decades, from its foundation in January 1805 to its demise at the end of 1868, the *Eclectic Review* was true to its title: it reviewed books in every field, including not only literature, history, theology, politics, and all the arts and sciences, but countless other more esoteric subjects, ranging from German philosophy to phrenology. Despite the nonconformist (chiefly Congregationalist) religious principles on which it was founded and by which its authors continued to be guided, its contents were not dominated by religious books or topics. Rarely in any of its more than 120 volumes is as much as a third of an issue devoted to theological topics and even then more likely than not in connection with contemporary scientific or philosophical questions. Using the same basic format established by review journals such as the *Monthly Review* * and the *Critical Review* * (for both, see *AAAJ*) in the eighteenth century—several long reviews, followed by a section of shorter notices in each issue—the *Eclectic* outlived the last of the surviving eighteenth-century journals and proved itself capable of competing with its more celebrated nineteenth-century counterparts, especially the *Edinburgh Review,* * *Quarterly Review,* * and *Westminster Review.* * Like Jeffrey's *Edinburgh Review,* which was both its most illustrious and its most antagonistic rival, the *Eclectic* offered sophisticated criticism that moved almost completely away from the old-fashioned techniques of quotation and abstract toward a genuine critical evaluation of books and their significance in the broader contexts both of the author's canon and of their formal or intellectual tradition. As in the *Edinburgh,* both the "review article" (in which several books on a given topic are reviewed together) and the "review essay" (in which the book is a pretext or starting point for a broader discussion of its topic) became staples in the *Eclectic.* In short, it offered recognizably modern review journalism. As the years passed, the

Eclectic grew to become what is now a massive and invaluable archive of the literary and intellectual history of the nineteenth century.

Few of its compilers were particularly famous, even in their own day. Of the more than sixty contributors who have been identified,[1] no more than two or three are still memorable a century later. James Mill, father of John Stuart Mill, was a regular contributor for many years, according to the *Eclectic*'s editor at that time, Josiah Conder (3d ser., 16:550). That Mill could do this while also involved with rival journals, especially the *Edinburgh Review* and the *Westminster Review,* is a result of the widespread practice of anonymity in reviewing. Robert Southey was a close friend of Conder's and he is known to have promised Conder repeatedly that he would write for the *Eclectic,* although whether he finally did so is still unclear (6th ser., 2:248). "The Bard of Sheffield," James Montgomery—a poet of some note and a friend of Byron's—contributed extensively for almost fifty years, from 1806 until well into the 1850s. It is reported that in his later years, Montgomery claimed to have reviewed in its pages "every contemporary of note except Byron."[2] And in the 1860s the *Eclectic* was conducted for eight years by Edwin Paxton Hood, author of more than twenty books (including full biographies of Milton, Cromwell, Swedenborg, Wordsworth, and Thomas Carlyle) and a respected figure in the mid-nineteenth-century world of letters.

Although the rest may be forgotten today, it is nonetheless true to say (as one of its editors said in the 1830s) that "the pages of the [*Eclectic*] have been enriched by the contributions of many of the most powerful intellects of the age" (4th ser., 1:1). One contributor, for example, was Olinthus Gilbert Gregory, a prominent mathematician, scientist, and theologian who helped to found the University of London in the 1820s. Another was Adam Clark, a protégé and biographer of John Wesley, a scholar of Hebrew, Syrian, Arabic, Persian, and Sanskrit and the author of a widely influential eight-volume *Commentary on the Holy Scriptures*. Many had comparable credentials. At least eight contributors were prominent enough to be themselves the subjects of biographies, including Conder, Montgomery, Thomas Binney, John Foster, John Pye Smith, Joseph Fletcher, W. H. Stowell and Robert Hall.[3] Others were important philanthropists and reformers, such as George Thompson, who toured the world and risked his life repeatedly to campaign for the abolition of slavery, and Andrew Reed, who was instrumental in founding the London Orphan Asylum, the Infant Orphan Asylum, and the Royal Hospital for Incurables. Another contributor, Thomas Chalmers, was a theologian, scientist, and philanthropist whose life-long efforts on behalf of poor relief touched the lives of thousands; it has been estimated that half the population of Edinburgh attended his funeral in 1847.[4] Many were involved with other periodicals and literary projects. Francis Augustus Cox helped found the *Baptist Magazine* in 1809; George Redford founded the *Congregational Magazine* in 1812 and contributed to it and three other journals; Josiah Conder edited the *Patriot* from 1832 on; Robert Vaughn founded the *British Quarterly* in 1845 and served as its editor for the next twenty years. At least two others besides Mill (Thomas Chalmers and Henry Rogers) were actively involved as contributors on the *Edinburgh Review,* despite the hostilities between it and the *Eclectic.* Finally, two regular contributors eventually published collections of their *Eclectic* reviews in book form—Robert Hall's *Polemical and Other Miscellanies, Consisting of Articles Orginally Inserted in the London "Eclectic Review"* (also reprinted in an American edition) and John Foster's *Contributions, Biographical, Literary, and Philosophical, to the "Eclectic Review"*—an indication, perhaps, of the regard in which both they and the *Eclectic Review* were held by the reading public.

The contributors were not without their foibles. Robert Hall was a hypochondriac who suffered occasional spells of insanity. John Foster, it is reported, "though a baptist minister . . . never once administered baptism."[5] And Adam Clarke, for all his erudition, held somewhat unusual views, including the idea that the serpent that tempted Eve was actually a baboon. But by and large, as the sustained quality of the *Eclectic*'s contents attests, its reviewers provided insightful criticism about individual books and thoughtful, often provocative, commentary on their relation to bigger artistic and intellectual issues.

The long publishing history of the *Eclectic* falls roughly into four periods. Although edited for most of its first year by Samuel Greatheed, the dissenting preacher best known for his widely-read sermon on the life of William Cowper, the *Eclectic* was really established in its early years by Daniel Parken, a fellow dissenter and cofounder of the *Eclectic* who served as editor from 1806 to 1812. It was Parken who attracted such important contributors as James Montgomery and John Pye Smith; it was Parken who first built up the *Eclectic*'s readership; it was Parken who first established the policy of enlightened, nondenominational (if not ecumenical) editorial policies and steered the *Eclectic* clear of theological disputes as far as possible. (For example, he carefully avoided assigning books written by churchmen to John Pye Smith to review because Smith held strong dissenting views and tended to excite controversy.) After Parken died in 1812, the *Eclectic* was edited for about a year by Theophilus Williams, another young dissenter who in later years conformed and took orders. The *Eclectic* faltered and nearly died before it was purchased in 1813 by Josiah Conder, who began what was to be twenty-three years as its proprietor and editor.

From 1814 to 1836 Conder poured money and energy into the *Eclectic,* though not always with success. At times he was reduced to compiling entire issues virtually by himself. By 1821 he was lamenting that "the sale does not increase" and complaining, "I am almost sick of the work" (6th ser., 2:248). Still, he persevered for almost a quarter of a century, only resigning what he called his "onerous responsibilities" in December 1836. That same month he composed a "Farewell Address" to his readers in which he looked back with pride on the performance of the *Eclectic* under his editorship. "Upon the whole," he wrote, "a more fair and complete view of the literature of the past five and twenty years is furnished by the Eclectic Review than by any contemporary publication'' (3rd ser., 16:552). Proprietary pride notwithstanding, his claim has merit.

From 1837 through 1855, except for a three-month interlude when William Linwood made an abortive attempt to take his place, the *Eclectic* was edited by Thomas Price. Price reinvigorated the *Eclectic*. He reaffirmed the journal's ''absolute neutrality'' in religious matters, a policy from which Conder and, more disastrously, Linwood had sometimes lapsed. He expanded its contents, introduced new sections on foreign (especially German) publications, and lowered its price from two shillings to eighteen pence—all part of a campaign to extend its circulation beyond ''Reading Societies and Literary Institutions'' and into more families (4th ser., 1:4). Plagued with illness in his last years, Price shared editorial duties with William Hendry Stowell from 1851 to 1855 and, for the last of those years, with his eventual successor Jonathan Edwards Ryland.

With Price's departure, the final and most unstable period of the *Eclectic*'s history began. Ryland was soon supplanted by an anonymous (and still unidentified) editor, and for two years (1859–1860) the *Eclectic* was transformed into a miscellany, combining features of both a review and a magazine. When Edwin Paxton Hood took over as editor in January 1861, he compared the *Eclectic* to ''an old and . . . disabled ship,'' but vowed that with ''new masts, and sails, and rigging, the old timbers might yet do a good deal of service.''[6] In the end, he coaxed almost eight more years out of the *Eclectic*. He increased the size of each issue (to 128 pages), lowered the price once more (to one shilling), and changed the *Eclectic* back into a straight book review journal—all in an effort to raise circulation to his stated goal of four thousand copies a month, the projected break-even point. His strategy apparently worked. Under Hood's spirited guidance, the *Eclectic* produced in its last eight years some of its finest review journalism.

Various incidental features distinguish the *Eclectic* from other periodicals. It was, for example, a nonprofit publication. From the beginning in 1805, its proprietors had arranged by a formal legal agreement to donate all profits to the British and Foreign Bible Society (1st ser., 1 pt. i:320). Also, although it steadfastly resisted denominational attachments, the underlying religious and philosophical tenets of its authors may have shaped its readership and affected its tone. Certainly there is in it a very high proportion of serious intellectual discussion and rather less than usual treatment of lighter literary forms such as drama and the novel. In the end, however, it is the extraordinary range and richness of the *Eclectic*'s sixty-five-year parade of literary history that most distinguishes it. The thousands of articles in its ten dozen volumes span the period from when the publication of the *Lyrical Ballads* was a recent event until three years after Dickens's last completed novel (*Our Mutual Friend*) was published.

It at once emerges that the *Eclectic* bestowed more attention on American literature (indeed, all books by or about Americans) than any other English periodical of the time. This was true even in its inaugural issue in January 1805, in which an obscure American work, John Blair Linn's *Powers of Genius,* was generously praised (1st ser., 1, pt. i:54–59). By mid-1806 the *Eclectic* had introduced a separate section devoted entirely to American publications. Over the course of the next few years, it presented articles on Webster's *Dictionary* (1st ser., 3, pt. 1:82–86), *Memoirs of the Philadelphia Agricultural Society* (1st ser., 5, pt. 2:629–38), Zebulon Pike's *Exploratory Travels through the Western Territories of North America* (1st ser., vol. 7, pt. 1:296–313), John Pickering's *Vocabulary of Americanisms* (2d ser., 13:356–63), as well as one article on a group of three books on emigration to America (2d ser., 20:529–49), and another on five books of travels in America (3d ser., 2:365–98). In 1832 it began reviewing issues of the *North American Review* (3d ser., 8:385–405) on a regular basis; in 1840 it examined de Tocqueville's *Democracy in America* in great detail (4th ser., 8:1–26); in 1853 it offered an article entitled "The American Poets," covering five books of American poetry, including volumes by James Russell Lowell, Oliver Wendell Holmes, and Edgar Allen Poe (5th ser., 6:307–21); in 1860 it even devoted a review to an American anthology, Charles Cleveland's *Compendium of American Literature,* discerning in its contents "the flighty, zig-zag, scintillating, daring style of thought which prevails in all modern American life" (7th ser., 4:219).

This continuing attention to American literature was far more than a condescending curiosity about the culture of the young republic. Rather remarkably, even as early as 1810, American authors were accorded the same serious treatment as the major authors in English and other European literatures. In 1810, for example, an *Eclectic* reviewer described Joel Barlow's *Columbiad* as "one of the most extraordinary productions of the age," adding (somewhat darkly) that "it is the work of an uncommon but very perverted mind" (1st ser., 6, pt. 1:416). In 1820 the *Eclectic* began reviewing Washington Irving's *Sketch Book of Geoffrey Crayon* while it was still appearing in serial installments (2d ser., 13:38–44). The reviewer hailed it as "the first purely literary production that has issued from the American press, which could claim to rank, in point of original talent and classic elegance of style, with the best English authors" (2d ser., 13:290). In later years, James Fenimore Cooper received comparable accolades (5th ser., 3:410–22); Harriet Beecher Stowe's *Uncle Tom's Cabin* was acclaimed as a "marvellous work" (5th ser., 4:719); and the poetry of J. G. Whittier was warmly welcomed because it came from "our well-loved farmer and Quaker poet" (8th ser., 1:362). Not surprisingly, the American author who proved most perplexing to the *Eclectic* reviewers was Ralph Waldo Emerson. Already in 1842, his *Essays* were described as "anti-pacific" and "Ishmaelitish" (4th ser., 12:667). Twenty years later, in an article dealing with six of his works, the reviewer welcomed Emerson's challenge to orthodox religion, but denounced (and demonstrated) his various plagiarisms from Novalis, George Herbert, Thomas Carlyle, and others. In summarizing Emerson, the reviewer offered a memorable characterization: "To most Englishmen, Ralph Waldo Emerson is a transcendant literary anomaly. The new world has developed a new man" (8th ser., 3:365).

Of course the major English authors received considerably more attention. Among the Romantic poets, Wordsworth was most favored, and his role as leader of a major new poetic movement readily recognized. "In this age of poetical experiment," wrote the reviewer of Wordsworth's *Poems* in 1808, "Mr. Wordsworth has distinguished himself, by his *Lyrical Ballads,* as one of the boldest and most fortunate adventurers in the field of innovation" (1st ser., vol. 4, pt. 1:35). Not all their judgments were so perceptive. The same reviewer went on to describe the "Ode: Intimations of Immortality" as a "wilderness of sublimity, tenderness, bombast, and absurdity." Coleridge fared less well with the *Eclectic.* Although his genius was evident, the reviewers distrusted his "mighty profusion and excursiveness of thought" (1st ser., 7, pt. 2:931) and with the publication of such poems as "Kubla Khan" they nearly despaired, calling on him "to break off his desultory and luxurious habits, and to brace his mind to intellectual exertion" (2d ser., 5:572). Although Shelley's works were discounted for his "prophanity" and atheism (2d ser., 5:391–93), Keats was judged to have shown "an immature promise of possible excellence" in his *Poems* published in 1817 (2d ser., 7:270). Byron's poetry received more attention than any other, save Wordsworth's, and while its shortcomings were duly mentioned, the reviewers did not hesitate to extol the virtues of a work such as *Child Harolde* in which the reader would "be dazzled even to tears" (2d ser., 7:292).

Among the major novelists, Sir Walter Scott was reviewed regularly, in acknowledgement of his vast popularity, but his novels were regarded with a certain ambivalence. The review of *Ivanhoe* is typical. Describing it as "one of the cleverest of all our Author's productions," the reviewer nevertheless pronounced it "a failure" as a romance (2d ser., 13:529). Virtually the whole of Dickens's career is covered in the *Eclectic.* Installments of the *Pickwick Papers* were reviewed as they appeared, for the reviewers already sensed Dickens's brilliance. They found his mastery of language "without a rival" and saw many of his characters as "master-pieces in their own way" (4th ser., 1:341–42). Over the years, reviews were also devoted to novels by the Brontës, William Thackeray, Anthony Trollope, Victor Hugo, and George Eliot. Trollope's *Barchester Towers* afforded the reviewers the rare but welcome opportunity to combine criticism of the established Church with the discussion of a masterly satiric novel (6th ser., 2:54–59). But in general, the *Eclectic*'s treatment of the novel was balanced, insightful, and sophisticated; the ability of its reviewers to put aside their own religious and moral views was never more evident than in their approach to Hugo's *Les Miserables,* about which, despite its dark and godless implications, they stated: "It is a great book [but] it cannot be called a good book" (8th ser., 3:451).

An array of other important literary figures received significant attention over the years: not only standard authors such as George Crabbe, Burns, James Hogg, Hazlitt, Stendhal, and Goethe, but problematic figures like De Quincey. The reviewer of his *Confessions of an English Opium Eater* admitted that the *Eclectic* had almost decided not to review the book because it was so "objectionable and positively disgusting," and then when it did, treated it primarily as a medical treatise and morality lesson on opium addiction (2d ser., 19:366–71). The *Eclectic* reviewed the works of Tennyson, both Brownings, John Henry Newman, Matthew Arnold, and the Rossettis. Its discernment was often acute. Although it described the more famous Elizabeth Barrett Browning as "the Schiller of our higher nature," it also presented a major article comparing Robert Browning's poetic achievement to that of Tennyson (8th ser., 7:361–89). Similarly, it prided itself on being the first journal to "discover" and "to notice at any length" Christina Rossetti's *Goblin Market and Other Poems* (8th ser., 2:499).

Beyond literature, the *Eclectic* covered books in every field imaginable. To take one very typical example, the issue for January 1845 contained seven major articles, of which three were on literary subjects: Dickens's *The Chimes,* Pascal's *Pensées,* and John Keble's *De Poeticae Vi Medica.* The rest were divided among theology, politics, education, and natural history. An article on "Aggressive Nonconformity" discussed six tracts on dissenting doctrine; "Naturalists and Natural History" covered two books, one on ornithology, the other on biology; a third article reviewed some thirteen pamphlets on private and religious academies and related pedagogical issues; the final article, "County Constituencies," dealt with eight books on the topic of electoral reform.

Attention was also paid to art. Ruskin's *Modern Painters,* for example, was pronounced "an English classic (7th ser., 4:480). Occasionally the *Eclectic* offered coverage of art exhibitions, such as its very long, thirty-five-page review of the Exhibition at the Royal Academy in 1848 (4th ser., 23:665–90). Contemporary scientific and philosophical topics were not slighted. Darwin's *On the Origin of Species* was carefully, albeit negatively, reviewed in 1860 (7th ser., 3:217–42). The debates over the Newman Movement and Anglo-Catholicism were also accorded extensive coverage. In general, over the years the *Eclectic* showed remarkable tolerance for other religious groups—not only the various denominations of Protestants, but also Roman Catholics and Jews. It was a steady and vociferous opponent of slavery and a supporter of various kinds of reform, political, social, and ecclesiastical.

Although clearly aimed at the highly literate and thoughtful reader, the *Eclectic* was anything but elitist about the audience it sought. Its founders had set the subscription price as low as possible, with the aim of "enlarging its circulation among various classes of people" (1st ser., 1, pt. 1:iii). Certainly articles such as its lead in the August 1830 issue, "Cabinet and Family Libraries," suggest that it was aimed primarily at the lower-middle and lower class literate; that article discusses the merits of some nineteen different encyclopedic home libraries such as *Lardner's Cabinet Cyclopedia* and the *Family Classical Li-*

brary (3d ser., 4:93–106). Ultimately, both for nineteenth-century families and for modern scholars, the *Eclectic* itself formed the most comprehensive and valuable encyclopedic repository of nineteenth-century *belles lettres,* science, and intellectual history.

At its height, the *Eclectic* enjoyed a wide readership in England, America, and presumably throughout the British Empire. It was for a brief period reprinted in America, under the auspices of Foster, Bisbee, and Co. in New York, whose name appeared in the imprint from January to December 1841. It is not to be confused with a later periodical, a medical journal called the *Eclectic Review,* published in New York from 1890 to 1915, or with any of the following American periodicals with similar titles: the *Eclectic Magazine* (Boston, 1844–1907), the *Eclectic Museum* (New York and Philadelphia, 1843–44), and the *Eclectic* (Portland, Maine, 1850–54).

Notes

1. See lists of contributors (past and current) in the *Eclectic,* 3d ser., 16:550–51; 4th ser., 1:3–4. (All subsequent references to the *Eclectic* are parenthetical in the text.)

2. *Dictionary of National Biography,* s.v. "Montgomery, James."

3. See bibliography below.

4. *Dictionary of National Biography,* s.v. "Chalmers, Thomas," "Reed, Andrew," and "Thompson, George."

5. *Dictionary of National Biography,* s.v. "Foster, John."

6. Advertisement sheet for the *Eclectic,* dated 1 May 1861, and bound into the *Eclectic,* 8th ser., vol. 1, as a preliminary.

Information Sources

BIBLIOGRAPHY

Conder, Eustace R. *Josiah Conder; A Memoir.* London, 1857.

Dictionary of National Biography. S.v. "Chalmers, Thomas"; "Foster, John"; "Montgomery, James"; "Reed, Andrew"; and "Thompson, George."

Fletcher, Joseph. *Memoirs of the Reverend Joseph Fletcher, D.D.* London, 1846.

Foster, John. *Contributions, Biographical, Literary, and Philosophical, to the "Eclectic Review."* London, 1844.

Hall, Robert. *Polemical and Other Miscellanies, Consisting of Articles Originally Inserted in the "London Eclectic Review" and Apology for the Freedom of the Press from the Seventh London Edition.* Boston, 1827.

Holland, John and James Everett, *Memoirs of the Life and Writings of James Montgomery.* London, 1854.

Hood, E. Paxton. *Thomas Binney, His Mind, Life, and Opinions.* London, 1874.

Medway, John. *Memoirs of the Life of John Pye Smith.* London, 1853.

Ryland, Jonathan Edwards, ed. *The Life and Correspondence of John Foster.* London, 1846.

Stowell, William, ed. *A Memoir of the Life and Labours of the Reverend William Hendry Stowell.* London, 1859.

INDEXES

Each issue indexed.

REPRINT EDITIONS
>   Microform: English Literary Periodicals (UMI), reels 545–576.
LOCATION SOURCES
> *American*
> >   Widely available.
> *British*
> >   Complete runs: British Museum, Manchester Public Libraries.
> >   Partial runs: Widely available.

Publication History

MAGAZINE TITLE AND TITLE CHANGES
>   *The Eclectic Review.* Single issues only change to: *The Eclectic Review: A Critical Journal of British and Foreign Literature,* January 1857–December 1858. *The Eclectic: A Monthly Review and Miscellany,* January 1859–June 1861. *The Eclectic and Congregational Review,* January 1864–December 1868.

VOLUME AND ISSUE DATA
>   1st series, volume 1, part 1–volume 8, part 2, January 1805–December 1812; volumes 9–10, January 1813–December 1813 (misnumbered on some single issues as volume 9, parts 1, 2); 2nd series, volumes 1–30, January 1814–December 1828; 3d series, volumes 1–16, January 1829–December 1836; 4th series, volumes 1–28, January 1837–December 1850; 5th series, volumes 1–12, January 1851–December 1856; 6th series, volumes 1–4, January 1857–December 1858; 7th series, volumes 1–5, January 1859–June 1861; 8th series, volumes 1–15, July 1861–December 1868.

FREQUENCY OF PUBLICATION
>   Monthly.

PUBLISHERS
>   1st series, volume 1–volume 2, part 1, January 1805–June 1806: C. Taylor, 108, Hatton-Garden. 1st series, volume 2, part 2–volume 7, part 2, July 1806–December 1811: Longman, Hurst, Rees, and Orme, Paternoster-Row. 1st series, volume 8, part 1–volume 9, January 1812–June 1813: Gale, Curtis, and Fenner, Paternoster-Row. 1st series, volume 10, July 1813–December 1813: Gale, Curtis, and Fenner, Paternoster-Row [and] Josiah Conder, 18, St. Paul's Church-yard. 2d series, volumes 1–10, January 1814–December 1818: Josiah Conder, 18, St. Paul's Church-yard. 2d series, volumes 11–30, January 1819–December 1828: B. J. Holdsworth, Successor to Josiah Conder, 18, St. Paul's Church-yard. 3d series, volumes 1–8, January 1829–December 1832: Holdsworth and Ball, 18, St. Paul's Church-yard. 3d series, volumes 9–16, January 1833–December 1836: Jackson and Walford, 18, St. Paul's Church-yard. 4th series, volumes 1–3, January 1837–June 1838: William Ball, Aldine Chambers, Paternoster-Row. 4th series, volumes 4–5, July 1838–June 1839: William Ball, 34, Paternoster-Row. 4th series, volumes 6–8, July 1839–December 1840: W. Ball, Arnold, and Co., 34, Paternoster-Row. 4th series, volumes 9–10, January–December 1841: Jackson and Walford, 18, St. Paul's Church-yard. 4th series, volumes 11–20, January 1842–December 1846: Thomas Ward & Co., Paternoster-Row. 4th series, volume 21–5th series, volume 4, January 1847–December 1852: Ward & Co., Paternoster-Row. 5th series, volume 5–7th series, volume 1, Jan-

uary 1853–June 1859: Ward & Co., 27, Paternoster-Row. 7th series, volumes 2–5, July 1859–June 1861: Judd and Glass, New Bridge Street, and Gray's Inn Road. 8th series, volumes 1–3, July 1861–December 1862: Ward and Co., 27, Paternoster-Row. 8th series, volumes 4–15, January 1863–December 1868: Jackson, Walford, and Hodder, 27 Paternoster-Row.

EDITORS

Samuel Greatheed, January 1805–sometime in early 1806. Daniel Parken, 1806–1812. Theophilus Williams, late 1812 or early 1813 until December 1813. Josiah Conder, January 1814–1836. Thomas Price, January 1837–December 1849. [William Linwood], January–April 1850. Thomas Price, May–December, 1850. Thomas Price and William Hendry Stowell, January 1851–December 1855. Jonathan Edwards Ryland, ?January 1854–December 1856. Unknown, 1857–1860. Edwin Paxton Hood, January 1861–December 1868.

James E. Basker

EDINBURGH MAGAZINE AND LITERARY MISCELLANY, THE

An account of the origin and decline of the *Edinburgh Magazine* forms one strand in the complex network of early nineteenth century Scottish journalism. Its first editors, Thomas Pringle and William James Cleghorn, edited a few numbers of an *Edinburgh Monthly Magazine* for William Blackwood in the first months of 1817. Dissatisfied with their performance, Blackwood soon dissolved his partnership with them and launched the new, staunchly Tory *Blackwood's Magazine.** Pringle and Cleghorn then turned to Archibald Constable, who was also the publisher of the strongly Whiggish *Edinburgh Review,** and undertook to bring out a fourth series of the *Scots Magazine* * (see *AAAJ*) under the new title of *Edinburgh Magazine and Literary Miscellany*. They replaced the familiar blue cover of the *Scots* with a new green one, improved the quality of the paper and printing, and raised the price to two shillings. In the first issue, dated August, which appeared on 1 September 1817, two title pages were used, one bearing the new title and the other the old.[1] These were eventually consolidated into a single title page: *"The Edinburgh Magazine . . . Being a New Series of the Scots Magazine."* Despite these surface changes, the contents of the "new" magazine were markedly similar to the third series of the *Scots Magazine* that had been edited by the geographer, Hugh Murray; its history during the ensuing nine years is that of a slow decline and loss of ground, both to *Blackwood's* and to Constable's own *Edinburgh Review*.

Original articles made up slightly less than half of the hundred or so pages in an issue; reviews and notes of new publications, original poetry, literary and scientific "intelligence," and a register of new books took up the rest, along with over twenty pages devoted to news about agriculture, meteorology, and commerce. This section was probably the work of William James Cleghorn, who had previously edited the *Farmers Journal* and later became a well-known actuary and accountant.[2] His partner, Thomas Pringle, was a copyist of old records at the registrar's office.

In the later years of the *Edinburgh Magazine* its editor became hard pressed to attract contributors and material was reprinted from other sources. Sometimes this was acknowledged, as in the printing of the Rev. Sydney Smith's strong speech in favor of the Catholic Emancipation Bill in the June 1825 issue. Often, especially where poetry was concerned, no indication of previous publication was made.

The magazine remained steeped in antiquarianism in an age which prided itself upon progress. Indeed, by April 1821, the *Edinburgh* itself was joking about its "high repute for soporific effects." Just previously, in February 1821, "The Genius of the Scots Magazine to the Reader" had appeared and analyzed the situation: "Among this load of vapid essays and puerile poetry, many gems are to be found which redeem my character from the unfounded charge of hopeless and persevering stupidity. . . . I was once fond of joking, though my Editors have long since moulded the muscles of my face into an almost imperturbable gravity" (ser. 4, 8:311).

By the spring of 1819 Cleghorn and Pringle had left the magazine, and the Rev. Robert Morehead, a Scottish Episcopalian, took over. *Blackwood's* had been taunting the *Edinburgh* for its "dullness."[3] Morehead made it livelier for a brief period, but eventually found himself hampered by the small amount Constable allowed him to pay contributors. Payment may have been instituted before Morehead's editorship, but no record of it exists, and such payment was a fairly new practice at that period. Morehead found the fifteen pounds allowed for each three issues insufficient to attract lively material and had to supplement payments out of his own salary of sixty pounds a year. Morehead also regarded his position as junior minister of St. Paul's Epsicopal Chapel in Edinburgh as a handicap to his editorship because he could not be "up in matters of daily interest." In addition, he was "neutral in politics," and the *Edinburgh Magazine* lacked the partisan bite that so often contributed to both the liveliness and the malice of the *Edinburgh Review* and *Blackwood's*.[4] In May 1824 the magazine printed a compliment which, intentionally or not, was indicative of its lack of vitality. First stating the magazine's historical function as "the oldest and most complete periodical record of our national history and literature since Scotland ceased to be a separate Kingdom," the writer then added: "It aspires at least to convey to sober-minded readers a rational and not inelegant repast for the mind."[5] In February 1825 Morehead had served without salary for three months owing to the sharp decline in sales. He announced in the July issue that circumstances had disorganized arrangements for the publication. Indeed, Constable was nearing the bankruptcy which would so severely affect the fortunes of Sir Walter Scott. Publication ceased the following June and *Blackwood's* purchased the copyright in July.[6]

In the *Noctes Ambrosianae* for November 1826 *Blackwood's* paid tribute in its own way to its unsuccessful rival and forerunner as "the worthy old woman

. . . the ancient lady with the green gown on whom the Shepherd [*Black-wood's*] was but too fond of playing off his jibes, his jeers and his jokes. Peace to her ashes."[7] It would be unfair not to mention several articles that were of some note and reflect a standard the *Edinburgh Magazine* could not sustain. Among the contributors who can be identified with any certainty, the best known is William Hazlitt. *Blackwood's* attacks on Hazlitt during this period increased his willingness to write for Constable. While these contributions are not among his best work, there is some evidence that he reviewed his own *Round Table* and *Characters of Shakespeare's Plays* in the November 1817 issue.[8] The other articles attributed to him are "Remarks on Mr. West's Picture of Death on the Pale Horse . . ." in December 1817, "On the Question of Whether Pope Was a Poet" in February 1818, and "On Nicknames" in September 1818. All are signed "W.H." His letter on "Historical Illustrations of Shakespeare," signed "W. Hazlitt," appeared in January 1819 and provided an example of Shake-speare's use of historical material beyond that discussed in his *Characters of Shakespeare*. In this letter he described historical documents which might have furnished Shakespeare with material for the trial of Anne Boleyn in *Henry VIII*.

Felicia Hemans on her own initiative contributed extracts from her poem "Dartmoor" to the July 1822 issue.[9] The English bibliographers Thomas Frog-nall Dibdin and Henry Cotton provided an exchange of views on the biblio-graphical problems surrounding a list of early English editions of the Bible. Cotton's rejoinder to Dibdin's criticism of his work attacked Dibdin on the ground that his criticisms were motivated by the feeling that Cotton had not paid him proper homage.[10] Material other than literary and antiquarian was included in the magazine, but became less and less frequent in later years. Between 1818 and 1820 Robert Stevenson, the civil engineer who had super-intended the construction of the Bell Rock Light House, published a series of letters on his tour in the Netherlands (ser. 4, 2:234ff.).

While satire was most definitely not the *Edinburgh Magazine*'s forte, it did print the bitterly ironic "Defence of Phrenology" by "Peter Petricranium" in the January 1825 issue. By this time, however, the *Edinburgh Magazine* was sinking under the rivalry of the livelier *Edinburgh Review* and *Blackwood's* and the desperate state of Constable's own affairs did not allow him to put more resources into the magazine. The "worthy old woman" went to her rest and survives as a footnote in the history of early nineteenth-century literary jour-nalism.

Notes

1. D.S.M. Imrie, "The Story of the *Scots Magazine:* III. The Final Struggle (1817–1826)," *Scots Magazine*, n. s. 30 (1939):446. For Cleghorn and Pringle, see *Dictionary of National Biography*. Pringle later emigrated to South Africa and on his return to London in 1827 became secretary of the British Anti-Slavery Society. He signed the document on 24 June 1834 proclaiming that the abolition of slavery in the British do-minions would be celebrated with a day of thanksgiving on 1 August.

2. Imrie, "The Story of the *Scots Magazine:* IV. Editors, Printers and Publishers (1826–1939)," *Scots Magazine,* n.s. 31 (1939):219–20.

3. Imrie, n.s. 30:447.

4. Quoted by Imrie, n. s. 31:226.

5. Imrie, n. s. 30:451.

6. Ibid., p. 452. See also G. W. Niven, "The Bibliography of the *Scots Magazine*," *The Library* 10 (1898):310. The sale was reported in the *Edinburgh Evening Courant* for 27 July 1826 but *Blackwood's* had no record of it in 1898.

7. *Blackwood's Edinburgh Magazine* 20 (1826):786; number 39 of the *Noctes Ambrosiae,* ser. 4, 1 (1817):352–61.

8. John O. Hayden, "Hazlitt Reviews Hazlitt," *Modern Language Review* 64 (1969):22. Hazlitt's other contributions may be found in 1 (December 1817):403–5; 2 (1818):99–101; 3 (1818):240; 4 (1819):39–43.

9. For the attributions in this paragraph, see Imrie, "The Story of the *Scots Magazine:* V. Contributors (1781–1826)," n. s. 31 (1939):149–50.

10. See Dibdin's review of Cotton's *A List of Editions of the Bible and Parts Thereof in English from the Year 1505 to 1720* . . . (Oxford, 1821), 4th ser., 9 (1821):411–14 and Cotton's reply in 4th ser., 11 (1822):431–33.

Information Sources

BIBLIOGRAPHY

Constable, Archibald. *Archibald Constable: and His Literary Correspondents: A Memorial By His Son Thomas Constable.* 3 vols. Edinburgh, 1873.

Dictionary of National Biography. S.v. "Cleghorn, James" and "Pringle, Thomas."

Gillies, Robert Pearse. *Memoirs of a Literary Veteran: Sketches and Anecdotes of the Most Distinguished Literary Characters from 1794–1849.* 3 vols. London, 1851.

Hayden, John O. "Hazlitt Reviews Hazlitt." *Modern Language Review* 64 (1969):20–26.

Imrie, D.S.M. "The Story of the *Scots Magazine*." *Scots Magazine,* n. s. 30 (1939):341–49, 445–52; n. s. 31 (1939):51–58, 141–50, 218–26.

Niven, G. W. "The Bibliography of the *Scots Magazine*." *The Library* 10 (1898):310.

INDEXES

Annual list of contents in Imrie, "The Story of the *Scots Magazine*," *Scots Magazine*. See bibliography above.

REPRINT EDITIONS

Microform: English Literary Periodicals (UMI), reels 68–72.

LOCATION SOURCES

American

Widely available.

British

Complete runs: Aberdeen University Library; Birmingham Public Library; Bodleian Library; British Museum; Dundee Public Library; Edinburgh Public Library; London University Library; New College, University of Edinburgh Library. Partial runs: Aberdeen Public Library; Cambridge University Library; Edinburgh University Library; Glasgow University Library; Manchester Public Library; National Library of Scotland; Queen's University of Belfast; St. Andrews University Library.

Publication History

MAGAZINE TITLE AND TITLE CHANGES
The Edinburgh Magazine and Literary Miscellany; A New Series of "The Scots Magazine."

VOLUME AND ISSUE DATA
Volumes 1–18, August 1817–June 1826. (Series 4, volumes 80–97, of the *Scots Magazine*.)

FREQUENCY OF PUBLICATION
Monthly.

PUBLISHER
Archibald Constable, Edinburgh.

EDITORS
William James Cleghorn and Thomas Pringle, August 1817–March 1819(?). Robert Morehead, April 1819(?)–June 1826.

Barbara J. Dunlap

EDINBURGH MAGAZINE, OR LITERARY MISCELLANY, THE. See EDINBURGH MAGAZINE, THE (1785) (AAAJ)

EDINBURGH MONTHLY MAGAZINE, THE. See BLACKWOOD'S EDINBURGH MAGAZINE

EDINBURGH MONTHLY REVIEW, THE

The prospectus of the *Edinburgh Monthly Review* set forth its aims clearly. It was "intended to be a review in the stricter sense of the word, avoiding all disquisition not essentially connected with a critical examination of the works noticed" (1.iii), thus removing itself from the practices of such reviews as the prestigious quarterly *Edinburgh Review*.*

The *Edinburgh Monthly Review,* nevertheless, had its own ambitions, namely to provide a view "of the existing state of Literature, Science, and the Fine Arts," as it must have done. For it provided, in a monthly minimum of seven sheets (112 pages), long reviews on general subjects occasionally running from twenty to thirty pages, as well as (after April 1819) a list of new publications and works in progress. In this regard it must have been a useful reviewing periodical for readers bent on staying abreast of publications; a modern equivalent would be the *Times Literary Supplement*.

The prospectus also announced political and religious policies. Politics was not to be pursued for its own sake, but "it will be treated, when it does occur, in a spirit of loyalty and patriotism." Religion likewise was not to be given "peculiar prominency." The *Edinburgh Monthly Review* seems to have been conservative but not partisan in its inclinations.

By such policies, the proprietors hoped to render ''their publication as inviolate tribunal of literary equity'' (1:iii), a hope also reflected in the motto that appears in each volume—*''Sunt hic etiam sua praemia laudi''* (Virgil's *Aeneid*, 1. 461: ''Even here worth wins her praise'').

The matter of equity became strained at times in the literary reviews, which covered all important new works as well as others of lesser note. Political considerations, for example, are evident in the unfavorable critique of Byron's *Mazeppa* (2 [August 1818]:214–18) and both political and religious issues colored the review of Hazlitt's *Political Essays* (3 [March 1820]:297–309). But despite serious moral objections, Byron's *Don Juan* received considerable praise, and on the whole the literary reviewers confined themselves to literary considerations.

One novelty of the review was the substitution of ''Analysis of Articles Contained,'' a list of abstracts of the reviews, for the usual simple index.

In July 1821 the monthly review changed its name to the *New Edinburgh Review* and became a quarterly. Each issue now contained about three hundred pages, but otherwise the format remained the same. One publisher quit the periodical by volume 2, and the *New Edinburgh Review* itself ceased publication after the fourth volume without any announcement.

Information Sources

INDEXES
Abstracts at beginning of each volume, 1–5; index with abstracts, new series, at end of volumes. *Poole's Index.*

REPRINT EDITIONS
Microform: Early British Periodicals (UMI), reel 190.

LOCATION SOURCES

American
Complete runs: Dickinson College Library; Harvard University Library; Wesleyan University Library; Yale University Library.
Partial runs: Amherst College Library; Boston Athenaeum; Bowdoin College Library; Detroit Public Library; New York Public Library; Queens College Library; Tufts University Library; U.S. Library of Congress.

British
Complete runs: British Museum; Edinburgh University Library; Magee University College Library.
Partial runs: Aberdeen University Library; Bodleian Library; St. Andrews University Library.

Publication History

MAGAZINE TITLE AND TITLE CHANGES
The Edinburgh Monthly Review, 1819–1821. *The New Edinburgh Review*, 1821–1823.

VOLUME AND ISSUE DATA
Volumes 1–5, 1819–1821; new series, volumes 1–4, 1821–1823.

FREQUENCY OF PUBLICATION
>   Monthly.

PUBLISHERS
>   Volumes 1–4: Waugh and Innes, Hunter Square, Edinburgh/G. & B. Whittaker, Ave Maria Lane, London/Rodwell and Martin, New Bond Street, London. Volume 5–new series, volume 1: same as above, John Warren (replaced Rodwell and Martin), Old Bond Street, London. Volumes 2–4: same as above, but John Warren was dropped.

EDITOR
>   Unknown.

John O. Hayden

EDINBURGH REVIEW, THE

In October 1802 Sidney Smith, Francis Horner, and Francis Jeffrey, assisted by Henry Brougham and others, began publication of the *Edinburgh Review*. Several factors combined to favor their enterprise. Edinburgh was a center of intellectual and publishing activity. At the university, Smith, Horner, and Jeffrey had been influenced by Dugald Stewart, himself influenced by Adam Smith and Thomas Reid. Smith, Horner, Jeffrey, and Brougham were members of the Academy of Physics and (except Smith) the Speculative Society. Both groups were devoted to discussion of scientific, literary, and political subjects and books.[1] In these groups the collaborators found opportunities to develop their ideas and the confidence and inspiration to seek a larger audience through publication of their opinions. And they were lucky enough to find a publisher willing to support them, Archibald Constable. They were further prepared for the enterprise by the unusually broad scope of Scottish university education, and especially by the emphasis on literature in legal education. Jeffrey, Horner, and Brougham had little employment and consequently much free time in a city whose courts were dominated by lawyers and judges of the opposing political Tories.

When the editors of the *Edinburgh Review* decided to emphasize their contributors' opinions on the subjects of books being reviewed, they departed radically from the formula used generally and by their initial chief rival, the *Monthly Review* * (see *AAAJ*). There, the purpose was usually description, and accordingly a large amount of space was used to present extracts from the work under review. Since the *Edinburgh*'s formula required longer articles, the broad coverage of the *Monthly Review* was dropped in favor of eight or nine articles in each issue, supplemented by a list of recently published books.

Of great importance to the success of the review was the decision to use as contributors only gentleman writers (at first unpaid) and to encourage them to develop their personal views and style. This again departed from the practice of the *Monthly Review* and other periodicals who used writers of lesser talent who were poorly paid and whose assignment was frequently to puff the books of the booksellers who employed them. The immediate success of the *Edinburgh* and the strength of its financial backing soon allowed it to pay its contributors on an admirable scale and so to attract even better writers. The result was a review of a new and exciting nature whose circulation rose to 13,000 by 1818 (196:289).

It was determined from the beginning that the review would serve as a vehicle for Whig views. This intention was apparent in the editors' choice of colors, buff and blue. During the 127 years of its existence, the *Edinburgh* took positions on every major issue in British politics.[2] Among those on which it frequently spoke were overpopulation, which it saw as a problem of distribution and labor mismanagement; slavery, which it opposed on all grounds; the Corn Laws, which it believed harmful to free trade; and the balance of power in Europe, which it thought depended upon strong British naval power and commercial interests. In matters of foreign policy the magazine consistently advocated the use of free trade, treaties, and all peaceful means of settling disputes, but backed up by a powerful British navy. The *Edinburgh* dealt frequently with the Irish and Catholic questions, which it said could be made less serious if landlords were made resident and all laws distinguishing among religions repealed. It supported parliamentary reform, but wished change to be undertaken on a moderate scale. Though it supported the need for better representation, the *Edinburgh* opposed universal suffrage and the secret ballot in 1818. In this same year it condemned the governments of Europe for denying their people's rights, comparing their regimes to Napoleon's. It called for reform of the game laws, and it favored higher wages for workers and gradual abolition of the Poor Laws in 1820. In 1831 it supported full citizenship for Jews. In 1844 it grudgingly praised Sir Robert Peele's reduction of interest on the national debt, lowering of customs duties, and reform of the currency through renewal of the Bank of England's charter. In 1880 it examined the problems of Great Britain's agriculture, concluding that increased productivity rather than protective legislation could solve most of the problems, and disagreeing with those who argued that the large size of British agricultural units made for efficiency.

The *Edinburgh*'s political nature is reflected in the careers of its editors and major contributors. Francis Jeffrey eventually became lord advocate and Henry Brougham lord chancellor. Editor George Cornewall Lewis, member of Parliament, served at various times as chancellor of the exchequer and member of the privy council, home secretary, and secretary for war. Henry Reeve had a long and influential career as clerk of appeal to the judicial committee of the privy council. Arthur R.D. Elliot, member of Parliament, founded the Liberal Union Club, and Harold Cox, also a member of Parliament, was like Elliot a strong advocate of free trade. Most of the political writers for the *Edinburgh* followed the ideas of Dugald Stewart, Thomas Reid, and Adam Smith, especially Stewart's emphasis on the importance of political economy. Again and again when offering explanations and considering questions across a broad spectrum of topics, they underscored the importance of economics and especially free trade.

Between 1802 and 1850 the *Edinburgh* published more than 250 articles on economics, favoring among other things more equitable taxation, the gold standard, and, of course, free trade. It opposed the Corn Laws, Poor Laws, and government regulation in general.[3] "Finance—The Budget" (51:211–24) is typical in its emphases. It favors reform of the kind and distribution of taxes, rather than an overall reduction, arguing that a selective reduction of duties and controls on imported products would produce more revenue and introduce more competition, improving the quality of products. The article opposes a property tax, favoring an income tax as more equitable.

The *Edinburgh* gave regular attention to travel and geography, science, medicine, and education. In education, as in politics and economics, it favored reform. In an 1826 article on London University, the *Edinburgh* argued for the exclusion of religion and for a more flexible curriculum, attacking Oxford and Cambridge for neglecting subjects such as chemistry, economics, and mineralogy for Greek, Latin, and mathematics. An 1830 article condemns the management of Eton for using worthless textbooks and for allowing fagging and flogging. In scientific matters the *Edinburgh*'s reviewers usually provide an encyclopedic survey of the subject, followed by the reviewer's opinion. This habit of offering a comprehensive treatment of the background is especially evident in the reviews of more significant publications. The April 1860 review of Darwin's *On the Origin of Species* is thorough in its presentation of earlier theories and the objections to Darwin's ideas, but firmly of the opinion that Darwin's theory is not adequately proven by his observations and hence is conjectural. The October 1890 review of Frazer's *The Golden Bough* is skeptical of the way Frazer links the customs of different peoples, saying that he did so on the basis of superficial similarities, that he oversimplified matters truly obscure and complex but preferred unnecessarily complex explanations where simpler ones would serve just as well. A 1920 article on an English translation of Einstein's *Relativity* provides a great deal of background and a thorough review of the challenges to the theory, concluding with an opinion supporting the theory.

The period of its largest circulation and influence, the first quarter of the nineteenth century, coincided with the appearance of the major works of the Romantic writers. Francis Jeffrey wrote the majority of the literary reviews during this time. In the very first issue he attacked the new writers for their use of the language of the lower classes and for their attempt to use common experience for expression of lofty and abstract ideas. They failed, he said, to follow "the established system of poetry and criticism." He condemned their lack of originality and their "splenetic and idle discontent with the existing institutions of society" (1:71). These criticisms and others like them are maintained throughout the period by Jeffrey and others, though not without exceptions and a gradual change toward acceptance, especially of Byron, Keats, and Leigh Hunt.[4] Though Jeffrey's review of Wordsworth is notorious, the review of Byron's *Childe Harold* (27:277–310) is a better example of his criticism. Jeffrey's reviews, collected first in 1833, have since been published in numerous editions.[5] His review of Archibald Alison's *Essay on the Nature and Principles of Taste* (2d ed., 1811) appears (revised) in the *Encyclopaedia Britannica* as the entry for "Beauty" through the eighth edition.[6]

After Jeffrey the most important of the contributors to the magazine was Thomas Babington Macaulay. Recruited by Jeffrey in 1824, Macaulay wrote forty articles for the *Edinburgh* between then and 1844 (196:296).[7] Among his subjects were Milton, Dryden, Johnson, Bunyan, Byron, and Machiavelli. He wrote against Bentham and Mill, founders of the *Westminster Review,** and he attacked Gladstone's ideas on church and state. His *Edinburgh* essays were collected in three volumes in 1843 and have been reprinted often since. Other better-known contributors were Walter Scott, G. H. Lewes, Thomas Carlyle, William Hazlitt, Sir James Stephen, Edward Bulwer-Lytton, and William Thackeray.[8] The *Edinburgh* did not follow the general trend after 1865 of publishing the names of its authors. It did not begin until July 1912 (211, no. 441).

When the *Edinburgh* began publication in 1802, its chief rival among the reviews was the politically liberal *Monthly Review*. The success of the *Edinburgh* in the Whig cause moved the Tories to establish the *Quarterly Review** in 1809. The final, determining event was the appearance in the issue for October 1808 of a particularly infuriating article on the Spanish revolt of the previous spring. Beginning in 1824 the *Westminster Review* took up the ground to the political far left of the *Edinburgh*. The elder John Mill's reviews of the *Edinburgh* and the *Quarterly* in the first and second numbers of the *Westminster Review* (January and April 1834), though of course strongly biased, provide a good view of the differences.[9] The *Annual Review* (1803), *Eclectic Review** (1805), and *London Review** (1809) were modeled after the *Edinburgh*. William Blackwood founded *Blackwood's Edinburgh Magazine** (1817) with the hope, not realized, of undercutting the *Edinburgh*. From this time on the magazines did become increasingly more competitive with the quarterlies and gave them serious problems after the middle of the century.[10] But when the *Edinburgh Review* ceased publication in October 1929 (250, no. 510), its last editor, Harold Cox, wrote that it did so not only because of the heavy competition from the monthlies, daily press, and radio, but also because there were no more Whigs.

Notes

1. John Clive, *Scotch Reviewers: The "Edinburgh Review," 1802–1815* (Cambridge, Mass., 1957), p. 21.

2. Many of the articles dealing directly with political matters can be found under the heading "Whigs" in the indexes.

3. See Frank W. Fetter, "Economic Controversy in the British Reviews, 1802–1850," *Economica,* n.s. 32 (1965):424–37.

4. Thomas Crawford, *The "Edinburgh Review" and Romantic Poetry (1802–29),* Auckland University College Bulletin no. 47, English Series No. 8 (Auckland, 1955), pp. 28–30.

5. The best of these is a school text, *Selections from the Essays of Francis Jeffrey,* ed. Lewis E. Gates. G. L. Kittredge and C. T. Winchester, gen. eds. (Boston, 1894).

6. Gates, p. 206.

7. Thomas Babington Macaulay, *Selected Writings,* ed. John Clive and Thomas Piney, in *Classics of British Historical Literature,* gen. ed. John Clive (Chicago, 1972), p. xiv.

8. The best guide to the identity of contributors is *The Wellesley Index to Victorian Periodicals, 1824–1900,* ed. Walter E. Houghton, vol. 1 (Toronto, 1966).

9. For the *Edinburgh*'s differences with the *Westminster Review*'s Utilitarianism, see 49 (March 1829):159–89; (June 1829):273–99; and 50 (October 1829):99–125.

10. John Gross, *The Rise and Fall of the Man of Letters* (London, 1969), p. 10.

Information Sources

BIBLIOGRAPHY

Brogan, D. W. "The Intellectual Review." *Encounter* 21, no. 5 (1963):7–15.

Cockburn, Lord Henry. *Life of Lord Jeffrey.* 2d ed. 2 vols. Edinburgh, 1852.

Cox, R. G. "The Great Reviews." *Scrutiny* 6 (1937):2–20, 155–75.

Crawford, Thomas. *The "Edinburgh Review" and Romantic Poetry (1802–29).* Auckland University College Bulletin No. 47, English Series No. 8. Auckland, 1955.

Elliot, Arthur R.D. "The *Edinburgh Review.*" *Edinburgh Review* 196 (1902):275–318.

Fetter, Frank W. "Economic Controversy in the British Reviews, 1802 1850." *Economica,* n.s. 32 (1965):424–37.

Gates, Lewis E., ed. *Selections from the Essays of Francis Jeffrey.* Gen. eds. G. L. Kittredge and C. T. Winchester. Boston, 1894.

Graham, Walter. *English Literary Periodicals.* New York, 1930.

Greig, James A. *Francis Jeffrey of the "Edinburgh Review."* Edinburgh, 1948.

Gross, John. *The Rise and Fall of the Man of Letters.* London, 1969.

Hayden, John O. *The Romantic Reviewers, 1802–1824.* London, 1969.

Horner, Leonard, ed. *Memoirs and Correspondence of Francis Horner.* 2 vols. London, 1853.

Macaulay, Thomas Babington. *Selected Writings.* Edited by John Cline and Thomas Piney. In *Classics of British Historical Literature.* Gen. ed. John Cline. Chicago, 1972.

Napier, Macvey. *Selections from the Correspondence of the Late Macvey Napier.* London, 1879.

Renwick, W. L. *English Literature 1789–1815.* Vol. 9 in *The Oxford History of English Literature.* Edited by F. P. Wilson and Bonamy Dobrée. Oxford, 1963.

Wellesley Index to Victorian Periodicals. Edited by Walter E. Houghton. Vol. 1. Toronto, 1966.

INDEXES

Volumes 1–20, 21–50, 51–80, 81–110, 111–140, 141–177, separately published, 1812–1891. Indexes to volumes 1–40 reprinted separately (Carrollton Press). 1802–1881 in *Poole's Index.* 1802–1900 in *Wellesley Index* 1.

REPRINT EDITIONS
>   Microform: Academic Archives, Raleigh, N.C. Bell & Howell Co., Wooster,
>   Ohio. Datamics Inc., New York. Early British Publications (UMI), reels 427–
>   457. Princeton Microfilm Corp., Princeton, N.J. U. S. Library of Congress Photo
>   Duplication Service, Washington, D.C.

LOCATION SOURCES
American
>   Widely available.
British
>   Widely available.

Publication History

MAGAZINE TITLE AND TITLE CHANGES
>   *The Edinburgh Review, or Critical Journal.*

VOLUME AND ISSUE DATA
>   Volumes 1–250, numbers 1–510, October 1802–October 1929.

FREQUENCY OF PUBLICATION
>   Quarterly.

PUBLISHERS
>   Volumes 1–44, October 1802–October 1826: Archibald Constable and Com-
>   pany, Edinburgh. Volumes 45–250, January 1827–October 1929: Longmans,
>   Green and Company, London.

EDITORS
>   Francis Jeffrey, January 1803–June 1829. Macvey Napier, October 1829–Janu-
>   ary 1847. William Empson, April 1847–October 1852. George Cornewall Lewis,
>   January 1853–January 1855. George Cornewall Lewis and Henry Reeve, April
>   1855. Henry Reeve, July 1855–October 1895. Arthur Ralph Douglas Elliot, Jan-
>   uary 1896–April 1912. Harold Cox, July 1912–October 1929.

Dickie A. Spurgeon

ENGLISHMAN'S MAGAZINE, THE

The *Englishman's Magazine* ran only briefly, from April to October 1831,
but it is of great interest both for the stature of its contributors and as an early
venture of the young publisher Edward Moxon. Moxon had already published
Lamb and Wordsworth and was shortly to make a great success publishing the
works of Coleridge, Keats, Landor, the Shelleys, and the Brownings, as well
as those of Tennyson at an early stage in the poet's career. Moxon was obviously a fine judge of current writing.[1]

Son of a woolen worker at Wakefield, Moxon enjoyed a good education at
the charity school there before his apprenticeship to a bookseller. He went to
London about 1817 and by 1821 was working for Longmans, the company that
published his first book of poems. In 1824 he met the Lambs and through them
the wealthy banker-poet Samuel Rogers. In 1828 he went to work for Hurst,

Chance, and Company, which published his second volume of poems. In 1830, with a five hundred pound loan from Rogers, he began as an independent publisher in a small shop at 64 New Bond Street. Lamb's *Album Verses* was his first production.

The founding of the *Englishman's* was apparently Moxon's project from the first, although the Irish poet William Kennedy, assisted by the Scottish novelist Leitch Ritchie, was probably co-founder and first editor.[2] The first four numbers were published by Hurst, Chance, and Company, but Moxon took over the publication of the magazine beginning in August.

Competition was heavy. Apart from the quarterly reviews, of which the *Edinburgh** represented the Whigs, there were *Blackwood's Edinburgh Magazine,** the Benthamite *Westminster Review,** William Jerdan's weekly *Literary Gazette,** and the weekly *Tatler,** for which Leigh Hunt wrote a regular essay. Immediate liberal competitors included Henry Colburn's *New Monthly Magazine,** edited by Thomas Campbell, and the *Athenaeum,** edited by Keats's friend Charles William Dilke.

The *Englishman's* first issue, which appeared in April, featured Daniel Defoe on its cover. In its lead article, "Our Principles," the new monthly announced that in Defoe's spirit it would battle "untrammelled" for the "inherent and inalienable rights of mankind" throughout the globe. In regard to literature it professed:

> Our trust-worthiness in literary matters may be inferred from a few facts. Possessing ample means to compensate talent, we despise the miserable restrictions of a *coterie,* and deride the ostentatious parade of a sounding catalogue of names. With assistants among the most illustrious ornaments of literature, the value of contributions is left to be determined by their absolute merit. From the unexhausted mine of rising genius we shall draw liberally and often.

In format the magazine was a 130-page (or so) octavo. Its April issue contained about twenty-five items, including articles on parliamentary reform; "Runic Rhymes" by William Kennedy, the editor; "The Incendiary: A Tale of the German Peasant Wars"; an article entitled "Napoleon's Tomb"; a satirical ode ostensibly by Sir Charles Wetherell, a vehement anti-Reformist M.P.; a lively and sympathetic review of two American novels, now forgotten; and a full-page engraving of the "Villa di Papa Giulio" in Italy. Three articles were the first installments of a series: Henry D. Inglis wrote about his travels in "Rambles in Spain"; the surgeon James Kennedy pleaded for public health measures to combat the cholera epidemic;[3] and Thomas Pringle, the secretary of the Anti-Slavery Society, wrote about his experiences in South Africa, where he had found the Europeans more barbaric than the "harmless women and children" they enslaved.[4] In addition, the issue provided commentary on current poetry. One suspects Kennedy or Ritchie of this flowery passage:

> It is pleasant for us, and well for our readers, that we are in pupilage to no particular school of the gentle art of poetry. . . . Our humanities rally at the strains of Burns—Coleridge wafts us in a dream of ethereal delight—away—away—away—wherever the pinions of imagination can exercise their power. Reflection pilgrimages with Wordsworth to worship in grand mountain solitude—the oratory of natural religion—we carouse with Scott, in the old baronial hall, and the desolate majesty of Byron, moody and mournful, flings its broad shadow over our brow.

This issue and succeeding ones also included sentimental poetry, often in ballad style, although none of it was outstanding. The "British and Foreign Monthly Literary Gazette," another recurring feature, varied in form every month but regularly listed some fifty new English books, as well as French and German publications. In the April issue warm praise was bestowed on the essays of Leigh Hunt, whose complimentary article, "Mr. Moxon's Publications," had recently appeared in the *Tatler* for 4 June 1831.[5] "The Drama" declared that all English play-writing was bedeviled by "incapacity and corruption" except for the work of James Sheridan Knowles, a friend of Lamb's and Tennyson's and the author of the popular *Virginius*. "Literary News" dwelt on Knowles's forthcoming production of (*King*) *Alfred*. Knowles's biography of the artist Henry Fuseli also received a listing in the issue.

The May issue provided more short fiction and poetry, more about the Reform Bill, another installment of "Rambles in Spain," and a "brief historical report of the Anti-Slavery cause," possibly written by Pringle. An eleven-page review praised Knowles's *Alfred*, starring Macready in the title role. James Kennedy provided a full-page map of the spread of the cholera epidemic, and his continuing plea for public health measures was no doubt one of the factors that soon sent a British investigatory commission to Eastern Europe. A "Yankee Oxonian" criticized British higher education. Another engraving of Italy appeared. "Black and White" urged equality in the West Indies. "Bird Nesting" was contributed by a "field naturalist." Clearly there was going to be continuity in the *Englishman's,* as well as balanced coverage of topics of intense current interest.

In June a "West Indian Manifesto" was tacked on to the magazine. This issue also included a protest of the cutting off of state literary pensions to the aging Coleridge, among others. The indignation expressed by this issue and the July issue was to no avail, although Coleridge eventually received a three hundred pound lump sum from the government, and J. H. Frere provided the missing pension. Sir James Mackingtosh's *History of England* received a warm review, although Hallam's "masterly treatise" on the subject was said to be of nearly equal merit. "The Miners of Bois-Monzil" showed concern for the victims of a mine explosion. A new series, "Our Early Patriots," is known to be the work of the nineteen-year-old John Forster, a friend of Dickens's and Lamb's. The July issue also contained articles on the Italian singer Madame Pasta and on scientific experiments with evaporation; a tribute to the actress

Sarah Siddons, just deceased; a memoir of Charlotte Corday, Duperret, and Marat; more information on the cholera epidemic and the political unrest in Poland; and the suggestion that the Royal Academy set up a paint-making scheme to improve the quality of available pigments. The drama column pointed out that although "theatricals" were said to be declining, London now supported five times the number of theaters it had twenty years ago. Clerical opposition to the Reform Bill elicited the firm suggestion that the Church also needed reform. Finally, bound with this issue was a paper from the Anti-Slavery Society "in reply to the West Indian Manifesto."

Moxon's industriousness resulted in a particularly impressive issue for August, even though it lacked the contributions he had hoped to get from Wordsworth and Southey. Many of the articles and poems were now signed with names, initials, or recognizable pseudonyms. The issue continued to report on the cholera epidemic and the Reform Bill, and there were travel articles and continuations of previous series. "The Mismanagement of the Library of the British Museum" castigated the library for not having enough books and not measuring up to the French equivalent. Charles Lamb contributed two essays on the actor Elliston (signed "Elia") and an unsuccessful poem entitled "Hercules Pacificatus" (signed "C. L."). The issue also contained Leigh Hunt's verses on the month of May, Thomas Hood's "The Death Bed," and John Clare's charming sonnet, "The swallow catkins, once all downy white." The honorable Mrs. Caroline Norton, best known for her friendship with Lord Melbourne (a current scandal, although the relationship was probably platonic) was represented by a ten-stanza poem entitled "The Minstrel's Warning." The "author of Atherton" was represented by a less exciting poem that discussed old maids. In the drama column an anonymous critic deplored the expression *blue-stocking* and praised women writers, some by name. "Epistles by De Foe, Junior, No. 1," possibly by Moxon, began a new series. Moxon also triumphantly announced a series entitled "Peter's Net," by the "incomparable ELIA."

Arthur Hallam had also been industrious in connection with the August issue. Since his friend Tennyson had not responded to his request for a poem, Hallam himself provided the poet's striking and original sonnet, "Check every outflash. . . ." Hallam also asked a friend to approach Moxon on Tennyson's behalf to see what the *Englishman's Magazine* would pay for regular contributions.[6] Hallam's own contribution to the August issue was a sincere but feeble effort entitled "Stanzas," whose subject was presumably his fiancée, Tennyson's sister Emily. More impressive if too worshipful is Hallam's long essay "On Some of the Characteristics of Modern Poetry, and on the Lyrical Poems of Alfred Tennyson." Later, in a laudatory essay on Tennyson that appeared in *Blackwood's*, John Wilson declared that Hallam's extravagant praise of Tennyson "awoke a general guffaw and it expired in convulsions. Yet the Essay was exceedingly well written."[7] Certainly the article stirred interest in a poet who had only one major volume behind him. W. B. Yeats thought the first half of Hallam's essay "criticism . . . of the best and rarest sort," and one can hardly credit it, as Wilson did, with killing the *Englishman's Maga-zine*.

The August issue represented a good start for Moxon, although the effort it required was more than a working publisher could sustain. The September issue did carry four items by Lamb: the first installment of "Peter's Net"; "Recol lections of a Late Royal Academician," which satirized George Dawe; "Lines Suggested by a Sight of Waltham Cross," which expressed sympathy for the late, ill-treated Queen Caroline; and the unsigned review "The Latin Poems of Vincent Bourne," which also managed to publicize Lamb's *Album Verses,* published by Moxon. "I have ingeniously contrived to review myself," Lamb had written to Moxon when he submitted the article.[8] The issue also contained the second of Thomas Pringle's two poems on Africa, Thomas Hood's poem "Anticipation," Mrs. Norton's poem "The Last of His Race," William Ken-nedy's "Song of Poland," and John Forster's autobiographical essay "Prodi-gious!" A poem to the musician Vincent Novello by "C. C." is surely the work of Charles Cowden Clarke, who had recently married Novello's daughter Victoria. Finally, there appeared a review of Thomas Moore's *Life and Death of Lord Edward Fitzgerald* and a laudatory article about Edmund Kean at the Haymarket Theatre.

The October issue was less illustrious than its two predecessors; its only widely known contributors were Lamb and John Clare. Nevertheless, Moxon was still eager to continue and had been advertising his magazine as he rarely did his books. In the *Athenaeum* for 1 October 1831 he asked for two new shareholders to come forward in support. Leitch Ritchie had fallen ill, and William Kennedy may have abdicated amicably. The shareholders did not ma-terialize, causing Moxon to discontinue the magazine for lack of funds. Lamb wrote Moxon an amusing consolatory letter.[9] In *Blackwood's* Wilson wrote, "*The Englishman's Magazine* ought not to have died, for it threatened to be a very pleasant periodical."[10] Moxon did begin another magazine in 1832 with the twenty-year-old John Forster as editor, but their less distinguished *Reflector* ran only for three issues. The two magazines represented Moxon's only "fol-lies," yet the *Englishman's* was in many ways a fine effort. As the editor-publisher who presented Lamb, Clare, Hunt, Hallam, and Tennyson in a single issue, Edward Moxon had provided a remarkable bridge between the Roman-tics and the Victorians.

Notes

1. The prime source of information about Moxon and the *Englishman's Magazine* is Harold G. Merriam, *Edward Moxon, Publisher of Poets* (New York, 1939).

2. See the *Dictionary of National Biography* on both. The *DNB* attributes the death of the magazine to Ritchie's poor health, but Ritchie's health was more likely only a cause of Moxon's assuming editorial duties in August. See also Merriam, p. 31n, and George Gilfallan, "Tennyson," in *A Gallery of Literary Portraits,* series 2 (New York, 1857), p. 206, which mentions Kennedy as the *Englishman's* moving force.

3. Merriam, p. 32.

4. Although articles were generally unsigned, some authors, like Pringle, can be traced. See Merriam, pp. 33, 75.

5. *Leigh Hunt's Literary Criticism,* ed. C. W. and L. H. Houtchens (New York, 1956), pp. 388–93.

6. Christopher Ricks, *Tennyson* (New York, 1972), pp. 68–69.

7. Philip Henderson, *Tennyson: Poet and Prophet* (London, 1978), p. 21. See also Arthur Hallam, *Writings,* ed. T. H. Vail Motter (New York, 1943), p. 21, for Hallam's comments on the essay.

8. *The Letters of Charles Lamb,* ed. E. V. Lucas (London, 1935), 3:319.

9. Ibid., 3:324–25.

10. Henderson, p. 20.

Information Sources

BIBLIOGRAPHY

Cecil, Lord David. *Melbourne.* London, 1955.

Charnwood, Dorothea. *Call Back Yesterday.* London, 1937.

Hallam, Arthur Henry. *Letters.* Edited by Jack Kolb. Columbus, Ohio, 1980.

———. *Writings.* Edited by T. H. Vail Motter. New York, 1943.

Hunt, Leigh. *Leigh Hunt's Literary Criticism.* Edited by C. W. and L. H. Houtchens. New York, 1956.

Jack, Ian. *English Literature 1815–1832.* Oxford, 1963.

Lamb, Charles. *Letters.* Edited by E. V. Lucas. 3 vols. London, 1935.

Lamb, Charles and Mary. *Works.* Edited by E. V. Lucas. 7 vols. London, 1903–1905.

Lucas, E. V. *Life of Charles Lamb.* London, 1921. Reprint. New York, 1968.

Merriam, Harold G. *Edward Moxon, Publisher of Poets.* New York, 1939.

Ricks, Christopher. *Tennyson.* New York, 1972.

Tennyson, Hallam Lord. *Alfred Lord Tennyson: A Memoir.* 2 vols. New York, 1897.

Wordsworth, William and Dorothy. *Letters.* 2d ed. Edited by A. G. Hill and E. de Selincourt. Oxford, 1979.

INDEXES
Volume 1 only, in the September 1831 issue.

REPRINT EDITIONS
Microform: English Literary Periodicals (UMI), reel 359.

LOCATION SOURCES

American
Complete runs: Harvard University Library; Henry E. Huntington Library; Library Company of Philadelphia; Newberry Library; U. S. Library of Congress. Partial runs: Boston Athenaeum; New York Public Library.

British
Complete runs: Bodleian Library; British Museum; Cambridge University Library; Glasgow University Library. Partial runs: Edinburgh University Library; St. Andrews University Library.

Publication History

MAGAZINE TITLE AND TITLE CHANGES
The Englishman's Magazine.

VOLUME AND ISSUE DATA
>Volume 1, numbers 1–5, April–August 1831; volume 2, numbers 1–2, September–October 1831.

FREQUENCY OF PUBLICATION
>Monthly.

PUBLISHERS
>Volume 1, numbers 1–4, April–July 1831: Hurst, Chance, and Company, 65 St. Paul's Churchyard, London. Volume 1, number 5–volume 2, numbers 1–2, August–October 1831: Edward Moxon, 64 New Bond Street, London.

EDITORS
>William Kennedy, Leitch Ritchie, Edward Moxon.

>*Winifred F. Courtney*

ENGLISH REVIEW, THE. See AAAJ

EUROPEAN MAGAZINE, THE. See AAAJ

EXAMINER, THE

In 1808 Leigh and John Hunt founded the *Examiner* primarily as a political journal. In early issues its major articles covered national and foreign affairs as well as Parliament, but the newspaper also contained columns on theater and the fine arts, and eventually on literature. Leigh Hunt founded, edited, or wrote for a dozen journals during his lifetime, but the *Examiner* remained the most successful of his enterprises. While John Hunt handled the business matters, Leigh wrote the editorials and many of the articles. The Hunts named their newspaper after the Tory journal that Jonathan Swift had conducted nearly a century earlier. "I thought only of (the) wit and fine writing" and not of Swift's political principles, Leigh Hunt explained in his autobiography. To be sure, the Hunts' *Examiner* espoused "reform in Parliament, liberality of opinion in general . . . and a fusion of literary taste into all subjects whatsoever."[1] This emphasis on political ideas accurately reflected the *Examiner*'s direction throughout much of its seventy-three years. Although the Hunts intended to avoid a specific party point of view, in the course of the first year their politics became identified as radical, and their legal troubles began.

During 1808 alone, Leigh Hunt attacked financial privileges of the English aristocracy; opposed several tenets of English criminal law, especially the large number of capital offenses; came out strongly for Catholic Emancipation; exposed cases of corruption among government ministers; questioned the abilities of government officials and military officers; and, ultimately to the detriment of his health and his pocketbook, attacked the king's behavior. Government and military officials rose to the bait. For the next four years they threatened, and several times actually filed, libel suits against the *Examiner* and the Hunts. Leigh Hunt's *ad hominem* attack on the Prince Regent on 12 March 1812 resulted in heavy fines and prison terms for the brothers. While Leigh's prison stay, in particular, was ameliorated by his family's joining him and by several parties thrown by his friends, he emerged financially and personally beaten. He still strongly believed in parliamentary reform, but the high-spirited, ringing prose of the first few years of the *Examiner* was gone. Circulation fell from over 7,000 in 1812 to under 3,000 in 1821. Leigh and John Hunt had a falling-out, and Leigh, who had already given up his share of the ownership, left even his editorial duties late in 1821 to meet with Shelley and Byron in Italy to plan a new periodical.[2]

During Leigh Hunt's tenure as editor the *Examiner* became a major force in public acceptance of Romantic literature, and in fact introduced Keats and much of Shelley to its audience. Hunt's 1 December 1816 essay, "Young Poets," on Shelley, Keats, and John Hamilton Reynolds, foreshadowed subsequent publication of articles on these authors, Keats and Shelley in particular. Some articles reviewed their work, some responded to attacks made on their poetry by other periodicals. Hunt published Keats's "O Solitude," his first appearance in print, and Shelley's "Hymn to Intellectual Beauty," "Ozymandias," and "To a Skylark." Hunt's diligence in supporting Shelley and Keats, and the appearance in the *Examiner* of some of Hunt's own poetry, caused the weekly to be viewed as the chief organ of what J. G. Lockhart in *Blackwood's* * labeled the "Cockney School of Poetry."

The *Examiner* also published poems by Wordsworth and essays by Lamb, Hazlitt, and Thomas Barnes (later to become editor of the *Times*), but, prior to 1816, the *Examiner* had included only one non-theatrical literary review, Hazlitt's 1814 discussion of Wordsworth's *Excursion*. Hazlitt, who became the *Examiner*'s regular dramatic critic in March 1815, also wrote most of the early "Literary Notices," the regular literary reviewing department that began in June 1816. Within a year, however, Hunt took over those duties. This section, and its eventual replacement, the "Literary Examiner," defined "literary" broadly enough to include works on politics, economics, science, travel, and the military, in addition to poetry and fiction. Hazlitt had also written sections of "Table Talk" in 1813 which, intended to be a series of short anecdotes or *bon mots,* actually became a section of brief essays, and sections of the "Round Table" discussions published throughout 1815, intended to be essays in the style of Addison and Steele. His contributions to this latter column are identifiable by his initials; Hunt's are indicated by the often-present pointing finger adopted as his own signature.

Thus, Leigh Hunt established a firm basis for both literature and literary criticism in the *Examiner* during the nearly fourteen years he served as editor. With Leigh's departure for Italy in 1821, brother John apparently moved his own son, Henry Leigh Hunt, into the position of editor. In 1828 John Hunt retired, leaving the entire management of the *Examiner* to his son. Financial problems continued to plague the weekly, however, and after the younger Hunt declared bankruptcy Dr. Robert Fellowes bought the copyright, gave a small share to John Hunt, and sold the rest to Albany Fonblanque, who had been chief political writer since 1826. The *Examiner* enjoyed a renaissance as Fonblanque surrounded himself with qualified critics and writers. In the 1830s, for example, Leigh Hunt and John Stuart Mill contributed reviews and articles, John Forster became literary editor, and William Thackeray briefly contributed and served as sub-editor in the next decade. Thackeray was succeeded first by fiction-writer Dudley Costello, then by Henry Morley.[3]

Under Fonblanque the *Examiner* became less politically radical and increasingly critical of the Philosophical Radicals' inflexibility. In fact, Fonblanque's editorial criticism of the Radicals eventually led to a break with Mill.[4] In 1847 John Forster, who had been literary editor for over a decade, became editor and maintained the high quality of literary criticism that the newspaper had become famous for under Fonblanque. But with Forster's departure late in 1855 the *Examiner* lost the last of its major literary figures. Its remaining editors, some of whose names have not yet risen from obscurity, failed to recapture the imagination of the reading public and, while the newspaper continued publication for another quarter of a century, it never again achieved either the power or the public it previously enjoyed.

Both Fonblanque and Forster expanded the literary review section. While they are less famous than Hunt is for having "discovered" major authors, the reviews appearing during their editorship helped to shape public opinion and to introduce young authors to a weekly reading public. Forster in particular showed his literary perspicacity. As an early supporter of Robert Browning, for example, he found in *Paracelsus* "poetical genius," and maintained that, even though a reader might find it difficult to read, "he will find enough of beauty to compensate him for the tedious passages." In particular, Forster praised Browning's "deep knowledge of humanity" and "subtle and inquisitive" intellect (no. 1440:563). This review, one of the longest to have appeared in the *Examiner*, indicated the significance that reviewer Forster and editor Fonblanque attached to the young Browning. Fonblanque himself apparently reviewed the young Dickens's *Sketches by Boz*. His only complaint about the work was Dickens's "excessive" hyperbole, apparently toned down in *Pickwick*, whose monthly numbers received very favorable notice (no. 1465:132).[5] Fonblanque used much of his space for lengthy quotations, often to prove his contention that Dickens was one of the finest comic writers in the language (no. 1492:563).

During the decade from the mid-1830s to the mid-1840s, however, the *Examiner*'s literary reviews were mainly Forster's creations. Reading his reviews, one becomes aware of the literary sensitivity that he brought to his reading, and recognizes the contrast his views form with the views of more partisan critics writing for other periodicals. During Forster's tenure as literary editor and then as editor, the pages of the *Examiner* were often filled with long passages from major works—enough to whet readers' appetites for the entire work. At least as important, its pages highlighted new works by young authors often before those works became more generally acknowledged and accepted. In addition to *Paracelsus* in 1835, Browning's *Pippa Passes, Dramatic Lyrics,* and *Dramatic Romances and Lyrics* received high praise. Forster acknowledged every "indication of the poet's continued advance in the right direction," and was positive that "Mr Browning will win his laurel" (no. 1817:756). In fact, Browning had asked his publisher to delay publication of *Dramatic Lyrics* in 1842 to allow Forster's to be the first review. His 1845 volume was even more highly praised. The reviewer was pleased that the poet was less often getting lost in "transcendental or other fogs," called his rhythm "poetical," and declared that his work had "the stamp and freshness of originality" (no. 1972:723).

To authors whom its reviewers particularly liked, the *Examiner* returned as frequently as it had works to review. Browning's works, therefore, were fit matter for discussion whenever he published them, or indeed whenever subsequent editions of previously published works appeared. So, too, reviews of new editions of Wordsworth's and Shelley's poetry and of Lamb's essays appeared frequently, keeping these Romantic authors constantly before the *Examiner*'s readers. Charles Dickens, whose works were serialized throughout this period, was also frequently discussed. With the serial publication of *Dombey and Son,* the reviewer, possibly Leigh Hunt, called Dickens "our greatest living master of humour and pathos," and he quoted the novel in four different articles in 1846.

Such extensive use of quotation—of Dickens, other English authors, and much of the foreign literature that the *Examiner* had begun to review as well— and the increasingly used Victorian commonplaces of praise, "manly" and "earnest," masked the development during this time of increasingly sophisticated critical approaches if not critical terminology. In its final review of *Dombey* as a completed volume, for example, the *Examiner* never used the word *motif* but recognized Dickens's extraordinary foreshadowing throughout the earlier parts of the novel: "The recurrence of particular thoughts and phrases . . . [runs] like the leading colour through a picture, or the predominant phrase in a piece of music" (no. 2126:692). The reviewer of *Bleak House* in 1853 praised the same quality, and held Dickens up as the standard by which to judge literature generally.

During these Fonblanque-Forster years, Alfred Tennyson also received considerable attention, especially after the success of his 1842 *Poems.* Forster acknowledged retrospectively that Tennyson's 1830 and 1832 volumes had generated some criticism but more praise, and that in his ten years of silence nothing else had appeared to match his best passages. In the 1842 volumes Forster particularly appreciated Tennyson's having eliminated "affectations" of diction, images, and rhythm (no. 1791:340).

Although *The Princess* was given a mixed review early in 1848, *In Memoriam* received unstinted praise in 1850. Despite the poem's having been published anonymously, the *Examiner* recognized Tennyson's authorship "by the tender melancholy, the full flowing music, the intensely English scenery and by the easy and natural manner in which profound truths are shed from delicate fancies." The structure of the entire work was one of its strongest qualities, as each section built upon previous ones. The reviewer also praised the poem's theme, "the record of a healthy and vigorous mind working its way, through suffering, up to settled equipoise and hopeful resignation," and the specific poetic techniques its author used, in particular the "numberless images of various beauty" (no. 2210:356).

Thus, while Forster was literary editor and then editor, Tennyson was the subject of several important reviews, and the *Examiner,* as it had been for Browning, was instrumental in creating both an audience and a reputation for him. In fact, several of his poems actually appeared first in its pages in the half-decade from 1849 to 1854. Most significant of them was "The Charge of the Light Brigade," which appeared on 9 December 1854 before being included in the 1855 volume, *Maud, and Other Poems.* The reviewer liked that volume particularly for the way in which Tennyson related his scenery to the shifting emotions of the narrator: "Every point of [the scenery] appears to be known to us, because it has been presented in connection with an emotion by which it was fixed in the mind—precisely as in nature all familiar objects become fixed there" (no. 2479:484). This last idea, the relationship between art and reality, became increasingly significant in the *Examiner*'s literary reviews in the 1850s.

It culminated in a review of the Cambridge essays of 1855. Although the review appeared after Forster had resigned, it reflected a concern that had developed under his guidance, and the example used certainly reflected his influence on the *Examiner*'s literary principles. One of the Cambridge essays had attacked novels for not portraying events realistically. But the *Examiner*'s reviewer carefully distinguished between "direct imitation" and "representation," clearly coming down on the side of representation: "Mr Dickens, in common with other great novelists, represents life, not as a copyist, but as an artist. . . . By recombinations of his own that are not, or even cannot be, transcripts of anything, [he] knows how to give the most distinct impressions of the spirit of the life he is describing" (no. 2502:20). The *Examiner* thus joined an impressive list of periodicals in the early 1850s that were discussing the shape and merits of literary realism.

Shortly after Forster resigned as editor, however, the shape and merits of literary criticism in the *Examiner* changed significantly. Except for a sharp but brief increase in the mid-1870s, the number of original poems included annually, already having begun to decline in the 1840s, declined even further. What had been a significant means of introducing young poets' works under Hunt became little more than filler after 1855. In addition, fewer books received lengthy reviews; in their place was a paragraph or two on each of several newly published books. This efficient means of introducing more works to its readers each week necessarily reduced the amount of detailed criticism and the number of quotations that had earlier allowed readers first-hand exposure to the works. The emphasis had thus shifted to covering more works superficially. During the 1860s the "Literary Examiner" section listed more works but discussed even fewer. Even reviews of significant works were shorter, and geared more, it seemed, to an increasingly mobile and hurried world.

Simultaneously, the *Examiner* was becoming less partisan in its reviews than it had been under Leigh Hunt. Indeed, even under Fonblanque it had railed less at its political foes. Under Forster, and even more noticeably under M. W. Savage and Henry Morley through the late 1850s and the 1860s, it made a special effort to praise well-written works with whose ideas or form it disagreed. Of the former, Matthew Arnold's *Essays in Criticism* gave the reviewer much with which to disagree. He especially disagreed with "a clever independent thinker" who, knowing the great literature that England has produced, still preferred a French Academy. Yet, the reviewer quickly added, Arnold's essays "aim at a true independence of criticism, desire to be and are honest, thoughtful, and precise in expression" (no. 2979:134). With A. C. Swinburne's *Atalanta in Calydon,* however, it was the form with which the *Examiner*'s reviewer disagreed: "Utterly mistaken" Swinburne was, the reviewer maintained, "when he applied his remarkable poetical powers to reproduce in English the tragic forms of Greece." Nonetheless, the reviewer acknowledged, the poem was the best of its kind, at least since Shelley's attempt in *Prometheus Unbound* (no. 2998:440).

Conversely, its approval of an author's abilities or technique did not guarantee a positive review. *The Mill on the Floss,* "one of the cleverest books of the day," was also "nearly the most tedious": for George Eliot was guilty of "over-elaboration," of spending too many pages on a "minute painting of a boy and a girl." Perhaps reflecting the decline in critical acumen among the reviewers and editors of the *Examiner,* this particular review concluded with the assertion that "among the female novelists of our day only Miss Bronte and Mrs Gaskell occupy a higher place than [George Eliot] is likely to retain" (no. 2733:372–73).

In its remaining decade-plus of existence, the *Examiner* expanded its reviews of other periodicals, which it had begun in the 1840s, and attacked them politically—whatever their party bias—when it determined that they had erred, but it as frequently praised their content when that content merited praise. It lamented the decline in Tennyson's performance; *Gareth and Lynette,* a reviewer noted morosely, would "add nothing to his reputation" (no. 3378:1056). But its reviewers tried desperately not to attack the laureate: *Queen Mary* would succeed, if at all, by its association with Tennyson's name, but its poetry was "like that of an uncultured novice first breaking the clods of language with a tool too heavy and wonderful for him" (no. 3517:717).

In this last decade several of the reviews were signed, or at least identified by initials, a return to the policy apparently governing some of the articles under Leigh Hunt's editorship. But circulation declined, and a plaintive note in the 26 February 1881 issue announced that publication would be "temporarily discontinued." The *Examiner* had lost its audience, in part because it no longer represented any political faction of significant numbers, in part because the rise of more purely literary publications had seized its literary audience, and in large measure because it had lost the fire and imagination of its early leaders. It had no more Leigh Hunts, Albany Fonblanques, and John Forsters to follow to notoriety and fame. The journal that Leigh Hunt helped found, and that became his most successful literary enterprise, never again appeared.

Notes

1. *The Autobiography of Leigh Hunt,* ed. J. E. Morpurgo (London, 1948), pp. 173, 175.

2. Information in this paragraph appears in George Dumas Stout, *The Political History of Leigh Hunt's "Examiner,"* Washington University Studies in Language and Literature, n.s. no. 19 (St. Louis, 1949), pp. 3–38 *passim.*

3. Darwin Bostick, "An Account of the *Examiner,"* *Victorian Periodicals Newsletter* 11, no. 1 (1978):19–21.

4. Joseph Hamburger, *Intellectuals in Politics: John Stuart Mill and the Philosophical Radicals* (New Haven, 1965), pp. 166, 203–4.

5. Alec W. Brice, "Reviewers of Dickens in the "Examiner": Fonblanque, Forster, Hunt, and Morley," *Dickens Studies Newsletter* 3 (September 1972):69, provides internal evidence that Fonblanque wrote the review.

Information Sources

BIBLIOGRAPHY

Blunden, Edmund. *Leigh Hunt and His Circle.* New York, 1930.
———. *Leigh Hunt's "Examiner" Examined.* New York, 1928.
Bostick, Darwin F. "An Account of the *"Examiner." Victorian Periodicals Newsletter* 11, no. 1 (1978):19–21.
Hunt, Leigh. *The Autobiography of Leigh Hunt.* Edited by J. E. Morpurgo. London, 1948.
Stout, George Dumas. *The Political History of Leigh Hunt's "Examiner." *Washington University Studies in Language and Literature, n.s. no. 19. St. Louis, 1949.
Thompson, James R. *Leigh Hunt.* Boston, 1977.
The Woman Question: Papers Reprinted from "The Examiner." London, 1872.

INDEXES

Each volume indexed, except final volume.

REPRINT EDITIONS

Microform: English Literary Periodicals (UMI), reels 210–248 and 188–192.

LOCATION SOURCES

American

Partial runs: Widely available.

British

Complete runs: Birmingham Public Library; Bristol Public Library.
Partial runs: Widely available.

Publication History

MAGAZINE TITLE AND TITLE CHANGES

The Examiner; a Sunday paper, on politics, domestic economy, and theatricals, 3 January 1808–27 March 1869. *The Examiner and London Review,* 3 April 1869 (merged with *London Review and Weekly Journal*) through 31 December 1870. *The Examiner,* 7 January 1871–26 December 1874. *The Examiner. Established 1808. An Independent Weekly Review of Politics, Literature, Science, and Art,* 2 January 1875–26 February 1881.

VOLUME AND ISSUE DATA

Numbers 1–3813, 3 January 1808–26 February 1881. "Literary Notices" section was published as a separate Saturday supplement, *Literary Examiner,* from 5 July 1823 (no. 1) to 27 December 1823 (no. 26) before being reincorporated into the Sunday *Examiner.* Sunday publication continued through number 1742, 20 June 1841; *Examiner* began Saturday publication with number 1743, 26 June 1841.

FREQUENCY OF PUBLICATION

Weekly.

PUBLISHERS (all London)

Number 1, 3 January 1808–number 991, 28 January 1827: John Hunt, 15 Beaufort Buildings, Strand (number 1, 3 January 1808–number 243, 23 August 1812)/21 Maiden Lane, Covent Garden (number 244, 30 August 1812–number 508, 21 September 1817)/19 Catherine Street, Strand (number 509, 28 September 1817–number 803, 15 June 1823)/38 Tavistock Street, Covent Garden (number 804, 22 June 1823–number 985, 17 December 1826)/4 York Street, Covent Garden (number 986, 24 December 1826–number 991, 28 January 1827). Number 992, 4 February 1827–number 1189, 14 November 1830: Henry Leigh Hunt, 4 York Street, Covent Garden (number 992, 4 February 1827–number 1155, 21 March 1830)/113 Strand (number 1156, 28 March 1830–number 1189, 14 November 1830). Number 1190, 21 November 1830–number 3326, 28 October 1871: George Lapham, 113 Strand (number 1190, 21 November 1830–number 1271, 10 June 1832)/5 Wellington Street, Strand (number 1272, 17 June 1832–number 1292, 4 November 1832)/210 Strand and 5 Wellington Street, Strand (number 1293, 11 November 1832)/5 Wellington Street, Strand (number 1294, 18 November 1832–number 1409, 1 February 1835)/Wellington Street, Strand (number 1410, 8 February 1835–number 1493, 11 September 1836)/5 Wellington Street, Strand (number 1494, 18 September 1836–number 2727, 5 May 1860)/9 Wellington Street, Strand (number 2728, 12 May 1860–number 3326, 18 October 1871). Number 3327, 4 November 1871–number 3348, 30 March 1872: Roderick Harding Lapham, 9 Wellington Street, Strand. Number 3349, 6 April 1872–number 3392, 1 February 1873: Gustavus Harding Lapham, 9 Wellington Street, Strand. Number 3393, 8 February 1873–number 3655, 16 February 1878: Edward Dallow, 7 Southampton Street, Strand (number 3393, 8 February 1873–number 3491, 25 December 1874)/136 Strand (number 3492, 2 January 1875–number 3655, 16 February 1878). Number 3656, 23 February 1878–number 3697, 7 December 1878: Arthur Percy Millar, 136 Strand. Number 3698, 14 December 1878–number 3705, 1 February 1879: James Williamson, 136 Strand. Number 3706, 8 February 1879–number 3711, 15 March 1879:

Robert Manson, 136 Strand. Number 3712, 22 March 1879–number 3718, 3 May 1879: Edward Rossiter, 136 Strand. Number 3719, 10 May 1879–number 3813, 26 February 1881: No publisher listed, 136 Strand.

EDITORS

Leigh Hunt, 3 January 1808–21 October 1821. (*Examiner*, 3 September 1859, p. 570, indicates that Leigh and John Hunt may have been joint editors; all other sources list only Leigh Hunt.) Henry Leigh Hunt(?), 28 October 1821–1830. Albany W. Fonblanque, 1830–1847. John Forster, 1847–(probably end of) 1855. Marmion W. Savage, 1856–1859. Henry Morley, 1859–1867(?). William Minto, 1874–1878.

Roger P. Wallins

F

FOREIGN QUARTERLY REVIEW, THE

After six numbers of the *Foreign Quarterly Review* had appeared, the *Athenaeum** observed in 1828 that "the establishment of an English Foreign Review marked . . . the commencement of a new era in our literature." Previously, the reviewer noted, the English had "regarded the literature of other countries as a subject of far-off contemplation, and scarcely realized . . . that any thing was required in the study of it besides a tolerable acquaintance with the words of the language."[1] Other reviews of foreign literature had been projected or actually commenced earlier in the 1820s, but they were narrow, shallow, and short-lived. From the start the *Foreign Quarterly* sought to offer review articles comparable to those in the *Edinburgh** and the *Quarterly.** It was the first successful review to devote itself exclusively to foreign literature (by which it meant books written in a foreign language, not belles lettres only). It was also the longest surviving foreign review in the nineteenth century, running for thirty-seven volumes and twenty years (1827–1846).

Although he privately doubted the success of the scheme, Sir Walter Scott in June 1826 suggested that Robert Pearse Gillies might earn "a regular and reasonable, though not a large income" by bringing out a "quarterly account of foreign literature, mixed with good translations, and spirited views of the progress of knowledge on the Continent." Gillies was described by Carlyle as "an unemployed Advocate . . . long . . . known as one of the most enthusiastic students of German, and as possessing the largest German Library of any man in Scotland or perhaps in Britain."[2] He had for some time written for *Blackwood's Magazine,** particularly on German and Danish literature, though he had never written as much as he proposed or as he later claimed. Fortunately the publisher he found for his new review was the London foreign bookselling firm of Treuttel and Würtz—fortunate because of two solid if unspectacular employees of the firm. These were John George Cochrane, like Gillies a Scot, and John Macray. Both had already published translations; later both were to be librarians, Cochrane of the newly founded London Library and Macray of the New Yaylor Institution at Oxford. From the start Cochrane was the real editor, and in 1830 he became the "avowed and ostensible Editor"[3] as well. He remained editor through 1834, when disagreements with the assignees of the now bankrupt publisher (Adolphus Richter & Co., successor to Treuttel and Würtz) led him to set up his own short-lived rival review. Macray functioned as a sub-editor, responsible chiefly through 1834 for writing "Miscellaneous Literary Notices," which concluded each issue, doing some of the translations that appeared in reviews, and choosing books to be reviewed.[4]

Cochrane set what was to remain general policy and format. The point was to introduce the English to foreign thought; therefore books by Englishmen on foreign subjects were not eligible for review. (Occasionally this rule was broken, and one or two reviewers went to comic lengths to include an ineligible title.)[5] Moreover, the magazine intended to review only books unavailable in English translation, which explains the relative neglect of American literature. One may cynically say that they were drumming up business for their publisher's trade in foreign books, and of course to some extent they were; but they were also eager to give a large number of their readers some knowledge of books which those readers, ignorant of the original languages, could never read except in the translated excerpts offered in the review. The review's various aims did sometimes trip over each other. An early reviewer explained the need for the *Foreign Quarterly* by pointing to a thirteen-year delay between the publication of Niebuhr's *History of Rome* and discussion of it in England (2:512). The *Foreign Quarterly* tried to let its readers know what was current on the Continent, and to this end each number included a list of books recently published abroad. But the magazine had to catch up as well, and in the early years summarized whole bodies of national literature. As John Bowring remarked, "Let it be remembered that we have had to lead the way to a new field, and to go over ground rather as literary topographers than literary critics" (3:66).

While Cochrane's contributors included such Whig and Benthamite figures as J. A. Roebuck, J. R. McCulloch, John Bowring, and Henry Southern, the review justly contends that it "has no party object to favour, no political bias to indulge" (14:299) and that its "pages . . . ever shall be open to any appeal that science makes to it, to any literary subject that comes within its sphere" (2:1). One is struck today by the authority of many of the reviewers, rather than by their political alliance. David Brewster, J. S. Henslow, and Dr. John Conolly were all, for example, of some importance in science and medicine; George Cornewall Lewis, John Ward, Charles Buller, and George Taylor sat on parliamentary commissions. Frequently the reviewers themselves alluded to their personal experience or to private sources of information. Essayists on literature included Walter Scott; George Moir, the translator of Schiller's *Wallenstein;* the Spanish and Italian political refugees Telesforo de Trueba y Cossio, Antonio Alcala Galiana, and Fortunato Prandi; as well as industrious hacks such as André Vieusseux, Mary Margaret Busk, and W. H. Leeds.

One internal dispute at the beginning lost important contributors. A young man named William Fraser wished to be or considered himself to be an assistant editor, to which Gillies agreed; Cochrane could not work with him; Fraser left to set up his own rival *Foreign Review* (1828–1830) and took with him or won Robert Southey, Pablo deMendibil, Anthony Panizzi, David Irving, and Thomas Carlyle. Of these only Irving returned wholeheartedly to the *Foreign Quarterly*. Carlyle, who in the *Foreign Review* had introduced a number of German writers to English readers, rejoined with the October 1831 issue, but he wrote little for it and he and the *Foreign Quarterly* were never comfortable with each other.

When Cochrane left at the end of 1834, he was succeeded as editor by Frederic Shoberl, a prince of puffers and hacks. His twelve numbers were less carefully edited than previous ones, and they contained considerably more hack work. Balance and variety were both lost. German literature received the most attention; French and Italian were also noted; but only one article appeared on Spanish literature, though some attention was paid to Spanish political affairs. Leeds, who had previously written on architecture and on Russian literature, now wrote only on architecture. Three important new contributors appeared: John Stuart Blackie, writing mainly on German literature; Thomas Wright, on medieval subjects; and David Urquhart, who directly or indirectly led the review to a violently pro-Turkish, anti-Russian position during the first two years of Shoberl's editorship. Urquhart contributed also to the *British and Foreign Review*,* praising in that review the essays he had published in the *Foreign Quarterly*. Under Shoberl the main essays varied more in length than before; some were no longer than earlier "Critical Sketches," and the "Critical Sketches" became little more than extended quotations within a brief explanatory framework. There was more quotation in the main articles as well, and, since Macray was gone, quotation without translation. The addition of Wright to the staff accounts for some of the new bibliographical and antiquarian interest; but articles also appeared on ancient Eastern literatures and on Egyptian and Mexican antiquities. Even such titles as "Steam Navigation to India" and "South America" camouflaged antiquarian articles. The style, which under Cochrane tended to the magisterial tone of the *Edinburgh* or *Quarterly*, now often rang of those magazines. Reviewers were ironic to the point of facetiousness, whether talking of volcanoes (15:74–83) or of "Homer, Aeschylus & Co." (17:123); they carefully noted where they were on a particular day, or what a famous murderer had said to a friend of theirs.

When the *Foreign Quarterly* and the *Foreign Review* merged in 1830, the review retained both former publishers. Black, Young, and Young had published the *Foreign Review;* in time they became Black and Armstrong and, after acquiring the bankrupt Richter's interest in 1838, became sole proprietors and publishers of the *Foreign Quarterly*. Whether for this reason or some other, the editorship changed again at this point, and the *Foreign Quarterly* continued its decline. Benjamin Edward Pote, who edited volumes 21–24 (1838–1840), was often referred to as the mad editor; it was neither a figure of speech nor hyperbole. He was also a poor editor. One intelligent reader wrote of having "been strongly impressed, in reading lately two or three numbers of the *Foreign Quarterly*, at the amount of ignorance which goes to the writing of some of the articles." [6] *Fraser's Literary Chronicle* * observed that the review "is rather foreign to its subject, as it generally gives little more than a collection of essays, to which the titles of foreign books serve as introductions. Till the appearance of the *Foreign Monthly Review* [May–October 1839], which, however, was a failure, we had no review of foreign literature, and knew little or nothing of what was going on abroad." [7]

Though foreign titles still headed the reviews, the books discussed were often English, and the review had become ultra-Tory. Its tone sometimes grew hysterical: to a claim that some people are inadequately housed, clothed, and fed, the *Foreign Quarterly* retorted, "How grossly untrue! Where is man thus circumstanced? . . . The benevolent spirit of Christianity had also long since met all exigencies of this character." Civil marriages can only "please the Unitarian; who sink it [marriage] below even the polygamist Milton's notion" (21:127–28). While it frequently referred to itself as a popular journal addressed to the masses (21:226; 22:390; 24:354), it quoted Greek and Latin without translation. Pote devoted article after article (sometimes much of an issue) to his own etymological hobbyhorses and to portentous questions: "WHO WERE THE ETHIOPIANS?" "WHO WERE THE PHOENICIANS?" and more quietly, "Who were the Etruscans?" He wondered, "How are so many peculiarities and provincialisms of the English tongue purely Eastern?—the same of the French and German?" (24:318). His writing was often tortured and unclear, and his editing careless. *Peru* became *Persia* (22:360–61), symptomatic of another hobbyhorse; parts of reviews seem to have been mislaid and printed separately later; articles were more than ever made up largely of quotations; German in particular was badly misspelled. Worse, Pote had his finger everywhere, by his own later admission: "I had fancied Editors shortened, altered, or varied, & curtailed always: in truth, I had . . . so acted myself, in every case." [8] He lengthened as well occasional paragraphs or whole pages sounding like editorial insertions. Sometimes two reviews, by different reviewers, were telescoped into one. Of the major reviewers only J. S. Blackie tolerated such interference and madness; he still contributed to most numbers, but wrote on classical or historical topics rather than on recent German literature. Pote did introduce one interesting new feature, "Music Abroad and at Home," but it could not atone for the harm he did the review.

Obviously the review could not long survive under such editorship, even had Pote not become seriously ill of "brain fever." His successor from April 1840 until April 1842 was the Rev. Dr. James William Worthington. Although he was described as "sitting on it as an incubus," [9] and though his numbers continued some of the earlier Tory hysteria and introduced a dullness all their own, he was a conscientious editor who tried to halt the downward progress of the review. Most of his new contributors were foreigners living in England or Englishmen living abroad. Perhaps the most notable of them was Antonio Gallenga. All in all, however, Worthington was a poor editor. He had no sense of variety; reviews of travels sometimes took up a disproportionate amount of space. He had little appreciation of literature, though he had a strong and narrow sense of moral and political worth. For a while he was successful with the *Foreign and Colonial Quarterly Review,* which he founded after losing the editorship of the *Foreign Quarterly,* but he could never understand its original formula of balance, authority, and liberal openness.

Finally that formula was again followed. Chapman and Hall acquired the magazine in October 1841 and set about immediately deposing Worthington. Thackeray hoped to be the next editor, but he spoke only of the languages he knew or might learn. John Forster actively recruited contributors who, even if they would be publishing anonymously, had reputations. Forster became editor, and Thackeray continued to contribute. Forster himself wrote on Greek philosophers and American journalists, some of the material probably being supplied by his friend Charles Dickens. He coaxed contributions from Bulwer-Lytton, John Sterling, Walter Savage Landor, Browning, Trollope, George Henry Lewes, Carlyle, George Stovin Venables, Frazer Corkran, John Oxenford, and others. Some of the essays dealt with history or current affairs, but the emphasis was on literature. "English Books on matters of Foreign concern" were no longer excluded. The announcement of the new management stressed that "the chief endeavour . . . will be to give *an English interest* to its treatment of general Foreign Literature," but this had been the *Foreign Quarterly*'s aim from the start. Forster dropped "Music at Home and Abroad" (Worthington's inversion of the original title) and added "Tables of Foreign Literature" and, more interestingly, "Foreign Correspondence." He may have been the "second worst critic of the age," as John Stuart Mill said, but he knew how to encourage better critics.[10] At this point he still had his reputation to make and undoubtedly felt that the *Foreign Quarterly* could help. He was also a person of great vitality and enthusiasm, and imparted those qualities to the review. Even if one smiles at a two-page review of nineteen German novels, the energy is impressive. Like Cochrane at the review's beginning, Forster could take pains, and once again the *Foreign Quarterly* was ably edited.

The criteria that reviewers applied were consistent with the new editor's views: an empiricist's preference for practice over theory; and "manliness," earnestness, "right-heartedness," sincerity, and healthiness as literary criteria. Unfortunately, physical healthiness was not Forster's lot at this time; he was ill for much of 1843 and often confined to his room. No doubt the illness was largely responsible for his giving up the editorship after the October 1843 number; but he also wanted a larger arena. In making a bid early in 1844 for admission to the *Edinburgh Review,* he acknowledged that "I felt the want of such circulation & character as those of the Edinburgh Review, in the effort I made some months ago, by articles in the Foreign Quarterly."[11]

The new editor was Walter Keating Kelly, a conscientious and hard-working translator published by Chapman and Hall.[12] He was a respectable editor, but unable to give the *Foreign Quarterly Review* the vitality that Forster had. Living with a second, bigamous family, he had to a considerable extent withdrawn from literary circles, whereas Forster had pushed (some said) his way into the most brilliant or most promising sets of the day; and Forster, who could nag, cajole, and flatter articles out of reluctant contributors, made good use of his circle. Landor, Carlyle, Frazer Corkran, and Forster himself no longer contributed, but some of Forster's acquisitions stayed, Venables and Lewes in particular. Thackeray stayed only for three numbers. Blackie, the St. Johns, Mrs. Sinnett, Thomas Wright, and T. A. Trollope all contributed more regularly than they had earlier (except for Wright when Shoberl was editor), or else Kelly was simply more willing to publish their articles regularly. These were all people rather like Kelly: interesting, competent, industrious journalists or scholars, writing in part out of enthusiasm for the subject, all desperately writing for the money as well.

German and French literature were given equal attention. Articles appeared on Dante (by Mazzini, intended for an earlier number under Forster's editorship), "The Antigone and its Critics," and Schiller, but emphasis was given to more popular literature. Wright's medieval interest fitted, and he contributed pieces on comic stories, monkish legends, and polemic, and either he or Kelly wrote on "Calendars and Almanacs." Essays treated "Popular Poetry of the Gretons," "The Rise and Progress of Culinary Literature and Cookery," "German Political Squibs and Crotchets," and "Recent Italian Political Poems." Many of Lewes's articles dealt with the French best-sellers by Balzac and George Sand.

Kelly's review aimed at a balance among literary, historical, and topical articles with emphasis on events in India and relationships between England and France. Some articles—Kirwan's on the French navy, for example—suggest modern reporting. The point of view was liberal, but a wide range of political sympathy was allowed. More articles dealt with the United States and with such issues of the day as "Ireland, its Evils and Their Remedies" and "Political Rights of German People." Kelly actively sought out Indian reviewers.

The July 1846 issue was the last as a separate review; the *Foreign Quarterly* then merged with the *Westminster Review,** which bore the double title for years, and which through October 1853 printed separate sections on foreign literature. Some *Foreign Quarterly* contributors continued to write these, and an editorial note claimed that the *Foreign Quarterly* editor was still editing the section. Kelly, however, never claimed an association with the *Westminster;* had the *Foreign Quarterly* changed editors again before the end?

The lasting value of the review, despite its editorial permutations, rests on its responses to various national literatures. Much of its criticism was dependent on political orientation, and judgments could swing wildly from one extreme to another as the magazine changed political coloration. In spite of such changes, however, a view of literature as the expression of national character provided a certain unity throughout its twenty years. By far the most attention was paid to French and German literature. Other English journals judged French literature on political and moral principles, and so did the *Foreign Quarterly* during its Tory middle period under the editorships of Shoberl, Pote, and Worthington. The reviewers writing for Cochrane, Forster, and Kelly usually judged literary works from literary criteria, reserving political and moral judgments for other French publications. This distinction they did not normally extend to books in any other language, perhaps because they were not as fluent in other languages. Typically they objected to the exaggeration of a German novel as immoral or to that of a French novel as inartistic.

Their literary principles were thoroughly English-Romantic. To them most pre-Revolutionary French literature (not Molière) seemed bloodless and artificial, while French Romanticism was too unrestrained to produce beauty. While the Tory years had lumped together Rousseau, Lafayette, St. Simon, and George Sand as "panders to abomination," during its closing years, and led by G. H. Lewes, the *Foreign Quarterly* was increasingly willing to think well of French literature. In George Sand's earlier, better novels her style was clear and pure, and therefore the novels were pure. Balzac, on the other hand, wrote with execrable style, and he coldly over-intellectualized character rather than creating it. This judgment turned upside down the *Foreign Quarterly*'s earlier assessments of the two writers—as Lewes's criticism generally and consciously turned things upside down. He also sought to rehabilitate French classical drama and, like the earlier reviewers, glimpsed the possibility that French literature must be classical in keeping with French character.

Carlyle's memorial article on Goethe in the August 1832 issue was too Teufelsdreckian for many readers, but later reviewers wrote on Goethe with little penetration. Abraham Hayward's obtuse reading of *Faust Part II* in volume 12 has been called the source of later English misinterpretation.[13] Blackie shifted and shifted about in numerous efforts to understand the Weimar sage. Pote's reviewers grew practically hysterical in writing about Goethe's works, "these loathsome carcases of putrifying abominations" (23:135). Surprisingly, in April 1840 Worthington published an interesting study of *Faust* that insisted on the unity of the two parts and argued for the significance of the work partly through reference to *Hamlet*. The level of this article was not maintained in subsequent volumes. G. H. Lewes, later Goethe's English biographer, made only casual reference to Goethe in the *Foreign Quarterly;* his major article appeared in the *British and Foreign*.

The reviewers were more comfortable with less Olympian Germans, though Schiller was the only one they consistently praised. Political sympathy often accounts for the interest in Italian literature; the presence of Italian political refugees in England both fed that sympathy and provided some of the contributors. Spanish literature was often read in terms of stereotypes of national character. In 1842 the review rightly claimed that it had "done perhaps more than any other publication in communicating intelligence relative to Russian Literature and Art" (30:242). That it had done so was the result of chance: W. H. Leeds, the architectural critic, somehow knew Russian. Although he was not a particularly perceptive critic, he drew readers' attention to a literature with which most would not have been familiar. This was Gillies's original aim, but when in later years the magazine became more political or more "English" or concentrated on more accessible foreign literatures, little mention was made of such literatures as the Russian. The founders of the review were excited by the discovery of little-known literatures; Gillies wanted to work "unopened mines" and "break down the hitherto insurmountable barriers of time and space."[14] Twenty years later the reviewers were more responsible, but they opened a smaller world to their readers. In March 1846, just before the *Foreign Quarterly* ended, Elizabeth Barrett wrote to Robert Browning of the need for "the establishment of an European review—journal rather—(the 'Foreign [Quarterly] Review,' so called, touching only the summits of the hills) a journal which might be on a level with the intelligent readers of all the countries of Europe, and take all the rising reputations of each, with the national light on them as they rise, into observation and judgment."[15] She asked of course for the impossible, but for something close to Gillies's original dream.

Notes

1. *Athenaeum,* 7 January 1829, p. 1.
2. See Walter Scott, *Journal,* ed. John Guthrie Tait and W. M. Parker (Edinburgh and London, 1950), 1:243; Robert Pearse Gillies, *Memoirs of a Literary Veteran* (London, 1851), 3:143–44; *The Collected Letters of Thomas and Jane Welsh Carlyle,* ed. Charles Richard Sanders et al. (Durham, N.C., 1970), 4:162.
3. Cochrane to Lord Brougham, 12 February 1833 (University College, London, Brougham Papers).
4. Later Macray claimed, "Some years ago I was much occupied, in London, in translating for the Foreign Quarterly Review." Letter to C. P. Cooper, 12 March 1838, Lincoln's Inn Library Miscellaneous Manuscript 274, folio 149. He also spoke of himself as "having been for many years engaged . . . in researches connected with the literary Biography & History of France & Germany, first in the Foreign Quarterly Review." Letter to Longman's, 15 February 1843, Univ. Coll., London, SDUK Mss. Here he may, however, refer only to his compiling of the "Miscellaneous Literary Notices."
5. "The appearance of a French translation of Mr. Herschel's admirable Essay on Light brings it within the scope of a Review devoted to foreign literature and science" (7:283).
6. Richard Chenevix Trench, *Letters and Memorials,* ed. Mary Trench (London, 1888), 1:244.
7. *Fraser's Literary Chronicle* 21 (February 1840): 198.
8. Pote to Macvey Napier, 10 September 1843, British Museum Additional Manuscript 34,624.

9. Apparently by his successor, John Forster. Quoted by Jane Carlyle to John Sterling, 19 January 1842. *Letters and Memorials of Jane Welsh Carlyle,* ed. Thomas Carlyle and James Anthony Froude (London, 1883), 1:135.

10. Ibid., 1:134.

11. Forster to Macvey Napier, 12 February 1844, British Museum Additional Manuscript 34,624, folios. 354–55.

12. One reference has been taken to show that James Relly Beard, a Unitarian clergyman, was editor from 1844 through 1846. However, not only did Kelly later claim to have been editor during this period, but he is referred to as editor by several writers of the period and is stated to have been editor by the publishers, Chapman and Hall.

13. William Frederic Hauhart, *The Reception of Goethe's "Faust" in England in the First Half of the Nineteenth Century* (New York, 1909), p. 43.

14. Gillies, 2:146.

15. *The Letters of Robert Browning and Elizabeth Barrett Browning 1845–1846,* ed. Elvan Kintner (Cambridge, Mass., 1969), 1:553.

Information Sources

BIBLIOGRAPHY
Curran, Eileen M. "The *Foreign Quarterly Review* (1827–1846): A British Interpretation of Modern European Literature." Ph.D. dissertation, Cornell University, 1958.

Houghton, Walter E., ed. *The Wellesley Index to Victorian Periodicals.* Vol. 2. Toronto, 1972.

INDEXES
Each volume indexed. *Poole's Index. Wellesley Index* 2. Partial author's index in Curran, "The *Foreign Quarterly Review.*"

REPRINT EDITIONS
Microform: Early British Periodicals (UMI), reels 70–75. Microcard Editions, Washington, D.C.

LOCATION SOURCES
American
Widely available.
British
Widely available.

Publication History

MAGAZINE TITLE AND TITLE CHANGES
The Foreign Quarterly Review. Merged in August 1846 with the *Westminster Review.**

VOLUME AND ISSUE DATA
Volumes 1–37, numbers 1–74, July 1827–July 1846.

FREQUENCY OF PUBLICATION
Quarterly.

PUBLISHERS
Volumes 1–5, July 1827–February 1830: Treuttel and Würtz, Treuttel, Jun. and Richter, Soho Square, London. Volumes 6–7, June 1830–April 1831: Treuttel

and Würtz, Treuttel, Jun. and Richter, 30 Soho Square, London/Black, Young and Young, Tavistock Street, London. Volumes 8–12, July 1831–October 1833: Treuttel and Würtz, and Richter, 30 Soho Square, London/Black, Young, and Young, Tavistock Street, London. Volumes 13–15, February 1834–July 1835: Adolphus Richter & Co., 30 Soho Square, London/Black, Young, and Young, Tavistock Street, London. Volume 16, October 1835 January 1836: Adolphus Richter & Co., 30 Soho Square, London/Black and Armstrong, Tavistock Street, London. Volumes 17–19, April 1836–July 1837: Black and Armstrong, 2 Tavistock Street, London/Adolphus Richter & Co., 30 Soho Square, London. Volumes 20–27, October 1837–July 1841: Black and Armstrong, 8 Wellington Street North, London. Volumes 28–37, October 1841–July 1846: Chapman and Hall, 186 Strand, London. A pirated American edition was also published, by J. M. Mason (late Lewer), New York. This was printed in double columns and had different pagination than the English edition.

EDITORS

Robert Pearse Gillies, nominal editor, volumes 1–5, July 1827–February 1830; perhaps actual editor of number 1, July 1827. William Fraser, unofficial co-editor, volume 1, number 1, July 1827. John George Cochran, volumes 1–14, July 1827–December 1834; actual editor almost from start, acknowledged editor from volume 6, June 1830. Frederic Shoberl, volumes 15–20, March 1835–January 1838. Benjamin Edward Pote, volumes 21–24, April 1838–January 1840. James William Worthington, volumes 25–29, number 57, April 1840–April 1842. John Forster, volume 29, number 58–volume 32, number 63, July 1842–October 1843. Walter Keating Kelly, volume 32, number 64–volume 37, January 1844–July 1846.

Eileen M. Curran

FRASER'S LITERARY CHRONICLE

Fraser's Literary Chronicle was edited by Percival Weldon Banks with the assistance of John Churchill and William Maginn.[1] All three were regular contributors to *Fraser's Magazine,* * but the editors were reluctant to acknowledge the connection. From the start in 1835 they modeled *Fraser's Literary Chronicle* closely on the *Literary Gazette,* * which had enjoyed considerable success since its appearance in 1817. Both were weekly reviews, and each number consisted of sixteen pages of three columns of text.

Fraser's Literary Chronicle also adopted its most important point of editorial policy from the *Literary Gazette*. It expressed the view that all works under review should be assessed exclusively on their literary merits: "A subcurrent of bookselling influence, and of personal interest, in authors and artists, too generally colours the essays, the reviews, and the strictures of those who deem themselves the best 'possible literary instructors' " (1:1). The two periodicals largely selected the same books for review, with *Fraser's Literary Chronicle* usually a week or two behind the *Gazette* in noticing new works. History, biography, and practical subjects such as politics or botany were most frequently discussed. The *Chronicle* published reviews of minor popular poets including Felicia Hemans (18:274–77). It printed notices of the first two installments of *The Pickwick Papers* (19:295; 23:359), treating it as a periodical, and devoted much attention to works of historical fiction. It carried several articles on Wordsworth and Coleridge. Thomas Allsop's *Letters, Conversations and Recollections of S. T. Coleridge* was the subject of a review in three parts, urging sympathetic understanding of a poet who had often been attacked by critics with no appreciation of his genius (6:81–84; 7:101–5; 8:119–22). The review encouraged T. Brockenhurst to submit Coleridge's "Essays on Genial Criticism" for publication in the periodical (12:184–85; 13:201–2; 14:217–18; 15:232–33; 16:248–49). Fragments of Coleridge's conversations were reprinted from Robert Aris Willmott's *Conversations at Cambridge* (19:291–92).[2] Wordsworth's critical reputation was defended in four essays which discussed his treatment of various themes, supported with quotations from his poems (3:42–43; 4:60–62; 19:297–98; 21:326–28).

In addition to reviews, the periodical printed original papers on a variety of subjects. Series of essays on phrenology, travels in Europe, historical topics, and political events were regular features. The most interesting series was "Adversaria" in which William Maginn brought his learning and wit to bear on literary subjects.[3] Foreign literature was represented by half a dozen translations, signed "W. J.," of poems by Goethe and Schiller. Essayists and reviewers generally felt free to quote passages in French, Italian, Greek, and Latin. New theatrical productions, exhibitions and fine art, and meetings of learned societies in London were discussed regularly. At a time when musical criticism in the periodical press was still in its infancy, concerts were reviewed along with newly published songs. One or two pages of advertisements, principally involving the book trade, concluded all numbers. The format remained unchanged for six months.

Fraser's covered a wide area of interest. The editors described their own circle of friends who represented potential readers of the review: "votaries of the Muses, or labourers in the stony fields of antiquarian or scientific love [*sic*], or cultivators of the flowery gardens of classical excellence; whom the love of their respective pursuits prompts from time to time to offer to the world, through a discriminating publisher, their midnight lucubrations" (1:2). The periodical enjoyed commercial success. A note on the front page of each number promised efficient nationwide distribution. It sold at three pence an issue versus eight pence for the *Literary Gazette* and four for the *Athenaeum*.[*4] The editors of *Fraser's*, however did not propose to compete with these well-established weekly reviews. They adopted the same format, but when they had attracted a circle of readers and subscribers they announced their intention to abandon literature as their main concern. They turned to political subjects: "Our politics are decidedly Tory, Conservative, Anti-Whig, Anti-Radical—any name, in short, which will suit those who are determined to support to the utmost the old Church-and-State policy of England" (26:401). The name of the weekly was changed to the *Carlton Chronicle of Politics, Literature, Science, and Art,* and it ran from 11 June 1836 to 13 May 1837.[5]

Fraser's Literary Chronicle had declared its commitment to the cause of independent reviewing. It frequently accused contemporary periodicals of printing hasty and casual criticism. "Is the public taste directed—the public feeling improved—or the public mind, in the slightest degree, instructed or delighted? Impossible! Nothing is gratified but the gross appetite of vulgar curiosity: the mere, and most contemptible, desire of prating, concerning the 'pretty passages' in the *last new* book"(6:81). Several of its reviewers displayed considerable knowledge of the book trade of the time, often having detailed information about minor literary figures and showing discrimination in their selection of extracts from the works under review. Spirited satire was a hallmark of *Fraser's Magazine.* Some of the reviews were written in a concise and fluent style suggesting the pen of William Maginn. Although flagrant bigotry and prejudice often formed part of these reviews, they spoke with authority and learning, and with time could have developed into criticism of considerable quality. In its short life *Fraser's Literary Chronicle* did not consistently apply the learning and critical acumen which were features of its best reviews, but often only printed angry attacks on contemporary reviewing. The editors converted the periodical into a forum or political discussion, and in the *Carlton Chronicle* reviews were relegated to the last pages of each issue. The spirited approach to literature never entirely disappeared, but the well-informed authority was lost and the style became more laborious as the reviewers limited themselves to faithful paraphrases and lengthy quotations from the works under review.

Notes

1. See Miriam M. H. Thrall, *Rebellious "Fraser's"* (New York, 1934), p. 58.
2. For further details of these publications see *Samuel Taylor Coleridge: An Annotated Bibliography of Criticism and Scholarship: Vol. 1: 1793–1899,* Richard and Josephine Haven, and Maurianne Adams, eds. (Boston, 1976), pp. 95, 97.
3. See Thrall, pp. 301, 309.
4. In his autobiography the editor mentioned a number of short-lived periodicals which copied the *Literary Gazette* in its first year of existence. He ascribed the success enjoyed by the *Athenaeum* to the lowering of its price from eight to four pence an issue. *The Autobiography of William Jerdan* (London, 1853), 4:213–11.
5. Two series of essays from *Fraser's Literary Chronicle* were continued in the *Carlton Chronicle:* "The Bystander" and "Adversaria."

Information Sources

BIBLIOGRAPHY

Ellis, S. M. *William Harrison Ainsworth and His Friends.* 2 vols. London, 1911.
Obituary of Percival Weldon Banks. *Gentleman's Magazine,* n.s. 34 (1850):665.
Thrall, Miriam M.H. *Rebellious "Fraser's".* New York, 1934.

"Varieties: *Fraser's Literary Chronicle.*" *The Literary Gazette*, 12 December 1835, p. 797.

INDEXES

Cumulative index at end of number 26.

REPRINT EDITIONS

None.

LOCATION SOURCES

American

Complete runs: Yale University Library.

Partial run: Duke University Library.

British

Complete runs: Bodleian Library; British Museum.

Publication History

MAGAZINE TITLE AND TITLE CHANGES

Fraser's Literary Chronicle, and Register of British and Foreign Literature, Sciences, and the Fine Arts.

VOLUME AND ISSUE DATA

Numbers 1–26, 5 December 1835–26 May 1836.

FREQUENCY OF PUBLICATION

Weekly.

PUBLISHERS

Numbers 1–4, 5 December 1835–26 December 1835: Thomas Hurst, 65 St. Paul's Church Yard, London. Numbers 2–26, 12 December 1835–26 May 1836: G. Berger, Holywell Street, Strand, London. Numbers 5–26, 2 January 1836–26 May 1836: S. Larkins, 5 Tavistock Street, Covent Garden, London.

EDITORS

Percival Weldon Banks, John Churchill, and William Maginn.

Karsten Engelberg

FRASER'S MAGAZINE

William Maginn, for many years a regular contributor to *Blackwood's* * and probably the originator of its famous *Noctes Ambrosianae*,[1] found in 1830 that the magazine no longer welcomed his articles. Exceedingly displeased, he determined to establish his own new periodical to rival, even to surpass "Maga," as *Blackwood's*, the most popular magazine of the time, was dubbed.[2] With no cash, but with a dozen years' experience as a magazine contributor, plus his Irish wit and charm, Maginn set out with a bundle of manuscripts and his friend Hugh Fraser, who did have the required capital, to find a publisher. Walking along Regent Street, they happened upon the shop of the publisher James Fraser. Maginn exclaimed, "Fraser! Here's a namesake of yours. Let's try him." Fortunately, James Fraser had been considering publishing a magazine of the sort that Maginn proposed. From such unlikely beginnings sprang *Fraser's Magazine for Town and Country*.

Modeled on *Blackwood's*, the new magazine, to be learned but also popular, was dubbed "Regina," Queen of the Magazines. The periodical was to be managed by a fictitious editor, Oliver Yorke, much like *Blackwood's* Christopher North. The inebriated Yorke was the collective editorial voice which delivered sarcastic and even libelous comments.

Within a year *Fraser's* claimed a circulation of 8,700, a figure near that of the prestigious *Edinburgh** and *Quarterly** and above *Blackwood's*. Malcolm Elwin says that *"Fraser's* definitely supplanted the now sobering *Blackwood's* as the *enfant terrible* of the literary world."[3] The reason for this success may lie in the curious blend of materials published, a blend that achieved a tone of both intellectualism and outrageous humor. In the first decade the magazine contained most of Carlyle's early writing, including *Sartor Resartus,* and Thackeray's *Catherine* and *A Shabby Genteel Story*. There were many reviews of current literature both of individual writings and collective pieces, such as "The Novels of the Season."[4] A regular feature during Maginn's tenure was "The Gallery of Illustrious Literary Characters," one-page accounts of prominent writers to accompany pen-and-ink sketches by Daniel Maclise. Maginn wrote eighty-one of these; among them were Thomas Carlyle, William Jerdan, John Gibson Lockhart, Thomas Moore, Sir Walter Scott, Benjamin Disraeli, Bulwer-Lytton, and William Hazlitt. The early *Fraser's* was a high-spirited creature complete with spoofs, such as "Presentation of the Magazine [*Fraser's*] to Their Majesties; Abbreviated from the Court Circular," and parodies like "On the Domestic Manners of the British," which ridiculed Mrs. Trollope's account of her travels in the United States.

The history of *Fraser's* falls into two parts. The first phase runs from 1830 until 1847 with Fraser and G. W. Nickisson as publishers, and Maginn, Thackeray, Carlyle, Father Prout (Francis Mahoney), John Galt, James Hogg, T. C. Croker, and Thomas Wright as regular contributors. Miriam Thrall sums up the first decade in her title *Rebellious "Fraser's"*, an apt description for a journal of progressive thought, absolutely independent of party or faction. Much of the content centered on politics and religion, but there were enough literary entries to qualify *Fraser's* as a literary periodical.

Friends and foes alike came in for ridicule in the pages of *Fraser's*. In one lampoon a Fraserian, John Wilson Croker, clearly identified by his Cork brogue, his lisp, and his tendency to repeat himself, objects to a demonstration "made against him in his own Alma Mater, Trinity College, Dublin: 'The young youths in Thwinity, Twinity, I mane, meen, waw going to thaws me in a blanket, which show'd their bad teest' " (2:246). The treatment of enemies of "Regina" was much more severe. A favorite pastime of the early Fraserians was "Bulwer-baiting," deflating the pomposity of the hapless Bulwer-Lytton and other dandies. Maginn constantly attempted to draw Bulwer, whom he referred to as "Mr. Edward Liston Bulwer," into a literary feud.

Surprisingly, the many libelous articles led to only three lawsuits, the last of which had near tragic results. In August 1836 Maginn reviewed *Berkeley Castle* by Grantley Berkeley, one of the detested fashionable novelists, stating that the only object of the book was to prove that the Berkeleys had once been great. Berkeley was enraged by Maginn's statement that "Mr. Grantley Berkeley's mother lived with Mr. Grantley Berkeley's father as his mistress . . . and had at least one child before she could induce the old and very stupid lord to marry her."[5] When James Fraser refused to identify the author of the review, Berkeley gave him a severe beating with a riding crop. Maginn and Berkeley then fought a duel in which no serious injuries were sustained. In September 1836 Maginn ended his official connection with the magazine, but Mahoney and then Kenealy kept up the spirited high jinks.

A decline of the magazine began with the death of Fraser in 1841. G. W. Nickisson, the new publisher-editor, simply could not maintain the traditional spirit of the periodical. Also, he lacked the aid of the Fraserians; some were dead, others had gone on to new pursuits.

Miriam Thrall declares that *"Fraser's* greatest service . . . was in the occasional introduction of esthetic theory into its reviews," aesthetic theory based for the most part on the ideas of Carlyle and Coleridge and pointing out their debt to German transcendentalism. Thrall says that "all told, there were approximately eighty articles which show the influence, however distorted, of some phase of transcendental ethics or metaphysics."[6] An equally significant service of the magazine was in championing writers practically neglected by their contemporaries but who have come to be seen as spokesmen for their age. *Fraser's* recognized the worth of Shelley, Coleridge, and Wordsworth when they were largely unnoticed by other critics, and the magazine was among the earliest admirers of Robert Browning.

The second phase begins with the William John Parkers, father and son, who took over in 1847 as publisher and editor, respectively. In a policy statement in 1849 the editor announced his intention for *Fraser's* to have a more sober, less combative tone: "The policy of calling hard names and imputing unworthy motives the Magazine has abandoned, and is not likely under its present management to return to it" (39:3). As compensation for the loss of its youthful rebelliousness Parker substituted high literary quality with the contributions of Edward Fitzgerald, J. A. Froude, Charles Kingsley (who published both *Yeast* and *Hypatia* in *Fraser's*), G. H. Lewes, and Thomas Love Peacock. Froude succeeded Parker as editor in 1860, switched the politics from liberal to conservative, and saw the magazine lose ground to the rising *Macmillan's** and *Cornhill** (for both, see *VEA*). In 1874 William Allingham took over but, lacking Froude's connections with men of letters, failed to attract distinguished contributors. Allingham did not grasp the fact that serialized novels were an important element in the success of his competitors. In July 1879 Principal John Tulloch of St Andrew's University was given the job of resusitating the magazine, but by September the circulation was down to 500. Finally owner

Charles James Longman assumed the editorship—to no avail. *Fraser's* ceased publication in October 1882.

Notes

    1. For discussion, see the entries for *Blackwood's* and also the *Dublin Review.**

    2. The account of the first decade of *Fraser's* history generally follows Miriam M. Thrall's *Rebellious "Fraser's"* (New York, 1934).

    3. *Victorian Wallflowers* (London, 1937), p. 113.

    4. Kathleen Tillotson in *Novels of the 1840's* (London, 1962), p. 16, says that the most interesting novel criticism of the decade is in *Fraser's*.

    5. "Mr. Grantley Berkeley and His Novel," *Fraser's* 14 (1836):243.

    6. Thrall, p. 88.

Information Sources

BIBLIOGRAPHY

Conway, Moncure. "Working with Froude on *Fraser's Magazine*." *Nation*, 22 November 1894, pp. 378–79.

Dunn, Waldo H. "Editing *Fraser's Magazine*." In *James Anthony Froude, A Biography*. Oxford, 1961–1963.

Elwin, Malcolm. *Victorian Wallflowers*. London, 1934.

Houghton, Walter E., ed. *The Wellesley Index to Victorian Periodicals*. Vol. 2. Toronto, 1972.

The Maclise Portrait-Gallery; or, Illustrious Literary Characters. Edited by William Bates. London, 1873.

Maurer, Oscar, Jr. "Froude and *Fraser's Magazine*, 1860–1874." *Studies in English* (University of Texas) 28 (1949):213–43.

Oliphant, Margaret. *A Memoir of the Life of John Tulloch*. Edinburgh, 1888.

Sadleir, Michael. *Bulwer: A Panorama*. Boston, 1931.

———. *Things Past*. London, 1944.

Skelton, John. "Reminiscence of James Anthony Froude." *Blackwood's* 156 (1894):756–76.

Thrall, Miriam M. H. *Rebellious "Fraser's"*. New York, 1934.

White, Edward M. "Thackeray's Contributions to *Fraser's Magazine*." *Studies in Bibliography* 19 (1966):67–84.

INDEXES

    Each volume indexed. 1830–1881 in *Poole's Index*. *Wellesley Index* 2.

REPRINT EDITIONS

    Microform: Early British Periodicals (UMI), reels 1–20. Microcard Editions, Washington, D.C. Princeton Microfilm Corp., Princeton, N.J.

LOCATION SOURCES

    American

        Widely Available.

    British

        Widely available.

Publication History

MAGAZINE TITLE AND TITLE CHANGES
Fraser's Magazine for Town and Country.

VOLUME AND ISSUE DATA
Volumes 1–80, 1830–1869; new series, volumes 1–26, 1870–1882.

FREQUENCY OF PUBLICATION
Monthly.

PUBLISHERS
February 1830–December 1841: James Fraser, 215 Regent Street, London. January 1842–June 1847: George William Nickisson, 215 Regent Street, London. July 1847–December 1860: John William Parker and Son, West Strand, London. January 1861–October 1863: Parker, Son, and Bourn, West Strand, London. November 1863–June 1865: Longman, Green, Longman, Roberts, and Green (no place of publication given). July 1865–October 1882: Longmans, Green, and Company (no place of publication given).

EDITORS
William Maginn, February 1830–September(?) 1836. Francis Sylvester Mahoney, October(?) 1836–December 1837(?). Editor unknown, 1838–1842. George William Nickisson, November or December 1841 or January 1842–June 1847. John William Parker, Jr., July 1847–October 1860. James Anthony Froude, November 1860–August 1874. William Allingham, September 1874–June 1879. John Tulloch, July 1879–January 1881. Charles James Longman, February 1881–October 1882.

J. Don Vann

G

GENERAL MAGAZINE AND IMPARTIAL REVIEW, THE. See AAAJ

GENTLEMAN'S MAGAZINE, THE. See AAAJ

GOSSIP, THE

True to the traditions of its name, the *Gossip* remains nearly anonymous, the reasons for its demise on 11 August 1821 as obscure as those for its emergence in March of that year. The weekly numbers list no editor, though the final issue directs all communications to D. Rymer. The contributions are signed throughout with one or occasionally two initials, the most frequent signature being "R." The first issue of the *Gossip: A Series of Original Essays and Poems* specifically eschews political and religious controversies: "As authors and editors of the Gossip, we have no opinion in regard to the politics of the day; for, though questions of general political economy may sometimes form the subject of our pages, we pledge ourselves carefully to exclude all reference whatever to tenets of Tories, Whigs, Moderate Reformers, or Radicals, High Churchmen, or Dissenters. . . . If we can amuse and interest—warm the heart, or expand the feelings, we shall have accomplished our aim."

To some extent literary politics do concern the *Gossip*, however. Published in the year of Keats's death, in April *Gossip* includes a letter purportedly from Laurence Sterne (in Elysium) criticizing harsh literary reviewers. This criticism continues. A June letter complains that the style of *Gossip* is too close to the invective of *Blackwood's;* * a July article is entitled "Honest Employment for the Writers in *Blackwood's Magazine*—Female Coal Porters," and an August

article proclaims "Quack Doctors and *Blackwood's Magazine* the Only Remedies We Have for a Superabundant Population." *Gossip* also targets the *Quarterly Review,** though not by name, in a July defense of the so-called Cockney
school.

Certainly not a Romantic journal despite its attack on Keats's critics, *Gossip*
demonstrates only the beginning of the transition from eighteenth- to nineteenth-
century sensibility. The first number discusses in "Scottish Dialect" the appropriateness of this vernacular to "express those feelings which arise in humble,
calm, and rural life . . . the milder and gentler emotions of the soul." Scots
dialect cannot, *Gossip* decides, aspire to the heroic. Such a critical viewpoint—
with a literary hierarchy culminating in the epic and a slightly patronizing attitude toward the emotions associated with rural life—shares more with the eighteenth century than with the *Preface* to *Lyrical Ballads,* published twenty-
three years previously.

The essays' attitude toward social change as well as their critical stance looks
backward approvingly if not longingly. The first issue indicates a growing
problem in education, a problem that Carlyle, Mill, and Dickens would later
address fully: "As virtue is the first and last lesson taught a girl, so is industry
the alpha and omega of a boy's education; with this we do not find fault, but
only to the meaning, which the tutors attach to the word industry. . . . This
mercantile spirit of our countrymen has been the cause of much evil, as well
as good." *Gossip* maintains that education ought to be naturally attractive—it
notes that "the father of periodical literature," Defoe, lost readers to the better-
educated Addison and Steele—but narrow, commercially oriented education
compromises its appeal and its usefulness by presumptuousness. Growing literacy has produced, *Gossip* claims, a clientele trained on newspapers and pamphlets alone, an audience which thus overvalues epigrammatic style. *Gossip*
indignantly distinguishes in the 7 April "Literary Celebrity" between mere
literacy and the ability to read poetry by acknowledging the worth of Byron's
poetry while dismissing the usual reason for praise—smooth versification—and
deploring the undervaluation of Thomson and Pope. However, true to its statement of purpose, *Gossip* remains genteelly reserved rather than truly conservative:

> This [preference for epigram and other "strong stimulating food"] is cer-
> tainly much owing to what may be in great degree a benefit, that is, the
> universal diffusion of the lower and necessary branches of learning. For-
> merly cultivation used to be bestowed with labour on particular patches
> of the field, and these brought forth abundantly, now it is spread thinly
> over the whole surface. Whether it will produce a more luxuriant harvest
> we shall leave to others to discover.

Gossip satirizes public taste in fields beyond poetry, particularly advertising.
It shrewdly observed, years before the publication of Herbert Spencer's *Study*

of Sociology, that the mindset of a nation is more readily inferred from advertising than from newspapers. Rymer laments the loss that modern scholarship has incurred because the ancients did not advertise. He then constructs "ancient" ads to prevent historical catastrophes such as the rape of the Sabine women, and (shades of Orwell) delights in the state of perfection which the language of current advertisements announces. *Gossip*, of course, sported no advertising and sought its audience among those appreciative of the lightly satirical essay. "Anticipation of Public Opinion in the Year Two Thousand Three Hundred, on the Poets of the Present Day" humorously criticizes the works, temperaments, and styles of Scott, Byron, Wordsworth, and Southey. One parody, "The Goose," after Byron's "Greece," appears in the issue for 9 June. Reviews are infrequent, but notable. The 14 July "Seraphina and Her Sister Clementina's Review of 'Epipsychidion' " ridicules Shelley's poem for vagueness and mixed metaphors. Given the rest of Gossip's content, the early criticism of *Blackwood's* and the *Quarterly Review* seems to have been not so much a defense of Keats as an attempt to build circulation by attacking established journals.

Gossip solicited manuscripts from its readers and seems to have had no consistent editorial policy to unify its theoretical essays and its poetry. Rather oddly, it published both a letter purportedly from Laurence Sterne in Elysium about "the present race of bards and bardlings, [who] appear to write for a weeping generation" (14 April) and several poems on hopeless romantic love and the death of a loved one. "Amor Exspes" details, for instance, the speaker's resolution not to give up his unrequited love. He wallows in his intense feelings, and disdains peace as unworthy. Poetry in *Gossip* inevitably takes conventional rather than organic forms. In both form and content the poems are reminiscent of the Graveyard School and the cult of sensibility.

The view of love developed in "Force of Misplaced Attachment" in the issue for 12 May neatly illustrates the position of the *Gossip* in the transition from one century to another. Love, it claims, is neither necessarily pure in itself nor purifying to the lover; further, women's love has no sexual component. Except for the devotees of sentimental feeling, eighteenth-century writers would by and large have accepted the first statement, so shocking to the Victorian sensibility. But, though some earlier writers might have assented to the notion of female asexuality, in the eighteenth century the idea never achieved its Victorian status as an article of faith. An 1821 attempt at wit and urbanity, *Gossip* records the fast-vanishing nostalgia for the world of social certainties reflected in Addison, Steele, and Pope in the world of increasing social uncertainties and changes in taste reflected in Keats, Shelley, and Wordsworth.

Information Sources

INDEXES
   None.

REPRINT EDITIONS
>None.

LOCATION SOURCES
>*American*
>>Complete runs: Newberry Library; University of Minnesota Library.
>>Partial run: State University of Iowa Library.
>
>*British*
>>Complete runs: Bodleian Library; British Museum.

Publication History

MAGAZINE TITLE AND TITLE CHANGES
>*The Gossip; a series of original essays and poems*, 3 March–30 June 1821.
>(Alternate title: *The Gossip; a series of original essays and letters, literary,
>historical and cultural; descriptive sketches.*) *The Literary Gossip*, 7 July–11
>August 1821.

VOLUME AND ISSUE DATA
>Numbers 1–24, 3 March–11 August 1821.

FREQUENCY OF PUBLICATION
>Weekly.

PUBLISHER
>D. Rymer, Broad Court, Long Acre, Chapple, Royal Exchange, London.

EDITOR
>Unknown.

Missy Dehn Kubitschek

H

HIBERNIAN MAGAZINE, THE. See AAAJ

HONEYCOMB

The early 1820s witnessed the birth of a number of reviewing periodicals, many of which did not survive the decade. One of the more modest and short-lived of these was *Honeycomb,* an eight-page, two-penny London weekly that appeared on consecutive Saturdays from 17 June to 20 August 1820. Its name was inspired by a song of Prospero's dainty Ariel, "Where the bee sucks, there lurk [*sic*] I."[1] *Honeycomb* was to be a source of "new and pleasant thoughts," and its primary purpose was to provide its reader with ideas and views to make him "better satisfied with himself and with his fellows." Occasionally "ancient matters" were to be discussed, but only if it seemed likely the reader might not be acquainted with them or if *Honeycomb* had something new to say about them. Despite the success that sometimes awaited journals of decided political views, *Honeycomb* promised to ignore all controversy, whether public or private: "As we shall never touch upon waspish politics or friendship-breaking polemics, our business will be with the better passions of the mind; and we shall discourse of Friendship, Love, and Charity, instead of battles, sieges, and auto-da-fes" (no. 1:2).

Most numbers consist of a single unsigned article; about half of the numbers include poems, either unsigned, initialed, or identified as by "a friend" (no. 8:64). Articles fall into three categories. One group consists of pieces indicative of *Honeycomb*'s interest in life and literature beyond contemporary England. "On Americanisms" discusses and, with a glossed fragment of a pastoral, demonstrates some lexical differences between American and British English (no. 4:25–29). "The Abbot" is the retelling of a novella from the *Cene* of Il

Lasca (pseudonym of a seventeenth-century Florentine imitator of Boccaccio, Antonfrancesco Grazzinia), and is offered to Walter Scott as material for *The Abbot,* which was appearing at the time (no. 6:41–46). "On the Virtues of Savage Life" extols the moral and physical courage of primitive peoples with examples derived from a number of works, including Jefferson's *Notes on Virginia* and Campbell's *Gertrude of Wyoming* (no. 8:57–63). A second group of papers relates the unhappy life of Hieronymous Neville, who, after twelve years in London as a failed poet, is reduced to streetsweeping and beggary. Numbers 2 and 3 consist of autobiographical fragments by Hieronymous, who vehemently denies, as some of his acquaintances have claimed, that he is Barry Cornwall, "a very servile copyist" (no. 3:20). Hieronymous disappears from the pages of *Honeycomb* until the last issue, when the editor meets him by chance while on a walking tour in North Wales. Hieronymous is now a gardener; he is preparing a treatise on Roman methods of cultivating parsnips and is only rarely writing poems, one of which is printed here: "The Song of the Lone Lady," in trimeter quatrains, the brief line having been forced on the poet by the narrowness of his sheets of paper (no. 11:81–88). And so, together, Hieronymous and *Honeycomb,* with the eleventh number, disappear, neither having enjoyed much success. Very little is known of the publisher and editorial staff of this weekly.[2]

Numbers 5 through 10 of *Honeycomb* are largely devoted to reviews of the work of four poets, Campbell and "Metropolitan Poets" Hunt, Cornwall, and Shelley. Similar measures of poetic accomplishment in these articles suggest that possibly all, and almost certainly those on the Metropolitan Poets, are from the same hand. Typical of most criticism of the time, *Honeycomb* asserts classical values derived from Dryden and Dr. Johnson: literature's mimetic nature and instructional responsibilities, correct diction, and reasonable imagery:

> We know that in Poetry as in every thing else, there will be a beginning, a middle, and an end—a superiority, the fortune of few—an excellence, to be attained by many—a mediocrity, by more—and a minimum, by no means rare. We do not quarrel with that—our object is to preserve these proportions in the public taste, and to range every individual in his proper station. [no. 10:73].

Both Campbell and Hunt are chastised for their faulty diction—Campbell for his "far-sought and quaint phrases" (no. 10:77), and Hunt for his vulgarity of expression (no. 5:33–35), a charge frequently leveled at Hunt.[3] Though Cornwall and Campbell (the first of whom the reviewer obviously appreciates more than Hieronymous does) are not guilty, as Hunt is (no. 5:37), of mean or affected thought (no. 7:51; no. 10:77), all three of these poets are at their best when they confine themselves to "the lighter, finer and more transient feelings of the heart" (no. 5:37). Neither Hunt nor Cornwall is capable of expressing "such feelings as fill the heart of Byron" (no. 5:37), and Hunt's error is to attempt on occasion just that kind of expression. The Metropolitan Poets "have gone mad *Italianly*" (no. 7:49), and in the case of Hunt, imitation accedes to caricature: "Dante in purgatory murmurs revenge for the fallen honours of Rimini, whose deep and sacred memory" Hunt has insulted (no. 5:38). Of the Metropolitan Poets, Hunt has been praised in the press about as much as he deserves, Cornwall more, and Shelley less (no. 9:67). There is about Shelley something too "mystical" (no. 9:67), something too high or too deep for common comprehension: "He knows that poetry is not composed of the language of common life as Mr. Wordsworth supposes, or its spirit of common feelings,—he knows that the nature of poetry is above the common nature of man, and that in reducing it to that level we are in fact depriving it of all its great characteristics" (no. 9:70).

These reviews are of particular interest for their outspoken criticism of the public behavior of poets and publishers (no. 9:65–71). *Honeycomb* condemns "literary hoaxing," whether of the kind perpetrated by certain literary journals or of the kind engaged in by certain poets, including the Metropolitans, who offer public compliments to one another in order to dupe the reading public and further their personal gain. Journals such as *Blackwood's,* the Edinburgh Review,** and the *Quarterly Review** behave more shamefully still, for not only do they exaggerate the artistic accomplishments of writers whom they stand to profit by, but they proffer false and malicious charges against other poets in order "to gratify a vitiated appetite for libel, and increase their monthly sale." Thus "Mr. C———k———r" was encouraged to inveigh against "poor Mr. Leigh Hunt." The allusion is to John Wilson Croker, a major contributor to the *Quarterly,* remembered especially for his review of *Endymion,* and probably the author of unfavorable reviews of Hunt in 1817 and 1818. "Mr. Gifford [editor of the *Quarterly*] and his coadjutors have poured out the vial of wrath with undistinguishing bitterness" on poets who, in turn, try to protect one another from critical barbs by entering into "combinations." The reviewer speaks scornfully of the recent appointment of the chief editor of *Blackwood's* as Edinburgh Professor of Moral Philosophy. The allusion is to John Wilson, who, with John Lockhart, wrote most of the important literary reviews for *Blackwood's* up to 1825, and who was thus at least partially responsible for the series of articles attacking Keats and Hunt, "On the Cockney School of Poetry." In the important war between the Northern reviews and London writers, *Honeycomb* records a brief attack which promised, in its ninth number, to develop into a major assault of a kind the first number of *Honeycomb* vowed to stay clear of. "We will," the Shelley review concludes, "unfold the secret springs of this poetical pantomime [of poets and publishers duping the public], and disclose the managers of the puppet show to view" (no. 9:71). Having broken one of its initial promises, *Honeycomb* also failed to keep another:

> By the bye, the ladies, if we don't take care, will get the mastery over us, for they are making most rapid inroads into those long-guarded territories of knowledge and learning in which we had so valiantly entrenched

ourselves. . . . Now, however, some of the most amusing and instructive writers among us are women. ... . this is a subject, however, which we should like to resume at another time and in another shape. [no. 11:15]

The subject was not resumed, and *Honeycomb,* without warning, ceased publication.

Notes

1. Theobald's emendation of *suck* by *lurk* prevails in this line, which serves as epigram of each issue of *Honeycomb:* see no. 1:1.

2. According to the *Union List of Serials,* the University of Iowa possesses the only complete run of *Honeycomb* in this country. Only *Honeycomb*'s remarks on Shelley appear to have survived in later publications: portions of the Shelley article appear in the 23 December 1821 issue of the *Champion,** over the signature, ''J. W.,'' which has not been identified; it is mentioned in J. P. Anderson's bibliography to William Sharp's *Life of Shelley;* it is briefly referred to in Theodore Redpath's *The Young Romantics and Critical Opinion, 1807–1827* (New York, 1973); and a portion of it is reprinted in N. L. White's *The Unextinguished Hearth* (Durham, N.C., 1938).

3. See, for example, *Blackwood's Edinburgh Magazine* 2 (1817)38–41; 4 (1819):70–76; *Edinburgh Review* 26 (1816):476–91; and *Quarterly Review* 18 (1818):324–35.

Information Sources

BIBLIOGRAPHY

Barcus, James E. *Shelley: The Critical Heritage.* London, 1975.

Brightfield, Myron F. *John Wilson Croker.* Berkeley, 1940.

Crawford, Thomas. ''The *Edinburgh Review* and Romantic Poetry (1802–29).'' *Auckland University College Bulletin* no. 47. 1955.

Hayden, John O. *Romantic Bards and British Reviewers: A Selected Edition of the Contemporary Reviews of the Works of Wordsworth, Coleridge, Byron, Keats and Shelley.* Lincoln, Nebr., 1971.

Marsh, George L. ''The Early Reviews of Shelley.'' *Modern Philology* 27 (1919)173–95.

Redpath, Theodore. *The Young Romantics and Critical Opinion, 1807–1827: Poetry of Byron, Shelley, and Keats as Seen by Their Contemporaries.* New York, 1973.

Wheeler, Paul Mowbray. ''The Great Quarterlies of the Early Nineteenth Century and Leigh Hunt.'' *South Atlantic Quarterly* 29 (1930):282–303.

White, Newman Ivey. *The Unextinguished Hearth: Shelley and His Contemporary Critics.* Durham, N.C., 1938.

INDEXES

None.

REPRINT EDITIONS

None.

LOCATION SOURCES

American

Complete run: University of Iowa Library.

Partial runs: Duke University Library; Harvard University Library.

British
  Partial run: Bodleian Library.

Publication History

MAGAZINE TITLE AND TITLE CHANGES
  Honeycomb.
VOLUME AND ISSUE DATA
  Numbers 1–11, 17 June–26 August 1820.
FREQUENCY OF PUBLICATION
  Weekly.
PUBLISHER
  R. Walker, 90 High Holborn, London.
EDITOR
  Unknown.

Carol de Saint Victor

_____ I _____

IMPERIAL MAGAZINE, THE

When at age fifty-four Samuel Drew became the founding editor of the *Imperial Magazine* in 1819 he was already well known among his fellow Methodists as a reformed criminal, lay preacher, and respected writer on doctrinal subjects. His best-known work, *The Immateriality and Immortality of the Human Soul* (1802) had earned him the label of "the English Plato" and "the Cornish Metaphysician" among the faithful; the book was translated into French and was to go through eight editions by mid-century. The son of a poor Cornish farmer, Drew had been by profession a shoemaker and by avocation (during his teens) a smuggler who was "born again" in 1785 at age twenty, probably as the result of the sermon preached at his brother's funeral. He became active in the Wesleyan movement and by 1788 had begun his lay preaching, which he was to continue the rest of his life. His first published work (1799) was, appropriately enough, a critique of Paine's *The Age of Reason*, and over the next twenty years he wrote miscellaneous religious works along with a history of Cornwall. Although he wrote briefly for the *Eclectic Review*,* after about 1820 his dual role as editor of the *Imperial* and business manager of the Caxton Press, its publisher, absorbed most of his energies and ultimately ruined his health. Throughout his adult life he was, as characterized by Leslie Stephen, "a very honourable and independent man, strongly attached to his family, and energetic as a preacher and writer."[1]

The first monthly issue of the *Imperial Magazine* (featuring an engraving of Drew) appeared in March 1819, composed of six octavo signatures in double columns numbered consecutively through the volume. Although the size and length of the magazine's issues remained constant, the second series, begun in January 1831 (no. 145), boasted "a more modern appearance," with numbered pages instead of numbered columns, each lead article in single-column format, and Drew's name on the title page as editor. The verbose subtitle of the first issue, which remained essentially unchanged though shortened in the second series, indicates the magazine's scope and its genteelly improving and spiritually uplifting purpose: "Compendium of Religious, Moral, and Philosophical Knowledge: Comprehending Literature, Moral Philosophy, or Ethics, Natural Philosophy, Chemistry, Review of Books, Historical Narrative, Antiquities, Domestic Economy, Trade, Miscellaneous Articles, Poetry." The emphasis, however, was on what P. G. Scott has called "timeless religious articles" rather than the topicality of the more famous quarterlies of the time.[2] Thus the annual prefaces by Drew frequently proclaimed the magazine's opposition to licentiousness and immorality while lamenting the advanced stage of both in society at large.

Drew also likes to reiterate the *Imperial*'s independence from party line in both politics and religion, though in the latter case the magazine clearly expresses the Dissenters' position. However, the magazine occasionally notes political events of moment: the May 1829 number approvingly prints the whole of the Catholic Emancipation Act along with an even-handed preface by Drew, though his Protestant stance is clear. The preface to the 1831 volume (written in late 1831/early 1832) refers uneasily to the political unrest surrounding the proposed Reform Bill; the preface to the next volume applauds its passage. And the magazine was staunchly anti-slavery from its inception. According to Drew, the magazine's independence of party and sectarian matters sometimes "subjected its conductors to a few impotent snarls," but such hostility, he claims, has actually increased rather than retarded circulation (preface to vol. 10). The purpose of the *Imperial*, he says a year later, is not to engage in disputes but "to defend religion, to discover truth, to improve morality, and to advance the interests of science."

The combination of religious uplift and practical knowledge that animates the *Imperial* is evident in a typical number like that of March 1820 (2, no. 13). The issue begins with an "Essay on Defamation" followed by an article on "The Wisdom of God in the Formation of Man" (concluded from the previous issue). Comprising the bulk of the number, other articles from "correspondents" cover agriculture, grammar, curiosities of natural history, attacks on geology (based on scriptural authority) and on popery, along with discussions of various doctrinal matters. There is also the monthly column on "Astronomical Occurrences," a forerunner of the horoscopes in today's newspapers. Reviews of books (which, following the usual custom, are mostly lengthy extracts) include those on ancient British history and several books of Christian instruction and doctrine. Literature is also represented via a poem reprinted from the January 1820 *Literary Gazette* * mourning in resolutely heroic couplets the death of George III. The practical interest of readers is piqued by an illustrated column on "Important Mechanical Inventions," dealing in this issue with a bilge pump and an improved printing press. The final article is a "memoir," with portrait, of Edward, Duke of Kent. (Such biographical sketches are an almost monthly feature throughout the fifteen years of the *Imperial*.) Rounding out the number, as is the case with each monthly issue from May 1819 through January 1823, is a "Commercial Report" for the previous month, giving market prices and import/export figures. Six years later this report was resumed as an annual "Commercial Retrospect" of the preceding year.

Other monthly columns were "Gleanings from Literature, Science, etc." and "Literary Notices," both of which were inaugurated as permanent features in the January 1823 issue. The former is a compendium of "useful knowledge" on the order of today's "Hints from Heloise"—for example, making glue from rice. The latter notices new and forthcoming books of probable interest to the readership. A representative issue might also contain solutions to mathematical problems, reports on missionary societies, queries on doctrinal and ethical matters, or requests for explanations of Biblical passages.

The "memoirs" of well-known figures were an especially important and, eventually, regular feature. The subjects were men (and very occasionally women) who "have rendered themselves conspicuous by their piety, their virtues, their literary talents, their scientific attainments, their distinguished situations, their unwearied researches, or their striking peculiarities" (preface to vol. 9). Most were Protestant divines (though not only Dissenters) or members of the royal family and other aristocrats; but others included Caxton, Wynken de Worde, the poet Thomas Campbell, Charles Lamb, Sir Walter Scott, and Henry Brougham, inventor and promoter of popular education through his Society for the Diffusion of Useful Knowledge. These biographical sketches frequently provided the lead article in a number, were apparently written by Drew, and were usually accompanied by an engraved portrait.

Though literature supposedly ranked high in the magazine's content, the *Imperial*, as one would expect from its lower-middle-class Dissenting readership, was strictly a literary lightweight. Though a few popular poets and other belletristic writers were the subjects of "memoirs," few books by the important authors of the time were reviewed in its pages. Of minor interest is a brief but spirited exchange in volumes 3 and 4 (1821–1822) in the form of letters and responses (pseudonymous or unsigned, like all other contributions to the magazine) about the relative merits of Wordsworth and Byron; the balance of the comment favored Wordsworth.

Having reached 144 monthly numbers without interruption by the end of 1830, it was felt that a new series and a somewhat modernized layout were called for beginning in 1831. The contents and purpose of the magazine, however, remained the same. Samuel Drew remained as editor until his death midway through 1833. The magazine continued to appear regularly, unchanged in content and editorial policy, for another year and a half, but it essentially died with him: with the December 1834 number it ceased publication after fifteen years—a little over half the length of the average run (twenty-eight years) of Victorian periodicals.[3]

Notes

1. S. Austin Allibone, *A Critical Dictionary of English Literature and British and American Authors Living and Deceased,* vol. 1 (London, 1872); Samuel Smiles, *Self-Help* (New York, n.d.), p. 141; *Dictionary of National Biography,* s.v. "Drew, Samuel."

2. P. G. Scott, "Victorian Religious Periodicals: Fragments that Remain," *The Materials, Sources, and Methods of Ecclesiastical History,* ed. Derek Baker (Oxford, 1975), p. 327.

3. *British Museum General Catalogue of Printed Books;* Scott, p. 325. Volumes 3 and 4 (1833–1834) of the *Imperial* were not available to this writer for examination.

Information Sources

BIBLIOGRAPHY

Allibone, S. Austin. *A Critical Dictionary of English Literature and British and American Authors Living and Deceased.* 3 vols. London, 1872.
British Museum General Catalogue of Printed Books, vols. 184–86.
Dictionary of National Biography. S.v. "Drew, John."
Scott, P. G. "Victorian Religious Periodicals: Fragments That Remain." *The Materials, Sources, and Methods of Ecclesiastical History.* Edited by Derek Baker. Oxford, 1975.
Smiles, Samuel. *Self-Help.* New York, n.d.
The Waterloo Directory of Victorian Periodicals, 1824–1900. Edited by Michael Wolff, John S. North, and Dorothy Deering. Elmsford, N.Y., 1980.

INDEXES
Each volume indexed.

REPRINT EDITIONS
Microform: Early British Periodicals (UMI), reels 50–52.

LOCATION SOURCES

American
Complete runs: Boston Public Library; Chicago Public Library; U. S. Library of Congress; Yale University Library.
Partial runs: Widely available.

British
Complete runs: British Museum; Cambridge University Library; National Library of Ireland, Dublin.
Partial runs: Bristol University Library; Cardiff Public Library; Edinburgh University Library; Glasgow University Library; Gloucester University Library; Liverpool Public Library; Sheffield Public Library; St. Andrews University Library; Trinity College Library.

Publication History

MAGAZINE TITLE AND TITLE CHANGES
The Imperial Magazine, or compendium of religious, moral, and philosophical knowledge, March 1819–December 1830. *The Imperial Magazine, and monthly record of religious, philosophical, historical, biographical, topographical, and general knowledge; embracing literature, science, and art,* January 1831–December 1834.

VOLUME AND ISSUE DATA

Volumes 1–12, numbers 1–144, March 1819–December 1830; second series, volumes 1–4, numbers 145–192, January 1831–1834. (The first two volumes contained only eleven numbers each; volumes 3 and 4 each contained two December numbers.)

FREQUENCY OF PUBLICATION

Monthly.

PUBLISHERS

March 1819–December 1820: Henry Fisher, Caxton Press, Liverpool/87 Bartholomew Close, London. January 1821–December 1830: Henry Fisher (and Son beginning August 1825), Caxton Press, 87 Bartholomew Close, London. January 1831–1834: H. Fisher, Son (R. Fisher), and P. Jackson, Caxton Press, 38 Newgate Street, London.

EDITOR

Samuel Drew.

Charles Brooks Dodson

IMPERIAL REVIEW, THE

The title of the *Imperial Review* was not mainly meant to convey grandeur or dignity, but rather was intended to partake of the denotation of the term *imperial:* of or relating to empire, and especially to the sub-definition, of or relating to the United Kingdom. For the proprietors of this monthly review made it clear in their prospectus that their magazine was to fill the absence of a reviewing periodical in Ireland and to further this aim would pay "a marked attention to the LITERATURE OF IRELAND" (1:iv–vi). This aim is further evidenced by the publishers listed; the main publishers were Cadell and Davies in London, but there were several others in London and in Dublin and lesser Irish cities. In the fourth volume the subtitle demonstrates imperial expansion by including Edinburgh.

The editors were simply "The Editors" in the few general addresses to the readers, and no further information has surfaced about the staff or reviewers of this short-lived review. The political and religious views they purveyed in any case seem to have been moderate; it is in fact difficult most of the time to determine what their own position is, and even when there are definite signs there is still some uncertainty. In the introduction to the first volume, "The Editors" promised never to "serve the views of a Party" (1:v) and apparently they were true to their word. Perhaps in an era of such political uncertainty and prejudice the lack of bias even insured the early demise of their journal.

The connotations of dignity and grandeur in the title are at least reflected in the reviews, which were usually long and weighty. Issues of the first three volumes of the *Imperial* were in fact longer than usual, running to 160 pages, and this size may show the influence of the quarterly *Edinburgh Review,** begun almost two years before. The form of the reviews was in any event not influenced by the *Edinburgh,* which tended to contain essays only suggested by the titles of the books under review; the *Imperial* on the other hand published only genuine reviews with analysis and evaluation. The selection, moreover, was less lively than the *Edinburgh*'s, running often to classical authors and profound scientific treatises. One original feature of the *Imperial* in fact was an occasional joint review of short scientific papers under the title "London Philosophical Transactions" (cf. 2:39–45).

The prospectus announced that the editors would not attempt to review every publication, as did some of the other monthly reviews, but would select only those considered important for one reason or another—here again the influence of the *Edinburgh* is evident. But there was a monthly catalogue of publications listed by general subject matter to keep the public up to date. In May 1804 short critical notices appeared with some of the listed books, but the fourth volume returned to a simple list.

The reviews of literary works are severely limited by the time-span of the review; the years 1804–1805 were too late for *Lyrical Ballads* and too early for other major Romantic writers such as Keats or Byron. (Reviews only noticed first editions at the time.) Scott's *Lay of the Last Minstrel* and Southey's *Madoc* were reviewed as were several novels by Maria Edgeworth. Otherwise, the literature reviewed was unimportant; but many of these literary works—in some volumes every one of them—were published by Cadell and Davies, the main London publishers of the *Imperial.* They were not, however, always favorably reviewed.[1]

In volume 4 a new feature uncommon in reviews at the time occurred— "Original Communications," which today we would call "letters to the editor." These letters were usually summarized by the editors and most often consisted of ponderous scholarly comments on past reviews.

In the same volume the size of the *Imperial Review* dropped from 160 pages to 120, suggesting perhaps that a long monthly reviewing periodical was a mistake. The reviews continued to be long and weighty, and after only one more volume the magazine folded.

Note

1. Later, these reviews appeared under different titles.

Information Sources

INDEXES
   Each volume indexed.
REPRINT EDITIONS
   Microform: English Literary Periodicals (UMI), reel 866.
LOCATION SOURCES
   American
   Complete run: Peabody Institute.

British
>   Complete runs: British Museum; Edinburgh University Library; Leeds University Library; National Library of Ireland, Dublin.

Publication History

MAGAZINE TITLE AND TITLE CHANGES
>   *The Imperial Review; or London and Dublin Literary Journal,* 1804–1805. *The Imperial Review; or, London, Edinburgh, and Dublin Literary Journal,* 1805.

VOLUME AND ISSUE DATA
>   Volumes 1–5, 1804–1805.

FREQUENCY OF PUBLICATION
>   Monthly.

PUBLISHERS
>   Volumes 1–5, 1804–1805: T. Cadell and W. Davies, The Strand, London; J. Archer, London; J. Cooke, London; M. W. Mahon, Dublin; A. Edwards, Cork. J. Barry, Limerick; W. Magee, Belfast.

EDITOR
>   Unknown.

>   *John O. Hayden*

INDICATOR, THE

Jailed for an attack on the Prince Regent in the *Examiner* * in 1812 and himself attacked in *Blackwood's* * as exemplifying the vulgar taste and moral depravity of the Cockney School of poets,[1] Leigh Hunt in September 1819 announced to the Shelleys his plan for a new publication:

>   It is to be called the *Indicator,* after a bird of that name who shows people where to find wild honey; and will, in fact, be nothing but a collection of very short pieces of remark, biography, ancient fictions, &c.; in short, of any subjects that come to hand, and of which I shall endeavour to *extract the essence* for the reader. It will have nothing temporary whatsoever in it, political or critical.[2]

The Indicator, an eight-page, two-pence weekly, first appeared on Wednesday, 13 October 1819.

"As far as the Editor is concerned," Hunt announced in the second number, for 20 October 1819:

>   the Examiner is to be regarded as the reflection of his public literature, and the Indicator of his private. . . . The Examiner is his tavern-room for politics, for political pleasantry, for criticism upon the theatres and living writers. The Indicator is his private room, his study, his retreat

from public care and criticism, with the reader who chuses to accompany him.

Hunt continues: "Here we are, then, this chilly weather, with a warm fire. How pleasant it is to have fires again!" (p. 9). No words could better illustrate the easy, colloquial tone of Hunt's writing, his presumption of friendship with the reader. The pieces that follow—in the first ten numbers, mostly short essays and notes, thereafter most often one essay filling the entire number—include tid-bits of information from the classics, from history or biography, translations, literary criticism, tales, and, most characteristically, familiar essays.[3] A point may be made in passing here and there, but Hunt writes primarily because he finds his material pleasant and interesting and believes his reader will too: a quiet evening's reading by the fire.

In "Pleasant Recollections Connected with Various Parts of the Metropolis," for example, Hunt begins by noting that "one of the best secrets of enjoyment is the art of cultivating pleasant associations," for such associations call us from the unpleasant sights around us. He then proceeds to a long catalogue, almost a directory, of places where various writers and historical figures were born, lived, and are buried. In "Hats, New and Ancient" Hunt confesses he is "not fond of a new hat": the insolence with which it puts itself forth, in all but appearance of less utility than an old hat (and that advantage problematical), to be worn with great risk in a mail coach. Hats are indeed "a very ancient part of dress," as Hunt documents by tracing them from ancient Chinese, Greek, and Roman times down to the present day. In "Spring.—Daisies.— Gathering Flowers" Hunt describes spring at this point in its progress, when it is complete, quiet, young, green, calling forth the idea of love. He then quotes Shakespeare and, noting that "we owe a long debt of gratitude to the daisy," quotes Chaucer, Jonson, Wither, and finally Wordsworth—regretting that "we cannot agree with him in thinking that it has a 'homely face.' " He ends by quoting in Italian, and then translating, Franco Sacchetti's "Gathering Flowers" (1, no. 3:19–24; 22:169–74; 28:217–24)—all interesting, informative essays, certainly, for the not impatient reader.

Hunt writes in the tradition of Wordsworth, with his emphasis on the poetic in the commonplace. His work in the *Indicator,* Hunt concludes, "may serve also to shew how much the cultivation of a natural chearfulness can do for the entertainment of itself and others, and what riches there must be in that ordinary world about us, whose veriest twigs and common-places want but the look of one's own eye to act upon them in sunshine" (2, no. 76:192). In retrospect, he was grateful for "the mixed colours of fancy and familiarity" he was able "to throw over some of the commonplaces of life."[4]

Cosmo Monkhouse typifies the critical response to Hunt's manner: "He talks to you—tells you his thoughts as they arise in his mind; we follow their meanderings as those of a stream, now broad now narrow, now breaking into sparkles of gentle merriment and now falling, but only for a moment, into a somewhat deeper pool—and the sun is always shining, and the water is always clear;

there are no torrents or spates in Leigh Hunt's brook, but it is never dry."[5]

Although the *Indicator* did not customarily print original poetry or literary reviews, Hunt did use it to promote Shelley, Keats, and Lamb. Shelley's "Love's Philosophy" first appeared (signed ϵ.) there in December 1819 (1, no. 11:88), and two entire numbers were devoted to the background and a review of *The Cenci*.[6] Hunt was the first to publish Keats's "La Belle Dame Sans Merci" and "A Dream, after Reading Dante's Episode of Paulo and Francesca" ("As Hermes once took to his feathers light"), over the signature Caviare; in two numbers he reviewed *Lamia,* retelling the stories in prose and giving long extracts.[7] Lamb's "Epitaph on a Dog (From the Latin of Vincent Bourne)," signed C.L., and "To My Friend The Indicator," signed ****, appeared in 1820—followed in December 1820 and January 1821 by five extracts from Lamb's work, four of these reprinted from Hunt's earlier use of them in the *Examiner*.[8]

This last fact points to the decline of the *Indicator*. Beginning in November 1820 Hunt was forced by ill health to suspend writing his essays and make up the paper with long reprints, translations, extracts, and contributions from correspondents. Hunt openly confessed his strategy, and the reason for it, to his readers; what seems remarkable is that he was able to satisfy his readers and put off the *Indicator*'s demise so long—until 21 March 1821.

In better times (23 August 1820) Hunt had written Shelley: "I speculate upon writing three [volumes] at least, if my health will hold out." There is no doubt but that the venture had been a success. Hunt had entered into it at least partly with a financial motive and, though his own retrospective accounts are somewhat contradictory, he noted in his *Autobiography* that he was helped by the income from the *Indicator*, "though it was but published in a corner, owing to my want of funds for advertising it, and my ignorance of the best mode of circulating such things."[9]

That the *Indicator* was financially successful is supported by the fact that two new publications vied for Hunt's readers when the *Indicator* ceased publication. The *Indictor* number 77 (no. 1, new series), published at two pence "by J. Onwhyn, No. 4, Catherine-street, Strand," appeared dated 28 March 1821 and ran to number 100, 13 October 1821; Onwhyn continued the pagination and format of Hunt's periodical, but freely admitted at the outset the difficulty of trying to follow Hunt. The second continuation, edited by Edward Hathway, lasted for three numbers only.[10]

The contemporary critical success is easier to document.[11] Perhaps Hunt himself, however, should have the last word: "The Indicator (*I fear*) is the best of my works:—so hard is it for one who has grown up in the hope of being a poet, to confess that the best things he has done have been in prose."[12]

Notes

1. See Clarence DeWitt Thorpe, "An Essay in Evaluation: Leigh Hunt as Man of Letters," in *Leigh Hunt's Literary Criticism,* ed. Lawrence Huston Houtchens and

Carolyn Washburn Houtchens (New York, 1956), pp. 1–73, for a good, if eulogistic, general introduction to Hunt and the controversies surrounding his life and work.

2. *The Correspondence of Leigh Hunt,* ed. by his Eldest Son (London, 1862), 1:149. Hunt emphasized again the lack of current information in a note in the second number (20 October 1819, p. 16): "As this publication is unstamped, it will not circulate by means of the general post without a heavy expense. Persons in the country who wish to become subscribers, should therefore order it of booksellers who send weekly or monthly parcels to their respective places of residence. The delay would be of little consequence with a work not containing any thing of merely temporary interest."

3. On the relation of Hunt's essays to those of the seventeenth- and eighteenth-century essayists, see Carl R. Woodring, *Prose of the Romantic Period* (Boston, 1961), p. 366; Melvin R. Watson, *Magazine Serials and the Essay Tradition 1746–1820* (Baton Rouge, La., 1956); and especially Marie Hamilton Law, *The English Familiar Essay in the Early Nineteenth Century: The Elements Old and New which Went into its Making as Exemplified in the Writings of Hunt, Hazlitt and Lamb* (Philadelphia, 1934).

4. Leigh Hunt, *Lord Byron and Some of His Contemporaries; with Recollections of the Author's Life, and of His Visit to Italy* (London, 1828), p. 433.

5. *Life of Leigh Hunt* (London, 1893), p. 143.

6. 1, no. 41 (19 July 1820):321–28; 1, no. 42 (26 July 1820):329–36. Reprinted in *The Romantics Reviewed: Contemporary Reviews of British Romantic Writers,* ed. Donald H. Reiman, "Part C: Shelley, Keats, and London Radical Writers" (New York, 1972), 2:471–79.

7. See 1, no. 31 (10 May 1820):248; 1, no. 38 (28 June 1820):304; 1, no. 43 (2 August 1820):337–44; 1, no. 44 (9 August 1820), 345–52. Reprinted in *The Romantics Reviewed,* Part C, 2:479–87.

8. 1, no. 30 (3 May 1820):241; 1, no. 51 (27 September 1820).402. Three of the reprinted extracts appeared in 2, no. 62 (13 December 1820): "Books with One Idea in Them" (pp. 73–74), "Gray's 'Bard' " (pp. 74–75), "Play-house Memoranda" (pp. 75–77). "A Sylvan Surprise" appeared in 2, no. 65 (3 January 1821):102. "Sir Thomas More," signed ****, not taken from the *Examiner,* appeared in 2, no. 63 (20 December 1820):81–87. Attributions: E. V. Lucas, ed., *The Works of Charles and Mary Lamb* (New York, 1903), 1:442, 443, 445, 471–72; 5:317, 325.

9. Hunt, *Correspondence,* 1:157. *The Autobiography of Leigh Hunt,* new ed., rev. by the Author, with a further revision and an introduction, by his Eldest Son (London, 1860), p. 273. See Hunt, *Correspondence,* 1:149, 161; and *Lord Byron and Some of His Contemporaries,* p. 432.

10. N.s. 1, no. 1 (28 March 1821): 197–98. See Louis Landré, *Leigh Hunt (1784–1859): Contribution à l'histoire du Romantisme Anglais* (Paris, 1936), 1:106–7; Alexander Mitchell, "Notes on the Bibliography of Leigh Hunt," *Bookman's Journal,* 3d ser. 15 (1927):7.

11. See Hunt, *Correspondence,* 1:153; Hunt, *Autobiography,* pp. 273–74; Landré, 1:106; and Alexander Ireland, *List of the Writings of William Hazlitt and Leigh Hunt* (London, 1868), pp. 130–31.

12. *Lord Byron and Some of His Contemporaries,* p. 432.

Information Sources

BIBLIOGRAPHY

Blunden, Edmund. *Leigh Hunt and His Circle.* New York, 1930.

Hunt, Leigh. *"The Indicator," and "The Companion";* *A Miscellany for the Fields* and the Fire-side. 2 vols. London, 1834 [and subsequent editions]. [Selections, with minor changes, and omissions.]

Landré, Louis. *Leigh Hunt (1784–1859): Contribution à l'histoire du Romantisme Anglais.* 2 vols. Paris, 1936.

Law, Marie Hamilton. *The English Familiar Essay in the Early Nineteenth Century: The Elements Old and New which Went into its Making as Exemplified in the Writings of Hunt, Hazlitt and Lamb.* Philadelphia, 1934.

Thorpe, Clarence DeWitt. "An Essay in Evaluation: Leigh Hunt as Man of Letters." In *Leigh Hunt's Literary Criticism.* Edited by Lawrence Huston Houtchens and Carolyn Washburn Houtchens. New York, 1956.

INDEXES
None.

REPRINT EDITIONS
"The Indicator" and "The Companion." 2 vols. 1834.

LOCATION SOURCES
American

Widely available.

British

Complete runs: Bodleian Library; Bristol Public Library; British Museum; Hampstead Public Library; Manchester Public Library.

Partial runs: Birmingham Public Library; Birmingham University Library; Cardiff Public Library; Sheffield University Library; University of Bristol Library.

Publication History

MAGAZINE TITLE AND TITLE CHANGES
The Indicator.

VOLUME AND ISSUE DATA
Volume 1, numbers 1–52, 13 October 1819–4 October 1820; volume 2, numbers 53–76, 11 October 1820–21 March 1821.

FREQUENCY OF PUBLICATION
Weekly.

PUBLISHER
Joseph Appleyard, 19 Catherine-street, Strand, London.

EDITOR
Leigh Hunt.

N. S. Bauer

INQUIRER, THE

The *Inquirer; or Literary Miscellany* (1814–1815), intended as a quarterly, appeared only three times. Very little has hitherto been known of its contributors. George L. Marsh suggested, in a 1928 article on "The Writings of Keats's Friend Reynolds," that it seems safe to identify certain entries as being "by the young Reynolds, from the fact that the publisher of the *Inquirer* was John Martin of Holles Street, Cavendish Square, who was one of the publishers of *Safie*" (one of Reynolds's major works).[1] In his edition of *Selected Prose of*

John Hamilton Reynolds Leonidas M. Jones notes, "It is a minor misfortune that these early prose pieces, first identified by George L. Marsh and never seen by this writer, seem lost irrecoverably, since bombing in World War II destroyed the volume in the British Museum, and the prospect of finding another copy is slight."[2]

Clearly neither Marsh nor Jones was aware of the existence of another copy of the *Inquirer* in the Bodleian Library at Oxford.[3] This was presumably John Martin's own copy since there are manuscript annotations and a flyleaf comment signed and dated from his home at Froxfield, near Woburn Abbey, where he was librarian to the Duke of Bedford, in 1843. He indicates that the essays originated from a group of young men who called themselves the Zetosophians, a group mentioned in the published correspondence of Reynolds but under the title "Letasophian." Reynolds writes to John Dovaston on 3 March 1813, "I am going this evening to my Literary Society, it is named the Letasophian; there are 14 members and most of them young men of very considerable genius; Every member must produce an Essay once a month, which he reads himself, the Society then discuss the topic generally. Wednesday is the Evening of Meeting here in each week."[4] Further independent confirmation of this society's activities is provided by the fact that a poem by Benjamin Bailey entitled "An Introductory Address to the Zetosophian Society" is among the papers deposited in the Leigh Browne-Lockyer Collection at the Keats Memorial Library in Hampstead.[5]

According to Martin's annotations in the Bodleian copy, the group included W. and F. Squibb, D. Bailey, J. Burchell, J. Reynolds, J. Cottle, Stanley, Archer, W. Seymour, and J. Martin; another less easily decipherable name may well be that of James Rice. Martin identifies authors for most of the anonymous articles, but given the possible distance in time between the appearance of the *Inquirer* and Martin's manuscript identifications, the assigning of specific articles needs to be accepted with caution. What can be said unequivocally is that Martin's copy was put together by, and contains some of the earliest work of, a number of those men who, for convenience's sake, have been styled the Keats circle.

Martin's annotations confirm Marsh's speculations about the Reynolds entries: Reynolds was responsible for "A Paraphrase of Catullus's Address to his Vessel," an essay "On the Character of Hamlet," and "Stanzas to ***," all of which appeared in the first issue, and "The Song of a Spanish Lover to His Mistress" in the third issue. Although his name does not appear on Martin's list of society members, C. W. Dilke is identified by Martin as being responsible for an article on drama in each issue. Bailey's contribution seems limited to an essay in the first issue on "Knowledge and Wisdom distinguished." Extended reviews of exhibitions, including those of the Royal Academy, are provided by Stanley. Martin himself seems to have avoided including any of his own material.

The *Inquirer* contains essays on general literary and historical subjects, poems, parodies and imitations, satirical essays, and reviews of galleries and, on occasion, theaters. The material's wit and contemporaneity reflects its origin in a society of lively and like-minded young men. While subsequent literary history indicates that the liveliness continued, the like-mindedness was not so enduring. Martin's note indicates that the Zetosophians broke up after "a deadly feud" and that the *Inquirer* consequently ceased publication after its third appearance.

Notes

1. George L. Marsh, "The Writings of Keats's Friend Reynolds," *Studies in Philology* 25 (1928):491.
2. *Selected Prose of John Hamilton Reynolds*, ed. Leonidas M. Jones (Cambridge, Mass., 1966), pp. 1–2.
3. See William S. Ward, *Index and Finding List of Serials Published in the British Isles 1789–1832* (Lexington, Ky., 1953), p. 74. *The British Union Catalogue* does not list the Bodleian copy.
4. John Clubbe, "The Reynolds-Dovaston Correspondence," *Keats-Shelley Journal* 30 (1981):176. In another letter to Dovaston (9 March 1813) quoted in the same article, Reynolds gives the variant spelling "Letosophian" (181).
5. Clayton E. Hudnall, "John Hamilton Reynolds, James Rice and Benjamin Bailey in the Leigh Browne-Lockyer Collection," *Keats-Shelley Journal* 19 (1970):15.

Information Sources

BIBLIOGRAPHY
Marsh, George L. "The Writings of Keats's Friend Reynolds." *Studies in Philology* 24 (1928):491–510.
INDEXES
None.
REPRINT EDITIONS
None.
LOCATION SOURCES
British
Complete runs: Aberdeen University Library; Bodleian Library; British Museum; London University Library.
Partial runs: Dr. William's Library; St. Andrew's University Library.

Publication History

MAGAZINE TITLE AND TITLE CHANGES
The Inquirer; or Literary Miscellany.
VOLUME AND ISSUE DATA
Numbers 1–3, 1814–1815.
FREQUENCY OF PUBLICATION
Quarterly.
PUBLISHER
John Martin, London.

EDITOR
John Martin.

Keith Wilson

INVESTIGATOR, THE (1820)

The *Investigator* bears the indelible mark of its three nonconformist editors. William Bengo Collyer ministered to a congregation in Peckham, London, of which Thomas Raffles became a member while still at school. Raffles became a clergyman in Liverpool where he was also engaged in organizing the education of independent ministers. In 1813 Raffles, together with James Baldwin Brown the elder, and the poet Jeremiah Holmes Wiffen, published *Poems by Three Friends*.[1] They became the three editors of the *Investigator*. Brown married one of Thomas Raffles's sisters and rose to become a judge in the north of England. Collyer, Raffles, and Brown were all active members of society and received many tokens of their fellow citizens' esteem. Their nineteenth-century biographers portrayed them as colorless but principled and energetic men.[2]

The *Investigator* was a quarterly magazine propagating the civic virtues that its editors exemplified. Humility and temperance were the hallmarks of all contributions to the periodical. Literature was discussed in light of "the connection which ought to be maintained between sound Literature and pure Religion" (5:iii). It is a tribute to the reviewers in the *Investigator* that their literary criticism did not descend to the level of bigoted castigation more often. Literature was presented as one of a number of human activities, and seen in a historical perspective was but an appendix to major political and social events.[3] Poets were characterized with an antiquarian's love of detail. Their various talents were described in long lists of epithets which were rarely synthesized, and considered verdicts were hardly ever given on the relative merits of their work (1:121; 2:367–68; 3:105; 4:391–92, 403–4). Minor poets were reviewed sympathetically: Jeremiah Holmes Wiffen, Cornelius Neale, and James Edmeston were praised for their poetic celebrations of virtuous themes and advised to polish their style (3:102–11; 4:391–404; 12:356–65; n.s. 4:449–71). William Cowper was often held up as a model for poets. The original poetry that formed a regular feature of the periodical exemplified the genre favored by the reviewers: meditative poems reflecting on the vanities and sufferings of human life glorified only by Divine Providence. The comprehensive quarterly bibliography of new books published in every issue of the first series included a separate section enumerating publications of this type of devotional poetry. Works of fiction were listed under "Miscellaneous," and drama was excluded altogether. In the early numbers of the periodical active disapproval of immoral literature was infrequent, its most forceful expression being occasional asides regretting "that talents supereminent as [Shakespeare's] give their most powerful and their

most dangerous attractions to the too fascinating amusements of the stage"
(1:122). But the urbanity disappeared in later numbers when the reviewers felt
compelled to warn their readers against literature which challenged established
ethical and religious ideas. In a review of *Don Juan* (6:353–60) the periodical
declared war on Byron and Shelley, "companions and fellow-workers in iniq-
uity, (if to debauch the mind and deprave the heart,—if to destroy the surest
safeguards of virtue here,—the only hopes of happiness hereafter, be iniqui-
tous)" (6:353). The attacks were continued in reviews of various works by
Shelley, Byron, and Charles Hanbury Willis (10:314–71) and of the first issue
of the *Liberal* * (11:76–108). The energetic and lively style characteristic of
these vituperative onslaughts contrasts sharply with the rather bland tone of
approval in earlier reviews. As the campaign against the Satanic School of
Poetry gained momentum the traditionally sympathetic reviews degenerated into
repetitions of formulae for acceptable literature (12:366–96). The reviewers'
inability to transfer this aggressive energy to unbigoted criticism indicates the
limitations of their approach to literature, and they were frustrated into silence
about imaginative literature in the last six issues.

The caustic tone of the later reviews resulted from an implicit realization of
the persuasive powers of literature. It was not characteristic of the *Investigator*
as a whole. Dogma was foreign to the missionary tradition in which the *Investigator* was written;[4] it sought to convert by individual example and evinced
an interest in a broad spectrum of human activities. Every issue of the first
series consisted of two parts: long original articles on a variety of subjects, and
a large section providing information on a diversity of recent events. A nonconformist interest in personal testimony recording religious experiences was
reflected in many of the articles. "Original Letters from Eminent Persons" was
a regular column of items copied from Thomas Raffles's large collection of
autographs.[5] Written mostly by provincial clergymen in the eighteenth century,
the letters described various specific, private occurrences in great detail. No
explanatory introductions or footnotes were supplied to set them in chronological and geographical context; they were valuable as universal statements of the
presence of God, which was reaffirmed to devout individuals in the minutiae
of their everyday lives.

The section of miscellaneous information regularly included "Philosophical
and Literary Intelligence," containing notices of recent discoveries and inventions. "Conversion of Rags into Sugar" (1:185), "Alleged Important Inventions in Hydraulics" (1:180–81), and other technical advances promising to
improve the material conditions of human life were applauded. The literary
intelligence consisted of reports from various literary societies, on discoveries
of ancient manuscripts, and on civic honors bestowed on artists. Anthropolog-
ical observations and expeditions to foreign parts were also noted in this column; many of these items were reprinted from the *Gentleman's Magazine* * (see
AAAJ). "Provincial and Miscellaneous Intelligence" and "Political Retrospect" recorded events, particularly in ecclesiastical institutions, of both local

and international importance. Occasional editorial comments provided no perceptive analyses but called for moderation and tolerance in all matters. "Religious and Philanthropic Intelligence" and "Summary of Missionary Proceedings" reflected most clearly the editors' motives for attaching importance to this miscellaneous section. The columns contained reports from a wide variety of religious and philanthropic organizations in Britain and abroad, which were given without denominational bias. They provided detailed insights into the living conditions of people who had been deprived of the comforting awareness of God's omnipresence. Such knowledge was essential to missionaries attempting to alleviate cruel human misfortunes. The editors were especially eager to establish contacts with reliable correspondents in India and America who could supply this information (3:iii). A by-product of this policy was an interest in American literature, which had been largely neglected in Britain at that time. The tone of "American Literature and Intelligence" was inevitably patronizing, but the column gave a sympathetic reception to American literature. Nonconformist hagiographies and accounts of missionary expeditions received particular attention, but a few works of literary interest were also introduced. The most notable example was Washington Irving's *The Sketch Book of Geoffrey Crayon, Esq.,*[6] which illustrated the motto of the column: "Why strive ye together, are ye not brethren?"

The *Investigator* was sold at two shillings an issue, which put it out of the reach of the working classes. Lowering the price, however, would have meant excluding the columns of miscellaneous information. The editors regarded them as an integral part of their quietly missionary periodical and insisted on retaining them (1:iv). But after the fourteenth issue they found that the pressure of other commitments made it necessary to reduce the scope of the periodical. The columns of miscellaneous information were omitted and the four issues of the new series were sold at half the original price. Even in its reduced form the *Investigator* demanded too much time from its editors and was finally abandoned. New publications had appeared to take over the task of spreading information to encourage tolerance and understanding and to fight vice and irreligion. The editors referred their readers to the *Philomatic Journal,* published by the Philomatic Institution, of which they were all honorary members and whose president was William Bengo Collyer (7:iii, 8:iii). To Brown, Raffles, and Collyer the *Investigator* was but one of a number of activities devoted to humble celebrations of God's omnipresence in man's life. To modern readers it offers unique insight into the integration of literature and a nonconformist philosophy of life.

Notes

1. *The British Museum General Catalogue of Printed Books* wrongly names his son as the third editor. James Baldwin Brown the younger was born in the same year as the *Investigator*.

2. See James Baldwin Brown the Younger, *Thomas Raffles, D.D.,LL.D.: A Sketch* (London, [1864]); John Morison, *Lessons Suggested by the Death of Venerable Pastors: A Sermon Preached at Hanover Chapel, Peckham, on the Evening of the Funeral of the Rev. William Bengo Collyer* (London, [1854]); Thomas Stamford Raffles, *Memoirs of the Life and Ministry of the Rev. Thomas Raffles, D.D., LL.D., Etc, Etc, Etc* (London, 1864). See also articles on the editors in the *Dictionary of National Biography*.

3. See the survey of the history of English literature in a review of *Specimens of the British Poets,* ed. Thomas Campbell (London, 1819–) in the *Investigator* no. 1 (1820):110–31.

4. See Robert E. Spiller, *The American in England During the First Half Century of Independence* (New York, 1926), pp. 201–45 for an interesting account of various activities within the nonconformist, missionary tradition.

5. The collection is described in detail by John Cordy Jeaffreson in the appendix to part 1 of the *Sixth Report of the Royal Commission on Historical Manuscripts* (London, 1877), pp. 468–75.

6. See William B. Cairns, *British Criticism of American Writings 1815–1833*, University of Wisconsin Studies in Language and Literature no. 14 (Madison, 1922), pp. 20, 34–36.

Information Sources

BIBLIOGRAPHY

Brown, James Baldwin. *Thomas Raffles, D.D., LL.D.: A Sketch*. London [1864].

Cairns, William B. *British Criticisms of American Writings 1815–1833: A Contribution to the Study of Anglo-American Literary Relationships.* University of Wisconsin Studies in Language and Literature no. 14. Madison, 1922.

Collyer, William Bengo. *The Reverend W. B. Collyer's Interesting Letter in Vindication of His Own Conduct, from the Calumnious Reports Circulated Against Him.* London [1823].

Morison, John. *Lessons Suggested by the Death of Venerable Pastors: A Sermon Preached at Hanover Chapel, Peckham, on the Evening of the Funeral of the Rev. William Bengo Collyer, D.D., LL.D., F.A.S.: Monday, 16th January, 1854.* London [1854].

The Philomatic Journal and Literary Review, 4 vols., 1824–1826.

Raffles, Thomas Stamford. *Memoirs of the Life and Ministry of the Rev. Thomas Raffles, D.D., LL.D., Etc, Etc, Etc.* London, 1864.

Sixth Report of the Royal Commission on Historical Manuscripts. London, 1877.

Spiller, Robert E. *The American in England During the First Half Century of Independence.* New York, 1926.

INDEXES

Each volume indexed.

REPRINT EDITIONS

Microform: British Museum Newspaper Library, London.

LOCATION SOURCES

American

Complete run: Boston Public Library.

Partial runs: American Philosophical Society; Cornell University Library; Harvard University Library; Library Company of Philadelphia; Newberry Library; Union Theological Seminary Library; U. S. Library of Congress; Williams College Library.

British

Complete runs: Bodleian Library; British Museum; Cambridge University Library; Edinburgh University Library.

Partial run: St. Andrews University Library.

Publication History

MAGAZINE TITLE AND TITLE CHANGES

The Investigator, May–August 1820. *The Investigator; or, Quarterly Magazine,* October 1820–October 1824.

VOLUME AND ISSUE DATA

Volumes 1–7, numbers 1–14, May 1820–October 1823; new series, volume 8, numbers 1–4, January 1824–October 1824.

FREQUENCY OF PUBLICATION

Quarterly.

PUBLISHERS

Numbers 1–new series 4, May 1820–October 1824: Thomas and George Underwood, 32 Fleet Street, London; Black, Kingsbury, Parry, and Allen, Leadenhall Street, London; Ogle, Duncan, and Co., Paternoster Row, London; F. Westley, Stationers' Court, London; B. J. Holdsworth, St. Paul's Churchyard, London; Waugh and Innes, Edinburgh. Numbers 1—8, May 1820–April 1822: Taylor, Church Street, Liverpool. Numbers 7–new series 4, January 1822–October 1824: Sherwood, Neely, and Jones (Sherwood and Co.: numbers 9–new series 4), Paternoster Row, London; Wood, Marlborough Street, Dublin; Manning, Chapel Lane, Belfast.

EDITORS

William Bengo Collyer, Thomas Raffles, and James Baldwin Brown the elder.

Karsten Engelberg

INVESTIGATOR, THE (1822). See CHAMPION, THE

J

JOHN BULL

In the last months of 1820 King George IV was finding little support for his attempt to divorce Queen Caroline. Whigs, Radicals, and most of the press defended the queen, and the king's own Tory government pursued his divorce without enthusiasm. But when the first issue of *John Bull* appeared on 17 December 1820 it was clear from its subtitle—"For God, the King, and the People"—and from its first article that the king was no longer without a champion:

> The shameful licentiousness of a prostituted Press, the infamous tendency of the caricatures which issue from every sink of vice and infamy in and near the Metropolis, the inflammatory speeches of knaves and fools, the absurd unmeaning Addresses to the Queen, and the libellous and treasonable answers given to them, are banes to our Constitution, which call loudly for an antidote. [p. 4]

The eight-page weekly contained the usual domestic and foreign intelligence; police, market, and court reports; and lists of births, deaths, and marriages. But the material that gave the paper its initial success and made it famous was its unrelenting attacks on the queen and her supporters. Each issue contained witty, often scurrilous poems about Queen Caroline and her friends. *John Bull* also copied the *Courier*'s idea of listing, together with unflattering comments, all of the ladies who called on the queen. In a short time few dared to do so.

The new periodical was immediately successful, achieving within six weeks a circulation of 10,000.[1] "The 'John Bull' is amusing," Emily Cowper told her brother, "for you see it is not written by a common hack, but by some man who knows society. Theodore Hook denies it, but is strongly suspected."[2]

As Lady Cowper and many others suspected, Theodore Hook was the founder, editor, and principal contributor to *John Bull*. The son of James Hook, a composer of popular songs for the theater, Theodore Hook was born in 1788.[3] At an early age he developed a flair for the extemporaneous composition of songs and poems which made him a favorite of society nearly all his life. As a youth he began to write farces and at nineteen published his first novel. In time he became known to the Prince Regent, who secured for him an appointment in 1812 as accountant general and treasurer of Mauritius. This fine opportunity turned out to be the great disaster of Hook's life. In 1819 he was brought back to England in disgrace, accused of malfeasance. Though exempted from criminal penalties, he was saddled with a debt to the government of 62,000 pounds, which he could never pay and which would later cause him to spend two years in prison.

In the spring of 1820, soon after his return from Mauritius, Hook, with his theater friend, Daniel Terry, founded a monthly periodical called the *Arcadian*. It ended after only two issues when the publisher withdrew. Hook then formed a partnership—apparently without Terry—with another printer, William Shackell, to put out a weekly paper, similar in tone and in content to the *Arcadian*. The new paper, *John Bull,* was to be published and distributed on Saturday afternoon, though dated from Sunday. It was widely believed at the time that powerful Tories had chosen Hook to edit the new paper and were aiding him financially. Various sources suggested that Sir Walter Scott had helped Hook gain the support of a major Tory figure, either the Duke of Wellington or John Wilson Croker, but there is no evidence to support those rumors.[4] Hook tried to keep his connection with the paper secret, even resorting to the ruse of having *John Bull* print a denial disdainful of himself (1, no. 6:44). But it was impossible to keep such a secret, and in time Hook no longer tried.

After the death of Queen Caroline in the summer of 1821, Hook turned his attentions to Whig and Radical leaders, especially Joseph Hume. The well-known Radical was repeatedly the victim of various forms of ridicule, most notably the free translations of lines from Horace in which cognates of the word *humus* appeared. Thus, "Hum-asse velit" became "Let no one call Hume an ass" and "Humili modo loqui" was said to mean "To talk Scotch like Hume."[5]

Radical writers were also subjected to venomous personal attacks. Not only was William Hazlitt's indiscreet *Liber Amoris* described as the "beastly trash of Billy Hazlitt the Cockney lecturer who is not able to write English," but *John Bull* revealed that it was based on Hazlitt's love affair with Sarah Walker, the daughter of a tailor in whose house he had lived. The paper even obtained and printed a long personal letter from Hazlitt to the woman.[6]

In 1824 Hook brought in William C. Maginn to edit a Wednesday edition of the paper, called the *John Bull Magazine*. It failed only after six numbers, but not before printing a vicious libel on Thomas De Quincey in the first of a series of articles entitled "The Humbugs of the Age."[7] Maginn and Hook remained close friends and collaborators for the rest of their lives; and both still live in

Thackeray's novels, Maginn as Captain Shandon in *Pendennis* and Hook as his friend, Mr. Wagg, in *Pendennis,* and in *Vanity Fair.*[8]

After the first few years *John Bull'*s circulation declined somewhat, and it ceased the more gross personal attacks that had made it infamous. Hook spent more time on his novels, and others assisted him with *John Bull.* Among them were his brother, Dr. John Hook, who wrote under the name ''Fitz-Harding''; Thomas H. Bailey; Richard Dalton Barham, author of *The Ingoldsby Legends;* and Samuel Carter Hall.[9] From 1836 until his death in 1841 Hook also edited the *New Monthly Magazine.**[10] By this time *John Bull* had become a relatively sedate literary paper which appealed to middle- and upper-class readers. Its circulation ranged from 1,600 in 1855 to 3,000 in 1870.[11] The paper remained politically conservative and ultra-Protestant, supporting the Orange cause and opposing Catholic Emancipation. In time the paper developed a special connection with High Church and Tory clergy. In its last years Mrs. Oliphant noted that *John Bull,* once so objectionable, was ''now the most irreproachable of weeklies.''[12] The paper ceased publication after 3,739 issues, the last on 16 July 1892. The title was revived in 1903 and again in 1906 under Horatio Bottomley.[13]

Notes

1. H. R. Fox Bourne, *English Newspapers: Chapters in the History of Journalism,* 2 vols. (London, 1887; reprint ed., New York, 1966), 2:6.

2. Emily Cowper to George Lamb, ca. February 1821, *The Letters of Lady Palmerston,* ed. Tresham Lever (London, 1957), p. 69.

3. The best accounts of Hook's life are: R. H. Dalton Barham, *Life and Remains of Theodore Hook,* new and rev. ed. (London, 1877) and [John Gibson Lockhart,] ''Theodore Hook,'' *Quarterly Review* 72 (1843):53–108.

4. Fox Bourne, *English Newspapers,* 2:5; Lockhart, ''Theodore Hook,'' pp. 74–75; Richard Garnett, ''Theodore Edward Hook,'' *Dictionary of National Biography,* 9:1168–70. For a good modern discussion of the issue, see Myron F. Brightfield, *Theodore Hook and His Novels* (Cambridge, Mass., 1928; reprint ed., St. Clair Shores, Mich., 1977), pp. 133–36.

5. Alexander Andrews, *The History of British Journalism,* 2 vols. (London, 1859; reprint ed., Grosse Point, Mich., 1968), 2:97.

6. Stanley Jones, ''Hazlitt and *John Bull:* A Neglected Letter,'' *Review of English Studies* n.s. 17 (May 1966):163–70.

7. Kenneth Forward, '' 'Libellous Attack' on De Quincey,'' *Publications of the Modern Language Association* 52 (March 1937):244–60; *Notes and Queries,* 5th series 8 (11 August 1877):108.

8. T. H. S. Escott, *Masters of English Journalism* (London, 1911; reprint ed., Westport, Conn., 1970), pp. 193–94.

9. Andrews, *History of British Journalism,* 2:98; Brightfield, *Hook and His Novels,* p. 145.

10. ''Hoaxer and Wit,'' *The Times Literary Supplement,* 23 August 1941, p. 408.

11. Alvar Ellegard, *The Readership of the Periodical Press in Mid-Victorian Britain* (Göteborg, 1957), p. 19.

12. Arthur Aspinall, *Politics and the Press, c. 1780–1850* (London, 1949), p. 346. C. A. Cranfield, *The Press and Society from Caxton to Northcliffe* (New York, 1978), p. 154. Margaret O. Oliphant, *The Victorian Age of English Literature,* (New York, 1892), 2:625.

13. See Walter Graham, *English Literary Periodicals* (New York, 1930), p. 387.

Information Sources

BIBLIOGRAPHY

Barham, R. H. Dalton. *Life and Remains of Theodore Hook.* New and rev. ed. London, 1877.

Brightfield, Myron F. *Theodore Hook and His Novels.* Cambridge, Mass., 1928. Reprint. St. Clair Shores, Mich., 1971.

Dictionary of National Biography. S.v. "Hook, Theodore Edward."

Forward, Kenneth. " 'Libellous Attack' on De Quincey." *Publications of the Modern Language Association* 52 (1937):244–60.

"Hoaxer and Wit." *The Times Literary Supplement,* 23 August 1941, p. 408.

Hook, Theodore. *The Choice Humorous Works, Ludicrous Adventures, Bon Mots, Puns and Hoaxes of Theodore Hook.* London, 1889.

Jones, Stanley. "Hazlitt and *John Bull:* A Neglected Letter." *Review of English Studies* 17 (1866):163–70.

[Lockhart, John Gibson.] "Theodore Hook." *Quarterly Review* 72 (1843):53–108.

INDEXES

Each volume indexed.

REPRINT EDITIONS

Microform: British Museum Newspaper Library, London. Datamics Inc., New York.

LOCATION SOURCES

American

Partial runs: Widely available.

British

Complete runs: British Museum; Edinburgh Public Library; London Library. Partial runs: Widely available.

Publication History

MAGAZINE TITLE AND TITLE CHANGES

John Bull. *"For God, the King and the People,"* 17 December 1820–18 June 1837. *John Bull. "For God, the Sovereign and the People,"* 25 June 1837–16 July 1892. (The words *"and Britannia"* were included in the title from 19 April 1856 until the 1860s, when they were dropped.)

VOLUME AND ISSUE DATA

Volumes 1–72, numbers 1–3,739, 17 December 1820–16 July 1892.

FREQUENCY OF PUBLICATION

Weekly.

PUBLISHERS

17 December 1820–20 January 1822: R. T. Weaver, 12 Johnson's Court, Fleet Street, London. 27 January 1822–10 December 1837: Edward Shackell, 40 Fleet Street, London. 17 December 1837–ca. 1860s (exact date unknown): John Cooper

Bunney, 40 Fleet Street, London (until September 1855)/9 Crane Court, Fleet Street, London (until May 1857)/112 Fleet Street, London (after May 1857). It is uncertain whether printers listed after Bunney were either publishers or proprietors of the paper.

EDITORS

Theodore Hook, 1820–1841. H. F. Cooper, Samuel Phillips, 1845–1846. Godfrey W. Turner, 1855. Charles G. Prowett, to 1865. George H. Smith.

Darwin F. Bostick

JOURNAL OF SCIENCE AND THE ARTS, THE. See QUARTERLY JOURNAL OF SCIENCE, LITERATURE, AND THE ARTS, THE

JOURNAL OF THE ROYAL INSTITUTION OF GREAT BRITAIN, THE. See QUARTERLY JOURNAL OF SCIENCE, LITERATURE, AND THE ARTS, THE

——— K ———

KNIGHT'S QUARTERLY MAGAZINE

Knight's Quarterly Magazine was one of the novelties of the London periodical press in 1823–1824, but it owed more to Windsor and Cambridge than to the capital city. Although it issued from the Northumberland Court press of William Clowes and the Pall Mall publishing office of Charles Knight, its leading writers were graduates of Eton and/or students at Cambridge, where plans for launching the quarterly were worked out. Containing "writing . . . of a very superior character,"[1] the magazine deserved to run far beyond its sixth issue, but any regret for its short life is to some degree palliated by the realization that *Knight's* fostered the work of several young men who would make significant contributions to the cultural life of nineteenth-century England.

Charles Knight, destined to become a major name in the Victorian book trade and in popular education, was publisher, editor, contributor, and later historian in this enterprise. Consequently, chapters 8–10 of his autobiography, *Passages of a Working Life,* remain the most detailed and authoritative account of the magazine.[2] Knight began his history by telling of his role as publisher and printer of the *Etonian,* an extraordinary magazine edited by the brilliant Eton students William Mackworth Praed and Walter Blunt. Fifteen persons, either students or alumni of the college, contributed, but "no one . . . in the extent or variety of his articles, approached Mr. Praed," who wrote a quarter of the miscellany. When he left Eton for Trinity College, Cambridge, in the summer of 1821, the *Etonian* was forced to conclude. But once having entered upon his studies at Trinity, Praed again turned to periodical writing, and again it was to Knight that he made a proposal, in a letter of December 1822: "I shall labour in no periodical vocation until you publish one in which I can be of service to you; and divers other Etonians long to hear of your happy establishment in town." Accordingly, Knight went up to Cambridge and spent a pleasant week getting acquainted with several of Praed's friends, and there "the general plan of 'Knight's Quarterly Magazine' was settled." Knight confessed that he "drifted into the editorship much against his will"; nevertheless, he found that his position had "its pleasures." Some of the articles sent to him he regarded as almost perfect, and, on the whole, he was greatly pleased with the contributions.[3]

On 1 June 1823 the first number was published in London. Not only were the compositions of high calibre; the pseudonymous writers were presented in a frame of vivacious interaction reminiscent of *Blackwood's* * and the *Etonian*. As Christopher North presided over the convivial meetings of his fictional Edinburgh coterie and Peregrine Courtenay "sate as chairman of a jovial meeting of congenial spirits" in the *Etonian*'s "King of Clubs," so the "knot of young men" who would support *Knight's Quarterly* gathered in the initial article at the imaginary court of a Lady Mary Vernon, "the Mistress of all Harmony, the Queen of all Wits, the Brightest of all Belles," a combination of medieval chatelaine, Petrarchan lady, and late-Georgian woman of fashion. The group of assembled contributors took her as their patroness, and resolved to write "a Book of some sort." They knelt before her ottoman, swore fealty, and gave their twenty-five *noms de plume* in pledge.[4]

The principals among these literary liegemen wrote for the first number, and Knight singled them out for identification in his autobiography. Praed signed his work with either "Peregrine Courtenay" or "Vyvyan Joyeuse"; "Courtenay" he had brought over from the *Etonian*, and "Joyeuse" "was the one he adopted for his gay and laughing moods in the 'Quarterly Magazine.'"[5] Another pseudonym of the *Etonian* circle, "Gerard Montgomery," was retained by poet John Moultrie. Samuel Taylor Coleridge's son Derwent kept his initials in "Davenant Cecil," and Derwent's cousin, Henry Nelson Coleridge, passed as "Joseph Haller." Other clues in initials can be seen in "Tristram Merton" (Thomas Babington Macaulay) and "Hamilton Murray" (Henry Malden). "Edward Haselfoot" was William Sidney Walker. Knight himself contributed under the names "Frederick Vernon" (brother of Lady Mary) and "Paterson Aymer."[6] All except Knight were students at Cambridge when the magazine began publication, and H. N. Coleridge, Moultrie, Praed, and Walker also had written for the *Etonian*. With Knight, who was about ten years older than most of them, they established in this first number a youthful verve and lightness of tone that showed keen sensitivity to the literary spirit of the age.

To begin, Praed's scintillating "Castle Vernon" (1:2) initiated the fictional framework of Lady Mary's court, where repartee and topical allusions made up much of the contributors' dialogue. Next, Knight's "The Editor" (1:13–16) advanced this fiction. In an open letter to his staff the supposed editor offered some criticisms of their recent contributions. Near the end of the issue "The Eton Montem" (1:193–200), also by Knight, showed Gerard Montgomery, Paterson Aymer, and other contributors participating in the Montem, a triennial fancy-dress assembly of Etonians on Salt Hill, Slough, to beg money for sending a senior to one of the universities.

In addition to creating this lively fictional medium for the succeeding five issues, the first number also established the genres that would comprise most of the volumes of *Knight's Quarterly*. Seven of the articles may well be classed as essays—some of them familiar, some analytical. Knight's "On Queues" (1:142–44) took up the style of Elia and lamented the passing of a fashion in men's hairdressing. More formally, Macaulay appealed idealistically for abolition in "On West Indian Slavery" (1:85–94), and in "On the Royal Society of Literature" (1:111–17) he clearly demonstrated the uselessness and the potential harm of that recently formed association, concluding with the irresistible "apologue" of King Gomer Chephoraod and the Royal Wine Society. Two essays of this number introduced reviewing into the *Quarterly Magazine*—W. S. Walker's easy-going, nonmagisterial review of novels by John Wilson and John Gibson Lockhart and Allan Cunningham's more conventional critique of Scott's *Quentin Durward* (1:200–14). At the same time, the magazine published some historical fiction of its own with Macaulay's "Fragments of a Roman Tale" (1:33–44); C. B. Taylor's "Rose Aleyn" (1:65–77), set in the England of the Civil War; Henry Malden's "Agostino della Monterosa" (1:117–42), a tale of passion, intrigue, and black magic in medieval Padua; and Knight's "the Burial of Charles the First" (1:106–11), a story of seventeenth-century Windsor. Most of the poetry of number 1 was concentrated in two sections. By far the more exceptional is "La Belle Tryamour, A Metrical Romance" (1:144–79), Gerard Montgomery's (John Moultrie's) bald but clever imitation of the style of *Don Juan*, down to the ottava rima and characteristic digressions, topical allusions, and infinitely open ended plot. The other major poetical section is the melange entitled "What You Will" (1:215–26), Vyvyan Joyeuse's arrangement of several of his own poems along with a few by Macaulay, Derwent Coleridge, and Henry Malden. Joyeuse closed the issue and the potpourri with a riddle, a piece of characteristic nonchalance, for he confessed, it was written in a rush merely to make up the copy, which the printer's assistant was waiting at the door to collect.

Not many readers, it seems, entered fully into the capricious spirit of this first number. According to Knight, few of "the intelligent public" appreciated the originality of the articles. Some criticism from the strait-laced may well have brought the response in number 2 of "Castle Vernon," which opened the second issue, for October 1823 (1:227–35). Arriving at Lady Mary's court, Joyeuse expressed his fear that Montgomery's "La Belle Tryamour" had offended the taste of the age, for,

> The great, the gay, the learned, and the fair,
> Return at last to prudence and formality;
> And reverence, as their fathers did before 'em,
> Dry bread, dry talk, cold water, and decorum.

[1:232]

He foresaw "that a great revulsion is taking place in the national feeling" (1:234) and recommended that they "cut Moore, and study the Fathers" (1:234).

One such fastidious reader was Zachary Macaulay, whose "great uneasiness" at the levity of the magazine led him to insist that his son Thomas cease writing for *Knight's*. On 20 June 1823 the younger Macaulay dutifully wrote from Leicestershire that he felt constrained to withdraw "to respect prejudices which I do not in the slightest degree share." Knight and his staff looked upon this "secession" as "an almost irreparable loss"; but Praed doubled his determination and wrote to Knight, "For myself, I will give night and day to the Magazine, rather than see it so assassinated." Keeping his promise, he wrote more than a fourth of the October number, including the second part of "Castle Vernon" quoted above. But Macaulay's absence was fortunately a brief one, and with the third number (January 1824) his contributions again appeared, as they would in each of the succeeding numbers until the end. He became, in fact, "unquestionably [the magazine's] leading spirit."[7]

Meanwhile, Knight "had also looked around [him] amongst [his] own old familiar friends," such as the barrister Matthew Davenport Hill, who wrote under the names "Martin Danvers Heaviside" and "William Payne."[8] The second number contained the entertaining account of his first appearance as a courtroom lawyer ("My Maiden Brief," 1:273–76) and his vivid description of the inhabitants and landscape of the country of the Staffordshire collieries (1:295–300). Thomas De Quincey, whose *Confessions of an English Opium-Eater* had appeared in 1821–22, perhaps wrote two articles for this issue.[9]

With the restoration of Macaulay to the staff and the enlistment of other contributors, the magazine carried on through 1824 with the same character of an inventive miscellany that had been established in its issue of June 1823. Although "Castle Vernon," originally the main receptacle of the magazine's fiction about itself, did not appear after October 1823, other articles were made to serve that purpose. "The Editor" (2,3) permitted Knight to carry on the earlier intimacy with readers and pseudonymous contributors. This fiction culminated in "The Anniversary," which celebrated the magazine's first and only "birthday." The long article comprised more than half of the fifth issue and seemed to follow *Blackwood's* lead in bringing the contributors and the editor together on an excursion to Garraway's tavern in Knight's beloved Windsor, where the reader was allowed to overhear their dialogue and reading of papers, embellished with songs, narration, and stage direction.[10] The issues of 1824 also carried narratives, notably "Narenor," a tale of conjuration set in Germany "in the days of fairies and necromancers" (2:274), an early work of Edward Bulwer (later Lord Lytton); De Quincey's imitation of German stories in "The Incognito" (3:143–56) and "The Somnambulist" (3:443—63); and the "Irish Stories" of William Maginn. The continued appeal of historical fiction is evident in the three-part "Lady Alice Lisle," which begins on the day of the execution of Charles I (2:46–53, 393–403; 3:395–406). A considerable portion of volumes 2 and 3 (about 175 pages) was given to literary criticism, either to general critical essays or to reviews. In the former category stand Macaulay's "Criticisms on the Principal Italian Writers" (Dante, 2:207–23; Petrarch, 2:355–68); W. S. Walker's "Shelley's Posthumous Poems" (3:182–

92); and the still unattributed "On the Poetry of Southey" (3:156–64). Among the reviews of new books or editions are the articles on *Digby's Broad Stone of Honour* (2:287–304), by Walker; Vieusseux's *Italy and the Italians* (3:9–16), unattributed; and Mitford's *History of Greece* (3:285–304), by Macaulay. There is one review by Walker of another periodical, the *Retrospective Review** (3:51–60). In addition to criticism, there were essays in the familiar and analytical modes (cf. 2:100–114, 446–60; 3:112–16, 169–72). Poetry came from many hands, including H. N. Coleridge, Bulwer, Macaulay, Knight, Vieusseux, and Mrs. M. D. Hill. But the principal contributors in this department remained Moultrie and Praed, who added a canto, respectively, to "La Belle Tryamour" (2:115–57) and "The Troubadour" (2:412–31) in the first half of 1824, before they began to withdraw their support of the magazine. The vacancy resulting from the loss of their aid was to some degree filled by William Maginn, who published a long poetical contribution in the last number ("Batrachomyomachia," 3:342–53).

This disagreement with Praed and Moultrie became, indeed, a principal factor in Knight's decision to terminate the magazine. A visit to Cambridge in October 1824 was chilled because "two of [the magazine's] first supporters were holding back their contributions. . . . some misunderstanding about the future editorship—had produced a coldness in those with whom I had been most intimate." During the same period, Knight's father was dangerously ill and "large undertakings in London" and "a divided duty at Windsor" were a serious distraction to the publisher. He later wrote, "The Magazine was a loss and a trouble. With the sixth number I determined to announce that its career was ended." Consequently, he introduced the last issue with the "Advertisement" apologizing for two delays in publication and expressing his "lingering anxiety of a severe domestic calamity" and "something like a heartless indifference to the consequences of wanton neglect" (3:viii). This announcement "led to a controversy" with Praed in the *Cambridge Chronicle* although the two men shortly resumed their friendship. The next year Knight attempted to revive the magazine, and with the aid of Henry Malden and Derwent Coleridge, he brought out one number of the *Quarterly Magazine, New Series* in August 1825. Its 240 pages were "much more sober" in tone "and of course less interesting . . . than its predecessor." Despite the proffered assistance of "one of the great wholesale houses in Paternoster Row," the new series did not survive the financial panic of 1825.[11]

In 1881 J. A. Picton, writing in *Notes and Queries** (see *VEA*) of the initial reception of *Knight's Quarterly,* described the contents as "caviar to the multitude," and Knight himself had commented on the scarcity of appreciative readers.[12] Nevertheless, several discriminating nineteenth-century critics recognized the exceptional quality of the magazine. In a review of 2 June 1823, the (London) *Courier* is typical. It observed that the first number "is certainly not inferior to any of those Monthly Miscellanies to which some of the best writers of the day are now contributors. In some respects we think it superior to them. Upon the whole it bears the evidence of a greater *variety* of talent than its contemporaries; and it has nothing of that sickly egotism which is the characteristic of one school, nor of that mere essay writing which is the besetting sin of another.''[13]

The acclamations of the talents that supported *Knight's* are sustained by the achievements of its contributors subsequent to their writing for the periodical. As one of his many ventures, Knight edited Shakespeare, as did William Sidney Walker. Malden distinguished himself as a classical scholar and furthered the development of University College, London. De Quincey, Bulwer, and Macaulay would enter or approach the ranks of the leading authors of the nineteenth century. Both Coleridges performed a service for English letters in editing the works of their famous kinsman. Moultrie became rector of Rugby and an associate of Dr. Thomas Arnold, and Hill was a leader in reforming the penal system. At least four of them (Bulwer, Hill, Praed, and Macaulay) took seats in Parliament, and Bulwer and Macaulay were elevated to the peerage.

Notes

1. J. A. Picton, *"Knight's Quarterly Magazine 1823–4,"* Notes and Queries, 6th series, 3 (1881):361.

2. Charles Knight, *Passages of a Working Life During Half a Century: With a Prelude of Early Reminiscences* (1864; reprint ed., London, 1873), 1:280–338.

3. Ibid., pp. 291, 294, 295, 301.

4. [W. M. Praed], "Castle Vernon," *Knight's Quarterly Magazine* 1 (1823):1–2. In March 1822 *Blackwood's* had begun *Noctes Ambrosianae*, a series of dialogues purporting to record the meetings of editor Christopher North and his principal contributors, Timothy Tickler, Morgan Odoherty, and the Ettrick Shepherd (James Hogg). Eight of the *Noctes* had appeared before June 1823.

5. Knight, *Passages of a Working Life*, 1:296.

6. Knight, *Passages of a Working Life*, 1:296–333, provides many attributions of authorship for specific articles; but an equally helpful source is the list published in G. J. Gray, *"Knight's Quarterly Magazine,"* Notes and Queries, 6th series 4 (1881):261–63. Gray's list was made from a copy of the magazine "in the possession of Messrs. Macmillan & Bowes, Cambridge, which has the authors' names filled in in manuscript, and, as far as I can see, correctly" (p. 261). These two sources form the basis for attributions throughout this profile.

7. See Knight, *Passages of a Working Life*, pp. 302–308, 317. Macaulay's contributions to *Knight's* comprise more than two hundred pages of volume 8 of *The Complete Works of Lord Macaulay* (New York, 1898), ed. Lady Trevelyan. A letter of Thomas Macaulay to his father (7 October 1824) indicates something of Knight's dependence upon his young contributor: "Knight is absolutely in our hands, and most desirous to gratify us all, and me in particular." George O. Trevelyan, *The Life and Letters of Lord Macaulay* (New York, 1909), 1:115.

8. Rosamond and Florence Davenport Hill, *The Recorder of Birmingham: A Memoir of Matthew Davenport Hill* (London, 1878), p. 67.

9. "The Raven: A Greek Tale" (1:349–52) and "The Black Chamber" (1:353–61), according to Gray's list only. In the magazine these are signed "A. F." for

"Archibald Frazer.'' They are not reprinted in David Masson's 1890 edition, *The Collected Writings of Thomas De Quincey,* nor are they mentioned in James Hogg's account of an interview that he had with Knight for the express purpose of ascertaining De Quincey's contributions to the magazine. *The Uncollected Writings of Thomas De Quincey,* ed. James Hogg (London, 1892):1:xiv–xv.

10. Most of the *Noctes Ambrosianae* of *Blackwood's Magazine* were set at Ambrose's tavern, Edinburgh; moreover, in August and September of 1819 the pseudonymous contributors had been shown at work and play in three lengthy accounts of fictional excursions into the Scottish countryside (*Blackwood's Magazine* 5:597–613, 627–719, 720–36).

11. See Knight, *Passages of a Working Life,* 1:334–36.

12. Picton, p. 361. Knight, *Passages of a Working Life,* 1:302.

13. For other reviews, see *Literary Gazette* * no. 333 (1823):366; "Periodical Literature," *The Literary Chronicle and Weekly Review* * no. 212 (1823):365; *Blackwood's Edinburgh Magazine* 14 (1823):487; 17 (1825):370; 18 (1825):508; *Noctes Ambrosianae,* rev. ed. (1863; reprint ed., New York, 1866), 1:361; *A History of Booksellers: The Old and the New* (London, 1873), p. 254.

Information Sources

BIBLIOGRAPHY

Coleridge, Derwent. "Memoir." In *The Poems of Winthrop Mackworth Praed.* Rev. ed. 2 vols. New York, 1885.

Curwen, Henry. *A History of Booksellers: The Old and the New.* London, 1873.

Gray, G. J. "*Knight's Quarterly Magazine.*" *Notes and Queries,* 6th ser. 4 (1881):261–63.

Hill, Rosamond, and Florence Davenport. *The Recorder of Birmingham: A Memoir of Matthew Davenport Hill; with Selections from His Correspondence.* London, 1878.

"Histories of the Publishing Houses. No. IV. The House of Charles Knight." *The Critic,* 18 May 1861, pp. 624–28.

Hogg, James, ed. *The Uncollected Writings of Thomas De Quincey.* 2 vols. London, 1890.

Hudson, Derek. *A Poet in Parliament: The Life of Winthrop Mackworth Praed, 1802–1839.* London, 1939.

Knight, Charles. *Passages of a Working Life During Half a Century: With a Prelude of Early Reminiscences.* 3 vols., 1864. Reprint. London, 1873.

Mackenzie, Robert Shelton, ed. *Noctes Ambrosianae.* Rev. ed., 5 vols., 1863. Reprint. New York, 1866.

Moultrie, John, *Poems.* London, 1838.

———, ed. *The Poetical Remains of William Sidney Walker . . . with a Memoir of the Author.* London, 1852.

Picton, J. A. "*Knight's Quarterly Magazine, 1823–4.*" *Notes and Queries,* 6th ser. 3 (1881):361–62.

Sadleir, Michael. *Bulwer and His Wife: A Panorama, 1803–1836.* London, 1933.

Trevelyan, George Otto. *The Life and Letters of Lord Macaulay.* 2 vols. New York, 1909.

Trevelyan, Lady. *Complete Works of Thomas Babington Macaulay.* 10 vols. New York, 1898.

INDEXES
>Table of contents for volume at beginning of each bound volume.

REPRINT EDITIONS
>Microform: English Literary Periodicals (UMI), reel 517.

LOCATION SOURCES

>*American*
>>Widely available.

>*British*
>>Widely available.

Publication History

MAGAZINE TITLE AND TITLE CHANGES
>*Knight's Quarterly Magazine,* June 1823–November 1824. *The Quarterly Magazine. New Series,* August 1825.

VOLUME AND ISSUE DATA
>Numbers 1–6, volumes 1–3, June 1823–November 1824; new series, August 1825 only.

FREQUENCY OF PUBLICATION
>Quarterly.

PUBLISHERS
>Numbers 1–6, volumes 1–3, June 1823–November 1824: Charles Knight, 7 Pall Mall East, London. New series, August 1825: Charles Knight, Pall Mall East, London/George B. Whittaker, Ave Maria Lane, London.

EDITOR
>Charles Knight, June 1823–November 1824, August 1825.

Douglas K. Morris

L

LADY'S MAGAZINE. See AAAJ

LEIGH HUNT'S LONDON JOURNAL

With *Leigh Hunt's London Journal* Hunt joined the journalistic movement begun in the late 1820s to reach an audience of readers with limited money, time, and literary sophistication. Charles Knight with his *Penny Magazine* (1832) and Robert and William Chambers with their *Edinburgh Journal* (*Chambers's Journal**) (1832) had proven that penny journalism could be as commercially profitable to its publishers as it was personally edifying to its readers. In size and variety of articles, the *London Journal* was an avowed imitator of *Chambers's Journal,* but with "a character a little more southern and literary" (no. 1:1). As *Chambers's Journal* was to provide working-class readers with "a meal of healthful, useful, and agreeable mental instruction,"[1] Hunt's enterprise was intended "to assist the enquiring, animate the struggling, and sympathize with all" (no. 1:1), particularly with those who sought knowledge and had little access to it. Typically, Hunt assumed here the role of his reader's intimate and teacher, but that he attempted this role among readers who were not of the middle class makes his *London Journal* a document of special interest.

As its name suggests, the writing of *Leigh Hunt's London Journal* was very much a one-person operation. Purposely shunning articles that might vex his readers (including political pieces and satire), Hunt envisioned his weekly as a miscellany of essays, criticism, and passages from and about books:

It is proposed, as the general plan of the Journal, but not without the power of change or modification, as circumstances may suggest, that it should consist of One Original Paper or Essay every week, from the pen of the Editor; of Matter combining entertainment with information, selected by him in the course of his reading, both old and new; of a weekly Abstract of some popular or otherwise interesting book, the spirit of which will be given *entire,* after the fashion of the excellent abridgments in *Johnstone's Edinburgh Magazine;* and, lastly, of a brief current notice of the Existing State of Poetry, Painting, and Music, and a general sprinkle of Notes, Verses, Miscellaneous Paragraphs, and other helps to pleasant and companionable perusal. [no. 1:1]

Within a few months of its commencement, Hunt reclaimed from advertisers the back page of his eight-page weekly in order to have more space for a variety of articles, which soon came to include occasional letters and contributions from readers and his messages to certain of them. Hunt's apparent effort was to make the *London Journal* a personal, useful exchange with readers "of all classes," including especially those readers who, for want of education and opportunity, had been deprived of "the pleasures of taste and scholarship" (no. 1:1).[2]

Hunt seldom failed to write an original essay as the leading article of each issue. At least twice he reprinted, with apology, articles he had published earlier in such publications as the *New Monthly Magazine.** Another time he offered as the leading article an essay on Horace by Egerton Webb, a young scholar and wit whom Hunt presented to his readers as one of a number of writers, including Keats and Shelley, whom he had introduced to the public and whose long article, "A Few Thoughts on Language," appeared serially in the *London Journal.* Of the many original essays Hunt wrote for this weekly were commentaries on literary works (including his important essay on "The Eve of St. Agnes") and a large number of personal essays ("Pleasure," "On a Pebble," "Spring," "Windows," "Breakfast in Summer," "A Pinch of Snuff"). Hunt republished a good selection of these essays, along with a few pieces originally published in other periodicals, as *The Seer; or Common-Places Refreshed* (1840–1841). A column, "The Week," was occasionally devoted to contemporary happenings in the fine arts, but more often it consisted of prose extracts and poems with notes celebrating anniversaries of eminent figures and the seasons. Extracts from Hunt's reading account for a good portion of each issue, whether under a specific column name or not. One column, "Romances of Real Life," a series "of those extraordinary real circumstances often found in the history of private individuals" (no. 1:5), provided Hunt with material for another book, *One Hundred Romances of Real Life* (1843). Among works Hunt abstracted for his readers were Mrs. Gore's novel, *The Hamiltons,* De Kock's novel, *Un Bon Enfant,* and Kerr's translation of Cuvier's *Theory of the Earth.* Though published and sold weekly, the *London Journal* was also sold in monthly numbers. In order to make those larger numbers uniform in size, Hunt wrote a series of supplements entitled "The Streets of the Metropolis," accounts of people and events associated with various London places. These articles also became a book: *The Town: Its Memorable Characters and Events* (1848). The death of Lamb occasioned the reprinting of a number of his essays in the *London Journal* as well as commemorative pieces by Hunt and others. Hazlitt's *Characters from Shakespeare* was reprinted serially in Hunt's weekly.

Perhaps the first published hint in the *London Journal* of the troubles that were to result in its early demise was the announcement in the issue for 18 June 1834 that the weekly, effective with this fourteenth issue, was in the hands of a new publisher. Though the *London Journal* was largely written by Hunt, he originally shared ownership of it with Thomas Littleton Holt. For reasons unknown, Henry Hooper bought the publication two months after it first appeared, and Hunt, no longer equal beneficiary of its profits, became its salaried writer.[3] A year later Hunt announced the "marriage" of the *London Journal* and the *Printing Machine,* a critical review of current writing established for the benefit of working-class readers by Charles Knight in early 1834. Knight assumed direction of the two periodicals.[4] From June until December 1835 both publications appeared, reduced but otherwise unchanged, as two separate parts of *Leigh Hunt's London Journal and the Printing Machine*. The *London Journal* had appeared on Wednesdays, in nostalgic deference to the *Indicator** and the *Tatler** and to Lamb's homage to the mid-week appearance of the former. The *London Journal and the Printing Machine* appeared on Saturdays—as the *Printing Machine* had done—a more suitable publication day, as Hunt acknowledged, for cheap periodicals and their worker-readers. At the end of 1835, abruptly and without warning, publication of the mechanically merged weeklies ceased altogether. In a letter to Thomas Weller written a year later, Hunt alluded to problems in the commercial marriage and explained why he had not warned his readers of its dissolution through the demise of both parties: "The *London Journal* was discontinued with an abruptness almost as surprising to me as to you, owing to some mysteries of partnership which I cannot explain; and I could not take leave of my readers, because I hoped, *beyond* the last moment, to be able to carry it on, in which hope, owing to the shortness of the time, I was unfortunately disappointed."[5]

In December 1850 what Hunt called "the revival, in another form" of *Leigh Hunt's London Journal* appeared under the name *Leigh Hunt's Journal: A Miscellany for the Cultivation of the Memorable, the Progressive, and the Beautiful*.[6] It lasted for only seventeen weekly numbers and disappeared as abruptly as its predecessor had, "partly, perhaps, from want of accordance with other pens concerned; but chiefly from the smallness of the means which the proposers had thought fit for its establishment."[7] Hunt had hoped to engage prominent writers as contributors, including two whom he apparently failed to persuade to write for the *Journal,* Mrs. Gaskell and Tennyson. Hunt began his weekly with an article strongly recommending that Tennyson be named laureate because he possessed, among living poets, the greatest imaginative power. The *Journal* did attract Carlyle, who contributed "Two Hundred and Fifty Years Ago," and Landor, who offered several "poemetti." Other writers whose work appeared in the *Journal* include William Allington, John Stores Smith, Parson Frank, Charles Ollier (publisher of some early works of Hunt, Keats, Shelley, and Lamb), and R. H. Horne (editor of the *Monthly Repository* and correspondent of Elizabeth Barrett Browning). In spite of its publication of articles and stories by many other writers, the *Journal* calls to mind the *London Journal,* and it does so chiefly through its inclusion of extracts from various writings and a number of essays and articles by Hunt, including a continuation from the *London Journal* of "The Town," and a serialization of his play, *Lovers' Arrangements.*

Both the *London Journal* and the *Journal* were plagued with operational difficulties; additionally, neither enjoyed the public favor their success depended on. Many years later Hunt offered an explanation for the failure of the *London Journal* that suggests he came to consider the endeavor ill-founded, its method ill-conceived: "The note which it struck was of too aesthetical a nature for cheap readers in those days."[8] Unfortunately for Hunt, "cheap readers" seem to have been even less appreciative of his *Journal* than of his *London Journal.*

Notes

1. "The Editor's Address to His Readers," *Chambers's Edinburgh Journal* no. 1 (1832):1.

2. For an indication of the tone of condescension Hunt on occasion permitted himself as intimate and teacher of heretofore neglected readers, see his leading article, "Letters to Such of the Lovers of Knowledge as Have Not Had a Classical Education" (no. 3:17).

3. Louis Landré, *Leigh Hunt (1784–1859): Contribution à l'histoire du Romantisme Anglais* (Paris, 1936), 1:204, 218–21.

4. Ibid., p. 221.

5. Leigh Hunt, *Correspondence,* ed. Thornton Hunt (London, 1862), 1:311.

6. Leigh Hunt, *Autobiography,* ed. Roger Ingpen (London, 1903), 2:243.

7. Ibid., 2:244. Also see "Editor's Address to the Reader," *Leigh Hunt's Journal* no. 1 (1850):1, for Hunt's statement of expectation that difficulties of this kind would not develop.

8. Leigh Hunt, *Autobiography,* 2:213.

Information Sources

BIBLIOGRAPHY

Chambers, William. *Memoir of Robert Chambers with Autobiographic Reminiscences.* New York, 1872.

Cross, Launcelot. *Characteristics of Leigh Hunt, as Exhibited in that Typical Literary Periodical, "Leigh Hunt's London Journal" (1834–35).* London, 1878.

Curwen, Henry. *A History of Booksellers, Old and New.* London, 1873.

Hunt, Leigh. *Autobiography.* Edited by Roger Ingpen. 2 vols. London, 1903.

———. *Correspondence.* Edited by Thornton Hunt. 2 vols. London, 1862.

Landré, Louis. *Leigh Hunt (1784–1859): Contribution à l'histoire du Romantisme Anglais.* 2 vols. Paris, 1936.

Scott, George Dumas. *Studies toward a Biography of Leigh Hunt*. Ph.D. dissertation, Harvard University, 1928.

INDEXES

Numbers 1–40 indexed at end of volume. Numbers 41–91 indexed by alphabetical list of articles.

REPRINT EDITIONS

Microform: Early British Periodicals (UMI), reels 191–192.

LOCATION SOURCES

American

Widely available.

British

Complete runs: Bodleian Library; British Museum; Cambridge University Library; Glasgow University Library; Guildhall Library; Manchester Public Library; Southport Public Library; University College (London) Library; University of Bristol Library.

Partial runs: Birkenhead Public Library; Birmingham Public Library; Edinburgh Public Library; Leeds Public Library; London University Library.

Publication History

MAGAZINE TITLE AND TITLE CHANGES

Leigh Hunt's London Journal, 2 April 1834–27 May 1835. *Leigh Hunt's London Journal and the Printing Machine*, 6 June–31 December 1835. (The 31 December 1835 issue, though titled *Leigh Hunt's London Journal and the Printing Machine*, consists only of the *Printing Machine*.) *Leigh Hunt's Journal: A Miscellany for the Cultivation of the Memorable, the Progressive, and the Beautiful*, 7 December 1850–29 March 1851.

VOLUME AND ISSUE DATA

Numbers 1–61, 2 April 1834–27 May 1835; numbers 62–91 (plus unnumbered 31 December 1835 issue), 6 June–31 December 1835; new numbers 1–17, 7 December 1850–29 March 1851.

FREQUENCY OF PUBLICATION

Weekly.

PUBLISHERS

2 April–11 June, 1834: Sparrow and Co., *Bell's Weekly Magazine* Office, 11 Crane Court, Fleet Street, London. 18 June 1834–27 May 1835: H. Hooper, 18 Pall Mall East, London. 6 June–31 December 1835, and 7 December 1850–29 March 1851: Charles Knight, 22 Ludgate St., London.

EDITORS

Leigh Hunt.

For the *Printing Machine:* Leigh Hunt, Charles Knight.

Carol de Saint Victor

LIBERAL, THE

The idea was Byron's. The nervous cultivation of the idea was Shelley's. The sweaty[1] implementation of the idea was Leigh Hunt's. The early impact of the fruit of the idea was sensational and the expiration of the idea was a relief to everybody connected with it. Simplistically encapsulated, so runs the brief but turbulent history of what one commentator calls the "periodical of the highest literary quality of the first quarter of the nineteenth century."[2] Appearing in four issues between October 1822 and July 1823, the *Liberal* is of undisputed historical significance. Modern appraisal might more cautiously suggest that the journal was important without being truly or at least uniformly distinguished—that it was, like the careers of its major participants, an event, a spectacle which from Italy set the London literary scene boiling and seething first in expectation of it, then over its contents, and briefly in its wake.[3] To be sure, it numbers among its 765 pages of text several acknowledged masterworks: Byron's "The Vision of Judgment," Hazlitt's "My First Acquaintance With Poets," and Shelley's translation from *Faust*, "May-day Night."[4] Just behind these in literary merit one might rank Byron's translation from Pulci, "Morgante Maggiore," his *Heaven and Earth,* Shelley's "Song, Written for An Indian Air" (afterward, "Lines To An Indian Air"), and two more of Hazlitt's essays. But thereafter comes a fairly sharp falling-off to what might be termed high-level mediocrity, including Leigh Hunt's four "Letters From Abroad," assorted translations, and some original prose and verse, perhaps the best of which is "Mahmoud"; Byron's "The Blues"; a tale and two essays by Mary Shelley; and mildly diverting prose by Thomas Jefferson Hogg, Charles Armitage Brown, and Horace Smith.[5] In addition are a dozen or so admittedly "minor pieces"—translations, dialogues, epigrams—forgettable to all but the specialists. In thus judging *Liberal* as qualitatively uneven, one should be mindful of Byron's rejoinder to his own publisher John Murray respecting *Don Juan:*

> You say the *one half* is very good—you are *wrong;* for if it were, it would be the finest poem in existence . . . if *one half* of the two new Cantos be good in your opinion—what the devil would you have more?—no—no—no poetry is *generally* good—only by fits & starts—& you are lucky to get a sparkle here & there—you might as well want a Midnight *all stars*—as rhyme all perfect."[6]

The *Liberal* does offer an abundance of sparkles, but it is a wonder that we have anything. Byron's enthusiasm for the enterprise, originally proposed by letter to Thomas Moore on Christmas Day 1820 and revived in conversations with Shelley during their Ravenna visit in August 1821, considerably waned between Shelley's transmission of the proposal to Leigh Hunt on 30 August and Hunt's arrival with his wife, Marianne, and six small children at Byron's Palazzo Lafranchi in Pisa on 3 July 1822. The chief purpose of Hunt's voyage was to undertake editorship of the projected journal. Occupied during the intervening months with work on "The Vision of Judgment," distracted by two cumbersome moves, tense relations with Shelley, and the disappointing reception of his *Sardanapalus* volume, Byron had little time or interest for fleshing out his original idea with specific plans for submission to the arriving editor. Although not dissuaded from continuing his participation, he must also have been influenced in his wavering attitude toward the project by the clamorous and somewhat hysterical protests of London intimates.[7] They pled with him to eschew association with one so likely to tarnish his reputation and jeopardize his future as Leigh Hunt. Nor was the press silent. While the *Examiner** alone supported, most other journalistic outlets fulminated against or remained non-commital about the Pisan alliance—even those periodicals of moderate or radical cast from which encouragement or at least tolerance might have been expected. From the Tory *Blackwood's Edinburgh Magazine** came bemused but contemptuous blast after blast, from February onward, with such unusual regularity that anxiety over the potential influence of the new journal has been suspected as a motive.[8] Other, less secure conservative spokesmen felt the moral and political threat more keenly, and did not hesitate to condemn the "academy of blasphemy" and "poetical school of immorality and profaneness" before it had published a word.[9] It was enough to know what harm Shelley, Hunt, and particularly Byron had already wrought by way of the printed page.

Into this inhospitable climate the *Liberal* was launched, and the situation swiftly and disastrously worsened. A mere six days after welcoming Hunt at Leghorn, Shelley drowned, thus striking the death knell of the project on the eve of its birth. With the guiding intelligence, philosophical shaping, and tempering influence of Shelley (who, however, had himself expressed doubts about the feasibility of the project even while nurturing it), the journal might have survived; without him, given the politically sympathetic but otherwise wildly incompatible Hunt and Byron, and their financial, domestic, and literary difficulties, it scarcely stood a chance.

Because of the vilification to which the unborn journal had been subjected by the British conservative press, Hunt felt "forced to be prefatory" in the first number. There he answered charges against the irreligion, immorality, and illegitimacy of the periodical, and urged that its name (which was Byron's suggestion) "be taken in its largest acceptation, old as well as new,—but always in the same spirit of admiring and assisting, rather than of professing" liberalism. He also sought to define aims and editorial policy. "The object of our work is not political," except insofar as "all writing now-a-days must involve something to that effect." As "advocates of every species of liberal knowledge," contributors would provide "liberalities in the shape of Poetry, Essays, Tales, Translations, and other amenities, of which kings themselves may read and profit, if they are not afraid of seeing their own faces in every species of inkstand." "Want of liberality in the assailants" of the journal and its friends, said Hunt, would determine the "force of our answers"; and, supported by the "Spirits" of liberal literary figures from Chaucer through Milton, Hunt vowed to champion man as a "thing of hope and freedom . . . a being progressive, instead of a creeping creature retrograde." A ringing and heady last paragraph thus summarizes: "Wherever . . . we see the mind of man exhibiting powers of its own, and at the same time helping to carry on the best interests of human nature . . . there we recognize the demi-gods of liberal worship." Modern commentators state that "the controlled beat of the preface represents Hunt at his best" and, alternatively, that the piece "was written in Leigh Hunt's most cocky and offensive vein."[10] Whatever the final verdict in that connection, more important is Hunt's vision of a journal which clothed its political points in literature of the first rank and of wide appeal. Beyond that, he "was clearly attempting to reconcile a political conception of liberalism with one that embraced intellectual freedom, but it seems that in his own mind his ardor for the former occasionally interfered with his full acceptance of the latter."[11] Nevertheless, relatively few items in the four issues exhibit an obvious or, without wrenching, even covert political slant, though those which do are some of the most memorable. The likelihood is that Hunt necessarily and in the strict sense abandoned, without betraying, the aims articulated in his preface in order to fill his pages.

Published on 15 October 1822 by John Hunt, Leigh's older brother, and marketed for five shillings, the first number of the *Liberal* came under almost instant fire from the press garrisons which had for months stood by, artillery loaded, aimed, and cocked. First to score were the newspapers, to be followed by the journals in November and December, but both media, with few exceptions, took the same line. Reviews in the *New European Magazine*,* the *Literary Speculum*,* the *Council of Ten*, the *Edinburgh Review*,* *La Belle Assemblée*,* the *Courier*, and the mighty *Blackwood's* were representative in characterizing the new journal as "evil and impotent," "imbecilic," an "atrocity," "obscene," "pestilential," "profligate," "fiendish," "depraved," "monstrous," "disgusting," "despicable," "indecent," rife with "blasphemy," "impurity," "wickedness," "profaneness," "lewdness," "nonsense," and, anticlimactically, "bad taste."[12] Under so heavy a barrage, the rare faint praise for Hunt's "Letter" and for Shelley's "May-day Night" was barely audible, though one newspaper, the *British Luminary and Weekly Intelligencer,* and one journal, Galignani's *Paris Monthly Review,* joined the *Examiner* in favorably noticing the new publication. The primary target of the conservatives was predictably Byron's "The Vision of Judgment," censured as morally horrific and artistically bankrupt, but Hunt himself and Byron's lamentable association with him were also the objects of savage pummelling. Quarrels with the title preoccupied yet other reviewers. Three independent works—critiques, parodies, and "antidotes" to the journal—appearing in late 1822 and early 1823 supply additional evidence of public outrage over the *Liberal*'s first number.[13]

This hostile and dismaying reception followed two other developments which had already endangered the enterprise and accelerated the deterioration of the relationship between Hunt and Byron. Murray, at Byron's request delivering "The Vision of Judgment" to John Hunt for publication in the *Liberal,* neglected to provide either the corrected proof copy or the essential "Preface," in the latter of which the poet, aware of "actionable passages" in his verses, had taken some pains to specify Southey, not the king, as the principal object of the satire.[14] Furthermore, because Leigh Hunt so earnestly desired the poem for his first number, he forfeited editor's prerogative (for Byron had no copy in Italy) and saw the poem only when the issue containing it arrived in Genoa in early November. Sagacious as he was in such matters, Hunt would undoubtedly have advised the toning down or deletion of politically explosive passages had he seen the manuscript. Second, on 9 October, Byron had written a letter to Murray from Genoa that was condescending toward the Hunt family and distorted his own participation in the journal, broadly hinting at readiness to give up the venture, and, "by some species of hallucination," conceiving himself "as a martyr to the enterprise."[15] The effect of the first of these developments was legally to imperil the *Liberal,* and the effect of the second was to render a split between Byron and Hunt almost inevitable, for Murray seized the letter as a weapon that might—and did—expedite the separation he had long advocated. Leaking its contents to associates, Murray apparently made certain that rumors, at least, of its more stinging parts found their way through John Hunt and his son Henry to Leigh, who graciously but firmly confronted the poet with them. Paradoxically, Leigh Hunt hoped, for the sake of the journal, to smooth away the incident with minimum public notice. At the same time, for the sake of his dignity, he wanted from Byron a public retraction, and sought Mary Shelley's active support to get it. But Leigh Hunt was not content with Byron's indirect, half-hearted, and privately expressed regrets. And Byron recognized that by "injudicious rudeness" English friends had cemented "a sort of connection which [Hunt] strove to prevent."[16]

Work was proceeding, nevertheless, on the second number, when word reached Genoa on 23 December that John Hunt had been indicted on charges of "contriving and intending to injure, defame, disgrace, and villify, the memory, reputation, and character of his late Majesty King George the Third" and furthermore of suggesting that His Majesty was "a person of mean and avaricious disposition," "an enemy to the liberties of his people and of other nations," and "a person of bad and vicious character."[17] Byron promptly offered to return to England and stand in John Hunt's place, but did not persist against the latter's objection. When the second edition of the first number of the *Liberal* appeared on 1 January 1823, it contained both John Hunt's "Advertisement" explaining the earlier omission of the "Preface" to "The Vision of Judgment," and now the "Preface" itself, but too late to stay or reverse the litigation. A guilty verdict against John Hunt was brought in on 15 January 1824.

Other problems persisted throughout the venture. Although the first number had enjoyed reasonably brisk sales (4,050 of 7,000 copies by February 1823 and a profit of 377 pounds, 16 shillings, of which Leigh Hunt received 291 pounds, 15 shillings),[18] because it had been largely discredited as a threat to conservative thought, less notice was accorded the second number (also published New Year's Day 1823). Hostility was milder (among exceptions were *John Bull,** the *British Critic,** the *Monthly Censor,** the *Gentleman's Magazine** [see *AAAJ*]), and a few reviewers even praised parts of the issue, particularly Byron's *Heaven and Earth. Blackwood's,* however, was moved to respond with some nastiness to Hazlitt's "On the Scotch Character." But negative reception was less stimulating to sales than previously, so that by June 3,300 of 6,000 copies remained, and John Hunt showed a second number deficit of more than fifty-eight pounds. Financial considerations, then, combined with Byron's flagging interest and reluctance to provide either supporting funds or substantial copy, constituted yet another blow to the tottering project. The poet now plainly wished to have done with it, but how to accomplish the break without additional insult, offense, or the appearance of irresponsibility escaped him. Greece, of course, eventually offered a way. Meanwhile, Leigh Hunt, anticipating failure if Byron withdrew, on 7 April 1823 wrote accusingly to the poet: "If it had failed, [that] is no doubt partly owing to its having contained, from your pen, *none* but articles of a certain character, however meritorious in themselves, and to a certain want of super-induced cordiality towards it on your part, which you unfortunately allowed to escape to the public."[19] The statement is not without truth.

The third number appeared on 26 April (with an announcement of the fourth for 1 July) to generally indifferent notices. Byron's "The Blues" was observed to be inferior. Reviewers split on the merits of Hogg's and Hazlitt's contributions, and others lamented the preponderance of Hunt and the scarcity of Byron (nine pieces to one). Later, the only monthlies to heed the issue were the *Edinburgh Magazine,** which liked Hazlitt's "My First Acquaintance With Poets," and *Blackwood's,* which applauded what it believed to be Byron's separation from the periodical. By 30 July, the publication date of the fourth, shorter and final number, the "sparkles" of which were Byron's Pulci translation, Hunt's "Mahmoud," and two Hazlitt essays, Byron was seven days into his Greek adventure and Hunt five issues into his new publishing enterprise, the *Literary Examiner.** Notices were slight. But the *Examiner's* 31 August official announcement of the demise of the *Liberal* excited new interest, and the *Gentleman's Magazine,* the *British Critic, Blackwood's,* and *John Bull,* among others, rushed to disinter and eviscerate the already mangled corpse, sometimes in vitriolic, sometimes in jocular terms, but altogether, like the surviving principals involved in its creation and perpetuation, with relief that the *Liberal* was finished.

Notes

1. Byron's apt descriptive. See his letter to Thomas Moore, 27 August 1822, in *Byron's Letters and Journals,* ed. Leslie A. Marchand (Cambridge, Mass., 1979), 9:197.

2. Walter Graham, *English Literary Periodicals* (New York, 1930), p. 286.

3. Newman Ivy White, *Shelley,* 2 vols. (London, 1947), who called the *Liberal* a publication of "four excellent issues" (2:387). William H. Marshall notes White's description in *Byron, Shelley, Hunt and The Liberal* (Philadelphia, 1960), p. 211n, and

comes close to echoing his estimate (pp. 212–13). To Marshall's meticulously detailed and scrupulously documented definitive study of the *Liberal,* the following account is heavily and gratefully indebted.

4. The *Liberal* would certainly have become an even weightier journal, qualitatively, had it carried, as it was scheduled to carry in its second and again in its third number, Shelley's "Defence of Poetry." Why it did not remains a mystery. Also intended for the *Liberal* but withdrawn at the author's request and published separately by John Hunt were Byron's "The Island" and "The Age of Bronze."

5. Smith's essay, "A Sunday's Fête At St. Cloud," in the third number was long thought (even by Hunt, because of a comment by his brother) to be Peter George Patmore's. See Edmund Blunden, *Leigh Hunt and His Circle* (New York, 1930), p. 181. It should here be mentioned that no articles in the *Liberal* were signed except, occasionally, pseudonymously.

6. 23 April 1820. Marchand, 7:83–84.

7. Principally, Thomas Moore, John Cam Hobhouse, John Murray, and Douglas Kinnaird. See Hazlitt's "On Jealousy and Spleen of Part," in *The Complete Works of William Hazlitt,* ed. P. P. Howe, 21 vols. (London, 1930–1934), 12:378–81.

8. See Marshall, p. 48.

9. [John Watkins], *Memoirs, Historical and Critical, of the Right Honourable Lord Byron, with Anecdotes of Some of His Contemporaries* (London, 1822), pp. 408–14. Quoted in Marshall, p. 49.

10. Cf. James R. Thompson, *Leigh Hunt* (Boston, 1977), p. 84; Graham, p. 287.

11. Marshall, p. 84.

12. Marshall reproduces selections from reviews of this and subsequent numbers of the *Liberal,* pp. 97 *passim.* The *Quarterly Review* * was curiously silent, possibly, suggests Marshall, at John Murray's request (p. 116).

13. *A Critique on "The Liberal,"* the *Liberal* and the *London Liberal.* Marshall reprints the *Illiberal* (pp. 217–27) and extracts from the *London Liberal* (pp. 228–37).

14. Byron to Douglas Kinnaird, 23 December 1822, in Marchand, 10:66.

15. Clemet Tyson Goode, *Byron as Critic* (Weimar, 1923), p. 172. For the letter, see Marchand, 10:13.

16. Byron to Kinnaird, 10 October 1822, in Marchand, 10:65.

17. From the *Examiner* no. 780 (5 January 1823):5–6. Quoted in Marshall, pp. 126–27.

18. Contributors to the first number were not compensated. For items in the second, authors were paid, according to Marshall's estimate, approximately a pound a page (p. 148). Financial details about the third and fourth numbers are sketchy, but Marshall assumes that contributors continued to be paid. These numbers also showed a tiny profit (p. 178), but by 1 January 1824 Leigh's indebtedness to his brother for the *Liberal* venture, including responsibility for unsold copies, had climbed to 1790 pounds, 19 shillings, ten pence (see pp. 203–5).

19. Blunden, pp. 183–84.

Information Sources

BIBLIOGRAPHY
Blunden, Edmund. *Leigh Hunt and His Circle.* New York, 1930.
Bostetter, Edward E. "The New Romantic Criticism." *Sewanee Review* 69 (1961):490–500.

Gates, Payson G. "A Leigh Hunt-Bryon Letter." *Keats-Shelley Journal* 2 (1953):11–18.

Goode, Clemet Tyson. *Byron As Critic*. Weimar, 1927.

Graham, Walter. *English Literary Periodicals*. New York, 1930.

Hartley, Robert A., ed. *Keats, Shelley, Bryon, Hunt and Their Circles: A Bibliography: July 1, 1962–December 31, 1974*. Lincoln, Nebr., 1978.

Hazlitt, William. *The Complete Works of William Hazlitt*. Edited by P. P. Howe. 21 vols. London, 1930–1934.

Madden, Lionel, and Diana Dixon. *The Nineteenth-Century Periodical Press in Britain: A Bibliography of Modern Studies, 1901–1971*. New York, 1976.

Marchand, Leslie A. *Byron: A Biography*. 3 vols. New York, 1957.

———. "John Hunt as Bryon's Publisher." *Keats-Shelley Journal* 8 (1959):119–32.

———, ed. *Byron's Letters and Journals*. Vols. 9–10. Cambridge, Mass., 1979–1980.

Marshall, William H. *Byron, Shelley, Hunt and the "Liberal."* Philadelphia, 1960.

Miller, Barnette. *Leigh Hunt's Relations With Byron, Shelley and Keats*. New York, 1910.

Pickering, L. P., ed. *Lord Byron, Leigh Hunt and the "Liberal."* London, 1925.

Reiman, Donald H., ed. and intro. *The Romantics Reviewed, 1793–1830: A Collection in Depth of Periodical Reviews of the English Romantic Writers*. New York, 1976.

Shelley, Percy Bysshe. *The Complete Works of Percy Bysshe Shelley*. Edited by Roger Ingpen and Walter E. Peck. 10 vols. London, 1926–1930.

Thompson, James R. *Leigh Hunt*. Boston, 1977.

Tillett, Nettie S. "The Unholy Alliance of Pisa—A Literary Episode." *South Atlantic Quarterly* 28 (1929):27–44.

Ward, William S. *British Periodicals and Newspapers, 1789–1832: A Bibliography of Secondary Sources*. Lexington, Ky., 1972.

White, Newman Ivy. *Shelley*. 2 vols. London, 1947.

White, Robert B., Jr. *The English Literary Journal to 1900: A Guide to Information Sources*. Detroit, 1977.

INDEXES
Lists of contents at beginning of bound volumes.

REPRINT EDITIONS
Microform: Early British Periodicals (UMI), reel 192.

LOCATION SOURCES
American
Widely available.
British
Widely available.

Publication History

MAGAZINE TITLE AND TITLE CHANGES
The Liberal. Verse and Prose from the South.

VOLUME AND ISSUE DATA
Numbers 1–4, October 1822–July 1823. (Numbers 1–2 and 3–4 separately bound as volumes 1 and 2 following original publication.)

FREQUENCY OF PUBLICATION
  15 October 1822 (2d ed., 1 January 1823); 1 January 1823; 26 April 1823; 30 July 1823.
PUBLISHER
  John Hunt, 22 Old Bond Street, London.
EDITOR
  Leigh Hunt.

W. Paul Elledge

LITERARY AND STATISTICAL MAGAZINE FOR SCOTLAND, THE

The formidable title of the quarterly *Literary and Statistical Magazine for Scotland* only begins to suggest the wide range of its interests. The contents, set out in departments, began with "Original Communications" (long essay-letters on various subjects) followed by "Extracts from Recent Publications" and then "Reviews." The next section, entitled "Statistics," delivered on the promise in the periodical's title; it contained statistics on various Scottish parishes—population, occupations, geography, and so on. "Scientific Information" followed, then "Poetry," and finally an unusual "Academical Intelligence," a collection of vital statistics from "various seminaries of education"— in fact from universities around the world. The customary catalogue of new publications and notes to correspondents brought each issue to a close. This was indeed an impressive magazine with extraordinary ambitions.

The poetry section contained both excerpts from other publications and original contributions. But what began as a sizeable department started to dwindle and was reduced to smaller print in volume 4. This movement was manifesting, not the problems of the magazine's wide ambitions, but rather the more general movement within the magazine toward religion.

The *Literary and Statistical Magazine* was in fact metamorphosing in volume 4 into the *Scottish Episcopal Review and Magazine*. The process is curious and perhaps unexampled in the history of periodicals, perhaps indicating some struggle within the magazine itself. Volume 4 saw a change from double to single column as if some more fundamental change had occurred. All issues of volume 4, however, were still entitled the *Literary and Statistical Magazine,* and yet the title page for the volume carries the changed title, and volume 2 of the *Scottish Episcopal Review and Magazine* begins with the fifth issue, as if the first four numbers of the previous volume preceded it regardless of the titles and numbers given on the issues. No announcement of the changes appeared.

The *Literary and Statistical Magazine* began as a secular journal. One contribution to volume 1 was rejected as "more suited for a religious Magazine" (1:336). But the *Scottish Episcopal Review and Magazine* was "in its object chiefly theological" (3:630), as the new title indicates. And yet, the editor continued, general science and literature were not considered inconsistent with that object.

By the third volume, nevertheless, the departments were mostly dropped and replaced by letter-essays on religious subjects and a few reviews. Apologies occasionally appeared promising the return of one or another department. The "Academic Intelligence" was, moreover, replaced in volume 3 of the new magazine with a "Quarterly Register of Religious and Ecclesiastical Intelligence." The change is perhaps likewise evident in the change of mottoes: *Simul et jucunda et idonea dicere vitae* (Horace's *Ars Poetica,* 334: "At the same time both pleasing and useful") was changed to the more solemn *Hic patet ingeniis campus: certusque merento / Stat favor* of Claudian's *Panegyric on the Consulship of Fl. Manlius Theodorus,* ll. 262–63: "[Here] the field of glory is open to the talented, and the man of merit is certain of reward."

The selection of an editor "for some time" for the *Scottish Episcopal Magazine and Review* also points toward the new religious disposition; he was Michael Russell, later Episcopal Bishop of Glasgow and Galloway (and previously connected with the *British Critic**).[1] The new title also suggests the theological alignment, the moderate High English party. There is much discussion of the Scottish Episcopal Church in the "Notes to Correspondents," and the second volume carried the long "Historical Outline of the Episcopal Church of Scotland" in two issues.[2] The religious views were temperate on the whole, although the magazine was distinctly opposed to the Evangelicals (3:478).

Volume 2 of the *Scottish Episcopal Magazine and Review* increased from the 112-page issues that had obtained under both titles to 160 pages, and the price was raised to three shillings, six pence. In the same volume we are told, "We steadily exclude politics" (2:630), and in fact there had never been much of a political nature in the magazine to give it more appeal. In the third volume there is a reference to "our sober pages" (3:480), as indeed they had become. The end of that volume saw the end of the magazine.

Notes

1. William Walker, *Three Churchmen* (Edinburgh, 1893), p. 42; *The Gentleman's Magazine,* n.s. 29 (1848):552.
2. Walker, p. 43, claims that the *Scottish Episcopal Review and Magazine* was not really actively interested in the Episcopal Church, but the evidence would indicate otherwise.

Information Sources

BIBLIOGRAPHY
The Gentleman's Magazine, n.s. 29 (1848):551–52 (obituary of Michael Russell).
Walker, William. *Three Churchmen.* Edinburgh, 1893.
INDEXES
Each volume indexed.
REPRINT EDITIONS
None.

LOCATION SOURCES

American

Complete run: Yale University Library.

Partial runs: Boston Public Library; Dickinson College Library; Trinity College Library.

British

Complete runs: British Museum; Mitchell Library (Glasgow); National Library of Ireland; National Library of Scotland; St. Andrews University Library.

Partial runs: Durham University Library; Edinburgh University Library: New College (Edinburgh) Library.

Publication History

MAGAZINE TITLE AND TITLE CHANGES

The Literary and Statistical Magazine for Scotland, 1817–1820. *The Scottish Episcopal Review and Magazine,* 1820–1822.

VOLUME AND ISSUE DATA

Volumes 1–4, 1817–1820 (volume 4 is also volume 1 of the new series); new series, volumes 1–3, 1820–1822.

FREQUENCY OF PUBLICATION

Quarterly.

PUBLISHERS

1817–1820: Skelly & Co., 52 Prince's Street, Edinburgh. 1820–1822: Macredie, Skelly, & Co., 34 Prince's Street, Edinburgh/F. C. & J. Rivington, T. & G. Underwood, London.

EDITORS

Unknown. (Michael Russell, "for some time" was editor of the *Scottish Episcopal Review and Magazine.*)

John O. Hayden

LITERARY CHRONICLE AND WEEKLY REVIEW, THE

An important journalistic development of the Regency period was the rise of hebdomadal book reviews like the *Literary Chronicle and Weekly Review,* which became one of the leading competitors during its decade of publication. Issued on Saturdays from May 1819 to July 1828, its sixteen quarto pages attempted to keep pace with the ever-burgeoning output of the publishers. Despite the sometimes contemptuous regard of established periodicals and despite the superior reputation of the *Literary Gazette* * among these weeklies, the *Literary Chronicle* was a proud and determined rival.

The "Address to the Public" of the first issue for 22 May 1819 offered the readers a low price that would place the *Chronicle* "within the reach of all classes of society." As a "leading feature" there would be "an Analytical Review of every new work of value or interest, as soon as published" which would "differ widely from its contemporaries" in *not* taking a title of a new book as a pretext for "long disquisitions" on other topics or for a splenetic attack on the author's "political opinions or private errors." The *Literary Chronicle* proposed, on the other hand, a presentation of "such an abstract as will, in some measure, enable [readers] to form their own opinion of the merits of the work under consideration." To these principles of economy, immediacy, and objectivity the periodical added its intention to be truly a miscellany and a chronicle by giving "a faithful register of every novelty in Literature, Philosophy, the Fine and Useful Arts, History, the Drama, &c." Throughout its ten volumes the *Literary Chronicle* remained remarkably true to its objectives, although it was necessary to raise the price of the stamped edition to cover postal expenses, and although a cautious conservatism can sometimes be detected in its pages. Moreover, the journal prided itself on its independence from publishers—in being "a Review of Books, but *not* a Bookseller's Review" (no. 33:1). The "Address to the Public" became an annual observance, with the first page of each new volume reiterating the essence of the statement of May 1819.

Between 1819 and July 1828 a succession of three editors conducted the periodical under two titles. During the first six years the editor was Thomas Byerley, whose literary engagements were numerous.[1] At the same time that he was conducting the *Literary Chronicle,* he edited the *Mirror of Literature, Amusement, and Instruction* * from 1823 to 1826, collaborated in the *Percy Anecdotes,* and assisted Dr. Tilloch in editing the *Star,* an evening newspaper. Upon Byerley's death in July 1826 he was succeeded by John Watson Dalby, whose poetical contributions had appeared in the pages of the *Chronicle* for many years, even before the publication of his *Poems* of 1822. Although little is known of Dalby's circumstances and activity during this period, he subsequently became an intimate of Leigh Hunt and survived the *Literary Chronicle* for half a century. At the beginning of May 1828 the editorship and part of the proprietorship passed to Frederick Denison Maurice until the merger (three months later) with James Silk Buckingham's *Athenaeum,* * which from 6 August 1828 (no. 41) through 30 December 1829 (no. 114) was entitled the *Athenaeum and Literary Chronicle.*[2]

Before the merger the *Literary Chronicle* had undergone variations in title, though more for practical considerations than for substantive differences. Its first fifty-eight numbers (through 24 June 1820) had appeared only under the title of the *Literary Chronicle and Weekly Review* at a cost of six pence. For the edition printed for city readers, this title was maintained to the end, but "in consequence of the wishes often expressed by many friends in the country, a stamped edition of the *Literary Chronicle,* . . . entitled the *Country Literary Chronicle,*" was begun with number 59 for 1 July 1820 at a price of ten pence per copy. The four pence surcharge allowed the proprietors to deliver the stamped edition directly to country readers without taxing city subscribers with an unfair postal expense. (At the outset readers received a solemn promise that there would be no rise in price [no. 2:32].) Beyond this practical advantage, the alternative title made very little difference in the content of the *Chronicle;*

indeed, the confusion caused by publishing the same copy under two titles for as many groups of readers eventually led to the discontinuation of the *Country Literary Chronicle* after number 260 for 8 May 1824. In number 261 the editor advised new subscribers "desiring our papers by post" to order *"the stamped edition* of the Literary Chronicle" (p. 318).

These shifts of editor and title scarcely affected the overall composition of the *Literary Chronicle,* which maintained a remarkable consistency of format from 1819 to 1828. Several departments that appeared in the first month were published weekly almost to the end: "Review of New Books," "Original Correspondence," "Literary and Scientific Intelligence," "The Bee," "The Drama," and "Fine Arts." To these may be added headings that appeared intermittently throughout most of the life of the *Chronicle,* such as "Biography" and "Foreign Literature." The department titles suggest the periodical's endeavor to be a chronicle and a miscellany, to record and evaluate the most recent developments in literature, science, the theater, and exhibitions of art. An almost infinite range of interests was possible in "Original Correspondence," which contained full-length articles and essays on a wide diversity of topics, and in "The Bee," which served as a repository of curious facts, anecdotes, and brief extracts from other sources.[3] The collection of such trivia was, of course, Byerley's forte, as is evident in his editing the twopenny *Mirror of Literature, Amusement, and Instruction,* in the collection entitled *Relics of Literature,* and in his collaboration with Joseph Clinton Robertson in the *Percy Anecdotes.*[4]

The first New Year's "Address" under Dalby's direction indicated his intention to maintain the original plan of Byerley's *Chronicle:* "With the present number, a new series of the *Literary Chronicle* may be considered as commencing, although the excellence of the original plan, (which makes every volume complete in itself, and in itself an Annual Register of every thing connected in art and literature) precludes the necessity of a new series of numbers" (no. 399:1). Dalby's format, then, remained essentially that established by his predecessor, even after the addition of such minor departments as "University Notices" and "Works Preparing for Publication." On the other hand, a few distinct changes in content can be observed in nothing more than a cursory reading of the issues for the months immediately preceding and following Dalby's assumption of the editorial post. There was an increased use of the column "To Readers and Correspondents," which Byerley had originated but had seldom resorted to in his last years. The *Chronicle* under Dalby showed more interest—and sometimes partisanship—in theological controversy, supporting an anti-Catholic viewpoint in more than one article of late 1826 (no. 390:702). The poetical Dalby also determined to elevate contributions in verse from the irregular and limited nook to which Byerley had been inclined to confine them at the close of his tenure. To the *Revue Encyclopédique*'s unfavorable estimate of the poetry published in the *Chronicle,* Dalby responded on 20 October 1826:

"It is due to ourselves to observe that the poetical department of *The Literary Chronicle* was never thought its embellishing characteristic by the late editor, whilst it is intended by the present arrangement to vie for rank of talent with any of its contemporaries" (no. 388:669). In the next volume, beginning in number 399, the poetical items were no longer printed all together under "Original Poetry" or "Original" but were interspersed with the prose. Among the poets frequently represented at this time was George James De Wilde, a known schoolmate and friend of Dalby.[5]

Frederick Denison Maurice apparently imagined a greater degree of innovation than Dalby, for after four issues he concluded volume 10 with only 336 pages and initiated the "new series" on 31 May 1828; but since only nine numbers made up this final stage of the *Chronicle,* there was scant opportunity for realizing the new emphases projected in the prospectus, namely the "notices of passing events" and the publication of "Tales."[6] There is some hint that the *Chronicle* had in Maurice its most liberal and tolerant editor, one who recognized "among our contributors persons of various shades of opinion" (n.s. no. 5:68). An editorial introduction to the leading article of the last issue opined: "We do not profess to reduce the writings of all our contributors to one standard of doctrine. . . . We must hear the many languages and accents of inquiry, or we shall fail to recognize the one overawing and melodious voice of Truth" (n.s. no. 9:129). The first (and only) installment of a serial entitled "Characters" was, significantly, the unflattering word portrait entitled "The Sectarian" (n.s. no. 5:73–74).

All three of the editors enriched the *Chronicle* by means of serials—titles which lacked the status of departments but which nevertheless ran for several weeks or months. Often these serials allowed for the widest scope of miscellany, leaving the writer or editor free to include trivia that could not be introduced elsewhere. Two of the longest-running of these were "Londiniana," in nineteen issues, a collection of historical, topographical, and social sketches about the metropolis; and the "Rambles of Asmodeus," in thirty-nine issues, the correspondence of a gossipy demon who could make himself invisible and gain entrance wherever he pleased. Similarly diverse in scope were "The Family Trunk," "The Peripatetic," and "Nil Admirari" (appearing in seven, six, and eighteen numbers respectively). Other serials, though of shorter duration, added still more variety to the *Chronicle* as a whole. "Americana" introduced transatlantic matter, such as excerpts from newspapers in the United States; "Casanoviana" summarized some of the adventures of the notorious libertine, ostensibly "to convince everyone what gross pictures of depravity and impurity are contained in a work which has been extolled as highly interesting for the eminent personages to which it introduces us" (no. 226:585); and "Enigmas in Prose" teased the reader with a riddle of several paragraphs which would be answered in the following number. The letters of Jonathan Oldworth permitted an elderly "correspondent" to comment leisurely from time to time on whatever interested him. The *Chronicle* often repeated its policy of completing such serials before the end of the volume in which it was begun, but the rule was bent for such useful series as "Rambles of Asmodeus" and "Nil Admirari."

As a journal of criticism the *Literary Chronicle* was seldom profound, for its usual approach to reviewing was merely to provide a brief introduction and conclusion that enclosed an abstract or series of excerpts to enable readers "to form their own opinion of the merits of the work under consideration" (no. 1:1). Although most of the commentary appears on the periphery of the articles, one can sense a tendency to be fair, especially to little-known writers who were publishing their first works. It appears that the *Chronicle* was sincere in its claim of taking care "not to crush the rising bud of genius by the chilling blast of criticism; nor in works of real merit to seek only for faults," a policy which led to some accusations "of lenity and good nature" (no. 138:1). Significantly, the motto chosen for the title page of several of the earlier volumes was a quotation from Pope's *Essay on Criticism* prescribing moderation:

> In ev'ry work regard the writer's end,
> Since none can compass more than they intend;
> And, if the means be just, the conduct true,
> Applause, in spite of trivial faults, is due.

[255–58]

Unfortunately, several of the adverse criticisms that did appear were directed at names now among the immortals of the Romantic movement. Novels by the author of *Waverley* were duly excerpted as they appeared, but the *Chronicle*'s criticism was almost formulaic in pronouncing several of them unequal to their predecessors. *Bride of Lammermoor* and *A Legend of Montrose* were found in 1819 to be not "so well written nor the subjects so interesting as the tales of *Old Mortality* and *The Heart of Mid-Lothian*" (no. 6:81). *Ivanhoe* (1820) was judged inferior "to all the productions attributed to the same author" (no. 34:24); and *Quentin Durward* (1823) was subsequently found to be "the worst" (no. 212:363) until supplanted in 1824 by *St. Ronan's Well*, "the worst of all the novels by the author of Waverley" (no. 243:24).

More often than not Wordsworth's works were negatively received. An early number predicted that he and the Lake School "will be entirely forgotten" and long outlived by "the lofty and impassioned diction of those whose works have stood the test of ages" (no. 2:21). The *Chronicle* chided him for his egotism (no. 33:12; no. 96:169). A curt review of 1822 looked quickly at two volumes by "this prince of the lake poets" and pronounced his *Ecclesiastical Sketches* "sad work" and *Memorials of a Tour on the Continent* "pure and unadulterated nonsense throughout . . . silly, absurd, or unintelligible" (no. 187:791–93). The notice concluded by wondering "that a person of Mr. Wordsworth's good sense, who has written some pieces worthy of immortality, and who consequently, has a reputation to lose, can ever give his name to such doggerel" (p. 793).

The younger generation of Romantics was also subjected to the *Chronicle*'s strictures. It could freely acknowledge the literary gifts of Byron and Shelley. Indeed, the *Chronicle* has the distinction of being the first to publish *Adonais* in England, and the death of Byron inclined the journal to defend his memory. But these poets were seldom praised without some reservation about tainted morals or infidelity. The announcement of Shelley's death judged the poet "a man of extraordinary but perverted talents" (no. 169:504). As for Keats, the principal notice came in the review of his 1820 volume, *Lamia, Isabella, The Eve of St. Agnes, and Other Poems,* where the reviewer took the occasion to instruct Keats in the means to becoming a better poet—by renouncing "all acquaintance with our metropolitan poets," by never writing "a poem of more than a hundred verses at the utmost," and by giving "us the English Language as it is taught and written in the nineteenth century" (no. 63:484–85). Keats's mentor, Leigh Hunt, fared even worse at the hands of the *Chronicle* reviewers, who often mentioned him with derision, especially during the years of Byerley's editorship. Hunt's *Liberal,** which was reviewed as each number appeared, was regarded as mawkish and tending toward atheism (no. 179:655). The *Chronicle* writer was dismayed to see in number 3 of the Pisan paper an increase in Hunt's part and a diminution of Byron's, a development judged to be "a serious injury to its literary reputation" (no. 206:257).[7]

The *Literary Chronicle* was supported by a considerable circle of contributors and "correspondents," a few of whom have been identified but most of whom remain either anonymous or nothing more than names. Some are yet concealed behind initials which may or may not provide a clue to their real names; others signed themselves in apparent pseudonyms like Beppo or Menippus. Several correspondents also brought out now long-forgotten volumes under the name signed to their *Chronicle* articles: Barton Wilford (no. 96:165), Jesse Hammond (no. 4:470), S. R. Jackson (no. 98:199; no. 142:70), and John Watson Dalby (no. 183:721; no. 338:709). Occasionally the journal gave some notice of the personal adversities of its contributors, as in the plea in the issues for May and June 1828 for donations for the poverty-stricken poet J. Wilmington Fleming, and the account of the wretched end of the suicidal Henry Neele (no. 457:108; no. 460:157). A few names are notable mainly because they appeared frequently during a certain period of the *Chronicle*'s life. Poetry or prose from a J. D. Newman was published almost every month in 1819–1820, and William Henry Parry and C. A Monck were recognized successors to "* * T" in the "Fine Arts" department. A Mr. Hatt was frequently published in "Original Poetry" in issues in 1821–1822 and occasionally thereafter; and the poetry and prose of a J. M. Lacey were often admitted in 1822–1825. George James De Wilde's poetry was much seen in the months following the succession of his friend Dalby to the editorship in July 1826.[8] From November 1827 through May 1828 many issues carried a poem by "Sforza."

Another much-published contributor of the Dalby period, John Doran, had been the French correspondent for the *Chronicle* for several years. Many of the

French articles during the Byerley years were probably from his pen, but it was only after Dalby became editor that Doran's identity was revealed, first in the signature "J. D——n" appended to his series "Recollections and Reminiscences" (in twelve numbers from 5 January to 19 April 1828). When these and one other article were published as *Sketches and Reminiscences,* the *Chronicle*'s review of the collection printed the author's name in full and owned him as a contributor. Dalby, in old age, recalled "how greatly young Doran, during his flying visits from Paris to London, contributed to the mirth and rather boisterous conviviality of certain suppers that were given to the staff of the short-lived journal in the editorial chambers in Serle's Place."[9]

From first to last the *Literary Chronicle* manifested a determination to achieve eminence in the ranks of the weekly reviews. Almost every new "Address to the Public" looked back over the accomplishments of the past year and forward to projected changes or additions that would better serve the readers. It noted that nearly 200 works had been reviewed in 1820, 250 in 1822, 300 in 1823, and 350 in 1824. Granted, some of these "reviews" were little more than paragraphs, but the lead articles were growing more substantial and the volume of letter press was increasing so that it was necessary to begin printing in smaller type and in three columns rather than two. At midpoint in its history, in the issue for January 1824, the "Address to the Public" commented on the steady increase of subscribers in each succeeding year and proudly added that its "literary connections have also been much extended."

Moreover, the *Chronicle*'s keen sense of competition with other weekly reviews is often evident. The journal harbored a special ill will toward the *Literary Gazette,* regarding it as a contemptible "bookseller's review," a tool for puffing forthcoming publications which it was to review from proof sheets provided by a leading publisher, with the consequent bias in criticism arising from such an arrangement. Longman's was the publisher controlling the *Gazette,* the *Chronicle* averred, and it snidely applied the epithet "Longuemanne's Cunnynge Advertyzer" to its rival (no. 305:188–89). The *Gazette* was also jeered for its claims to originating the format of the weekly review, and the *Chronicle* seized several opportunities for demeaning William Jerdan's journal (no. 291:797 and no. 292:813, for example). This rivalry drew attention near the conclusion of a contemporary satire, David Douglas's *Visions of Taste,*[10] where the poet recorded his "vision" of three feuding cocks on a dunghill. In case the reader should misunderstand, Douglas wrote notes to explain his allusions. The *Literary Gazette,* the *Literary Chronicle,* and the *Literary Museum,** he observed, "may fairly be considered *the three Literary Cocks* of the day." The *Chronicle* "cock," after subordination to the other two, is finally knocked down and crushed "with Justice" by a book from which a scroll uncurls and reveals this inscription:

> The CHRONICLE is price *sixpence,*
> I am the Editor—a dunghill cock!—
> And with my party scribblers fly in flock!

> And when reviewing what an author wrote,
> We've just enough of learning to misquote!

The other two cocks then resume fighting until with the passing of time they both sink down and moulder, each "on his own peculiar dunghill."[11]

Douglas was only partially correct in his prophecy. The *Gazette* did long outlive the *Chronicle,* but the *Museum* perished three years before the *Chronicle*'s merger with the *Athenaeum London Literary and Critical Journal.* The "new series" of the *Literary Chronicle* was, indeed, a kind of prelude to the merger, its nine numbers sharing several features of format with the *Athenaeum.* "This being the case," wrote the editor of the *Chronicle* in its final issue, "the conductors of these two papers have come to an agreement, the effect of which will be to unite . . . in the production of one Weekly Literary Journal." The editor further assured his readers "that the coalition . . . is a *bona fide* one . . . as there is not a contributor to the old work whom they will not recognize as a contributor to the new one" (n.s. no. 9:143).[12] Four days later, on Wednesday, 30 July 1828, the partnership was confirmed in the title: the *Athenaeum and Literary Chronicle.* The last three words were dropped at the end of 1829, but the *Athenaeum* survived throughout the century and twenty years beyond, outlasting the *Literary Gazette* by more than fifty years. Indirectly, then, the *Chronicle* gained the supremacy that it had always coveted.

Notes

1. *Dictionary of National Biography,* s.v. "Byerley, Thomas." "Necrology: Thomas Byerley, Esq.," *Literary Chronicle* no. 377:493.

2. See J(ohn) C(ordy) J(eaffreson), "Dr. Doran, F. S. A.," *Temple Bar* 52 (1878):468; Luther A. Brewer, *My Leigh Hunt Library: The Holograph Letters* (Iowa City, 1938), pp. 308–10; *The Correspondence of Leigh Hunt,* ed. Thornton Hunt (London, 1862); Frederick Maurice, *The Life of Frederick Denison Maurice Chiefly Told in His Own Letters* (London, 1884), pp. 78–79; John C. Francis, *John Francis, Publisher of "The Athenaeum": A Literary Chronicle of Half a Century* (London, 1888), 1:31.

3. "Original Correspondence" became "Original Communications" in number 18 and eventually simply "Original." After the death of Byerley, the title "Varieties" was substituted for "The Bee," which was dropped at the end of 1826.

4. Byerley published *Relics of Literature* (London, 1823) under the *nom de plume* Stephen Collett. In the "Advertisement" he explained that this collection of more than 250 excerpts grew out of "a course of reading somewhat desultory and extensive," during which he "extracted for his private portfolio such articles as at the time he deemed curious or interesting" (p. i).

John Timbs, "Preface" to *The Percy Anecdotes Collected and Edited by Reuben and Sholto Percy* (London, 1868), pp. v–vi.

5. *The Correspondence of Leigh Hunt,* 1:286n.

6. The last issue of the original series of the *Chronicle,* number 471 for 24 May 1828, gave notice that "a New Series" was about to begin and that a prospectus would appear in the next issue (336). The copy of this issue available for examination did not contain any such prospectus, but the final number of the new series recalled the prom-

ises that had been made in it (n.s. no. 9:143). Unlike the original *Chronicle*, the new series apparently intended to carry serialized fiction, like the two parts of "Lionel: A Tale," carried in the issues for 19 and 26 July.

7. Although the *Literary Chronicle*'s treatment of Hunt was censorious as a whole, he was occasionally defended in its pages, as in the letter to the editor in number 120:552–53. See also number 120:558, number 164:426, number 454:50. *The Correspondence of Leigh Hunt* shows that from 1834 to 1858 both Dalby and his friend De Wilde were admirers and benefactors of the indigent Hunt.

8. In his youth De Wilde was intimately acquainted with Leigh Hunt and Cowden Clarke. Upon the recommendation of Sir James Stephen, De Wilde became editor of the Northampton *Mercury,* a position he held for forty years. He contributed also to the *Gentleman's Magazine** (see *AAAJ*), *Notes and Queries** (see *VEA*), the *Mirror,* and the *Casket,* under the *noms de plume* of Sylvan Southgate, Camden Somers, and Vandyke Brown.

9. Doran was hardly twenty-one when he completed his work for the *Chronicle*. He died on 25 January 1878, at seventy-one years of age, having been editor of *Notes and Queries* for the last five years. William J. Thoms, "In Memoriam," *Notes and Queries,* 5th ser. 9 (1878):81.

10. David Douglas, *Visions of Taste* (London, 1823).

11. Ibid., pp. 87, 92.

12. Maurice could speak with such confidence because he was also to be editor of the *Athenaeum and Literary Chronicle* for the next ten months.

Information Sources

BIBLIOGRAPHY

Brewers, Luther A. *My Leigh Hunt Library: The Holograph Letters.* Iowa City, 1938.

Dicey, Edward. "In Memoriam." In George James De Wilde, *Rambles Roundabout and Poems.* Northampton, England, 1872.

Dictionary of National Biography. S.v. "Byerley, Thomas."

Douglas, David. *Visions of Taste, a Satire.* London, 1823.

Francis, John C. *John Francis, Publisher of "The Athenaeum": A Literary Chronicle of Half a Century.* 2 vols. London, 1888.

Hunt, Thornton, ed. *The Correspondence of Leigh Hunt.* 2 vols. London, 1862.

J(eaffreson), J(ohn) C(ordy). "Dr. Doran, F. S. A." *Temple Bar* 52 (1878):460–94.

Maurice, Frederick. *The Life of Frederick Denison Maurice Chiefly Told in His Own Letters.* 2 vols. London, 1884.

"Necrology: Thomas Byerley, Esq." *Literary Chronicle and Weekly Review,* 5 August 1826, pp. 493–94.

Thoms, William J. "In Memoriam." *Notes and Queries,* 5th ser. 9 (1878):81.

INDEXES

Each volume indexed.

REPRINT EDITIONS

Microform: English Literary Periodicals (UMI), reels 510–514.

LOCATION SOURCES

American

Partial runs: Buffalo and Erie County Public Library, Grosvenor Reference Division; Rice University Library; St. Louis Public Library; University of Illinois Library; University of Minnesota Library; Yale University Library.

British

Complete run: British Museum.

Partial runs: Bodleian Library; London Library; National Library of Scotland.

Publication History

MAGAZINE TITLE AND TITLE CHANGES

The Literary Chronicle and Weekly Review, 22 May 1819–24 June 1820. *The Literary Chronicle and Weekly Review/The Country Literary Chronicle and Weekly Review* (a stamped edition for subscribers receiving the journal by post), 1 July 1820–8 May 1824. *The Literary Chronicle and Weekly Review*, 15 May 1824–24 May 1828. *The Literary Chronicle, New Series*, 31 May–26 July 1828. (Merged with *The Athenaeum and Literary Chronicle* on 30 July 1828.)

VOLUME AND ISSUE DATA

Numbers 1–471, volumes 1–10, 22 May 1819–24 May 1828; new series, volumes 1–9 (also numbered 472–480), 31 May–26 July 1828.

FREQUENCY OF PUBLICATION

Weekly (Saturday).

PUBLISHERS

Numbers 1–19, 22 May–24 September 1819: J. Sidebethem, 287 Strand, London. Numbers 20–215, 2 October 1819–23 June 1823: John Limbird, 53 Holywell Street, Strand, London (numbers 20–45); 355 Strand, London (numbers 46–215). Numbers 216–480, 5 July 1823–26 July 1828: G. Davidson, 2 Surrey Street, Strand, London (joined by his son G. H. Davidson in early 1824).

EDITORS

Thomas Byerley, 22 May 1819–July 1826; John Watson Dalby, probably July 1826–April 1828 (numbers 376–467). F. D. Maurice, May–July 1828 (numbers 468–480).

Douglas K. Morris

LITERARY EXAMINER, THE

The *Literary Examiner* was John Hunt's idea, proposed to his brother Leigh while the latter was living in Italy: the new periodical was to serve as a companion to the *Examiner*,* made up of literary reviews and original essays, and Leigh "might resume the *Indicator* [*] in it."[1] It was announced in the *Examiner* of 29 June 1823 and first appeared dated Saturday, 5 July 1823.

The sixteen-page weekly was published for twenty-six numbers, ending 27 December 1823, by Henry Leigh Hunt, John's son; the first four numbers were unstamped and cost five pence; thereafter, the unstamped periodical cost four pence, and a stamped version (for posting) cost seven pence.

The venture began promisingly enough. Leigh Hunt contributed characteristically reminiscent and associative essays in the manner of the *Indicator,* under the heading "The Indicator":[2] "My Books" (in nos. 1–2), "On the Suburbs of Genoa and the Country about London" (in nos. 7–8), "On the Latin Poems of Milton" (in nos. 9–11). Although it was clearly announced from the outset that others besides Hunt would write "The Indicator,"[3] the columns not by Hunt were headed "For the Indicator," giving the expectation that Hunt would fill those pages. Hunt's inability to write more than three essays for this series was instrumental in the periodical's demise: in the final number the editor remarked the absence of "The Indicator" and confessed that

> while there was a prospect of the continuance of these papers, we filled up, in the best manner we could, the vacuum occasioned by their suspension; but that prospect no longer exists. This publication was set up *chiefly* as a vehicle for the resumption of the *Indicator*—ill-health and other circumstances now prevent anything like regular contribution from its Author; and we are therefore compelled, notwithstanding the very promising degree of support it has obtained, to discontinue it. [No. 26:412][4]

The *Literary Examiner* is perhaps most noteworthy for the disproportionate attention devoted by its editor to Byron's *Don Juan*. The notices begin in the first number, with introductory remarks in which the reviewer attacks Byron's attackers: it is because he is a nobleman championing the oppressed that Byron is pilloried; *Don Juan* has drawn the fire of critics not because of its amorous scenes, as they claim, but because of its satire (no. 1:6–9).[5] There follow, in this and in numbers 2, 5–8, and 19–22, copious extracts as the reviewer advances the plot of *Don Juan* from Canto VI to Canto XIV.

Although the treatment of the other, less enduring works reviewed in the *Literary Examiner* is strictly routine, the themes of political liberty, social equality, and freedom from religious superstition come through again and again in the reviews, the short essays, the "Table Talk," and the aphoristic "Commonplaces" that make up the numbers. Tyrants and emperors are attacked, though Napoleon is praised as a great man. Freedom of the press and liberty are hailed. French court etiquette is ridiculed. Lord Gower's comment that he has omitted from his translation of *Faust* passages that he finds "revolting" is greeted by the reviewer with the sneer that "we hope it is not fear of the precious 'Societies' which has operated; for if so, we can assure his Lordship, that, being a Lord, he has nothing to fear from *them*" (4:61; 10:150–56; 22:352; 2:29; 10:156; 6:85–87; 3:39). The reviewer of a book on insanity notes with interest the incidence of "religious fanaticism" among mad women surveyed; another announces that "our purpose . . . is merely to show that the Catholic is not the only church which can exhibit superstitious puerility." The Inquisition is described as an "institution a bigotted faction in France would have restored," "most likely" in the "gay and festive originality" of the auto-da-fé. "The Vicar-General of Christ upon earth is evidently the same political plaything in Europe, as the Dalai Lama in Asia, and a like decline usually attends mere priestly power in all places"; a true God would not love flattery, which in fact arises from human conceit (1:13; 6:88, 91; 11:170; 19:302). In sum, "political truth is libel; religious truth, blasphemy" (11:173).

When the *Literary Examiner* ceased publication, the editor announced, " 'Literary Notices' will be resumed in the *Examiner* Newspaper" (26:412).

Notes

1. John Hunt to Leigh Hunt, 25 February 1823; unpublished letter, quoted by William H. Marshall, *Byron, Shelley, Hunt, and the "Liberal"* (Philadelphia, 1960), p. 166.

2. The first "Indicator" essay is given as "No. LXXVII," pointing up the continuity with the earlier *Indicator,* which ended with number 76.

3. See the *Examiner* no. 805 (29 June 1823):424.

4. Hunt cites ill health again as the reason for his inability to contribute in *Lord Byron and Some of His Contemporaries; with Recollections of the Author's Life, and of His Visit to Italy* (London, 1828), p. 498.

5. The reviews of *Don Juan* are reprinted in *The Romantics Reviewed: Contemporary Reviews of British Romantic Writers,* ed. Donald H. Reiman, part B (New York, 1972), 3:1358–64, 1370–90.

Information Sources

BIBLIOGRAPHY
Landré, Louis. *Leigh Hunt (1784–1859): Contribution à l'histoire du Romantisme Anglais.* 2 vols. Paris, 1936.
Marshall, William H. *Byron, Shelley, Hunt, and the "Liberal."* Philadelphia, 1960.
INDEXES
  None.
REPRINT EDITIONS
  Microform: English Literary Periodicals (UMI), reel 148.
LOCATION SOURCES
  American
    Widely available.
  British
    Complete runs: Birmingham University Library; Bodleian Library; British Museum; Edinburgh University Library; London Library; Manchester Public Library.

Publication History

MAGAZINE TITLE AND TITLE CHANGES
  The Literary Examiner: consisting of the Indicator, a review of books, and miscellaneous pieces in prose and verse.
VOLUME AND ISSUE DATA
  Numbers 1–26, 5 July–27 December 1823.
FREQUENCY OF PUBLICATION
  Weekly.
PUBLISHER
  H . L. Hunt, 38 Tavistock Street, Covent Garden, London.
EDITOR
  Henry Leigh Hunt.

N. S. Bauer

LITERARY GAZETTE, THE

The *Literary Gazette* was started on 25 January 1817 by Henry Colburn, a publisher known for aggressive advertising. He shrewdly perceived that there was a general and unsophisticated readership that the dominating *Edinburgh Review** and the *Quarterly Review** were not reaching, and he also saw an opportunity to promote his own stable of writers. In July he appointed one of his contributors, William Jerdan, as editor. Jerdan's principal interest was literature, but he also had a journalistic bent. He had worked on the short-lived *Sun* and *Aurora,* and had an eye for a scoop. The weekly *Gazette* had an immediacy which the monthlies and quarterlies could not acquire; Jerdan's Saturday paper consistently reviewed new works as soon as they were published and, with Colburn's books, even before they reached the stationers. Jerdan maintained the editorship for thirty-three years, first as a shareholder, until 1841, and later as sole owner. He lost control and resigned in 1850.

The value of the weekly for scholarship is vitiated by the lack of an office record. In Jerdan's woefully uninformative autobiography he names 200 contributors, with only a few of importance.[1] The list of the better-known includes William Blackwood, William Lisle Bowles, Edward Bulwer-Lytton, George Grote, Benjamin Haydon, James Hogg, Thomas Hood, Theodore Hook, J. G. Lockhart, William Maginn, Sir Francis Palgrave, Walter Scott, William Sotheby, and Robert Southey. No ascription to specific articles can be made safely. Jerdan himself wrote the bulk of the articles; in many of them his mannerisms of style and imagery are monotonously evident. Cardinal weaknesses in the magazine included Jerdan's reluctance to get innovative managerial assistance and the dearth of first-rate writers, especially after the decline in the early 1830s. He made no effort to share the editing, except for the brief period in the late 1820s when he collaborated with the popular poet, Letitia Landon. Miss Landon only mirrored his own tastes.

Nevertheless, the *Gazette* was impressively successful during its first fifteen years. It was a greater literary authority than the respectable reviews for a large number of readers. A piece on a new novel insured a good sale if favorable, and a poor one if condemnatory. The weekly catered to the simpler tastes of the novel-reading public, and frequently included lengthy book sections, sometimes continuing through several issues. Both writers and publishers protested this practice, because they feared that it diminished book sales.

The general index to the bound copies of the 1817 run is a fair summary of the content during Jerdan's editorship:

Original Correspondence, foreign and domestic; Critical Analysis of New Publications, English and Foreign; Varieties on all Subjects connected with Polite Literature—Discoveries and improvements—Phaenomena of

Nature and Mind—Philosophical Researches—Rural Economy—Scientific Inventions—Sketches of Society, Manners, and Morals—Proceedings of Universities, Public Societies, &c. &c; Biographical Memoirs of Persons distinguished by their talents and public merits; Original Letters and Anecdotes of remarkable Personages; Essays on the Fine arts, which shall be conducted with due regard to Science and Liberality; Review of British and Foreign Drama, including the Italian Opera, with New Music, &c; Miscellaneous Articles of Literary Intelligence: Notices of Works projected and in a state of forwardness; Announcements of New Publications, and New Editions; Works of Art, &c.

In addition to literary news and reviews, the *Gazette* carried articles on mesmerism, developments in agriculture, archaeological discoveries, inventions, and exhibitions of new paintings. The only significant change in format occurred in 1846, when the price dropped from eight pence to four: an expansion from sixteen to twenty-four pages that could not be sustained. An earlier price change, from a shilling to eight pence, was made in 1826, when Jerdan began to feel the threat from other periodicals.

The weekly enjoyed a wide circulation until about 1830. In 1823 the sale was 4,000 a week or 16,000 a month, which compared favorably with the two great quarterlies—the *Edinburgh Review* at 7,000 and the *Quarterly Review* at 17,000. No firm figures are available, but Jerdan's autobiography makes it clear that there was a severe drop in 1830 when Maginn's *Fraser's Magazine* * and the *Athenaeum* * boomed into the scene. The latter was the venture of Jerdan's partner, Colburn, who broke with him over unsatisfactory reviewing of the publisher's books, but still maintained a share in the production of a weekly. Colburn installed Charles Wentworth Dilke as editor of the *Athenaeum,* and he made great changes in it. Its emphasis shifted to reviews rather than original articles, and the price was reduced from eight to four pence. Its sales rose from a few thousand copies to eighteen thousand. The *Gazette* never recovered from the blow of the *Athenaeum*'s competition, and in circulation and authority it was relegated to a minor role until Jerdan's bankruptcy in 1850. It staggered on for twelve more years under nine successive editors, and finally merged with a new paper called *Parthenon,* which died in 1863.

During the early years, the *Literary Gazette* was often accused of puffery. Until Dilke of *Fraser's* took over the journal in 1830, few reviews could be considered innocent of this charge. Probably because of Colburn's more blatant use of pressure and Jerdan's generosity toward personal friends and new writers, the *Gazette* became known for this practice. The *Athenaeum* and *Fraser's* cited it as the prime offender. The *Athenaeum* charged that Colburn and Bentley, his partner, withheld new publications from periodicals not under their control until their own papers had blessed them. In defense of Charles Lamb, who was the butt of a nasty review in the *Gazette,* the poet laureate himself, Robert Southey, offered his sympathy to the poet in verse, concluding: "I ween, old

Friend! thou art not worse bested/ When with a maudlin eye and drunken aim/ Dullness hath thrown *a jerdan* at thy head.''[2] When Jerdan recalled the complaint of favoritism in his *Autobiography,* he fell between two stools attempting the impossible. He defended himself against the accusation that he supported puffery, but he was so sensitive to the charge of Colburn and others that he had not supported them that he tried to prove that he had adequately cooperated with them.

The reviews of Jerdan and his contributors tended to be appreciative or condemnatory, rather than analytical. His remark in the *Autobiography* indicates the weekly's principle of prose criticism: ''If I were writing a romance or a novel, I could make my principal character to suit the tastes of those who admire perfect heroes.''[3] His admiration of Dickens began with the Boz sketches and never faltered. Dickens honored Jerdan at a banquet for urging him to develop the character of Sam Weller after the first few numbers of *Pickwick Papers*. Although the *Gazette* faulted Thackeray for cynicism, *Vanity Fair* was commended with a prediction that it would become a ''great favorite.'' The reviewers continued to seed the articles with obligatory moral objections, but generally praised the novels of Mrs. Trollope, Jane Austen, Elizabeth Gaskell, Mary Shelley—especially *Frankenstein*—Douglas Jerrold, and G.P.R. James. But Carlyle's *Sartor Resartus* was described as a ''patch-work . . . made repulsive by form and manner,'' and Maturin's *Melmoth* was unacceptable because it touched dangerously on religious matters. The *Gazette*'s loyalty to the tastes of its audience continued: the popular novels of fashion were given serious treatment long after the reputable journals were contemptuously dismissing them.

Byron's free-thinking made a reviewer—the style suggests Jerdan—uncomfortable, although his great talent was generously acknowledged. On the whole, the philosophical subtleties of Coleridge and Wordsworth were beyond the interest of the reviewers, and only grudging praise was offered. In contrast, Southey offered no mysteries and was duly admired for his dignity and range, although he was accused of verbosity.

The charge that the *Gazette* under Jerdan was anti-American is an unfair oversimplification.[4] While it is true that his Tory principles led him to fear that liberalism would give power to a rabble, and that like other British critics he found the practice of slavery a hypocrisy, he approved heartily when American writers such as Cooper objected to the habits and customs of the British. There was seldom any significant prejudice in the *Gazette*'s articles, and no indication of a desire to assume inferiority in American writers. Jerdan's reviews of Washington Irving's works were warm, complaining only about his essay on English writers. He hailed Benjamin Franklin with the highest of encomium. He praised Cooper as well as Melville, Bryant, Longfellow, Dana, and James Kirke Paulding. When qualifications were made, and they were rare, it was never suggested that a New World writer was in any way limited because he was an American. Indeed Bryant was exhorted to exploit the potential of the new country, to seek fame by using the rich resources at hand rather than derived materials. He found Emerson too fine-spun for his tastes, and did not care for Carlyle.

Like many other critics, the *Gazette* reviewer praised Melville's *Redburn* as a welcome departure from his previous obscurity, but found his other novels puzzling. Of *Mardi* he wrote, in the issue for 29 May 1847, "The images are brilliant, and upon the whole you wonder how aught so luminous can be so dark. We never saw a book so like a Kaleidoscope. . . . As for giving any idea of it, we have none ourselves." In its treatment of American writers, as in the treatment of British writers, the *Gazette,* especially under Jerdan, reflected popular attitudes toward literature without offering its readers any depth of perception.

Notes

1. William Jerdan, *Autobiography* (London, 1852–1853).
2. *Athenaeum,* 7 August 1830, p. 491.
3. Jerdan, 2:3.
4. William B. Cairns, *British Criticism of American Writings 1815–1833* (Madison, Wis., 1922), p. 17.

Information Sources

BIBLIOGRAPHY

Ashton, Helen. *Letty Landon.* New York, 1951.
Dictionary of National Biography. S.v. "Jerdan, William."
Duncan, Robert W. "William Jerdan and the *Literary Gazette.*" Ph.D. dissertation, University of Cincinnati, 1955.
Jerdan, William. *Autobiography.* 4 vols. London, 1852–1853.
———. *Men I Have Known.* London, 1866.

INDEXES

None.

REPRINT EDITIONS

Microform: English Literary Periodicals (UMI), reels 907–920. Kraus Microform, Millwood, N.Y. New York Public Library. Princeton Microfilm Corp., Princeton, N.J. Three M-IM Press, Washington, D.C.

LOCATION SOURCES

American

Complete runs: California State Library, Sutro Branch; New York State Library; North Texas State College Library; Stanford College Libraries; Yale University Library.

Partial runs: Widely available.

British

Complete runs: Birmingham Public Library; British Museum; Chetham's Library (Manchester); Leeds University Library; London Library; Sunderland Public Library.

Partial runs: Widely available.

Publication History

MAGAZINE TITLE AND TITLE CHANGES
  The Literary Gazette, and Journal of Belles Lettres, Arts, Sciences. (Caption title sometimes "London Literary Gazette.")
VOLUME AND ISSUE DATA
  Numbers 1–2162, 26 January 1817–26 June 1858; new series, volume 1, 3 July 1858–1863.
FREQUENCY OF PUBLICATION
  Weekly.
PUBLISHERS
  London, various addresses, some unknown. The first printer was Valpy, followed by Pinnock and Maunder, publishers of catechisms and history books.
EDITORS
  William Jerdan, July 1817–December 1850. I. A. Reeve, 1851–1856. J. M. Jephson, 1856(?)–1858. Shirley Brooks, Henry Christman, W. R. Workman, Frederick Arnold, John Morley, C. W. Goodman, 3 July 1858–1863.

Robert Duncan

LITERARY GOSSIP, THE. See GOSSIP, THE

LITERARY GUARDIAN, THE

Throughout its short life the *Literary Guardian and Spectator of Books* was important, as Walter Graham says, for its reviews of contemporary works.[1] From the first issue, which appeared 1 October 1831, through the last, for 4 August 1832, it offered a broad sampling of reviews of works written on subjects ranging from fiction to science, and paid attention as well to autobiography, travel literature, medical theory and practice, history, biology, music, psychology, and so on. Most reviews consisted of brief introductory remarks provided by an unidentified editor and followed by long extracts from the books being considered. Because of the brevity of its analytical comments, the *Literary Guardian* did not establish a reputation as a force in the history of periodical criticism, but the wide range of its interests and the lengthy extracts included in its pages make it a vital source of information about intellectual history in the early 1830s. The word *sampler* best describes this periodical. Not only did it sample books as a means of reviewing them; it also gave extracts from other periodicals from England and America, and it gave choice passages from many important literary annuals popular at the time. Furthermore, its pages of advertisements complement the *Literary Guardian*'s role as mirror of the reading interests of the age.

Edited by Messrs. Book-Worm, Glow-Worm, and Silk-Worm, the *Literary Guardian* throughout most of its nearly ten months of publication had sixteen quarto pages and sold for two pence. According to its own account of its circulation, the weekly *Literary Guardian* reached three thousand readers. The monthly collection of the four preceding weekly issues, bound together for distribution across the British Isles—and for a time in Paris as well as in unspecified locations in America—sold 12,000 copies. Evidently the magazine was well received; in one issue the editors puffed it by printing commendations taken from fourteen newspapers from all over England, Ireland, and Scotland.

The contents of a typical issue demonstrate the *Literary Guardian*'s character as sampler and miscellany and suggest that it is a worthy ancestor of the *Saturday Review* * (see *VEA*), the *New Yorker*, the *Book Digest Magazine*, and the *Reader's Digest*. The front page of each issue contained the masthead with the title that remained essentially unchanged throughout the magazine's life: *The Literary Guardian, and Spectator of Books, Fine Arts, Public Amusements, and Fashions*. In the first months of publication, a sketch of the contents for each issue also appeared on the front page, but this useful feature soon disappeared. Following the contents were the various sections which were to appear somewhat regularly in succeeding issues. Most of the reviews were in the leading section: "Spectator of Books." The issue for Saturday, 8 October 1831 reviewed the following books: Moore's *Life of Byron* (an excerpt from a previously published review in the *Edinburgh Review* *); *Campaign Cruises in Venezuela and New Grenada* (excerpted from the contemporary *Literary Gazette,* * for, as the editors explained, they had not seen the book); Michael Mitford's *The Smuggler: A Tale, The Life of John Ledyard—The American Crusoe, Insect Miscellanies* (a biology treatise); and *The Familiar Law Adviser.* All of these reviews contained brief introductory comments followed by long excerpts.

This issue also included brief assessments of periodicals such as *Blackwood's* * and reprinted from it a poem by Felicia Dorothea Hemans—"The Freed Bird." Mentioned next were the following: the *New Monthly,* * from which was reprinted a delightful essay attacking progress in any form ranging from steam locomotives to new types of boots and shoes; the *Metropolitan,* * which was praised for its variety; then *Fraser's Magazine,* * which was condemned for its grumbling nature and its lack of taste; the *Union Monthly,* which as a new journal was encouraged; the *Ladies' Museum,* which was criticized for having serials; the *Diamond Magazine,* which was praised for its neatness; and the *Magnet,* which was labeled diminutive but praised for being inexpensive.

Following this illuminating assessment of literary periodicals, there was a section headed "Foreign" which included a mildly satiric extract from *Le Roi des Ribauds, Histoire du Temps de Louis XII,* recounting the solemn entry of Mary, Princess of England, into Paris to be the bride of Louis. Following this extract was a section which appeared only sporadically thereafter: "Ladies' Fashions." Excerpts here from Townsend's *Parisian Fashions* enlightened fashion conscious readers.

In the "Fine Arts" section a new print of Henry Welling depicting Westminster Palace and St. Stephen's Chapel received a favorable review, but in the "Music" section some new piano pieces were soundly condemned for being overly imitative. The "Drama" section listed plays being produced at the major theaters and offered brief analyses. In the issue for 15 October 1831 Wycherley's "Country Girl" received harsh criticism and a prophecy of failure because of the coarseness of its language. An excerpt from Hunt's *Tatler* * recounted Edmund Kean's ability to portray death scenes.

A delightful but soon abandoned section titled "Miscellanea" contained friendly gossip about Sir Walter Scott's impending voyage aboard a royal yacht to the Mediterranean for his health's sake. A section under the heading "Paris Gossip" gave details about two royal exiles, Pedro of Brazil and Hussein of Algiers, who then lived in Paris.

The issue concluded with an intriguing advertising section which contained notices of other magazines such as the *Diamond Magazine* and the *Calendar and Universal Mirror* (a soon to be published miscellany which was seeking subscriptions); of books such as *The Printer's Manual* and *The Book Binder's Manual;* of new and old novels; of books on health problems ranging from cholera to childhood consumption; of voyage and travel literature; of new textbooks on algebra, French, sports (physical education); and of an English composition manual. The variety of books advertised grew as the magazine became better established, and in later issues the venerable firm of Sotheby's listed estate collections of fine books and objects of art to be sold at auction.

With but few exceptions the *Literary Guardian*'s editors rarely attempted critical reviewing or interpretive analysis. Whoever Messrs. Book-Worm, Silk-Worm, and Glow-Worm were, they did not often demonstrate a strong critical bent, but in the few essays in which they did address either theoretical or practical aspects of criticism their observations were perceptive. A long discussion in the issue for 14 July 1832 on the nature of reviews lamented the prevalence of literature designed merely to appeal to popular tastes at the expense of literature which contained lasting, universal qualities. Furthermore, the essay challenged standards and techniques employed by reviewers in other periodicals.

Although the scarcity of criticism similar to that found in analytical journals is lamentable, the *Literary Guardian* was keenly aware of the major trends in fiction, poetry, and drama, as well as of major developments in science and industry; and its editors had noteworthy interests in matters of literary history. The magazine's initial publication of five of Byron's letters to John Hunt in their entirety (four transcribed and a fifth as a lithographically reproduced facsimile), plus an extract from a sixth letter, exemplifies this interest. The first letter, in the issue for Saturday, 3 December 1831, indicated Byron's desire to have the publication for six cantos of *Don Juan* handled by Douglas Kinnaird rather than by John Murray and to have "Werner" and "Heaven and Hell" published in the *Liberal*.* Kinnaird was described in the second letter as "my trustee in all matters of business'' (Saturday, 10 December 1831). In the same letter Byron also referred to aspects of Leigh Hunt's trial and advised John Hunt to "employ good writers and to pay them handsomely.'' A third letter, which appeared Saturday, 17 December 1831, stressed that Byron wanted no part of the "stoppage of *'The Liberal'* '' and explained his belief that the possible dangers his reputation might cause to the magazine led him to "crave permission to withdraw.'' The fourth letter, appearing Saturday, 7 January 1832, noted Byron's having sent the proofs of "The Blues'' and furthered the argument that for him to continue to be associated with the *Liberal* would endanger the magazine's chances for success, but he promised not to withdraw without "mature consideration.'' Byron also added some criticism of Murray to the earlier complaints. He concluded by asking Hunt to send him "by land'' *Peveril of the Peak,* and by noting that attempting to send the "prohibited *Liberal*'' would be pointless. The final letter to Hunt, the lithographed facsimile attached to the issue for Saturday, 16 June 1832, is primarily valuable for its revelation of Byron's strong insistence that ten remaining cantos of *Don Juan* be set and proofs forwarded for his corrections. Byron also wrote that he wanted to have the proofs for "The Island'' immediately.

The sixth of the group of letters in the *Literary Guardian* appeared in the issue for Saturday, 30 June 1832, and was an extract from Byron's celebrated defense against charges made about his father in Amédée Pichot's "Essai sur le Génie et le charactère de Lord Byron,'' which had been published in a French translation of Byron's works begun in Paris in 1821.[2]

The publication of these five letters and of the lengthy extract from the sixth gives a clue to the *Literary Guardian*'s place in the political spectrum associated with periodicals, and defines its side in the still-raging controversies about Byron. Although the editors maintained admirable objectivity during an age in which political factions and differences of opinions about writers' personalities influenced the content of reviews just as such elements often had done since the eighteenth century, their biases in favor of Byron are obvious.

For its publication of the Byron letters alone, the *Literary Guardian* deserves a significant place in any comprehensive history of British literary periodicals. Of course, the many additional contributions the magazine made in reflecting as well as chronicling cultural history assure its importance. The *Literary Guardian,* and many other such small journals, caught the temper of the early 1830s when England was between declining Romanticism and the advent of a new mode, Victorianism. Its attempts to provide balanced coverage of older works as well as its focus on contemporary writing show that its editors knew well the nineteenth-century readers' preferences. Among the first of many periodicals to review Charles Lyell's *Principles of Geology* (Saturday, 11 February 1832), the magazine gave the public—in what was soon to be the age of evolution as well as the age of Victoria—a preview of a new scientific era. Although the excerpts included in the review did not center specifically on the evolutionary principles suggested in even this early example of Lyell's observations, the selected passages pointed to concepts that later influenced development of the Victorian dilemma. With its Byron letters and its attention to new editions of popular eighteenth-century novelists, the *Literary Guardian* harkens back to a recent as well as to a somewhat more distant past; and with its attention to contemporary works and to a work eventually to be as significant as was Lyell's *Principles of Geology,* the magazine serves as a harbinger of the Victorian Age.

Although no reasons are given in its own pages for its demise, and although its obscurity has caused it hitherto to enjoy only cursory mentions in literary histories, one suspects that financial problems prompted its cessation. Near the end of the magazine's life its editors reduced its size and price by half—apparently in hopes of increasing sales. To provide literary news and reviews at a low cost was noted as a major aim of the editors in the opening essay. Of the first issues—a sort of Pickwickian colloquy among Messrs. Book-Worm, Silk-Worm, Glow-Worm, and the harried printer—the point was stressed that a need existed for a literary journal sufficiently inexpensive to allow readers with limited incomes to purchase and enjoy it. That their laudable efforts failed is unfortunate, but this competently edited periodical continues to reward the intelligent readers who have access to it.

Notes

1. Walter Graham, *English Literary Periodicals* (New York, 1930), p. 325.
2. Leslie A. Marchand, ed., *Byron's Letters and Journals* (Cambridge, Mass., 1980), 10:208.

Information Sources

BIBLIOGRAPHY

Altick, Richard D. "Nineteenth Century English Periodicals." *Newberry Library Bulletin,* 2d ser., no. 9 (1952):255–64.
Graham, Walter. *English Literary Periodicals.* New York, 1930.
Marchand, Leslie A., ed. *Byron's Letters and Journals.* Vol. 10. Cambridge, Mass., 1980.
Prothero, Rowland E., ed. *The Works of Lord Byron.* Vol. 6. New York, 1966.

INDEXES

The index for 4 August 1832 is cumulative.

REPRINT EDITIONS

Microform: English Literary Periodicals (UMI), reel 725.

LOCATION SOURCES

American

Partial runs: Newberry Library; Princeton University Library; University of Illinois Library.

British
> Complete runs: Bodleian Library; British Museum.

Publication History

MAGAZINE TITLE AND TITLE CHANGES
> *The Literary Guardian, and Spectator of Books, Fine Arts, Public Amusements, and Fashions,* volume 1, numbers 1–25, 1831–1832.
> *The Literary Guardian, and Spectator of Books, Science, the Arts, Drama, Etc.,* volume 2, numbers 26–45, 1832.

VOLUME AND ISSUE DATA
> Volume 1, numbers 1–24, 1 October 1831–24 March 1832; volume 2, numbers 25–45, 31 March 1832–4 August 1832.

FREQUENCY OF PUBLICATION
> Weekly.

PUBLISHERS
> Numbers 1–14, 1831: F. C. Westley, 165 Strand, London/21 Paternoster Row, London/3 Wellington Street, Strand, London. Numbers 15–45, 1831–1832: William Tyndall, 3 Wellington Street, Strand, London.

EDITORS
> Unknown (Messrs. Glow-Worm, Book-Worm, Silk-Worm, 1831–1832).

> *Kenneth W. Davis*

LITERARY JOURNAL, THE

The *Literary Journal* was founded and edited by the philosopher James Mill. Like many of his fellow Scots, Mill had come to London hoping to make a career in literary pursuits. In addition to the *Literary Journal* and the highly successful Utilitarian organ, the *Westminster Review,** which he founded in 1824, he printed single articles in the *Anti-Jacobin Review** and the *British Review,** as well as numerous articles in the *Edinburgh Review,** the *Monthly Review** (see *AAAJ*), the *Eclectic Review,** the *Philanthropist,* and other assorted publications, including important essays in the *Encyclopedia Britannica.* Most of these were prior to his monumental *History of India* (1817), which established his reputation and fortune. The subtitle of the *Literary Journal,* "A Review of Literature, Science, Manners, Politics," accurately reflects the contents in its early issues. Mill had at least three highly professional and experienced writers as assistants. Thomas Thomson, an eminent chemist, wrote the scientific columns; his brother James wrote on philosophy and contributed to the third edition of the *Encyclopedia Britannica;* and David Macpherson, the literary reviewer, had edited various Scottish materials.[1]

Throughout its brief life, the *Literary Journal* seemed to be in search of an audience, for it made frequent and radical changes of format and content. It survived as a weekly for only six months, from 6 January to 30 June 1803. It then changed to twice-monthly publication because of the prohibitive newspaper stamp duty. The long essay on "Physics" which began each issue was dropped entirely. As the "To Our Reader" column at the end of volume 1 explained, it had been found too difficult for the general reader and too brief for the scientific specialist. Twice-monthly publication continued through volumes 2 and 3, from 16 July 1803 through 1 July 1804. The sections on "Literature" were expanded, and the section on "Manners" underwent continuous change. In volume 1 this section, written by "R. S.," hoped to emulate Addison and Steele by laughing readers out of their absurdities (1:16–20). Some of the discussions give interesting sidelights to contemporary manners, but their heavy-handed irony and general tone of moral stricture often grate on the reader. In volume 3 "R. S." is replaced by "The Nabob," a middle-aged onlooker of the current social scene obviously based on the characters in the *Spectator* (see also *AAAJ*).[2] Gradually "The Nabob" was replaced by a series called "The Classic" and then by "Letters" from "Dr. Noehden." These permutations indicate a radical change in the editor's perception of the *Literary Journal*'s readers. While the two earlier features were aimed at a general audience, both Dr. Noehden and "The Classic" required highly erudite readers, versed in Greek and Latin, and interested in philology and textual arguments.

The *Literary Journal* continued to change in other ways. With volume 4 for July 1804 it became a monthly magazine with the subtitle "Or, Universal Review of Literature Domestic and Foreign." "Manners" and "politics" were both abandoned. The *Literary Journal* became exclusively a review journal of contemporary literature, through volume 5 and volumes 1 and 2 of the new series. Mill's biographer, Alexander Bain, suggests that it failed because in its monthly form it was so much like other magazines that it did not command a large public, and that, "moreover, it had a large tincture of Mill's own severe views both in politics and religion."[3]

An address "To the Reader" at the end of volume 5, announcing the new series, states the political and doctrinal independence of the journal, and its freedom from party support. But throughout its four years' run the *Literary Journal* reflected Mill's liberal views, which included the need for Catholic Emancipation, for the abandonment of civil and criminal discrimination against the native Irish, for changes in the Poor Laws, for freedom of trade and manufacture, and for freedom of the press. Moreover, the emphasis on serious publications continued. The first issue of the new series (January 1806) contains major reviews of Horne Tooke's *Diversions of Purley,* a discourse on grammar (this review was written by Mill); *An Essay on Sovereign Power;* Cumberland's *Memoirs;* Mangourit's *Journey in Hanover;* Dugald Stewart's *Pamphlet . . . the Election of a Mathematical Professor in the University of Edinburgh;* Gallet's *Political Gallery;* Good's *Lucretius;* Dr. Hamilton on *Purgative Medicines;* and, finally, a review of what we would now call "literature'': R. C. Dallas's *The Morelands.* The "Monthly Catalogue," which follows, has brief critiques of books on all kinds of issues, as well as novels, poetry, and drama. Novels thus briefly reviewed in volume 1 of the new series are: T. Surr's *A Winter in London; or Sketches of Fashion;* Madam Cottin's *The Saracen; or Matilda and Malek Adhel, a Crusade Romance;* and W. H. Rayner's *Virtue and Vice.*

"Literature," therefore, signified anything that had been recently published, on any subject, fictional or nonfictional. The four novels and three poems that are reviewed—all the poems are anonymous effusions on the death of Nelson—also reveal another characteristic of the *Literary Journal.* Because of the accident of its publication dates, 1803–1806, nothing now thought of as a major work of the English Romantic period was available for review. Minor fictional works reviewed include Edgeworth's *Popular Tales* (3:605–7) and *Lenora* (n.s. 1:459–65); Joanna Baillie's *Miscellaneous Plays* (5:49–64); Godwin's *Fleetwood* (5:238–49); Southey's *Metrical Tales* and *Madoc* (5:157–66, 621–36); Scott's *Lay of the Last Minstrel* (5:271–80); and Thomas Moore's *Epistles, Odes, and Other Poems* (n.s. 1:646–57). Perhaps of interest to Blake scholars is his blistering two-part condemnation of Thomas Taylor's translation of Plato (3:444–61, 577–89); and a sympathetic article on Davies's *Celtic Researches* (3:526–37).

The few comments that the *Literary Journal* made on major contemporary writers were negative. Although the review of Benjamin Heath Malkin's *A Father's Memoirs of His Child* is highly favorable, the reviewer writes, "We cannot extend our approbation to the irrelevant panegyric upon Mr William Blake, painter and engraver." Mr. Blake's engravings may be all very well,

> but what can Mr. Malkin mean by introducing his friend to us as a poet? He allows that Mr. Blake's attempts are "unfinished and irregular"—and he asserts him to have ventured on the "ancient simplicity"—*illa priorum simplicitas*—but with due submission to the judgment of our readers, should we not say that Mr. Blake has successfully heightened the "modern nonsense?" We conclude our critique with an extract

—and they print "Laughing Song" from *Songs of Innocence* (n.s. 2:28, 34–35).

Wordsworth fares equally badly. In reviewing Southey's *Metrical Tales* the reviewer praises Southey's genius and industry but wishes it were more happily directed:

> When Mr. S. attempts to write for the *people* . . . the opinion which he seems to entertain of the reach of his countrymen is little less degrading than that which is held forth by the author of "Goody Blake and Harry Gill." If *Tam O'Shanter,* and the other poems of Burns and Ramsay are adapted to the capacities of the common people of Scotland, and express

their ideas and sentiments in their own language; and if the ballads and tales of Wordsworth and Southey do the same by the common people of England; what a mortifying comparison for the latter! . . . But, indeed, nothing can be more wide of the real sentiments and language of the common people than *every thing* that Mr. S. or Mr. Wordsworth, or Mr Coleridge have written. [4:160]

Since these strictures are from a journal which finds James Montgomery's *The Wanderer of Switzerland* "by no means deficient in poetical merit," and quotes approvingly the following stanzas:

> Shep.   "WANDERER! whither would'st thou roam?
> To what region far away,
> Bend thy steps to find an home,
> In the twilight of thy day?"

> Wand.   "In the twilight of my day,
> I am hastening to the west;
> There my weary limbs to lay,
> Where the sun retires to rest,"

[n.s. 1:433]

the reader might have serious doubts about its critical discrimination.

However, the *Literary Journal* did have some critical discrimination. It had a sharp eye for genuinely bad writing, and was often wickedly tart in deriding it. For example, "Mrs. Anna Maria Smallpiece is one of those devotees of the sentimental muse who have a ready effusion of sensibility for every occasion. She weeps over a rose, sighs over a lily, bewails the tree in St. Paul's Churchyard, and is particularly pathetic on a periwinkle" (n.s. 1:329). And an excerpt from a long and hilarious plot summary of Eliza Nugent Bromley's *The Cave of Cosenza* reveals the kind of literature it felt compelled to review:

> The captain of the banditti turns out to be a man of the strictest honour, integrity, principle, and sentiment. He feeds the hungry, clothes the naked, and never murders travellers, unless they attempt to defend their property. To be sure this excellent man had begun his career by robbing his father, and murdering his tutor: after which he marries a lady for her fortune, suspects her of infidelity, and murders herself, her gallant, and attendant. He afterwards by mistake, assassinates his father in his bed, and a woman who was sleeping with him. But what of all this? His father was a tyrant, his tutor a sour fellow, and his wife not sufficiently circumspect in her conduct. [3:30]

Given a plethora of novels such as this, its strong moral tone, and its editor's life-long commitment to education, it is not surprising that the *Literary Journal* welcomed Maria Edgeworth's three-volume series of *Popular Tales,* whose avowed intention was to amuse and instruct those 70,000 readers in Great Britain who were not members of the learned orders or who did not belong to polite society.[4] One plot summary after another reveals Miss Edgeworth's emphasis on the virtues of prudence and industry: "The story of 'Rosanna,' is an admirable example of the blessings of industry and contentment, contrasted with the miseries of ill-gotten wealth, accompanied with malice, envy, and other vices" (3:606). Miss Edgeworth's *Tales,* tediously didactic as they may seem, found a sympathetic response in a journal that believed *Tom Jones* too indelicate to be read aloud before ladies (1:15), and Joanna Baillie superior to Shakespeare and Otway because of her avoidance of obscenity (5:63).

In its strongly moralistic tone the *Literary Journal* is a product of its time, but its insights into the state of literary endeavor are frequently illuminating. For example, it argues that the reason for absurd plots, such as the one summarized above, is that novels confined themselves to courtship and marriage and thus had long since exhausted incidents from real life (2:429–30). It also explained the deficiencies of contemporary drama as owing to the deplorable excess of sensibility also found in the novel and poetry: "Sentiment, commonplace tame misapplied sentiment has been made to supply the place of wit and humour, the play of language and brilliance of comic incident which once so greatly distinguished the English stage" (3:590).

The *Literary Journal* may perhaps be of most significance in its insights into the developing ideas of its editor, James Mill, and early Utilitarian theory, as can be seen in Donald Winch's edition of Mill's *Selected Economic Writings.* It is surprising, however, that Winch seems to have been the only writer since Bain in 1882 to investigate the contents of the journal for insight into Mill's concerns between his coming to London in 1802 and his meeting with Bentham in 1808.[5] For instance, familiarity with the *Literary Journal* would have modified the categorical statement by a recent writer that few Englishmen of Mill's day knew much about the Industrial Revolution, and that "nowhere in Mill's private correspondence or published writings do we find any reference to these matters."[6] The *Literary Journal* has such references, one of the more interesting being in a review of James Grahame's *The Birds of Scotland and Other Poems.* The reviewer praises the title poem, but takes issue with Grahame's views on commerce, saying that sensibility has led him into false political notions:

He observes a number of children employed in manufactures, improperly educated and ill attended to, and from thence, and similar abuses, he concludes that manufactures and commerce themselves are a great curse to mankind, and that things will never go well till we become an agricultural nation again. But if he delights to see mankind well cloathed, fed, and supplied with the various necessaries and comforts of life, why

> should he thus reproach the only means by which these benefits can be brought about? [N.s. 1:528]

This is not only knowledge of the Industrial Revolution, it is a glorification of it.

James Mill almost certainly did not write this review, but it expresses ideas that he is known to have had, and that occur throughout the *Literary Journal*.[7] In the background of the argument against Grahame's ideas is a concept of Mill's which Elie Halevy terms "the theory of indefinite perfectibility."[8] That theory receives clear expression in the "Politics" section of the second issue: "What extraordinary, and important changes have taken place in Europe during the last hundred, nay the last fifty years, which in their progress were never reflected upon, but which now, when viewed collectively, present an object of such magnitude! That changes of equal, nay of superior magnitude will take place during the next fifty years is what the experience of human affairs gives us reason to expect" (1:60). When the new war with France broke out, it was deplored because it interrupted this "favourite expectation" (1:671).

Furthermore, it is not known when Mill first began reading Bentham, but the *Literary Journal* has many references to "utility," a concept that also lies behind the criticism of Grahame. In an essay written by James Thomson on the "Philosophy of Mind," "utility" becomes the standard of all value judgments: "The object of Intellectual Philosophy is to collect, classify, and name all the important facts which relate to the intellectual part of man, in order to enable us to ascertain by what methods it can be carried to the highest degree of improvement. For we should never forget that the object of every science is utility" (1:72).[9] The standard of utility, moreover, is applied to natural as well as mental science. In a review of James Parkinson's *Organic Remains of a Former World,* the reviewer disagrees with Parkinson's theory on the formation of coal, and comments:

> Indeed, we look upon all such gratuitous hypotheses as nothing else than trifling. It is going beyond our sphere, and cannot be productive of much advantage to Science. Even if a person were lucky enough to hit upon the very way in which coal was actually formed, still unless he could adduce evidence that it was actually so formed, or that it might be artificially so formed from vegetables, it would be of little or no utility." [4:570]

So much for pure science.

The *Literary Journal* reflects Mill's countless ideas and shows a mind in transition. The journal regarded "utility" as a standard of value and noted that many philosophers agreed that "promoting general utility is the only laudable and virtuous motive that ought to influence our conduct." But the magazine also held that "utility" should be a secondary principle and not "permitted to usurp the place of conscience, the supreme principle.'' It cited the French Revolution, where the greatest excesses were perpetrated not out of passion but on the principle of the greatest utility for all (1:724–25), as evidence of the horrors that would ensue. James Mill was later to repudiate such beliefs but his advocacy of ''Revolution without Violence'' in his agitation for the Reform Bill of 1832 certainly grew out of his knowledge of the excesses of the French Revolution.[10] He realized that any advocacy of ''utility'' would also need to take its excesses into account.[11] Much may be learned about James Mill and early Utilitarianism by reading the *Literary Journal.*

Notes

1. For details, see the entries for these three men in the *Dictionary of National Biography;* and Alexander Bain, *James Mill: A Biography* (1882; reprint ed., New York, 1967). For identification of articles by Mill not in Bain, see *James Mill: Selected Economic Writings,* ed. Donald Winch (Edinburgh and London, 1966), pp. 445–48.

2. It is not known who wrote this section. Bain paraphrases a letter from Mill to Thomas Thomson saying that he does not know who has been engaged by the publisher, Baldwin, for the post. The inspiration of trying to emulate Addison and Steele may have come from James Thomson, who edited an eight-volume edition of the *Spectator* * in 1799 (see *Dictionary of National Biography*).

3. Bain, *James Mill,* p. 61.

4. See Richard Lovell Edgeworth's ''Preface'' to *Popular Tales* (London, 1804), 1:ii–iii (the estimate of possible readers comes from Burke). James Thomson's essay on ''Philosophy of Mind'' praises the Edgeworths' educational efforts (1:82).

5. In addition to the works cited below, see John Plamenatz, *The English Utilitarians,* 2d ed. (Oxford, 1958); Jack Lively and John Rees, eds., *Utilitarian Logic and Politics: James Mill's ''Essay on Government'', Macaulay's critique and the ensuing debate* (Oxford, 1978); and J. H. Burns, ''The Light of Reason: Philosophical History in the Two Mills,'' in *James and John Stuart Mill/Papers of the Centenary Conference,* ed. John M. Robson and Michael Laine (Toronto, 1976), pp. 3–20. Leslie Stephen mentions the journal, but his only comment about its contents is that ''His [Mill's] own contributions show that, although clearly a rationalist, he was still opposed to open infidelity.'' See *James Mill,* vol. 2 of *The English Utilitarians* (London, 1900), p. 5.

6. W. H. Burston, *James Mill on Philosophy and Education* (London, 1973), p. 4.

7. See, for example, Mill's pamphlet, *Commerce Defended. An Answer to Arguments by which Mr. Spence, Mr. Cobbett, and others, have attempted to prove that Commerce is not a Source of National Wealth* (1807; 2d ed., 1808), which argues that manufacture should be free, unrestricted, and encouraged, and as a corollary, that more workers would then be employed and earning wages which they could in turn expend for more goods. In an early issue of the *Literary Journal* the restrictive apprenticeship practices of the woolen trades are inveighed against for similar reasons. The Industrial Revolution is coming into full swing, and the *Literary Journal* and James Mill see it as of inestimable value to England.

8. Elie Halevy, *The Growth of Philosophic Radicalism,* trans. Mary Morris (1928; reprint ed., London, 1972), p. 256. Winch, however, notes that this ''roseate doctrine'' is not a feature of Mill's later writings, although he never lost the notion of progress (see *Selected Writings,* p. 6).

9. Authorship attributed by Bain in *James Mill,* p. 49.

10. See Mill, *Autobiography and Other Writings,* ed. Jack Stillinger (Boston, 1969), pp. 25–27; Joseph Hamburger, *James Mill and the Art of Revolution* (New Haven, 1963), pp. 20–21.

11. His son certainly tried to come to grips with the problem. See Edward Alexander, "The Principles of Permanence and Progress in the Thought of J. S. Mill," in *James and John Stuart Mill,* pp. 126–42.

Information Sources

BIBLIOGRAPHY

Bain, Alexander. *James Mill: A Biography.* 1882. Reprint. New York, 1967.

Burston, W. H. *James Mill on Philosophy and Education.* London, 1973.

Edgeworth, Maria. *Popular Tales.* 3 vols. London, 1804.

Halevy, Elie. *The Growth of Philosophical Radicalism.* Translated by Mary Morris. 1928. Reprint. London, 1972.

Hamburger, Joseph. *James Mill and the Art of Revolution.* New Haven, 1963.

Lively, Jack, and John Rees, eds. *Utilitarian Logic and Politics: James Mill's "Essay on Government", Macaulay's critique and the ensuing debate.* Oxford, 1978.

Mill, James. *Essays on Government, Jurisprudence, Liberty of the Press and Law of Nations.* 1825. Reprint. New York, 1967.

Mill, John Stuart. *Autobiography and Other Writings.* Edited by Jack Stillinger. Boston, 1969.

Plamenatz, John. *The English Utilitarians.* 2d ed. Oxford, 1958.

Robson, John M., and Michael Laine, eds. *James and John Stuart Mill/Papers of the Centenary Conference.* Toronto, 1976.

Stephen, Leslie. *The English Utilitarians.* 3 vols. London, 1900.

Winch, Donald, ed. *James Mill: Selected Economic Writings.* Edinburgh and London, 1966.

INDEXES

Each volume indexed.

REPRINT EDITIONS

Microform: English Literary Periodicals (UMI), reels 525–526.

LOCATION SOURCES

American

Complete run: Amherst College Library.

Partial runs: Newberry Library; U. S. Library of Congress; University of Illinois Library; Yale University Library.

British

Complete run: British Museum.

Partial runs: Aberdeen University Library; Edinburgh Public Library; Literary Philosophical Society Library; London University Library; Manchester Public Library; Stepney Public Library.

Publication History

MAGAZINE TITLE AND TITLE CHANGES

The Literary Journal, a review of literature, science, manners, politics.

VOLUME AND ISSUE DATA
Volume 1, 6 January–30 June 1803; volumes 2–3, 16 July 1803–1 July 1804; volumes 4–5, July 1804–December 1805; second series, volumes 1–2, January–December 1806.

FREQUENCY OF PUBLICATION
Weekly, 6 January–30 June 1803 (volume 1); twice-monthly, July 1803–July 1804 (volumes 2–3); monthly, July 1804–December 1806 (volumes 4, 5; new series 1–2).

PUBLISHER
C. & R. Baldwin, New Bridge-Street, London.

EDITOR
James Mill.

Helen B. Ellis

LITERARY JOURNAL AND GENERAL MISCELLANY, THE

Realizing that in the swirl of periodicals circulating in 1818 there would need to be some "peculiarity in the attempt" to attract readers to a new journal, the proprietors of the weekly *Literary Journal and General Miscellany* emphasized in their address "To the Public" the novelty of their undertaking: "The plan of the LITERARY JOURNAL is new—the OBJECTS, PRICE, and the TIMES OF PUBLICATION, taken together, the plan is NEW. Its objects will be chiefly literary; its price will be Sixpence only; and its times of publication will be Sunday mornings" (1 [28 March 1818]:1) It was to contain "an innocent, amusing, elegant, and instructive miscellany" and would regularly communicate "all novelties in Literature, Science, and Arts, and every branch of knowledge, carefully and industriously collected from English and Foreign publications." This would be no easy task the proprietors added, "in this era of discovery and research."

The contents were as miscellaneous as promised by the above address and by the subtitle (General Miscellany of Science, Arts, History, Politics, Morals, Manners, Fashion, and Amusements). But there were several prominent features. A reviewing section led off every issue and there was always a selection of "Original Poetry." Some of the verse was signed, which may have stimulated vanity, for apparently there had been an attempt to bribe the editor to include a verse contribution (1:[10 May 1818]:111). But on the whole the *Literary Journal* was, as vowed in the opening address, "pregnant with variety." Most issues were filled with letters to the editor, anecdotes, bits of information, and an occasional illustration.

At first, the ambition of the magazine was "to please Female readers and Youth" but this aim seems to have been a matter of maintaining modesty, of avoiding "unappropriate topics," rather than of circumscribing the readership (1 [29 March 1818]:1). For, soon after, the real aim of the *Literary Journal* was spelled out, and it was in one sense revolutionary. It is true that every periodical would like as large a number of subscribers as possible, but the proprietors of the *Literary Journal* wished it to become "A PAPER FOR ALL" on philosophical grounds: "There is a middle point, at which all mankind, of every rank, of every condition, and of every degree of information, may meet and may understand each other," and the proprietors hoped to promote such understanding (1[19 April 1818]:63). That this was no passing fancy, but a deeply felt aim, is clear from the reiteration of the philosophy just before the weekly paper folded: the proprietor "is endeavouring to adapt to popular use a publication devoted to the higher branches of literature, science, and the arts; the scheme is new and has its apology in the circumstances of a new age," one in which literacy was expanding (2[3 April 1819]:218).

This populist urge was behind the early price of six pence and for the later return to that price after an increase. One month after its inception the *Literary Journal* may have already felt the pinch of pursuing such a policy, for ads for books began to take up the last page of each issue.

There was also an attempt to increase country subscriptions by producing "a Monday's Edition" on stamped paper at ten pence (1[12 April 1818]:48). It was to have a different title, the *Literary Chronicle,* but on 1 August 1818 we learn that the different name with exactly the same contents ran afoul of the policy of the Stamps Office and that the special country edition would be discontinued (1:302).

The ambition for social diversity in the readership was matched by a dispersion of authorship: "The truth is, that we are rarely, ourselves, the authors of six lines in any one number of the *LITERARY JOURNAL*" (1 [19 April 1818]:63). Put more whimsically later, the proprietors claimed, "Our paper is not only a PAPER FOR ALL, but a PAPER BY ALL. . . . For ourselves, we have only to sit at the helm, and hold the tiller and cast a look, from time to time, at the compass and the sails; and our little bark performs, as it were, by herself, her modest and careless voyage" (1[23 January 1819]:63). Many periodicals relied for a large part of their contents on donations from readers, but no other journal is known to have made this exaggerated a claim.

The readership must in any case have been curtailed to some extent by the "Politics" promised in the subtitle and contained in small doses in the paper itself. One early anonymous correspondent (1 [12 April 1818]:46) hoped the politics of the *Literary Journal,* not yet recognizable, were "on the right side— that of well-regulated popular liberty." No comment by the editor followed, but apparently the "well-regulated" correspondent was not disappointed. The journal soon attacked the Radicals (1 [18 July 1818]:267) and later characterized the Whigs as "a busy, noisy, ambitious, and unprincipled party" (1 [5 December 1818]:587).

But this conservative weekly paper was not to last long anyway. The price of six pence, the key to wider dissemination, was raised in volume 2 (2 January 1819) to nine pence because of printing costs. On 3 April 1819 the proprietors announced a return to the price of six pence so that it could again be a "PA-

PER FOR ALL'' (2:218). What wasn't announced was that the pages (quarto) would decrease from sixteen to twelve and that two of the publishers would back out. J. Limbird, possibly the force behind the populist philosophy, continued alone for the last two issues.

Information Sources

INDEXES
> Index at end of volume 1.

REPRINT EDITIONS
> Microform: English Literary Periodicals (UMI), reel 518.

LOCATION SOURCES
> *American*
>> Partial runs: American Philosophical Society; Boston Public Library; Harvard University Library; Yale University Library.
>
> *British*
>> Complete runs: Bodleian Library; British Museum.

Publication History

MAGAZINE TITLE AND TITLE CHANGES
> *The Literary Journal, and General Miscellany of Science, Arts, History, Politics, Morals, Manners, Fashion, and Amusements.*

VOLUME AND ISSUE DATA
> Volumes 1–2 (59 issues), 28 March 1818–8 May 1819.

FREQUENCY OF PUBLICATION
> Weekly.

PUBLISHERS
> 29 March 1818–5 April 1818: A. Christie, 362 Strand, London. 12 April 1818–17 October 1818: A. Christie, E. Wilson, 88 Cornhill, London/J. Chapell, 98 Cornhill, London. 24 October 1818–24 April 1819: J. Limbird, 53 Holywell Street, Strand, London/E. Wilson, J. Chapell, London. 1 May–8 May 1819: J. Limbird, London.

EDITOR
> Unknown.

John O. Hayden

LITERARY MAGNET, THE

In an introductory address to readers, ''Tobias Merton,'' pseudonymous editor of the *Literary Magnet,* takes as his models the great British essayists in the tradition extending from Bacon to the creators of the *Adventurer,** the *World,** and the *Connoisseur** (for all, see *AAAJ*). In the ''Plan and Arrangement of the 'Magnet,' '' with which the first number concludes, the projectors confirm the priority of the essay and prose literature by giving first place to the publication of ''Original Papers'': ''Essays, Fictions, Sketches of Character,

Delineations of Manners, notices of the Belles Lettres, at once light, and interesting" (1:16). Reviews of new books, "with copious Extracts," are cited next
in order of importance, while poetry and a "choice selection of Jeux d'Esprit"
are consigned to "Miscellaneous Matters" (1:16). The first series of the *Magnet* (1824–1825) adheres to this format; the *Magnet*'s new series (1826–1827)
reverses the priorities and gives precedence to poetry. The *Literary Magnet*
initiated its four-year career as a "delicate unpresuming *weekly* magazine,"
before it grew into a "sturdy pugnacious *monthly*" (2:iv). Editorial comments
suggest that December 1824 was the magazine's first monthly number; the arrangement in monthly parts is clear in volume 3. In this volume, too, the
experiment was made of dividing each number into two segments: "Original
Papers" and a "Monthly Journal," featuring reviews of new books, drama,
fine arts, and public events, the parts of which were joined to form a separate
section in the annual volume.[1]

The anonymity of most of the leading contributors to the first series of the
Magnet has been preserved.[2] The "Plan and Arrangement of the 'Magnet' "
boasts of the "acknowledged talents" of the magazine's regular correspondents, including "several Scholars in the Universities of Oxford and Cambridge," who "have the assistance and co-operation of writers distinguished
by their eminence in the literary world" (1:16). The transiency of university
students may account for the frequent turnover in editors and regular contributors during the magazine's first two years. At any rate, only a few of these
writers can be named. Sir Samuel Egerton Brydges, a well-known bibliographer, has been identified as the author of two essays in volume 2 that are signed
"B."[3] He may have written two other essays and two poems in volume 2 as
well as five essays in volume 1, all of which are signed "B." His son, Egerton
Anthony Brydges ("E.A.B."), a student at Trinity College, Cambridge, is represented by two poems in each of the first two volumes. There is some evidence that the Brydges, father and son, were "Tobias Merton, Gent." and
edited the *Magnet* during its first eight months.[4] Edward George Ballard ("Γ")
is the author of four poems and a prose sketch in the first volume. J. Gans
("J. G——ns"), a translator of German literature, wrote several prose pieces
for the second and third volumes. Miss A. Selwyn ("A. S.") published three
prose sketches in the second volume, in which her novel, *Emily, or Traits of
Principle*, is reviewed favorably. Felix McDonough (the "Hermit") contributed prose sketches to the second and third volumes, and two poems by
William Harrison Ainsworth, using the *nom de plume* "Cheviot Ticheburn,"
appear in volume 4.

The most significant "Original Papers" in the first series of the *Literary
Magnet* are its general articles on literature and its evaluations of leading writers of the day. The essays by Samuel Brydges are the most philosophical in
theme and tone. In "The Vagaries of the Imagination" Brydges speaks in
general terms of the creative faculty that has "dominion, not only . . . over
every thing that exists, . . . but when it has exhausted one world, it has the

power to form another; and can clothe and people it with objects of its own formation'' (1:246). In ''Fiction in Poetry'' he examines more particularly the role of the imagination in writing poetry: ''The grand art in poetry . . . is to give a vent to all the vagaries of fancy; never to appear studied or affected, never to seem anxious to obtain an effect; but depend upon cause (the exciting of pleasing emotion and the enkindling of fancy) to obtain those objects'' (2:55). Like Brydges's essays, observations ''On Painting, Poetry and Music'' by ''EDGAR'' (2:44–45) are more philosophical than critical in developing the aesthetic affinities of the sister arts.

Several essays examine a dilemma in British drama that was not resolved until the end of the century. The author of ''Observations on the Modern Drama'' regrets that the success of a play depends more on the ''combined efforts of the scene painter, and the mechanic'' than on ''all the vigour and energy of the author's imagination'' (1:195). However, two other essays, ''Remarks on Dramatic Literature and Performance,'' by ''EDGAR'' (1:241–42), and ''Poetry and Drama,'' by ''T:AM,'' quoted below, deplore the absence of action in contemporary poetic drama:

> Too much attention has undoubtedly been bestowed by our tragic writers on mere decoration of style, and too little to the more indispensable requisites of action and passion. . . . We go to a tragedy, not to hear a poem repeated, but to have our sympathies awakened, and our passions brought into play by energetic action and moving incidents;—and which of our modern dramatists has been able to accomplish this? [2:95]

The critical essays on individual writers are more uneven in quality than the general essays on literature. An extended essay ''On the Genius and Poetry of Wordsworth'' (3:26–29, 67–72, 156–60) offers the most perceptive critical judgments: ''In the most simple of Wordsworth's poems there is something that displays a deep sense of things beyond the immediate subject in hand. . . . He mingles the simplicity of a child with the feelings and understanding of a man and a philosopher'' (3:71–72). The remaining essays tend to discuss the writer's reputation, usually in defense or eulogy, and neglect the works themselves. Lord Byron draws the most attention, and the assessments of his poetry are consistently ambivalent. In ''Lord Byron'' (1:305–6) and ''Lord Byron's Works'' (2:353–54), both critics admire Byron's ''genius'' and deplore the moral ''failings'' of his life and his later works. In ''The Literature of the Nineteenth Century'' the critic ranks Byron as the ''first poet of the age'' and awards him the ''crown of excellence'' for his ''intensity of feeling, grasp of thought, and power of description'' (3:161). The same critic finds that the ''name of Shelley and Genius have become synonymous,'' accords him second place, and concludes that his ''want of popularity'' is due ''to the profundity and subtleness of his philosophical reveries'' (3:163–64). Washington

Irving is eulogized by "J.H.H." in a fifteen-page "Essay on the Genius and Writings of Washington Irving, Esq." The article reviews each of Irving's works, beginning with *The Sketch Book*—"perhaps, the sweetest production that ever came from the press" (2:253), and concluding with a summary of Irving's talents: "He far surpasses any other writer of his own country, and, certainly equals the most celebrated in ours" (2:266).

In November 1825 a change in the *Magnet* is foreshadowed by the publication of Letitia Landon's poem, "Lines to Alaric A. Watts, Esq." Watts's new influence in the magazine is even more strongly indicated in the December number, which prints a ten-page notice of his annual, the *Literary Souvenir* for 1826. Alaric Watts confirms his purchase of the *Literary Magnet* in a letter of 16 December 1825 to William Blackwood: "I forgot to mention that I have just bought the copyright of a little work called the 'Literary Magnet' of which between eighteen and nineteen hundred are sold monthly and I hope in a month or two to increase very materially its circulation."[5] Watts was evidently not the editor of the first volume of the new series, although he may have performed many of the editorial functions. The *Magnet* for February 1826 publishes a denial that the owner of the magazine is its editor (n.s. 1:112). The editor was evidently the unidentified "literary friend" whom Watts mentions in a letter of 9 January 1826 to William Blackwood: "I have purchased as I think I mentioned the Lit. Magnet partly with a view to employ a very clever young literary friend and partly because . . . it is likely to yield me some profit."[6] A letter of 12 July 1826 to Blackwood suggests that Watts may have taken over the magazine's editorship after the completion of the first volume in June: "I have just been trying my hand at the same subject [the "book trade"] for my little magazine which has now fallen into my hands entirely."[7]

At the time he purchased the *Magnet* Watts had edited two volumes of his popular annual, the *Literary Souvenir; or, Cabinet of Poetry and Romance*. Strong ties developed between the annual and the monthly, since Watts advertised and excerpted the *Literary Souvenir* at length in the *Magnet* and actively recruited the annual's writers for the magazine. In his letter to Blackwood of 9 January, Watts says that he has "written all persons with whom [he has] any connection on the subject of the Magazine."[8] John Clare, a contributor to the *Literary Souvenir,* responded to Watts's invitation on 19 March 1826: "I shall be very happy to assist your new work of the 'Literary Magnet' if any contributions of mine will do anything for it."[9] Three of Clare's poems appear in the *Magnet*. Watts succeeded in attracting many other *Souvenir* writers, including the most popular poets of the day: William Lisle Bowles, Felicia Hemans, Mrs. Cornwall Baron Wilson ("C.B.W."), William Howitt, Cornelius Webb, Thomas Hood ("T.H."), Margaret Hodson, Derwent Conway (Henry David Inglis), and J. H. Wiffen, his brother-in-law. However, the most frequent contributors of verse were lesser-known poets—John Malcolm ("J.M."), George Fleming Richardson ("G.F.R."), Mrs. Henry Rolls, and Charles Swain ("C. S——n"). Mary Howitt ("M.H."), Mary Russell Mitford, and Maria Jane Jewsbury ("M.J.J.") wrote prose and poetry for the *Magnet*. Only four poems and two prose sketches are identified as Watts's by name or initials ("W" or "A.A.W."), but he undoubtedly authored a number of the unsigned pieces.

Under Watts's ownership the *Literary Magnet* achieved a better overall balance between fiction and poetry. However, unlike the critical essays in the first series, the articles in the new series focus on poets of the second rank, poets of Watts's own circle—Felicia Hemans and provincial poet Letitia London,—and Robert Franklin, J. F. Pennie, and Ismael Fitzadam (John Macken), who are considered under the heading of "neglected genius." There is also a two-part essay on Wordsworth. All of these essays may have been written by Watts, who for some years had been compiling materials for "Specimens of the Living Poets." The essays on Hemans, Landon, and Wordsworth are particularly interesting, since, taken together, they reflect the aesthetics of the early nineteenth-century poetry of sentiment. A. Alfred Watts, Alaric's son, has described the *Souvenir* and *Magnet* poetry more precisely as the "poetry of taste"—the "poetry of an often powerful, but always refined and cultivated sentiment."[10] Mrs. Hemans's poems are judged superior "for their picturesque delineations, vivid imagery, exquisite taste, and absolutely superb fancy" (n.s. 1:121). Letitia Landon "breathes an intensity of feeling, a passionate earnestness of manner" (n.s. 1). The observations on Wordsworth's poetry are more revealing, however, because the critic contrives to discover in Wordsworth the "peculiar excellencies" of the poetry of taste: his "unswerving regard to the dignity and happiness of man"; "his high standard of the female character"; and "his treatment of the passion of love," which he makes the "sweetening influence, not the engrossing business of life" (n.s. 1: 18–19, 21–22). The last two stanzas of Watts's poem, "Remember Me," which appears on the page following the Wordsworth essay, illustrate the poetry of taste that prevails in the *Magnet* in 1826 and 1827:

> Remember me, and oh! when fate hath 'reft thee,
>   Of fame and fortune, friends, and love, and bliss,
> Come back to one, thou know'st would ne'er have left thee,
>   And she'll but chide thy falsehood with a kiss!
> But no, no, no, I feel that life is waning,—
>   That what I was I never more can be;—
> That I am fast on that sweet haven gaining,
>   Where there is rest for even a wretch like me.
>
> Remember me! thou canst not sure refuse me
>   The only boon from thee I've sought or seek;
> Soon will the world with bitter taunts accuse me,
>   Yet wake no blushes on my bloodless cheek!
> But I would have thee tender to my fame,
>   When I have 'scaped life's dark tumultuous sea;
> And, howsoever unkinder spirits blame,
>   As what thou know'st I was REMEMBER ME!

[1:23]

In his letter of 16 December 1825 Watts tells Blackwood that the *Magnet* will print a "good deal of gossip of one kind & the other," and he kept his word.[11] Two regular columns, "Notices of New Publications" and "Chit-Chat: Literary and Miscellaneous," are devoted to literary news, gossip, and occasional puffery. Ironically, Watts and several other *Magnet* writers were victims of the most sensational bit of gossip reported in the magazine. In May 1826 there is an announcement, without comment, of the first number of the *Star Chamber*. In July 1826 the *Magnet* published a bitterly angry denunciation of Benjamin Disraeli as the author of *Vivian Grey* and as the reputed editor of the *Star Chamber*. The *Star Chamber* not only published a "key" to Disraeli's novel, but directed satirical gibes at Watts, Landon, Hemans, and other writers of their circle in "The Dunciad of To-Day" (10 May 1826, pp. 76–84). The *Magnet*'s counterattack is launched in "Nuisances of the Press. No. 1 The 'New Unknown.' " In ridiculing Disraeli, the tactic is to identify him with his hero, Vivian Grey, and damn them both:

> Vivian Grey is quite a love of a man; wears violet-coloured slippers, and *kisses,* or rather slobbers *Italian greyhounds until they bite his lips.* In his own estimation he is "devilish clever"; and in every one else's, to borrow his own gentlemanlike phraseology, "devilish blackguard." Report says, that this would-be-exquisite,—this fashionable cutpurse, is intended by the author as a picture of himself. [N.s. 2:3]

The direct response to the *Star Chamber* satire is more defensive, and the sarcasm does not completely conceal the hurt feelings: "Would he [the "young Israelite"] have Mr. Watts and Miss Landon, cut each other's throats, because they are read and purchased, whilst he, the 'New Unknown,' . . . loses 120 pounds by a contemptible catchpenny in nine weeks?" (n.s. 2:4–5).

The *Literary Magnet* will continue to have a footnote in Disraeli biography and criticism. The essays and criticism in the first series of the *Magnet* may deserve more attention than they have received; the new series, which under Watts's ownership preserved many specimens of the most popular poetry of the early nineteenth century, should be of more interest to cultural historians.

Notes

1. Bibliographies have perpetuated the error of George C. Boase, who identifies the *Magnet* as a monthly in *Notes and Queries** (*see VEA*): "Vol. i. contains 452 pages, brought out in six monthly numbers; vol. ii. 416 pages, published in the same manner" (3 May 1879, p. 350). During the first eleven months of 1824, the *Magnet* was published as a sixteen-page weekly (28 numbers in volume 1 and 22 numbers in volume 2). The first weekly number of the magazine may actually have appeared in mid-December 1823; the first monthly number was issued December 1824. Boase also fails to indicate the third series of the *Magnet* in 1828. William Charlton Wright, who published the first two volumes of the magazine, describes himself as the "PUBLISHER and SUPERINTENDANT" of the final series (5:141). There is a sharp decline in the quality

of the literature in these final months of the *Magnet,* and Robert Shelton Mackenzie is the only contributor of note. The third series ended after the publication of only three numbers (January–March). Bibliographies that show six monthly numbers are incorrect.

2. Anonymity is turned to humorous account in the "Round Table," a regular column in the second and third volumes. The Round Table purports to record the proceedings of the gathered contributors: "Tobias Merton, Editor," "Irwin Alleyn," "Timothy Oakley," "Paul Clutterbuck," "J.H.H., Secretary," and William Charlton Wright, the publisher.

3. Mary Katherine Woodworth, *The Literary Career of Sir Samuel Egerton Brydges* (Oxford, 1935), p. 183.

4. "Tobias Merton, Gent." may be read as an anagram, the solution of which reveals the names of the editors: SAM / EGERTON / TONI(Y) / B. / T. (The extra "T" may be taken as an abbreviation of Trinity).

5. *The Letters of Alaric Alexander Watts from the Blackwood Papers in the University Library of Scotland,* ed. Estus C. Polk, Kentucky Microcards, Series A. Modern Languages Series no. 17 (Lexington, Ky., 1957), pp. 330–31.

6. Ibid., p. 339.

7. Ibid., p. 355.

8. Ibid., p. 339.

9. *The Letters of John Clare,* ed. J. W. and Anne Tibble (New York, 1970), p. 187.

10. Alaric Alfred Watts, *Alaric Watts: A Narrative of His Life* (London, 1884), 1:13.

11. *Letters of Watts,* p. 331.

Information Sources

BIBLIOGRAPHY

Watts, Alaric Alfred. *Alaric Watts: A Narrative of His Life.* 2 vols. London, 1884.
———. *The Letters of Alaric Alexander Watts from the Blackwood Papers in the National Library of Scotland.* Edited by Estus Cantrell Polk. Kentucky Microcards, Series A: Modern Languages Series no. 17. Lexington, Ky., 1957.
Woodworth, Mary Katherine. *The Literary Career of Sir Samuel Egerton Brydges.* Oxford, 1935.

INDEXES

Each volume indexed.

REPRINT EDITIONS

Microform: English Literary Periodicals (UMI), reels 515–516.

LOCATION SOURCES

American

Widely available.

British

Complete runs: British Museum; St. Andrews University Library.

Partial runs: Athenaeum (Liverpool); Bodleian Library; Cambridge University Library; Glasgow University Library; Manchester Public Library; Manchester Unitarian College Library; National Library of Ireland.

Publication History

MAGAZINE TITLE AND TITLE CHANGES
> *The Literary Magnet of the Belles Lettres, Science, and the Fine Arts,* 1824–1825.
> *Literary Magnet; or, Monthly Journal of the Belles Lettres,* 1826–1827.
> *Wright's London Magnet,* January–March 1828.

VOLUME AND ISSUE DATA
> Volumes 1–2, December (?) 1823–December 1824; volumes 3–4, January–December 1825; new series, volumes 1–4, January 1826–December 1827; volume 5, January–March 1828.

FREQUENCY OF PUBLICATION
> Weekly, December 1823–November 1824; monthly, December 1824–March 1828.

PUBLISHERS
> Volumes 1–2, December 1823–December 1824: William Charlton Wright, 65 Paternoster Row, London. Volumes 3–4, 1825: George Wightman, 46 Fleet Street, London.
> New series, volumes 1–2, 1826: Charles Knight, Pall Mall East, London. Volumes 3–4, 1827: F. G. Moon, 20 Threadneedle Street, London. Volume 5, January–March 1828: William Charlton Wright, 65 Paternoster Row, London.

EDITORS
> Samuel Egerton Brydges and Egerton Anthony Brydges, December 1823–August 1824. "J. H. H.," September 1824–June 1825. Unknown, July–December 1825. Unknown, January–June 1826. Alaric A. Watts(?), July 1826–December 1827. William Charlton Wright(?), January–March 1828.

Ted R. Ellis III

LITERARY MUSEUM, THE

Beginning first as the *London Museum* and then as the *Museum,* this weekly periodical eventually took over another journal called the *Literary Register* in August 1823 and thus finished its short life as the *Literary Museum.* Its aims can be fairly detected in the remainder of its full title—a "Record of Literature, Fine Arts, Science, Antiquities, The Drama, etc." The "Introductory Address" in the first issue for 27 April 1822 by the (deliberately) anonymous editor, actually P. Bayley, announces its mild ambition of "diffusing a knowledge of literature, and of the arts and sciences" without "carrying a party spirit into literary topics," and in fact the journal seems simply to have been a kind of cultural potpourri aimed at the general reader and chiefly valuable today as a reflection of popular taste of the early 1820s.

The journal's first issue is a generally accurate revelation of what was to come in all issues, and of the kind of audience it had in mind. Sixteen pages long (as every issue was to be), it begins with a major book review which runs for more than five pages and stops in order "to be continued" in the next two issues. This serialization of reviews is most typical, as is the fact that the "review" is almost entirely a plot summary of the book. The next section of the journal is called "Original," and consists of three anonymous essays: "The Relative Advantages of Beauty and Accomplishments," which is about beauty in women, defined as "the quality of being pleasing in the eyes of men," and which offers advice to its lady readers to be good listeners, graceful, attentive, and cleanly; "On the Building and Management of Churches and Chapels" ("to be continued"); and "Paris—A Sketch," part of a projected series of descriptive essays called "The Picture Book." Page 10 begins a two-page section called "The Fine Arts" with an essay in praise of Wilkie's "Chelsea Pensioners Receiving the News of the Battle of Waterloo." There is then a two-page section called "The Drama," and finally a section called "Varieties," containing anecdotes, university news, interesting information, small poems and puzzles, weather reports, announcements, letters, and other trivia. Another section, called "Original Poetry," does not appear in the first issue but is frequently present in subsequent issues.

In all of this the actual literary value is small. Invariably the writers for the *Literary Museum* are bland, banal, stilted, and—by design—anonymous. For the editors of the journal harkened back to what they called "the prudence of the olden time" before the "period of the revolution effected by the Edinburgh [*Review**] and its rival the Quarterly [*Review**]" in insisting that their writers appear anonymously or pseudonymously, in opposition to the "vanity of the younger school" which tries to "circuit abroad . . . the name of every author of every article in every periodical" (no. 41[1823]:77–78). This "pre-revolutionary" attitude is carried over into even larger areas of taste as well, so that the journal actually becomes interesting to the modern reader as a sample of how steadfastly late eighteenth-century morals and attitudes lasted throughout the Romantic period into the 1820s among the general public. Besides their preference for genteel anonymity and decorum, for instance, both the editors and the reviewers show an evident distaste for the current literature of personal self-expression and displays of emotions, and they even exhibit more than a slight disdain for such a "new" genre as the novel.

The major names that preoccupy the pages of the *Literary Museum* are, as one might expect, those of Sir Walter Scott and Lord Byron—the two most popular writers of the day. Toward Scott the journal seems respectful but ambivalent. Each of his latest novels—*St. Ronan's Well, The Fortunes of Nigel, Quentin Durward*—is given a front-page summary continuously from issue to issue, but the accompanying comments can be mixed. The reviewer of *The Fortunes of Nigel,* for instance, says in 1822 (no. 6) that Scott has "lost something of his early favor with the public," and adds that he will still tell his readers about the book "to satisfy the curiosity of our readers, though, perhaps, it might be directed to better objects." "These Scotch novels," the reviewer mutters, have "a baleful effect on the literary character of our times." But the reviewer of Scott's *Quentin Durward,* in issue 54 of 1823, says that Scott's novels have "delighted and improved the world" and have rescued the genre itself. "A department of literature which had gradually sunk as low as dulness could drag it down," he proclaims, "has been suddenly elevated to an eminence equal, at least, to its brightest periods" (p. 273).

The reviewers of Byron, however, are uniformly unhappy with him, though they cannot ignore him. Byron's *The Age of Bronze* occasions the general complaint that "modern writers" exhibit a sort of "mental nudity" in which "every author strips his mind bare to the public" to reveal "much that is disgusting, and even more that is absurd." Byron is the worst among these, the reviewer says, "for he not only bares his mental deformities to the public gaze, but he actually makes a boast of them; and . . . is an humble imitation of Milton's Satan" (no. 50 [1823]:209). Byron's *The Island* is dismissed curtly in a review of 1823 as "miserably inferior" to his former productions. And *Don Juan* is at first presented without comment in an extract called "The Shipwreck" in issue 58 for 1823; but eventually its twelfth, thirteenth, and fourteenth cantos are reviewed with disdain. "They are," the reviewer says, "very ordinary stuff," full of "baldness and nonsense"; and Byron is denounced as "a peer who is forever perking his coronet in the public's face (no. 85 [1823]:768).

As for the other major writers of the day, Wordsworth is barely mentioned, Keats is ignored, and the only recognition of Shelley is a surprising article prompted by the poet's death. In it the author dissents fully from Shelley's opinions, but regards the treatment that Shelley received from the critics of the day as "extremely disgraceful to them," and he ends by regarding Shelley as a "misguided young man who was indeed highly gifted" and had "great powers" (no. 27[1822]:417–18). De Quincey's *Confessions of an English Opium-Eater* is given a fairly respectful review-summary in 1822 (pp. 433ff.), as is Hazlitt's *Table-Talk* in the same year (pp. 177, 195); but Hazlitt's *Liber Amoris* is dismissed as an incredible "disgusting mass of profligacy and dulness" (no. 58[1823]:337). Even the fairly famous work *Italy,* by the "banker-poet" Samuel Rogers, is given the same denunciation as "a mass of dulness, unenlightened by a single ray of wit or imagination" (no. 55[1823]:289). The only other major writer to receive commendable notice is James Fenimore Cooper, whose *The Pilot* is reviewed with the comment that he is not so good as Scott and Smollett, but comes closer than anyone else of the day (n.s. no. 5[1824]:60).

Most of the poetry favorably reviewed in the *Literary Museum* is of the kind of Mrs. Hemans's "The Siege of Valencia" or Winthrop Mackworth Praed's "Lillian: A Fairy Tale" (both 1823). The poetry published in the "Original Poetry" sections of the journal is mostly by anonymous or (deservedly) unknown authors, and is occasional, comic, or sentimental—such as, in the last issue in 1824, the imitation ballad "St. Valentine's Complaint," or the sonnet "Spanish Vintager's Chores." There are several prize poems such as "Palmyra" by Ambrose Barbee of Wadham College, Oxford, or "Australasia," by the young and ubiquitous Winthrop Mackworth Praed of Trinity College, Cambridge. The only other poem of any possible distinction is William Lisle Bowles's "The Grave of the Last Saxon" in issue 4 for 1822.

In its last issue in 1824 there is a review of "a new periodical work," the subsequently famous *Westminster Review.* The reviewer calls it respectable and solid, but says that "the great fault is heaviness" (n.s. no. 7:98)—a singular instance of a pot calling a jeroboam black.

Information Sources

INDEXES
> Each volume indexed.

REPRINT EDITIONS
> None.

LOCATION SOURCES
> *American*
>> Complete runs: Iowa State University of Science and Technology Library; Harvard University Library; U. S. Library of Congress.
>> Partial run: Newberry Library.
>
> *British*
>> Complete runs: Bodleian Library; British Museum.

Publication History

MAGAZINE TITLE AND TITLE CHANGES
> *The London Museum,* numbers 1–6. *The Museum; or, Record of Literature, Fine Arts, Science,* numbers 7–66. *The Literary Museum and Register of Arts, Sciences, and General Literature,* numbers 67–new series number 7.

VOLUME AND ISSUE DATA
> Numbers 1–88, 27 April 1822–27 December 1823; new series, numbers 1–7, 3 January 1824–14 February 1824.

FREQUENCY OF PUBLICATION
> Weekly (Saturdays).

PUBLISHERS
> Numbers 1–67: John Miller, 69 Fleet Street, London. Number 68–n.s. 7: John Warren, 7 Brydges Street, Strand, London.

EDITOR
> P. Bayley.

George Allan Cate

LITERARY PANORAMA, THE

The *Literary Panorama* was published monthly in London from October 1806 to September 1814, with a new series running from October 1814 to July 1819, when it merged with the *New Monthly Magazine.* Its editor was Charles Taylor, who had also edited the *Literary Annual Register.* Taylor was by profession an engraver who had studied under Bartolozzi. He also wrote treatises on perspective and drawing, translated Fenelon and anonymously revised and published the highly successful Calmet's *Dictionary of the Bible.*[1] The word *literary,* as in other journals of the period—*Literary Journal,* for instance—is very broadly interpreted to cover practically anything written, published, reported, or said. The *Literary Panorama* was a general purpose news magazine which gave an overview of political events; reviewed notable books on all subjects from *The Elements of Land Surveying* to *Essays on the Anatomy of Expression in Painting,* criticized under the title "Didascalia" the current productions at Covent Garden and Drury Lane; gave anecdotes about the famous; reported on exhibitions at the Royal Academy and the British Institution; listed bankruptcy proceedings and obituaries; published in each issue two to four pages of bad poetry by long-forgotten poets; gave details of British trade around the world; listed current and proposed publications under the title "Literary Register"; and generally tried to be all things to all people. For this reason, and also because of reviewing habits of the day, which run to plot summary and copious quotations, the *Literary Panorama* has little to offer to the specialist in literature. Reviews of fiction, drama, poetry, and essays comprise less than 10 percent of the total content of the journal. It is most useful, however, in giving the reader a feeling for the important issues of the day.

The very first issue, for instance, reports on a proposal by Lord Suffolk to alleviate the condition of the poor by having employers deduct a small amount from their wages to establish a fund to provide for workers when out of work, ill, or old—essentially a combination social security and unemployment income scheme (1:102–3). In the same issue "Proposita Philanthropica," a regular feature, reports from the British and Foreign Bible Society that 2,000 copies of the New Testament in Spanish have been contributed to Spanish prisoners of war, and that an edition of the Gospel of St. John, in Mohawk, has been sent to Canada for distribution (1:173). A review of James Montgomery's "The Chimney-Sweeper's Boy" says that a society is being founded to relieve these boys, and recounts the true story of Mrs. Montague of Portland Place who found her stolen child among the chimney sweeps (2:1195–97). Blake's account of the fate of sweeps is once again shown to be no exaggeration.

One is also impressed, on reading the *Panorama,* by the world-wide interests of England. During the early years of its publication, England was at war, and the magazine is filled with reports of battles, victories, defeats, army lists of promotion, etc. This is to be expected, as are the many reports from North America. But one is also made vividly aware of England's interest in the East: the magazine published diaries, memoirs, and travel reports from India and the Orient, and grammars, dictionaries, and accounts of the mythology and literature of Middle Eastern and Oriental countries. Southey's *The Curse of Kehama* and Moore's *Lalla Rookh,* both of which receive lengthy reviews (9:1044–59; n.s. 6:897–913), reflect this popular interest in exotic Near and Far Eastern culture, language, and myths.

William S. Ward states that journals of the period are characterized by patriotism, and by emphasis on the moral, religious, and instructional aspects of poetry.[2] The *Literary Panorama* adheres to all of these principles. Its dislike of "Jacobin" ideas is evidenced in its review of *The Life of Thomas Paine* by

James Cheetham in October 1818, for it worries that Paine's ideas might spread: "We have not room to notice Mr. Cheetham's able exposure of the detestable tendency of Paine's political writings; but we commend them to the attention of our readers, as particularly worthy of notice, at the present crisis, when the leaven of similar principles is fermenting, under the watchword of Reform" (n.s. 8:1099). Although it deplores such tendencies, the *Literary Panorama* is generally a moderate, not an extremist journal, and argues for freedom of the press against F. von Gentz's advocacy of censorship in *Reflections on the Liberty of the Press in Great Britain* (n.s. 9:217–22).

The *Literary Panorama*'s patriotism is also evidenced in its strong interest in British history and culture. This is especially shown in the early series on "British Antiquities," which reprints Welsh laws, history, and poetry (1:1048–55, *et seq.*). Some insight into Blake's belief that the Druids were allied to the patriarchs of the Old Testament is found in a similar argument, and the *Literary Panorama* also finds similarities in Greek and Hindu religion. In the review of Sir James Hall's *Essay on the History and Origins of Gothic Architecture* the connection is not only made, but the reader is reminded that Dr. Clarke found Druid structures on Mt. Ida facing Mt. Olympus, proving the antiquity and extensiveness of Druidism (14:388).

Hall's book on Gothic architecture is only one of many volumes that were being published on the churches and cathedrals of England. The kind of debate recorded in Humphrey Repton's *Fragments on the Theory and Practice of Landscape Gardening* on the unsuitability of Greek designs for houses in the British climate reminds us that this is the period of the Greek Revival in British architecture (n.s. 5:401–09). The many reviews of various expeditions to the Greek mainland and islands, and the reprinting of the Report of the Parliamentary Select Committee on the Elgin Marbles (n.s. 4:440–46, 705–25) also reminds us that this is the period when the marbles were brought to England. The British Museum is regularly reported on, and its expenses are justified as adding to the literary merit and reputation of the British at home, and as impressing on foreign governments "the politeness as well as the power of our country" (2:980).

The editor's strongly moral tone is primarily shown in reviews of productions at Covent Garden and Drury Lane. The very first volume prints a letter stating that no lady of character dare leave her box because of the dubious morals of the audience (1:388–91). A production of *The Tempest* is castigated because of the "silly and indecent scenes" that were introduced (1:769), but Kemble's revival of *Two Gentlemen of Verona* is praised because "the comedians did not disgrace it by a single oath" (4:304). The reviewer was horrified by productions in which women dressed in men's clothes and men in women's (4:924), and even more by a female gymnast (n.s. 4:145). The Rev. James Plumptre's *English Drama Purified,* which provided suitably purified acting versions of such plays as *The Gamester, Jane Shore, The Conscious Lovers,* and *The Good-Natur'd Man,* was thus enthusiastically welcomed (12:610–16).

Given its highly moral tone, it is not surprising to find a feature, which ran for a number of issues, entitled "Morality of the English Novel and Romance, Illustrated by Selections of Sentiment, Characters and Description." The novels rifled by the "Selector," Samuel Jackson Pratt—the only contributor to the literary aspects of the journal mentioned by name—were standard works from the preceding century—*Tristram Shandy, Tom Jones, The Vicar of Wakefield,* and such contemporary authors as Miss Porter, Mrs. Hunter, and Mrs. Hanway (see 9:97–103, *et seq.*).[3] In its own words, however, "the Panorama reviews very few novels, having happily, or unhappily, works of greater estimation, if not importance, under consideration" (3:72).

One of the few novels it reviewed is *Emma,* and this review is a good introduction to the quality of its critical acumen. The author first commends the recent trend toward emphasis on character in the novel at the expense of plot, and then describes Jane Austen's contribution to the genre: "*Emma* presents the history of a young lady, who, after allowing her imagination to wander towards several gentlemen, and almost to mislead her affections, fixes them, at last, on the proper object. This, we are persuaded, is no uncommon case. The story is not ill conceived; it is not romantic but domestic. To favour the lady, the gentlemen are rather unequal to what gentlemen should be" (n.s. 6:418). The author of this review obviously misses Austen's irony and humor, viewing *Emma* as yet another domestic love story of a young girl with a succession of suitors.

Unfortunately, scanty as the *Literary Panorama's* reviews are in proportion to its other concerns, these reviews only occasionally rise above the quality of the comments on *Emma,* and even when they do, rarely escape the critical commonplaces of the age. Like all the magazines of the time, it regularly reviews Scott's poetry and as regularly deplores his haste, lack of revision, careless rhymes, and faulty plots. Of *Rokeby* it concludes that "Mr. Scott can do much better *if he will*" (13:743), another critical commonplace. Byron is also reviewed at length, and generally unfavorably.[4] The only review in the *Literary Panorama* whose author has been identified, that of *Childe Harold I and II,* by C. Dallas, praises his *English Bards and Scotch Reviewers* as "Satire . . . of which the lash possesses a keenness, and the versification a nerve not surpassed, and rarely equalled, since the day of Pope."[5] Further, *Childe Harold's Pilgrimage* is "a poem in which narrative, feeling, description, sentiment, satire, tenderness and contemplation, are happily blended" (11:418–19). But Dallas perhaps did not write the review of *Beppo,* for Byron's skill at satire is forgotten: "From the uniformity of its *appearance* with Lord Byron's poems, as well as on account of its ardent praise of foreign beauty, this poem has been ascribed to his Lordship. It is, however, too sprightly to be the production of his sombre muse" (n.s. 8:242).

The *Literary Panorama* ceased publication before Byron began producing *Don Juan,* but given its general moralizing attitude, it would undoubtedly have expressed the same horror as other contemporary reviews. This is evident by its condemnation of Moore's *Lalla Rookh*. Parts of it the review praises highly, especially the concluding section, "The Fire Worshipper":

> But if ever he attain a fame beyond the admiration of the fashionable world, it will be . . . by entirely altering his mode of writing, and his way of thinking. . . . sensuality is the deep-rooted vice which imparts a flat and disgusting sameness to all his productions, a coarseness to all his sentiments . . . however calm and pure the surface may appear, venom and mischief lurk at the bottom. [N.s. 6:912]

This attitude toward Moore's "depravity" is another critical commonplace.[6] Of more interest is the comparison of his poetry to Leigh Hunt's: "The best part of many passages in these poems, remind one of Leigh Hunt's Rimini; not that they equal the lively, firm, and natural expression of feeling, in that performance; the joyousness, energy, and freshness of nature in it are here wanting" (n.s. 6:906). This commendation of Hunt reveals one of the more attractive attributes of the *Literary Panorama*'s generally insipid criticism: with the rare exception of authors such as Moore and Paine, and its horror at the licentious drama of the preceding period, it generally does not attack authors or classes of people; it does not use epithets such as "Lake School" or the "Satanic School" or the "Cockney School."

The writers reviewed by the *Literary Panorama* were the fashionable writers of the day, most of whom have long since, deservedly, been forgotten. Any search for comments on those poets whom we now think of as the giants of the period, with the exception of Byron, is in vain. There is a sensible review of *The Works of Charles Lamb* (n.s. 8:1646–53); a commendatory and lengthy review of A. W. Schlegel's *A Course of Lectures on Dramatic Art and Literature* (n.s. 8:1271–87); and lengthy excerpts from Hazlitt's lecture series, *Characters of Living Poets* (n.s. 8:673–81, *et seq.*). Otherwise there is largely silence. The publication of Keats's *Endymion,* of Shelley's *Alastor,* of Coleridge's *Christabel* volume and *The Statesman's Manual,* of Wordsworth's *The Excursion* and *The White Doe of Rylstone* are announced, but none of these works is reviewed. Wordsworth's *Poems, in Two Volumes* is given a one and one-half page "review" which has not a word of comment, only reprints of the "sonnet," "The Sun Has Long Been Set" (which is not a sonnet at all!), and "The Red Breast and Butterfly" (3:271–72). Not surprisingly, in a survey of contemporary reviews of Wordsworth, William S. Ward is unable to decide whether this notice is favorable or unfavorable.[7] And its brevity and lack of any comment are in strong contrast to the ten-page review of William Sotheby's *Saul, A poem,* in the preceding issue (pp. 32–42).

The last few issues contain many more reviews than the earlier ones; there is much more analytical commentary (see especially n.s. 8); and one must conjecture that a new reviewer with some understanding of the contemporary scene had been hired. In a brief essay, "On Modern Poetry," the writer argues that "it cannot be denied that the habit which living Poets cultivate, of dealing only in those impressions which have affected them most strongly as individuals, contributes much to the warmth, intensity and enthusiasm of their compositions." Further, poets should be allowed their own ideas and inspiration and not be bound by metaphysical rules: "We therefore think Mr. Coleridge should be allowed to introduce his owls, and mastiff, in his old Christabel, without molestation" (n.s. 8:827). Similarly, in a review of *The Banquet* (Hans Busk) the author questions "whether the new works are to be judged by the old established rules, or whether new rules are to be framed and adapted to these fresh-raised fabrics of romantic *inspiration*" (n.s. 9:211).

These new trends in its literary criticism come at the end of the *Literary Panorama;* until then it aptly illustrates Ward's judgment that most poetic reviewing of the period is sickly and timid.[8] As a journal it is largely free from polemic political, religious, and literary partisanship, attributes that may account for John O. Hayden's statement that "of all the regular magazines published in the period . . . *Literary Panorama* . . . was surely the least important or influential."[9] But, for present-day readers, its failure to take a stand on critical principles or values is its chief weakness. In a statement that Ward quotes to summarize many contemporary reviewers' attitudes, its failure to see the *form* of a literary work as important is manifest:

> We shall ever be ready to apply the lash to injurious, useless, or ill-written books: but we agree with the skilful and amiable judge who says— "true critics enquire, does the work relate to the interests of mankind? Is its object useful, and its end moral? Will it inform the understanding, and amend the heart? Is it written with freedom and impartiality?—Does it bear the marks of honesty and sincerity? If it inspire noble sentiments and generous resolutions, our judgment is fixed." [8:229]

Notes

1. *Dictionary of National Biography,* s.v. "Taylor, Charles."
2. William S. Ward, "Some Aspects of the Conservative Attitude Toward Poetry in English Criticism, 1798–1820," *Publications of the Modern Language Association* 60 (1945):396–98.
3. See *DNB* for details of Pratt's extraordinary career as actor, poet, playwright, editor, and hack writer.
4. Donald H. Reiman, however, finds an increasing harshness toward Byron after his marital break-up. See *The Romantics Reviewed: Contemporary Reviews of British Romantic Writers,* part B (New York, 1972), 5:1533, 1535.
5. See John O. Hayden, *The Romantic Reviewers 1802–1824* (Chicago, 1969), p. 271.
6. See H. E. Haworth (Helen B. Ellis), " 'The Virtuous Romantics'—Indecency, Indelicacy, Pornography and Obscenity in Romantic Poetry," *Papers on Language and Literature* 10 (1974):287–306; Cyrus Redding, *Fifty Years Recollections, Literary and Personal, with Observations on Men and Things* (London, 1858), 1:61–62.

7. William S. Ward, "Wordsworth, the 'Lake Poets,' and Their Contemporary Magazine Critics, 1798–1820," *Studies in Philology* 42 (1945):110.

8. Ward, "Some Aspects," p. 398.

9. Hayden, p. 59.

Information Sources

BIBLIOGRAPHY

Dictionary of National Biography. S.v. "Taylor, Charles."

Haworth, H. B. (Helen B. Ellis). " 'The Virtuous Romantics'—Indecency, Indelicacy, Pornography and Obscenity in Romantic Poetry." *Papers on Language and Literature* 10 (1974):287–306.

Hayden, John O. *The Romantic Reviewers 1802–1824*. Chicago, 1969.

Reiman, Donald H. *The Romantics Reviewed: Contemporary Reviews of British Romantic Writers*. New York and London, 1972.

Ward, William S. "Some Aspects of the Conservative Attitude Toward Poetry in English Criticism, 1798–1820." *Publications of the Modern Language Association* 60 (1945):386–98.

———. "Wordsworth, the 'Lake Poets,' and Their Contemporary Magazine Critics, 1798–1820." *Studies in Philology* 42 (1945):87–113.

INDEXES
Each volume indexed.

REPRINT EDITIONS
1816, Boston.

Microform: English Literary Periodicals (UMI), reels 736–740.

LOCATION SOURCES

American

Complete runs: Newberry Library; U. S. Library of Congress; Yale University Library.

Partial runs: Widely available.

British

Complete runs: Bodleian Library; British Museum; London University Library.

Partial run: University of Bristol Library.

Publication History

MAGAZINE TITLE AND TITLE CHANGES
The Literary Panorama (subtitle varies), October 1806–September 1814. *The Literary Panorama and National Register,* October 1814–July 1819. (Merged into *New Monthly Magazine.*)

VOLUME AND ISSUE DATA
Volumes 1–15, October 1806–September 1814; new series, volumes 1–9, October 1814–July 1819.

FREQUENCY OF PUBLICATION
Monthly.

PUBLISHER
Volume 1–new series, volume 9, October 1806–July 1819: Cox, Son, and Baylis, Great Queen-Street, London.

EDITOR
    Charles Taylor.

                                                              Helen B. Ellis

LITERARY SKETCH-BOOK, THE

A small sixteen-page, octavo-size Saturday paper, the *Literary Sketch-Book*
sold "for the price of *two-pence,*" and the proprietors made a great fuss about
the low price (1:1). Indeed, everything about the *Literary Sketch-Book* was
slight, including most of the contents, as suggested by the Popean motto poem
appearing on every issue:

> To wake the soul by tender strokes of art,
> To raise the genius, and to mend the heart;
> To make mankind, in conscious virtue bold,
> Live o'er each scene, and be what they behold.

The proprietors wished, as they said, to provide "such reading as may divert
[their readers] in their leisure hours" with "innocent amusement" (1:2).
    Because of problems of space (and, one would think, problems of editorial
consistency), the proprietors did not "intend . . . to meddle" with politics,
but they did intend to produce a periodical "worthy of the perusal of the KING
(God bless him!)" (1:1). Moral concerns loomed larger than political: subscribers "may safely give their wives and daughters our little periodicals to read
without fear of injury to their morals; for the improvement of the *heart* will be
as much studied as the edification of the mind" (1:2).
    The matter of heart shows up in the contents, especially the poetry and prose,
which is light and sentimental.[1] Largely the submission of correspondents, the
verse can be found in "Poetry," a regular department of the magazine.
    Other departments also appeared. "Scrapiana" continued through the first
half of the issues as a receptacle of jokes and anecdotes. One of the heavier
items, which ran as a ten-part series, was "Lectures on History" by "J. W.,"
a correspondent. There was also a "Letter Box" set aside for notes to correspondents, showing clearly that the *Literary Sketch-Book* was largely a vehicle
for aspiring writers. Engravings also appeared occasionally.
    The "reviews" were largely excerpts without comment. The most important
of the few that were actually critiques were the somewhat favorable reviews of
later cantos of Byron's *Don Juan,* which are said to have gone beyond the
"spirit of licentiousness and hardened libertinism" of the early cantos (1:56).
But, the reviewer noted honestly, cantos 9–11 and 12–14 were not as good
poetically (1:56, 297).
    The editors of the magazine were anonymous, but a change in editorship
was announced on 10 January 1824 (p. 352). Several issues later the new editor

attacked his predecessor for printing ''The English Clergyman: A Sketch,'' which described the typical minister of the Church of England as ambitious and unconcerned. The article does seem curiously out of place in such a light-hearted periodical and could well have been the reason for the change in editors.

In any event, the new editor announced on 17 April 1824 that the last issue of volume 1 would appear ''on Wednesday next'' and the first issue of volume 2 would begin ''on Saturday next'' (p. 348). The last issue of volume 1 appeared a week from that Wednesday and volume 2 never began at all.

Note

1. Sometimes the contributions are signed. ''L. E. L.'' (Letitia Elizabeth Landon) and ''Geoffrey Crayon'' (Washington Irving) apparently submitted work or had material lifted from other places.

Information Sources

INDEXES
   Indexed by genre at end of number 37.
REPRINT EDITIONS
   None.
LOCATION SOURCES
   American
      Complete runs: Public Library of Cincinnati; Yale University Library.
   British
      Complete runs: Aberdeen University Library; British Museum.

Publication History

MAGAZINE TITLE AND TITLE CHANGES
   The Literary Sketch-Book, for the Education and Amusement of All Ranks of Society.
VOLUME AND ISSUE DATA
   Numbers 1–37, 16 August 1823–28 April 1824.
FREQUENCY OF PUBLICATION
   Weekly.
PUBLISHER
   W. Crawford, Jun., 124 Cheapside, London.
EDITORS
   Unknown, but changed 10 January 1824.

John O. Hayden

LITERARY SPECULUM, THE

The first number of the *Literary Speculum* opens with neither an address to readers nor with introductory remarks of any kind. Instead, the magazine launches its fifteen-month career with a review article on Byron's *Don Juan* and immediately establishes its serious tone and its focus on literary criticism. The *Speculum*'s clearest statement of purpose appears in an address that introduces its third volume—ironically, only a month before the magazine ceased publication: "The *Literary Speculum* was commenced in November, 1821, with the honest intention of endeavoring to keep pace with the general improvement of periodical literature" (3:ii). The magazine's attempts to attain this modest goal had already attracted "three thousand readers" by January 1822 (1:215).

The *Literary Speculum* was conducted by a small group of writers who only rarely accepted the work of outside correspondents:

> The articles are *entirely original,* and contributed expressly for the work by a select literary association, who are united in the promotion of its interests. It is thus totally independent of all anonymous assistance, at the same time that it does not invidiously exclude the occasional insertion of papers of merit, written by unknown hands. [3:iii]

With only one exception, the earliest members of the "literary association" are introduced by initials or pseudonyms in the second number in the "Editor's Coterie" (1:144), which becomes a regular column of notices for correspondents and readers. The editor was evidently "Star" (*), "as dear in our regard as ourselves, and we are assured he will never desert us." "J.G.G.," a leading contributor, may also have been one of the proprietors "With J.G.G. . . . , we have contracted a debt which we shall scarcely ever be able to repay." "H.," "Adam Winterton," and Mary Leman Rede ("M.L.R.") round out the initial group of writers. In the months that follow, "S.R.J.," "C.W.," and "R." are admitted to the "coterie." Mary Leman Rede, the sister of William Leman Rede and Leman Thomas Rede, is the only regular correspondent who identifies herself.[1] Edward Reginald, whose poems are printed occasionally in later numbers, is the only other writer to give his name.

The average seventy-two-page number of the *Speculum* offers a balanced selection of poetry, fiction, essays, and criticism. The magazine relies on Rede and "J.G.G." for verse until they are joined by "S.R.J.," "C.W.," and occasional versifiers, including Reginald. Although five or six poems appear in each number, the *Speculum*'s poetry is mediocre and adds nothing to its reputation. The magazine's humorous tales and its satirical and non-satirical sketches are much more appealing and were evidently popular, judging from the number of regular columns devoted to them: "The Letter Sylph," "Epistles from the Shades," "The Stage Coach," and "Scotiana." The leading contributors of prose satire, sketches, and tales were "Star" (*), "H," and "R," and they also wrote the *Speculum*'s non-critical essays. The magazine features a number of essays, formal and informal, serious as well as humorous, on a wide range of universal and domestic topics: antipathies, apparitions, auctions, balls, death, dress, duelling, eccentricities, fatalism, genius, music, noses, old age, old furniture, poverty, self-esteem, speculative felicity, visitors, and war. As the following passage from the essay "On War" demonstrates, the *Speculum* writers were not necessarily bound by a conventional *"pro patria"* attitude:

> What glory is there in the blood-stained wreath that encircles the warrior's brow, where every fibre in every leaf is purchased with a human life?—The glory of the soldier is false glory; . . . it is the reward of a demon who grins exultingly at the destruction of the human race; humanity abhors it; virtue shudders at it; nature disowns it. [1:29]

The *Speculum's* essays belong to the *Spectator*-*Tatler** (see *AAAJ*) tradition, which, in the nineteenth century, was giving way to fiction and newer forms of the essay.

It is one of the newer forms, the critical essay, that is the *Literary Speculum's* most distinctive feature. The magazine's literary criticism appears in two styles—the review article on a particular literary work and the survey article on a writer's canon of works. There are review articles, for instance, on Byron's *Don Juan, Childe Harold, Cain,* the *Liberal,** and *Werner;* on Walter Scott's *Fortunes of Nigel* and *Hallidon Hall;* and on Washington Irving's *Bracebridge Hall* and *The Sketch Book.* There are survey articles on the writings of Bernard Barton, Robert Bloomfield, Thomas Campbell, Coleridge, George Colman, the younger, George Crabbe, Hazlitt, James Hogg, Charles Maturin, James Montgomery, Thomas Moore, Lady Sydney Morgan, Samuel Rogers, Scott, Southey, and Wordsworth. In addition, there is a series of "Brief Notices of Eminent Authors," by "H.," which reviews the careers of seventeenth- and eighteenth-century writers. The magazine's critics, "Star" (*), "J.G.G.," "H.," and "R.," took their work seriously, and in the preface to the first volume the editor claims that they have written with "justice and impartiality": "Totally *uninfluenced* by that narrow and partial policy, . . . the strictures of the *Literary Speculum,* will at least possess the distinction of being honest, but unwarped by the prejudices either of literary envy, or personal predilection" (1:iv).

However, it is the *Speculum's* "warped" judgments that provided A. William Ellis with material for his facetious backward look—" 'The Literary Speculum': Critical Opinions a Century Ago."[2] What Ellis finds comically ironic about the *Speculum's* criticism are its blunders in conferring the title of "genius" on Robert Bloomfield and George Colman and in denying the claims of Hazlitt and Wordsworth to the title. Ellis may be correct in assuming that the *Speculum's* negative attitude toward Hazlitt reflects the influence of *Blackwood's,*[3] but, of course, it is an attitude echoed in many other magazines of the day. A different bias apparently motivated the hostile responses to Wordsworth, who is linked with Bernard Barton and the "silly school of minute poetry" (2:48). Wordsworth's violations of decorum draw the mixed reactions to the *Lyrical Ballads*—"productions which abound with glaring defects and exquisite beauties, deeply pathetic traits of character, intense passion and elegant descriptions, mixed up with much that is mean, uncouth, and absurd'' (1:435). The *Speculum* reviewers also share a moral "predilection" that contributed to harsher judgments of Byron's later poetry and to overly positive assessments of the works of Bloomfield, Campbell, and Montgomery. In his essay "On the Moral Character of Authors," "H." evidently expresses the assumptions of his *Speculum* colleagues as well as his own conviction of the moral qualifications of authorship: "It is of the last importance, that a writer should be a good as well as a learned and talented man. . . . And if fame be an author's object, surely there are no paths to it so pleasing as those of rectitude" (2:316–17).

At its best, the *Speculum*'s criticism focuses on the literary work, and not on its author's reputation, and points to both strengths and weaknesses in its style. When this focus and balance are maintained, as they are in several essays by "J.G.G." and "Star," the magazine's critical approach is strikingly modern. In an essay "On the Genius and Writings of Sir Walter Scott," there is praise for Scott's characters, as "vigorously drawn and consistently preserved," his description of scenery and events, and the "fidelity" of "his pictures of ancient manners and habits." He is chided for "reprehensible carelessness" in his "general style" and in the "rhyme, measure and diction" of his poetry. However, a tendency toward "amplification" is cited as his greatest fault: "He quits a subject with reluctance, and seldom till its grandeur is weakened by unnecessary extension" (1:83). Thomas Moore's poetry is described as resembling "the Peris it has celebrated: . . . it has a mingled delicacy and uprightliness, to which we can attach no term more appropriate than *aerial*" (1:218). Several flaws are observed in Moore's style: "He is not always careful to avoid a confusion of metaphor. . . . Such repetitions as, *do, do; come, come*, &c. may suit the colloquial homeliness of Crabbe, but harmonise ill with the light and elegant pictures of Moore" (1:225). Colman's plays are appreciated generally for being "cheerful and rational" and for teaching "the secret of despising folly, without malevolence, and admiring virtue without envy" (2:217). But the literary merit of Colman's plays is questioned: "With all his excellence, . . . there is no single play of Colman's which can be pointed out as a model. . . . He seems to have shrunk from the labour of revision, to have obeyed his first impulses . . . without much reference to the general effect" (2:220). In his essay "On the Prose Writings of Maturin," "Star" manages to suggest both the attractions of popular literature, which defies the "coldness of criticism," and its artistic shortcomings: "[Maturin's] skill in dialogue is indifferent, and all his characters have this glaring defect,—they speak one language. There is little distinction in their sentiments, and none in their mode of expressing them" (2:461, 465).

The *Literary Speculum*'s efforts to carry on the tradition of the periodical essay may be of interest to literary historians. In its judgments of the reputations of contemporary authors, the magazine merely reflects current opinion. In its attempts to achieve balance and a critical method, however, the *Literary*

Speculum participates in the development and refinement of nineteenth-century periodical criticism.

Notes

1. R. Inglis, "Names of Authors and Editors," *Notes and Queries,* 6th ser. 10 (22 November 1884):408.
2. A. William Ellis, "The 'Literary Speculum': Critical Opinions a Century Ago," *Bookman* 85 (October 1933):20–22. Ellis does not pretend to offer either a faithful or a complete profile of the *Literary Speculum.* He saw only the second volume of the magazine, which he treats as an antique curiosity, and his observations are slanted, and frequently inaccurate or distorted, to create his own humor.
3. Ibid., p. 20.

Information Sources

BIBLIOGRAPHY
Ellis, A. William. " 'The Literary Speculum': Critical Opinions a Century Ago." *Bookman* 85 (October 1933):20–22.
Inglis, R. "Names of Authors and Editors." *Notes and Queries,* 6th ser. 10 (22 November 1884):408.
INDEXES
Each volume indexed.
REPRINT EDITIONS
Microform: English Literary Periodicals (UMI), reel 527.
LOCATION SOURCES
American
Complete runs: Harvard University Library; U. S. Library of Congress; Yale University Library.
Partial run: Duke University Library.
British
Complete run: British Museum.

Publication History

MAGAZINE TITLE AND TITLE CHANGES
The Literary Speculum.
VOLUME AND ISSUE DATA
Volume 1, November 1821–May 1822; volume 2, June–December 1822; volume 3, January 1823.
FREQUENCY OF PUBLICATION
Monthly.
PUBLISHER
Thomas Richardson, 98 High Holborn, London.
EDITOR
"Star" (*)?

Ted R. Ellis III

LOITERER, THE

In January 1789 James Austen, the eldest brother of Jane Austen, began an essay serial entitled the *Loiterer*. Of the sixty issues that were published weekly between 13 January 1789 and 20 March 1790, James, then a Fellow of St. John's College, Oxford, wrote twenty-seven. His younger brother Henry wrote ten, and an Austen family friend, the Rev. Benjamin Portal, contributed part or all of three essays. The remaining issues were the work of various friends of James Austen, who for one reason or another wished to remain anonymous.

In the first issue James was at some pains to indicate that the weekly essay would be in the *Tatler*-Spectator,* Idler*-Rambler** (for all, see *AAAJ*) tradition, commenting on all the foibles and vanities of both human beings and literature while avoiding politics and faction. The *Loiterer* was published every Saturday morning at three pence an issue, and, in the best Johnsonian manner, contained "as much learning, sense, and wit, as we can possibly afford for the money" (no. 1). The first publisher, C. S. Rann, was ordered to make the paper available at 9 A.M. so the *Loiterer* might be "served up" with breakfast. James also remarked that the name was deliberately chosen to pay "a compliment to four-fifths of the English nation." Its weekly motto, with very occasional variation, was "Speak of us as we are."

The essays, all of which were anonymous, were mostly written in the epistolary style. Virtually all aspects of human society and literature are satirized by "Mr. Loiterer" or his correspondents. Such popular Oxford sports as fox-hunting, skating, and shooting are lampooned (no. 3), and even an ironical discussion on the virtues of boxing makes an appearance (nos. 22 and 43). Another favorite topic of the *Loiterer* is indolent Oxford students, especially those who spend great sums of money studying fashion rather than books (nos. 4, 15, 21, 24).

If the *Loiterer* had contained nothing but satires on such trivia as mentioned above, it could be dismissed as simply one more of a great many eighteenth-century satirical essay serials. However, there are two recurring themes that were concerns of Jane Austen later—the marriage of interest, and most particularly, excessive sentimentality in literature and its baneful effect on human behavior.[1] The discussions of the marriage of interest are often accompanied by descriptions of London life as opposed to country life, to the detriment of the former. Essays 38 and 39 contain a letter from Agrestis (James Austen) that attacks both the marriage of interest and those people who leave good country estates "in order to enjoy the expensive and empty pleasure of a luxurious and overgrown Capital." In Agrestis' opinion, country manners are much to be preferred over those of fashionable Londonites. In the country "saw I a husband and wife actually fond of each other, I saw young women beautiful without vanity, and improved without affectation." Numbers 29, 40, 41, and

44 also deal with the marriage of interest; number 54 attacks the migration to London from the country with the resultant vulgarization of these rural transplants.

However, the most sustained pictures of the miseries of the marriage of interest come from two letters written by women who have endured such marriages. In numbers 52 and 53 the fair Cecilia (James Austen) mourns that she learned too late the sorrows attendant upon a marriage which is not based on affection, and concludes her letter: "Though a Union of Love may have some misery, a Marriage of Interest can give no happiness." Likewise, in number 57 an aptly named Clarissa M. (Henry Austen is both imitating and satirizing the Richardson style) recounts the story of yet another unhappy marriage and ends by stating: "Indifference is a frail foundation for marriage. . . . The Woman, who loves not her husband, must love someone else"—in this case, her husband's nephew.

Another equally prominent target for Mr. Loiterer and his correspondents is excessive sentimentality in literature and its evil consequences for human behavior. Indeed, the very style of the *Loiterer* itself is a sustained attack on excessively sentimental writing styles. In number 9 a certain Sophia Sentiment (a parody by Jane Austen herself?) criticizes the *Loiterer* on two points: unlike the *Spectator* and the *Tatler,* it contains nothing of interest to women, and it does not have "one sentimental story about love and honour and all that." Miss Sentiment, who professes to be a "great reader" of "some hundred volumes of novels and plays" as well as periodicals, denounces the *Loiterer* "as the stupidest work of the kind I ever saw" and threatens not to buy any more issues unless the *Loiterer* begins to print something for ladies of sentiment. In his reply Mr. Loiterer defends himself against the charge of male chauvinism and states that he doubts that the majority of his women readers "would be much amused with Novels, Eastern Tales, and Dreams" and suggests that these themes are completely hackneyed and of no interest to people of genuine feeling. Here and elsewhere the *Loiterer,* as did Jane Austen later, makes a careful distinction between true and false sentiment.[2]

A lengthier attack on excessive sentimentality is provided in numbers 47 and 48 in a letter from Aurelius (Henry Austen). Aurelius recounts that, while a young man, he made the Grand Tour. In France, he narrowly escaped fighting a duel over a marquise, who had too passionately imbibed the doctrines of Rousseau and Madame de Genlis. As a result of his experience with this kind of sentimentality, Aurelius returns to England, marries happily, and refuses a political career in favor of an ecclesiastical one. Thus Aurelius is presented as a man of true sentiment.[3]

By Saturday, 13 March 1790, James Austen and his contributors apparently realized that publication of the *Loiterer* must cease. Evidently, Henry and the Rev. Portal decided to have one last shot at the fashionable literary excesses of the time. Thus number 59 ironically defends overly pompous and sentimentalized writing styles and presents a lengthy list of rules governing both diction and syntax in writing proper prose. From this witty and extensive list, one example must suffice: no author should write "the country lying round" when he can use the phrase "the country circumjacent." This essay provides both a particularly good example of everything that James, Henry, and Jane Austen detested in contemporary prose style and of the *Loiterer*'s method in general: to attack by ironically pretending to defend something.

On 20 March the *Loiterer* issued its last number. In the final essay, which he signed, James Austen, in typical fashion, facetiously suggests that the *Loiterer* was ceasing publication because all the vices which it had denounced had been abolished as a result. He then states the real reason for the *Loiterer*'s demise—a reason not unknown to more modern periodicals: "the short list of my subscribers and the long bill of my publishers." He also identifies the authors of the various essays whenever possible: his own were signed with the letters C or S; those by Henry were coded with the letter E, and the letter F identified the contributions of the Rev. Portal. In his concluding remarks Austen notes that the *Loiterer* had used an approach different from that of other periodicals in drawing its "sources principally from academical life." The first volume was devoted almost entirely to Oxford scenes. The second was expanded, but with the purpose still of offering the general public "a rough, but not entirely inaccurate sketch of the character, the manners, and the amusements of Oxford, at the close of the eighteenth century."[4] Finally, at the end of this last essay, Austen restates the overall satirical purpose that had governed the *Loiterer* from its inception: the classic definition of satire as the promotion of reform through the castigation of folly.

Notes

1. A. Walton Litz, *"The Loiterer:* A Reflection of Jane Austen's Early Environment," *Review of English Studies* 12 (1961):251–61, discusses the *Loiterer* in relation to Jane Austen's juvenilia and novels.

2. In a letter to her niece Anna, dated 28 September 1814, Jane Austen criticizes Anna's use of the phrase "vortex of dissipation," as "novel slang" as old as Adam. See James Edward Austen-Leigh, *Memoir of Jane Austen,* ed. R. W. Chapman (Oxford, 1926), p. 97.

3. Essays 27 and 33 of the *Loiterer* respectively discuss proper forms of education and affectation in both men and women.

4. James apparently changed his mind later concerning the value of the *Loiterer* and "spoke very slightingly of this early work," according to his son, James Edward. *Memoir,* p. 12.

Information Sources

BIBLIOGRAPHY

Austen-Leigh, James Edward. *Memoir of Jane Austen.* Edited by R. W. Chapman. Oxford, 1926.

Austen-Leigh, William, and Richard Arthur. *Jane Austen: Her Life and Letters.* 1913. Reprint. New York, 1965.

Chapman, R. W., ed. "Preface to Juvenilia" In *Oxford Illustrated Jane Austen*. Vol. 6. Oxford, 1952.

Graham, Walter. *English Literary Periodicals*. New York, 1930.

Hopkins, Annette B. "Jane Austen's 'Love and Friendship': A Study in Literary Relationship." *South Atlantic Quarterly* 24 (1925):34–49.

Litz, A. Walton. *Jane Austen: A Study of Her Artistic Development*. New York, 1965.

———. *"The Loiterer:* A Reflection of Jane Austen's Early Environment." *Review of English Studies,* 12 (1961):251–61.

INDEXES
> None.

REPRINT EDITIONS
> Dublin, 1792.

LOCATION SOURCES
> *American*
>> Widely available.
>
> *British*
>> Complete runs: Bodleian Library; British Museum; University of Bristol Library.

Publication History

MAGAZINE TITLE AND TITLE CHANGES
> The Loiterer, A Periodical Work in Two Volumes, First Published at Oxford in the Years 1789 and 1790.

VOLUME AND ISSUE DATA
> Volume 1, numbers 1–30, 31 January–22 August 1789; volume 2, numbers 31–60, 29 August 1789 20 March 1790.

FREQUENCY OF PUBLICATION
> Weekly.

PUBLISHERS
> Numbers 1–43: C. S. Rann, Oxford. Numbers 44–60: Prince and Cooke, Oxford.

EDITOR
> James Austen.

Larry L. Bronson

LONDON AND WESTMINSTER REVIEW, THE. See WESTMINSTER REVIEW, THE

LONDON MAGAZINE, THE (1791). See NEW LONDON MAGAZINE, THE (AAAJ)

LONDON MAGAZINE, THE (1820)

Despite its short life, 1820–1829, with the exception of its last four years *London Magazine* is one of the most important journals of the nineteenth century. Its outstanding qualities include the editing and writing brilliance of John Scott, its first editor; the excellence and fairness of its reviews; the important works first published in its pages—Lamb's Elia essays, Hazlitt's *Table-Talk*, De Quincey's *Confessions of an English Opium-Eater;* and its fine list of contributors: Octavius Gilchrist, Horace Smith, W. H. Reynolds, T. G. Wainewright, P. G. Patmore, Barry Cornwall (B. W. Proctor), T. N. Talfourd, John Clare, H. F. Cary, Thomas Carlyle, Thomas Hood, George Darley, and Allan Cunningham, among others.[1]

London Magazine was founded by the publishers Baldwin, Cradock and Joy, and was known in its first year as "Baldwin's *London Magazine*" to distinguish it from "Gold's *London Magazine,*" which was established the same year. Its editor for the first fourteen months was John Scott, who had founded the *Champion** and edited it from 1813 to 1817. Scott was fatally wounded in a duel with J. H. Christie in February 1821, and after a search for another editor the journal was sold in April to the publishers Taylor and Hessey, who also bought Gold's magazine in July. Unfortunately, Taylor chose to edit the magazine himself. Although he brought De Quincey and other fine writers into its pages, his procrastination (worsened by frequent illness), his timidity in editorial and critical policy, and his custom of altering his contributors' submissions led to a gradual but steady decline of the magazine.[2] Sub-editor Thomas Hood kept some of John Scott's brightness in the magazine, but he was gradually replaced by less lively and original sub-editors.[3] At the end of 1824 Henry Southern became editor. Southern bought the journal in September 1825 and it increasingly reflected his radical Utilitarian philosophy until he sold it in April 1828 to Charles Knight. Under Knight's supervision the journal became even more sober, and expressed his interest in popular education. It ceased publication in June 1829.[4]

John Scott's death, at the age of thirty-eight, was a serious loss to English criticism and publishing as well as being a personal tragedy for his family. A special fund had to be started for the benefit of his penniless widow and children.[5] The quarrel that led to Scott's death arose from a series of attacks he made against *Blackwood's Edinburgh Magazine.** The attacks were occasioned by that journal's repeated scurrilous personal abuse of contemporary writers. Scott's criticism of *Blackwood's* was certainly merited. "High spirits" is no justification for reviews that refer to "pimpled Hazlitt"[6] and Haydon's greasy hair, that say Leigh Hunt's poetry "is that of a man who has kept company with kept-mistresses," that urges Keats to give up poetry and return to his apothecary's shop, to his "plasters, pills, and ointment boxes," and that boasts of its "salutary" criticism of Keats after his death.[7] *Blackwood's* invited and gloried in such recriminations as Scott's. Action was taken only when Scott accused John Gibson Lockhart, an "anonymous" but known contributor to the magazine,[8] of being *Blackwood's* editor and the author of many of these scurrilous passages, and of cowardly hiding behind his anonymity. Lockhart's direct challenge to Scott fell through, but his second, J. H. Christie, took the quarrel upon himself, and a meeting occurred. The first round of shots, which should have been sufficient to satisfy the code of honor, hit no one, but bungling seconds insisted upon a further series of shots and Scott was fatally wounded.[9]

Despite the violence of his attack on *Blackwood's,* Scott was not a blind partisan of those whose cause he espoused: Humphrey House states the case accurately when he argues that "Scott can seriously be looked on as a martyr to honest book-reviewing."[10] Often reviewing consisted of puffery for books being published by the proprietor of the journal—Taylor indulged in this practice during his editorship of *London Magazine*. Reviewers also often judged an author almost solely on the basis of his political affiliation (Scott notes in his review of Keats's *Lamia* volume that this was as much a fault of Hunt in the *Examiner** as of *Blackwood's* and the *Quarterly Review** [3:315]). Scott stood for a fair and honest assessment of a writer's content and style. Thus, in one of his major attacks on *Blackwood's,* he finds similar faults with the poetry of John Wilson, a writer equally responsible with Lockhart for the virulence of *Blackwood's* criticism, and Leigh Hunt. "The mawkishness of Wilson's poetry betrays its hypocrisy; it shows the want of genuine sentiment"; Hunt's "philosophy is as petty as his taste—and poisonous in a worse way. He would convert life into a child's play, in which sweetmeats represent everything desirable" (2:516). These comments reveal Scott's gift for the telling critical phrase, his ability to make critical judgments independent of partisanship, and his strong moral standards. The contemporary writer he most admires is Walter Scott, whose writing he describes as healthy, urbane, and manly. In the first of his "Living Author Series"[11] he praises Scott for all these virtues, and for giving his readers a favorable view of human nature and society:

> More than any other writer, except Shakespeare . . . he renders the reading of his works encouraging to human nature, by putting us in good humour with whatever he offers to our attention: and this beautiful result, in consequence of the power and comprehension of his genius, and the truth and vigour of his moral constitution, he effects without ever shocking the principles of conscience, or violating any one rule of civil or sacred authority. [1:12]

Because he valued Scott's novelistic genius and his salutary effects on readers, he included him in his condemnation of *Blackwood's*. Scott apparently encouraged the tactics of that journal (in part because Lockhart was Sir Walter's son-in-law), and vigorously promoted Wilson to the Chair of Moral Philosophy at the University of Edinburgh at the expense of the most eminent philosopher of the day, Sir William Hamilton (2:518–20).

John Scott's commitment to strict moral principles, however, does not blunt his critical common sense; in the face of contemporary critical hysteria over Byron's depravity and irreligion, his judgment of Byron's character in the fourth of the Living Author Series is the sane opinion of a man of the world:

> We dare say he has done nothing sufficiently worse than other people, if all were known, to justify, or even render excusable, his rhymed remorse . . . really our own strong suspicion is, however mortifying it might be to his lordship to know it . . . that, notwithstanding his numerous hints, which have set his admirers on hunting out *deeds without names* to lay to his door, he is not distinguished by one unpardonable or abominable vice; that his private history is by no means enriched by crimes of deep dye. [3:53]

Byron does not escape strong critical censure for the content of his poetry, for the sickly sentimentality and morbidity of much of his verse, and most of all for "the quick alternation of pathos and profaneness,—of serious and moving sentiment and indecent ribaldry,—of afflicting, soul-rending pictures of human distress, and absolute jeering of human nature" (3:56). Nevertheless, Byron is praised as one of the most powerful of living poets, of wide sensibility, glowing descriptions, and great eloquence. Scott's criticism of Byron is independent, perceptive, and balanced.[17]

Scott's review of Keats's *Lamia* volume is equally perceptive. He finds the stanzas on Isabella's brothers "no better than extravagant school-boy vituperation of trade and traders," which "dreadfully mar[s] the musical tenderness of its general strain," and suggests that if Keats wishes to express such viewpoints, he write "in the bold indignant style of Wordsworth's glorious Sonnet! The world is too much with us!" (2:316–17). But he quotes and praises for nobility and beauty the last two stanzas of "Ode to a Nightingale," the description of Madeline's disrobing in "The Eve of St. Agnes," and the depiction of Asia and the opening seventy-one lines of *Hyperion,* which he characterizes as "one of the most extraordinary creations of any modern imagination" (2:319). Given the sureness of Scott's own critical perceptions, it is unfortunate that he chose to print P. G. Patmore's gush on *Endymion:* "It is as if the muses had steeped their child in the waters of Castaly, and we beheld him emerging from them, with his eyes sparkling and his limbs quivering with the delicious intoxication, and the precious drops scattered from him into the air at every motion, glittering in the sunshine, and casting the colours of the rainbow on all things around" (1:381). As Scott himself says, Keats has suffered almost as much from over-praise as from the savage attacks in *Blackwood's* and the *Quarterly Review* (2:315).

The reviewing of current literature was only one of *London Magazine*'s many interests. Its Prospectus announced, "The *spirit* of things generally, and, above all, of the present time, it will be our business, or at least our endeavour, to catch, condense, and delineate" (1:v). Hazlitt may well have gotten the title of *The Spirit of the Age* from this manifesto, and his article on Crabbe, the fifth of the Living Author Series (3:484–90), appeared in this later work. The most famous series to emerge from the pages of *London Magazine* were Hazlitt's *Table-Talk,* Lamb's Elia essays (which continued until very late in the journal's career), and De Quincey's *Confessions of an English Opium-Eater,* which was commissioned by Taylor. All reveal the very spirit of the age, its bustle, its high spirits, its everyday concerns and habits, no matter how trivial, and occasionally its darker moments, as in De Quincey's memoirs. But above all these essays, and *London Magazine* in general, have two major characteristics: a lively humor and an urbane and sophisticated prose style (despite the occasional excesses of Patmore and the uncharacteristic shrillness of Scott's attacks on *Blackwood's*). Scott's editorial comments under "The Lion's Head" are always a delight, and Thomas Hood kept up their liveliness. Both use the feature as a means of communication with their contributors. Thus Hood:

> H.L. is always correct in his rhymes, but sometimes with the sacrifice of his sense; for example:
>
> > Dark, dark is the sky, the thunder rolls,
> > The lightning *follows,*
> > The tempest *hollows.*
>
> We would suggest also that Noah's three-decker was not provided, as in our naval *ark*itecture, with wings; and, besides, that it is contrary to all seamanship to say:
>
> > Spread, spread your sail, for there *blows a gale.*

[5:403]

But of all the personalities who romp through the early pages of *London Magazine* none is more ebullient, extravagant, or bizarre than Thomas Griffiths Wainewright. Known to connoisseurs of British crime as "Wainewright the poisoner" for his later habit of feeding strychnine to relatives whose inheritances he wanted, in his *London* days Wainewright contributed innumerable articles and notes to the *London Magazine* under the preposterous pseudonyms of Janus Weathercock, Egomet Bonmot, and Van Vinkbooms. Wainewright's life and personality, his strange combination of dandy, wit, and mass murderer, have fascinated later writers. He is the model of Varney in Bulwer-Lytton's *Lucretia,* the basis of Dickens's "Hunted Down,"[13] the subject of Oscar Wilde's brilliant essay, "Pen, Pencil and Poison," and more recently the inspiration for the Australian novelist Hal Porter's *The Tilted Cross,* which was based on Wainewright's life in Van Dieman's Land, where he was transported for forgery and later died. In addition to his personae and gossip, Wainewright's contributions included theatrical and art criticism. An artist himself, Wainewright knew Blake and bought several of his illuminated books.[14] In his character of Janus Weathercock he makes one of the few contemporary comments on Blake's *Jerusalem* in his usual facetious manner:

> Talking of articles, my learned friend Dr. Tobias Ruddicombe, M.D. is, at my earnest entreaty, casting a tremendous piece of ordnance,—*an eighty-eight pounder!* which he proposeth to fire off in your next. It is an account of an ancient, newly discovered, illuminated manuscript, which has the name "JERUSALEM THE EMANATION OF THE GIANT ALBION!!!" It contains a good deal anent one *"Los,"* who, it appears, is now, and hath been, from the creation, the *sole* and fourfold dominator of the celebrated city of *Golgonooza!* The doctor assures me that the redemption of mankind hangs on the universal diffusion of the doctrines broached in this M.S. [2:300]

Wainewright's most celebrated remark, moreover, also involves aesthetic judgment. When a friend asked him how he could be so barbarous as to kill his wife's half-sister, Helen Abercromby, whose life he had insured, he answered, "Upon my soul, I don't know, unless it was because she had thick ankles."

The interests of *London Magazine* are wide and varied. In its first year it was fortunate in having Hazlitt as its drama critic, and he was succeeded by two other good critics, T. N. Talfourd and W. H. Reynolds. Music is fully reported; productions, artists, and composers are discussed, and critics travelled outside of London to visit various musical festivals. For art criticism it was able to draw on Hazlitt, Wainewright, and John Scott, and occasionally on Haydon and Horatio Smith. The current interest in antiquity is reflected by engravings and comments on three ancient sculptures in the British Museum. In the first three issues of volume 2, the Apotheosis of Homer, the Head of Memnon, and Theseus from the Elgin Marbles are featured. With Scott's death these cease, and are feebly succeeded by two insipid contemporary paintings, Haydon's "Christ's Agony in the Garden" (frontispiece, May 1821), and Hilton's "Nature Blowing Bubbles for her Children" (frontispiece, August 1821). There are a number of stories based on original literature, beginning with "Old Stories" in volume 2, followed by "Traditional Literature" and "Twelve Tales of Lyddalcross." These were all enormously popular.[15] There were also extensive notices of Continental literature, both ancient and modern. John Scott began a series of "Notices of Some of the Early French Poets" (1:241–44), which was continued by Francis Cary. There also appeared Stendhal's reviews and a series entitled "Grimm's Grandson," which began in the new series in 1825.[16]

The *London Magazine* never achieved a high level of circulation, even under Scott, and under Taylor's editorship it gradually declined into dullness. De Quincey, whose *Confessions* had caused enormous interest and skepticism as to its authenticity (see 4:584–86), continued his contribution with a pedestrian series, "Letters to a young man whose education has been neglected" (7:84–90, *et seq.*), and other articles. Even in 1824, however, he caused a small flurry of replies and counter-replies to his assertion that women are inferior to men not only in powers of reason but in imagination as well: "No, no! good women: it is sufficient honour for you that you produce *us*—the men of this planet—who produce the books (the good ones, I mean)" (9:643).[17] Contributors slipped away, and Taylor and Hessey, although they had appreciated Keats, alienated, among others, Hazlitt, who wished to have his liberty in *Table Talk*. In the same letter in which he wondered why the magazine was not selling well, Taylor stated with some scorn that he would not have published "The Fight," one of Hazlitt's most famous essays.[18]

Under Southern the journal continued to deteriorate. Conventional criticism can be found, but a letter to the editor on Washington Irving's *Tales of a Traveller* expresses a frankly Utilitarian view of the novel: "What have I gained by such an expense of time and eyesight? Am I wiser? Very little. Or better? Not much. What have I gained, then? Why, so many hours' amusement. And is this all? All:—what would you more?—Instruction." If he cannot have instruction, the writer asserts, echoing Jeremy Bentham, "I would nearly as soon spend my time at a billiard table. Indeed altogether as soon; for a good game of billiards invigorates the body, whilst a novel, such as I speak of, debilitates the mind" (10:401).

There are interesting articles to be found under Knight's editorship also, but perhaps *London Magazine*'s fatal decline can best be seen through its art criticism. In the early days of the magazine Etty's paintings are condemned by Wainewright with nice precision:[19] "The heads of Amor and Psyche would be vulgar if they were not mawkish, and disarm critical severity by meek imbecility. The drawing is feeble; the handling and colouring of the figures shadowy, and consort ill with the common unraised humanity of their forms, which are little better than Albert Durer's famous *Adam and Eve,* only more fleshy, gristly, or rather woolly" (3:441). In 1825, under Southern's editorship, the same painter is praised in meaningless generalizations: "This is a very noble picture. It is always gratifying to those who feel for the honour and independence of painting, when, as in the present instance, an artist successfully relies on nature and the resources of his own mind for his subject, and on the appreciation of congenial minds for his mode of treating it" (2d series, 2:256).

By 1829, under Knight's editorship, the reviewer again returns to particularities, but Etty arouses only moral disapproval: "Of the visitors of the fair sex who aid in making the gallery so delightful a lounge, we observe that few venture to give more than a glance at Mr. ETTY's 'Subject from Ovid's Metamorphoses.' What is not proper to be seen, we apprehend it would not be quite correct to describe. The style is perfectly in character with the *petit-soupe* cabinet of some splendid voluptuary; but it is not a fit subject for public exhibition'' (3d series, 3:293).

One can sympathize, on varying grounds, with the artist for all three of these reviews, but the critical acumen, the liveliness, the originality that made the early *London Magazine* such delightful reading are greatly diminished by the time of the last review.

Notes

1. *London Magazine* has received much critical notice, but this essay is primarily indebted to Josephine Bauer's painstaking study, *The London Magazine 1820–29* (Copenhagen, 1953). For identification of authors of reviews, see also John O. Hayden, *The Romantic Reviewers 1802–1824* (Chicago, 1968); and Donald Reiman, *The Romantics Reviewed: Contemporary Reviews of British Romantic Writers,* 9 vols. (New York, 1972).

2. See Bauer, pp. 80–89; Edmund Blunden, *Keats's Publisher: A Memoir of John Taylor* (London, 1936), pp. 123–49; Peter F. Morgan, "Taylor and Hessey: Aspects of Their Conduct of the *London Magazine*," *Keats-Shelley Journal* 7 (1958):61–68.

3. Bauer, p. 84.

4. Knight says amazingly little about his editorship of *London Magazine* in his autobiography, dismissing it as having "furnished us [himself and his co-editor Barry St. Leger] very agreeable employment from the spring of 1828 till the summer of 1829. My occupations, in connexion with the Useful Knowledge Society, had then become too engrossing and too important to allow of a continuance of my part of those pleasant excursions into the field of light periodical literature." See Charles Knight, *Passages of a Working Life* (1864; reprint ed., New York, 1973), 2:109.

5. See the appeal in *London Magazine* 3 (1821):359.

6. Hazlitt's biographer, Herschel Baker, says that this phrase "infuriated Hazlitt until the day he died." See Herschel Baker, *William Hazlitt* (Cambridge, Mass., 1962), pp. 370–81.

7. See *Blackwood's,* 2:38–41; 2:194–201; 2:414–17; 3:196–201; 3:453–56; 3:519–24; 5:97–100; 5:639–42; 6:70–76; 7:775–82; 14:220–27; 16:67–73; 19:xxvi–xxvii. These citations, which primarily focus on Hunt and Keats, do not exhaust *Blackwood's* comments.

8. There is an amusing broadside, apparently written before the duel, that in its references to various pseudonyms reveals how public the knowledge of *Blackwood's* affairs, and of the tenor of Lockhart's criticism, were:

> For Lokhearte was ane cruelle prince,
>   Ane snake coyl'd in the grasse,
> Who darted venom on all goode
>   And great that hap'd to passe.
>
> And ever it was his delighte,
>   The unwarie to surprise,
> And plunge ane dagger in their breast,
>   Wrapp'd up in quaint disguise.

See Alan Lang Strout, *"Blackwood's Magazine,* Lockhart, and John Scott. A Whig Satirical Broadside," *Notes and Queries* 180 (1941):22–24.

9. Accounts of this "affair of honor" vary widely: Scott himself, before his death, exonerated Christie and his second. It was his own second, P. G. Patmore, who insisted that the duel be continued. For the whole wretched quarrel and its tragic conclusion, see *London Magazine,* 3:1–8; Bauer, pp. 75–80; Marion Lochhead, *John Gibson Lockhart* (London, 1954), pp. 82–85; Edgar Johnson, *Sir Walter Scott: The Great Unknown* (New York, 1970), 1:724–27; and Jacob Zeitlin, "The Editor of the *London Magazine,"* *Journal of English and Germanic Philology* 20 (1921):340–54. Zeitlin's is the fullest account, and one that explains in great detail precisely the kind of reprehensible reviewing behavior that Scott attacked.

10. Humphrey House, "A Famous Literary Periodical," *All in Due Time* (London, 1955), pp. 246–47.

11. Scott also wrote on Wordsworth (1:275–85), Godwin (2:163–69), and Byron (3:50–61).

12. For a complete discussion of Scott's criticism of Byron, see Elmer L. Brooks, "Byron and the *London Magazine,"* *Keats-Shelley Journal* 5 (1956):49–67.

13. Dickens's two-part fictionalized version of Wainewright's story appeared in *All the Year Round* 4 (11 July 1860). For De Quincey's view of Wainewright, see "Charles Lamb," in *The Collected Writings of Thomas De Quincey,* ed. David Masson (London, 1897), 5:246–51. For an unbiased biography which explodes many of the more extravagant accusations made against Wainewright, see Jonathan Curling, *Janus Weathercock* (London, 1938).

14. See Alexander Gilchrist, *Life of William Blake* (1880; reprint ed., New York, 1969), 1:322–26; G. E. Bentley, Jr., *Blake Books* (Oxford, 1977).

15. Bauer, pp. 146–52.

16. For Cary see Bauer, pp. 295–99; for Stendhal, pp. 299–301.

17. For replies, see 10:3–4, 53–55, 184–88, 333. De Quincey was using the pseudonym "X,Y,Z."

18. Blunden, *Keats's Publisher,* pp. 137–38; Bauer, p. 85.

19. This article is unsigned, but is attributed to Wainewright on the basis of style by W. Carew Hazlitt; the attribution is accepted by Curling, p. 380.

Information Sources

BIBLIOGRAPHY

Baker, Herschel. *William Hazlitt.* Cambridge, Mass., 1962.

Bauer, Josephine. *The London Magazine 1820–29.* Copenhagen, 1953.

Bentley, G. E., Jr. *Blake Books.* Oxford, 1977.

Blunden, Edmund. *Keats's Publisher: A Memoir of John Taylor.* London, 1936.

Brooks, Elmer L. "Byron and the *London Magazine." Keats-Shelley Journal* 5 (1956):49–67.

Curling, Jonathan. *Janus Weathercock.* London, 1938.

De Quincey, Thomas. "Charles Lamb." In *The Collected Writings of Thomas De Quincey.* Vol. 5. Edited by David Masson. London, 1897.

Gilchrist, Alexander. *Life of William Blake.* 1880. Reprint. New York, 1969.

Hayden, John O. *The Romantic Reviewers 1802–1824.* Chicago, 1968.

Hazlitt, William. "The Periodical Press." In *The Complete Works of William Hazlitt.* Vol. 16. Edited by P. P. Howe. London, 1933.

House, Humphrey. *All in Due Time.* London, 1955.

Johnson, Edgar. *Sir Walter Scott: The Great Unknown.* New York, 1970. Vol. 1.

Knight, Charles. *Passages of a Working Life During a Half Century: With a Prelude of Early Reminiscences,* 3 vols. 1864. Reprint. New York, 1973.

Lochhead, Marion. *John Gibson Lockhart.* London, 1954.

Morgan, Peter F. "Taylor and Hessey: Aspects of Their Conduct of the *London Magazine.*" *Keats-Shelley Journal* 7 (1958):61–68.

Reiman, Donald. *The Romantics Reviewed: Contemporary Reviews of British Romantic Writers.* 9 vols. New York, 1972.

Strout, Alan Lang. *"Blackwood's Magazine,* Lockhart, and John Scott. A Whig Satirical Broadside." *Notes and Queries* 180 (1941):22–24.

Zeitlin, Jacob. "The Editor of the *London Magazine.*" *Journal of English and Germanic Philology* 20 (1921):340–54.

INDEXES

Each volume indexed. *Poole's Index.*

REPRINT EDITIONS

Microform: English Literary Periodicals (UMI), reels 79–84.

LOCATION SOURCES

American

Widely available.

British

Complete runs: British Museum; Guildhall Library; London Library; Manchester Public Library.

Partial runs: Widely available.

Publication History

MAGAZINE TITLE AND TITLE CHANGES

The London Magazine.

VOLUME AND ISSUE DATA

Volumes 1–10, 1820–1824; new series (2d series), volumes 1–9, January 1825–March 1828; third series, volumes 1–3, April 1828–June 1829.

FREQUENCY OF PUBLICATION

Monthly.

PUBLISHERS

Volumes 1–3, January 1820–June 1821: Baldwin, Cradock and Joy, London. Volumes 4–10 and new series (2d series), volume 1, July 1821–April 1825: Taylor & Hessey, London.

Second series, volumes 2–9, May 1825–March 1828: Hunt and Clarke, London.

Third series, volumes 1–3, April 1828–June 1829: Henry Cooper, London.

EDITORS

John Scott, January 1820–February 1821. John Taylor, April 1820–November(?) 1824. Henry Southern, November(?) 1824–July 1828. Charles Knight and Barry St. Leger, August 1828–June 1829.

Helen B. Ellis

LONDON MUSEUM, THE. See LITERARY MUSEUM, THE

LONDON QUARTERLY REVIEW, THE. See QUARTERLY REVIEW, THE

LONDON REVIEW, THE (1809)

The English reader confronted a broad range of periodicals in 1809. Along with daily newspapers and monthly magazines as diverse as the genial *Gentlemen's,* * the liberal *Universal,* * (for both, see *AAAJ*), and Leigh Hunt's fierce *Reflector,* * the great quarterly reviews had begun to lead debate and dominate taste in literature. Ian Jack observes that, "the prestige of the Reviews was very great. In an age of discussion they were among the chief channels of discussion. At times their influence was comparable to that of Parliament itself." [1] "Literature" in these early nineteenth-century quarterlies included works of the imagination as well as philosophical, religious, pedagogical, biographical, historical, medical, and scientific texts. The reviewers embraced books on all these subjects. Most often, however, the book under review became merely the starting point for a reviewer's own pointed essay. Partisanship, sometimes extreme and often unfair, was fostered in part by the absence of attribution. Most readers at the time associated a review with its known party or bias rather than with the identities of its anonymous editor or contributors. Indeed, readers "had more faith in the mysterious oracle than in the known critic." [2] Severely stung by criticism during his lifetime, the seventy-seven-year-old dramatist Richard Cumberland sought to redress the real and potential hazards of anonymous or pseudonymous reviewing. His *London Review* identified each contributor. No other periodical heretofore did so and no other would for many years to come. Cumberland's strict policy, in fact, died with the *London Review* in its infancy and would not be resurrected until late in the nineteenth century. Signed reviews are not necessarily interesting, of course, and the dearth of sharp commentary along with the publisher's bankruptcy limited the *London's* run to four half-crown issues published in 1809.

In the *London's* "Introductory Address" Richard Cumberland defends his revolutionary commitment to identifying contributors. He invokes military metaphors to describe cowardly competing reviews' "operations under casemates or by ambuscade," and concludes poignantly, "When the enemy veiled himself in a cloud, honest Ajax only prayed for light" (1:ii). Cumberland then shifts from the language of the battlefield to the familiar eighteenth-century stance of honest, impartial—indeed, beneficent—critic, the reading public's servant:

> The man, who in the genuine spirit of criticism impartially distributes praise or blame to the writer he reviews, has no more need to hide his name than the tradesman has, who records himself over his shop-door; for whom has he to fear, or of what to be ashamed? . . . Every one must confess, that there is dangerous temptation, an unmanly security, an unfair advantage in concealment: Why then should any man, who seeks not to injure but to benefit his contemporaries, resort to it?'' [1:ii]

In an age of warring reviews, self-consciously political periodical authors, and socially active poets and novelists, Cumberland's theoretical support for his policy of identifying contributors seems naive at least: "Literature is of no party; the critic should not let his politics appear" (1:v). Despite such anachronistically sweet reasonableness, Cumberland freely acknowledges that by naming authors, his *Review* runs the "risk of an experiment" (1:vi).

Cumberland's contemporaries agreed. Upon hearing of the idea at least one informed reader, Walter Scott, immediately declared that the "extraordinary proposal that each contributor shall place his name before his article . . . must prove fatal to the undertaking."[3] Cumberland's novel idea challenged a long and virtually unbroken history of anonymous periodical writing, an eighteenth-century legacy. "Except for La Crose's voluntary assumption of responsibility at the beginning of the eighteenth century," Walter Graham observes, "there is no other example of such critical frankness in periodicals before the middle of the nineteenth century."[4] The general practice of nameless contributions to periodicals persisted well into the Victorian Age, with signed articles and stories beginning to appear in the 1860s. "Most articles and stories in the Victorian periodicals were anonymous or pseudonymous—before 1870 about 97 percent, for the whole period probably 90 percent."[5] Only the "star system" of the 1870s finally insured signatures after most articles written subsequently. The controversy over signed versus anonymous reviewing which was "intermittent through most of the nineteenth century" also became hotly debated "after 1860."[6] Arguments on each side were very strong. Consider also the impact of anonymity and powerful editors upon the composition of periodical writing beyond the obvious freedom and potential authority authors enjoyed writing under a review's aegis. First, most essays in the early reviews easily became collaborations between an unnamed—unknown—author and an editor who quietly emended contributions; and second, prolific contributors—Henry Brougham in the *Edinburgh Review,** for example—could silently contribute several articles to an issue, in effect dominating it, without readers becoming aware of such a pervasive single voice. Hence, Cumberland's bold experiment in 1809 radically altered the status of the previously anonymous author, the fashioning of a typical review essay, and the character of the entire review. Despite submissions from well-known London professionals, however, signatures alone could not ensure the *London*'s success. And its failure inevitably helped perpetuate the tradition of anonymity in reviews.

For many years before beginning his *Review* Richard Cumberland was known as a playwright whose characteristic work was the sentimental domestic comedy, and as author of two novels and a translation of Aristophanes' *The Clouds*. He embarked upon his theatrical career in 1761; his best-known play is *The West Indian* (1771), produced by Garrick. Cumberland's circle included Foote, Reynolds, Garrick, and Goldsmith, all of whom he would meet at the British Coffee-House. Fame brought with it feuds, and he was caricatured by Sheridan in *The Critic* (1779) as "Sir Fretful Plagiary," supposedly in revenge for Cumberland's reception of *School for Scandal*.[7]

In 1808, anticipating "an aera . . . I am bold to promise no past period will eclipse" (1:4), and with Hewson Clarke as partner and assistance from Henry Crabb Robinson, Cumberland commenced his challenge to the enormously successful *Edinburgh Review*. For the enterprise, he assembled a competent group of contributors including a few writers of distinction. Among them was James Smith, whose parodic *Rejected Addresses* (1812) and *Horace in London* (1813), both written with his brother Horace, would win him fame. He reviewed *A New System of Domestic Cookery* in the first number. Horace Twiss, a politician and lawyer, evaluated Scott's *Marmion* (no. 1) and Campbell's *Gertrude of Wyoming* (no. 3). Poet Laureate Henry James Pye reviewed, among other books, Scott's edition of Dryden (no. 1) and Inchbald's *British Theatre* (nos. 2, 3). G. W. Crowe reviewed Hannah More's *Caelebs in Search of a Wife* (no. 2) and Bowles's *Poems* (no. 3). John Landseer considered two volumes of engravings (nos. 2, 4). Henry Crabb Robinson surveyed four works "On the Spanish Revolution" (no. 4), including Wordsworth's *Concerning . . . the Convention of Cintra*.

The Review's four numbers now seem quite miscellaneous. The length and number of reviews in each issue show that Cumberland modeled his quarterly on the *Edinburgh Review*. The *London* was, in fact, its first imitator. The first issue, published in February 1809, occupies 222 pages containing the "Introductory Address," eleven reviews, a "Concluding Address" (pp. 203–6), and a "Quarterly List of New Publications" (pp. 207–22). Each issue featured the "List" with its nineteen categories ranging from "Agriculture" to "Education," "Medicine" to "Navigation," and "Poetry" to "Topography." Running titles appear throughout both volumes. Cumberland wrote four of the twelve articles, including the first of a two-part rambling and digressive essay on Fox's *History of . . . James II* and a brief review and printing of George Townsend's *Plan of an Epic Poem . . . to be entitled "Armageddon."* James Smith contributed a hilarious tongue-in-cheek review of *A New System of Domestic Cookery . . . "by A Lady."* "It may be stated, as an indisputable fact," Smith declares, "that man is a cooking animal, and increases in civilization in proportion to the beauty and variety of the produce of his saucepans" (1:29). Smith delights in mocking the author's bathetic piety: "Talents here find themselves placed in the same sentence with treacle; custards are coupled with conjugal fidelity, and moral duties with macaroni" (1:33). Horace Twiss attacks

Scott's "vicious style" (1:82)—his reliance on archaisms—in *Marmion*. And the jest book *New and Old Joe Miller, or the Tickler* receives a sober appraisal here as well.

The second number appeared on 1 May 1809. Its 241 pages contain ten reviews, the "Quarterly List of New Publications" (pp. 445–56), and an analytical index to the volume (pp. 457–64). Cumberland here concludes his review of Fox (and recent British history). The Rev. Dr. Symmons discusses John Davis's *Life of Chatterton*, first sketching Chatterton's brief existence and then concluding that this youth could not have been the author of the Rowley poems. He has examined the manuscripts in the British Museum and affirms their antique authenticity. John Landseer, father of the famous Victorian wildlife painter and a noted engraver and painter in his own right, reviews George Dance's *Portraits,* considering initially the technology involved with producing them (p. 303) and then their aesthetic effects (pp. 306ff.). Henry James Pye examines Mrs. Ichbald's headnotes and principles of selecting plays for *The British Theatre,* and G. W. Crowe warmly praises More's *Caelebs in Search of a Wife.*

Volume 2, number 3 appeared in August. Occupying 230 pages, it contained eleven reviews and the "Quarterly List" (pp. 215–30). A note promises optimistically that an index to the volume "will be inserted in No. V which will be published on the First of March, 1810." Cumberland did not foresee his publication's end after its next number. To this issue he contributes three essays. The most important and lead article reviews Leigh Hunt's first book of criticism, *Critical Essays on the Performers of the London Theatres* (published in 1807, it collected pieces originally printed in his brother John's *The News*). Cumberland applauds the young Hunt's good sense and sharp eyes: "These Essays abound in a variety of judicious observations and remarks, which . . . will afford general entertainment and delight." They mark Hunt's "sincere and manly character" (p. 1). But Cumberland soon abandons Hunt's volume to pursue his own reminiscences of life in the theater. Horace Twiss composes an encomium to Campbell's *Gertrude of Wyoming*. Reviewing R. H. Cromek's *Reliques of Robert Burns* with some prescience, he predicts that "Burns's fame, the orb that now glares so broadly and so brightly, seems destined to fade from its glittering greatness" (p. 138).

The *London Review*'s final number contains its most important essay. Cumberland devotes 44 of its 233 pages to the lead article, titled boldly "ON THE SPANISH REVOLUTION"—a review of four books by Henry Crabb Robinson. Robinson had assisted Cumberland in editing the *London*. In his only written contribution to it he considers effects of the peninsular war by focusing particularly on Wordsworth's *Convention Cintra* pamphlet.[8] He begins by reviewing European history from 1792 to the present, emphasizing along with Wordsworth that unity of "a people" in individual nations cuts across class barriers and emerges with unexpected strength at times of national stress. Quickly shifting attention to Wordsworth's moral essay, Robinson rightly characterizes its subject, which is not current politics, but the human spirit oppressed by war:

> It is not a political pamphlet, but an ethic essay on a political subject, in which the philosophy of human nature, and the principles of an high-toned and pure morality, are applied to the Conduct and fate of nations. . . . in this work the author displays a warm or as some will say, a romantic attachment to the cause of liberty. [Pp. 250–52]

Robinson quotes liberally from Wordsworth's pamphlet. He demonstrates the poet's hatred of both the imposing "I" of Napoleon's decrees and Britain's expedient abandonment of principles—indeed, its failure to comprehend a symbol's powerful significance. A simple citation fairly represents Wordsworth's idealism and Robinson's thrust: "We combated for victory in the empire of reason, for strong-holds in the imagination. Lisbon and Portugal, as city and soil, were chiefly prized by us as a *language; but our generals mistook the counters of the game for the stake played for*" (pp. 254–55). Robinson glories in Wordsworth's "sentiments eloquently enforced by a great variety of illustrations" (p. 255), though he acknowledges that the poet "seems content to be understood and relished by a few like himself: his thoughts are great, but sometimes obscure; his genius is original, and therefore unaccommodating" (p. 266). Robinson displays his own critical acumen as he contrasts Burke with Wordsworth: "The imagery of Burke is more varied and dramatic, that of Wordsworth more intense and lyric: the one receives a coloured glare from his objects; the other reflects the pure light of his own mind" (p. 265). They become, for a prophetic Robinson, the mirror and the lamp.

The *London Review* also includes in its final issue Mr. Pye on *An Orthöepical Analysis of the English Language,* Hewson Clarke on Joel Barlow's *Columbiad,* John Landseer reviewing William Green's *Studies from Nature,* and G. W. Crowe on Shee's *Elements of Art: A Poem.* This range typified early reviews, but reviewers' treatments in the *London* failed to generate excitement. Despite Robinson's particularly lucid, impassioned review and a few other worthy essays, the *London Review* failed "as much because of its dulness as because the public was not ready for signed articles."[9] The *London* concludes its run quietly, bearing no word of impending expiration. The bankruptcy of its publisher, Samuel Tipper, at the end of 1809 was connected with the public's disdain for the lackluster and the known. Cumberland's courageous experiment in signed periodical publication remains a singular anomaly.

Notes

1. Ian Jack, *English Literature 1815–1832,* vol. 10 of the *Oxford History of English Literature* (Oxford, 1963), p. 8. Jack underscores his point by devoting more than half of his first chapter, "The Literary Scene in 1815," to periodicals.
2. Walter Graham, *English Literary Periodicals* (New York, 1930), p. 240.

3. *Letters from and to Charles Kirkpatrick Sharpe,* ed. Alexander Allardyce (Edinburgh, 1888), 1:351; cited in Stanley Thomas Williams, *Richard Cumberland: His Life and Dramatic Words* (New Haven, 1917), p. 273. Williams's book remains the best study of Cumberland to date.

4. Graham, p. 239.

5. Walter Houghton, "Introduction" to *The Wellesley Index to Victorian Periodicals* (Toronto, 1966), 1:xvi. On the journals initiating signed contributions, including *Macmillan's Magazine** (1859), the *Fortnightly Review** (1865), and the *Nineteenth Century** (1877) (for all, see *VEA*), see pp. xviii–xix.

6. Oscar Maurer, Jr., "Anonymity vs. Signature in Victorian Reviewing," in *The University of Texas Studies in English* 27 (1948):1. Maurer studies representative arguments on both sides of the issue. He notes that "as early as 1831" when Bulwer assumed editorship of the *New Monthly** he became a fierce proponent of signature. On the controversy, see also Houghton, "Introduction," pp. xvii–xviii.

7. I derive much of this biographic information from Williams, *Richard Cumberland,* and the *Dictionary of National Biography.*

8. Robinson's review is reprinted in *The Romantics Reviewed: Contemporary Reviews of British Romantic Writers,* ed. Donald H. Reiman (New York, 1972), part A, 2:631–53. The Convention of Cintra (30 August 1808) resulted in great part from the British military's "personal squabbles"; it allowed a beaten French force to surrender in Portugal but return to France with all its arms and equipment. For the history of the period, see J. Steven Watson, *The Reign of George III 1760–1815,* vol. 12 of *The Oxford History of England* (Oxford, 1960), pp. 459–61. For a thoroughly detailed personal and historical background to Wordsworth's *Concerning . . . the Convention of Cintra* and a reprint of its text, consult *The Prose Works of William Wordsworth,* ed. W.J.B. Owen and Jane Worthington Smyser (Oxford, 1974), 1:193–415.

9. Maurer, p. 19.

Information Sources

BIBLIOGRAPHY

Cumberland, Richard. *Memoirs of Richard Cumberland.* London, 1807.

Dircks, Richard. *Richard Cumberland.* Boston, 1976.

Graham, Walter. *English Literary Periodicals.* New York, 1930.

Hayden, John O. *The Romantic Reviewers: 1802–1824.* London, 1969.

Houghton, Walter, ed. *The Wellesley Index to Victorian Periodicals.* Vol. 1. Toronto, 1966.

Jack, Ian. *English Literature 1815–1832.* Vol. 10 of the *Oxford History of English Literature.* Oxford, 1963.

Maurer, Oscar, Jr. "Anonymity vs. Signature in Victorian Reviewing." *The University of Texas Studies in English* 27 (1948):1–27.

Morley, Edith J., ed. *Henry Crabb Robinson on Books and Their Writers.* 3 vols. London, 1938.

Reiman, Donald H., ed. *The Romantics Reviewed: Contemporary Reviews of British Romantic Writers.* 3 vols. New York, 1972.

Williams, Stanley Thomas. *Richard Cumberland: His Life and Dramatic Works.* New Haven, 1917.

INDEXES

Each volume indexed.

REPRINT EDITIONS
>   Microform: English Literary Periodicals (UMI), reel 529.
LOCATION SOURCES
American
>   Complete runs: Boston Athenaeum; Library Company of Philadelphia; State University of Iowa Library; Yale University Library.
British
>   Complete runs: Birmingham University Library; Bodleian Library; British Museum; London University Library.

Publication History

MAGAZINE TITLE AND TITLE CHANGES
>   *The London Review.*
VOLUME AND ISSUE DATA
>   Volumes 1–2, numbers 1–4, February–November 1809. (Number 1 appeared in February 1809; number 2 on 1 May 1809; volume 2, number 3 appeared in August 1809; number 4 in November 1809.)
FREQUENCY OF PUBLICATION
>   Quarterly.
PUBLISHER
>   Samuel Tipper, Leadenhall Street, London.
EDITOR
>   Richard Cumberland.

Mark L. Greenberg

LONDON REVIEW, THE (1835). See WESTMINSTER REVIEW, THE

LOUNGER's MISCELLANY, THE. See AAAJ

M

McKAY's NEW BRITISH LADY'S MAGAZINE. See BRITISH
LADY'S MAGAZINE, THE

METROPOLITAN MAGAZINE, THE

Under the direction of its ablest editor, Captain Frederick Marryat, the *Metropolitan Magazine* became the first nineteenth-century British periodical to provide serial fiction in its monthly numbers. In the pages of the magazine between 1832 and 1837 appeared two complete novels by Marryat (*Jacob Faithful* and *Japhet, in Search of a Father*), as well as excerpts from three more (*Peter Simple, Mr. Midshipman Easy,* and *Snarleyyow*), and various pieces later gathered in *Pacha of Many Tales* and *Olla Podrida*. Marryat's associations with the navy led to the publication of three other nautical tales in the early period of the magazine, the best known of which is *Rattlin the Reefer* by Edward Howard.[1] Lesser-known works by such fashionable authors as Lady Morgan, Miss Mitford, and Mrs. Trollope also appeared before the *Metropolitan* ceased publication in 1850.

The publisher James Cochrane began the *Metropolitan: A Monthly Journal of Literature, Science, and the Fine Arts* in May 1831, with Thomas Campbell as editor, and Marryat as one of several major investors. However, Campbell's qualifications as a well-known poet did not prepare him for the business of editorship, and in 1832 Marryat took over responsibility as editor and chief proprietor.[2] He transferred publication to the established firm of Saunders and Otley, and in 1833 renamed the periodical the *Metropolitan Magazine*. In addition to fiction by Marryat and others, and poetry by Campbell and James Montgomery, early issues of the magazine offered reviews and notices of a wide range of events in science, commerce, politics, the fine arts, music, drama, horticulture, learned societies, works in progress—even the weather.

Despite Marryat's own aristocratic proclivities, the magazine, in the "To Our Readers" of its first issue, described itself as an "unflinching advocate of a Reform in State and Church; not on a wild, theoretical, abstract plan, but a rational reform. . . . we therefore hail the cause of liberty everywhere—in the lofty and noble-minded Poland—in France—in the boastful and noisy Belgium" (1:iv). In this vein the magazine published an extensive feature on the debates of the First Reform Bill (3:95–101) and in volume 13 (1835) reviewed Shelley's works favorably, noting that the poet's reputation had suffered from critics who had attacked him for his radical political views.

But it was the *Metropolitan*'s publication of serial fiction in the early 1830s— before Dickens, Thackeray, and others began arousing the Victorian appetite for the magazine serial—that confers a significant place in literary history upon the periodical. Before the *Metropolitan*'s experiments in magazine serialization of fiction, *Blackwood's Edinburgh Magazine* * had presented numerous tales as well as a dozen or more longer works of fiction published in installment parts. However, with one or two exceptions, few of these magazine serials before Marryat's contributions to the *Metropolitan* had consciously or skillfully exploited the aesthetic possibilities inherent in serial publication.[3] Though Marryat rather abruptly suspended serial publication of *Peter Simple* before its denouement, in 1833 he provided in the last installment of the novel one of the first nineteenth-century defenses for "the system of having one or two of the papers in the magazine as continuations" (8:69). In a formulation which anticipates Dickens's conception of serialization both as an aesthetic form and a marketing technique, Marryat wrote that, in 1833:

It is impossible, in one short sketch, to delineate character truly, and give that effect which, as writers, we feel that our reputation demands. . . . Perhaps there is another reason which we, as story-tellers, claim as our privilege, that of imparting a degree of prospective interest to our work, and inducing the public to look forward to the ensuing number. When the Kessehgou, or story-teller of the East, has entered upon the most effective part of his narrative, and his audience are breathless with interest and impatience, he drops his cap and his story at one and the same time, and until he perceives that his cap is replete with the small coin of the country . . . he proceeds no further. Why, then, may we not claim the same privilege, and wish to excite that interest which will occasion the purchase of the ensuing number? [8:69–70]

As a magazine editor Marryat clearly sensed the value of "prospective interest" in maintaining the audience's involvement. Thus, after the incomplete *Peter Simple* ceased publication in September 1833, readers of the magazine encountered a serial installment of at least one of Marryat's works in every monthly number for almost the next four years.[4] These serial novels do not disclose evidence of the careful planning—so necessary to contriving suspenseful endings—that characterizes the work of Dickens, Hardy, and later masters of serial fiction. On the other hand, Marryat did possess the ability to keep an adventure story moving, and his serials do not fall into self-contained and unrelated episodes like the anecdotal assemblages of many of *Blackwood's* serialized tales. Occasional "cliffhangers" provided fillips for the reader. His daughter's biography records that, as with Dickens's works, the periodic interruption of the narrative kept avid readers in a proper state of enthusiastic anticipation: "The general interest excited by this tale [*Japhet, in Search of a Father*] whilst it was running in the pages of the magazine was so great that an American vessel meeting an English one in the broad Atlantic, instead of a demand for water or supplies, ran up the question to her masthead, "Has Japhet found his father yet?"[5] *Rattlin the Reefer,* often falsely attributed to Marryat, actually was the work of Marryat's sub-editor, Edward Howard, who began serializing the novel in the *Metropolitan* in September 1834 as *The Life of a Sub-editor*.[6] Howard took over the editorship when Marryat resigned his position in 1836 to accept command of a naval vessel.[7] To herald the new management, the January 1837 issue began with a collection of introductory puffs by Campbell, Thomas Moore, Lady and Sir Charles Morgan, James Montgomery, John Banim, Mrs. Gore, and Marryat himself.

However, the scope of the magazine began to diminish under Howard. Marryat's serials ceased, and the political notices and features declined in number in the late 1830s. The list of the *Metropolitan*'s advocates mentioned above tells the tale of the magazine's decline. All but Marryat were fashionable writers of the Regency whose popularity did not last long into the Victorian period. Indeed, the newer writers like Dickens who were to dominate the mid-nineteenth century were noticed (if at all) by the *Metropolitan* only in terms of pallid imitations, like the parody of *Pickwick Papers* which appeared in October 1838. Howard himself left for the *New Monthly Magazine* * in 1839. After 1846 the numerous reviews and notices disappeared from the magazine; with the monthly length severely cropped, it was sold by Saunders and Otley (who had purchased it from Marryat) to the lesser-known firm of Kent and Richards. The only noteworthy publications of the 1840s were Mrs. Trollope's serial, *Blue Belles of England* (January 1841–January 1842), and the first British magazine publication of two of Hawthorne's tales: "Dr. Heidegger's Experiment" (February 1849), and in the last number, "Peter Goldthwaite's Treasure" (April 1850). With number 228, the *Metropolitan Magazine* ceased publication.

Notes

1. The importance of Marryat's friendship with a number of other sailor-authors is examined by Oliver Warner in *Captain Marryat: A Rediscovery* (London, 1953), pp. 90–92. In addition to nautical tales by Marryat and Howard, Captain Chamier's *Life of a Sailor* appeared from May 1831 to April 1832, and the anonymous *Scenes from the Life of Edward Lascelles, Gent.,* from March 1834 to July 1837.

2. See Warner, pp. 89–90, for a more detailed account of the founding of the magazine.

3. William G. Kilbourne, Jr., "The Role of Fiction in *Blackwood's Magazine* from 1817 to 1845" (Ph.D. dissertation, Northwestern University, 1966), helpfully surveys *Blackwood's* fiction. Lance Schachterle, *"Oliver Twist* and Its Serial Predecessors," *Dickens Studies Annual* 3 (1974):1–13, examines Marryat's serials in relation to earlier and later magazine installment fiction. His article is the basis for this survey of Marryat's work.

4. *Jacob Faithful* appeared from September 1833 to October 1834; Marryat assured his readers in January 1834 that the novel would run to completion. *Japhet, in Search of a Father* ran from November 1834 to January 1836, and thirty-nine of the sixty-five chapters of *Snarleyyow* appeared from January 1836 to June 1837. The first four chapters only of *Mr. Midshipman Easy* were published in August 1836.

5. Florence Marryat, *Life and Letters of Captain Marryat* (London, 1872), 1:213–14.

6. A publication history of the novel and an account of Howard's and Marryat's literary relations are provided by Arthur Howse in his edition of *Rattlin the Reefer* (London, 1971), pp. vii–x and 401–4.

7. Warner, p. 110.

Information Sources

BIBLIOGRAPHY
Howard, Edward, *Rattlin the Reefer,* ed. and intro. by Arthur Howse. London, 1971.
Kilbourne, William G., Jr. "The Role of Fiction in *Blackwood's Magazine* from 1817 to 1845." Ph.D. dissertation, Northwestern University, 1966.
Marryat, Florence. *Life and Letters of Captain Marryat.* 2 vols. London, 1872.
Schachterle, Lance. *"Oliver Twist* and Its Serial Predecessors." *Dickens Studies Annual* 3 (1974):1–13.
Warner, Oliver. *Captain Marryat: A Rediscovery.* London, 1953.

INDEXES
Each volume indexed.

REPRINT EDITIONS
Microform: English Literary Periodicals (UMI), reels 312–325.

LOCATION SOURCES
American
Partial runs: Widely available.

British
Complete runs: Birmingham Public Library; British Museum; Cambridge University Library.
Partial runs: Widely available.

Publication History

MAGAZINE TITLE AND TITLE CHANGES
The Metropolitan: A Monthly Journal of Literature, Science, and the Fine Arts, May 1831–December 1832. *The Metropolitan Magazine,* January 1833–April 1850.

VOLUME AND ISSUE DATA
>Numbers 1–20, volumes 1–5, May 1831–December 1832; Numbers 21–228, volumes 6–57, January 1833–April 1850.

FREQUENCY OF PUBLICATION
>Monthly.

PUBLISHERS
>Numbers 1–12, May 1831–April 1832: James Cochrane and Co., 11 Waterloo Place, Pall Mall, London. Numbers 13–192, May 1832–April 1847: Saunders and Otley, Conduit Street, London. Numbers 183–228, May 1847–April 1850: Kent and Richards, 51 & 52 Paternoster Row, London.

EDITORS
>Thomas Campbell, 1831–1832. Frederick Marryat, 1832–1836. Edward Howard, 1836–1839 (sub-editor 1832–1836). Subsequent editors unknown.

Lance Schachterle

MIRROR MONTHLY MAGAZINE, THE. See MIRROR OF LITERATURE, AMUSEMENT, AND INSTRUCTION, THE

MIRROR OF LITERATURE, AMUSEMENT, AND INSTRUCTION, THE

On 2 November 1822 John Limbird, a stationer and printer in the Strand, published the initial number of the *Mirror of Literature, Amusement, and Instruction,* thus inaugurating "the first long-lived cheap periodical."[1] Limbird specialized in inexpensive reprint sets of popular novelists, poets, and various classics, much to the dismay of larger publishers and the bookselling establishment. So it was entirely consistent with his general practice that his new weekly magazine should be offered to the public for only two pence. And the public, eager for inexpensive if superficial edification in short and varied doses, responded by buying 150,000 copies of the first issue. In 1825 the weekly circulation was still as high as 80,000, and the magazine's success was such that when Limbird died in 1883, an obituary referred to him as "the father of our periodical literature."[2]

The formula that Limbird used was a simple combination: the two-penny price and sixteen pages of miscellaneous contents reprinted from books and other periodicals. The *Mirror* was similar to today's *Reader's Digest* except that longer articles were simply excerpted verbatim rather than "condensed" entire. A typical issue of the *Mirror* contained, as Lord Brougham noted approvingly, "much matter of harmless and even improving amusement, selected with very considerable taste," along with "information of a most instructive kind."[3] The subtitle to volume 5 (1825) illustrates the magazine's scope: "Original Essays; Historical Narratives; Biographical Memoirs; Sketches of

Society; Topographical Descriptions; Novels and Tales; Anecdotes; Selected Extracts from New and Expensive Works; Poetry, Original and Selected; The Spirit of the Public Journals; Discoveries in the Arts and Sciences; Useful Domestic Hints; & c., & c., & c."

The contents of two typical issues ten years apart illustrate not only this miscellaneous nature but also its almost monotonous consistency over the years. The number for 1 October 1831 features a lead article, with an engraving, on Tunbridge Wells. Other articles are on "London Illuminations" (the festive, decorative night-lighting of public buildings), the Scottish peasantry, musicians named Paganini, the English fondness for wine, and China. There are excerpts from articles on Byron, from a forthcoming book on the H.M.S. *Bounty* mutiny, and from *Duke Christian of Luneburg,* a novel by Jane Porter. Other miscellaneous features include a character sketch of "The Old Dutchman," a poem, four brief humorous anecdotes, a humorous epitaph, and a chronological list of England's kings and queens, with coronation dates. Seven of the entries are credited to other publications, six are putatively written for the *Mirror,* and four are unattributed. The issue for 8 May 1841 opens with an article on the Place de la Concorde (with engraving) along with articles on household antiques and "The Pains of Authorship"; an excerpt from Balzac's *The Dangers of Misconduct;* a description of the magazine *George Cruikshank's Omnibus*; reviews (with extracts) of two new books, a report of a conversation with a Thames waterman (operator of a boat/taxi) about his objections to steamboats; and "The Gatherer," a miscellany of trivia, which was by this time a regular feature. In this issue only two contributions are supposedly written expressly for the *Mirror.* The two issues, though separated by ten years, are thus practically interchangeable in content.

By the early 1840s the *Mirror* was only one of dozens of similar magazines that flourished during the Victorian era, especially among the middle and working classes; John W. Dodds describes the *Mirror* and its siblings as "politically innocent, unless an iteration of the theme 'be content with your lot' could be construed as propaganda on behalf of the ruling classes. They all stressed education, piety, and industriousness."[4]

Limbird chose as his first editor Thomas Byerley, who was already known in the trade as the co-compiler, with Joseph Clinton Robertson, of the popular *Percy Anecdotes,* a miscellany supposedly written by the brothers Sholto (Robertson) and Reuben (Byerley) Percy, "Percy" being the name of the London coffee house Byerley and Robertson frequented.[5] Following Byerley's death, the editorship was assumed for the next eleven years by John Timbs, whose career as a journalist and compiler spanned fifty-five years and over 150 publications. Timbs left the *Mirror* in 1838 to begin *The Year Book of Science and Art,* but he resumed the editorship in early 1841, when the *Mirror* changed owners. He may have left again as early as 1842 to become sub-editor of the *Illustrated London News,* a position he held until 1858.[6] However, he was used to pursuing more than one editorship at a time, for during his first period with the *Mirror* he had also compiled *The Arcana of Science* (1828–1838) and *Knowledge for the People* (1831–1832) and produced five other books.[7]

During the hiatus in Timbs's editorship from 1839 to 1841, the post was filled by John A. Heraud, who was later to become dramatic critic for the *Athenaeum* * (1843–1868) (see *VEA*) and the *Illustrated London News* (1849–1879). An acquaintance of Wordsworth, Coleridge, Southey, Lockhart, and the Carlyles, Heraud had been educated for a business career but began writing for the magazines in 1818. He was assistant editor of *Fraser's* * from 1830 to 1833 and edited the *Sunbeam* (1838–1839) and *Christian's Monthly Magazine* as well as the *Mirror*. In addition to his career as a journalist, he published twenty volumes of poetry, plays, lectures, essays, fiction, and scholarship.[8]

The year 1846 saw a major change in the *Mirror*'s format, content, and editorship. In July of that year the *Mirror* became a monthly under a new publisher, the sixth since Limbird's departure only five years before. The new editor was Percy Bolingbroke St. John, a prolific writer of adventure stories and travel books whose lengthy but unremarkable career as a journalist also included contributions to *Chambers's Journal* * and numerous other newspapers and magazines and, in 1861, the editorship of the *London Herald*.[9] Henceforward, the *Mirror* would no longer be a miscellany compiled from other publications but would print only "original material"; moreover, its new content was essentially belletristic, mostly tales and serializations of novels along with some poetry, book reviews, and reports on concerts and the theater.

Though the old weekly *Mirror* had occasionally reprinted works by major writers (for example, Lamb's "Melancholy of Tailors," and Hazlitt's "The Maid-Servant"), its contents were largely forgettable; the same is true of the new monthly "literary" version. The number for February 1847, for instance, leads off with some chapters from "The Miser's Will; or, Love and Avarice," a potboiler by St. John himself, followed by an extract from an anonymous naval officer's South American journal. The anonymous oriental tale "Habbakuk Sallenbacha; or, the Merchant of Jericho" is concluded and "My Uncle's Diary," by one "Ion, D.D., Cambridge," is continued. There are five other stories (sentimental, moralistic, and/or faintly exotic), an essay lightly debunking old wives' tales about the moon, and an article on Lloyd's Coffee House; about half of these contributions are anonymous or pseudonymous. Poems are contributed by Frances Brown, Fanny E. Lacy, C. T. Browne, and Stuart Farquharson, the first two being regular contributors who also wrote two of the tales in the issue. Two articles propose new educational projects, one a workingman's "scientific association" and the other (by Douglas Jerrold) a mercantile college. The issue is rounded off with brief reviews of a potpourri of ten books and short descriptions of three London theaters, a charity concert, and Mme. Tussaud's wax museum. None of the contributions is attributed to other magazines or newspapers. If the literary content of the new *Mirror* is lightweight, it at least shows the general reading public's taste in escapist and miscellaneous literature at that time.

It is not clear how long St. John continued as editor; after only one year the magazine changed hands again, and this may have also meant a change in the occupant of the editor's chair, as had been the case in 1841 and 1846. From its first monthly issue, the new *Mirror* featured stories by St. John, and it continued to do so until its demise. However, if St. John remained as editor beyond 1846, he was guilty of shamelessly puffing his own works in the book review section, because several of his books were praised in numbers appearing as late as October 1848.

As a monthly literary magazine, the *Mirror* had a relatively short life in comparison to that of its venerable and miscellaneous forbear, which had gone through 1,324 weekly numbers over a period of almost twenty-four years. In 1850, after only four years with the new format and content, the *Mirror* was renamed the *London Review* and expired after only six monthly numbers.

Notes

1. Richard D. Altick, *The English Common Reader* (Chicago, 1963), p. 266.
2. Altick, pp. 266–67, 321, 393. Henry Peter Brougham, "Practical Observations Upon the Education of the People" (1825), in *Speeches* (Edinburgh, 1838), 3:107.
3. Brougham, 3:106–7.
4. John W. Dodds, *The Age of Paradox: A Biography of England 1841–1851* (New York, 1952), p. 116.
5. *Dictionary of National Biography*, s.v. "Byerley, Thomas."
6. Ibid., s.v. "Timbs, John."
7. S. Austin Allibone, *A Critical Dictionary of English Literature and British and American Authors Living and Deceased* (London, 1872), 3:2422.
8. *Dictionary of National Biography*, s.v. "Heraud, John Abraham."
9. Ibid., s.v. "St. John, Percy Bolingbroke."

Information Sources

BIBLIOGRAPHY

Allibone, S. Austin. *A Critical Dictionary of English Literature and British and American Authors Living and Deceased*. 3 vols. London, 1872.
Altick, Richard G. *The English Common Reader*. Chicago, 1963.
Brougham, Henry Peter. "Practical Observations Upon the Education of the People." In *Speeches*, vol. 3. Edinburgh, 1838.
Dodds, John W. *The Age of Paradox: A Biography of England 1841–1851*. New York, 1952.
Timbs, John. "The 'Percy Anecdotes.' " *Notes and Queries* 7 (1853):214.
The Waterloo Directory of Victorian Periodicals, 1824–1900. Edited by Michael Wolff, John S. North, and Dorothy Deering. Elmsford, N.Y., 1980.

INDEXES

Each volume indexed.

REPRINT EDITIONS

Microform: Early British Periodicals (UMI), reels 488–494.

LOCATION SOURCES

American

Complete runs: Brown University Library; New York Public Library.
Partial runs: Widely available.

British
> Complete runs: British Museum; Cambridge University Library.
> Partial runs: Widely available.

Publication History

MAGAZINE TITLE AND TITLE CHANGES
> *The Mirror of Literature, Amusement, and Instruction*, November 1822–June 1847. (The original title was retained through the first two volumes of monthly numbers.) *The Mirror Monthly Magazine*, July 1847–December 1849. *The London Review*, January–June 1850.

VOLUME AND ISSUE DATA
> Volumes 1–38, 2 November 1822–25 December 1841; new series, volumes 1–9, 1 January 1842–27 June 1846 (also called vols. 39–49 in 2d–4th series); third series, volume 1, July/August 1846–December 1846; fourth series, volumes 1–6, January 1847–December 1849.

FREQUENCY OF PUBLICATION
> Weekly, 2 November 1822–27 June 1846; monthly, July/August 1846–December 1849, January–June 1850.

PUBLISHERS
> Volumes 1–37, 2 November 1822–30 January 1841: John Limbird, 355 Strand, London. Volumes 37–n.s. volume 2, 6 February 1841–24 September 1842: Hugh Cunningham, 1 St. Martin's Place, Trafalgar Square, London. New series, volumes 2–4, 1 October 1842–4 November 1843: Hugh Cunningham and John Mortimer, Adelaide Street, Trafalgar Square, London. N.s., volumes 4–5, 11 November 1843–4 May 1844: John Mortimer, Adelaide Street, Trafalgar Square, London. N.s., volumes 5–9, 11 May 1844–28 March 1846: Aird and H. A. Airstall, 2 Tavistock Street, Covent Garden, London. N.s., volume 9, 4 April–18 April 1846: Hayward and Adam, 48 Paternoster Row, London. N.s., volume 9, 25 April–27 June 1846: T. Croxo, 42 Newgate Street London. Third series, volume 1, July–December 1846: H. Hurst, 27 King William Street, Strand, London. Fourth series, volume 1, January–June 1847: Charles Ollier, 18–19 Southampton Street, Strand, London. Fourth series, volumes 1–6, July 1847–December 1849: Kent & Richards, 51–52 Paternoster Row, London.

EDITORS
> Thomas Byerley, 1823–1826. John Timbs, 1827–1838. John A. Heraud, 1838–1841. John Timbs, 1841–1846(?). Percy B. St. John, 1846(?)–1849.

Charles Brooks Dodson

MONTHLY CENSOR, THE

A 120-page review first published in June, 1822, the *Monthly Censor* was a rather ponderous publication with individual reviews of books separated into four sections of approximately equal length: theology, polity, physics, and philology. These categories were interpreted with enough scope to include any sort of book; education, for example, was included under "Theology" and mathematics under "Physics." Each section initially began with a handy list of works reviewed therein, but it was dropped after the second issue.

The politics of the review seem to have been conservative but partisan. William Hazlitt's *Table Talk* was attacked (in an otherwise favorable review) for obtruding "the rankness of faction" (1:835). On the same page the proprietor's own political proclivities are suggested in the rejection of Hazlitt's politics as "not in the best taste, nor in any degree such as men, sincerely attached to the hallowed institutions, and real liberties of their country, can approve." Such sentiments are in keeping with the unfavorable attitude toward parliamentary reform evidenced elsewhere (1:378–83).

The literary reviews for the most part were contained under the category "Philology." In fact, there were sub-categories of "Poetry," "Tales" (all types of fiction), and "Criticism" (satire, comedy, and literary criticism), but biographies of literary figures appeared in the category "Polity." The critiques themselves are on the whole defensible as, for example, the unfavorable verdict that Scott's *The Fortunes of Nigel* was flawed by excessive haste in composition (1:216–24). When a review is not defensible, as in the case of the condemnation of Byron's "The Vision of Judgment" (2:453–58), it is at least understandable, in this instance in view of Byron's treatment of the recently deceased, blind, mad king. An interesting defense of Wordsworth's career occurs in a joint review of his *Ecclesiastical Sketches* and *Memorials of a Tour* (2:324–35).

The names of the Rivingtons, one of the two sets of original publishers, were still carried on the cover of the second volume, but their tenure as proprietors probably ended by the issue of April 1823, which sported a new list entitled "Literary Information of Works Preparing for Publication." A smaller version of the list occurred in the next, and last, issue of this short-lived journal.

Information Sources

INDEXES
>Each volume indexed.

REPRINT EDITIONS
>None.

LOCATION SOURCES
>*American*
>>Partial run: Harvard University Library.
>*British*
>>Complete runs: Bodleian Library; British Museum; Cambridge University Library.
>>Partial runs: Edinburgh University Library; Trinity College Library.

Publication History

MAGAZINE TITLE AND TITLE CHANGES
>*The Monthly Censor; or General Review of Domestic and Foreign Literature.*

VOLUME AND ISSUE DATA
        Volumes 1–2, June 1822–May 1823.
FREQUENCY OF PUBLICATION
        Monthly.
PUBLISHERS
        Volume 1, June–November 1822: F. C. & J. Rivington, St. Paul's Church-Yard,
        and Waterloo Place, Pall Mall, London. Volume 2, December 1822–May 1823:
        G. & W. B. Whittaker, Ave Maria Lane, London.
EDITOR
        Unknown.

John O. Hayden

MONTHLY MAGAZINE, THE

Richard Phillips founded and published the *Monthly Magazine* for twenty-eight years from 1796 to 1824. In politics, the *Magazine* was antiministerial; in religion, Dissenting and Unitarian; and in literature, in its early years, sympathetic to young writers such as Coleridge, Southey, and Lamb. The purpose of the *Magazine,* announced in the preface to the first volume, was to give the public "various objects of information and discussion, both amusing and instructive, which have not usually made a part of the contents of similar Publications" and also to propagate liberal principles: "an enterprise on behalf of intellectual liberty against the forces of panic conservatism."

Phillips was the guiding force of the *Monthly Magazine* and actively secured contributions and decided what to publish. He employed Dr. John Aikin as his editor until 1806, when a dispute led to Aikin's resignation, but Phillips's duty was always "that of literary editor. All the original correspondence came under his inspection; articles were inserted or rejected according to his judgment, and the proof sheets underwent his revision."[1] Phillips compiled material from newspapers and was responsible for accounts of public affairs. Aikin also wrote extensively for the *Magazine* and secured contributions from friends such as Joseph Priestley, William Enfield, William Taylor, Joshua Toulmin, and Thomas S. Norgate. Enfield wrote fourteen essays for the important "Enquirer" series from 1796 until September 1797, and Norgate contributed the "Half-Yearly Retrospect of Literature" from 1797 to 1807.

The *Monthly Magazine* followed the pattern of the *Gentleman's Magazine** (see *AAAJ*), publishing letters to the editor, short essays, poetry, statistical tables on the weather, lists of bankruptcies, births, deaths, new books, and a half-yearly Retrospect of Literature which provided brief descriptive-critical notices of most of the new books. The letters and essays covered a wide range: classical antiquity; Biblical criticism; accounts of tours in Britain, the Continent, and the United States; essays on Spanish, German, Italian, and oriental literature; letters advocating reforms on such topics as the position of women, the treatment of the insane, and the need for a redistribution of land. Many letters dealt with scientific, medical, and mathematical questions: Aikin and Dr. Thomas Beddoes were M.D.s, and Priestley a chemist. In the fifth volume for 1798 Beddoes wrote on nitric acid (5:55), Dr. C. H. Parry on Bell's *Anatomy* (5:348–51), and Priestley on the "New Theory of Chemistry" (5:158–59), and Beddoes described the Pneumatic Institution, which he and Humphry Davy had established in Bristol.

A feature of each issue of the *Magazine* was a section of "Original Poetry" of two to four pages. A few authors signed their names, but most left their poems unsigned or used initials or pseudonyms. Coleridge contributed several poems during 1796–1797 under the signature of Nehemiah Higginbotham: "On a Late Connubial Rupture in High Life" (2:647); "Reflections on Entering into Active Life" (2:732), later published as "Reflections on Having Left a Place of Retirement"; and "Sonnets Attempted in the Manner of Contemporary Writers" (4:374). Charles Lamb during the same period contributed six poems, and Robert Southey contributed nine poems as well as a series of translations from Spanish and Portuguese poetry.[2] Other members of this circle were also contributors: George Dyer, Charles Lloyd, Amos Cottle, and John Thelwall. Other familiar names were William Taylor, Anna L. Barbauld, Amelia Opie, Mary Robinson, and Gilbert Wakefield. The best-known and most influential poem to appear in the *Monthly Magazine* was certainly William Taylor's translation of Bürger's "Lenore," (1:135–37), which aroused the interest of Walter Scott in that genre and enjoyed a contemporary popularity of its own. But the *Magazine* owed its prominence for poetry not so much to original poems as to translations from German, Spanish, and oriental languages in special essays.

Phillips, who was committed to the liberal cause and who had endured imprisonment for selling Paine's *Common Sense,* had a keen interest in profits and sensed that there was a profitable market for a magazine appealing to the growing Dissenting, liberal, and literate reading public. This sense was accurate, and the *Magazine* at its peak achieved a circulation of 5,000, only slightly below that of the more successful *Edinburgh Review,* * *Quarterly Review,* * and *Blackwood's.* * Later, when public taste changed, Phillips sold his magazine in 1824 to Cox and Baylis. The picture that emerges of Phillips is that of a person not especially liked and one who drove hard bargains, a picture derived from passing references in the correspondence of authors whom he published, the article on him in the *Dictionary of National Biography,* and George Borrow's unflattering portrait in *Lavengro.*[3] Phillips was elected a sheriff of London in 1807 and was knighted in 1808.

The main interest of the *Magazine* lies in the picture it gives of the liberal reading public during the years 1796 to 1824—roughly the lifetimes of Keats, Shelley, and Byron; its antiministerial policies ensured an audience among educated Dissenters and Unitarians, and its miscellaneous articles appealed to a wide reading public. Its important features were the "Enquirer" series, its articles on Continental literature by Southey and Taylor, and, finally, the many pages devoted to economics and the work of the humanitarians. "The merits of the magazine should not be exaggerated," Geoffrey Carnall reminds us. "Its contributions are often hastily written and superficial. Yet it expresses some of the intellectual vitality of the early nineteenth century to an extent which makes it worth study. . . . It was a reading public primarily interested in the diffusion of useful knowledge and the improvement of society. . . . Poetry was justified in their eyes if it could be shown that it promoted the welfare of the community."[4]

The political ideas of the *Magazine* are the expression of a liberal, proparliamentary reform group of Unitarians, addressed not to a sectarian coterie but to a wider public. The *Magazine* was an advocate of religious toleration and expressed concern for the poor and those suffering from legal and economic injustices. Articles and letters discussed the treatment of the insane, the deplorable conditions among the very poor—specifically chimney-sweepers— and the condition of prisons. Industrial pollution in the cities was a special concern of the *Magazine* and its publisher Richard Phillips. Practical economic issues loom large in every issue, where accounts of improved methods of agriculture mingle with accounts of new discoveries in mechanics and engineering. Reports of travellers from home and abroad, usually in the form of journals or letters, were another prominent feature of almost every number. Almost every town or district in Britain and Ireland was the subject of at least a brief account. The United States was of especial interest, and the pages of the *Magazine* are a mine of informaion about America as seen by travellers. Particular mention should be made of the articles by Harry Toulmin from Kentucky. After 1826, however, the *Magazine* radically changed its focus and political direction, and its frequent changes of ownership attest its growing unprofitability and declining influence. The second series (1826–1838), which incorporated the *European Magazine* * (see *AAAJ*), published as a new feature short fiction, including the first sketch of Dickens, and works of Mitford, Galt, Hazlitt, and G.W.M. Reynolds. The third and final series (1839–1842) was the organ of the Syncretic Association under the editorship of J. A. Heraud.[5]

Who were the contributors to the *Monthly Magazine?* Although many have been identified together with their contributions, much remains to be done. A useful, but monumental, undertaking would be the determination of the authors of the contributions in the *Magazine,* and a start could be made with the first decade, in some ways its liveliest period. Phillips himself seemed not to know the identity of all his contributors as, of course, many letters came unsolicited and with pseudonymous signatures. Such well-known authors as Coleridge, Lamb, Southey, Dickens, and Hazlitt have had their works identified, but interesting groups of writers found the pages of the *Magazine* hospitable to their contributions. An alert reader can identify such authors by their initials and places of residence: J. T. of Taunton is Dr. Joshua Toulmin of Taunton, the Dissenting minister; A.S.C. of Clifford's Inn is Amos Cottle, who lived at Clifford's Inn; and T.S.N. is T. S. Norgate. Other contributors later published their essays and poems in books. George Burnett during 1807 published anonymously in the *Magazine* a series of letters, "Particulars of the present State of Poland, by an English Gentleman," which he later republished under his own name as *View of the Present State of Poland* (London: Longman, 1807). Two important groups of contributors were the Norwich group, centered about Taylor and Aikin, and the Bristol group, apparently centered about the physician Dr. Thomas Beddoes, but also including Southey, Coleridge, Humphry Davy, and their friends. Would it be possible to identify "A. B." of Bristol? Elisabeth Schneider (*Coleridge, Opium and Kubla Khan*) discovered his essay on Bristol and its citizens in the magazine and raised the question. Many essays come from Bristol and seem to originate within the Beddoes-Coleridge-Southey-Cottle group.

The *Magazine* offers less to the literary student than to the social and political historian, but some of its reviews of literary works deserve mention. Byron's liberal political views, as they accorded with those of the publisher, ensured a warm welcome for his poetry, and the unidentified reviewers in the *Magazine,* almost alone among other reviewers, were not shocked by the "immorality" of *Don Juan*.[6] At the same time, however, the *Magazine* had turned against the older generation of poets because of their changed politics. But the reviewing of books, especially of belles lettres, was a minor concern of the *Magazine*. Its section entitled "Original Poetry" offers on the whole rather poor fare despite the fact that Coleridge, Southey, Lamb, and Dyer were contributors during the early years. A prospective researcher will find that the pages of the *Magazine* will yield valuable results, but it is more likely to be in tracing the trends of social, political, and intellectual history as they are intertwined with each other than in the pursuit of exclusively literary themes.

Notes

1. Lucy Aikin, *Memoir of John Aikin, M. D.* (London, 1823), 1:188.
2. E. V. Lucas, ed., *The Works of Charles and Mary Lamb* (London, 1903), 5:14–19. Lamb's poems appeared between December 1796 and October 1797 and were signed either with his full name or with initials. Kenneth Curry, "The Contributions of Robert Southey to the *Monthly Magazine* and the *Athenaeum*," *Wordsworth Circle* 11 (1980):215–18.
3. Thomas Boyle, in "A Portrait in *Lavengro*," *Notes and Queries* 196 (1951):211–13, works out the details for the portrait of Phillips and some of his writers as depicted in the novel.
4. *"The Monthly Magazine,"* *Review of English Studies* n.s. 5 (1954):158–64.
5. Richard L. McGuire's dissertation is the best source of information for the several continuations of the *Monthly Magazine* after Phillips's proprietorship ended. McGuire lists many of these writers and their fictional works when the new proprietors turned to fiction and changed the politics of the *Magazine*. The notes to the *Letters of Charles Dickens*, ed. Madeline House and Graham Storey (Oxford, 1965), 1:32, identify the nine sketches Dickens contributed at the beginning of his career (1833), and record also several changes in the ownership and editorship of the *Magazine*. There is, however,

limited information on the post-Phillips years so that we know very little of the last years of the *Magazine* and its dwindling prosperity and influence.

6. W. S. Dowden, "A Jacobin Journal's View of Lord Bryon," *Studies in Philology* 48 (1951):56–66.

Information Sources

BIBLIOGRAPHY

Aberdeine, Jennie W. *John Galt*. Oxford, 1936.

Aikin, Lucy. *A Memoir of John Aikin, M. D.* 2 vols. London, 1823.

Boyle, A. "Portraiture in *Lavengro.*" *Notes and Queries* 196 (1951):211–13; 361–66; 410–12; 453–56; 477–79.

Carlton, W. J. " 'Captain Holland' Identified." *Dickensian* 57 (1961):69–77.

———. "Charles Dickens, Dramatic Critic." *Dickensian* 56 (1960):11–27.

Carnall, Geoffrey. "A Hazlitt Contribution." *Times Literary Supplement,* 19 June 1953, p. 397.

———. "*The Monthly Magazine.*" *Review of English Studies,* n.s. 5 (1954):158–64.

———. *Robert Southey and His Age.* Oxford, 1960.

Christiansen, Merton A. "Taylor of Norwich and the Higher Criticism." *Journal of the History of Ideas* 20 (1959):179–94.

Coldicutt, Dorothy. "Was Coleridge the Author of the 'Enquirer' Series in the *Monthly Magazine* 1796–9?" *Review of English Studies* 15 (1939):45–60. Cf. Lewis Patton's reply, ibid., 16 (1940):188–89.

Curry, Kenneth. "The Contributions of Robert Southey to the *Monthly Magazine* and the *Athenaeum.*" *Wordsworth Circle* 11 (1980):215–18.

Dowden, Wilfred S. "A Jacobin Journal's View of Lord Byron." *Studies in Philology* 48 (1951):56–66.

Hecht, Hans. *Robert Burns: The Man and His Work.* London, 1936.

Howe, P. P., ed. *The Complete Works of William Hazlitt.* 21 vols. London, 1930–1934.

Knapp, William I. *Life, Writings and Correspondence of George Borrow.* 2 vols. London, 1899.

Landré, Louis. *Leigh Hunt (1784–1859): Contribution à l'histoire du Romantisme anglais.* 2 vols. Paris, 1935.

McGuire, Richard L. "The *Monthly Magazine* (1796–1843): Politics and Literature in Transition." Ph.D. dissertation, Rice University, 1968.

Mineka, Francis. *The Dissidence of Dissent: The "Monthly Repository" 1806–38.* Chapel Hill, N.C., 1944.

Pollin, B. R. "Mary Hays on Women's Rights in the *Monthly Magazine.*" *Etudes Anglaises* 24 (1971):271–87.

Robberds, J. W. *A Memoir of the Life and Writings of the Late William Taylor of Norwich.* 2 vols. London, 1843.

Schneider, Elisabeth. *Coleridge, Opium and Kubla Khan.* Chicago, 1953.

Seton-Anderson, James. "Robert Burns." *Notes and Queries* 194 (1949):107.

INDEXES

Each volume indexed.

REPRINT EDITIONS

Microform: English Literary Periodicals (UMI), reels 448–475.

LOCATION SOURCES

American

Complete runs: Boston Athenaeum; Library Company of Philadelphia; Trinity College Library; University of Chicago Library.

Partial runs: Widely available.

British

Complete run: British Museum.

Partial runs: Widely available.

Publication History

MAGAZINE TITLE AND TITLE CHANGES

The Monthly Magazine and British Register, volumes 1–60, February 1796–January 1826. *The Monthly Magazine: or British register of literature, science, and belles lettres,* new series, volumes 1–26, 1826–1838. (Incorporates *European Magazine.*) *The Monthly Magazine of politics, literature, science, and belles lettres; Monthly Magazine,* 3d series, volumes 1–9, 1839–1843.

VOLUME AND ISSUE DATA

Volumes 1–60, February 1796–January 1826; new series, volumes 1–26, 1826–1838; third series, volumes 1–9, 1839–1843.

FREQUENCY OF PUBLICATION

Monthly.

PUBLISHERS

Volumes 1–57, 1796–1824: Richard Phillips. Volumes 58–60, 1824–January 1826: George B. Whittaker. New series, volumes 1–6, 1826–1829: George B. Whittaker. Volumes 7–13, 1829–1832: Whittaker, Treacher, and Company. Volume 14, 1832: J. Lewer. Volume 15, 1833: Charles Tilt. Volume 16, 1833: A. Robertson. Volume 17, 1834: W. Cochrane and M'Crone. Volumes 18–20, 1834–1835: James Cochrane and Company. Volumes 21–26, 1836–1838: Sherwood, Gilbert, & Piper. Third series, volumes 1–2, 1839: J. W. Southgate. Volumes 3–6, 1840–1841: Sherwood, Gilbert & Piper. Volumes 7–8, 1842: C. Mitchell. Volume 9, 1843: Sherwood, Gilbert & Piper.

EDITORS

John Aikin, 1796–1806. George Gregory, 1806–1808. John Thelwall, 1824–1825. George Croly, 1826–1833. J. B. Holland, 1833–1836. James Grant, 1836. G.W.M. Reynolds, 1837–1838. Francis F. Barham and J. A. Heraud, 1839–1840. J. A. Heraud, 1840–1841. Benson E. Hill, 1842–1843.

Kenneth Curry

MONTHLY MIRROR, THE

The *Monthly Mirror* advertised itself as an independent voice of taste and judgment. Its contents included the typical sections of a miscellany, with an appeal to a polite and fashionable readership. Each issue contained a biographical sketch or memoir of a public figure, primarily of the theater, but also including writers, together with an engraved portrait. On its title page, the

Monthly proclaimed to be "embellished with superb engravings"; on occasion an issue contained two plates. Over the years, the prefaces to the semi-annual volumes praised the quality of the paper and engravings and the introduction of new type faces.

The first preface announced the *Mirror*'s principle of honesty, morality, and impartiality, to the exclusion of party politics (pp. iii–xii). The sections of the magazine became established by volume 3 and lasted throughout its existence. The preface to volume 3 stated the aims of "blending elegance with utility, and entertainment with profit" (pp. v–viii).

The first section, "Miscellaneous," of fifteen to twenty pages, began with the biographical sketch and included letters and essays by correspondents, short fiction, anecdotes, and social or moral commentaries. Next, the "Review of Literature" treated ten to twenty titles in ten to fifteen pages, often merely noting a work with a brief, generalized paragraph. Toward the middle of the new series, this section covered fewer reviews with greater elaboration. There were two sections devoted to theater. The "British Stage" contained reviews of dramatic publications, historical essays, and criticism. "Memoranda Dramatica" reviewed current productions in and out of London. "Original Poetry" ran two to six pages. The contributions were not memorable. At times there were large quantities, filling up to ten pages. In March 1808 a seventy-page "Supplementary Number" was needed to print the backlog of poetry. "The British Parliament" became an irregular section after volume 6. It contained an impartial report of debates and other legislative actions. A final section, entitled "News" or "Domestic Events," included notices under the heads of marriages, births, and deaths. For the first few months, through March 1796, there was a stock report, with prices of stocks, grain, sugar, and tallow in London and other markets.

The first two issues in volume 1 are dated December 1795. The first, however, lists stocks as of November, and the second as of December. Volume 1 ends with April 1796, and volume 2 with December, after which the volumes regularly appeared semi-annually. Each issue includes a contents page, and each volume an index, usually divided into four sections: "Prose," "Review," "British Stage," and "Poetry." Pages of these features are sometimes included in the pagination. There are no consecutive numbers for the monthly issues. In the first ten volumes, each issue had sixty-four pages. With volume 11, beginning in January 1801, the price increased to eighteen pence as a result of adding a half-sheet to increase reviews and drama criticism. From that time, each issue averaged seventy-two pages until 1810, when another half-sheet was added, making each issue eighty pages until publication ceased.

Because the *Mirror* attempted comprehensive coverage in its reviews, it sacrificed extended analysis and lengthy extracts. There were reviews on a wide range of subjects, including history, travels, translations, topical controversies, politics, and a few on religion. As a result, not many reviews of novels or poetry by major writers were featured. Current works by Ann Radcliffe and

Charlotte Smith were briefly noted (November 1796, March 1797, January 1798, August 1798); a one-paragraph review of *Elegiac Sonnets* praised Mrs. Smith's "merit" as "always simple" and "elegant." Coleridge's early poems were praised, despite his political sentiments, although later, with a change of editor, he was severely abused for *The Friend* and "The Three Graves" (n.s. 8:26–31, 98–105, 186–96, 322, 402). Southey's works were treated at greater length, with the reviewer of *Thalaba* acknowledging his effort to be fair and impartial despite his "censure" of Southey's political opinions (12:243–47). *Lyrical Ballads* (1798), assumed to be the work of one author, was briefly noted in a paragraph and praised for its successful experiment. The 1800 edition was attributed to Wordsworth in a relatively long three-and-a-half-page review and judged in a balanced manner. The reviewer noted that Wordsworth's sentiments may not be shared by readers and that "obscurity too often arises from a romantic search after simplicity" (6:224–25; 11:389–92). Scott's *Lay of the Last Minstrel* received a ten-page review as the *Monthly Mirror* shifted to fewer reviews with more detail (12:385–95). There was a continuing series of Cowper's letters and anecdotes, at times called "Cowperiana."

In keeping with its political neutrality, the *Mirror* featured a sympathetic biographical sketch of Mary Wollstonecraft, a review of her "Letters" from her Scandinavian travels, and a two-part review of Godwin's memoirs of her life. Later, however, it praised Mrs. Wakefield's "Reflections on the present condition of the female sex," because "reformation, not revolution is her system," in contrast to Mary Wollstonecraft (1:131–33; 285–89; 5:153–57, 210–13; 11:37). One issue praised Burke's style but criticized his "weak . . . often fallacious" arguments, and followed with a review of Thelwall's attack on Burke's pamphlet, commenting that the readers could decide the issues for themselves. Later, a volume of the "beauties" of Burke's writings was favorably reviewed, as was a "life" (2:421–25; 5:352–53; 6:36–37).

Its political neutrality did not prevent the *Mirror* from publishing a number of items of humanitarian concern, social criticism, and reform. One correspondent contributed an essay, signed "Recluse," against cruelty to animals. Another described the "wretched situation of the chimney sweeps," and in conclusion attacked "ye senseless accumulators of wealth." Later there was a letter on the "defects and imperfect administration of the poor laws." Also Brewer's *Rights of the Poor* was reviewed as "a publication of very superior interest, . . . worthy of the serious attention of the legislature" (2:208–9; 10:301–3; n.s. 1:173–76). The magazine catered, however, to patriotism and "public attention" at the death of Lord Nelson after the victory of Trafalgar, with an unusually rapid response from a reviewing magazine. Much of the November 1805 issue was devoted to the events at the end of October, including lengthy "dispatches" and a portrait and memoir of Nelson.

The tone of the *Mirror* was one of elevation, propriety, and "respectability." The preface to volume 2 (1796) stated: "We have endeavoured to give variety and interest, without the introduction of *ribaldry,* a species of humour

which we are sorry to remark is too often looked for in a work of this kind"
(pp. v–vi). In an article, "General Reflections on What Is Called Taste," the
conventional standards were asserted, including the ideas of "conformity" with
"exact decorum," that "all men possess at their birth the first principles of
taste," that taste is "depraved" by "corrupt education" or "prevailing customs," and that Gothic architecture lacks taste, "rule," and "proportion"
(1:265).

Such were the romantic suppositions that guided the magazine and influenced
its choice of subjects and format.

Information Sources

BIBLIOGRAPHY
Hayden, John O. *The Romantic Reviewers: 1802–1824*. Chicago, 1969.
INDEXES
  Each volume indexed.
REPRINT EDITIONS
  None.
LOCATION SOURCES
  American
    Complete runs: Cornell University Library; Harvard University Library; Rice
    Institute Library; University of North Carolina; Yale University Library.
    Partial runs: Widely available.
  British
    Complete run: Manchester Public Library.
    Partial runs: Birmingham Public Library; Birmingham University Library; Bod-
    leian Library; British Museum; London University Library.

Publication History

MAGAZINE TITLE AND TITLE CHANGES
  *The Monthly Mirror: reflecting Men and Manners, with strictures on their epit-
  ome, the stage.*
VOLUME AND ISSUE DATA
  Volumes 1–22, December (November) 1795–December 1806; new series, vol-
  umes 1–9, January 1807–June 1811 (sometimes referred to by consecutive vol-
  ume numbers 23–31).
FREQUENCY OF PUBLICATION
  Monthly.
PUBLISHERS
  Volumes 1–6, December (November) 1795–September 1798: Thomas Bellamy,
  Monthly Mirror Office, King Street, Covent Garden, London. Volumes 7–21,
  October 1798–January 1806: Vernor and Hood, In the Poultry. Volumes 21–
  n.s. 2, January 1806–December 1808: Vernor, Hood, and Sharpe, The Poultry.
  New series 3–9, January 1808–June 1811: J. Murray, Fleet Street, London/A.
  Constable & Co., Edinburgh.

EDITORS
   Thomas Bellamy, December 1795–late 1798. Unknown, 1799–1807. Edward
Dubois(?), January 1807–June 1811.

                                                              Nathaniel Teich

MONTHLY REVIEW, THE. See AAAJ

N

NATIONAL MAGAZINE, THE. See DUBLIN LITERARY
GAZETTE, THE

NEW BON TON MAGAZINE, THE

In October 1818 appeared the *New Bon Ton Magazine,* the old *Bon Ton*
apparently being the *Bon Ton Magazine, or Microscope of Fashion and Folly*
of some twenty-two years in the past, although no reference is made to the
predecessor.

The satiric aim of the old *Bon Ton,* suggested by the subtitle (*Microscope of
. . . Folly*), is in any event present in the motto poem that graces each volume
of the *New:*

> To lash the follies—vices—of mankind;
> To mend the morals, and instruct the mind;
> This is our object—this our sole endeavour;
> By this we hope to keep in public favour.

But the *New Bon Ton* was less Juvenalian than the *Satirist,** the other major
satirical periodical of the time; several contributors were even rejected for being
immoderate or inflammatory in their satiric offerings, or so at least the letters
to correspondents claimed (1:64). As the proprietors put it (3:iv), they wished
the magazine to be "a monitor of moral instruction, as well as an agreeable
companion."

The layout of the magazine at least was agreeable. The monthly sixty-four
pages appeared in single-column, clear print with bold-faced captions; a colored cartoon began each issue. The articles were of general interest, designed

"towards forming a complete body of useful information, arts, sciences, and fashionable life" (2:iii).

Only one department survived through all issues, "The Stage." Even that section began to dwindle in volume 2 and reappeared in the next volume in smaller print but with longer critiques of the current theater. The verse, said to be "wholly original" (3:v), was mainly satirical, but occasionally serious pieces appeared. One satiric poem, "Fashionable Life, or Bon Ton," continued over a number of issues. The prose tales as well were sometimes non-satirical and were sometimes continued from issue to issue (cf. 1:34). Many satirical articles appeared as letters to the editors, as they probably were. Short anecdotes and jokes, always modest, were also a common feature of the magazine. The proprietors claimed to have employed "men of the first talent" (1:iv) and boasted that not only had they themselves reprinted earlier numbers, "a thing unexampled in periodical publications" (ibid.), but that other periodicals had reprinted some of their material (3:v). As flattering as they may have been, however, both forms of reprinting were not really all that unusual.

The literary reviewing began as a department in the first volume, then disappeared until volume 3, in which cantos 1 and 2 of Byron's *Don Juan,* the only important literary piece critiqued, were attacked with moral indignation. No reviews appeared in subsequent volumes, but oddly enough canto 3 of *Don Juan* appeared in eight installments in volumes 5 and 6 without comment. Another policy that distinguished the *New Bon Ton* from the *Satirist* and other periodicals was that it contained no criticism of other journals as a matter of policy (2:iv).

Absent also is the political virulence of the *Satirist.* Perhaps any periodical that considered itself to "have accomplished that desideratum in polished society, which Montesquieu calls 'a book for a parlour window' " (3:iv) could not have been politically engaged. In any event, it claimed a kind of independence in the motto attached to its "Address to the Public" in volume 2: "Open to all, influenced by none." The *New Bon Ton* was not violent even on the subject of Radicals like William Cobbett; it had itself attacked the rich in early issues (cf. 1:v).

The maverick quality of its political views is evident in comments on Cobbett: "Whatever Cobbett's character may be, those of his prosecutors are not an atom better" and "it is difficult to tell whether a Whig or a Radical be the most trustworthy" (6:172–73). Even the Tories receive their share: "Bad as I conceive our present rulers to be"—but here there were qualifications—"I prefer them to Whigs" (6:174). But the *New Bon Ton* did not favor Reform (6:321–25).

The magazine stood aside on the issue of Catholic Emancipation, becoming instead a forum on the subject. One favorable letter on the issue by a Protestant is a model of liberality and common sense (3:192–94). Methodism, on the other hand, received the abuse customary at the time, especially in a series entitled "Confessions of a True Methodist." As "a rational follower of the doctrines of the Church of England" (1:174), the *New Bon Ton* aimed "to support the Established Church." As such, the magazine was well ahead of its time in favoring divorce (1:85–88).

Perhaps in an age of factionalism and sectarianism such flexibility was simply not welcome. Whatever the reason, this very appealing magazine produced its last issue in April 1821, less than three years after its first.

Information Sources

INDEXES
Indexed (labeled "Contents," incomplete) at the beginning of each volume.
REPRINT EDITIONS
None.
LOCATION SOURCES
American
Complete runs: Boston Athenaeum; Brooklyn Public Library; Buffalo and Erie County Public Library, Grosvenor Reference Division; Henry E. Huntington Library; University of Minnesota Library.
Partial runs: U. S. Library of Congress; University of California (Berkeley) Library.
British
Complete runs: British Museum; London Library.

Publication History

MAGAZINE TITLE AND TITLE CHANGES
The New Bon Ton Magazine; or Telescope of the Times.
VOLUME AND ISSUE DATA
Volumes 1–6, October 1818–April 1821.
FREQUENCY OF PUBLICATION
Monthly.
PUBLISHER
J. Johnston, Cheapside, London.
EDITOR
Unknown.

John O. Hayden

NEW BRITISH LADY'S MAGAZINE, THE. See BRITISH LADY'S MAGAZINE, THE

NEW EDINBURGH REVIEW, THE. See EDINBURGH MONTHLY REVIEW, THE

NEW EUROPEAN MAGAZINE, THE

When James Asperne, respected London bookseller and longtime proprietor of the *European Magazine* * (see *AAAJ*), died on 1 November 1820,[1] his successors intended some moderate changes in that staid periodical. In the November 1820 number, the first after Asperne's death, the editor gave notice that the miscellany would continue to be "published as usual" but with some "improvements . . . about to be introduced" in the method of communicating with correspondents through the pages of the magazine (78:471). The nature of this "new proposed plan" became evident in the alterations of format in the issue for January 1821, especially in the inauguration of "The Editor's Conversazione," an intimate and diverse monologue for readers and contributors which self-consciously mentioned "this new mode of corresponding" with friends of the magazine "by the way of having all the conversation to ourselves" (79:2). In the succeeding months at the *European* office, the contention about this innovation would play some part—if not the principal part—in the genesis of the *New European Magazine,* with the *new* suggesting a rival to rather than a revival of its parent journal.

The *conversazioni* appeared throughout 1821 and into 1822, as the *European* continued to be "printed for the Proprietors and Sold at the Late James Asperne's . . . where Communications for the Editor are requested to be addressed," that is, at 32 Cornhill, London. Then, in the spring of 1822, the proprietorship changed, the connection with the Asperne firm was severed, and Lupton Relfe of 13 Cornhill became the publisher of the *European.* The April issue made a clean break with the past by publishing the last of the "Editor's Conversazione" (briefly associated with the pseudonymous editor Alfred Beauchamp) and by informing the public that "the Editorial department" would now be "conducted by one of the New Proprietors," who "feeling that a Conversazione forms no necessary part of a monthly publication, that the term is at variance with the subject to which it refers, and that it has already entailed considerable ridicule on the European Magazine, has determined to relinquish that *vehicle of wit and humour* after the present number, and confine himself to the usual Notices to Correspondents" (81:291).

This reactionary announcement is indicative of the kind of disparity of tastes among the conductors of the *European* in the first half of 1822 and is at least one possible provocation for the establishment of the *New European,* which was first issued under date of July 1822, by "John Letts, Jun. (late Asperne), Bible, Crown, and Constitution, 32, Cornhill."[2] The first number opened with "The Court of Claims," some pages of jocular communications to correspondents much like the *conversazioni* banished three months before from the *European Magazine.* The editor assumed the new pseudonym of Percival Somerset, but a later issue would name as contributor Alfred Beauchamp, Jun., the "junior" appendage pointing to his erstwhile though brief connection with the parent magazine. Thus, in a singular sequence of shifts, the "old" *European* moved with its conservative format to a new address shortly before the *New European* began issuing its mildly innovative monthly from the address where Asperne had published his magazine for more than fifteen years.

It was evident from the first that the editor of Letts's magazine admired the type of coterie of imaginary contributors that had succeeded in *Blackwood's* * and the *Etonian* during the preceding five years. The monthly department entitled "The Court of Claims," with its chatty review of the magazinists' concerns, shows this kinship most clearly. Following no consistent format, these "Court of Claims" articles appear half serious, half humbug, and they sustain the fiction of an editor who meets with his council to vote on magazine policy. The December 1822 issue, for example, reported a discussion of "the preliminary arrangements of our new Volume," an occasion where much oil and wine were consumed, "our 3,715 subscribers" were toasted, plans and papers for the following six months were examined and decided upon, and four new members were added to the council and "took their seats accordingly" (1:486). In addition, the editor could comment there on correspondence from readers and contributors, sometimes including their poetry and prose.

The *New European*'s identification with other magazines that made use of the modish coterie device is further suggested by its recognition of *Blackwood's* Christopher North (1:196) and Timothy Tickler (4:414), by its praise of that Edinburgh monthly (3:296), and by its acknowledgment of characters created for the "court" of Lady Mary Vernon in *Knight's Quarterly Magazine.* * [3] Certainly Letts's magazine regarded itself as belonging to a species of journalism that had advanced beyond the old *European*. In February 1824 one writer in the *New European* observed: "The Old European;—any further discrimination is quite out of the question: it is all *alter et idem,* the same joint of meat differently dressed. . . . [It] has changed masters, as well as managers; and truly not before it was required. Very dull, and very heavy, were it's [*sic*] contents; and, between ourselves, I do not yet see much improvement under the new *regime*" (4:145). Three months later another correspondent tersely noted, "The Old European gets worse, that I thought impossible" (4:386).

For all its condescension, the *New European* actually held a conservative position, little if at all removed from that of the old *European*.[4] The old Asperne sign of the Bible, Crown, and Constitution adorned the title page along with citations of Scripture admonishing obedience to authorities. "Official memoranda" listing high government officials prefaced the bound volumes. In keeping with its allegiance, the magazine seldom mentioned Byron, Shelley, or Hunt without a tone of condemnation.[5] And on the score of content and composition, the *New European,* pleasant and sometimes entertaining, was seldom exceptional. Like other miscellanies of the day, it carried biographical memoirs, character sketches, mediocre poetry, reviews of books, essays, descriptions of travel, and fiction.[6] Approximately twenty of the ninety-five pages of an issue were filled by a gazette, with sections on the fine arts, the theater, books recently published, literary and scientific intelligence, and the quotidian concerns of the record offices—births, deaths, marriages, patents, bankruptcies, etc.

The editor and most of the contributors who filled these pages for two years remain unknown. A majority of the attributions appear to be pseudonymous—from the editorial comments of Percy Somerset to poetry and prose by such writers as Tyro, Niccolo, Peter Patterson, Stafford Claverton, Tudor Anwyl, and Arthur M. Templeton, Jun.[7] Many articles and poems were signed only with initials. The name of William Wordsworth therefore stands conspicuously at the head of "Wallace's Tower, at Cora Lynn" (3:74), a poem which had been published in a collection of 1820. The most frequent known contributor was William Branwhite Clark, mentioned in the "Court of Claims" for August 1823 as "our excellent friend the Rev. W. B. Clarke . . . gifted author of 'The River Derwent' " (3:99), the same who contributed the poem "Wake, Love, Awake!" to the issue for November 1822. Several other works of prose or poetry are initialed *W.B.C.* in various issues of the *New European*.[8]

Of publisher Letts's role in the composition of the magazine still less is known, and even his identity can be only tentatively deduced. He was apparently the oldest son of John Letts, stationer of 95 Cornhill and founder of England's first commercial diary company, in 1812, a business which passed into the management of Thomas Letts, younger brother of John Letts, Jr.[9] After the failure of the *New European* in 1824, John Jr. seems to have given up the publishing business; and in 1830 one finds him matriculating at Sidney College, Cambridge, from which he took a B.A. in 1835 and an M.A. in 1838. He was Rector of St. Olave's, Hart Street, London, from 1837 until his death in 1857, and author of a history of that parish.[10]

Notes

1. James Asperne, "Memoir of the Late James Asperne," *European Magazine* 79 (1821):5–6.

2. The plans to begin publication of the *New European* were noticed in the *Literary Gazette** for 13 July 1822: "On Thursday, Aug. 1, will be published, pr. 2s. embellished with a Portrait and Frontispiece, No. 1 of the NEW EUROPEAN" (p. 445).

3. In October 1823, with the second number of *Knight's Quarterly,* a *New European* writer mentioned "our juvenile Contemporary of *Knight's Quarterly*" who has "essayed to render Enigmas once more fashionable" (3:292). A correspondent in the next issue (3:400) asked if he might not "coin words as well as Edmund Bruce, or Marmaduke Villars" (characters of the imaginary "court" of contributors in *Knight's*).

4. In "Pulpit Oratory, No. III," printed in *The Yellow Dwarf,** 28 February 1818, John Hamilton Reynolds had snidely referred to the *European Magazine* as "Brother Asperne's Magazine." Reprinted in *Selected Prose of John Hamilton Reynolds,* ed. Leonidas M. Jones (Cambridge, Mass., 1966), p. 222.

5. See especially the attacks on the *Liberal** (1:354–63) and *Don Juan,* cantos 9–11, which the *New European* called "a display of vileness, wickedness, and stupidity" (3:195).

6. A description of contemporary essays that appeared in the second number of the *New European* applies well to many of the essays which would be published in the magazine itself: "In the style of an Essay, now-a-days, the matter is not so much an object of interest as the colouring and the display. Most compositions are now imbued with a certain tone of poetical feeling, caught from the writer" (1:138).

7. Like Alfred Beauchamp, Jun., Arthur M. Templeton, Jun. is a name brought over from the old *European* with the appendage of *Jun.*

8. The *Dictionary of National Biography* credits Rev. William Branwhite Clarke with the authorship of "The River Derwent" (1822) and, after his emigration in 1839, with the discovery of gold and tin in Australia, where he became a distinguished clergyman, geologist, and civic leader of Sydney.

9. John Letts, stationer of 95 Cornhill, is listed in the eleventh edition of the *Triennial Directory* for London and environs for the years 1822–1824 (London, 1822) and on page 230 of *Robson's London Commercial Directory, Street Guide, and Carrier's List for 1826–27* (London, 1825). Both of these sources also list a John Letts, Jun. as a bookseller of Cornhill. (Robson locates him at 32 Cornhill, the address of the *New European* and of Asperne's.)

10. The author is indebted to Mr. Anthony A. Letts, whose letter of 16 September 1981 enclosed a genealogical table and other information confirming the relationships explained here. At the time of his letter, Mr. Letts was chairman and managing director of Charles Letts & Company Ltd., Diary House, Borough Road, London. See also J. A. Venn's *Alumni Cantabrigienses, Part II (1752–1900)* (Cambridge, 1951), 4:155, and Arthur Jewers and A.W.H. Clarke's *Monumental Inscriptions and Heraldry in St. Olave's* (London, 1929), pp. 10, 61. The Rev. John Letts's history of the parish remains in manuscript in St. Olave's Church.

Information Sources

BIBLIOGRAPHY

"The Editor's Conversazione." *European Magazine* 79 (1821):2; 81 (1822):194, 291.
Jewers, Arthur J., and A. W. Hughes Clarke. *Monumental Inscriptions and Heraldry in St. Olave's, Hart Street, London.* London, 1929.
"Memoir of the Late James Asperne." *European Magazine* 79 (1821):3–6.
Robson's London Commercial Directory, Street Guide, and Carrier's List for 1826–27. 7th ed. London, 1825.
Venn, J. A., comp. *Alumni Cantabrigienses.* 6 vols. Cambridge, England, 1940–1954.

INDEXES
Each volume indexed.
REPRINT EDITIONS
None.
LOCATION SOURCES
American
Complete run: University of Minnesota Library.
British
Complete runs: Bodleian Library; British Museum; Cambridge University Library; Edinburgh University Library.
Partial run: Aberdeen University Library.

Publication History

MAGAZINE TITLE AND TITLE CHANGES
   The New European Magazine.
VOLUME AND ISSUE DATA
   Volumes 1–4, July 1822–June 1824.
FREQUENCY OF PUBLICATION
   Monthly.
PUBLISHER
   John Letts, Jr., 32 Cornhill, London.
EDITOR
   Unknown.

Douglas K. Morris

NEW LADY'S MAGAZINE, THE. See AAAJ

NEW LONDON MAGAZINE, THE. See AAAJ

NEW MONTHLY MAGAZINE, THE

Surveying and evaluating periodical literature for the *Edinburgh Review* * in May 1823, William Hazlitt ranked Henry Colburn's *New Monthly Magazine* alongside Taylor and Hessey's *London Magazine* * as the best of a crowded field.[1] In 1846 Cyrus Redding claimed that during the 1820s the *New Monthly* "stood alone among periodical works . . . then, as now, the widest circulated at the highest price [three shillings, sixpence] of all works of its class" (77:333). William Harrison Ainsworth, prefacing the one-hundredth volume in January 1854, wrote that with Thomas Campbell's assumption of the editorship in 1821 the magazine "became a planet of the first importance in the system of periodical literature."[2] Remarkably enough, modern estimates echo this appraisal.[3]

   The *New Monthly* began in 1814 as a Tory, anti-Jacobin, anti-Napoleonic journal, an antidote to the "poison . . . ribaldry and irreligion" (1:ii) of Richard Phillips's *Monthly Magazine.* *[4] Politically, it was cousin to the *Quarterly Review,* * staunchly supporting the monarchy in some of its most repressive and restrictive policies; and in the youthfully extravagant acrimony of *Blackwood's* * the journal found both inspiration and pattern for such literary pieces as an 1818–1819 series "On the Cockney School of Prose."[5] Between 1814 and 1819, forced by its competitors, the *Scots Magazine* * (see *AAAJ*), *Blackwood's Edinburgh Magazine,* and the *Literary Gazette,* * it noticed, reviewed and quoted at length from no fewer than fourteen of Byron's works.[6] Hunt, Shelley, Coleridge, Keats, and Wordsworth were also critiqued, though as a

rule not so favorably as Crabbe, Campbell, and Moore.[7] The exceptions, however, are noteworthy. A perceptive and distinctly favorable review, possibly by
Thomas Noon Talfourd, of Keats's *Lamia* volume appeared in the September
1820 number; and in the November and December numbers of the same year
came Talfourd's "On the Genius and Writings of Wordsworth," an intelligent,
courageous, and prophetic defense against continuing general attacks on the
Lake poets' "systems" and particular ones on Wordsworth's characters, subjects, and language.[8] Such attentiveness on the part of the *New Monthly* to the
British literary scene—Mrs. Radcliffe, Scott, Burns, Southey, Maturin, Godwin, and Clare also appeared as subjects of biographical sketches or evaluative
essays—heralds the coming change in editorial policy which itself attests to the
publishing expertise and commercial savvy of Henry Colburn. Ever alert to
shifts in public interest, he was not loath to reshape his journal, in years of
becalmed political passions, to take advantage of them.[9]

With the 1821 appointment of Thomas Campbell to the editorship of the now
retitled *New Monthly Magazine and Literary Journal,* Colburn's periodical lost
its reactionary stamp[10] and acquired literary respectability, legitimacy, and
prestige, not to mention twice as many subscribers. Among these subscribers
were young liberals who soon became contributors.[11] Campbell, however tem-
peramentally unsuited to the task, was a popular, widely respected poet of
Whiggish coloring.[12] Colburn paid well for his acquisition. In exchange for his
annual 500 pounds, Campbell promised six pieces in prose and six in verse
over the contracted three-year period and got in the bargain an assistant to
manage the ubiquitous and vexing editorial choices. Cyrus Redding was already
on board as compiler of the "Historical Register" section, a fifty-page potpourri of everything from current events to obituaries.[13] It was bound and issued separately from the "Original Papers" as a third volume each year until
1833, and after 1837 was eliminated. Redding replaced Edward DuBois as sub-
editor after one issue, and quickly proved himself a nearly indispensable hand
to the volatile, hypersensitive Campbell.

The fame of his titular editor, the skills of his actual one, and the publisher's
own largesse,[14] then, combined to attract as contributors what Redding was
pleased to call "the first among the literary men [and, one should add, women]
of the time" (77:333), and the result was a frequently distinguished, always
interestingly diversified publication. Articles ranged from Campbell's own
weighty, learned lectures on Hebrew, Greek, and Roman poetry to James
Smith's witty "Grimm's Ghost," a monthly series of letters to Hermes on
"whatever takes place worthy of note in that forest of chimneys" which is
London (1:345). Other articles included Hazlitt's excellent "Table Talk" series
and his profiles, "The Spirits of the Age," on such figures as Bentham, William Tooke, Scott, and Lord Eldon; R. L. Sheil's (and, occasionally, W. H.
Curran's) "Sketches of the Irish Bar"; Stendhal's "Sketches of Parisian Society" and dispatches from Rome; at least one piece (probably) by Mary Shelley
on the latter city; Thomas Wyse's "Walks in Rome," and James Blanco White's

"Letters From Spain" and other foreign parts; often lengthy and penetrating reviews of the recent publications of de Musset, Scott, Cowper, Byron, Pepys, Moore, Thomas Medwin, Hunt, Ugo Foscolo, D'Israeli, Landor, Samuel Rogers, John Galt, and Godwin as well as several informed and still pertinent essays. Among these were Mrs. Radcliffe's "On The Supernatural in Poetry"; Mary Shelley's "Byron and Shelley on the Character of Hamlet"; Foscolo on Italian poets Michel Angelo, Frederick II, Pietro delle Vigne, and Guido Cavalcanti; T. C. Grattan on the living French poets Beranger and Lamartine; an anonymous author on German artists Korner, Goethe, and Schiller; various hands on Shakespeare, Malthus, Quevedo, Machiavelli, Milton, and, inescapably then as now, "The Classics and Romantics." Additionally, one finds the travelogue and tourist literature of Sydney Morgan (signed "Lady Morgan"); Clark and Sherwill's detailed account of their Mont Blanc assault; unpublished letters of Evelyn, Prior, Swift, and Burke; biographical sketches of assorted notables; stories, tales (one an "improvisation" by Buonaparte), and a substantial amount of verse, much of it Campbell's but including Elizabeth Barrett Browning's first periodical contribution[15] and the Keats-Brown collaboration, "Stanzas on Some Skulls in Beauley Abbey, Near Inverness." Finally, it would seriously disfigure the character of the *New Monthly* to omit from this survey such lightweight but engaging and often spicy items as "Ante and Post-Nuptial Journal," "Advantages of Having No Head!" "The Last of the Pigtails," "Memoirs of a Haunch of Mutton," and "Miss Hebe Hoggins's Account of a Literary Society in Houndsditch" (afterward, "The Houndsditch Album"), all by Horace Smith; "H. Lackrhyme's" "A Vision of Judgment, in Prose"; and "Robin Goodfellow's" (probably Leigh Hunt's) "Men, Women, and Nimmen, or a New Sex Discovered." Regular contributors, along with those already mentioned, were Talfourd, P. G. Patmore, Cornelius Webb, E. E. Crowe, Sismondi, Lamb, Felicia Hemans, Letitia E. Landon, W. S. Landor, Mary Russell Mitford, and, prominently toward the end of Campbell's tenure, Edward Bulwer-Lytton. How these and their articles were received may be judged by the previously noted circulation increase. One "in-house" writer, probably T. C. Morgan, conceived that reception, in a clever twitting of the British journalistic audience. This may be gathered from his January 1823 "Letter To The Editor":

First, sir, you are to know that the New Monthly Magazine is conducted with a vast deal of spirit, very lively and wittily written, but—as dull as an oyster; devilish clever, but—d——d stupid; full of variety, with—too much sameness; in most extensive circulation, but—does not sell. (G——d help Mr. Colburn, then, *"Thinks I to myself,"* for he must soon be ruined.) Mr. Campbell's Lectures are the only things worth reading in the book; but what is Greek literature to us? There's nothing amusing but Grimm's Ghost, except Peter Pindarics and the Irish Bar. Doblado's Letters [from Spain] are highly interesting by the air of verity they possess,

> though—they are evidently fictitious, and not a word of them true. The great merit of the publication is, that it does not meddle in politics; but— it is too decidedly a Tory work, the editor is a reputed Whig, and half the contributors downright Radicals. The public rejoice that the editor is no saint, but they would like the publication much better if it were a shade more *"Serious."* . . . There is "a constant reader" who thinks it does not *"look like a magazine,"* for want of double columns; and two maiden ladies, with whom I sometimes drink tea, who would think much better of the publication if it were stitched in a blue cover. [7:4]

Oddly enough, the division of opinion Morgan humorously describes here seems latterly to have infected the *New Monthly* editorial offices and, combined with personality clashes and power struggles, led by 1828 to a rapid deterioration of what had been, despite Campbell's testiness and Colburn's money-mindedness, a reasonably stable and certainly productive arrangement among the three principals. With Redding's gratefully accepted resignation in 1830 the alliance dissolved, for Campbell found himself unable to continue alone.

If Samuel Carter Hall during his first (ten-month) stint as editor brought little save a commercial, conservative, and conforming mentality to the *New Monthly*, along with occasional engravings of the subjects of its articles and the moderately interesting "Living Literary Characters" series,[16] his successor, Edward Bulwer, restored to the position not only fame but something of the passionate, partisan fervor, though now whipped up in the cause of radical reform, that had distinguished the earliest days of the journal. Colburn should not have been surprised, nor Hall (now sub-editor) fractious and vengeful, nor readers unsettled by the relatively heavy interlarding of political with other copy, nor indeed Bulwer sternly reproached for it, for reform or anti-reform was the universally obsessive issue of the day. (Even under Hall had appeared such anonymous pieces as "Will the Lords Pass the Bill, the Whole Bill, and Nothing but the Bill?" and "If The Lords Reject the Reform Bill, What Will Follow?") Bulwer commenced his January 1832 number thus:

> The New Year—and when, within our memory, did the year open with such omen of ill, and yet with such promise of good? . . . At this moment a certain weariness—a certain apathy pervades the higher classes of society. The little great world is sick of the eternal Reform, *blasé* with the cholera, and tired of the more novel horrors of the dissecting room and the Italian Boy. But slowly, darkly, fearfully rolls the great current of Opinion, among those orders who have no leisure for weariness

and he proceeds to assure readers "that we have every cause to be *convinced* that Ministers are resolved on carrying the Bill, the next time, through the Lords" (34:1).

But the magazine by no means sacrificed literary matter or quality to political cause. Bulwer's own "Asmodeus at Large," while in sections bluntly political and emphatically prejudicial, is also a fascinating literary curiosity. More important, of course, are T. J. Hogg's lengthy "Percy Bysshe Shelley at Oxford," Lady Blessington's complete "Journal of Conversations with Lord Byron," essays on Sir Thomas Elyot, Sir Thomas More, and Roger Ascham, Godwin's "Fragment of a Romance," Carlyle on the death of Goethe, and the editor on that of Scott in a four-page, black-bordered tribute. In addition to Bulwer's column "The Lion's Mouth"—"answers to our corresponding friends" and multifaceted editorial comment—plus an unusually large proportion of other material from his pen, readers could expect to hear regularly from John Poole, Hunt, Thomas Haynes Bayly, Letitia Landon, Harriet Martineau, Isaac D'Israeli, Benjamin Disraeli, "Barry Cornwall" (Bryan Waller Procter), Ebenezer Elliott, and even Thomas Campbell. By August 1833, however, after a year and nine months, the energetic Bulwer found himself spent by the stress of (in his view) almost single-handedly preserving the magazine's status as a spirited, provocative, and popular journalistic enterprise. Depending upon whose testimony one heeds, Bulwer's politicization of the *New Monthly* increased circulation, as he claimed, or decreased it, as Hall insisted.[17] But at all events Colburn appears to have greeted his editor's withdrawal with satisfaction that his magazine, now returned to Hall's editorship, could lapse into the generally unremarkable, sometimes bland, and always inoffensive character provided it by contributors Mitford, Hemans, Landon, Pardoe, Scargill, Willis, and the editor's wife. Again, of course, there are exceptions. Campbell continued to submit, as did Hunt, Lamb, and Landor. Coleridge is represented in previously unpublished letters, M. G. Lewis in a "mono-drama," "The Captive," and James Hogg in a three-part essay about the Ettrick Shepherd. But the major exception is Theodore Hook, an already popular humorist destined for the editorship. The subject matter and tone of his many articles for Hall presage the change in the nature and title of the journal to the *New Monthly Magazine and Humorist*.

In late 1836 Colburn once more altered the title when he found alteration in public taste. When a former partner, Richard Bentley, began *Bentley's Miscellany* * (see *VEA*) in 1737, Colburn hired Theodore Hook and instructed him to add a section of humor to rival *Bentley's*. Although the addition of "Humorist" to the title lasted only a year, Hook remained editor until 1841, attracted as contributors Trollope and Thackeray, and increased the number of serials. At Hook's death Colburn courted Dickens, who refused the editorship. Thomas Hood then became nominal editor under Colburn's control for two years. In June 1845 William H. Ainsworth, formerly editor of *Bentley's* and at that time of *Ainsworth's* * (see *VEA*), purchased the *New Monthly*. The best days of the magazine were over. Although it was published until 1884, the *New Monthly* never enjoyed the stature or success it had known under Campbell and Bulwer.

Notes

1. "The Periodical Press," *Edinburgh Review* 76 (May 1823):370.
2. "Prologue to the Hundredth Volume," quoted in *The Wellesley Index to Victo-*

rian Periodicals, 1824–1900, ed. Walter E. Houghton (Toronto, 1979), 3:163. I am grateful to this indispensable resource tool which supplies much of the information in my account. Mary Ruth Hiller, with the assistance of Linda Dobbins and Linda Jones, has supplied a survey and index for the years 1821 to 1854 (3:161–302). My account focuses on the years 1814–1836, which include Campbell's editorship. The magazine ran until 1884. See "Publication History" below.

3. Walter Graham notes that "in the original nature of its letterpress it was, from 1820 on, one of the most progressive of periodicals." *English Literary Periodicals* (New York, 1930), p. 286. Neil S. Grill described the *New Monthly* as "a significant force in the literary world of London." "The *New Monthly Magazine* and American English, 1814–1824," *American Speech* 47 (1972):256n. Linda B. Jones classifies the *New Monthly* with *Blackwood's* and *London Magazine* as one of the three leading magazines of the 1820s. "The *New Monthly Magazine:* 1821–1830," Ph.D. dissertation, University of Colorado, 1971, p. 1.

4. Myron F. Brightfield notes that the "dishonest practice of taking the name of a rival publication with the prefix 'New', in order to share its popularity and perhaps confuse its subscribers, was not infrequent then, although it was condemned by many." *Theodore Hook and His Novels* (Cambridge, Mass., 1928), p. 152n.

5. Cf. John Lockhart's "On the Cockney School of Poetry," in *Blackwood's* 2, nos. 1, 2 (October, November 1817); 3, nos. 4, 5 (July, August 1818).

6. See Donald H. Reiman, ed., *The Romantics Reviewed: Contemporary Reviews of British Romantic Writers,* 9 vols. (New York, 1972), part B, 5:1897. The reviews themselves appear on pp. 1886–1905 of the same volume.

7. Neil S. Grill, "The *New Monthly Magazine:* 1814–1820," Ph.D. dissertation, New York University, 1970, p. 441.

8. See William S. Ward, "An Early Champion of Wordsworth: Thomas Noon Talfourd," *Publication of the Modern Language Association* 68 (1953):998.

9. See Houghton, 3:161–62.

10. Campbell's "Preface" to the January 1821 issue (numbered volume 1, number 1) signals the new direction:

It is better, with all its drawbacks, that political zeal should be alive than dead. . . . But it does not follow, from the general utility of political discussion, that it should invariably pervade every species of literary compilation, or that there should be no calm spot in the world of periodical literature where all minds of common charity and candour may meet without the asperities of party feeling. There is no scarcity of polemical writers on political subjects, and there is no call for any man to add himself to their number, unless he is conscious of his habits and pursuits having peculiarly fitted him to come with power into the context. Impressed with this consideration, the present Editor the more willingly undertook this work, as the Proprietors declared their wish for its main object to be literary, not political. . . . [The Editor] thinks himself more likely to be usefully employed in stamping the WORK with a purely literary character, than by coming forward in the arena of politics." [v–vi]

11. Reiman, part A, 2:796.
12. On this issue, P. G. Patmore writes:

In temperament indolent, capricious and uncertain, yet hasty, sensitive, wilful, and obstinate in giving will its way; his habits of composition slow to a degree of painfulness; his literary taste refined, even to fastidiousness; and, above all, his personal position as the friend and associate of nearly all the distinguished litterateurs of the day, and his almost morbid sensitiveness on the point of giving pain, or even displeasure to any of them;—Campbell was, and knew himself to be, the ideal of what the proffered office required its occupant *not* to be. [*My Friends and Acquaintances*, 3 vols. (London, 1854), 1:109–10]

13. This representative table of contents for the "Historical Register" comes from volume 12 (1824):

Political Events; The Drama [normally done, says Houghton, 3:164, by Talfourd]; Music; Fine Arts [initially Robert Hunt's column, later taken over by Samuel Beazley: see Houghton, 3:164]; Varieties—Great Britain; Foreign Varieties; Rural Economy; Useful Arts; New Patents; New Publications, British, With Critical Remarks; ———Foreign . . . ; Literary Reports; Meteorological Reports; Agricultural Reports, Prices of Corn and Markets; Commercial Reports, Stocks, &c; Bankrupts, Dividends, and Sequestrations; Prices of Canal Shares; Incidents, Appointments, Marriages, and Deaths, with Biographical Notices of Distinguished Persons Deceased; Provincial Occurrences.

14. Houghton (3:165) defines the usual compensation as twelve guineas per sheet, four less than that paid by the *Edinburgh* and *Quarterly;* but some authors earned sixteen guineas, and a few considerably more if Colburn thought their work likely to hike sales. For submitting whatever he pleased, Horace Smith annually received the equivalent of 40 percent of the editor's salary.

15. So identified by Gardner Taplin, "An Early Poem by Mrs. Browning," *Notes and Queries* 195 (1950):252–53. The poem, "Stanzas, Excited by Some Reflections on the Present State of Greece," appears in 1 (May 1821):523.

16. Variously authored by Allan Cunningham, John Poole, Hall, Letitia Landon, Mary Mitford, and often anonymously. See Houghton, 3:215–16.

17. See Houghton, 3:166.

Information Sources

BIBLIOGRAPHY

Brightfield, Myron F. *Theodore Hook and His Novels*. Cambridge, Mass., 1928.
Cox, R. G. "The Reviews and Magazines." In *From Dickens To Hardy*. Vol. 6 of *The Pelican Guide To English Literature*. Baltimore, 1958.
Graham, Walter. *English Literary Periodicals*. New York, 1930.
Grill, Neil G. "The *New Monthly Magazine* and American English, 1814–1824." *American Speech* 47 (1972):256–60.
———. "The *New Monthly Magazine:* 1814–1820." Ph.D. dissertation, New York University, 1970.
Houghton, Walter E., ed. *The Wellesley Index To Victorian Periodicals, 1824–1900*. Vol. 3. Toronto, 1979.
Jones, Linda B. "The *New Monthly Magazine,* 1821–1830." Ph.D. dissertation, University of Colorado, 1970.

Lombard, C. "Portrait of Lamartine in the English Periodicals (1820–1870)." *Modern Language Review* 56 (1961):335–38.

Marchand, Leslie A. *The Athenaeum: A Mirror of Victorian Culture*. Chapel Hill, N.C., 1941.

Mayer, S.R. Townshend. "Leigh Hunt and the *New Monthly Magazine*," *Notes and Queries* 7 (1877).265–66.

Patmore, P. G. *My Friends and Acquaintances*. Vol. 1. London, 1854.

Pollin, Burton Ralph. "William Godwin's 'Fragment of a Romance.' " *Comparative Literature* 16 (1964):40, 54.

Reiman, Donald H., ed. *Contemporary Reviews of British Romantic Writers*. Vol. 5. New York, 1972.

Rosenberg, Harry and Sheila. "Newspapers and Magazines." In *The New Cambridge Bibliography of English Literature,* ed. George Watson. Cambridge, England, 1969.

Scott, Winifred. *Jefferson Hogg*. London, 1951.

Taplin, Gardner. "An Early Poem by Mrs. Browning." *Notes and Queries* 195 (1950):252–53.

Ward, William S. "An Early Champion of Wordsworth: Thomas Noon Talfourd." *Publications of the Modern Language Association* 68 (1953):992–1000.
INDEXES
Each volume indexed. 1821–1881 in *Poole's Index*. 1821–1854 in *Wellesley Index* 3.

REPRINT EDITIONS
Microform: English Literary Periodicals (UMI), reels 249–264.

LOCATION SOURCES
American
Partial runs: Widely available.
British
Complete runs: British Museum; Leeds University Library; London Library; Victoria and Albert Museum Library.
Partial runs: Widely available.

Publication History

MAGAZINE TITLE AND TITLE CHANGES
The New Monthly Magazine and Universal Register, 1814–1820. *The New Monthly Magazine and Literary Journal,* 1821–1836. *The New Monthly Magazine and Humorist,* 1837–1852. *The New Monthly Magazine,* 1853–1881. *The New Monthly,* January–October 1882. *The New Monthly Magazine,* December 1882–January 1884.

VOLUME AND ISSUE DATA
Volumes 1–14, 1 February 1814–1 December 1820; second series, volumes 1–149, January 1821–December 1871; third series, volumes 1–15, January 1872–June 1879; fourth series, volumes 1–8, July 1879–January 1884.

FREQUENCY OF PUBLICATION
Monthly.

PUBLISHERS
1814–1828: Henry Colburn, Conduit Street, Hanover Square, London/New Burlington Street, London (in 1825). 1829–1831: Henry Colburn and Richard Bent-

ley, same as above. 1832–1834: For Henry Colburn by Richard Bentley, same as above. 1835–November 1845: Henry Colburn, same as above. December 1845–1869: Chapman and Hall, London. 1870–1873: Adams and Francis, London. 1873–1884: E. W. Allen, London.

EDITORS

Frederic Shoberl, volume 1–(?), February 1814–(?). Dr. John Watkins, volumes 1–10, February 1814–December 1818. A. A. Watts, volume 11, January 1819–May or June 1819. Thomas Campbell, 2d series, volumes 1–29, January 1821–December 1830. (Sub-editors: Edward DuBois, volume 1, January 1821; Cyrus Redding, volumes 1–29, February 1821–September 1830; S. C. Hall, volume 29, October 1830–December 1830.) S. C. Hall, 2d series, volumes 31–32, January 1831–October 1831. E. L. Bulwer (later Bulwer-Lytton), 2d series, volumes 32–38, November 1831–August 1833. (Sub-editor: S. C. Hall.) S. C. Hall, 2d series, volumes 39–48, September 1833–December 1836. Theodore E. Hook, 2d series, volumes 49–62, January 1837–August 1841. (Sub-editors: Benson E. Hill and Robert Folkestone Williams.) Robert Folkestone Williams, 2d series, volume 63, September 1841. Thomas Hood, 2d series, volumes 63–68, October 1841–September 1843. (Sub-editors: P. G. Patmore, William Shoberl, and D. E. Williams or R. F. Williams.) Henry Colburn, with his clerks, P. G. Patmore, William Shoberl, and D. E. Williams, 2d series, volumes 69–74, September 1843–June 1845. William Harrison Ainsworth, 2d series, volumes 74–96, July 1845–December 1852. (Sub-editor: William Francis Ainsworth.) William Harrison Ainsworth, 2d series, volumes 97–147, January 1853–December 1870. (Sub-editor: William Francis Ainsworth.) William Francis Ainsworth, volumes 148–3d series, volume 15, January 1871–December 1879. Joshua Hatton ("Guy Roslyn"), 3d series, volume 16–(?), January 1880–1884(?).

W. Paul Elledge

NEW REVIEW, THE

By 1813 both the *Edinburgh Review** and the *Quarterly Review,** as well as a raft of monthly reviews, had already developed the procedures and standards of reviewing in what must have seemed every possible fashion. But in that same year the *New Review* was founded and earned its title with a number of innovations that now seem reasonable and useful.

Most of the innovations were proclaimed in the prospectus attached to volume 1. But the first mentioned, and perhaps the most important, was actually a throwback to an eighteenth-century practice long since abandoned as impractical: the *New Review* intended "to analyze *every* publication (1:iii). Every book, moreover, was presented first with a large-print version of what looks like the title page; then the analysis was to proceed "by giving a view of the *Contents,* the *Preface,* when it explains the subject; and *Extracts* of prominent and striking parts of the book; thus enabling the reader to exercise a judgment unprejudiced by the sentiments of the Reviewer" (1:iii).[1] Finally, the proprietors intended "to state what other works each Author has Published, or Edited."

In the process, the reviews sometimes ran to ten double-column pages, but most were one- or two-page critiques. To cover the flow of books, the *New Review* resorted to another innovation: the size of each issue would "be proportioned to the press of the matter" (1:iv). The issues ran approximately 100–120 pages a month, but the number of books was still great enough to turn the *Review* away in March from its original intention of leisurely analyzing all books from the previous year (1:359).

The *New Review* also proposed to pay more attention to other reviewing periodicals than had ever been done before; every month it printed the table of contents of every such periodical for the preceding month. It carried, moreover, *"Defenses of Authors* against Criticisms," that is, against reviews of their works printed in other magazines. And as an attempt to be an indisputable center of information on general literature, the proprietors likewise proposed to carry prospectuses of new works ("at a moderate charge") and advertisements of those already published. A catalogue of new publications was of course unnecessary, since all new publications were to be criticized in the *New Review* anyway.

To give access to the mass of information on publications and reviews, elaborate indexes were provided in supplements to each volume, which listed all books by author, title, subject matter, and categories. In August 1813 the *New Review* began an additional "List of Living Authors and Other Persons in any way noticed in the reviews and Magazines Published on the 1st of [the previous month]" (1:222–24). If the *New Review* had had a longer life span, we would today have a very valuable reference tool.

The reviews themselves are not especially valuable as judgments of the works. The reviews of literature of importance are mainly of works by Byron, who was very prolific at the time in question; they are not without critical comments, but the reviewers are generally hesitant to make judgments, preferring rather to outline plots and provide excerpts.[2]

At first the *New Review* seems to have fulfilled some contemporary need; about halfway through the first volume there are six pages of correspondence praising the new periodical (1:355–60). But soon it appeared that something was amiss. Perhaps it was the absence of critical rigor that one comes to expect in a reviewing organ and that cannot be replaced by completeness of coverage and elaborate indexes. Whatever the cause, the *New Review* filled only three volumes before its early demise.

Notes

1. Late in 1813 the proprietors promised to add a half-sheet so that no one would object to the "full titles" (1:613).
2. Donald H. Reiman, in *The Romantics Reviewed,* part B (New York, 1972), 5:1935, claims in his introduction to the review of Byron's *The Bride of Abydos* in the *New Review* that "the reviewer indicates that the 'plan' of the *New Review* forbade any attempt to judge the 'intrinsic merit' of the books it reviewed." As far as is known, the *New Review* had no such policy. What the reviewer said was as follows: "In these

preliminary remarks, we are not transgressing the plan of our *Journal,* or stating our opinion with regard to the intrinsic merit of the poetry of this work'' (3:112). Praise and adverse criticism do occur in the reviews; see, for example, the review of Scott's *Rokeby,* 2 (September 1813):230, and Byron's *Giaour,* 2 (December 1813):674.

Information Sources

INDEXES
> Cumulative index for volumes 1 and 2 in a supplementary number.

REPRINT EDITIONS
> Microform: English Literary Periodicals (UMI), reel 952.

LOCATION SOURCES
> *American*
>> Partial runs: Boston Athenaeum; New York Historical Society; University of Minnesota Library.
>
> *British*
>> Complete runs: London University Library; St. Andrews University Library.

Publication History

MAGAZINE TITLE AND TITLE CHANGES
> *The New Review, or Monthly Analysis, of General Literature.*

VOLUME AND ISSUE DATA
> Volumes 1–3, 1813–1814.

FREQUENCY OF PUBLICATION
> Monthly.

PUBLISHERS
> Sherwood and Co., Paternoster Row, London/Underwood, Fleet Street, London/Munday and Slatters, Oxford/Deighton, Cambridge.

EDITOR
> Unknown.

John O. Hayden

NEW UNIVERSAL MAGAZINE, THE. See UNIVERSAL MAGAZINE, THE (AAAJ)

NIC-NAC, THE

The *Nic-Nac* was Thomas Wallis's second venture in the field of cheap weekly magazines. In 1818 he had started the *Modern Spectator, or, Wallis's Minor Magazine,* which ran to eighteen issues. He was editor and printer for the *Nic-Nac* throughout its existence (30 November 1822 to 26 April 1828). In February 1824 Wallis moved his press (cf. 65:104), presumably to Finchley, but he retained his shop in Camden Town.[1] This division of his business created practical problems affecting the publication of the *Nic-Nac.* Wallis remained one of the publishers, but maintaining contact between editor, publishers, and printer became time-consuming and cumbersome. On 15 May 1824 J. Harris of Bow Street, who was then Wallis's co-publisher, started receiving communications for the editor. This arrangement was abandoned on 23 April 1825, when Wallis in Camden Town resumed sole responsibility for the publishing. There followed a period of considerable turmoil for the *Nic-Nac,* and the fact that most of the issues published between 23 April 1825 and 7 January 1826 have been lost indicates that the publishing arrangements were still far from satisfactory. The *Gentleman's Magazine* * (see *AAAJ*) remarked that the *Nic-Nac* ''cannot possibly continue long as it is not met with at more than three shops in London, and is not published till about three months after date.''[2] Numbers 123–125 were published by J. Harris alone, but he was again joined by Wallis on 16 July 1825. The last period of uninterrupted publication enjoyed by the *Nic-Nac* lasted from 7 January to 29 July 1826, during which time Wallis was sole publisher. However, the gap in extant copies between 29 July 1826 and 21 July 1827 suggests that the familiar problems of publication still remained unsolved, and the final volume contains nineteen issues published at irregular intervals solely by J. Harris. Wallis, having then presumably given up his shop in Camden Town, handled the printing of the last issues from his premises in Finchley.

There are few clues to the identity of the editor. The prefaces to volumes 1 and 2 are signed ''T. W.'' and the nature of the periodical makes it unlikely that it ever had any other editor. It contained extracts reprinted from published material, and the editor's task was one of selecting appropriate passages for inclusion. Furthermore, a periodical selling at one pence an issue could hardly afford an external editor. Even when Wallis finally gave up publishing the periodical and completed moving his business, he must have retained the editorship. A poem entitled ''Sweet Little Mary'' was printed in issue 220 (p. 88). Under ''To Correspondents'' in the next issue there appeared a note from the editor to Alphus refusing insertion of that same poem, followed by a note in which ''the printer begs to state that he inserted the poem by mistake'' (p. 96). Such a mistake was most likely to occur if the editing and printing took place under the same roof.

The *Nic-Nac* was primarily a commercial venture permitting Thomas Wallis to maximize the use of his press. The rapid expansion of its circulation is evident from the number of booksellers who were involved in the enterprise during the first two years, and from the number of reprints, which were in continuous demand (cf. no. 18:144; no. 23:184; no. 76:192; no. 113:72; no. 117:104; no. 175:144). In his preface to the first volume, written in November 1823, Wallis proudly compared the *Nic-Nac* to a number of weekly periodicals that had started publication at the same time. Apart from a few spectacular successes such as the *Mirror of Literature, Amusement, and Instruction* * and the *Pulpit* none of the periodicals ran for more than two years. Wallis's selection revealed his lack of concern for the distinctive features of the periodicals: the *Mechanic's Magazine,* the *Literary Sketch-Book,* * the *Sabbath,* and the

Anti-Infidel reflected widely different editorial policies, but their commercial performance was the only point of interest to Wallis.

The *Gentleman's Magazine* thought little of the *Nic-Nac;* it made the depreciatory remark that the *Nic-Nac* was "bought by the plebeian herd for a penny."[3] But Wallis maintained in the first issue that he was proud to see his periodical take part in "the universal diffusion of education and intelligence among all classes of the community" (p. 6). As an editor he took a conservative stand: "We are old-fashioned fellows, who fear GOD and honour the King; go to Church and not to the Meeting-house; prefer Port and Ale to Champagne and Burgundy; and would rather inhabit a cottage in Old England, than the finest Chateau in all France" (no. 2:iii; cf. no. 164:56). He allowed no discussion of controversial subjects:

> Whatever may be our political opinions, we never trouble our readers with them, and expect them, in return, to display the same courtesy towards us. It is our aim to render the Nic-Nac a miscellany entirely free from offensive matter, so that in the perusal of it the purchaser may for a time forget the turmoils, asperities, and harassing conflicting passions which are too generally suffered to mar the comfort of man's existence. [68:128]

The editorial tone reflected the commercial nature of the periodical. Brusquely optimistic, Wallis was never loath to display the success of his venture, and he had clear and unsophisticated ideas concerning suitable items for inclusion in the *Nic-Nac*. Novelty and sensation were important qualities in contributions, which should not duplicate recently published material (9:72). Old publications and publications not readily available in London became his main hunting ground. His wish to amuse and startle his readers led him to include series on such subjects as ancient methods of torture, often illustrated with woodcuts. The stage provided a similarly fascinating subject, and the periodical ran an illustrated series on the history of the English theater covering more than 200 years in an erratic manner, but with considerable detail.[4] Other dramatic items included a series of four essays on English dramatists (no. 111:49–51; no. 113:67–69; no. 115:82–83; no. 116:90–93) and a reprint of Hazlitt's essay "On Actors and Acting" (no. 93:321–25).

In this context poetry provided a soothing counter-balance. A weekly column of "Original Poetry" contained short verses of immutable character: occasionally humorous, but most frequently lyrical, sentimental, and picturesque, supplied by such minor poets as H. S. Van Dyk, Mrs. Cornwell Baron Wilson, and John Chalk Claris. Reviews were never included, but the periodical carried various articles of literary interest. "Poetry and Poets" ran to eleven installments giving selections of short anecdotes about poets from Milton to Coleridge.[5] No literary criticism was attempted, but there was occasional evidence of an antiquarian's interest in pointing out sources and textual variants of particular lines (cf. no. 22:172–73). The articles grew somewhat less extravagant as the series progressed; the extracts became longer and were prefaced with brief remarks setting them in critical or biographical traditions. On rare occasions when a literary subject offered surprising details the *Nic-Nac* responded promptly; Byron's death received immediate attention, and numbers 78, 79, and 80 devoted an unusual amount of space to commemorative articles.

Wallis's policy of relying for extracts on publications not readily available to London readers generated an interest in America unprecedented in England at the time. One correspondent known as Clio supplied material for a column entitled "Transatlantic Varieties." It first appeared on 3 May 1823 and remained a regular feature of the periodical till it ceased publication. Short clippings from American journals on extraordinary events, unusual facts, and marvellous discoveries provided information on American society to an audience largely ignorant of the new country. American literature was introduced in eight installments of "The American Muse" by reprinting poems from periodicals such as the *New York Commercial Advertiser*, *Philadelphia Gazette*, and *Baltimore Advertiser*.[6] The poems were frequently anonymous, but the columns included contributions by two minor poets who were active members of nonconformist sects in America: William Bigham Tappan and William B. Walters.

The *Nic-Nac* was designed for readers of fixed habits. When Wallis wished to capitalize on his commercial success by publishing the periodical twice weekly, the angry reactions from his readers startled him into returning to the familiar pattern of publication (no. 60:64). The format of each issue remained the same throughout, providing easy and untroubled reading. Efficient publishing and distribution were essential because the *Nic-Nac*'s readers valued ready access to entertainment, and the difficulties inflicted on circulation by Wallis's move to Finchley proved the bane of the *Nic-Nac* (no. 169:96). Nevertheless, it enjoyed a brief commercial success; and although it has been largely ignored by modern scholars, it remains a fascinating document of early interest in American affairs and in the history of the stage. It reflects the various interests of a group of readers who were rapidly gaining importance in the 1820s as a target group for publishers of both literature and periodicals.

Notes

1. William B. Todd, *A Directory of Printers and Others in Allied Trades: London and Vicinity: 1800–1840* (London, 1972), p. 203.

2. "On Cheap Periodical Literature," *Gentleman's Magazine* 95 (1825):485.

3. "On Cheap Periodical Literature," p. 483.

4. In twenty-seven installments published between 12 April 1823 and 24 September 1824.

5. They were published between 26 April 1823 and 15 September 1827.

6. The series was published between 19 April 1823 and 18 August 1827.

Information Sources

BIBLIOGRAPHY

Gohdes, Clarence. *American Literature in Nineteenth-Century England*. New York, 1944.
Landré, Louis. *Leigh Hunt (1784–1859): Contribution à l'histoire du Romantisme Anglais*. 2 vols. Paris, 1936.
The Modern Spectator, or, Wallis's Minor Magazine, nos. 1–18, 19 December 1818–29 May 1819.
PAN. "On Cheap Periodical Literature." *Gentleman's Magazine* 95 (1825):483–86.
Todd, William B. *A Directory of Printers and Others in Allied Trades: London and Vicinity: 1800–1840*. London, 1972.

INDEXES
Volumes 1, 2 indexed. The copy of volume 5 in the Birmingham Public Library includes an incomplete manuscript index for volumes 1–3.

REPRINT EDITIONS
None.

LOCATION SOURCES
American

Complete runs: Lloyd Library and Museum; U. S. Library of Congress.
Partial runs: Cornell University Library; Yale University Library.

British

Complete run: British Museum.
Partial runs: Birmingham Public Library; John Rylands Library (Manchester). (The copies of the *Nic-Nac* held in Birmingham Public Library contain a few MS notes identifying authors of anonymous poems and a MS index to volumes 1–3.)

Publication History

MAGAZINE TITLE AND TITLE CHANGES
The Nic-Nac; or, Oracle of Knowledge, 30 November 1822–29 November 1823.
The Nic-Nac, or Literary Cabinet, 6 December 1823–26 April 1828. Titlepages of volumes 1–2, 30 November 1822–27 November 1824: *The Nic-Nac; or, Literary Cabinet: Containing an Amusing Assemblage of Tales, Anecdotes, Poetry, Biography, Epigrams, Enigmas, Oddities, Receipts, Wonders of Nature and Art, The Spirit of the Periodical Press, and Gleanings from Foreign Journals; Together with a Comprehensive History of the English Stage: With Numerous Engravings.*

VOLUME AND ISSUE DATA
Volume 1, numbers 1–52, 30 November 1822–29 November 1823. No issue was published on 18 October 1823. Volume 2, numbers 53–104, 6 December 1823–27 November 1824. (Numbers 53–58 were published twice weekly. No issues were published between 24 December 1823 and 3 January 1824, on 14 February 1824 and 29 May 1824, and between 27 November 1824 and 1 January 1825.) Volume 3, numbers 105–139, 1 January 1825–27 August 1825. (No copies of numbers 122, 126–132, and 140–157 are extant.) Volume 4, numbers 158–187, 7 January 1826–29 July 1826. (No copies of numbers 188–209 are extant.) Volume 5, numbers 210–228, 21 July 1827–26 April 1828. (Numbers

210–219 were published fortnightly, and numbers 220–228 were published very irregularly.)

FREQUENCY OF PUBLICATION
Weekly; frequently irregular.

PUBLISHERS
Numbers 1–121, 30 November 1822–23 April 1825; numbers 133–187, 16 July 1825–29 July 1826: Thomas Wallis, 4 Upper Pratt Place, Camden Town, London. Numbers 13–18, 22 February 1823–29 March 1823: John Fairburn, 13 Broadway, Ludgate Hill, London. Numbers 53–120, 6 December 1823–16 April 1825; numbers 123–125, 7 May 1825–21 May 1825; numbers 210–228, 21 July 1827–26 April 1828: J. Harris, Bow Street, Covent Garden, London. Numbers 112–117, 19 February 1825–26 March 1825: G. Gifford, Paternoster Row, and Newgate Street, London. Numbers 118–120, 2 April 1825–16 April 1825; numbers 133–139, 16 July 1825–27 August 1825: Dunbar, Wych Street, Drury Lane and Archer, London.

EDITOR
Thomas Wallis.

Karsten Engelberg

_____ **P** _____

POETICAL MAGAZINE

On 1 May 1809 the *Poetical Magazine*, "dedicated to the Lovers of the Muse," was available at booksellers and stationers in the United Kingdom for two shillings. Rudolph Ackermann, the publisher, established his business at the Repository of Arts (101 Strand, London) as a dealer in prints, art supplies, fabrics, and fancy goods, but by 1809 he had become a publisher of prints and fine books. In January, four months before the *Poetical Magazine* appeared, Ackermann brought out a monthly miscellany with a title that incorporated his business name—the *Repository of Arts, Literature, Commerce, Manufactures, Fashions, and Politics*. The early numbers of the *Repository* print very little poetry and are filled, instead, with prose literature; music reviews; articles on art, commerce, politics, furniture, and fashions; literary and scientific news; medical, agricultural, and market reports; and meteorological tables. As W. J. Burke suggests in an article on Ackermann's career, the *Poetical Magazine* was founded, in part, to take "care of the surplus verse submitted to the already overcrowded *Repository of Arts*." [1] The editor of the *Poetical Magazine* was probably Frederic Shoberl. He edited the *Repository* during its entire twenty-year run, and the ties between the two magazines were particularly close at the outset. Manuscripts for both magazines were directed to the same London address, and contributors to the first four numbers of the *Repository* were among the earliest writers for the *Poetical Magazine*. These included William Combe, Samuel Blake Frome, James Murray Lacey, Thomas Marshall, J. Hamilton Roche, and "Azeli." The prospectus for the *Poetical Magazine* was appended to the April number of the *Repository*, and in the May number the editor apologizes to "Lovers of Poetry" for the absence of poems and recommends Ackermann's new magazine to them. Occasionally thereafter, throughout 1809 and 1810, the *Repository*'s notes to "Readers and Correspondents" inform contributors that poems submitted to the *Repository* will be published instead in the *Poetical Magazine*.

Ackermann's innovative ideas for the *Poetical Magazine* transcended both its function as a receptacle for the *Repository*'s "surplus verse" and its own avowed purpose of keeping "flights of fancy" from being lost. The "Introductory Address," evidently written by Ackermann, declares the magazine's intention to democratize poetry by expanding its scope and by recruiting new poets. In calling for verse in "all varieties of mode, measure, and subject," Ackermann includes not only the traditional subjects of "poems, descriptive, moral and satiric," but subjects that had been excluded previously from poetry: advertisements, "accounts of public events or domestic occurrences," announcements of births, marriages, and deaths, and even law cases, "if any rhyming Barrister will favour us with such a novelty" (1:iii). Interest in obituaries and advertisements in verse soon dissipated, but "greeting-card" verse, marking birthdays, anniversaries, and other personal occasions, appears in the magazine until the end of the second volume. It was also at this time (May 1810) that the magazine tightened its editorial policy. In the "Introductory Address," however, Ackermann invites the "exertions of every rank and degree of poetic talent." He evidently believed poetic talent to be "so generally diffused . . . that almost every class of people, except those who live by manual labour, [has], more or less, a tincture of it" (1:ii). The assumption that a poet need only be literate accounts for the magazine's "open-door" policy toward contributors. The policy did not owe to the financial motive attributed to Ackermann by J. G. Merle, a corresponding clerk at the Repository of Arts, who claimed that Ackermann, instead of giving "liberal payment" for contributions of established poets, "trusted chiefly to gratuitous communications, most of which were interesting when in print only to their authors."[2] An end to the magazine's lenient editorial policy and a new concern for quality are signaled in the May 1810 number, which for the first time prints notes "To Readers and Correspondents" and announces that medals will be offered by the "Proprietor" to "encourage poetical merit in its fullest extent" (3:48).

Although Ackermann failed to expand the subject matter of poetry, the *Poetical Magazine* does achieve variety in "mode" and "measure." Between seven and eight hundred poems were printed in two years, and they encompass many types: impromptus, epigrams, acrostics, apostrophes, enigmas and solutions, anagrams, anacreontics, elegies, epitaphs, monodies, canzonets, hymns, eclogues, dramatic prologues and epilogues, dialogues, fables, narratives, epistles, pastorals, parodies, translations and imitations of classical odes, and poems in French, Latin, Greek, and Italian. Many different stanza forms are also represented in the four volumes of poetry, and the poems frequently display ingenuity and sophistication in their metrical and rhyming patterns. It is no surprise, however, that in rank order the most frequently used stanzas are those associated with light verse and narrative poetry: heroic couplet, iambic tetrameter couplet, ballad, sonnet, heroic quatrain, long ballad, ode, and blank verse.

The four volumes of the *Poetical Magazine* preserve poems of more than 200 writers. Judging from the careers of those regular correspondents who can be identified, the contributors varied widely in their life situations, and writing was no more than a passing interest or a diversion for most of them. Only a few of the writers whose verse appeared regularly in the *Poetical Magazine* ever published their own collections of poetry. This group included both professional writers in mid-career or beyond, such as William Combe, Thomas Clio Rickman, and Thomas Vaughan, and young writers who had not yet chosen careers, such as George Daniel, Samuel Elsdale, S. B. Frome, John Gwilliam, James Murray Lacey, and Samuel Miller Waring.[3] The contributions of four of these writers—Vaughan, Rickman, Daniel, and Gwilliam—illustrate the scope and variety of verse that they and their more obscure or anonymous colleagues published in Ackermann's magazine.

Thomas Vaughan, clerk of the peace for the city of Westminster, regularly supplied the magazine with witty epigrams and *vers de société*. Vaughan authored at least three comic plays between 1776 and 1784, and his friend R. B. Sheridan may have modeled Dangle in *The Critic* after him. His novel, *Fashionable Follies*, first issued in 1782, was revised and republished in 1810. Vaughan's poems are signed "V——" or "Lambeth Road" or "V——, L——b——th R——d." The following epigram is typical of Vaughan's style:

MAN AND WIFE.—A CONSOLATORY DUET AT PARTING

> HE,—"Bone of my bone, and flesh beside,
>   Attend my dying words," he cried:—
>   "As Death, at length, will make us twain,
>   I hope we ne'er may meet again."
> SHE.—"If that's the blessing which you give,
>   I beg you'll hear me in reply;
>   My fears are only lest you live,
>   So, quickly, John, I pray you—die."

[1:131]

James Murray Lacey ("J.M.L."), J. Lilly, Eliza (?) St. Claire ("Azeli"), and Thomas Wilson ("T.W.") as occasional correspondents furnished light verse in the same vein.

Thomas Clio Rickman ("Clio") was a bookseller by trade and a reformer by conviction, and by 1809 he had already achieved some notoriety for his political verse satire and republican songs. His most important publication was yet to come—a biography of his friend Tom Paine, who composed the second part of *The Rights of Man* in his house. The poems that Rickman wrote for the *Poetical Magazine* between May 1809 and November 1810 are neither political nor satirical. His best effort is probably a "Sonnet, Written in a Favourite Chair of Dean Swift's":

> Here seated,—erst where Swift oft musing sat,
>   And form'd his Gulliver's immortal tale;
> Or entertain'd his friends in witty chat,
>   Or bade sublimer topics to prevail;—
> Here seated,—deep Reflection takes her range,
>   And contemplates the altering hand of Time;
> With retrospective eye marks ev'ry change,
>   Since Swift here wrote his prose, or sportive rhyme;—
> Here seated,—while enamour'd Mem'ry dwells
>   On Genius, Talent, Learning most profound,
> With mortified regret the bosom swells,
>   And proud Humanity receives a wound,
> That Swift, endow'd with gifts the wisest crave,
> Should sink a senseless madman to the grave.

[1:209]

George Daniel ("G——E D——N——L"), who was only twenty when his first poems were printed in the *Poetical Magazine,* includes Rickman in his later satirical poem, *The Modern Dunciad:* "Hoarse Clio Rickman's sonnets bay the moon, / Clio, a poet, patriot, and buffoon."[4] The poems that Daniel wrote for the magazine between September 1809 and April 1811 are rather conventional, academic exercises. He had not yet developed the biting style of *The Modern Dunciad* and was partial to odes, elegies, and verse epistles. His contributions to the magazine were collected in *Miscellaneous Poems* (1812), and a reviewer in the *Critical Review* (see *AAAJ*) cites an "Ode to Contentment" as one of Daniel's best (ser. 4, 1.554). The following lines from the ode give some idea of Daniel's style:

> Let not my humble Muse despise
> To seek where true Contentment lies:
> O! Let her (train'd in rustic lore)
> The peasant's lowly cot explore:
> In sweet content and peace he lives,—
> What blessings bounteous Nature gives!
> . . . .
> In harmless joys his life is spent
> With ruddy Health, and sweet Content.

[3:106]

Daniel's apprentice verse is marred by affected pathos and stilted diction, but it is still superior to the magazine's more extreme didactic, patriotic, and religious effusions, which were amply supplied by Samuel Elsdale, S. B. Frome, and the Quaker brothers, Elijah and Samuel Waring.

With the single exception of William Combe, the most frequent contributor to the *Poetical Magazine* was John Gwilliam, who as a writer for *Scourge* * also earned a place in Daniel's *Modern Dunciad.*[5] Like Daniel, Gwilliam was a novice, but he had published poetry regularly in the *Cabinet* * between June and December 1808. Forty-eight of his poems appear in the *Poetical Magazine* between May 1809 and January 1811, and, although he favored the sonnet, a variety of stanza forms, themes, and moods are represented in his verse. His most ambitious production is "Tears of Sympathy," which recounts Napoleon's conquest of the Austrians. The first of a series of poems Gwilliam composed on Napoleon and the Napoleonic Wars, it was revised, expanded, and published privately in 1813 as *The Battles of the Danube and Barossa*. The faults that the critic in the *Eclectic Review** discovers in this battle poem are flaws to be found not only in Gwilliam's style, but in much of the serious verse in the *Poetical Magazine:*

> Among the most prominent of these [faults] is a total disregard of *discipline* in the thoughts, which have frequently a good deal of individual strength, but nothing more. Another offence, is a strange propensity to apostrophise: to summon the reader's attention in almost every stanza. . . . No sort of writing is more provoking than this, or more opposed to the genuine spirit of poetry. [8:321]

The efforts of Vaughan, Rickman, Daniel, and Gwilliam notwithstanding, the *Poetical Magazine* would have collapsed after a few numbers if it had not been kept alive by Dr. Syntax. William Combe and Thomas Rowlandson, the artist, were the magazine's most important contributors, since together they created its most popular and original feature, "The Schoolmaster's Tour." Dr. Syntax, the schoolmaster, began his adventures in the opening number, and an episode of his story appears in each succeeding number until his "tour" ends abruptly with the termination of the magazine in April 1811. In a note to the 1812 edition of the poem, Combe describes the unique working relationship with Rowlandson that eventually produced close to 10,000 lines of verse: "An Etching or Drawing was . . . sent to me every month, and I composed a certain proportion of pages in verse, in which, of course, the subject of the design was included: the rest depended upon what my imagination could furnish."[6]

The popularity of "The Schoolmaster's Tour" depended largely on both the pictorial and poetical depictions of its central character. Dr. Syntax is described in the poem by Squire Hearty, his patron, whose speech also suggests the schoolmaster's genealogy as a character: ". . . in this Divine, / Quixote and Parson Adams shine: / An hero well combin'd you'll view / For *Fielding* and *Cervantes* too" (2:244). The amiable satire in the poem is directed at travel literature, very much in vogue, and at the picturesque school of popular artists with which Syntax identifies himself:

> "Nature, dear Nature, is my goddess,
> Whether arrayed in rustic bodice,
> Or when the nicest touch of Art

> Doth to her charms new charms impart;
> But still I, somehow, love her best,
> When she's in ruder mantle drest:
> I do not mean in shape grotesque,
> But when she's truly *picturesque.''*

|3:49|

There is irony in Combe's gibes at the picturesque, however good-humored, since he is the author of many of the poems that accompany the magazine's second monthly engraving, which invariably features a picturesque landscape. ''The Schoolmaster's Tour'' is the only poem that enjoyed an extended life beyond the pages of the *Poetical Magazine. The Tour of Doctor Syntax in Search of the Picturesque* went through nine editions between 1812 and 1819, and Combe, who was sixty-eight when he began the Syntax series, wrote two sequels to the *Tour* in 1820 and 1821.[7]

According to Joseph Merle, the monthly circulation of the *Poetical Magazine* never ''exceeded seven or eight hundred copies'' and ''would not have reached three hundred'' without Combe's Syntax.[8] With only the success of ''The Schoolmaster's Tour'' to show for its two-year run, the *Poetical Magazine* was of limited value as a showcase or a repository of poetry. The magazine is more interesting now for its experiment in the democratization of poetry, for which it may deserve a footnote in the history of nineteenth-century popular culture.

Notes

1. W. J. Burke, ''Rudolph Ackermann, Promoter of the Arts and Sciences,'' *Bulletin of the New York Public Library* 38 (1934):817. Other information on Ackermann and Frederic Shoberl comes from the *Dictionary of National Biography*.

2. Joseph G. Merle, ''A Newspaper Editor's Reminiscences,'' *Fraser's Magazine* 23 (1841):699.

3. There were three regular contributors to the *Poetical Magazine* who never published their own verse: Charles Shrubsole Bonnett (''C.S.B.''), William Cove (''W. C——E''), and Elijah Waring (''E. W——G''). Ackermann also published the poetry of two deceased writers, Phillis Wheatley, the Boston slave poet, and Bryan Edwards, a Jamaican official and apologist for slavery.

4. George Daniel, *The Modern Dunciad, Virgil in London, and Other Poems* (London, 1835), pp. 8–9.

5. Daniel, p. 104.

6. ''Advertisement'' to *The Tour of Doctor Syntax in Search of the Picturesque* (London, 1813), pp. i–ii.

7. Harlan W. Hamilton, *Doctor Syntax: A Silhouette of William Combe, Esq.* (Kent, Ohio, 1969), p. 260.

8. Merle, p. 700.

Information Sources

BIBLIOGRAPHY

Burke, W. J. ''Rudolph Ackermann, Promoter of the Arts and Sciences.'' *Bulletin of the New York Public Library* 38 (1934):807–23, 939–53.

Hamilton, Harlan W. *Doctor Syntax: A Silhouette of William Combe, Esq.* Kent, Ohio, 1969.

Merle, Joseph G. "A Newspaper Editor's Reminiscences." *Fraser's Magazine* 23 (1841):699–710.

INDEXES
Each volume indexed.

REPRINT EDITIONS
Microform: English Literary Periodicals (UMI), reel 693.

LOCATION SOURCES

American
Widely available.

British
Complete runs: Bodleian Library; British Museum.
Partial run: London University Library.

Publication History

MAGAZINE TITLE AND TITLE CHANGES
Poetical Magazine; dedicated to the lovers of the Muse, by the Agent of the Goddess, R. Ackermann (in volume 4, "Humble Servant" replaces "Agent").

VOLUME AND ISSUE DATA
Volumes 1–4, May 1809–April 1811.

FREQUENCY OF PUBLICATION
Monthly.

PUBLISHER
Rudolph Ackermann, Repository of Arts, 101 Strand, London.

EDITOR
Frederic Shoberl(?).

Ted R. Ellis III

PRINTING MACHINE, THE. See LEIGH HUNT'S (LONDON) JOURNAL

—— Q ——

QUARTERLY JOURNAL OF LITERATURE, SCIENCE AND THE ARTS, THE. See QUARTERLY JOURNAL OF SCIENCE, LITERATURE AND THE ARTS, THE

QUARTERLY JOURNAL OF SCIENCE, LITERATURE AND THE ARTS, THE

Sir James Chettam explains to Dorothea in *Middlemarch* that he is planning to make over one of his properties into a model farm. He has been reading Sir Humphry Davy's *Agricultural Chemistry,* the book based on Davy's research and popular lectures at the Royal Institution. It was the aim of the Royal Institution, founded in 1799 by Count Rumford, Sir Joseph Banks, and others, to disseminate knowledge about the useful arts and the improvements of the condition of life in England. The Royal Institution rapidly evolved into an organization for the practical application of science to the management of the landed estates, estates owned by gentlemen such as Sir James Chettam. Sir Humphry Davy, through his experiments in an improved agriculture, in tanning, and in mine safety, and through his popular lectures, became an important spokesman for science in the early decades of the nineteenth century. In addition to his books and lectures, Sir Humphry Davy published in scientific journals. He was also the co-editor of an early, short-lived journal published by the Royal Institution and a frequent contributor to the early issues of the more substantial *Quarterly Journal of Science, Literature and the Arts* sponsored by that same institution between 1816 and 1830. Davy achieved immense success in popularizing science, in part because his audience of rich and powerful landlords were eager to learn new ways to improve their farms, mines, and transportation, but also in part because of his ability to communicate with his audience.

His flair for imagery led Coleridge to claim (so it is said) that had Davy not been the age's most important chemist, he would have been its first poet. Southey, too, saw his poetic talents.[1] More to the point, Davy advocated and practiced a simple, clear, and serviceable prose style. "In detailing the results of experiments, and in giving them to the world," he wrote, "the chemical philosopher should adopt the simplest style and manner; he will avoid all ornaments as something injurious to the subject." He asked scientific writers to remember the saying of James I: "The tropes and metaphors of the speaker were like the brilliant wild flowers in a field of corn; very pretty, but which very much hurt the corn."[2]

The other contributors to the *Quarterly Journal,* although lacking Davy's flair, followed his advice in writing plain, clear, accessible prose. The major contributors, those who contributed ten or more articles, included the editor, William Thomas Brande; the chemist and physicist John Frederic Daniell; Davy's successor as director of the Royal Institution Laboratory and Brande's editorial assistant, Michael Faraday; the physiologist Marshall Hall; the Scottish geologist John MacCulloch; and the Scottish doctor and chemist Andrew Ure. They were all prominent men of science, and some, like Davy, Daniell, and Faraday, have earned a distinguished place in the history of science.

The goals of the *Quarterly Journal,* as expressed in the first number, were to add to the "common stock of knowledge and experience." Too many records of scientific experiments were confined to the members of learned societies and published only in transactions, the editor noted. The *Quarterly Journal,* he promised, will make "useful information respecting the Sciences and Arts of Life" more accessible and "will candidly present to the public every useful discovery and every promising novelty" (1, no. 1:iii–iv). In pursuing these goals the editor included reports of experiments and lectures at the Royal Institution, narratives of travels, and observations of flora, fauna, and geological formations from all over the world. He also published summaries of the transactions of other scientific societies in England and abroad, and descriptions of scientific activity in Europe and America as well as in England. The writings of important Continental scientists, such as the German naturalist Alexander Baron von Humboldt and the French mathematician and astronomer Pierre Simon Laplace, were translated and discussed.

Each number was issued in 1,000 copies and contained ten to fifteen long articles and twenty to fifty short notes, comments, or news items. The notes were divided, in the later issues, under the headings "Mechanical Science," "Chemical Science," and "Natural History." In 1823 the category "Literature and Miscellaneous Intelligence" joined the three others, but it was dropped several years later.

Because the *Quarterly Journal* had many contributors and lasted more than a decade, one finds a variety of opinions and a large range of subjects. Despite this variety, there is a consistent core of attitudes about the role of science in human life. The unifying force was provided by the editor, William Thomas

Brande, who presided over the periodical from 1817 to 1830. He was an ambitious man of definite if not imaginative opinions, and of energetic if not far-sighted actions. Although he accepted articles of antiquarian interest (he even wrote an article on the history of alchemy) and reported the results of pure research, he consistently promoted a view that science was a practical tool capable of improving the standard of life. He was very much the scientist that Carlyle portrayed in an article, "Signs of the Times," in the *Edinburgh Review* * of 1829. The new scientist, Carlyle wrote, was no Newton who by silent meditation discovers the system of the world in the fall of an apple. Instead he stands in "his Scientific Institution, and behind whole batteries of retorts, digesters and galvanic piles, imperatively 'interrogates Nature.' "[3]

Brande appealed to a group of middle-class men who saw scientific knowledge not as a dilettantish pursuit, but as part of their professional background. The landlords were not the only ones who welcomed such scientific pursuits as those of Sir Humphry Davy; doctors, bureaucrats, manufacturers, colonial entrepreneurs, and barristers were also interested in science and technology. Not only could science penetrate the mysteries of the universe; it could, on a practical level, improve agriculture and the efficient production of goods. Science could even solve those problems of pain, poverty, and ignorance that disturbed the order of society. The *Quarterly Journal* thus also dealt with social issues. Gas illumination was not just a matter of deciding if coal or oil were the best source of fuel (although this was discussed at length), but also a matter of discussing the improvements that it allowed in the quality of life and the social effects of its use. Science, too, could collect and analyze statistics about population growth. We need not fear the predictions of Malthus, one article informed the readers: modern science can solve the problems of increased population.

Literature and art, despite their prominence in the title of this journal, did not obtain as large a place in its pages as did the world of science. The editors, in commenting on a paper presented to the Liverpool Royal Institution by William Roscoe, gave the arts a minor role. The author, Roscoe, in "On the Origin and Vicissitudes of Literature, Science and Art," argues for the importance of literature as our basic means of expression, but the editors claim the arts are merely "objects of request of the rich and refined" and, therefore, are not basic or essential to society. They are, the editors add, only amusements of a "secure establishment." Furthermore, taste involves so much disagreement that it cannot be a precise measure of excellence. The purpose of poetry, the commentators assert, is to present scenes of nature and the passions of mankind, but, they add, these scenes are already observed by us and present in our senses. Nature, therefore, should be sufficient; art is not needed. Nor can art be justified on the grounds that it amuses, fills up leisure time, or sharpens the intellect, since science, the commentator assures the readers, can perform these functions quite as well as art (5, no. 9:1–25).

Most of the articles on art in the *Quarterly Journal* (there were only a few) were of an antiquarian or archaeological nature. C. R. Cockerell, for example, contributed two articles on classical sculpture, but both do little more than discuss the original position of the fallen statues in the tympanum. Cockerell describes the "scientific" accuracy with which he notes the original position when each piece was excavated. His arguments for his reconstruction of the position of the figures are based on measurements of the pieces and observations on the finish. Only marginally is his artistic sense of a viable compositional grouping employed in his argument. George Rennie gives an even more elaborate factual description of the aqueduct of Alcantara in Portugal. Rennie includes full measurements, a list of extant documents, reports of early descriptions of the aqueduct, a complete history, detailed descriptions of materials, recordings of inscriptions, and even a chemical analysis of the water. The Royal Academician R. R. Reinagle used many diagrams of lines and patterns for his lecture described in the *Quarterly Journal,* "On the Beauties Contained in the Ovals and in the Elliptical Curves." He hoped to prove that a curved line was beautiful in and of itself as an abstraction, without reference to nature.

Most of the notes on literature have an antiquarian interest and deal with descriptions of inscriptions, discoveries of manuscripts, and the attempts to decipher hieroglyphics. A few articles, however, do deserve special attention, such as the one that describes the various manuscript and book collections, including those of Lord Fitzwilliam and Francis Bourgeouis. Another article, written by Samuel Parkes and continued through two issues, describes twenty-three literary periodicals published between 1681 and 1749. Also significant are William Sankey's article "On Some Points Connected with the Analysis and Structure of the Greek Tongue" and an anonymous article "On Proper Names." Both demonstrate the early efforts to develop a science of philology. Although the *Quarterly Journal* left some room for literature and art in its pages, these articles were "scientific" in their approach to the fine arts.

The managers of the Royal Institution decided in 1830 to remove Brande as editor of their journal and to take editorial decisions into their own hands. It was not that they were dissatisfied with him, since he did continue to be a contributor, nor that they desired to make great changes, for they made few, but rather that they wished the *Quarterly Journal* to have a closer connection with the Royal Institution. Popularly the *Quarterly Journal* had been called *Brande's Journal;* even the binder had adopted this title on several copies examined. The issue for October 1830 thus boasted a new name, the *Journal of the Royal Institution,* and began numbering with "Volume the First." Only two volumes, however, were published under the new arrangement.

The *Quarterly Journal* documents important years in the formation of British science, and helps to define the attitudes that these early scientists had toward the role of science in the nineteenth century. Although concerned with experimental science, the *Quarterly Journal* brings science out of the laboratory into the farms, mines, and streets, and even into the artist's studio and the scholar's study.

Notes

1. Martin Thomas, *The Royal Institution* (London, 1942), p. 12.
2. *Journal of the Royal Institution* 1 (1831):355; quoted in a review of J. A. Paris's biography of Davy.
3. As quoted in Morris Berman, *Social Change and Scientific Organization: The Royal Institution, 1799–1844* (Ithaca, N.Y., 1978), p. 133.

Information Sources

BIBLIOGRAPHY
Berman, Morris. *Social Change and Scientific Organization: The Royal Institution, 1799–1844*. Ithaca, N.Y., 1978.
INDEXES
Volumes 1–20, separately published, 1826.
REPRINT EDITIONS
2d ed., 1817.
LOCATION SOURCES
American
Widely available.
British
Widely available.

Publication History

MAGAZINE TITLE AND TITLE CHANGES
The Journal of Science and the Arts, volumes 1–6. *The Quarterly Journal of Literature, Science and the Arts*, volume 7. *The Quarterly Journal of Science, Literature and the Arts*, volumes 8–20, 22. *The Quarterly Journal of Science and the Arts*, volumes 21, 23–29.
The Journal of the Royal Institution of Great Britain, new volumes 1–2.
VOLUME AND ISSUE DATA
Volumes 1–29, 1816–July 1830 (vols. 23–29 also n.s. 1–7); new volumes 1–2, October 1830–1831.
FREQUENCY OF PUBLICATION
Quarterly.
PUBLISHERS
Volumes 1–24: J. Murray, London. Volumes 25–29: Henry Colburn and Richard Bentley, London. New volumes 1–2: Royal Institution of Great Britain, London. (Volumes 1–5 also published in an American edition, New York, James Eastburn & Co.)
EDITOR
William Thomas Brande.

Helene E. Roberts

QUARTERLY MAGAZINE, THE. See KNIGHT'S QUARTERLY
MAGAZINE

QUARTERLY REVIEW, THE

Throughout the nineteenth century the *Quarterly Review* appealed to the basic conservatism of the British reading public. In literary criticism, it defended Augustan literary theory; despite its ultimate acceptance of Wordsworth and Coleridge (the latter after his death), it generally disapproved of subjective, Romantic literature. In political and social articles, it supported traditional English morality, paternalism, aristocratic authority, and the supremacy of the Anglican Church against the infidels who authored attacks on these institutions.

Although neither its publisher, John Murray, nor one of its initial guiding lights, Walter Scott, had wanted it to be partisan, in its early years the *Quarterly* nonetheless based much of its literary criticism on political and social considerations. It applauded the archetypal Tory, Robert Southey; it spoke highly of Byron, who was after all a lord (and whose works John Murray published), at least until his poetry became too "immoral" and his democratic utterances insufferable (and until Murray was no longer his publisher); it even praised Whigs "with classical proclivities," like Thomas Campbell and Samuel Rogers.[1] On the other hand, Leigh Hunt, "low-born" and radical, was denigrated; authors suspected of associating with Hunt were similarly tarred.

The *Quarterly*'s politicizing even of its literary criticism can be explained by its origins. As the *Edinburgh Review** became stridently Whig in its articles, Walter Scott stopped contributing to it; when the *Edinburgh* attacked his *Marmion* in 1808, he began to think seriously of forming another journal to oppose it. Simultaneously, George and Stratford Canning, good Tories both, were also considering an opposition review; Stratford introduced John Murray to William Gifford, a satirical poet and former editor of the *Anti-Jacobin,** and Murray arranged to meet with Scott. What prompted this activity, in addition to its review of Scott, were the *Edinburgh*'s political articles stressing England's need to make peace with France at any cost. Scott and Murray knew that any new review, though a rival to the *Edinburgh,* had to copy its Whig antagonist in some ways: it must pay well, be independent of booksellers and not "puff" its publisher's books, and provide articles that were fair-minded, enlightening, and interesting. As Scott, who declined the editorship, emphasized to William Gifford, who accepted, the new review must not support the government blindly.[2] Scott promised to contribute articles on an irregular basis; in fact, in addition to lining up other contributors, he wrote four essays for the first number.

However, the *Quarterly*'s publisher, editor, and writers were unable to create even a facade of impartiality. In order to attack the *Edinburgh,* the *Quarterly* naturally assumed a conservative air; many early political articles were the collaborative efforts of George Ellis, George Canning, and John Wilson Croker. Both Scott and Southey, though avid supporters and contributors, found the early numbers to be too savage for their taste. Yet that very savagery helped make it an immediate success in Edinburgh and, gradually, a moderate success in London. Besides, the new review had extremely close ties with the government: Croker was secretary to the Admiralty; Sir John Barrow was assistant secretary; Canning, Sir Robert Peel, the Duke of Wellington, and Lord Stanley also contributed.[3]

William Gifford was in his early fifties when he became editor of the new periodical, a position he held until illness forced his retirement in 1824. His one major problem with the *Quarterly* was a result of his developing bad health: several issues were published three to six months late, and only two appeared in 1824 (210:759). Nonetheless, the *Quarterly* thrived under Gifford's leadership, its circulation nearly tripling in its first decade; each copy sold was read by scores of people.[4] The Tory ideals it espoused were popular, and, like the *Edinburgh,* its policy of strict anonymity allowed celebrated individuals to write with impunity.

Because critical and political judgments often merged, authors with whose political views the *Quarterly* disagreed were often subjected to intemperate attacks. Its review of Leigh Hunt's *The Story of Rimini* is a case in point. Angered at Hunt's continued attacks upon the government while living off public funds during his imprisonment for libel, the reviewer (probably Croker) began his attack, "A considerable portion of this poem was written in Newgate." The tone was thus set for the entire essay, as much an *ad hominem* attack as a piece of literary criticism (14:473–81). Shelley fared only slightly better. John Taylor Coleridge was his first reviewer in the *Quarterly,* and found *Laon and Cythna,* Shelley's atheism, and his lack of moral scruples unacceptable; furthermore, the poem was "unsupportably dull and laboriously obscure." In this essay, one literary historian states, the *Quarterly Review* achieved the distinction of being the only periodical to say that literary considerations were less important than political considerations.[5] But Coleridge's acknowledgment was tempered by his claim that, in this particular case, "the freight is so pernicious" (21:460–71). William Sydney Walker's October 1821 review of *Prometheus Unbound* found Shelley's poetry to be unmusical, "absolutely and intrinsically unintelligible," and "drivelling prose run mad" (26:168–80).

Probably the most famous attack in the *Quarterly*'s pages was John Wilson Croker's censure of Keats's *Endymion* in the April 1818 issue (which did not appear, however, until September). In his four-page review, Croker claimed that he found incomprehensible the one part he had read. After denouncing the obscurity of book 1—generally acknowledged to be a legitimate criticism— Croker did point to some strengths, some "rays of fancy, and gleams of genius," but found fault with Keats's diction. Croker seemed to object most to the possibility of Keats's being Hunt's disciple (19:204–8). Whether this review "killed" Keats, as it was subsequently accused of doing, is debatable; the idea carries less weight once one has read both the poem and the review for, while Croker's rhetoric may be offensive, his criticism does not seem unreasonable.[6]

While some authors found themselves excoriated in the pages of the *Quarterly* in part for the quality of their writing and in part for their political leanings—or their friends' political leanings—subscribing to Tory principles was not sufficient in itself to guarantee a positive review. Walter Scott, despite his politics and his special position with the *Quarterly,* came in for his share of lukewarm, even slightly negative, comments. In reviewing some of Scott's anonymously published novels, Croker and and Ellis did not effuse over them.[7] In fact, Scott's first truly positive review in the *Quarterly* was the one he wrote for *Tales of My Landlord,* to which Gifford editorially added strong praise (16:430–80).

In the early years of the *Quarterly* William Wordsworth and Samuel Taylor Coleridge received mixed reviews. The *Quarterly*'s first review of Wordsworth was its discussion of *The Excursion* in 1814, written, at Wordsworth's request, by Charles Lamb. Even as modified by editor Gifford, it was—not surprisingly—strongly positive (12:100–111).[8] The only other review of Wordsworth's poetry during Gifford's tenure appeared the next year, a much less laudatory analysis of the 1815 *Poems.* In fact, this reviewer attacked Wordsworth's style, rejected his major premise that "incidents of low and rustic life" were better suited to become poetry than were other subjects, and praised instead the neoclassic ideal of poetry "addressed to our reason" (14:201–25). Coleridge fared no better while Gifford was editor: only one work of his, *Remorse,* was reviewed (11:177–90). The poet may have been unaware that his nephew, John Taylor Coleridge, was his critic, when he claimed that the review was injurious. It may have been criticism in this review, in fact, that led Coleridge the poet to begin work on the *Biographia Literaria* less than a year later.[9] After Gifford resigned, and as the two poets grew more conservative, the *Quarterly* more strongly praised Wordsworth and Coleridge.

One of the more interesting footnotes in the history of the *Quarterly Review* as a literary periodical (which it never was primarily) while Gifford was editor was its role in the "Pope Controversy" of the second and third decades of the nineteenth century. William Bowles, churchman, poet, and literary critic, had published an edition and life of Alexander Pope in 1806, which led to a pamphlet war including, among others, Byron and Campbell. Bowles defended Romantic principles and attacked Pope's moral character. The *Quarterly Review* could not allow such views to stand without answering them, which it did through Isaac D'Israeli in a July 1820 review, nominally of Spence's *Anecdotes of Books and Men* (23:400–34). Bowles, believing the anonymous attack to be by a different critic, responded; in time, all authors mentioned also responded, and the controversy erupted into what would have been a comedy of errors had it not been for the abuse on all sides.[10]

In 1826 John Taylor Coleridge, who had replaced William Gifford as editor, was himself replaced by John Gibson Lockhart, one of the renegade writers of *Blackwood's Edinburgh Magazine.** Lockhart had been largely responsible for that magazine's biting but humorous tone, and had solid credentials as anti-

Whig and anti-"Cockney"; he was also Walter Scott's son-in-law. Nonetheless, Lockhart did not become editor easily. John Wilson Croker opposed his appointment, in part because Croker himself may have wanted to be editor, in part because Croker disliked Lockhart's performance at *Blackwood's*. John Murray was so distressed at Croker's opposition to Lockhart that Croker was kept out of the *Quarterly*'s pages until 1831. Significantly, by that time the review opposed Catholic Emancipation, a position opposite to the one it might have taken had Croker been active on the staff.[11]

For over twenty-seven years John Gibson Lockhart guided the *Quarterly*'s fortunes, and for much of that time they both did well. Lockhart retained several of the review's major contributors and developed significant new ones. Thus, the *Quarterly* began to develop a regular staff of writers: Southey kept contributing until 1839; Barrow, who had written all or part of 112 articles during Gifford's editorship, mainly on travel and exploration, continued to write until his death in 1848; Croker returned to the staff for more than another two decades; Abraham Hayward began fifty years of writing for the *Quarterly* in 1834; Henry Hart Milman, Washington Irving, Elizabeth Rigby (later Lady Eastlake), and others also contributed for long periods of time.

If the *Quarterly Review* under Gifford had made some errors in its literary judgments, under Lockhart it became more interesting and more reliable as a judge of literature. Lockhart brought with him from *Blackwood's* his love of German literature, a love he continued to develop in the *Quarterly*. He also brought to his new home a quality he might have developed at his previous periodical had he matured there: under his leadership, the *Quarterly*'s literary review articles were notable less for their political vituperation than for sound critical judgments. Despite occasional viciousness, John Wilson Croker, for example, was in many respects an astute critic. His review of Tennyson's 1832 *Poems* was one reason for the major revisions Tennyson undertook on them, as the poet was able to look beyond Croker's scathing irony to the legitimate criticisms (49:81–96). Tennyson's revisions excited *Quarterly* reviewer John Sterling in 1842, who particularly praised the "fusion of [Tennyson's] own fresh feeling with the delightful affections . . . of others, and with the fairest images of the real world as it lies before us all today" (70:385–416). This emphasis on increased realism in literature was a feature of *Quarterly* criticism for the next two decades.

In view of the attention paid by Croker's 1833 review, Sterling's 1842 review, and even a generally unfavorable review of Tennyson's *The Princess* by Lockhart in 1848, it is surprising that the *Quarterly* had nothing to say about *In Memoriam* and the laureateship in 1850 and *Maud* in 1855. It was left to William Gladstone, who was to become prime minister within a decade, to discuss all of Tennyson's major volumes in a mammoth article in 1859, when Lockhart was no longer editor. With one exception (*Maud*, which "may be good frenzy, but we doubt its being good poetry"), Gladstone strongly approved of Tennyson's poems (106:454–85). Although fifty years later another

Quarterly reviewer called Gladstone's comments "brief, trite, and obvious" (211:295), Tennyson always believed that this review was one of the best that *Idylls of the King* had ever received.

The comments about Tennyson's poetry while Lockhart was editor have turned out to be critically just. Such has not been the case with the criticism by Elizabeth Rigby of two novels late in 1848. While she found some of the characters and events in *Jane Eyre* to be "masterly in conception," she also decided that "the hero and heroine are . . . singularly unattractive . . . and they do things which, though not impossible, lie utterly beyond the bounds of probability." The test of realism that Sterling had applied favorably to Tennyson six years earlier here condemned a novel. Miss Rigby was particularly offended by the character of Rochester: the pseudonymous author committed the "highest moral offense a writer can commit, that of making an unworthy character interesting in the eyes of the reader." Miss Rigby feared that lady readers would be enchanted by Rochester, who "deliberately and secretly seeks to violate the laws both of God and man." The other novel, *Vanity Fair,* received high praise for Thackeray's "keen observation," "deep wisdom," and "consummate art." In fact, Miss Rigby believed this novel to be one of the finest ever written. The problem that she identified was its too great realism: the characters are too much like people we know, she claimed, for us to "draw any distinct moral from" (84:153–85).

This review of *Jane Eyre* and *Vanity Fair* has become Elizabeth Rigby's most widely read essay. She was important to the *Quarterly Review,* however, for the wide range of topics she could write about. From 1842 to 1891 she contributed three dozen essays on evangelicalism, children's books, German language and literature, travel, biographies, and women's subjects, in addition to English fiction. Her essay on "The Art of Dress" in March 1847 was the first *Quarterly Review* article on "anything so wholeheartedly feminine" (298:65).

Miss Rigby is a useful symbol of the *Quarterly*'s problems in much of the second half of the nineteenth century. After 1853, when Lockhart relinquished the editorship, the *Quarterly*'s literary criticism, while less politically motivated, became unexceptional as well. In addition, the review had lost some of its major, earlier writers: Barrow, Scott, and Southey were dead; John Taylor Coleridge, his legal duties taking most of his time, contributed only eight articles between 1824 and 1860; Croker continued his work until 1856 when he was forced out by what he viewed as unacceptable editorial policy. Important Victorian authors who contributed to the *Quarterly* in the second half of the century did so sparingly: Mark Pattison published five articles from 1853 to 1865; William Thackeray reviewed one book, in December 1854; John Forster wrote two articles in the mid-1850s; Bulwer-Lytton was responsible for five or six articles from the mid-1850s to the mid-1860s; Harriet Martineau published one article, in April 1860; J. A. Symonds wrote a review for the October 1878 issue; and Matthew Arnold published three articles between 1877 and 1879.

Henry Hart Milman, having become dean of St. Paul's in 1849, nonetheless was heavily represented through the middle of 1865; Samuel Wilberforce contributed sixteen articles from 1849 to 1873.

In its literary criticism during the second half of the nineteenth century, however, the *Quarterly Review* did have a few flashes of insight, if not brilliance. In March 1854, for example, Whitwell Elwin analyzed some of the techniques employed in Laurence Sterne's fiction, including the "art of selecting and grouping the details of his finished scenes" (94:303–53). Although Elwin contributed until 1885, he published more than half of his forty-two articles during his seven years as editor. In his January 1860 article on William Cowper, he discussed, as had Sterling and Rigby before him, the realism of an author's work: Elwin found Cowper's images to be "not more vivid than true"; Cowper "had blended the accuracy of the topographer with the picturesqueness of the poet" (107:168–220).

The decline in the quality of literary criticism in the *Quarterly Review* reflected the change in the nature of its editors. Gifford and Lockhart had been particularly strong, impressing their views onto the journal. By the 1860s, the editors were less forceful: for example, William Smith, editor from 1867 to 1893, was a lexicographer, and was less concerned with leaving his own imprint on the *Quarterly*. External forces were also operating to reduce the influence of all quarterly publications during the second half of the century. As the tempo of Victorian life quickened, monthly reviews were more able to keep pace with publications and other developments significant to the growing masses of readers. The circulation of the monthlies surpassed that of the quarterlies.

By the last two decades of the century, the *Quarterly* reviewers talked of "poetic force" and "poetic susceptibility," the generalizations of an age unable to come to grips with the major changes occurring in its poetry. In 1890 Rowland E. Prothero, who was to become editor four years later, used just such terms to discuss the late Robert Browning's work, which had long been an enigma to the *Quarterly*'s writers. Despite Browning's "defects of manner and form" and the obscurity of his subjects, Prothero wrote, his poetry is necessary as "a counter-irritant to that poison of subjectivity which impels poets to shut themselves up in the maze of their own personal experiences" (170:476–502). The Aesthetes of the 1880s found no sympathetic audience in Rowland E. Prothero. Mowbray Morris, another *Quarterly* contributor near the end of the century, had difficulties understanding Matthew Arnold's essays. Arnold's reputation would be "higher," Morris maintained, if he had not strayed from literary criticism into theological and social criticism. Morris had particular trouble with one of Arnold's main terms, and complained that the author's "universal panacea for the failures and shortcomings of our nation was something he called *culture*" (167:398–426).

As Elizabeth Rigby symbolizes the difficulties of the *Quarterly Review*'s critics for much of the second half of the nineteenth century, the Rev. William F. Barry and J. Churton Collins may represent two *fin de siècle* problems the

Quarterly experienced. In some ways, both men could have been fine critics: Barry had read widely, exhibited a fine literary sensibility when he actually discussed literature in his thirty-four articles from 1889 to 1900, and wrote well; Collins possessed a strongly analytical mind capable of piercing through the cant of other, lesser critics. But too often Collins's attention was diverted from literature itself to what other people had written about literature. In 1885, for example, he attacked J. A. Symonds's scholarship in pre-Shakespearean drama; in the next year he found Edmund Gosse's published lectures on English poetry to be grossly inaccurate. In both articles Collins listed errors at length and provided his own, presumably correct, discussion (156:330–81; 158:289–329). William Barry, tying literature and ethics in an inextricable knot, too often digressed into moralizing: Heine's poetry was beautiful, he believed, but was not based on Christian principles; French literature was obscene; Ibsen's themes were anarchistic; J. A. Symonds and Walter Pater were hedonists.[12] George W. Prothero, who became editor in April 1899, might have found Barry's views too reactionary or too religious for literary essays; in either case, Barry soon stopped contributing.

By the end of the nineteenth century, then, the *Quarterly Review* had clearly lost the fire of its youth. That was a mixed blessing because along with Croker's vicious but literate irony had gone his literary insight. The knowledgeable writers who had graced the *Quarterly*'s pages in its first decades—Scott in literature; Barrow in travel; Croker and Southey in literature, politics, and other fields—had been replaced by craftsmen, intelligent and well-read, but craftsmen nonetheless. The still-conservative journal faced an uncertain future as it entered the twentieth century.

Notes

1. Josephine Bauer, *The London Magazine, 1820–29,* Anglistica vol. I (Copenhagen, 1953), p. 47.

2. John Gibson Lockhart, *Memoirs of the Life of Sir Walter Scott* (Boston, 1901), 2:84–101.

3. Edgar Johnson, *Sir Walter Scott* (London, 1970), 1:311; Walter Graham, *Tory Criticism in the "Quarterly Review," 1809–1853* (New York, 1921), p. 7.

4. Richard D. Altick, *The English Common Reader* (Chicago, 1957), p. 392.

5. John O. Hayden, *The Romantic Reviewers, 1802–1824* (London, 1969), p. 251.

6. Hayden, pp. 192–93, discusses "couplet construction," versification, and specific diction.

7. Graham, p. 32, points out that Croker and Ellis may not have realized that Scott was the author.

8. Scott's review of his own work may have been his attempt, at least in part humorously, to persuade Murray that he was not the author of the *Tales;* in the review, Scott approved of the work but wrote deprecatingly of its construction and characterization.

9. James D. Wilson, "A Note on Coleridge and *The Quarterly Review,*" *The Wordsworth Circle* 6 (1975):51–53.

10. A complete discussion of the controversy appears in Jacob Johan Van Rennes, *Bowles, Byron and the Pope-Controversy* (Amsterdam, 1927). According to "The Late Isaac D'Israeli, Esq.," in *Bentley's Miscellany* 23 (1848):224, it was D'Israeli's review that actually "gave rise to the great Pope controversy."

11. Charles C. Nickerson, "Disraeli, Lockhart, and Murray: An Episode in the History of the 'Quarterly Review,'" *Victorian Studies* 15 (1972):306; Scott Bennett, "Catholic Emancipation, the 'Quarterly Review,' and Britain's Constitutional Revolution," *Victorian Studies* 12 (1969):283–304.

12. The following articles by Barry are represented: "Heinrich Heine," 169 (1889):399–430; "The Modern French Novel," 170 (1890):287–317; "Realism and Decadence in French Fiction," 171 (1890):57–90; "Anarchist Literature," 178 (1894):1–30; "Latter-Day Pagans," 182 (1895):31–58.

Information Sources

BIBLIOGRAPHY

Bennett, Scott. "Catholic Emancipation, the 'Quarterly Review,' and Britain's Constitutional Revolution." *Victorian Studies* 12 (1969):283–304.

Brightfield, Myron F. *John Wilson Croker*. Berkeley, 1940.

(C.E.L.) "Retrospect: Numbers 1–500." *Quarterly Review* 253 (1929):117.

"The Centenary of 'The Quarterly Review.' " *Quarterly Review* 210 (1909):731–84; 211 (1909):279–324.

Graham, Walter. *English Literary Periodicals*. 1930. Reprint. New York, 1966.

Grosskurth, Phyllis. "Churton Collins: Scourge of the Late Victorians." *University of Toronto Quarterly* 34 (1965):254–68.

Hayden, John O. *The Romantic Reviewers, 1802–1824*. London, 1969.

Johnson, Edgar. *Sir Walter Scott*. Vol. 1. London, 1970.

Lang, Andrew. *The Life and Letters of J. G. Lockhart*. 2 vols. London, 1897.

Lloyd, Christopher. *Mr. Barrow of the Admiralty: A Life of Sir John Barrow, 1764–1848*. London, 1970.

Lochhead, Marion. "Miss Rigby and *The Quarterly Review*: Pioneer Woman Journalist." *Quarterly Review* 298 (1960):59–69.

Lockhart, John Gibson. *Memoirs of the Life of Sir Walter Scott*. Vol. 2. Boston, 1901.

McCready, H. W. "The 'Quarterly Review' in 1898 and 1919." *Victorian Periodicals Newsletter* 7 (1974):18–24.

Nickerson, Charles C. "Disraeli, Lockhart, and Murray: An Episode in the History of the 'Quarterly Review.' " *Victorian Studies* 15 (1972):279–306.

Paston, George (Emily Morse Symonds). *At John Murray's: Records of a Literary Circle, 1843–1892*. London, 1932.

Smiles, Samuel. *A Publisher and His Friends: Memoirs and Correspondence of John Murray*. 2 vols. London, 1891.

Tye, J. R. "Malleus Maleficorum: The Reverend W. F. Barry, D. D., 1849–1930." *English Literature in Transition* 16 (1973):43–56.

INDEXES

Volumes 1–20, 21–40, 41–50, 51–80, 81–100, 101–121, 122–140, 141–160, 161–180, 181–201, 202–222, 223–243, separately published, 1820–1925. Indexes to volume 1–80, reprinted separately (Carrollton Press). 1809–1881 in *Poole's Index*. 1824–1900 in *Wellesley Index* 1. 1809–1824 in Hill and Helen C. Shine, *The "Quarterly Review" under Gifford*. Chapel Hill, N.C., 1949.

REPRINT EDITIONS

Microform: Bell and Howell Co., Wooster, Ohio. Princeton Microfilm Corp., Princeton, N.J. Early British Periodicals (UMI), reels 646–675.

LOCATION SOURCES

American

Widely available.

British

Widely available.

Publication History

MAGAZINE TITLE AND TITLE CHANGES

The Quarterly Review.

VOLUME AND ISSUE DATA

Volume 1, number 1–volume 305, number 654, February 1809–October 1962.

FREQUENCY OF PUBLICATION

Quarterly. (Nominally so under Gifford and early in Lockhart's editorship: for example, under Gifford, issues were frequently two to five months late, and only two issues were published in 1824 when he was very ill; during the first five years under Lockhart, some issues were dated and published one or two months apart, and others five months apart. By the early 1830s, issues were normally published in January, April, July, and October.)

PUBLISHER

John Murray, 32 Fleet Street/50 Albemarle Street, London. American publisher: Leonard Scott Publication Co., New York (dates unknown).

American edition: Theodore Foster (vol. 52, August 1834–vol. 192 [October 1900 and beyond]) (different pagination throughout). Title from 1834–1883: *London Quarterly Review;* title from 1884–: *The Quarterly Review. American Edition.*

EDITORS

William Gifford, February 1809–April 1824 (numbers 59, 60, and 61—the last three under Gifford—were edited at least in part by John Murray, John Barrow, and John Wilson Croker). John Taylor Coleridge, March–December 1825. John Gibson Lockhart, March 1826–June 1853. Whitwell Elwin, September 1853–July 1860. William Macpherson, October 1860–January 1867. William Smith, April 1867–July 1893. John Murray, October 1893–January 1894. Rowland E. Prothero, April 1894–January 1899. George Walter Prothero, April 1899–   .

Roger P. Wallins

R

REFLECTOR, THE

"The Reflector," declares Leigh Hunt in the 1810 "Prospectus" to his new quarterly, "will be an attempt to improve upon the general character of Magazines. . . . Reform of periodical writing is as much wanted in Magazines, as it formerly was in Reviews, and still is in Newspapers" (1:iii). With characteristic optimism, Hunt projects the reformist course, in politics as in writing, that the *Reflector* would pursue. Indeed, Hunt perceives an intimate connection between politics and literature as social institutions.[1] "Politics," he argues, "should naturally take the lead in periodical discussions, because they have an importance and interest almost unexampled in history, and because *they are now, in their turn, exhibiting their re-action upon literature, as literature in the preceding age exhibited its action upon them*" ("Prospectus," 1:iv–v; italics are Hunt's). Each issue embodies this unified vision. Familiar essays, literary and linguistic debates, articles on religion, psychology, education, and medicine, along with the quarterly "Retrospect of the Theatre" counterpoint the regular "Retrospect of Public Affairs," articles on "War" (1, no. 1), the "Character of the Prince Regent" (2, no. 3), and "The Reformers . . .—A Fragment of a Political Dialogue" (1, no. 1).

Leigh Hunt and his brother John published the *Reflector* for only fifteen months. Its four issues appeared from about 1 January 1811 to 23 March 1812; they occupy 989 pages containing eighty-seven articles and poems and twenty-five short miscellaneous pieces. The magazine sold for six shillings, the price of many books in 1811. Shortly after 23 August 1812 remaining issues were bound into two volumes, entitled *The Reflector: A Collection of Essays.*

In his "Prospectus" to the magazine published in April 1810, Hunt follows a familiar Romantic paradigm. His remarks advance from criticism of the superficial and antiquarian character of recent periodicals to a vision of what a magazine should be. His claims were to prove prophetic: "The old Magazines are notoriously in their dotage; and as to the new ones, . . . they have returned to the infancy of their species—to pattern-drawing, doll-dressing, and a song about Phillis." Rejecting such ephemerality, Hunt declares that "a Magazine should properly be a *Chronicle for Posterity*"; it does so by rendering unflinchingly "*the character of the times*" as revealed in "*mind, which the Reflector* will endeavour to pourtray" (1:iv; ix). Four areas especially concern Hunt: politics, the theater, fine arts, and literature. In each, the *Reflector* was to achieve Hunt's ambitious goal, principally through his energetic and wide-ranging contributions, and his prescient cultivation of good writing. Hunt had gathered about himself a circle of intelligent, literate friends whom he could call upon to contribute to the new journal. Foremost among them was Charles Lamb. Indeed, enduring interest in the magazine resides both in Hunt's editorial judgments and in the essays and poetry of both Hunt and Lamb. The numerous reprints of these writings demonstrate the regard that posterity has for the *Reflector*.

In the spring of 1810 the twenty-six-year-old Leigh Hunt had the world before him; his brother John "projected a quarterly magazine of literature and politics, entitled the *Reflector*," which Hunt edited.[2] Hunt's *Juvenilia* had appeared in 1801 and had gone to five editions by 1804. Some of his theatrical reviews for his brother's papers, the *News* and the *Statesman*, were published in a volume in 1807, and from 1808 to 1821 he edited and wrote for the weekly *Examiner*.* In 1810 Hunt seemed energized by the "Prosecution Commenced by the Duke of York" against the *Examiner* (as the *Political Examiner*'s headline boldly declared on 1 January 1809), as well as by another unsuccessful legal attack upon him in 1810 for reprinting in the *Examiner* an outcry against military flogging. A year earlier the *Examiner* had achieved a moderately good circulation of 2,200, permitting Hunt to quit his clerical job with the War Office, to marry (in 1809), and to devote his full energies to reading, writing, attending the theater, and socializing.[3]

Hunt's large circle of friends, many of whom remained from his Bluecoat days at Christ's Hospital School, contributed significantly to the *Reflector*. Hunt recalls that "Lamb, Dyer, Barnes, Mitchell, the present Greek Professor Scholefield [all Christ Hospital men], together with Dr. Aikin and his family wrote in it."[4] Octavius Gilchrist and Barron Field of the *Times* also authored essays. The miscellaneous flavor of the *Reflector* derives from contributions by this group. For example, Aikin writes the rambling "Comparison between Thomson and Cowper as descriptive Poets" (2, no. 3), a "Letter" to a "young friend" on "biography" (2, no. 4), and most likely the long, historical, Augustan "On the Origin, Progress, Corruptions, and Gradual Improvement of Medical Science" (2, no. 4). Gilchrist reflects "On the Origin of Shakespeare's Tempest" (1, no. 1); Dyer discourses "On Defects and Abuses in Public Institutions" (1, no. 1); and an unknown author dilates "On the Pernicious Effects of Methodism . . ." (1, no. 1). Hunt paid authors generously;

and his circle assured him of capable and willing contributors for the new periodical. Yet the *Reflector* grew out of Leigh Hunt's own literary ambitions. It reflects the historical perspective in which he understood politics and literature, as well as his brother John's expectations of increased profits through fuller utilization of his printing plant.[5]

Leigh Hunt craved a more spacious format than the *Examiner* afforded for his discursive and familiar essays and poetry. A quarterly would allow Hunt to expatiate freely on interacting literary and political subjects, and the length of a quarterly (he projected 240 pages in each number) would permit him to fashion essays that reflected his cast of mind. Hunt conceived present predicaments as emerging from a demonstrable history of blunders, a perceptible decline in "thinking" that repressed "by neglect the intellectual character of the nation," as he argues in the lead essay of the *Reflector*'s first issue (1:8). The causes for political and artistic disintegration can only be understood within the context of historical process, Hunt advocates implicitly in each "Retrospect of Public Affairs" and "Retrospect of the Theatre," and in several occasional essays. He urges this necessary perspective explicitly in the "Prospectus": "Each number . . . will endeavour to view the times in that *historical* light, which striking in broad and centrical masses . . . gives prominence, clearness, and effect to the principal objects" (1:v). In each of the political, theatrical, and literary essays written for the *Reflector,* Hunt glances back in order to comprehend the present. True to the magazine's carefully considered title, Hunt's writings both reflect his times and represent his reflections about them over a period of time.

Hunt expresses his expansive intellectual interests in five kinds of compositions framed for the *Reflector:* personal essays; poetry and translations; essays on the fine arts; theatrical criticism; and political commentary. These writings constitute fully one-quarter of the *Reflector*'s pages. Hunt's four personal essays, which he signs with the familiar printer's indicator, range freely over philosophy, literature, and history to comment on the state of contemporary civilization.[6] In the periodical essay tradition of Addison, Hunt's "Account of a Familiar Spirit, who visited and Conversed with the Author . . ." (1:86–99) and "PSUKES IATREION: or an Analogical Essay . . ." (2:144–56) invoke a dream vision whose speaker voices Hunt's highly allusive, often ironic and comic interpretations of history. The "Familiar Spirit," for example, recalls for "Mr. Reflector" the pains excessive eating visits upon the great. Food, under the "Spirit's" jurisdiction, punishes potentates and eminent literary figures alike, from "Dionysius and Henry VIII" to "Napoleon" and "Your Edinburgh Reviewers." "Fish crimped alive, lobsters boiled alive, and pigs whipped to death, became the most active and formidable spirits" (1:96–98). In "A Day by the Fire" (2:400–419), perhaps his finest writing in the *Reflector,* Hunt abandons the fictive persona of the traditional essay for the unselfconscious revelations of his own mind intimately shared with the reader. Diurnal rhythms gently guide a reflective day spent dining, reading, and musing by the fire. Hunt meditates on the days of past writers, and he cites passages from

Tasso, Cowper, Shakespeare, and Spenser. Like the greater Romantic lyric, the literary mode of this essay becomes the movement of the speaker's mind within the "snug" enclosure of a fire-warmed living room. Hunt's observation of minute particulars, akin to that of Coleridge in "Frost at Midnight," draws the reader to his fireside: "How observed with the smallest effort is every trick and aspect of the fire! A coal falling in,—a fluttering fume,—a miniature mockery of a flash of lightning,—nothing escapes the eye and the imagination" (2:411). The dynamics of the eye, repeatedly attracted to the unifying motif of the hearth, and of imagination, fired by the flux of the flames, draw reader to speaker in this remarkable poetic essay.

For Hunt, the theater cries for reform. In each of his four "Retrospects of the Theatre" Hunt surveys the general state of the drama, pausing at times to attack or, on one occasion, commend a particular production. "Drama, with respect to intellect, is at the lowest point of degradation," he observes. Authors lack intellectual substance, "character has been degraded into caricature, plot and sentiment into common-place, wit into punning, and composition into sheer ignorance of the language. Comedy has become . . . mere farce, and the serious drama . . . mere floweriness" (1:232). The sound is forced, the notes are few. Only once, concerning Thomas Moore's "M. P. or the Blue Stocking," Hunt praises "touches of genuine wit and poetry" (2:430). Hunt attributes the generally sorry state of drama to advancing commerce, which has filled increasingly large theaters with audiences unable to appreciate good drama; concomitantly, greedy managers have aimed productions at the expanding, crude middle class, while critics have gradually migrated "from pit to boxes" (1:234). Yet he stipulates that the theater's decline augurs opportunity: "Never has the history of the drama presented so fine an opening for rising talent." Like Shelley's apocalyptic "Glorious Phantom," Hunt views "the rising generation" as promise for bursting the theater's slumber (1:236).

Hunt's reformist spirit is implicit in almost everything he wrote and is the overt subject of his political essays. These include specifically one "Retrospect of Public Affairs" in each issue, and five occasional essays.[7] Hunt forecast in his "Prospectus" that the *Reflector*'s "opinions will be exactly those of the *Examiner*"; for he is "most anxious for reform" (1:v). But Hunt's tone is less strident in the *Reflector* essays than in the political columns of his weekly. Consequently, Hunt would never be prosecuted for any *Reflector* writing, although he was repeatedly prosecuted for attacking the government in the *Examiner*. In the seminal "The English considered as a Thinking People" (1, no. 1), Hunt viewed the worst effects of "political corruption" as radical disruptions of the body politic as well as of the body: they "gradually deaden our sensations and at last unsettle our powers of reason" (1:2). George III lapsed into madness in 1811 and did not recover. Thereupon the Prince of Wales was declared Regent. In "The Character of the Prince Regent" (2, no. 3), Hunt attacks the forty-seven-year-old Prince's unseemly "youthfulness," his retention of inept and corrupt ministers, his restoration of the Duke of York as commander-in-chief after the Duke had been accused of selling military commissions, and his staging of ostentatious parties in a time of economic hardship. Indeed, as Hunt specifies, terrible inflation, widespread bankruptcies, and unemployment had resulted from Continental and American markets barring British goods. Hunt's "Retrospects" voice mild approval for British gains in the Peninsular war in 1811, while simultaneously calling for peace in order to restore prosperity at home. Overall, Hunt's political opinions in the *Reflector* mirror those of the *Examiner,* though they are expressed more reasonably, and with greater reserve.

Hunt anticipated and advocated the later nineteenth-century development of art history and aesthetics as disciplines. His "Remarks on the Past and Present State of the Arts in England" (1, no. 1), calls for evaluation of the fine arts according to standards for "poetry, music, and other works of genius . . . by its invention, its harmonious agreement, and its nature" (1:207). Establishing criticism of the visual arts—painting, sculpture, and architecture—constitutes Hunt's project. To understand and judge cultural artifacts, he argued, one must first order their history. Hunt thus devotes eleven pages of his long essay to the tradition of British art before focusing on contemporary artists. These include Benjamin West, Fuseli (whose imagination Hunt valued), Stothard, Northcote, and Westall. Although Robert Hunt wrote the fine arts criticism for the *Examiner* and probably contributed several essays to the *Reflector,* in this single article Leigh Hunt demonstrates his own flexible critical ability, broad purview, and scholarly prescience regarding the need to give "painting and sculpture their due share in the social honours of poetry" (1:209).

Hunt's translations exhibit his facility with ancient and modern languages. His original "Feast of the Poets" shows his lively wit and a rashness of judgment Hunt would later revise. In the first number of the *Reflector* Hunt translates Voltaire's *Travels of Reason* and "Atys the Enthusiast" from Catullus. Hunt displays a creative freedom with length of line in "Atys," urging in a brief preface that the translation should reflect the original's changes in mood. Hunt's original and amusingly autobiographical "Politics and Poetics" (1, no. 2) treats the difficulties Hunt experienced meeting deadlines, attending to poetry when politics pressed upon him, and fighting off the law "court." He wrote "they swear and curse, / And din me with hard names; and what is worse, / 'Tis now three times that I have miss'd my purse" (1:362). The *Reflector* first printed Hunt's "Feast of the Poets," one of his most famous—and successively revised—poems. Reminiscent of Byron's "A Vision of Judgment," and expressed in the rush and flow of a Byronic poetic voice, the "Feast" figures Apollo summoning worthy bards to a traditional wreath crowning. Beginning in 1814, and again in 1815 and 1859, Hunt altered his judgments as to who merited the honor.[8] But in 1811 "Apollo" dismisses Coleridge "by his idling, and gabbling, and muddling in prose" and Wordsworth whose "second childhood with him had come close on the first" (2:319). The god crowns Southey, Campbell, Scott, and Moore while also rejecting Landor and never mentioning

Burns or Blake. For the young Hunt, an eager combatant in the nineteenth century's lively critical wars, literature like politics became the subject of fierce and often overstated debate.

As E. V. Lucas, Lamb's biographer, observes, the *"Reflector* gave Lamb his first encouragement to spread his wings with some of the freedom that an essayist demands."[9] Lamb's work spanned both discursive and personal essay forms as well as poetry in the fourteen items he wrote for the last three numbers of the *Reflector*. All have subsequently been reprinted. His critical appraisal, "On the Genius and Character of Hogarth . . ." (2, no. 3), stands as a touchstone of the Romantic revaluation of art and a seminal expression of Lamb's own critical sense. Lamb asserts that Hogarth's *"Harlot's and Rake's Progresses"* advance beyond the comic to the serious and salutary satiric mode: "They resemble Juvenal['s]" and Shakespeare's satires (2:61). "His graphic representations are indeed books: they have the teeming, fruitful, suggestive meaning of *words*. Other pictures we look at,—his prints we read" (2:62). Furthermore, sounding a characteristic Romantic note, Lamb refuted those who deprecated Hogarth because of his choice of "common or vulgar" subjects by stating that treatment determines an art work's worth, not subject matter: "The quantity of thought which Hogarth crowds into every picture, would alone *unvulgarize* every subject. . . . Everything in the print . . . *tells"* (1:64). Continuing the emphasis on reading as the highest form of intellectual intercourse a spectator may have with an art work, Lamb claims that in staging Shakespeare rather than reading him "we have let go a dream, in quest of an unattainable substance"; the mind's "free conceptions" become "crampt and pressed down to the measure of a straitlacing actuality" (2:300). Shakespeare's plays, for Lamb, are "less calculated for performance on a stage, than those of almost any other dramatist whatever" because Shakespeare's speeches represent "only a medium . . . for putting the reader or spectator into possession of that knowledge of the inner structure and workings of mind in a character" (2:300–301). The silent text, like Keats's Urn, pipes to the reader's spirit unheard melodies, ditties of no tone.

Lamb's personal essays and poetry display his facility for adopting protean personalities. His personal essay's epistolary form, exaggeration, literary allusions, and occasional didacticism hark back to eighteenth-century tradition; their dramatic rendering of character and often comic unselfconsciousness, calling forth our sympathy and judgment, look ahead to Tennyson, Browning, and Dickens. In the *Reflector* he slips easily from plangent victim of wrongful hanging (1, no. 2) to "Damned Author"—damned "after that memorable season of dramatic failures, 1806–7" (2:122). The "author" thereupon analyzes the varieties of "Hissing at the Theatre" and ultimately launches into a mock-bombastic attack on the hissing public. Lamb also satirizes those who aspire to fancy funerals, and delivers an ironically grandiloquent encomium to funeral directors in "On Burial Societies" (2, no. 3). In "A Bachelor's Complaint of the Behaviour of Married People" (2, no. 4), Lamb's speaker laments couples' "too loving" closeness which leaves him feeling neglected: "these married monopolists thrust the most obnoxious part of their patent into our faces" (2:350). Adopting another mask, that of an inveterate smoker "by sour physician / . . . debarr'd the full fruition" of tobacco's "favours," Lamb's speaker poetically bids a reluctant "Farewell to Tobacco." Lamb also creates light drama. A pair of his interacting personae write separately to the *Reflector*. "Edax" sadly tells that his enormous, uncontrollable "appetite" has made him the recipient of cruel jests. Again adopting the mask of the helpless victim, Lamb's "Edax" pleads for tolerance (2, no. 4), while in the subsequent, companion item, a missive from one vegetarian "Hospita" to "Mr. Reflector," the writer complains of the "immoderate indulgence"—"eating . . . particularly of animal food"—exhibited by her husband's "obnoxious young relation" (2:398–99). Throughout the three numbers of the *Reflector* to which Lamb contributed, and especially in this exchange, one witnesses him developing confidence in this dramatic style as he shifts voices and points of view. Indeed, Lamb owes to experiments with various masks here some of the subsequent success he enjoyed in the "Essays of Elia" (1820–1823; 1833), first published in the *London Magazine*.*

Although the quality of the *Reflector*'s writing improved demonstrably, in part benefitting from Lamb's increasing freedom with the essay form and steady stream of contributions, the magazine ceased publication precipitously after the fourth number. (Hunt had, in fact, promised in an editorial notice to the third number that "with the commencement of 1812, the *Reflector* . . . will put on more staid and quarterly habits.") Hunt attributed its demise to lack of funds, recalling years later that the "radical reformers in those days were not sufficiently rich or numerous to support such a publication."[10] Also, the British economy had been especially depressed during the *Reflector* years, 1810–1812. An introductory paragraph to the second binding of the magazine, written late in 1812 (and reprinted in full by Kendall, pp. 29–30), cites as cause for the *Reflector*'s cessation the "Editor's uneditorial want of attention to regularity of publication, but *chiefly* on account of those limited means," along with the considerable expense of paying contributors "well . . . out of policy and justice." As Kendall shrewdly observes, "another event of March 1812 . . . may have caused the retrenchment": the Hunts' expectation of prosecution expenses for publishing the censorious "Prince on St. Patrick's Day" in the *Examiner* the day "before the last *Reflector* appeared" (p. 29). Though events coalesced to end this quarterly, a legacy of lively and reflective writing remains, the partial fulfillment of Hunt's promise, voiced in the "Prospectus" for the *Reflector*.

Notes

1. Increasingly, politics became a prominent subject in early nineteenth-century periodicals paralleling the increase in literacy, improvements in paper-making and print-

ing, and popular agitation for political reform. Cobbett's weekly *Political Register,* for example, was widely read; Wooler's radical *Black Dwarf* reached a circulation of 12,000 in 1819; and, of course, the great critical reviews each represented a distinct political bias, the Tory *Quarterly Review** circulating 5,000 copies in 1810 and the Whig *Edinburgh Review** printing 7,000 copies in 1807. For further details and the source of these figures, see Richard D. Altick, *The English Common Reader* (Chicago, 1957), chap. 14 and "Appendix C: Periodical and Newspaper Circulation."

2. Leigh Hunt, *The Autobiography of Leigh Hunt; with Reminiscences of Friends and Contemporaries* (London, 1850), 2:83.

3. Hunt records this figure in *The Correspondence of Leigh Hunt,* ed. Thornton Hunt (London, 1862), 1:40. According to Ian Jack, "By 1812 Bentham calculated that the *Examiner* was selling between 7,000 and 8,000 copies" (*English Literature 1815–1832,* vol. 10 of *The Oxford History of English Literature* [Oxford, 1963], p. 320).

4. Hunt, *Autobiography,* 2:83. For the authorship of *Reflector* articles, see Kenneth E. Kendall, *Leigh Hunt's "Reflector"* (The Hague, 1971), appendix 1. I have profited especially from this portion of the only book-length study of the *Reflector.*

5. Concurrently, John Hunt printed and published the *Examiner* and the *Reflector.* For his probable role in starting the *Reflector,* see Kendall, p. 20.

6. The fourth essay, not discussed here, is "The True Enjoyment of Splendour:— A Chinese Apologue" (2:195–97).

7. Kendall, pp. 31–32, lists specific titles.

8. For analysis of Hunt's changing aesthetics, see Clarence De Witt Thorpe, "Leigh Hunt as Man of Letters: An Essay in Evaluation," in *Leigh Hunt's Literary Criticism,* ed. Lawrence Huston Houtchens and Carolyn Washburn Houtchens (New York, 1956), pp. 1–73.

9. E. V. Lucas, *The Life of Charles Lamb* (New York, 1905), 1:417.

10. Hunt, *Autobiography,* 2:84.

Information Sources

BIBLIOGRAPHY

Blunden, Edmund. *Charles Lamb and His Contemporaries.* Cambridge, England, 1933.
———. *Leigh Hunt and His Circle.* New York, 1930.
———. *Leigh Hunt's "Examiner" Examined.* New York, 1928.
Fogle, Stephen F. *Leigh Hunt's Autobiography, The Earliest Sketches.* Gainesville, Fl., 1959.
Houtchens, Lawrence Huston, and Carolyn Washburn Houtchens, eds. *Leigh Hunt's Dramatic Criticism.* New York, 1949.
———, eds. *Leigh Hunt's Literary Criticism.* New York, 1956.
Hunt, Leigh. *The Autobiography of Leigh Hunt; with Reminiscences of Friends and Contemporaries.* 3 vols. London, 1850.
———. *The Correspondence of Leigh Hunt.* Edited by Thornton Hunt. 2 vols. London, 1862.
Kendall, Kenneth E. *An Index to Leigh Hunt's Magazine, "The Reflector."* Gainesville, Fl., 1970.
———. *Leigh Hunt's "Reflector."* The Hague, 1971.
Landré, Louis. *Leigh Hunt (1784–1859): Contribution à l'Histoire du Romantisme Anglais.* 2 vols. Paris, 1936.

Law, Marie Hamilton. *The English Familiar Essay in the Nineteenth Century*. Philadelphia, 1934.

Lucas, E. V. *The Life of Charles Lamb*. 2 vols. New York, 1905.

INDEXES

An Index to Leigh Hunt's Magazine, *"The Reflector."* Comp. Kenneth E. Kendall. Gainesville, Fla., 1970.

REPRINT EDITIONS

After the *Reflector* ceased publication in 1812, remaining sheets were bound into two volumes, octavo. New title pages were printed which read: "The Reflector: A Collection of Essays, on Miscellaneous subjects of Literature and Politics; originally published as the commencement of a Quarterly Magazine, and written by the Editor of the Examiner, with the assistance of various other hands."

LOCATION SOURCES

American

Widely available.

British

Complete runs: Birmingham Public Library; Birmingham University Library; Bodleian Library; British Museum; London University Library; Manchester Public Library; National Library of Scotland.

Publication History

MAGAZINE TITLE AND TITLE CHANGES

The Reflector, A Quarterly Magazine, On Subjects of Philosophy, Politics, and the Liberal Arts. Conducted by the Editor of the Examiner.

VOLUME AND ISSUE DATA

Volumes 1–2, numbers 1–4, October 1810–December 1811. ("Prospectus," published April 1810. Volume 1 bears the dates "October 1810 to March 1811"; volume 2, "March to December 1811." Actually, number 1 appeared about 1 January 1811; number 2, about 27 July 1811; number 3, on 25 October 1811; number 4, on 23 March 1812.)

FREQUENCY OF PUBLICATION

Quarterly.

PUBLISHER

John Hunt, Examiner Office, Beaufort Buildings, Strand, London.

EDITOR

Leigh Hunt.

Mark L. Greenberg

REPOSITORY OF ARTS, THE. See POETICAL MAGAZINE

RETROSPECTIVE REVIEW, THE

In 1820 Henry Southern, a twenty-one-year-old M.A. candidate at Trinity College, Cambridge, assumed the editorship of a new journal, the *Retrospec-*

tive Review, which appeared quarterly, apparently under his editorship, from 1820 through 1826.[1] Southern, as did all the contributors, wrote anonymously during these seven years, although a lithograph of the Great Gate of Trinity College on the title page associated the review with Southern's college. According to Walter Graham, Charles Wentworth Dilke was one of the chief supporters of the *Retrospective* for several years after its introduction.[2] In 1827 Nicholas Harris Nicolas became co-editor with Southern. At this time the title of the periodical was changed to the *Retrospective Review and Historical and Antiquarian Magazine,* and the number of issues per year was reduced from four to three. Southern's and Nicholas's names appeared on the title pages as editors, but all of the contributors remained anonymous. In effect, the new arrangement meant a reduction in effort for Southern. He edited only the *Review* section and the number of reviews in each issue was reduced to a range of five to seven from a range of nine to thirteen. Nicolas edited essays on historical and antiquarian subjects. After two years this double-natured periodical ceased publication. The 1827 and 1828 volumes were called volumes 1 and 2, second series, but are sometimes referred to as volumes 15 and 16 of the *Retrospective Review.* In November 1852 the *Retrospective Review* was reestablished under unknown editorship (Henry Southern was an emissary to the Court of the Brazils at this time; he was dead before the first volume appeared a year later), and it was published quarterly for two years, 1853–1854. It contained a total of fifty-eight reviews and essays on predominantly literary subjects, plus a concluding section in each issue called "Anecdota Literaria."

The object of the *Retrospective Review,* as stated in the introduction to volume 1, was "to recal [*sic*] the public from an exclusive attention to new books, by making the merit of old ones the subject of critical discussion" (p. viii). The author of the introduction assumed that the intellectual vigor of the English people was being vitiated by too much reading of current, ephemeral literature and commentary. He intended that the *Retrospective* please the public by employing "the interesting form and manner of the present Reviews" (p. viii), but also that it correct the reading habits of the public by focusing attention upon "the history of literature,—which is, in fact, the history of the mind of man" (p. viii).

Of the books reviewed in the volumes from 1820 through 1828, 6 percent were published during the sixteenth century; 37 percent during the seventeenth century; 55 percent during the eighteenth century; and 2 percent during the nineteenth century. It had been a policy from the beginning not to review books published in the nineteenth century, but a footnote to a review of a contemporary study of medieval dramas in volume 13 states: "We have, in this instance, and shall, in future, depart from our former practice, of noticing only such books as were *printed* before the commencement of this century. When the matter is purely *Retrospective,* and relates to either the literature or history of past times, an adherence to our rule only narrows the interest of the Review, and cramps its influence over its legitimate province.—Ed" (p. 297). The new privilege was exercised very infrequently, however, even in the new series of 1827–1828. The most interesting of the nineteenth-century publications reviewed was a book entitled *Poetry Contained in the Novels, Tales, and Romances of the Author of "Waverley,"* 1822 (2d ser. 1:16–39).

More significant than the nineteenth-century exceptions are works which had never been printed but were reviewed in manuscript. There are about seven of these, including Sir Thomas Browne's *Letters* (1:161–66); Fedusi's "Sháh-Námeh, a Heroic Poem," a Persian manuscript (4:200–223); and "Life of Rice ap Thomas" (11:252–72). The last of these, written during the reign of James I, is described by the reviewer as a manuscript "mouldering on the dusty shelves of an unfrequented library, but which, from the historical value of its contents, and from the quaint and amusing manner in which those contents are registered, merits especial attention of all those who are attached to the study of the earlier history of our country" (11:253).

The books selected for review were not used as excuses for writing essays on chosen subjects, as was the case in some nineteenth-century periodicals. Although many of the reviews began with a paragraph or two of generalized context, the true subject of the review was almost always the book named in the title. Summaries of contents and generous extracts from texts were usually included, and the tone was usually appreciative. Several foreign works were included, for example, Ariosto's *Orlando Furioso* (8:145–70; 9:263–91), Charles Brockden Brown's *Arthur Mervyn* (9:304–27), Dorat's *Poésies* (10:198–219), Lessing's *Nathan the Wise* (10:265–85), Vincenzo da Filicarja's *Filicaia* (10:314–28), and Michelangelo's *Rime* (13:248–65). Reviews of translations of classical, modern Continental, and Arabian works were also included, for example, Charles Cotton's translation of Montaigne's *Essays* (2:209–27), George Sale's translation of the Koran (3:1–22), William Cooper's translation of *The Iliad* and *The Odyssey* (3:167–94), Sir William Jones's translation of *The Moâllakát, or Seven Arabian Poems* (5:332–42), and Phaer and Twyne's translation of *The Aeneid* (5:342–49). But the emphasis was on British books, as the author of the introduction had pledged that it would be: "The literature . . . of our own country, the most rich, varied, and comprehensive, of any in the world, and replete with more interest to the English reader than any other, will have peculiar claims on our attention—and to it will the pages of the 'Retrospective Review' be zealously devoted" (p. xi).

Many of the masterpieces of British literature were reviewed, including Browne's *Hydriotaphia: Urn Burial* (1:83–94), Sidney's *Arcadia* (2:1–44), Bacon's *Novum Organum* (3:141–67; 4:280–315), Defoe's *Journal of the Plague Year* (6:1–21), Walton's *Compleat Angler* (6:353–63), Milton's *Areopagitica* (9:1–18), Sidney's *Defense of Poesy* (10:43–60), and Berkeley's *Siris* (11:239–52). The *Works* of a considerable number of prominent poets were included, for example, Ben Jonson (1:181–200), Crashaw (1:225–50), Davies (5:44–56), Herrick (5:156–80), Carew (6:224–37), Skelton (6:337–53), Shakespeare (7:378–406), Donne (8:31–54), Daniel (8:227–46), Chaucer (9:172–206;

14:305–57), Marvell (10:328–43; 11:174–96), Spenser (minor poems) (12:142–65), Milton (14:282–305), and Cowley (2d. ser. 1:351–87).

The *Retrospective* specialized in the history of English drama, from medieval times through the Restoration. There is hardly an issue that does not contain an essay on a type of drama, a period of the drama, or a dramatist's works. An essay entitled "The Latin Plays Acted before the University of Cambridge" (12:1–42), written from archives, must be one of the best sources on the subject. There is also a distinct concentration on travel books. Furthermore, students of women would find several interesting pieces in the *Retrospective:* "Amory's *Memoirs of Several Ladies of Great Britain*" (6:100–112); "Privileges of Women," based on four seventeenth- and eighteenth-century works, including *Women Not Inferior to Men,* by Sophia, a Person of Quality, 1739 (10:88–112); "The Knight of Towre's Advice to His Daughters," on two translations of a treatise written in French in 1371 (2d ser. 1:177–94); "Mrs. Behn's Dramatic Writings," the first review in the revived *Retrospective,* 1853 (1:1–18); and "The Duchess of Newcastle (Margaret Cavendish) and Her Works," 1853 (1:332–50). The historical figure treated in most detail is Charles II: "Character and Anecdotes of Charles II" (7:183–218; 8:1–30); "Contemporary Notices of Charles II, and Certain Individuals of His Court" (13:167–80); and "Narrative of the Concealment of Charles II at Boscobel," a manuscript (14:47–68). There are several reviews of biographies of clergymen and statesmen.

Although the great majority of the pieces in the *Retrospective* are reviews, there are some thematic essays that cite several works as sources, including "Witchcraft," based on fifteen books published between 1584 and 1726 (5:86–135); "On the Prolongation of Life," based on five books, published between 1683 and 1778, concerned with preserving health and retarding age (7:64–87); "The Holy Bible" (as a literary work) (11:197–220); "Acts and Ordinances of the Long Parliament" (12:48–70); and "Memorials of the Civil War in the County of Devon in the 1640's" (12:179–216).

The author of the introduction to volume 1 avowed that the *Retrospective* would not be a partisan organ: "From the nature of the work, and from our unfeigned horror of either political or personal invective, we shall neither pamper the depraved appetites of listless readers, by piquant abuse—nor amuse one part of the public, by holding up another to scorn and mockery" (pp. viii–ix). Indeed, the *Retrospective* seems in general to have been beyond religious and political chauvinism; its bent was toward psychological and sociological interpretation, and its contributors, as a general rule, attempted scientific objectivity. In his review on Cardan's autobiography, Henry Southern neither glorifies nor condemns Cardan for his plagiarism, thefts, and lies, but treats the man and the author as an extremely interesting psychological phenomenon (1:103–7). William Johnson Fox treats the biography of Sethos, an Egyptian heir to the crown of Memphis born a few decades before the time of the Trojan War, with admirable disinterestedness, explicating but not arguing for or against the thesis of the author of the biography—"that the mythological fables and sacred rites of Greece were all derived from Egyptian customs" (3:84). The reviewer of *The Annals of Newgate* treats the criminals described in the annals as personalities, and his ruminations upon what he has learned from reading it are without moral or religious rancor. He concludes that capital punishment, especially public hanging, is not a deterrent to crime, since "the public exhibition of a young man dying resolutely, is rather a fearful display of courage, than an awful warning against crime" (7:290). Once nonpartisanship is violated. "The Sacrifice of the Mass," a review of the *Missale Romanum* (12:70–96), is self-conscious invective against the rituals of the Roman Catholic Church, which are judged to be stupid and barbarous (p. 73)—"strikingly different from the splendid, the beautiful, the poetical superstition of antiquity" (p. 72); and it is instinct with hatred for Irish Catholics (p. 70).

There seems to be no complete list of contributors to the original *Retrospective,* and the only clue to the authorship of reviews in the revived series, 1853–1854, is the statement that "the papers in this series were chiefly written by Thomas Wright, Esq., J. O. Halliwell, Esq., and M. A. Lower, Esq."[3]

The rationale of the revived *Retrospective* was different from that of the original. The author of the 1853 preface did not share with the author of the 1820 introduction the assumption that literature of the past was more edifying than modern literature. He seems to have been very much in tune with the mid-Victorian idea of evolutionary development, in spite of apparent antiquarian instincts:

> A retrospect of this kind is useful, as well as agreeable. Even while in the contemplation and enjoyment of modern improvements, we can learn something by comparing them with what was defective years ago, and by contemplating their past progress which may encourage us to look forward to new advances in the future. . . . to cull from forgotten books the beauties or the useful facts which are worthy of preservation, to restore forgotten knowledge, as well as to give our readers bibliographical notices of old books, is the particular object of our RETROSPECTIVE REVIEW.

The optimistic expectation that the author expresses in the conclusion of this preface—"we trust that we shall be enabled, by encouragement from the public, to carry out our design continually more effectively through each succeeding volume"—was not to be realized, since the second volume was the last.

Notes

1. Origins of the *Retrospective* are speculative. The *Gentleman's Magazine*'s* (see *AAAJ*) obituary of Southern in 1853 (7:547) reports that he was "the originator and editor of the Retrospective." An article by John E. Bailey in the *Manchester Guardian* in 1874 (reprinted in *Notes and Queries,** 5th ser. 2 (1874):159) suggests evidence that

the *Retrospective* was derived from the Society of Gentlemen, who contributed essays to the *Manchester Exchange Herald*. The society was founded by William Ford, a bookseller in St. Ann's Square. Although Southern is always referred to as sole editor of the *Retrospective* before 1827, the introduction refers to "editors" (p. viii), and William Ford seems the most likely to have been an initial co-editor.

2. Walter Graham, *English Literary Periodicals* (New York, 1930), p. 248.

3. *Poole's Index to Periodical Literature,* comp., ed. William Poole with the assistance of William I. Fletcher, rev. ed. (1891; reprint ed., Gloucester, Mass., 1963), has attributions for slightly more than 40 percent of the articles for volumes 1–7, part 1, or fifty-eight attributions.

For the series in 1853–1854, see William Thomas Lowndes, *The Bibliographer's Manual of English Literature,* rev. Henry Bohn, part 8 (London, 1864), p. 2074. See also *The Wellesley Index to Victorian Periodicals,* ed. Walter E. Houghton (Toronto, 1979), 3:530–31; and the *Dictionary of National Biography* entries for Thomas Wright and Mark Anthony Lower.

Information Sources

BIBLIOGRAPHY
Graham, Walter. *English Literary Periodicals*. New York, 1930.
Houghton, Walter E., ed. "The Westminster Review." In *The Wellesley Index to Victorian Periodicals*. Vol. 3. Toronto, 1979.
Lowndes, William Thomas. *The Bibliographer's Manual of English Literature*. Revised by Henry G. Bohn. Part 8. London, 1864.
Notes and Queries, 5th ser. 2 (1874):159; 7th ser. 2 (1886):328; 7th ser. 12 (1891):169.
INDEXES
Each volume indexed. *Poole's Index.*
REPRINT EDITIONS
Microform: University of Waterloo (Ontario, Canada) Micropeer Reproductions.
LOCATION SOURCES
American
Widely available.
British
Widely available.

Publication History

MAGAZINE TITLE AND TITLE CHANGES
The Retrospective Review, volumes 1–14, 1820–1826. *The Retrospective Review and Historical and Antiquarian Magazine,* second series, volumes 1–2, 1827–1828. *The Restrospective Review, Consisting of Criticisms upon, Analyses of and Extracts from Curious, Valuable, and Scarce Old Books,* volumes 1–2, 1853–1854.
VOLUME AND ISSUE DATA
Volumes 1–14, 1820–1826; second series, volumes 1–2, 1827–1828; volumes 1–2, 1853–1854.
FREQUENCY OF PUBLICATION
Quarterly, 1820–1826; thrice yearly, 1827–1828; quarterly, 1853–1854.

PUBLISHERS

Volumes 1–10, 1820–1824: Charles and Henry Baldwin, Newgate Street, London. Volume 11, 1825: Baldwin, Cradock, and Joy, Paternoster Row, London. Volumes 12–14–second series, volume 1, 1825–1827: Payne and Foss, Pall Mall, London/Baldwin, Cradock and Joy, Paternoster Row, London. Second series, volume 2, 1828: Baldwin and Cradock, London. Volumes 1–2, 1853–1854: John Russell Smith, 36 Soho Square, London.

EDITORS

Henry Southern (anonymous), 1820–1826. Henry Southern, Esq., M.A. of Trinity College, Cambridge, and Nicholas Harris Nicolas, Esq., of the Inner Temple, Barrister at Law, 1827–1828. Unidentified (perhaps John Russell Smith), 1853–1854.

Billie Andrew Inman

S

SATIRIST, THE

In the summer of 1807 "an unusual crop of pestiferous nuisances"—radicals such as Thomas Hague and William Cobbett—"threatened to destroy all social confidence, annihilate domestic happiness, and bring into contempt our monarch and our altars."[1] Confronted by such pests and the absence of any resistance to them, it occurred to one Englishman "that a periodical publication, devoted to the purposes of exposing and castigating every species of literary and moral turpitude, would, if conducted on honest principles, materially promote the interests of society."[2] Such at least is the high-flown description of the founding of the *Satirist* written by the Englishman in question, George Manners, a lawyer and minor author who was later to become British consul in Boston from 1819 to 1839.

The indignant, swollen rhetoric became one of the characteristics of the *Satirist* from its first issue in October 1807. The social and political dangers of the time, however, were real enough. With war against Napoleonic France raging abroad and with considerable political disaffection at home caused by economic stress and an unreformed Parliament, the situation in England was turbulent and anxieties made tempers run high. Political, often very personal, attacks were met by counter-pamphlets and libel suits.

The law required only that the publisher's name appear in every issue; the editor was in fact seldom specified in periodicals, especially of the volatile sort represented by the *Satirist*. "It was obviously desirable that the parties concerned in such a work should not be generally known," added Manners to his description of the periodical's founding, but admitted that such a secret would be impossible to keep.[3] A number of attempts were nevertheless made to cover tracks: a letter was sent "To the Editor of The Satirist" signed "George Manners,'' and a writer in the *Satirist* in another issue playfully questions whether Manners is the editor (3:517; 4:373).

As the reference to defense of "our monarch and our altars" would suggest, the *Satirist* represented the conservative wing of the Tories. In its early years it ridiculed the compromise "Ministry of All the Talents," and the Whigs in general (cf. 1:131–33). In its first issue it rather honestly declared, "We have strong *partialities*, and . . . we cling stubbornly to our inveterate *prejudices*" (1:4). But while guilty of directing some invective against the Whigs, the journal had considerable tolerance for the opposite party as such. When surveying the work of "Living Satirists" in the second number, for example, the *Satirist* noted "the brilliant wit and classical attainments which have been eminently enjoyed by the rival parties of this eventful reign," including the Foxite writers of the *Rolliad* (1:126).

The *Satirist* saved its spleen for revolutionaries, for radical reformers, and, especially later on, for Napoleonic sympathizers. The nonaligned radicals denounced so monotonously by Manners and his successor form in fact a kind of radical roll-call of the period: Horne Tooke, Samuel Whitbread, Sir Francis Burdett, Sir Richard Phillips, and William Cobbett. As for issues, parliamentary reform was the central proposal rejected stridently by "Mr. Satirist," with Catholic Emancipation second. The political cartoons contained in each issue were drawn by "W. H. Ekoorb" until September 1813, when George Cruikshank took over the task.

But the *Satirist* was not merely a political organ; it was a magazine and shared many of the features of the magazines of the period. In the first few years there were a number of departments such as "Le Bouquet" (which discussed various inventions), "Anecdotes," a book review section, and "Domestic Occurrences" (which was a section relaying vital statistics for London and then by counties). As the years passed only a few features, notably the review of new books and the theatrical criticism, survived.

The name *Satirist* was earned in many random articles, often in epistolary form addressed to "Mr. Satirist." Sometimes they were undoubtedly genuine letters from correspondents; at other times there is no reason to suppose they were not simply written by the editor or one of the staff using the fiction as a cover against libel. Satire itself seems to have interested Manners, for, besides the article "Living Satirists" already mentioned, the journal contained occasional essays on the theory and function of satire, such as "On the Utility of Ridicule" in the third volume. Social satire was clearly part of what Manners intended to purvey, for he considered the staff the "guardians of the public morals" (1:413). In the first volume he attacked the *"naked mania"* of current female fashions (p. 136), and the *Satirist* for years opposed adultery and dueling, both said to be condoned by high society as it entered the Regency period.

Such campaigns suggest the influence of new religious trends, especially the new, more puritanical sects, such as Methodism and Evangelicalism, as indeed may have been the case as far as general influence goes. But the campaigns were actually directed from the point of view of the Established Church, said to be "the most pure . . . that has been revealed by the kindness of Heaven for the benefit and happiness of man" (1:6). Evangelicals and especially Methodists in fact came in for a good deal of abuse.

Education received considerable scrutiny as well. Many of the newest educational experiments were ridiculed, but even such holy ground as Cambridge University was trampled on. A particularly interesting series entitled "Cantab" examined the educational ineptness, corruption, and bad writing at Cambridge, all of which suggests that Cambridge life as described by William Wordsworth in *The Prelude* a few years before had not yet changed.

The *Satirist* was not merely a political organ or a satirical journal; it had pretentions to being a literary magazine. Early on Manners published some serious, if sentimental, original verse, and although such contributions became rare by 1811, there was a return of such poetry in the years after the journal passed to other hands.

Even so, the verse contained in the *Satirist* was, like some prose fiction and dramatic fragments, mostly of a satirical nature. And most of this satirical material was fairly crude and of limited, topical interest. There was, nevertheless, some attempt to imitate the satires of Johnathan Swift and Alexander Pope and their combined effort as Martin Scriblerus. In the first volume there began the correspondence between two brothers about a "hitherto undiscovered island" called "Mormonia," with obvious satirical implications for the English à la Swift (pp. 31–40). A Popean "Art of Sinking" appeared in several numbers in volumes 6 and 7, and an article entitled "The Death and Funeral of Sir Francis Burdett" appeared to be modeled on a similar fictional death of a living Englishman manufactured a hundred years before by the Scriblerians (7:97–116). Some of the literary parodies which appeared from time to time, moreover, were of high quality.

The reviews of books were almost totally confined to political works and literature, unlike other reviewing periodicals of the time that looked at works of general interest in all fields. Although the motto "Fiat Justitia" (Let justice be done) was prefixed to every reviewing section, the reviews were with rare exceptions unfavorable, not to say scathing, especially in the earlier years. In fact there was a policy which led to this circumstance: "Our readers will recollect, that it is our peculiar duty to guard the public against literary imposters, and we are therefore under the necessity of selecting those works which merit exposure and castigation" (2:336; cf. 6:399). To fulfill this duty the better, the *Satirist*, the editor added, reviewed books as soon as they were published.

Reviewing periodicals of the time sometimes showed an interest in competing reviews, but the *Satirist* went well beyond the others in this regard. There were, for one thing, many articles on contemporary periodicals and their editors, ranging from the *Edinburgh Review* * to *Le Beau Monde* * to the *Evangelical Magazine*. One department that ran for years in every issue was "Comparative Criticism," which quoted one opinion of a book from one journal and then a directly opposite opinion from another. The logic of this procedure is not entirely clear since presumably the opinions of the *Satirist* itself might be added to the comparisons, but the point seems to have been to destroy *"confidence* in [the] learned arbiters of literary taste" (4:373). Another department with obvious relevance that appeared occasionally was "Comparative Criticism Extraordinary," where a journal was shown to contradict itself about a work in two different issues (cf. 4:519–20).

"Theatrical Criticism" was an item that survived for the full history of the journal. Appearing originally in double columns and smaller print, it began as a clearly less important review of the few licensed London theaters but it received better treatment in later years. Theodore Hook, a writer and wit of the time, may have been a reviewer in earlier volumes.[4]

In July 1812, at the beginning of volume 11, the *Satirist* changed hands. William Jerdan, an earlier contributor to the *Satirist* and later editor of the *Literary Gazette,** became editor of the *Satirist* in what amounted to a new series, although the old volume numbers were also retained. Most of the regular departments of the journal were soon dropped, including "Comparative Criticism." Jerdan introduced an unnumbered department, "The Moon," which contained light reading, and each issue began with an "Explanation of the Caricature," that is, the cartoon that continued to appear at the beginning of every number. The conservative bias of the *Satirist* remained constant, and the attacks on Napoleon took up increasing space for the last few volumes. It is even possible that Napoleon's defeat in 1814 contributed as much as anything to the demise of the journal, for it must have left a large void.

A still more likely reason was the less scurrilous tone assumed by the *Satirist* under Jerdan's editorship. Jerdan himself seems to have thought as much: "To confess the truth its literary merits did not suffice to qualify the public appetite so much as when it was seasoned with the spices I had repudiated."[5] Jerdan, moreover, had also become editor of the *Sun*, a newspaper, and thus had less time for the *Satirist*.[6]

The end in any case was apparently near by volume 12. In a move unusual for monthly periodicals of the time, the *Satirist* printed an advertisement (p. 394) for "Ladies Riding Habits" along with an announcement that such ads would become a regular feature. Even that ploy seems to have failed; no more ads appeared, but with the fourteenth volume (July 1814) the *Satirist* was transferred to new, unknown proprietors and changed its title to the *Tripod or, New Satirist*. The periodical shrank from its usual 112 pages to 80, and several features continued, but it did not survive long. According to Jerdan, "The 'Tripod' had soon hardly a leg to stand upon, and so was kicked over";[7] the last issue appeared in August 1814.

Notes

1. George Manners, *Vindiciae Satiricae* (London, n.d.), p. 3.
2. Ibid., p. 5.

3. Ibid.
4. Hook's participation is implied in *Satirist* 2 (1808):274–75.
5. William Jerdan, *Autobiography* (London, 1852), 2:315.
6. Ibid.
7. Ibid.

Information Sources

BIBLIOGRAPHY

Jerdan, William. *The Autobiography of William Jerdan, with His Literary, Political, and Social Reminiscences and Correspondence During the Last Fifty Years.* 4 vols. London, 1852.

Manners, George. *Vindiciae Satiricae.* London, n.d.

INDEXES

Each volume indexed.

REPRINT EDITIONS

Microform: English Literary Periodicals (UMI), reels 123–126.

LOCATION SOURCES

American

Complete runs: Harvard University Library; U. S. Library of Congress; University of Texas Library.

Partial runs: Widely available.

British

Complete run: British Museum.

Partial runs: Widely available.

Publication History

MAGAZINE TITLE AND TITLE CHANGES

The Satirist, or Monthly Meteor, 1 October 1807–1 June 1814. *The Tripod; or, New Satirist,* July–August 1814.

VOLUME AND ISSUE DATA

Volumes 1–14, 1 October 1807–1 June 1814 (volumes 11–14 also known as new series, volumes 1–4).

FREQUENCY OF PUBLICATION

Monthly.

PUBLISHERS

Volumes 1–5: Samuel Tipper, no address cited. Volumes 6–7: William Naunton Jones, no address cited. Volumes 8–14: "The Proprietors," London. (The address given in volume 13 is "Satirist" Office, 267 Strand.)

EDITORS

George Manners, volumes 1–10, October 1807–June 1812. William Jerdan, volumes 11–14, July 1812–June 1814.

John O. Hayden

SCOTS MAGAZINE, THE. See AAAJ

SCOTTISH EPISCOPAL REVIEW AND MAGAZINE, THE. See LITERARY AND STATISTICAL MAGAZINE FOR SCOTLAND, THE

SCOURGE, THE

The *Scourge, or monthly expositor of imposture and folly* followed the format of a miscellany. As was typical of monthly magazines in the first two decades of the nineteenth century, it included reviews of books and theater; character sketches of theatrical and other prominent people; short fiction and poetry; letters, anecdotes, and opinions submitted by readers; and briefs on fashions, politics, and gossip. The latter mostly appeared under the heading "Scourgiana," which became a regular section. Of particular significance are the literary and theatrical reviews, a series on contemporary periodicals and their proprietors, and the fold-out frontispiece illustrations for each number, many of which were the work of the young George Cruikshank.

In the seventy-two numbers of *Scourge,* forty-two of the frontispiece plates are authoritatively attributed to Cruikshank.[1] Most were signed "G" or "G. Cruikshank fect." *Scourge* was one of the first magazines to which he regularly contributed. In the plate for November 1811, ridiculing religious enthusiasts, Cruikshank placed his brother, himself, radical bookseller William Hone (for whom he later worked), and William Naunton Jones, printer and publisher of *Scourge,* in the lower left.[2] Each frontispiece plate in the entire run of the magazine was hand-tinted, a feature instituted by several magazines, indicating the importance of this practice for their success. *Scourge* advertised that it was "embellished with a humorous caricature." The editor noted in the first number, and occasionally thereafter, that each number would feature a "caricature" and a brief "explanation" of the satiric political or social cartoon.

Scourge's editorial sympathies were generally Whiggish, as seen in its supporting the *Edinburgh Review** and "detesting the subservence of the Ministerial Journals" (2:iv). One of its chief competitors, the *Satirist,* for which Cruikshank also worked, was Tory. *Scourge*'s editorial policy affected its literary and theatrical reviews; however, the miscellaneous contributions reflected the broader range of opinion held by the "correspondents" among the readers, who were requested to submit "original information."

Like the correspondents in other monthlies, *Scourge*'s correspondents presented moralistic and sententious as well as humanitarian opinions on issues of the moment. Short articles entitled "A Female Profligate," "Adultery in High Life," or "History of a Profligate" are indistinguishable as fiction or report, given the generalized and decorous style of writing suitable for the readership. The latter story described "the progress of a woman . . . whose mind naturally pure, was contaminated by too early an intercourse with the world, and whose ruin was completed by the imprudence and folly of her friends." Other overt social criticism deplored the seduction of female apprentices by the masters to whom they were indentured, and the cruelty and misery in lunatic asylums (2[Sept. 1811]; 4[Sept. 1812]; 6[Sept. 1813]:243; 11[March 1816]; n.s. 1[Dec. 1816]).

The editor, in the "Introduction" to the first number, expected to be greeted with "personal obloquy"; however, he pledged not to soften the "ridicule" of those who "persist . . . in defying the scorn and insulting the judgment of the theatrical world" (1:1–2). In following the literary fashions, *Scourge* reviewed mostly popular writers like Scott and Byron. Byron's life as well as his works occupied the reviewers, as in "The Wrongs of Lady Byron . . . and Lord Byron's Farewell to England" (n.s. 1:9–18). On Byron's *English Bards and Scotch Reviewers,* the reviewer defended the *Edinburgh Review*'s "views of English literature" as "to a certain degree original and unbiased" (1:195–96).

Scourge consistently supported the *Edinburgh Review* and attacked the *Quarterly Review* * at one extreme and Leigh Hunt and his *Examiner* * at the other. From number 4 (April 1811) to number 21 (September 1812), nine articles under the heading of "The Hypercritic" were published. They included discussions of major periodicals and their proprietors. Especially informative is a brief history of the reviews, signed "E," covering such major periodicals as the *Monthly Review,* * the *Critical Review,* * the *Analytical Review* * (for all, see *AAAJ*), and the *British Critic.* *

With number 40 for April 1814, the title changed to the *Scourge, or literary, theatrical and miscellaneous magazine,* with an accompanying editorial note "To Correspondents" promising increasing emphasis on literary and theatrical reviews. However, the contents remained relatively the same. One series, under the heading "Modern Poets," perpetuated the attacks against the Lake School, and Wordsworth in particular, for his subject matter, diction, and sentiments, which violated established decorum and taste. In the article entitled "Wordsworth," the reviewer, signed "C," concluded: "It is not our intention to assert that the merits of Mr. Wordsworth by any means counterbalance the amount of his defects" (6:375–81; 10:266–75).

In a review of Coleridge's 1816 volume, which included "Christabel" and "Kubla Khan," the reviewer repeated not only all the familiar charges, but also stressed the revolutionary "conspiracy" among the poets "against the authority of legitimate criticism" and aiming "to undermine the foundations of taste and common sense." A key paragraph of general criticism in this review is copied exactly from the previous one on Wordsworth (n.s. 1:60–72; cf. p. 62 and 1:270).

The announcement of a new editor in July 1816 was accompanied by an appeal to correspondents for all manner of contributions and an apology for the "political inconsistencies and literary imperfections that vitiated the tenor" of the "later numbers of the first series." Although new principles were enunciated, the new series did not survive beyond six numbers. Because a title page was not issued for these six numbers, it is uncertain whether they would have formed volume 12 or a new series.

There are no cumulative indexes, but each number has a contents page, which is sometimes included in the pagination. Numbers average over eighty pages each, with about ten pages of theater and opera reviews, and slightly fewer for book reviews. Some articles in extended series, such as "The Hypercritic" and "Modern Poets," ran up to ten pages each.

From the outset, and continuing intermittently, there were several pages of display advertisements at the end, not included in the pagination. An accompanying note to the "General Monthly Advertiser" for number 25 (January 1813) claimed "regular perusal by more than ten thousand persons . . . among the opulent and respected classes of the community." Among the ads were some for pills and syrups perhaps not unlike those in the "Table of Quack Medicines" that appeared in the first few numbers. Listed in the table under the "real effects" of one remedy were "internally, colic, palsy, death; externally, madness" (1:174).

Jerrold describes one editor of *Scourge* in terms fitting a moralistic anecdote in the magazine; however, the accuracy of this information is unsubstantiated. "The editor of the *Scourge*, 'Jack' or 'Mad' Mitford . . . had been an officer in the navy, but fell, through infamous conduct, to be the rhymester of running patterers. His principal work, 'Johnny Newcome in the Navy,' was written in the gravel pits near Bayswater, where he had hidden, and whither his publisher sent him a shilling daily to buy gin and cheese in return for 'copy.' He died in St. Giles's Workhouse."[3]

Notes

1. Albert M. Cohn, *George Cruikshank: A Catalogue Raisonné of the Works Executed During the Years 1806–1877* (London, 1924), pp. 206–10. Previous sources identify only the thirty-eight signed plates in volumes 1–11.

2. Ruari McLean, *George Cruikshank, His Life and Work . . .* (New York, [1948]), p. 13 n. 2; John Wardroper, *The Caricatures of George Cruikshank* (Boston, 1978), p. 12.

3. Blanchard Jerrold, *The Life of George Cruikshank* (London, 1894), 1:71.

Information Sources

BIBLIOGRAPHY

Catalogue of the Works Illustrated by George Cruikshank in the Harry Elkins Widener Collection, Houghton Library, Harvard Univerity.

Cohn, Albert M. *George Cruikshank: A Catalogue Raisonné of the Works Executed During the Years 1806–1877*. London, 1924.

INDEXES

None.

REPRINT EDITIONS

Microform: English Literary Periodicals (UMI), reels 597–598.

LOCATION SOURCES

American
>   Complete runs: Harvard University Library; New York Public Library; Princeton University Library.
>   Partial runs: Johns Hopkins University Library; U. S. Library of Congress; University of Minnesota Library; Yale University Library.

British
>   Complete run: British Museum.
>   Partial runs: Birmingham Public Library; Cambridge University Library; London Library.

Publication History

MAGAZINE TITLE AND TITLE CHANGES
>   *The Scourge, or monthly expositor of imposture and folly,* January 1811–March 1814. *The Scourge, or literary, theatrical and miscellaneous magazine,* April 1814–June 1816. *The Scourge and Satirist, or literary, theatrical, and miscellaneous magazine,* July–December 1816.

VOLUME AND ISSUE DATA
>   Volumes 1–11, numbers 1–66, January 1811–June 1816; new series, numbers 1–6, July–December 1816.

FREQUENCY OF PUBLICATION
>   Monthly.

PUBLISHERS
>   Volumes 1–9: W. N. Jones, Green Arbor Court, Old Bailey, London (for M. Jones, 5 Newgate Street). Volume 10: Jones & Company, London. Volume 11–n.s. number 6: James Johnston, 98 Cheapside.

EDITORS
>   Unknown.

Nathaniel Teich

SPECTATOR, THE

In the first issue of the *Spectator*, dated "For the Week Ending Saturday, July 5, 1828," editor Robert S. Rintoul announced that

> the principal object of a Newspaper is to convey intelligence. It is proposed in the Spectator to give this, the first and most prominent place, to a report of all the leading occurrences of the week. In this department, the reader may always expect a summary account of every public proceeding, or transaction of interest, whether the scene might lie at home or abroad, that has taken place within the seven days preceding the termination of our labours; which, we wish it to be remarked, close on *Saturday* at midnight.

Through the rest of the nineteenth century, the general format never varied; the paper always began with several colums of "News of the Week," followed by various departments: Parliament, the press, essays on various subjects collected under the general title "Topics of the Day," literary reviews, a military gazette, a list of births and deaths, a commercial report (including stock reports and East India shipping), and advertising. Departments were changed or dropped; some appeared on an occasional basis; but the leader was always "The News of the Week." Although the *Spectator*'s reputation was established by its fine writing, its liberal stance in politics, its reason and good judgment, and its political independence, it always remained a news magazine.

For about three years after arriving in London from Edinburgh, Rintoul edited the London *Atlas,* a general journal resembling the *Spectator* in content. However, in 1828 he broke with the proprietors of the *Atlas* and, with several *Atlas* writers, he established the *Spectator* with the financial backing of Douglas Kinnaird and Joseph Hume (among others). Although the paper's sales were not particularly high in the first forty years, it had a large readership among the influential members of the upper middle class—Rintoul often complained that five times as many people read his paper as bought it. It adopted a liberal, sometimes radical position on the great political issues of the day. Its ardent support of parliamentary reform—it was the *Spectator* which made popular the cry "The Bill, the Whole Bill, and Nothing but the Bill"—was probably instrumental in the passing of the Reform Bill. Its support of Edward Gibbon Wakefield's program for colonial reform persuaded the government to institute a sweeping revision of colonial policy. Naturally, the *Spectator* was also one of the leading advocates of Corn Law Repeal.

Through the thirty years of Rintoul's editorship, the paper often adopted positions unpopular with a number of its readers. However, it maintained a relatively stable circulation and prospered. Perhaps the reason that the *Spectator* could oppose itself to its readers' views without alienating them involved the nature of the readers themselves. The *Spectator* said of its own readers in the issue for 1 May 1858 that "by far the greater part of the regular readers of the *Spectator* have always been of a class that is not affected by partisan culture, who like to listen to all sides of controversies, provided the argument is conducted with fairness and moderation" (31:466). The *Spectator* argued with passion for reform and warned of dire consequences in the event that reform was not accomplished, but it never took the fatal step of advocating a new *form* of government. Indeed, for a journal as radical as it appeared to be in the 1830s, it was remarkably levelheaded in 1848, when all the world was in revolution and the Anti-Corn Law movement seemed to be moving England toward upheaval also. On 1 April 1848, in an article entitled "Treason in Ireland," the *Spectator* noted that, although armed rebellion might be necessary in the despotic states on the Continent, lawful methods of changing the government were available in Great Britain.

Rintoul, in failing health, sold the *Spectator* to a Mr. Scott in 1858. From

1858 to 1861 the paper struggled under the editorship of Thornton Hunt, Leigh Hunt's son. In 1861 Scott sold the paper to Meredith Townsend, who shortly afterwards took Richard Holt Hutton on as a partner. The two set the tone for the paper until 1897, when Hutton died and Townsend retired.

Townsend and Hutton got off to a rocky start, in part because of the paper's decline under Hunt and in part because of their championship of the North in the American Civil War. Alvar Ellegård notes that circulation declined from 3,000 in 1860 to 2,000 in 1865, then doubled to 4,000 in 1870 after the American issue was settled.[1] In its advocacy of the North, the *Spectator* was continuing the long-established policy of supporting its view of the morally right cause, no matter how unpopular that cause might be. In times past, the *Spectator* had advocated freedom for the colonies, freedom for working men, freedom for West Indian slaves, and freedom for oppressed peoples on the Continent. Advocating the cause of the Union, which it identified with emancipation, came naturally to the paper. Its faithful readers should have expected nothing less.

Naturally, Townsend and Hutton set the style for the *Spectator*, both in the positions that it adopted and in the very style in which it was written. Sir William Watson said that Hutton's style was the *Spectator*'s style, and that all *Spectator* contributors naturally wrote in that style, not because of Hutton's insistence, but because of his force of personality.[2] Certainly the arguments over who wrote which articles (all were anonymous) indicate that the style and thought of the paper were of an unvarying consistency. The moral earnestness and heavy arguments brought about charges of dullness, but the *Spectatorial* style was still widely admired and imitated.

Under Townsend and Hutton the paper continued to lead off with several columns of news. However, its old emphasis on politics was supplemented by more fully developed reviews of books, mainly because of Hutton's interest in literature. Also, whereas Rintoul had not shown any particular interest in religion beyond advocating Catholic Emancipation, the new *Spectator* began to adopt a Broad Church position in religious questions; Hutton was a friend of F. D. Maurice and Maurice's religious views heavily influenced Hutton's.

In the controversy brought about by Darwin's *Origin of Species,* the *Spectator* opposed the Darwinists, not merely because of the specific arguments over evolution, but because of a general opposition to contemporary science. Hutton, who led the paper's fight, perceived the new science as being fundamentally materialist, and therefore opposed to the spirituality of the Christian religion. However, he was not simply and dogmatically a Christian. He distrusted private religious judgments, and felt that only the Church of England had the authority to interpret scripture. Yet he also felt free to oppose church authorities over a prayer issue—specifically, over the efficacy and morality of the prayers against affliction.[3] In a series of articles in 1872, the *Spectator* attacked a proposal by Tyndall, published in the *Fortnightly Review**(see *VEA*), to prove the efficacy of prayer in a scientifically designed experiment. Such an experiment, said the *Spectator* in the issue of 6 July 1872, could not be properly carried out, nor would any results be conclusive. Private prayer is an effective power, "a power which alters the external course of the world as well as its internal course; but we believe in it on precisely the same kind of evidence on which every sane man believes that the passionate desires of individuals so often realize themselves, and that the hopes of multitudes create the great historic changes for which they cry" (45:847).

The *Spectator* was not particularly daring in its literary tastes, evidence which supports a view that journals liberal in politics are often conservative in the arts. It is true that Rintoul hired Rosetti as arts editor, and that the *Spectator* was an early supporter of the Pre-Raphaelite Brotherhood. Later, Swinburne wrote several critical articles and reviews for Hutton. However, the Rintoul *Spectator,* when it did take a literary position, felt that the artist was "a public servant, whose existence could only be justified if he did good to others through his art."[4] The Hutton and Townsend *Spectator* also subscribed to the general Victorian tenets on literature and art: art was to deal with contemporary humanity and contemporary problems; art was to be moral; art was to have a purpose. Swinburne's experiences with the *Spectator* illustrate the paper's general critical position. In the early 1860s Swinburne attempted to hoax Hutton with a review of an imaginary Baudelairean French poet named Ernest Clouet. Swinburne's reviews were quite daring because he always skated on the thin ice of immorality. Hutton refused to print the review on moral grounds, causing Swinburne to attack the prudishness of the press.[5] In a review of Swinburne's *Atalanta in Calydon,* the *Spectator* admired the poem's "very considerable imaginative power," its "fertility of fancy," and its "fine passages." But it found the poem ultimately unsatisfactory because "there is usually something a little perverse in the mind of a man who can find nothing real enough whereon to nourish his imagination within two thousand years of his own time, and who [therefore] must go back to Greece" (38:412–13).

Hutton felt that good literature required the addition of Christian ethics to a Coleridgean imagination. He sought an original faculty of the mind, which could not be accounted for by any external source (that is, education or experience). He also sought simplicity and naivete without self-consciousness. Value for him lay not so much in form as in imagination, in art as in genius. He condemned simple didacticism, saying that it must be melded into a tracing of human nature, the proper province of fiction. Through the 1870s and 1880s, the *Spectator* opposed naturalism, in part because it left no room for the imagination, and in part because naturalism's insistence on determinism conflicted with Hutton's belief in free will. The *Spectator* also opposed impressionism because of its extreme subjectivity and rejection of the controlling intellect.[6]

As might be expected, the *Spectator* was not always successful in its literary judgments. It reflected the prevailing tastes of the day in its support of Kingsley, Thackeray, Longfellow, Tennyson, and George Eliot. It accepted Dickens early, but later criticized him for his inability to create living characters. The

Brontës were criticized for lack of taste, as was Swinburne. Browning was attacked for his vague language and Carlyle for his worship of despotic kings and physical force. Pater and Wilde were dismissed later on, and Stevenson was never thoroughly approved. Matthew Arnold, like Swinburne, was criticized for not choosing contemporary English themes and settings for his poems.

The *Spectator*'s occasional failures of literary judgment cannot be laid solely at Hutton's door. Some of the finest essayists of the day contributed to the literary columns, including Bagehot, Morley, Thomas Hughes, F. D. Maurice, John Dennis, Daniel Lathbury, Talbot Baines, Herman Merrivale; A. C. Swinburne, D. S. MacColl, Alfred Church, C. J. Cornish, Eric Parker, Mrs. Oliphant, and, of course, Townsend. It is generally conceded that the *Spectator* spoke for "educated mid-Victorian critical opinion."[7] The opinion that its critical theories were representative of the time is supported by comments by Gladstone and Morley, among others, that Hutton was the finest critic of the century.[8] If the paper sometimes slept, it was because many people of contemporary influence also dozed.

In 1897 J. St. Loe Strachey took over sole proprietorship and editorship of the *Spectator*, and, in effect, began the twentieth-century period of the journal. He increased the circulation markedly while continuing the paper's traditions of political independence and outspoken advocacy of human freedom. By the end of the nineteenth century, the *Spectator* had become, as the *Nation and Athenaeum* (*Athenaeum* *) later expressed it, "a timeless institution, like the City Corporation, the Bank of England, and the House of Lords."[9]

Notes

1. Alvar Ellegård, *The Readership of the Periodical Press in Mid-Victorian Britain* (Göteborg, 1957), pp. 24–25.
2. Sir William Watson, *Excursions in Criticism* (London, 1893); see esp. the chapter on Hutton.
3. Frank Miller Turner, *"Rainfall, Plagues, and the Prince of Wales:* A Chapter in the History of Science," *Journal of British Studies* 13 (May 1974):47.
4. O. Maurer, "My Squeamish Public: Some Problems of Victorian Magazine Publishers and Editors," *Studies in Bibliography* 12 (1959):35.
5. Ibid.
6. Robert A. Colby, " 'How It Strikes a Contemporary': The 'Spectator' as Critic," *Nineteenth Century Fiction* 11 (1956):182–206.
7. John Gross, *The Rise and Fall of the Man of Letters* (London, 1969), p. 83.
8. W. V. Harris, "The Critics," in *Victorian Prose,* ed. David DeLaura (New York, 1973), pp. 440–43.
9. "The Spectator," *Nation and Athenaeum* 44 (1928):168.

Information Sources

BIBLIOGRAPHY
The following bibliography of secondary sources covers the most representative twentieth-century material written about the *Spectator*. Because of the *Spectator*'s influence

and long life, almost all histories of journalism and periodical publishing include some mention of it, usually standard bibliographic material. This bibliography lists several, but not all, such histories. The last year of publication for entries in this bibliography is 1979.

Altick, Richard. *The English Common Reader: A Social History of the Mass Reading Public 1800–1900*. Chicago, 1957.

————. "Nineteenth Century English Periodicals." *Newberry Library Bulletin*, 2d ser. 9 (1952):255–64.

Armytage, W.H.G. "The Editor Reflects: Newly Discovered Letters of R. H. Hutton, Editor of the *Spectator* 1861–1897." *Journal of English and Germanic Philology* 49 (1950):566–69.

Aspinall, A. "The Circulation of Newspapers in the Early Nineteenth Century." *Review of English Studies* 22 (1946):29–43.

————. "Statistical Accounts of the London Newspapers 1800–1836." *English Historical Review* 55 (1950):372–83.

Chew, Samuel C. "Swinburne's Contributions to the *Spectator* in 1862." *Modern Language Notes* 35 (1920):118–19.

Colby, Robert A. " 'How It Strikes a Contemporary': The 'Spectator' as Critic." *Nineteenth Century Fiction* 11 (1956):182–206.

Ellegård, Alvar. *The Readership of the Periodical Press in Mid-Victorian Britain*. Böteborg, 1957.

Graham, Walter James. *English Literary Periodicals*. New York, 1930.

Hogben, John. *Richard Holt Hutton of "The Spectator."* Edinburgh, 1899.

Jordan, H. D. "The Daily and Weekly Press of England in 1861." *South Atlantic Quarterly* 28 (1929):302–17.

Jump, John D. "Matthew Arnold and the *Spectator*." *Review of English Studies* 25 (1949):61–64.

————. "Weekly Reviewing in the Eighteen-Fifties." *Review of English Studies* 24 (1948):42–57.

————. "Weekly Reviewing in the Eighteen-Sixties." *Review of English Studies*, n.s. 3 (1952):244–62.

Lee, Alan J. *The Origins of the Popular Press in England, 1855–1914*. Totowa, N.J., 1976.

Maurer, Oscar. "My Squeamish Public: Some Problems of Victorian Magazine Publishers and Editors." *Studies in Bibliography* 12 (1959):21–40.

"One Hundred Years of the *Spectator*." *Living Age* 335 (1929):369.

Porter, Alan. "Dickens and the *Spectator*." *Spectator* 141 (1928):320.

Roberts, F. D. "Early Victorian Newspaper Editors." *Victorian Periodicals Newsletter* no. 14 (1971):1–12.

"6,000th *Spectator*." *Spectator* 170 (1943):586–87.

————. "The *Spectator*'s Attack on Trollope's *Prime Minister*: A Mistaken Attribution." *Notes and Queries* 213 (1968):420–21.

Spectator, Anniversary Issue, 125 (May 1953).

Spectator, Centennial Supplement, 141 (November 1928).

"The *Spectator*." *Nation and Athenaeum* 44 (1928):168–69.

Strachey, Amy. *St. Loe Strachey: His Life and His Paper*. London, 1930.

Strachey, J. St. Loe. *The Adventure of Living: A Subjective Autobiography*. London, 1922.

Tener, Robert H. "An Arnold Quotation as a Clue to R. H. Hutton's *Spectator* Articles." *Notes and Queries* 216 (1971):100–101.

———. "A Clue for Some R. H. Hutton Attributions." *Notes and Queries* 207 (1967):382–83.

———. "Hutton and 'Agnostic.' " *Notes and Queries* 209 (1964):429–31.

———. "Hutton's Essays Theological and Literary: A Bibliographical Note." *Notes and Queries* 205 (1960:185–87.

———. "More Articles by R. H. Hutton." *Bulletin of the New York Public Library* 66 (1962):58–62.

———. "R. H. Hutton: Some Attributions." *Victorian Periodicals Newsletter* no. 20 (June 1973):14–31.

———. "R. H. Hutton's Editorial Career: The 'Economist' and the 'Spectator.' " *Victorian Periodicals Newsletter* no. 8 (April, 1970):6–17.

———. "Richard Holt Hutton." *Times Literary Supplement,* 24 April 1959, p. 241.

———. "The *Spectator* Records 1874–1897." *Victorian Newsletter* no. 17 (1960):33–36.

———. "Spectatorial Strachey." *Times Literary Supplement,* 31 December 1964, p. 1181.

Thomas, Sir William Beach. *The Story of the "Spectator."* London, 1928.

INDEXES

Some reprint editions contain indexes.

REPRINT EDITIONS

Widely available, *BUCOP* lists seventy-six editions.

Microform: Bell and Howell, Wooster, Ohio; British Museum Newspaper Library, London; English Literary Periodicals (UMI), reel 961; Microcard Editions, Washington, D.C.

LOCATION SOURCES

American

Widely available.

Reprint editions: Widely available.

British

Complete runs: Bodleian Library; Nottingham Public Library; University College (Oxford) Library.

Partial runs: British Museum; Cambridge University Library; Durham University Library; Glasgow University Library; Leeds University Library; National Library of Scotland.

Reprint editions: Widely available.

Publication History

MAGAZINE TITLE AND TITLE CHANGES

The Spectator.

VOLUME AND ISSUE DATA

Volume 1, 5 July 1828–1925.

FREQUENCY OF PUBLICATION

Weekly (Saturday).

PUBLISHERS AND EDITORS

Except for one brief period (noted), the proprietors and publishers were also the editors. Address remained the same throughout the nineteenth century: 1 Wellington Street, London. 1828–1858: Robert S. Rintoul, ed. and prop. 1858–1861: Scott (first name not available), prop., and Thornton Hunt, ed. 1861–1897: Meredith Townsend and Richard Holt Hutton, eds. and props. 1897–1925: J. St. Loe Strachey, ed. and prop.

Richard D. Fulton

SYLPH, THE

The *Sylph* takes its name from the character Ariel in Pope's *Rape of the Lock*. He reappears in literary history as the conductor of a single-essay type periodical which ran for forty numbers, from 22 September 1795 through 30 April 1796. Eight pages long, the periodical was originally published twice a week on Tuesdays and Saturdays through number 16; thereafter, it was published on Saturdays only.

Ariel has returned to earth, he tells the reader, "in order that we may by our advice, authority, and influence bring about a reformation of morals and manners, so much wanted in the degeneracy of the present times. . . . It is our desire not only to make men good (as far as we can) but amiable" (p. 12).

The method proposed to achieve these ends is gentle satire. Finding severity both fatiguing and ineffective, the Sylph says, "We shall, in general, give our communications an air of gaiety; which is also more congenial to our own temper and habits." However, he may be severe when necessary to correct men's crimes. His observations on men and manners are conveyed sometimes in person (he has assumed the appearance of an ordinary mortal) and sometimes through his secretary, "Alato Caerulielli" ("Winged Creature of the Blue").

Essays in the *Sylph* discuss a wide range of topics. Several of them play on the identity and appearance of the Sylph himself, and the efforts of readers to identify him on the street or in bookshops. At least half a dozen essays deal with relationships between the sexes, both before and after marriage. Several others attack cheap popular novels, which convey romantic unreal pictures of life and under the guise of irresistible love glorify lust and marital infidelity. Flirtatious young ladies, bawdy old ladies, and idle, empty-minded young men are satirized. Reason, filial piety, and love of freedom are extolled. The author in separate essays discriminates politeness of manners (external) from politeness of sentiments (internal); self-love from selfishness (echoing Pope in *An Essay on Man*); and a *great* name (popular fame) from a *good* name (the reward of virtue). Elsewhere the effects of poverty are described, especially the effects on men of genius; and the universal duty of benevolence is enforced.

Frequent touches of humor and satire enliven the essays. For example, one essay chiding the ogling of women by men during church services, describes in detail the various stages of ogling: the Sweep, the Peep, the Glance, the Leer, the Ogle Oblique, and the Ogle Direct (no. 14).

Later, in one of several essays satirizing modern novels, the Sylph proclaims rules which should govern such writing:

1. That no novel in future be published with a preface (since the preface contains the only moral and beneficial part). He will thus strip novels of their false colors.

2. That none of the "emphatical words" (sentimental emotings uttered by young lovers in moments of romantic feeling, and usually italicized) be used more than seven times per page, except in certain specified cases.

3. "That not more than *one pair in fifty* shall be united together by the pure ties of *disinterested love;* and that all the rest shall act like *people of the world,* viz., connect themselves from interest and convenience. This will render all their love-affairs so *common* and *natural,* that there will be neither novelty nor interest in them, and they will, of course, fall into neglect." [No. 19]

A unique feature of the *Sylph* is a series of courts of justice, to which all men may have recourse in cases not cognizable by any human jurisdiction. The Court of the Fan, under Sylphid Zephyretta, presides over cases of love and gallantry. The Court of the Passions, under the sylph Flagello, presides over men's crimes, foibles, and follies. The Court of Dispatch, under Chief Justice Momentilla, takes cognizance of the use and abuse of time. A fourth court, not named, is given jurisdiction over all causes not cognizable by the other courts. Able casuists are available as counsel, gratis, to plead for the plaintiffs. Though the courts are introduced in an early number (7) the only one to be much invoked in later numbers is the COURT OF THE FAN (nos. 9, 10, 18, 23).

Another unusual feature is the long laudatory elegy on naval captain Robert Faulknor (1763–1795), whose thirty-six-gun ship *La Blanche* defeated the French thirty-eight-gun ship *La Pique* in the West Indies on 5 January 1795. Faulknor died leading the attack, and his heroism was widely publicized. The elegy, in iambic pentameter quatrains, describes the battle and Faulknor's death, contrasts his sacrifice with the behavior of selfish politicians who "only court their country for her dower," criticizes the ministry for denying him a monument, and predicts that his name will live in history. The unsigned *Elegy* is one of the few references to contemporary historical events to be found in the periodical, and the only poem. A long allegorical pseudo-Eastern tale, "The Tablets," and two essays on the Sylph's education of his beloved Eliza round out the contents.

While the imaginative framework for the periodical was derived from Pope, much of the substance and format suggests its derivation from such essay periodicals as Addison's *Spectator** and Johnson's *Rambler** (for both, see *AAAJ*). Many of the same features and devices characterize all three: the imaginary conductor, the strongly moral and didactic aim, the half-serious tone of mild satire, an occasional "letter to the Editor," even the use of a brief classical quotation at the beginning of each number.

None of the essays in the *Sylph* are signed, or ascribed to a contributor. Conceivably they may all be the work of the editor or proprietor, whose identity remains unknown. Since Ariel dictated his observations to his bookseller, George Marr implies that the bookseller, Thomas Longman, may be the author of the *Sylph;* [1] but direct evidence of authorship is lacking.

Note

1. George S. Marr, *The Periodical Essayists of the Eighteenth Century* (New York, 1924), pp. 238–40.

Information Sources

BIBLIOGRAPHY
Graham, Walter. *English Literary Periodicals*. New York, 1930.
Marr, George S. *The Periodical Essayists of the Eighteenth Century*. New York, 1924.
INDEXES
None.
REPRINT EDITIONS
1796.
LOCATION SOURCES
American
Complete runs: Library Company of Philadelphia; University of Minnesota Library.
British
Complete run: British Museum.
Partial run: Bodleian Library.

Publication History

MAGAZINE TITLE AND TITLE CHANGES
The Sylph.
VOLUME AND ISSUE DATA
Volume 1, numbers 1–40, 22 September 1795–30 April 1796.
FREQUENCY OF PUBLICATION
Biweekly, numbers 1–16; weekly thereafter.
PUBLISHERS
Thomas Longman, Paternoster Row, London/John Debrett, Piccadilly, London.
EDITOR
Unknown.

Daniel L. McCue, Jr.

T

TAIT'S EDINBURGH MAGAZINE

Begun in April 1832, *Tait's Edinburgh Magazine* became the organ of advanced liberalism in Scotland during the era of the First Reform Bill. It continued the work of London's *Westminster Review* * north of the Tweed and countered the conservatism of *Blackwood's Edinburgh Magazine*.* Although it was a monthly miscellany (in the first issue, a funny "Essay on Kissing" is followed by a serious study of the "True Causes of the Late Insurrection of the Slaves in Jamaica," and a "Sonnet by Gertrude" precedes "The Scottish Reform Bill"), its initial impulse was political. As the prospectus said, "A change has come over the spirit of the Time; mighty questions have been stirred; deep interests have been created; vast masses of men, formerly inert and passive, have suddenly begun to heave to and fro with the force of a newly-inspired animation; old things are passing away—all things are becoming new" (1:57).

In the second article of the first number, "A Tete a Tete with Mr. Tait," the founder and editor set forth his goals for the new publication: liberality, spirit, utility. By "liberality," he meant a sympathy with the perpetual changes in European civilization and an attempt to "join them in their progress towards something yet more desirable, which we always have in prospect and never in possession." By "spirit," he meant "my magazine will be distinguished for its life and living interest. . . . It cannot smack too much of the day . . . the anecdotes, events, biographies, and *livingnesses* of the day." Finally, by "utility," he meant "everything that contributes to the enjoyment of our being, and the perfection of our nature" (1:9–16). But "utility" was also a code word for "Utilitarianism" or "Philosophic Radicalism." Among the early contributors to *Tait's* were John Stuart Mill, Richard Cobden, and John Bright.

Two crucial changes occurred in 1834. First, the price of *Tait's*, which had been a half-crown, was reduced to a shilling. In an article of January 1834, which announced the change, *Tait's* explained that cheap publications sell far more copies, "the circulation proportionately rising as the price decreases." *Tait's* itself claimed to be in third place among the six expensive magazines, with a circulation of about twenty-five hundred (14:490–500). But as the *Christian Reformer* suggested, *Tait's* was only being read in coffee houses and reading rooms, because it was priced beyond the means of its intended middle- and working-class audience.[1] After the price reduction, it became the largest selling magazine in Scotland and a surprisingly popular magazine in England.[2] Second, in June 1834, *Johnstone's Edinburgh Magazine* was incorporated into *Tait's*. Mrs. Christian Isobel Johnstone became the literary editor, and under her reign *Tait's* enjoyed its dozen finest years.

Mrs. Johnstone was an accomplished writer and an indefatigable worker. Although William Tait still corresponded with contributors, Mrs. Johnstone became the working genius of *Tait's* and judged the articles that were submitted. She herself was a major contributor of fiction and criticism. For example, she often wrote the entire "Literary Register," the concise notices of current literature that took up approximately 20 pages of the 138-page publication. Most important, under the editorship of Mrs. Johnstone a major shift in emphasis took place. William Tait was a businessman and a political figure. Like his "great master" (2:56), Jeremy Bentham, he expressed considerable skepticism about the value of literature: "Poetry will not do, the world has outgrown it" (1:15). This attitude is reflected in the pages of *Tait's* during its first two years. Thus, an article on Rousseau begins, "Although mere literature appeared during the first years of this remarkable period to occupy the general attention, by degrees there arose discussions on the gravest and most important subjects. To Corneille, Boileau, Racine, succeeded Diderot, D'Alembert, and Voltaire" (1:339). The literature that did appear in *Tait's* often had direct social relevance, like the radical poems of Ebenezer Elliott, the author of the "Corn-Law Rhymes." But then Mrs. Johnstone made her own radical changes, and on the whole, *Tait's* became "more of a literary than a political organ."[3]

Mrs. Johnstone may have been responsible for the appearance of a large number of women writers in *Tait's*, including Harriet Martineau, Lady Blessington, Mrs. Gore, and Miss Mitford. It is also believed today that many of the subscribers to *Tait's* were women.[4] Among literary men, John Galt, Ebenezer Elliott, Leigh Hunt, William Edmondstoune Aytoun, Theodore Martin, and George Gilfillan were frequent contributors. But the greatest and most popular writer in *Tait's* was undoubtedly Thomas De Quincey. He contributed some forty articles between 1833 and 1841, some thirty between 1845 and 1848, and three as late as 1851. These include several of his most prized works. For example, in February 1834, in the first number of the new series of *Tait's*, De Quincey began his remarkable series, *Sketches of Life and Manners; from the Autobiography of an English Opium-Eater,* which ran on for seven years and included some twenty-seven papers. *Tait's* also published several of De Quincey's most famous "Reminiscences," including his four-part essay on

Coleridge and his five-part study of Wordsworth. Wordsworth resented the personal references so much that he refused to allow *Tait's* in his house again. In 1846 alone, De Quincey published in *Tait's* two essays on Sophocles's *Antigone,* two on Christianity, and two on Gilfillan's *Gallery of Literary Portraits,* and one each on Keats, Sir James Mackintosh, and the Marquis Wellesley, a notable demonstration of the versatility of the author and the magazine.

Although *Tait's* consistently advocated an advanced liberal position in politics, it was free, undogmatic, and inconsistent in literature.[5] *Tait's* went with the flow, publishing the best and most timely pieces it could get and not worrying much about literary principles. Its two finest writers, De Quincey and John Galt, also wrote for its great rival, the conservative *Blackwood's.* Perhaps the most consistent literary feature of *Tait's* was its broad, rollicking, subversive humor. Parody, burlesque, and farce enlivened its pages throughout its career. From 1841 to 1844, for example, William Edmondstoune Aytoun and Theodore Martin published nine articles in *Tait's,* in which appeared prose parody and burlesque, social criticism, literary discussion, coarse jokes, and parodic ballads and songs. Each article had a unity of its own. One, for instance, was a review, with extracts, of the *Topaz,* "the quintessence of all possible Annuals," and it attempted to demolish "those periodical visitants of our drawing rooms and boudoirs" (n.s. 8:749–56). Another was entitled "Lays of the Would-Be Laureates" and contained poetic applications for the post left vacant by the death of Southey (n.s. 10:273–76). Eventually, the best poetic parodies were published as *The Book of Ballads,* under the pseudonym Bon Gaultier. Saintsbury characterized it as "that admirable book of light verse, the equal of anything earlier and certainly not surpassed since."[6] George Kitchin, the author of the authoritative work on English parody and burlesque, began his discussion of these ballads, "Never have parodists more consciously striven to correct the bad taste of their day," and ended by speaking of "the deliberate crusade its authors intended against inferior literary manners."[7] Thus, it may be argued that in its irreverent, subversive, anti-establishment laughter, *Tait's* found the literary counterpart of its "radical" politics.

The second half of the career of *Tait's* was less successful. Ownership was transferred to Glasgow by 1847 when Alexander Alison, an influential ironmaster who believed in educating the working classes, purchased the proprietary rights. George Troup became the editor, the lead writer, and in 1849, after Alison suffered heavy financial losses, the new owner. Troup was an able and hard-working man who spread himself too thin. Besides controlling the destiny of *Tait's,* Troup was an important newspaperman, lecturer, and political writer. Still, "he would sometimes write almost the whole of the magazine himself, with the help of a clever Irishman, Jemmy Withers."[8] But Troup was more of a political than a literary man, and the literary quality of *Tait's* declined throughout the fifties. Apparently the readership also declined because Troup "lost much money in *Tait's.*"[9] Thus, it is hardly surprising that in 1861, after nearly thirty years of service, *Tait's Magazine* ended.

Notes

1. R. J. Morris, "The Unitarian View of Fifteen Periodicals in 1834," *Victorian Periodicals Newsletter* no. 18 (1972):32.

2. *Dictionary of National Biography*, s.v. "Tait, William"; Susan Dean, "The 1979 RSVP Conference," *Victorian Periodicals Review* 12, no. 4 (1979):142.

3. James Bertram, *Some Memories of Books, Authors and Events* (Westminster, 1893), p. 30.

4. Dean, p. 142.

5. The *Christian Reformer* described *Tait's* as "advocating popular sentiments not far removed from republicanism." Quoted in Morris, p. 32.

6. Quoted in Rosaline Masson, *Pollok and Aytoun* (Edinburgh, 1898), p. 153.

7. George Kitchin, *A Survey of Burlesque and Parody in English* (Edinburgh, 1931), pp. 290, 295.

8. James W. Scott, *"Tait's Edinburgh Magazine,"* *Scottish Notes and Queries* 6 (1893):150.

9. George Elmslie Troup, *Life of George Troup, Journalist* (Edinburgh, 1881), p. 118.

Information Sources

BIBLIOGRAPHY

Bertram, James. *Some Memories of Books, Authors and Events*. London, 1893.

Boucher, Odile. "Le Discours sur le Roman dans *Tait's Edinburgh Magazine*, 1832–1850." Ph.D dissertation, Univ. of Nancy, 1980.

Scott, James W. *"Tait's Edinburgh Magazine,"* *Scottish Notes and Queries* 6 (February 1893):129–32; 6 (March 1893):150.

Troup, George Elmslie. *Life of George Troup, Journalist*. Edinburgh, 1881.

INDEXES

Wellesley Index 4 (projected).

REPRINT EDITIONS

Microform: English Literary Periodicals (UMI), reels 492–506.

LOCATION SOURCES

American

Complete run: U. S. Library of Congress.

Partial runs: Widely available.

British

Complete runs: Birmingham Public Library; British Museum; Cambridge University Library; Edinburgh Public Library; Greenock Library; London Library.

Partial runs: Widely available.

Publication History

MAGAZINE TITLE AND TITLE CHANGES

Tait's Edinburgh Magazine.

VOLUME AND ISSUE DATA

First series, volumes 1–4, April 1832–January 1834; new series, volumes 1–28, February 1834–May 1861.

FREQUENCY OF PUBLICATION

Monthly.

PUBLISHERS
    1832–1846: William Tait, Edinburgh. 1847–1848: Alexander Alison and George
    Troup, Glasgow. 1849–1861: George Troup, Glasgow.
EDITORS
    William Tait, 1832–May 1834. Christian Isobel Johnstone, June 1834–1846.
    George Troup, 1847–1861.

Mark A. Weinstein

TATLER, THE

Leigh Hunt was seldom without a journal to edit. In all, he conducted (and
contributed massively to) a dozen periodicals during his life; simultaneously he
wrote for other journals and composed poetry, volumes of criticism, and fiction.[1] The two-year period beginning in 1830 was particularly fertile for Hunt's
periodical writing and editing. During the spring and summer of that year he
began (on 5 June) the *Chat of the Week* which, he tells us, "was to talk,
without scandal, of anything worth public notice. The Government," however,
claiming that the publication was a newspaper, "put a stop to this speculation
by insisting that it should have a stamp; which I could not afford."[2] Hunt
ceased publishing the *Chat* on 28 August. But a week later, on 4 September,
Hunt responded to this temporary setback positively by beginning a new periodical whose purview and format would render it far more important than its
immediate predecessor.

The *Tatler,* initially subtitled *A Daily Journal of Literature and the Stage,*
ran under Hunt's direction until 13 February 1832 and was continued by Robert
Seton, who also initiated a new series from 2/4 April to 6 October 1832. Charles
W. Reynell, printer of the *Examiner* *—and subsequently of the *Tatler*—noting
the modern revival of old titles such as *Spectator* * (see *AAAJ*) and *Examiner,* *
(see *AAAJ*) suggested that Hunt adopt the venerable name for his daily (see the
Tatler, AAAJ).[3] But the enterprise was almost entirely Hunt's. Although each
number consisted "but of four folio pages," as Hunt recalled his remarkable
labor,

> I did it all myself, except when too ill; and illness seldom hindered me
> either from supplying the review of a book, going every night to the play,
> or writing the notice of the play the same night at the printing office. The
> consequence was, that the work, slight as it looked, nearly killed me; for
> it never prospered beyond the coterie of play-going readers, to whom it
> was almost exclusively known; and I was sensible of becoming weaker
> and poorer every day. When I came home at night, often at morning, I
> used to feel as if I could hardly speak. . . . Such nevertheless, is a habit
> of mind, if it be but cultivated, that my spirits never seemed better, nor
> did I ever write the articles so well, as in the pages of this most unre-
> munerating speculation.[4]

Despite Hunt's rhetorical upswing in recollecting this "most unremunerating speculation" after two decades, and the genuine exuberance and pungent detail in the reviews to which it alludes, one should not discount its cost to him. The undertaking did nearly kill him, "probably injured his health permanently, and it reduced him to a condition of poverty and indebtedness"—including prosecution by creditors—from which he did not recover for several years.[5]

Yet Hunt's legacy seems to us at a safe distance worth the price: at its best, the *Tatler* combines Hunt's extraordinary prescience for literary talent with a daily reporter's sense of immediacy. During most of his editorship, Hunt reviews a new production—and evokes the theater's ambience—the night he has witnessed it, considers a different book almost every day, and assembles several theatrical play-bills in each issue, six days a week.[6] Hunt's pace proved his undoing. And in one sense the *Tatler* traces the "failure of an attempt to issue a daily literary journal," especially at a time when the literacy rate was below 50 percent and few readers could afford books or evenings at the theater.[7] But for students of the Victorian stage especially and of nineteenth-century culture generally, the *Tatler*'s brief run yields important information and the judgments of one of the age's keenest practical critics. The *Tatler* recaptures the rush and flow of theatrical performances and developing literary events in early Victorian England.

Early in the *Tatler*'s life Hunt shrewdly introduced a feature that was to prove very popular with theater-goers: number 12 contained play-bills from the London theaters. Introducing the new feature, Hunt expresses his hope that *Tatler*s will be " 'frequent and full' in the pit and boxes" as they will now be "sold at the play-house doors, as well as by the newsmen" (1:45). Appealing to readers' purses, Hunt reasons, "A Tatler . . . cost two-pence whereas the common play-bill is a penny. But if the latter be worth what it costs, will it be too great a stretch of modesty to suppose that our new play-bill is worth it also? Our criticisms, we will be sworn, have . . . a relish in them . . . and then there is the rest of the matter, in the other pages, to vary the chat between acts" (1:45). We are reminded that financial exigencies were very much on Hunt's mind. At first, Hunt prints play-bills from the Haymarket and English Opera, Adelphi. Subsequently, the feature expands: it occupies each issue's entire last page, continuing notices from those two theaters along with play-bills from Drury Lane and Covent Garden; beginning with number 60 (12 November) the newly titled "Performances of this Evening" page also includes notices from the Surrey, Coburg, Tottenham Street, and Sadler's Wells Theaters; finally, reflecting the new "Public Amusements" subtitle of volume 3, the feature opens to notices for circuses and amphitheaters as well as those for the Surrey, Queen's, and City Subscription theaters. In the greatly reduced new series, however, beginning 4 June 1832, Robert Seton separated the *Tatler Play-Bills* from the periodical. His misguided attempt to increase revenues quickly failed: only twelve of the independent notices were published.

Unlike the generally successful play-bills, several new features introduced mid-way in the *Tatler*'s run never developed significantly. A "Fine Arts" column begins appearing in number 230 (30 May 1831). It includes notices of current exhibitions and inaugurates a series entitled "The Living Painters." Its anonymous author may well have been Robert Hunt, Leigh's brother and the art critic for the *Examiner*. He concludes crankily that though modern art congratulates itself on bettering past creations, art has actually degenerated as a result "undoubtedly . . . of the multitude of pictures that exist" (2:918). In subsequent installments this writer considers Westall and Phillips (no. 232); Collins, Cooper, and Daniel (no. 238); and Turner, Martin, and Stothard (no. 241). He judges Turner "a genius" who towers above the others. Beginning with number 233 (2 June 1831) a brief and sporadic "Music" column first appears. Its author focuses upon Paganini in one of the few notable columns, praising him warmly (on 9 June); Hunt again lauds the composer's achievements in long essays of 23 and 25 June 1831. When Hunt commences publishing advertisements in *Tatler* number 164 (12 March 1831), he apologizes tongue-in-cheek. Typically, a few advertisements appeared for clients like *Fraser's Magazine* * and purveyors of new books and of ostrich feathers.

The most important—and enduring—writings in the *Tatler* include some of Hunt's theatrical reports and book reviews and a few occasional essays. Mute are the fierce political thrusts familiar to readers of the early *Examiner* and *Reflector,* * though Hunt's libertarian and democratic ideals occasionally ring out. Hunt mildly promises in the *Tatler*'s inaugural issue "entertaining extracts from books, with occasional criticism" and "theatrical criticism, written with a love of the subject . . . suitable to a breakfast-table" and "published the first thing in the morning. . . . The town will thus have, for the first time these many years, a regular daily paper devoted to literature and criticism" (1:1). Despite this emphasis upon arts criticism, in the fourth and fifth numbers Hunt attacks the appellations "Lord" and "My Lord" as unseemly in a democratic nation. Ten issues later he prints in bold type the words and music for the Marseilles Hymn while also mourning the death (on 18 September 1830) of William Hazlitt, "one of the profoundest writers of the day, an admirable reasoner . . . the best general critic, the greatest critic on art that ever appeared" (1:53). Hunt's political essay supporting Hazlitt's objections to the Utilitarians' mechanism, to their disregard of feelings and emotions, and to their denigration of poetry, appears in number 21. And Hunt prints for the first time Hazlitt's 1830 essay on the "Emancipation of the Jews" (in number 176). In it Hazlitt advocates such freedom as "but a natural step in the progress of civilization," arguing that if the Jews are "vicious, it is we who have made them so" (1:701). When the *Quarterly Review* * castigates the French Revolution of 1830, Hunt attacks the reviewers as "slaves of church and state," unrepresentative of most English who view events in France "with feelings of the greatest consolation and the most glorious hope" (1:157).[8] Such political outbursts, however, are rare. Generally, Hunt reserved most of his energy—and space in the *Tatler*—for reviews of the theater and of books.

Most of the books Hunt reviews have been long forgotten; a few, however, along with his reviews of them, endure. "The Reader" reads the range of nineteenth-century writings—travel literature, histories, memoirs, and miscellaneous writings such as Lady Morgan's *France in 1829–30* (considered by Hunt in numbers 7, 8, and 9, with copious extracts printed), and Walter Scott's *Letters on Demonology and Witchcraft* (number 17). The most important reviews center on imaginative literature and literary figures. Across five issues of the *Tatler* (nos. 111–15), for example, Hunt battles with Thomas Moore, whose *Letters and Journals of Lord Byron: with notices of His Life* (1831) he considers under the heading "Lord Byron—Mr. Moore—and Mr. Leigh Hunt, with Original Letters *NOT* in Mr. Moore's Work." Hunt reproduces numerous missives from Moore to him, many praising Hunt's work. According to Hunt, during the period of the Byron–Shelley–Hunt collaboration on the *Liberal* (1822–1823), a hypocritical Moore had flattered Hunt to his face while simultaneously berating Hunt's contributions to the "unworthy alliance" as "dead weight" in letters to Byron (2:442). Such behavior typifies Moore for Hunt, who concludes that the biography's "author is an insincere man of the world, and . . . neither he nor his hero has a right to scatter charges of vulgarity and unworthiness" (2:441). Hunt spices his counter-offensive with reminiscences showing that Byron was well aware of Moore's affectations and shortcomings and that he confided his feelings to Hunt. Moreover, Hunt declares that Byron's reputation is slipping; and Moore emerges from the *Tatler* as petty, jealous, and a liar. Hunt's memoirs of other literary figures, especially Keats and Shelley, remain happy. Throughout the *Tatler* Hunt frequently but briefly recalls them and their works reverentially. Indeed, he reserves comparison with them, his greatest praise, for only one young poet, Alfred Tennyson.

In a belated review, Hunt lauds without reservation Tennyson's *Poems Chiefly Lyrical* and Charles Tennyson's *Sonnets and Fugitive Pieces* (both 1830).[9] "We have seen," Hunt declares unequivocally, "no such poetical writing since the last volume of Mr. Keats"; the "authors . . . may take their stand at once among the first poets of the day. We mean that Mr. Wordsworth and Mr. Coleridge may give them the right hand of fellowship; and that all who love genuine poetry, will . . . like to live in the world of their thoughts" (2:593). Hunt decries the inadequacy of "common critical prose" to express the "least glimpse of such truth and beauty" that he finds in these volumes. Further comparing the Tennysons to Keats and Shelley moves Hunt to survey poets' predicaments over the last few decades. In language that prefigures later aestheticism, Hunt concludes that these Victorians "come at a happier time, when they need not fight against worldly assumption, nor become martyrs to the faith in truth and beauty" (2:593). At first (in number 149) Hunt cannot decide which of the brothers is the greatest poet; in the final installment of his review, however, Hunt's usually sharp instincts guide him to declare for Alfred, "because he seems less disposed to tie himself down to conventional notions" (2:618). Hunt reprints Alfred's "Lilian," "Marianna," and "The Merman" (in number 149); "Supposed Confessions of a Second-rate Sensitive Mind not in Unity with Itself"; lines from "Burial of Love"; all of "Owl Song," "Recollections of the Arabian Nights," "A Character," "The Poet," "The Poet's Mind," "The Mystic," and "The Deserted House"; and part of "Love and Sorrow" (in number 151). Hunt cites Charles Tennyson's poems in the last two parts of the review. But he had already bestowed his greatest praise upon one of Alfred's compositions: "If Mr. Keats had seen . . . 'The Poet's Mind', he would have felt it as a magic circle, drawn round him to repulse the assaults of worldliness and folly" (2:602).

When Mary Shelley's *Frankenstein* appeared in its third edition (as one of Colburn and Bentley's standard novels) with the author's newly penned "Introduction" (1831), Hunt seized the occasion to remark upon the novel as "an invention which appeals to some of the most universal, and yet least vulgarized feelings of mortal man" (3:449; no. 371). He summarizes approvingly manifestations of its hold upon readers' imaginations, its "rare lot in the history of books": "It has been dramatized at the theatres, quoted in Parliament, made a familiar illustration everywhere, and almost become a proverb" (3:449). Hunt helps perpetuate the book's sway by reprinting Shelley's "Account of the Circumstances that gave rise to *Frankenstein*" (3:449–50). Extracts from Hunt's own attempt at fiction, *Sir Ralph Esher,* also appear in the *Tatler* (no. 432), by this time increasingly miscellaneous in its purview. Overall, the beacons of Hunt's *Tatler* book reviews are few, but they glow with the fire of one who recognized enduring literature at first glance and broadcast his firm judgments persuasively

Surveying its run shows the *Tatler*'s principals struggling against difficult conditions, trying to accommodate the needs of a small readership. Changes in format and price record a losing battle. Prominently announced variations in the price charged for each issue reflect the editors' struggle to attract and retain readers. From its inception through number 300 (August 1831) the *Tatler*'s price had remained twopence. Thereafter, as Hunt declares proudly in number 295, he will offer "A Daily Paper, for a Penny a Day" since he is "desirous of not being outdone by a clever contemporary." Hunt proclaims this reduction with great fanfare in number 301 and continues the self-advertisement in notices printed in the next three issues. Still, Hunt continued to lose money. The new series, occasioned by these losses, also reduced its prices. These reductions adumbrate its rapid failure. At the end of March 1832 when Seton offers eight-page quarto issues thrice weekly, he announces with satisfaction that the price for each will remain a penny; three months later (13/14 June) he reduced the periodical to four pages, quarto, "for financial reasons"; and the weekly *Tatler,* which began on 28 July at a price of threepence, is finally cut to twopence in the penultimate issue 58, published on 29 September. Nevertheless, none of the price manipulations—effects of the journal's failure, rather than causes—rendered it profitable.

The additions and permutations of regular features exhibit an increasing diffuseness, due to the loss of Hunt's singular voice and of the journal's original purpose. These alterations exemplify the modest rise and fall of the *Tatler*. Hunt's journal began featuring "The Play-Goer By the Original Theatrical Critic in the *Examiner*," with its appropriately titled, recognizable personality reporting first-hand on that evening's theater, evaluating plays, performers, and performances, and sketching audience responses. During Hunt's periods of illness and increasingly near the end of his tenure, however, others write bland critiques under this heading; in the inferior new series, the column's new title reflects its loss of individual vision: it is denominated, vaguely, "Theatricals." "The Reader," another initial feature whose title aptly describes a column centered on an individual's—Hunt's—response to current literature, becomes the impersonal "Notices of New Books" in number 111, and beginning in number 449 it is further reduced to "Glances at New Books," a title retained throughout the new series. Where Hunt had critically evaluated a text, or joined a literary skirmish, or predicted with unusual accuracy a popular or a neophyte author's fate in his early writing for the *Tatler*, after mid-November 1830 miscellaneous correspondence often replaces the book reviews. Or when a review appears, one encounters in place of detailed and lively literary discussions by one who was friends with Byron, Shelley, Keats, and Hazlitt a mere summary of a book followed by lengthy, unevaluated extracts from it. As the new title indicates, finally we just "Glance at New Books." Indeed, after roughly 325 daily numbers, the character of the journal becomes increasingly miscellaneous: Hunt writes fewer "Play-Goer" columns and book reviews; letters on diverse topics appear increasingly; reprints of articles published elsewhere also increase. Correspondents debate digestion and mastication (after number 380), and articles on tea, coffee, and lobsters appear beside an essay on education (all in the representative number 432).

At the conclusion of his editorship Hunt cites illness as the principal cause for his withdrawal from the *Tatler*. "I commenced it in ill health, and quit it in worse. It was the necessity of going to the theatre night after night, and of writing the criticisms before I went to bed, that broke me down" (4:146). His creditors were also beginning to prosecute. Yet Hunt believes the paper has "done one good" for him: "It has enabled me to shew . . . that a life accustomed to hostility in politics does not prevent a man from having a habit of mind inclining to peace and good will" (4:146). Robert Seton, the new editor, explains that since Hunt had been gradually disengaging from his duties for "some time past," the changeover is "but nominal" (4:149). The newly edited journal remains committed to reform in the Commons following the resignation of ministers (12/14 May 1832). Seton publishes Hunt's poem, "The Late Mr. Bentham" (in n.s. no. 30:234–35); and a few other original compositions are scattered among remaining issues. Unfortunately, changes in publishing schedule, size, and length of each issue, along with the disappearance of timely reviews of theatricals, fundamentally destroy the periodical's unique character. It lacks focus and, without Hunt's personality at its center, quickly approaches its end. In a little over seven months after taking over Seton announced the

Tatler's cessation under his editorship. In its final number he states that "in about a fortnight" a new publisher, "Mr. Bucknall, King Street, Covent Garden," will continue the journal. His prediction, however, remained unfulfilled.

Notes

1. Titles and dates of Hunt's periodicals are recorded along with his bibliography in *The New Cambridge Bibliography of English Literature,* vol. 3, ed. George Watson (Cambridge, England, 1969), cols. 1216–23.

2. Leigh Hunt, *The Autobiography of Leigh Hunt; With Reminiscences of Friends and Contemporaries* (London, 1850), 3:215.

3. Hazlitt demurred at the new title upon learning of it and drew Reynell, who was also Hunt's brother-in-law, "into a window, and said, roguishly, 'What do you think, sir, of the ESOTERIC—or the EXOTERIC?' " W. Carew Hazlitt, *Memoirs of William Hazlitt, With Portions of His Correspondence* (London, 1867), 2:304–5.

4. *Autobiography,* 3:215.

5. Cosmo Monkhouse, *Life of Leigh Hunt* (London, 1893), p. 189. Monkhouse prints a letter of 1 May 1832 to an unnamed friend in which Hunt details his miserable health and poverty (pp. 189–91); the biographer attributes Hunt's "comparatively unproductive . . . next years" to lasting problems wrought by the demands of producing the *Tatler.* Edmund Blunden details "the dreary period after the fall of *The Tatler*" in *Leigh Hunt: A Biography* (London, 1930), pp. 244–47, 247 for the quotation.

6. Hunt began printing play-bills on 17 September 1830. Students of nineteenth-century theater might also wish to consult other theatrical papers, especially Nolan's forthright daily *Theatrical Observer* (1821–1823), the *Drama: or Theatrical Pocket Magazine* (monthly, 1821–1825), the 1828 weekly serial, the *Theatre,* and the important monthly *Dramatic Magazine* (1829–1831). For other titles, see Carl Joseph Stratman, *A Bibliography of British Dramatic Periodicals 1720–1960* (New York, 1962), James Fullerton Arnott and John William Robinson, *English Theatrical Literature 1559–1900: A Bibliography* (London, 1970), and the "Bibliographic Note" in Joseph W. Donohue, Jr., *Dramatic Character in the English Romantic Age* (Princeton, 1970), pp. 349–78.

7. The judgment cited belongs to Walter Graham, *English Literary Periodicals* (New York, 1930), p. 328. In his own day, Graham points out, as in ours, not one such daily periodical exists. For the best general discussion of literacy in nineteenth-century England, see Richard D. Altick, *The English Common Reader: A Social History of the Mass Reading Public 1800–1900* (Chicago, 1957), pp. 141–72.

8. In number 68 (21 November 1830) Hunt calls upon the "few" in France to "acquiesce" as the "many pronounce"; boldly, he prints "La Parisienne," words and music, across two pages. "Christmas Day," Hunt's occasional essay reminiscent of "A Day by the Fire" (*Reflector* 2, no. 4), voices hope that "present tribulations of Europe" will result in "glorious advances in the well-being of society" (1:385).

9. The review of the Tennysons appears in four issues, nos. 149 (24 February), 151 (26 February), 153 (1 March), and 155 (3 March 1831).

Information Sources

BIBLIOGRAPHY

Altick, Richard D. *The English Common Reader: A Social History of the Mass Reading Public 1800–1900.* Chicago, 1957.

Arnott, James Fullerton, and John William Robinson. *English Theatrical Literature 1559–1900: A Bibliography*. London, 1970.

Blunden, Edmund. *Leigh Hunt: A Biography*. London, 1930.

Graham, Walter. *English Literary Periodicals*. New York, 1930.

Hazlitt, W. Carew. *Memoirs of William Hazlitt, With Portions of his Correspondence*. 2 vols. London, 1867.

Houtchens, Lawrence Huston, and Carolyn Washburn Houtchens, eds. *Leigh Hunt's Dramatic Criticism 1808–1831*. New York, 1949.

———, eds. *Leigh Hunt's Literary Criticism*. New York, 1956.

———, eds. *Leigh Hunt's Political and Occasional Essays*. New York, 1962.

Hunt, Leigh. *The Autobiography of Leigh Hunt; with Reminiscences of Friends and Contemporaries*. 3 vols. London, 1850.

Landré, Louis. *Leigh Hunt (1784–1859): Contribution à l'Histoire du Romantisme Anglais*. 2 vols. Paris, 1936.

Monkhouse, Cosmo. *Life of Leigh Hunt*. London, 1893.

Stratman, Carl Joseph. *A Bibliography of British Dramatic Periodicals 1720–1960*. New York, 1962.

INDEXES

Volumes 1–3 and new series volume indexed.

REPRINT EDITIONS

None. Three volumes edited by Lawrence Huston Houtchens and Carolyn Washburn Houtchens and published in New York by Columbia University Press reprint articles from the *Tatler*. *Leigh Hunt's Dramatic Criticism 1808–1831* (1949), pp. 232–88, contains sixteen *Tatler* articles—most of which originally appeared in the regular column entitled "The Play-Goer"; *Leigh Hunt's Literary Criticism* (1956), pp. 275–400, reprints eight items, including the important "Mr. Hazlitt and the Utilitarians," the five-part "Lord Byron—Mr. Moore—and Mr. Leigh Hunt," and the four-part "A Review of Poems by Alfred and Charles Tennyson." *Leigh Hunt's Political and Occasional Essays* (1962), pp. 253–57, contains "Christmas Day."

Microform: English Literary Periodicals (UMI), reel 539.

LOCATION SOURCES

American

Complete run: Columbia University Library.

Partial runs: Widely available.

British

Complete runs: Bodleian Library; British Museum; Manchester Public Library; Victoria and Albert Museum Library.

Partial run: Hampstead Public Library.

Publication History

MAGAZINE TITLE AND TITLE CHANGES

The Tatler. (Subtitle varies: numbers 1–229 are subtitled "A Daily Journal of Literature and the Stage"; numbers 230–300, "A Daily Paper of Literature, Fine Arts, Music, and the Stage"; numbers 301–415, "A Daily Paper of Literature, Fine Arts, & Public Amusements"; and numbers 416–493, "A Daily Paper of Literature, Fine Arts, Music, and the Stage"; new series, vol. 1 is subtitled "A

Miscellany of Literature, Fine Arts, Music, and Theatricals,'' though through number 30 each issue's subtitle reads ''A Record of Books, Fine Arts, Music, Theatricals, and Improvements''; from number 31 to number 59 no subtitle appears.)

VOLUME AND ISSUE DATA

Volumes 1–3, numbers 1–415, September 1830–December 1831; volume 4, numbers 416–493, January–March 1832; new series, volume 1, numbers 1–59, 2/4 April–6 October 1832. (New series issue numbers appear in the upper left corner of each first page; entire series numbers are continued at lower left of each first page, numbers 494–552.)

FREQUENCY OF PUBLICATION

Daily.

PUBLISHERS

Volumes 1–2: J. Onwhyn, 4 Catherine Street, Strand, London. Volumes 3 and 4, and new series, volume 1: R. Seton, Tatler Office, 26 Brydges Street, Covent Garden, London.

EDITORS

Leigh Hunt, numbers 1–452. Robert Seton, numbers 453–493, new series 1–59.

Mark L. Greenberg

THEATRICAL INQUISITOR, THE

The *Theatrical Inquisitor,* first published in September 1812, underwent frequent changes of editors and format in its eight years of existence as a miscellany. Despite its emphasis on dramatic subjects, it carried a number of long literary reviews of Scott, Wordsworth, Coleridge, and, in particular, Byron. At the close of volume 1, an ''Address to Public'' promised a new arrangement with the ''strictest impartiality,'' to include: a biographical sketch of a dramatic personality with an engraved portrait; ''tales and romances,'' ''classic essays,'' ''original and fugitive poetry''; ''an ample review of literature''; ''notices of the fine arts, music, etc.''; and ''criticisms on the London and provincial theatres'' (1:2–3). The index to volume 1, divided into the headings ''Prose,'' ''Review,'' ''Stage,'' and ''Poetry,'' resembled that of the earlier *Monthly Mirror,** as did the format.

With volume 2 and the change of title to the *Theatrical Inquisitor, and Monthly Mirror,* a new editor stated in the preface that the original title ''precluded the miscellaneous communications of several valuable correspondents.'' Thus the format was broadened from theater to include ''essays on manners and literature,'' ''reviews of popular publications,'' ''literary curiosities,'' ''anecdotes,'' and other miscellaneous contributions (2:iii–iv). An alphabetical index accompanied this and subsequent volumes.

Early issues contained much theatrical material, as well as a list of theaters and their managers in England, Ireland, Scotland, Wales, and America; series, such as "Historical Sketch of the English Stage" and "History of Grecian Theatre"; a ranking of "the comparative merits of the principal tragedians and comedians of the present day, together with one formerly published of those of the time of Garrick" (1 [Oct. 1812]; 2 [1813]; 4 [May 1814]). Although striving for impartiality, the editor lamented that "memoirs of performers, it is well known, are generally supplied by their friends; of course impartiality is not to be looked for; accuracy . . . is all that can be expected" (7:iii).

The lead article for November 1813, signed "E. B. Inner Temple," presented "thoughts on the present state and moral effect of the drama." It was judged to be "rapidly on the decline" because the commercial and bureaucratic demands of the stage led to the production of primarily what pleased and drew crowds. Although the stage was reported free from the "immorality, licentiousness, [and] indecent language" of the Restoration, another cause of its decline was "the rage for novelty." The "love of bombast, show, and splendor" was criticized, along with bringing "horses, elephants, dogs, and *nondescripts*" on stage. An "indication of the improving taste . . . especially among the middling classes" was evident in the "rage for pantomime and buffoonery declining" in favor of "dramatic dialogue" (3:195–200). However, another correspondent wrote that *"burlesquing* folly is generally more efficacious than *seriously censuring"* those displaying "selfish views, egotism, and ostentation" in public life (2:344).

The tone of the *Theatrical,* despite its desire for "rigorous impartiality," was often cutting and vituperative (cf. 2:iv). On two occasions it attacked Methodism and the *Evangelical Magazine.* It also engaged in a controversy with a correspondent for a letter asserting the identity of Cerberus as "G. S." (1 [Oct.–Nov. 1812]). Its literary reviews were usually marked by a hostile tone and stereotypical judgments. "Rejected Addresses," parodying contemporary poets, was reviewed in seven pages with lengthy extracts. Reviews of popular writers were often long, but primarily made up of extracts, as in the twelve pages on Scott and nine on Hogg. Burns, however, was praised for his "natural simplicity" in a ten-page analytical essay, signed "H."

In a two-part review of Wordsworth's *Peter Bell* and *The Waggoner,* which ran to a total of fifteen pages, of which nine were extracts, the reviewer's comments and judgments were mostly derivative. Although Wordsworth's works were praised for "that genuine merit, which secures for them a large body of admirers, amongst people of undoubted taste, and a permanent station amongst our standard poets," the familiar charge of "affectation of simplicity" was stressed (14:369–76, 441–49).

Almost all of Byron's publications from *The Giaour* (1813) to *Childe Harold IV* (1818) were reviewed, each receiving the conventional mixture of praise and censure. The reviewer of *The Giaour* judged that Byron was sacrificing "the prospect of lasting fame, to the desire of immediate notoriety." The reviewer of the *Prisoner of Chillon* volume regretted that Byron's reputation was falling. In a two-part review of *Childe Harold IV,* however, Byron was compared favorably with Rousseau, for "tenderness and susceptibility of feeling" and "egotism" which nevertheless produced "a mysterious kind of sorrow" (3:48–50; 10:43–48; 13:217–21, 289–94). Byron's *Manfred* was condemned as "repulsive" and "incestuous poison," a bad influence on youth. "This book must either be suppressed or we shall proscribe it altogether." In contrast, Shelley's *The Cenci* was not condemned for the theme of incest. The thirteen-page review, with nine pages of extracts, concluded: "As a first dramatic effort, *The Cenci* is unparalleled for the beauty of every attribute with which the drama can be endowed" (11:120–27; 14:205–18).

Towards the end of its run, for its last eleven numbers, the *Theatrical Inquisitor* merged with the *London Magazine, and Monthly Critical and Dramatic Review,* one of the rival publications it had earlier criticized (16:32–38).

Information Sources

BIBLIOGRAPHY
Hayden, John O. *The Romantic Reviewers: 1802–24*. Chicago, 1969.
INDEXES
Each volume indexed.
REPRINT EDITIONS
Microform: English Literary Periodicals (UMI), reels 591–593.
LOCATION SOURCES
American
Complete runs: Brooklyn Public Library; Harvard University Library; U. S. Library of Congress; University of Michigan Library.
Partial runs: Widely available.
British
Complete run: British Museum.
Partial runs: Birmingham Public Library; Bodleian Library; Cambridge University Library; Edinburgh University Library; John Rylands Library (Manchester); National Library of Scotland; St. Andrews University Library.

Publication History

MAGAZINE TITLE AND TITLE CHANGES
The Theatrical Inquisitor; or Literary Mirror. By Cerberus, September 1812–January 1813. *The Theatrical Inquisitor, and Monthly Mirror,* February 1813–June 1819. *Theatrical Inquisitor,* July–December 1819. *Theatrical Inquisitor, and Monthly Mirror,* January–November 1820. (In January merged with *London Magazine, and Monthly Critical and Dramatic Review.*)
VOLUME AND ISSUE DATA
Volumes 1–16, September 1812–June 1820; new series, numbers 1–5, July–November 1820. (Among the many errors in pagination and dating are: 1 [January 1813] misdated December 1812; two issues dated January 1814, the first ending volume 3, the second beginning volume 4 [regular semi-annual volumes begin with volume 4]; volume 7 [November 1815] misdated June 1815; title page of volume 15 [July–December 1819] misdated to January probably because of

the "Supplementary Number" added to December; and volume 16 [April 1820] misdated May.)

FREQUENCY OF PUBLICATION

Monthly.

PUBLISHERS

Volume 1: Sherwood, Neely and Jones, Paternoster Row, London. Volumes 2– n.s., number 5: C. Chapple, Pall Mall, London.

EDITORS

Unknown, but internal evidence suggests changes in February 1813, January 1814, August 1814, January 1818, and July 1819.

Nathaniel Teich

TRIPOD, THE. See SATIRIST, THE

U

UNIVERSAL MAGAZINE, THE. See AAAJ

——— W ———

WATCHMAN, THE

When Coleridge began the *Watchman*[1] in 1796—serving as its publisher, editor, and chief contributor—he had just married Sara Fricker and was living in Bristol, casting about for funds after his plan to set up "Pantisocracy" in a Utopian community in America had failed. In addition, he and Robert Southey were lecturing in a fiercely antigovernment vein. On 29 October 1795 King George III had been booed and threatened with stones, and his carriage all but demolished by a mob crying out against the war. Other demonstrations against the bread shortage and against Prime Minister William Pitt the Younger alarmed Pitt and caused his Tory ministry to introduce the Seditious Meetings and Treasonable Practices bills in Parliament; the "Gagging Acts" became law on 18 December 1795.[2] Not only radicals, but many prominent Whigs as well protested. Such events provided the impetus for the magazine Coleridge had been pondering both to support himself and to fill a need in the English Midlands. Birmingham and Manchester were still unfranchised, and industrialists and workers alike tended to be Dissenters, alienated from the English war. Except for the *Cambridge Intelligencer,* edited by Coleridge's friend Benjamin Flower, local publications in the Midlands generally reported only the news provided in government communiqués.

In addition to political impetus, there was also a religious one. Coleridge was deeply involved in Unitarianism, whose most prominent ministers included Joseph Priestley and Richard Price. Both had written and spoken strongly against government policies. Coleridge himself was preaching sermons in Unitarian chapels, often in a political vein. Unitarians opposed the war, pleaded for the poor, called for a private boycott of the West Indian rum and sugar produced by slave labor, decried Anglican clerical support for the war, and favored the liberal Whigs, led by Charles James Fox, in opposition to Pitt.

All these ideas found outlet in the *Watchman,* whose name was perhaps derived from the Old Testament or from a speech of the great Whig advocate Thomas Erskine.[3] Coleridge's prospectus indicated that his "Miscellany" would be published every eighth day (to avoid the Stamp Tax and its contribution to war) for fourpence, or a halfpenny less than a four-page London newspaper. It would comprise thirty-two pages octavo, bindable as an "Annual Register." Besides news it would contain "original Essays and Poetry, chiefly or altogether political," and no advertisements. A principal aim was to oppose the Two Acts (although the *Watchman* did not pursue this purpose). The motto, derived from John 8:32, was to be "That All may know the Truth; and that the Truth may make us Free!!" The editor offered himself to the public "as a faithful WATCHMAN, to proclaim the State of the Political Atmosphere, and preserve Freedom and her friends from the attacks of Robbers and Assassins!!" The excited tone is only occasional in the *Watchman* itself.

Coleridge hoped to have contributions from friends, but he could not pay them; the physician Thomas Lovell Beddoes and the Unitarian minister John Edwards provided most of the original pieces not written by Coleridge. Other contributors included William Frend, deprived of his Cambridge fellowship for a "blasphemous" pamphlet; Thomas Poole, a tanner friend of Coleridge; and William Gilbert, a Bristol poet. In the manner of the time, much was reprinted from literary anthologies and London newspapers, chiefly the *Morning Chronicle* and the *Star,* which were closest to Coleridge's own views. These views bordered on the "Jacobin" or pro-French, but Coleridge's attitude toward the French was to cool as the *Watchman* proceeded.[4] He travelled through the Midlands in January, culling, he claimed, nearly a thousand subscribers.

The first number appeared on 1 March 1796. The leading essay elaborated on what the prospectus had claimed—that knowledge is power—and deplored the cost of information to the poor. Fair book reviews were promised, and in this issue appeared Coleridge's own critique of Burke's *Letter to a Noble Lord.* The many vain "Motions for Peace" made in Parliament over the preceding few years were cogently summarized. "Foreign Intelligence," from London papers, touched on recent events in France and noted Coleridge's "deep concern" at a French bill limiting press freedom. George Washington's thanks for a French flag, an official gift from France, was printed verbatim. "Domestic Intelligence" described the arrival home of an English regiment decimated by yellow fever in the West Indies, quoted antiwar sentiments from Southey's *Joan of Arc,* attacked Pitt via the *Morning Post,* and reported on the Lords debates and the Commons debate on the high cost of the war.

Despite this brave start, Coleridge never exactly determined his audience and tended to publish what was of interest to himself.[5] As a miscellany, much of the *Watchman* is entertaining to the modern reader (aided by Lewis Patton's notes); it reveals that Coleridge was well versed in the issues and personalities of the day. Light-hearted items, often satirical, and love poems are interspersed with more serious items, such as several dispatches from General Buonaparte on his Italian victories, harbingers of a threatening future. Number 8 for 27 April prints Coleridge's "Remonstrance to the French Legislators," which shows Coleridge's growing disillusion with the French for having rejected British peace overtures for reasons that seemed to him and many others spurious. Few crucial issues, except parliamentary reform, escaped Coleridge's busy patchwork. These issues included the slave trade, the Irish question, Catholic emancipation, poverty, trade, government expenditure, arrests under the Gagging Acts, liberty at home and abroad, game laws, the dog tax, erection of military barracks, famine, taxation, and drunkenness, as well as tyranny and the aristocracy. There also appeared some interesting anecdotes, a piece on hydrophobia, one on the new canals, and another on cockfights as a substitute for war. In the first issue he dispensed with "Court News" with the remark, "On Thursday the Queen had a drawing-room at St. James's Palace, *and all that—.*"

As for the "literary" content of the *Watchman,* number 1 contains the poem "To a Young Lady, with a Poem on the French Revolution," regretting the terrible toll of the war, and Coleridge's review of Burke's *Letter to a Noble Lord,* the best of the *Watchman* run. In number 2 appears an extract from Coleridge's poem "Religious Musings," attacking the "Kings and Chief Captains of the World" who are bringing "black Ruin" on the peaceful pursuits of pious men and women; an English imitation of a nonpolitical Latin poem by a contemporary Polish writer; a French verse lampoon; and an excerpt from the popular sonneteer William Lisle Bowles: all to illustrate certain aspects of the news.

Number 3 includes a "Historical Sketch" of the Germans by Coleridge and Southey, based upon their lectures, and a lengthy editorial discussion of new Shakespearean manuscripts that had supposedly been unearthed by the son of the bookseller, Samuel Ireland. They were treated cautiously in case of forgery, which was later proved. *Votrigern,* the alleged discovery, was already in London rehearsal. Coleridge's "Elegy" demonstrates through the story of two lovers that riches are not all; his "Hour When We Shall Meet Again" and "Lines on the Portrait of a Lady" are love poems, followed by "The Braes of Yarrow" by the Scottish poet John Logan, perhaps sent in by Charles Lamb. "Supposition" is political verse satire by a Birmingham contributor. Also in this issue are a strong editorial essay on "Modern Patriotism," and a review of Beddoes's *Letter to . . . Pitt* on how to feed the poor, a work cited as humane but impractical.

Number 4 provides another excerpt from "Religious Musings," and a further short poem of Coleridge's is embedded in his fine essay "On the Slave Trade." "A Morning Effusion" may also be his. "Invocation to Liberty" and an epigram represent political verse by minor contemporaries. Number 5 contains two sonnets with political overtones by Coleridge's brother-in-law Robert Lovell, Coleridge's sonnet "To Mercy" attacking "Iscariot" Pitt, and his "Recollection" of childhood, an attractive lyric. His review of Count Rumford's *Essays* shows his interest in Rumford's experiments in providing occupation for returned soldiers. An antiwar poem by William Crowe, previously rejected for reading at the Duke of Portland's installation as chancellor of Oxford University, finds a place here. Two verse epigrams are reprinted from an eighteenth-century Irish anthology that Coleridge used as a source. In the previous issue "Modern Patriotism" had been a veiled attack on the controversial William Godwin, author of the *Enquiry Concerning Political Justice* and the novel *Caleb Williams*. "To Caius Gracchus" is Coleridge's prose answer to a pro-Godwin critic; it promises a series of articles on Godwin's weaknesses that never appeared.

Number 6 includes only two "literary" items—an uncredited political sonnet on a whale and Coleridge's fine lines on observing a blossom in February: "This dark, freeze-coated, hoarse, teeth-chattering month." Number 7 contains only "An Irregular Ode to the Moon" by Thomas Dermody, from the Irish anthology. "To a Primrose," from the same source, appears in number 8. Here Coleridge also reprints a delightful spoof by his friend Richard Porson, the great classics professor of Cambridge, claiming, under the pseudonym of "S. England," to have discovered some fragments of Sophocles. The piece was inspired by the failure of *Vortigern* at the Drury Lane on April 2, as reported by Coleridge in number 6.

Number 9 reviews Beddoes's hostile *Essays on the Public Merits of Mr. Pitt*, to which Coleridge gives considerable space and thought, and quotation. A piece on the French poet Louis de Boissy proves merely pathetic anecdote. A four-line epitaph on an infant is Coleridge's, but prose translations from Esthonian ballads come from the same source as the de Boissy piece. Two juvenile nature sonnets by Dermody are reprinted from the Irish anthology. Number 10 includes a poem on love by William Gilbert, reprints from the *Monthly Magazine** a memorial to one deceased, and provides a sonnet on Lord Shelburne by Beddoes.

With the tenth issue, for Friday, 13 May, the *Watchman* came to an end. "The reason," Coleridge announced, "is short and satisfactory: The work does not pay its expences." Hoping it will not be said of him, "O Watchman! thou hast watched in vain!," he recommends his readers to Flower's *Cambridge Intelligencer* and the new *Monthly Magazine* of Richard Phillips, which, close in philosophy to the *Watchman,* had ample funds and paid its writers. With these—to Coleridge's barely concealed relief—he finds it impossible to compete. Some of the *Watchman*'s readers, like William Roscoe, regretted its going; others had been irked by the absence of local news and the heavy use of second-hand material. The number of original pages fell steadily from twenty-eight in number 1 to less than two in number 10, and numerous borrowings, even from Coleridge himself, were not acknowledged in every case. Interest in the *Watchman* must be centered, then, on the kind of material Coleridge chose to print, borrowed or not. Enormous work went into the reading, copying, production, and shipping involved. Apart from his book publisher Joseph Cottle's help with production and shipping, the rest was entirely Coleridge's enterprise.

The *Watchman,* though a valiant effort produced by its editor amid all kinds of domestic upset, is important now chiefly to students of Coleridge and the Romantics. It reveals how deeply and in what way politics was part of their outlook. In view of Coleridge's later and continuing recognition as a seminal influence in English literature and thought, the *Watchman* may be said today to have a scope and significance hardly evident in its brief lifetime.

Notes

1. The most useful edition of the *Watchman* is Lewis Patton's edition, in S. T. Coleridge, *Collected Works* (Princeton, 1970), which has an excellent introduction and notes, and to which this discussion is much indebted.
2. See Patton, pp. xxxviii–xli.
3. Ibid., p. xxix.
4. Ibid., p. xl. Coleridge claimed later never to have been a Jacobin, though John Thelwall disputed this. See Burton R. Pollin, "John Thelwall's Marginalia in a Copy of Coleridge's *Biographia Literaria*," *Bulletin of the New York Public Library* 74 (1970):81.
5. John Colmer, *Coleridge, Critic of Society* (Oxford, 1959), pp. 37, 50.

Information Sources

BIBLIOGRAPHY

Albrecht, W. B. "An Annotated Copy of *The Watchman*." *The Wordsworth Circle* 9 (1978):106–7.
Bate, W. J. *Coleridge*. New York, 1968. [See also Coleridge biographies by Chambers, Cooke, Hanson, and Lefebure, all of which discuss the *Watchman* from slightly different points of view.]
Coleridge, E. H. "Chapter V" of his unpublished life of Coleridge. In E. C. Blunden and E. L. Griggs, *Coleridge: Studies by Several Hands on the One Hundredth Anniversary of His Death*. 1934. Reprint. New York, 1970.
Coleridge, Samuel Taylor. *Biographia Literaria*. Edited by John Shawcross. 2 vols. Oxford, 1907.
———. *Collected Letters, Vol. 1, 1785–1800*. Edited by E. L. Griggs. 1956. Reprint. Oxford, 1966.
———. *Collected Works: Number 2, The Watchman*. Edited by Lewis Patton. Princeton, 1970. [On Coleridge as journalist, see also the introduction to number 3, *Essays on His Times*. Edited by D. V. Erdman. Princeton, 1978.]
Colmer, John. *Coleridge, Critic of Society*. Oxford, 1959.
Cottle, Joseph. *Reminiscences of Samuel Taylor Coleridge and Robert Southey*. 1847. Reprint. Highgate, 1970.
Erdman, D. V. "Coleridge as Editorial Writer." In *Power and Consciousness*. Edited by C. C. O'Brien and W. D. Vanech. New York, 1969.
Johnson, S. F. "Coleridge's *The Watchman*: Decline and Fall." *Review of English Studies*, n.s. 4 (1953):47–48.
Lamb, Charles and Mary. *The Letters of Charles and Mary Anne Lamb*. Edited by Edwin W. Marrs, Jr. Ithaca, N.Y., 1975.
Miller, J. T., Jr. "Ideology and Enlightenment: The Political and Social Thought of Samuel Taylor Coleridge." *Dissertation Abstracts International* 38 (1977):3519–A.

Paul-Emile, B. "Samuel Taylor Coleridge as Abolitionist." *Ariel* 5 (April 1974):59–75.

Priestley, Mary Ellen. "English Syntax in the Early Prose of Samuel Taylor Coleridge: A New Reading of the *Watchman,* 1796." Ph.D. dissertation, University of Alabama, 1967.

Raskopf, F. J. "Samuel Taylor Coleridge's Concept of Freedom of the Press as Revealed in *The Watchman* and *The Friend.*" *Dissertation Abstracts International* 40 (1979):1079–A.

Watson, George. "The Revolutionary Youth of Wordsworth and Coleridge." *Critical Quarterly* 18 (1976):49–66.

Whalley, George, "Coleridge and Southey at Bristol." *Review of English Studies,* n. s. 1 (1950):324–40.

Woodring, Carl. *Politics in the Poetry of Coleridge.* Madison, Wis., 1961.

INDEXES

Indexed in S. T. Coleridge, *Collected Works,* ed. Lewis Patton, Princeton, 1970.

REPRINT EDITIONS

Volume 2 in S. T. Coleridge, *Collected Works,* ed. Lewis Patton, Princeton, 1970.

LOCATION SOURCES

American

Complete runs: Boston Public Library; Harvard University Library; Ohio State University Library; U. S. Library of Congress; University of California at Los Angeles Library; University of Texas Library; Yale University Library.

Partial runs: Newberry Library; Western Kentucky State College Library.

British

Complete runs: Athenaeum Library (Liverpool); Bristol Public Library; British Museum; John Rylands Library (Manchester).

The London copy has Coleridge's manuscript notes and the prospectus.

Partial run: Bodleian Library.

Publication History

MAGAZINE TITLE AND TITLE CHANGES

The Watchman.

VOLUME AND ISSUE DATA

Numbers 1–10, 1 March–13 May 1796.

FREQUENCY OF PUBLICATION

Weekly.

PUBLISHER

S. T. Coleridge, Bristol. (Also listed is Coleridge's agent: Parsons, Paternoster Row, London.)

EDITOR

Samuel Taylor Coleridge.

Winifred F. Courtney

WESTMINSTER REVIEW, THE

In the highly politicized world of nineteenth-century quarterlies, the *Edinburgh Review** spoke for the Whigs, the *Quarterly Review** for the Tories, and, from its opening issue in January 1824, the *Westminster Review* allegedly for the Benthamites. Consequently, literary historians have emphasized that the *Westminster* considered literature unworthy of serious attention. There is some truth to this view, especially during the *Westminster*'s first decade. An article in the first issue, for example, claimed that a poet was, by his very nature, *"not a reasoner"* (1:18–27). Those poets were praised whose work provided "instructions" for something useful, as Dante's was for providing ideas for Italian political regeneration (7:153–69). One reviewer indicated that the sciences—of politics, law, economy, commerce, mathematics, and mechanics—and not "mere literature" had brought civilization to its heights; in fact, "to be literary . . . is the disease of the age" (4:147–76). Similarly, when John Stuart Mill attacked English literature as "mere amusement" calculated to show off "beauties of style," he appeared to be condemning his subject for being useless or trivial (6:62–103).

But such a view is oversimplified. Mill in particular was increasingly aware of the importance of literature in an individual's emotional and psychological development, and even indicated that many of the *Westminster*'s reviewers enjoyed reading poetry and fiction.[1] In much of his criticism, in fact, he valued literature for more than Utilitarian reasons. His defense of Tennyson's poetry against John Wilson Croker's attack in the *Quarterly,* for example, was decidedly non-Utilitarian: he found a strong "creative" power in the young poet, a "high degree of excellence in the art of painting a picture to the inward eye."[2]

Among *Westminster* authors Mill was not alone in his enlightened approach to literature. W. J. Fox praised Coleridge's work by indicating that the Benthamite concerns of utility and pleasure "exist in union" with the imaginative concerns of poetry. Fox further emphasized "the truth of the emotions" in Coleridge's poems (12:1–31). When Mill became less active on the *Westminster* after 1840, the review's literary criticism adhered even less to a strict Utilitarian point of view.

Ironically, perhaps, the very first article to appear in the *Westminster* was a literary review, by Fox, of J. S. Boone's poem, "Men and Things." After questioning why Boone had chosen that genre for his "didactic exposition," Fox concluded that Boone's ideas would have been "altogether unpalatable" in prose (1:1–18). There was for Fox, then, a validity to verse; even this early, in the *Westminster*'s first article, literature was not viewed as trivial. Each issue of the early *Westminster Review* contained at least one major review article on literature. Its literary tastes were catholic: throughout its existence, besides British literature ranging from Anglo-Saxon poetry to contemporary fiction, it also discussed foreign literature from ancient Greek tragedies to modern French novels. In his review of *The Memoirs of Vidocq* in July 1829, furthermore, Henry Southern offered this witty but trenchant observation on Utilitarian literary critics: "Those benevolent individuals who would regulate the world after the best possible methods, may learn that there may be instruction in a pleasant work, in a book of an agreeable style, and written in a light, and sometimes even in a picturesque manner" (11:162–80).

But the *Westminster Review* was not intended to be a literary journal, nor indeed did it ever become one. Jeremy Bentham had approved including literary articles because they were expected in a review seeking prominence and influence. For years before they founded the *Westminster,* in fact, Bentham and James Mill had discussed the need for a quarterly publication that would be "liberal" in its discussions, that would, in other words, propound the ideals of Benthamism on political, social, and economic issues. When Bentham was able to finance such a venture, James Mill was unable because of his position at India House to become editor. Bentham then asked John Bowring, his protégé, and a merchant and linguist. Much to the consternation of James Mill and his son John Stuart, Bowring accepted. The Mills viewed Bowring as a sycophant, and their dislike for him festered during the four years that they were initially associated with the review. Henry Southern became literary editor and for a few years was co-editor with Bowring.

The Mills were pleasantly surprised by the success of the first issue, which quickly sold out its original 2,000 copies. A major reason for this early success was James Mill's article about the *Edinburgh Review*—in keeping with Bentham's desire to review competing reviews—which actually became a Radical manifesto on the British political system (1:206–49). But the Mills still had serious reservations about Bowring's ability to reflect their ideas; to compensate, John Stuart Mill became the periodical's most prolific early contributor. But he also became increasingly aware that the *Westminster* was "unsatisfactory to those whose opinions on all subjects it was supposed specially to represent."[3] Until 1828 he and his father wrote for the review, much of the time (because of its financial problems) without pay.

Their contributions soon ceased. Knowing of their unhappiness with him, Bowring allegedly negotiated for them to take control of the *Westminster* without him as editor. Instead, he concluded a business arrangement with Colonel Thomas Perronet Thompson which transferred control to Thompson. The Mills were furious, and immediately began to plan their own periodical in opposition to the *Westminster*. Not until mid-1834 were they able to take action, however, when Sir William Molesworth asked the younger Mill to direct the forthcoming *London Review*. Like his father before him, John Stuart Mill was unable to become the official editor; but he did control editorial policy for the *London*'s four issues in 1835 and 1836. In 1836 Molesworth bought the *Westminster* from Thompson and Bowring, and Mill served as *de facto* editor of the newly named *London and Westminster Review*.

It is impossible to discuss the *Westminster Review* under any of its titles without emphasizing the significant contributions of John Stuart Mill. Some of those contributions took the form of particular reviews that he wrote. His 1835 review of Tennyson's 1830 and 1832 volumes of poetry, for example, helped establish Tennyson as an author worthy of serious consideration. His early review of Carlyle's *The French Revolution*, "not so much a history, as an epic poem," successfully pre-empted some of the negative criticism Mill anticipated the work would have received from "commonplace critics, all whose rules and modes of judgment it set at defiance" (27:17–53).[4] His literary influence extended beyond these and other important reviews, however. Under Mill's guidance, the *London Review* in 1835 and 1836 included more discussions of literature than did the *Westminster Review* during the same time. And with Mill in charge of the combined *London and Westminster Review*, literary criticism remained an important part of each issue.

It was common practice in the major reviews to use "review articles" less as a means of discussing other works (though they were discussed) than as the starting point for the reviewers' own ideas. Mill acknowledged this fact by introducing the "non-review" article in the first issue of the *London*, and continued the practice through the April 1837 issue of the *London and Westminster*. It was, however, an idea before its time; the experiment was discontinued. But the time was more propitious in July 1867, the next appearance of a non-review article. Thereafter, such articles became more common in the *Westminster*, which eventually eliminated all reviews except for brief paragraphs in each issue-ending "Belles Lettres" section: in January 1885, for example, sixty-nine books were "reviewed" in twenty pages.

While writing for the original *Westminster*, Mill had recognized the need to broaden the review's appeal by eliminating what he had come to see as the narrowness of strict Benthamism; under his guidance, the *London* and then the combined *London and Westminster* became a home for liberal thought generally, rather than for any particular brand of liberalism. He made it so in two ways, through some of his own essays and through an important editorial policy change.

In its first decade, the *Westminster Review* had jealously guarded the identity of authors of its reviews. Like its two great rivals, the *Edinburgh* and the *Quarterly*, it enforced a policy of anonymity that allowed each reviewer to speak with the authority of the entire publication. When Mill helped establish the *London Review* he required every article to be signed, by name, pseudonym, initial, or picture (Leigh Hunt used the *Examiner*'s hand-with-pointing-finger), in some consistent manner. Thus, though a particular writer's identity might not be made known, all articles by the same writer would be identifiable, and the views expressed would thus be known to be the writer's and not the editor's. Although strict adherence to this revolutionary policy lasted only as long as Mill controlled editorial policy, some *Westminster Review* articles were "signed" in each issue into the early 1850s.

Besides any immediate effect of some of the reviews that Mill wrote, two of his essays were particularly calculated to broaden the *London and Westminster's* audience. In his essays on Bentham in 1838 and Coleridge in 1840, Mill subsequently admitted that he might have been too extreme, that he might have overemphasized the weaknesses of Bentham's ideas and the strengths of Coleridge's in order to compensate for what he knew were his readers' predilections (29:476–506; 33:257–302).[5] The issue which contained his essay on Coleridge was Mill's last as *de facto* editor. In 1840 William E. Hickson and Henry Cole bought the periodical, became co-editors, and adopted the original name. Mill continued to contribute occasionally, but his major influence on the *Westminster Review* was over.

In 1846 the *Westminster* absorbed the *Foreign Quarterly Review,** and for five years each volume carried an unwieldy title, the *Westminster and Foreign Quarterly Review*. But the publication was always the *Westminster* in spirit, "an organ of enlightened radical thought"; the former *Foreign Quarterly* was relegated to a small section of "Foreign Literature," in smaller print, at the end of each issue.[6] Although the volumes' titles reverted to the shorter *Westminster Review* in 1852, when John Chapman bought it, individual issues retained the longer title until 1887.

While no one could take Mill's place, Hickson brought to the review a young man who was to exercise a significant influence on the periodical's literary standards, George Henry Lewes. Over the next two decades, for Hickson and then for Chapman, Lewes contributed articles on scientific and other non-literary subjects, but even more on literature, including selections for the newly established "Critical and Miscellaneous Notices," a section of brief reviews of recent publications. Lewes developed standards for literary criticism that indicate a surprisingly mature critical sense in so young a critic. In one of his earliest articles, on Shelley, he attacked the biographical approach to literary criticism, in favor of what has since been called the New Criticism: "The poems of every great man ought to, and do, speak for themselves with the most perfect completeness, needing no knowledge of the poet to make them clear." He also emphasized the concept of critical relativism: poets mirror, not eternal truths, but contemporary truths, he wrote; they reflect their age as their contemporaries view it; "critical evaluations, to have any validity, must reflect the changes" (35:303–44). And he employed a theory of realism, which had occasionally been mentioned in the *Westminster* and in other periodicals but had never been developed (cf. 6:103–12). Lewes may indeed have been the first among his contemporaries to use the test of realism as a significant criterion by which to judge the quality of fiction.[7] Writing for the *Westminster Review* for nineteen years, Lewes refined his ideas and applied them over a wide range of subjects, from "The Lady Novelists" in particular to "Realism in Art" generally. Because "realism" was the "basis of all art," as he wrote in 1858, he ultimately denied the distinction between art and reality. In fact, he maintained, art should intensify experience, not distort or falsify reality (70:488–518). This view of realism was important not only in itself but for the influence it apparently had on one of Lewes's co-workers at the *Westminster*, a woman who wrote for the periodical during the early and mid-1850s.

One of John Chapman's most important actions for literary posterity was his hiring of Marian Evans as sub-editor from January 1852 to January 1854. She was apparently the first woman to serve in that capacity for an English review.[8] Her initial task was to write the prospectus for the new series of the *Westminster Review* that Chapman, as proprietor and publisher, was also to edit. During the next five years, Miss Evans wrote at least sixteen reviews, including several for the "Belles Lettres" section, and revised many essays by other reviewers. Under her guidance, the short notices on contemporary literature that had been included in each issue were replaced by lengthy and coherent essays on current literature in England, America, Germany, and France.

Marian Evans and George Henry Lewes came to know each other during her years at the *Westminster*, and she was simultaneously developing the skills and literary theories underlying her eventual success as George Eliot. Lewes's discussions of realism in fiction apparently impressed her, perhaps because she was already thinking similarly. In her reviews of fiction, her chief test of merit was realism; she rarely discussed theme, plot, and character, except as they were "true to life."[9] In one of her most famous reviews, "Silly Novels by Lady Novelists," she found that most lady novelists—Jane Austen, Charlotte Brontë, Elizabeth Gaskell, and Harriet Martineau were exceptions—failed the test of realism, failed to provide "genuine observation, humour, and passion" (66:442–61).[10]

The confluence of these two intellects, Lewes's and Evans's, enabled the *Westminster Review* to regain in the 1850s the stature that it had enjoyed in the late 1830s under John Stuart Mill. And, like Mill's, Lewes's and Evans's influence was evident for years to come. Three decades later, in fact, realism was a dominant standard for *Westminster* writers. "The *accidents* of good novels are fictitious; the *essentials* are all real," and from "real men and women" in novels readers must be able to generalize "true types," one reviewer wrote in 1885 (123:53–100). A year later, a reviewer maintained that Flaubert's *Salambô* was "a story even more hideous and revolting than 'Madame Bovary' . . . without the redeeming merit of intense reality" (126:560–61). And the next year realism was still the standard: "Novels of 'life and manners' are all very well, but the novels that live the longest are those which place life first and foremost, and leave the manners pretty much to take care of themselves" (128:840–49).

By that time, the *Westminster Review* had adjusted to the changing realities of periodical publication: new monthly publications, more able to keep pace with rapid developments in all areas of Victorian life, and especially with the spate of books being published, had for years been drawing readers away from some of the quarterlies. John Chapman, finally unable to continue juggling his finances to support the *Review,* sold it to the newly formed Westminster Review Company. From April 1887 until its death in January 1914 it was published monthly, its articles shorter and less noteworthy than previously.

What is surprising is not that the *Westminster Review* failed in 1914, but that it lasted as long as it did. During much of its existence, it demanded radical reform—of Parliament in particular and the political process in general, of education, of sanitation. Its essays were well written, its points logically argued, its influence significant. But it was always in financial trouble. Early owners Bentham and Thompson each spent thousands of pounds of their own money to support it, and both Molesworth and Mill finally found the *London and Westminster Review* impossible to finance. Hickson and Chapman were more successful in reducing some expenditures, but apparently no one was able to increase circulation, and hence income, appreciably.

Despite its money problems, the *Westminster Review* under its various incarnations was always able to attract excellent writers and thinkers. In fact, the history of the *Westminster* is the history of illustrious men and women of the nineteenth century. Besides the individuals already mentioned, contributors included Edward Bulwer-Lytton, Thomas Carlyle, Edwin Chadwick, Albany Fonblanque, J. A. Froude, Edmund Gosse, W. R. Greg, T. H. Huxley, Harriet Martineau, George Meredith, Richard Monckton Milnes, Walter Pater, Mark Pattison, Thomas Love Peacock, J. A. Symonds, Herbert Spencer, John Sterling, and William Thackeray.

Yet, despite its "radical" positions (by nineteenth-century standards) on social and political issues, the *Westminster Review* was nonetheless a product of its age. Like the *Edinburgh* and the *Quarterly,* it often was politically motivated in areas where politics should not have been allowed to enter; the *Westminster* was, in other words, guilty of occasionally allowing non-literary concerns to affect its literary judgments. Its discussion of two authors may serve to exemplify the *Westminster*'s politicizing. In the early *Westminster,* Walter Scott received the most negative reviews of his career. While the criticisms had some basis in fact, the extent of the reviewers' vituperations was politically motivated: Scott was a leading Tory, an erstwhile contributor to the *Edinburgh Review,* and party to the development of the *Quarterly Review. Redgauntlet,* for example, was both damned and used as the damning agent for his other works: the story "is absurd in itself, and rendered more heavy by the clumsy way in which it is told. But still it contains particular passages of merit, and so far it is superior to its immediate predecessors" (2:179–94).

Charles Dickens, on the other hand, was generally well received by the *Westminster* early in his career. Although Dickens had trouble "developing character in action," Charles Buller wrote in 1837, Dickens's popularity was the legitimate result of his "great intrinsic powers of mind" (27:194–215). For William E. Hickson six years later, Dickens was "not a mere novelist" but an author who could "diffuse knowledge [and] promote happiness" (39:149–60; 40:446–60). However, the *Westminster*'s criticism took on a distinctly unfriendly tone after *Hard Times* attacked Utilitarianism in education and industry. Dickens was blamed as "the main instrument in the change which has perverted the novel from a work of art to a platform for discussion and argument" (82:24–49). In part, the change in attitude toward Dickens may have been due to shifting critical standards, especially the influence of G. H. Lewes and Marian Evans; in part, it may also have been the result of the reviewer's reaction to at least one of Dickens's subjects.

By the end of the nineteenth century, the *Westminster Review* itself had changed considerably. Although each issue still included "Belles Lettres," that section had become much shorter. The rest of the publication was devoted to colonial affairs, politics, and social questions, including an increasing number of articles on women's rights and women's place in a male-dominated society. In the second decade of the twentieth century, financial troubles, which had plagued the *Westminster* from its inception in 1824, finally provided the death blow: Nellie Chapman, a niece of Hannah Chapman who had helped her edit the review, failed to pay personal bills which she had, however, charged to the periodical.[11] With no indication to its readers that it would no longer appear, the *Westminster Review* quietly ceased publication with the January 1914 number.

Notes

(Old series volume numbers are used throughout.)

1. John Stuart Mill, *Autobiography* (Indianapolis, 1957), pp. 72–73, 86–118.
2. John Stuart Mill, "Tennyson's Poems," *The London Review* 1 (1835):402–24.
3. Mill, *Autobiography*, p. 63.
4. Mill discusses his purposes: ibid., p. 139.
5. Mill explained his reservations about these essays: ibid., pp. 140–141.
6. Walter E. Houghton, ed., *The Wellesley Index to Victorian Periodicals, 1824–1900* (Toronto, 1979), 3:540.
7. Lewes has been accorded that position by Edgar W. Hirshberg, *George Henry Lewes* (New York, 1970), p. 7.
8. Gordon S. Haight, *George Eliot and John Chapman* (New Haven, 1940), p. 46; George L. Nesbitt, *Benthamite Reviewing: The First Twelve Years of the "Westminster Review," 1824–1836* (New York, 1934), p. 172.
9. See William J. Hyde, "George Eliot and the Climate of Realism," *Publications of the Modern Language Association* 72 (1957):147–64.
10. For a good discussion of this article, see Richard Stang, "The Literary Criticism of George Eliot," *Publications of the Modern Language Association* 72 (1957):952–61.
11. *Wellesley Index*, p. 552 n. 111.

Information Sources

BIBLIOGRAPHY

de Groot, H. B. "The Status of the Poet in an Age of Brass: Isaac D'Israeli, Peacock, W. J. Fox and Others." *Victorian Periodicals Newsletter* no. 10 (1977):106–22.

Graham, Walter. *English Literary Periodicals*. 1930. Reprint. New York, 1966.

Haight, Gordon S. *George Eliot and John Chapman*. New Haven, 1940.

Hirshberg, Edgar W. *George Henry Lewes*. New York, 1970.

Houghton, Walter E., ed. *The Wellesley Index to Victorian Periodicals, 1824–1900.* Vol. 3. Toronto, 1979.

Hyde, William J. "George Eliot and the Climate of Realism." *Publications of the Modern Language Association* 72 (1957):147–64.

Nesbitt, George L. *Benthamite Reviewing: The First Twelve Years of the "Westminster Review," 1824–1836.* New York, 1934.

Stang, Richard. "The Literary Criticism of George Eliot." *Publications of the Modern Language Association* 72 (1957):952–61.

INDEXES

Each volume indexed, except final volume. Volumes 1–24, in volume 24; volumes 25–33 in volume 33. Volumes 1–13, separately published, in 1832. Series 1, volumes 1–24, separately published, 1836. Volumes 25–33, separately published, 1840. 1824–1881 in *Poole's Index.* 1836–1900 in *Wellesley Index* 3.

REPRINT EDITIONS

Microform: Academic Archives, Raleigh, N.C. English Literary Periodicals (UMI), reels 827–829. EP Group, Wakefield, England. Microcard Editions, Washington, D.C. Princeton Microfilm Corp., Princeton, N.J.

LOCATION SOURCES

American

Widely available.

British

Widely available.

Publication History

MAGAZINE TITLE AND TITLE CHANGES

The Westminster Review, January 1824–January 1836. *The London Review,* April 1835–January 1836 (republished as volumes 30 and 31 of the *Westminster Review*). *The London and Westminster Review,* April 1836–March 1840. *The Westminster Review,* June 1840–June 1846. *The Westminster and Foreign Quarterly Review,* October 1846–October 1851. *The Westminster Review,* January 1852–January 1914.

VOLUME AND ISSUE DATA

(*The Westminster Review*) Volume 1, number 1–volume 24, number 47, January 1824–January 1836.

(*The London Review*) Volume 1, number 1–volume 2, number 4, April 1835–January 1836 (republished as volumes 30 and 31 of the *Westminster Review*).

(*The London and Westminster Review*) Volume 25, number 48–volume 29, number 57, April 1836–August 1838 (double-numbered as volumes 3–7 to provide continuity with the *London Review*). Volumes 32–33, December 1838–March 1840 (by volume 33, issues are no longer cumulatively numbered, but instead are numbered 1 and 2 in each volume; thereafter, some volumes return to cumulative numbering of issues and others do not: volume 42, for example, contains numbers 82 and 83).

(*The Westminster Review*) Volumes 34–45, June 1840–June 1846.

(*The Westminster and Foreign Quarterly Review*) Volumes 46–56, October 1846–October 1851 (an edition of volume 46 with identical subject matter was also published as the *Foreign Quarterly and Westminster Review*).

(*The Westminster Review*) New series, volumes 1–71 (old series, volumes 57–127), January 1852–January 1887 ("The Westminster and Foreign Quarterly Review" is on each issue's title page through new series volume 70). Volumes 128–181, April 1887–January 1914. (Through volume 127, each volume consisted of two quarterly issues—volume 24 contained only the January 1836 issue, and volume 127 contained only the January 1887 issue. Volume 128 contained nine monthly issues, April–December 1887; thereafter, each volume contained six monthly issues, except for the final volume, which contained only the January 1914 issue.)

FREQUENCY OF PUBLICATION

Quarterly through January 1887; monthly from April 1887–January 1914.

PUBLISHERS (All addresses are in London)

Volumes 1–8, January 1824–July 1827: Baldwin, Cradock, and Joy. Volume 9, October 1827 and January 1828: Baldwin and Cradock. Volume 10, April 1828 and January 1829: J. C. Stevens, 4 York Street, Covent Garden. Volumes 11–20, July 1829–April 1834: Robert Heward, 2 Wellington Street, Strand/113 Strand/No. 5 Wellington Street, Strand. Volume 15, July and October 1830: information unavailable. Volume 21, July and October 1834: Robert Heward, No 5 Wellington Street, Strand. Simpkin and Marshall, Stationers' Court, Ludgate Street. Volume 22, January and April 1835: Simpkin and Marshall, Stationers' Court, Ludgate Street. T. C. Hansard, 32 Paternoster Row. Volume 23, July and October 1835: T. C. Hansard, 32 Paternoster Row. John Macrone, 3 St. James's Square. Volume 24, January 1836: information unavailable. Volumes 25–26, April 1836–January 1837: John Macrone, St. James's Square. Volumes 27–38, April 1837–October 1842 (except for volumes 30 and 31 below): Henry Hooper, 13 Pall Mall East. Volumes 30–31, April 1835–January 1836: Simpkin, Marshall, & Co., Stationers' Hall Court. Volumes 39–43, February 1843–June 1845: Samuel Clarke, 13 Pall Mall East. Volumes 44–53, September 1845–July 1850: George Luxford, 1 Whitefriars' Street. Volumes 54–56, October 1850–October 1851: Groombridge and Sons, 5 Paternoster Row. Volumes 57–72, January 1852–October 1859: John Chapman, 142 Strand/8 King William Street, Strand. Volumes 73–76, January 1860–October 1861: George Manwaring, 8 King William Street, Strand. Volumes 77–132, January 1862–December 1889: Trübner & Co., 60 Paternoster Row/8 and 60 Paternoster Row, 57 and 59 Ludgate Hill/Ludgate Hill. Volumes 133–137, January 1890–June 1892: Edward Arnold, 18 Warwick Square, Paternoster Row, E. C./37 Bedford Street, Strand, W. C. Volumes 138–141, July 1892–June 1894: Henry and Company, 6 Bouverie Street, Fleet Street, E. C. Volumes 142–151, July 1894–June 1899: Frederick Warne and Company, 15 Bedford Street, Strand. Volume 152, July–December 1899: information unavailable. Volume 153, January–June 1900: no publisher cited, 15 Bedford Street, Strand. Volumes 154–155, July 1900–June 1901: information unavailable. Volumes 156–162, July 1901–July 1904: R. Brimley Johnson, 8 York Buildings, Adelphi, W. C./4 Adam Street, Adelphi, W. C. Volumes 162–181, July 1904–January 1914: E. Marlborough and Co., 51 Old Bailey, E. C.

American edition: Leonard Scott & Co., New York (dates unknown).

EDITORS

The Westminster Review: John Bowring, editor or co-editor, January 1824–January 1836; Henry Southern, co–editor, January 1824–April or October 1827 or April 1828; Thomas Perronet Thompson, co-editor, January 1829–January 1836 (much of this time Thompson was actually in charge).

The London Review: Thomas Falconer, April 1835–January 1836.

The London and Westminster Review: Thomas Falconer, April 1836–April 1837; John Robertson, July 1837–March 1840. (John Stuart Mill was handling the actual editorial duties for *London Review* and *London and Westminster Review*.)

Westminster Review (and *Westminster and Foreign Quarterly Review*): William Edward Hickson and Henry Cole, June 1840; William Edward Hickson, September 1840–January 1851; Henry James Slack, April 1851; William Edward Hickson, June-October 1851; John Chapman, January 1852–November 1894 (George Eliot was sub-editor, January 1852–January 1854). Hannah Hughes Chapman, December 1894–January 1914(?) (her niece, Nellie Chapman, assisted her near the end of this period).

Roger P. Wallins

WRIGHT'S LONDON MAGNET. See LITERARY MAGNET, THE

————— Y —————

YELLOW DWARF, THE

The *Yellow Dwarf* represents a brief but fruitful collaboration between two friends, John Hunt and William Hazlitt. When John Hunt began the *Yellow Dwarf* in 1818 he was known as either a great or a notorious radical publisher. His progressive weekly paper, the *News*, commenced in 1805 and ran until 1839. Hunt started publishing the *Examiner** in 1808 with his younger brother Leigh Hunt, who continued as editor and principal contributor until 1821. And from 1811 to 1812 John published and Leigh edited the quarterly *Reflector*.* The brothers were such effective critics of the government that one of many printed attacks in the *Examiner*—"On the Character of the Prince Regent"—resulted in the imprisonment of each separately from 1813 to 1815. Undaunted, they continued work on their popular weekly in jail. For his political writing, John was again jailed in 1821–1822; and he was prosecuted in 1822–1823 for publishing Byron's "The Vision of Judgment" in the first number of the *Liberal** when a cautious John Murray had refused to print it. Thanks to the brothers' political activity and friendships with other writers, John became publisher of books by Byron, Shelley, Hazlitt, Bentham, and Leigh Hunt. By the time John Hunt retired from the publishing business and from the *Examiner* in 1826, his honesty, sincerity, and selfless dedication to principles of progressive, democratic government had earned the respect of many contemporaries. When in 1819 Hazlitt collected his *Political Essays, With Sketches of Public Characters,* many of which appeared in the *Yellow Dwarf,* he dedicated the volume to "John Hunt, . . . The tried, steady, zealous, and conscientious advocate of the liberty of his country, and the rights of mankind;—One of those few persons who are what they would be thought to be; sincere without offence, firm but temperate; uniting private worth to public principle; a friend in need, a patriot without an eye to himself; who never betrayed an individual or a cause he pretended to serve—in short, that rare character, a man of common sense and common honesty.''[1]

Precisely those qualities first attracted Hazlitt to John Hunt during Hazlitt's association with the *Examiner* (1815–1817). Indeed, throughout, Hazlitt's "main attachment to the *Examiner* had been to John Hunt.''[2] When the collaborators commenced the *Yellow Dwarf*, William Hazlitt was recognized as a zealous philosophical and political writer. He had written books on public affairs and on Malthus, and was the author of *The Eloquence of the British Senate* (1807), *Memoirs of the Late Thomas Holcroft* (1816), and most recently *The Round Table* (1817), a collection of essays mostly from the *Examiner*. He was also becoming famous as a frequent and controversial contributor to the *Morning Chronicle*, and *Champion*,* and the *Examiner*. During the *Examiner* years Hazlitt's career was in transition. He began turning toward the subjects for which we remember him: astute literary criticism and essays on contemporaries charged with the powerful political vision of his earlier writing. Hazlitt punctuated his new direction by beginning a series of lectures on the English poets in January 1818. His shifting, expanding interests and growing reputation united Hazlitt with his friend in 1818 when John Hunt gave "Hazlitt's political force and his own indomitable but undramatic liberalism a new medium of appeal.''[3]

That medium, the *Yellow Dwarf*, functioned predominantly as a political, and secondarily as a literary adjunct to the *Examiner*, which Hunt published simultaneously with it. Hazlitt's numerous contributions to the *Yellow Dwarf*, many valuable in themselves, illuminate also his transition from strictly political writing to literary and cultural criticism. Yet his treatments of most literary subjects in the journal, from Wordsworth and Coleridge to Moore and Byron's "Childe Harold," were informed by fiercely held political ideals. The *Yellow Dwarf*'s politics, like those of the *Examiner*, were reformist and democratic: Hunt and Hazlitt hated tyranny, and supported Catholic Emancipation and the abolition of slavery, reform of criminal law, and fundamental, democratic changes for Parliament. Although Hunt reflected self-consciously at the conclusion of the *Yellow Dwarf*'s first issue that it "has assumed a character more entirely political than it was in the contemplation of its projectors to give it" (no. 1:8), the journal maintained that character throughout its brief run. And despite that brevity and each number's diminutive, eight-page length, Hunt's *Dwarf* published articles by John Hamilton Reynolds, a portion of Keats's *Endymion* prior to the poem's full publication, and important essays by Hazlitt and excerpts from his current lecture series on the English poets.

The *Yellow Dwarf* now occupies a slim folio volume and complete runs of it are quite rare. Its twenty-one numbers were published within less than five months, from 3 January to 23 May 1818. Two columns of print, surrounded by a thin black border and separated by a central vertical line, appeared on each page. The journal sold each Saturday for fourpence.

The periodical's amusing and unusual title generally arrests contemporary readers. But in the early nineteenth century several popular and extremely serious political journals included "Dwarfs" of various hues in their titles. The association between political action and the little folks seems appropriate once we recall their traditional deportment. In folklore and mythology dwarfs dwell underground and love feasting and dancing at night, while they are busy at forges and ovens during the day. In Germanic mythology *Dockalfar*, or dark-skinned elves, were unsurpassed as craftsmen. They were said to have forged Thor's hammer and Odin's spear. Traditionally, dwarfs taught people to bake, tailor clothes, and fashion metals. Though sometimes mischievous, dwarfs were believed to possess prophetic powers and to give good advice. They could also become invisible and divide themselves in half. Dwarfs often express hatred against manifestations of superior power.[4] Mischievous, creative, self-transforming, trustworthy advisors committed to debunking the powerful, whom they constantly ridicule—these characteristics expressed perfectly qualities of several journals that embraced the dwarf in their name. The first, Thomas J. Wooler's enormously popular, radical *Black Dwarf* (1817–1824), depicts in its frontispiece a *Dockalfar* leading a satyr past the scattered symbols of authority: whips, shackles, bills and proclamations, and a crown satirically surmounted by a foolscap. Wooler declared in its introduction that his *Dwarf* would actively expose vice and folly, holding up a glass for fools and knaves.[5] Wooler's *Dwarf* drew a quick, contrasting response from Gibbons Merle's Tory *White Dwarf* (1817–1818). And a *Blue Dwarf*, published in Yarmouth, appeared in 1820. Hunt emphasized his *Dwarf*'s potency by taking its motto from Shakespeare's *Troilus and Cressida* (2. 3. 146): "A stirring Dwarf we do allowance give Before a sleeping Lion."

The *Yellow Dwarf* stirred with a political zeal that determined and shaped virtually every subject it raised. Under the heading "Politics of the Day," Hunt, like Cobbett, embraces American representative government as a club with which to beat England's aristocracy (no. 3). Even reviews of travel books, such as Morris Birkbeck's *Notes on a Journey in America . . .*, become occasions for warmly praising the United States at the expense of Britain's ruling elite (nos. 12–13). With quiet effectiveness, Hunt's article "United States" prints the elective franchise in each of the extant nineteen states, concluding that this list contains a "lesson to the friends of Parliamentary Reform in this country" (no. 6:44). Hunt extended his call for governmental reform in a projected ten-part essay, which began in number 12 and remained unfinished when the *Dwarf* ceased publication, advocating "Universal Suffrage and Annual Parliaments." Over fifty years before England provided for mandatory public education (in 1870) Hunt argued in "Workhouses" that "civil government does not consist in executions, but in making . . . provisions for the instruction of youth" and, furthermore, in "support of age." Instead of such services, Hunt declares, the "resources of a country are lavished upon courts, upon hirelings, upon imposters, and prostitutes. . . . Why is it," he demands in a timeless interrogative, "that scarcely any are executed but the poor?" (no. 5:39). John Keats, concluding a letter to his brothers in February 1818, commends John

Hamilton Reynolds's "two very capital articles in the Yellow Dwarf on popular Preachers."[6] Entitled "Pulpit Oratory," the scornful attacks on clerics ultimately extended to four articles printed on 7, 14, and 28 February and 4 April (pp. 46–48, 51–53, 67f., and 108f.). Reynolds composed the first three pieces, signed "Caius"; when he took ill in April, William Hazlitt anonymously concluded the series by ridiculing "The Rev. Herbert Marsh."[7] Keats himself contributed to the *Yellow Dwarf* of 9 May (no. 19:51–52) the "Hymn to Pan" from *Endymion* (1. 232–306) ten days before he registered the poem for publication.

Hazlitt was the *Yellow Dwarf*'s leading spirit, its most frequent and expansive contributor. He published at least fourteen items in its pages: eleven reviews or articles and excerpts from three lectures on the English poets then in progress. Three of his articles were reprinted from other journals. All but the relatively recently attributed "Pulpit Oratory 4" have been reprinted in P. P. Howe's edition of Hazlitt's *Complete Works*.

"The temptation to men in public life to swerve from the path of duty" (no. 3:10) constitutes the subject of Hazlitt's moral essay "On Court-Influence." In various forms, this concern extends throughout his substantive writings for the *Yellow Dwarf*. Former libertarians veering into complacency or cultivating a comfortable life among the powerful suffer Hazlitt's sharpest rebukes. Such ethical and political interpretations of behavior permeate virtually every review and essay. Many of these essays are well known, and all but one have been reprinted; the brief sampling here yields the flavor of contributions by the *Dwarf*'s principal contributor and consequently of the journal as well.

For Hazlitt, none have lapsed more completely, or with greater consequences for the nation's spirit, than the poets of his generation. Writing upon Wordsworth, for example, Hazlitt essentially rotates his metaphoric swerve ninety degrees, whence it becomes a slide: "From the elevation of his former well-timed enthusiasm against tyrants and conquerors, he slid into a place: and he will never rise out of it" ("The Press—Coleridge, Southey, Wordsworth, and Bentham," no. 1:4).[8] The other Lake poets, former revolutionaries fallen into official favor and reveling in it, according to Hazlitt, receive similar treatment. Only Bentham emerges in this essay as committed to a free press. Hazlitt specifically attacks Coleridge in "Mr Coleridge's Lectures" as a libertarian who has lost sight of his ideals. First the *Dwarf* reprints from the *Courier* of 9 February a report of Coleridge's first lecture on Shakespeare, followed by Hazlitt's critique of the lecturer. The *Courier* claims that Coleridge described Caliban as a prototype of Jacobinism. Hazlitt responds, "Whatever may be . . . his metaphysical hypercriticisms, his religious and political opinions seem pretty transparent . . . he speaks of mobs with contempt, and of Courts with kindness" (no. 8:60–61). Byron fares no better. Hazlitt terms "Childe Harold's Pilgrimage," Canto 4, a "falling off"—again, that swerve—from the previous cantos; "an indigestion of the mind." The poem's problems for Hazlitt reside in Harold's social class: Byron's hero embodies "arrogance of birth . . . idle wants, the haughty airs . . . the contempt for others . . . common to exalted birth'' (no. 18:142). Hazlitt could also praise, though only when he perceived a poet dedicated to democratic justice—and usually at the expense of most contemporary poets. Reviewing Thomas Moore's "The Fudge Family in Paris," Hazlitt declares that Moore "unites in himself two names that were sacred, till they were prostituted by our modern mountebanks, the Poet and the Patriot" (no. 17:138). A fall into "prostitution" even characterized for Hazlitt the experience of attending the opera. Writing idiosyncratically as the "Little Hunch Back," he argues that the art form overloads the senses: "To sit at the Opera for a whole evening, is like undergoing the process of animal magnetism for the same length of time. . . . It is a species of intellectual prostitution; for we can no more receive pleasure from all our faculties at once than we can be in love with a number of mistresses at the same time" (no. 21:166).

When the subject becomes organized religion or the state, Hazlitt's writing soars with the passion of complete moral commitment. In "On the Clerical Character" (no. 4) an occasionally shrill Hazlitt fixes upon religious garb as a cause for excessive egotism among clergy, the manifestation of their hypocrisy. (Hunt, in fairness, prints a lengthy "Defence of the Clerical Character" in numbers 7 and 8.) Hazlitt harangues the "legitimacy" of the throne in his two-part "What Is The People?" (nos. 10 and 11). Attacking "exclusive and invidious privileges" (no. 10:75), arguing that "intellect" and "greatness" derive from common people and not from institutions (no. 11:86), Hazlitt warns tyrants that arrogating all power to themselves ultimately results in self-annihilation. Eventually, a people "trod down" rebels: "They do not turn upon their tormentors till they are goaded to madness" (no. 11:86). Hazlitt perceives such goading in government's false claims of legitimacy, which he mocks. His well-modulated prose debunks the aristocracy's airy fictions by figuring the mighty as they actually exist, grounded firmly upon the earth: "Legitimate Governments . . . do not feed on ambrosia or drink nectar; but live on the common fruits of the earth, of which they get the largest share, and the best. The wine they drink is made of grapes: the blood they shed is that of their subjects: the laws they make are not against themselves: the taxes they vote, they afterwards devour" (no. 10:76).

Essays for the *Yellow Dwarf* represent Hazlitt's farewell to predominantly political writing as they adumbrate his future literary criticism and penetrating analyses of contemporaries in the brilliant *Spirit of the Age* (1825). Although the *Yellow Dwarf* ceases publication precipitously and without explanation, presumably Hazlitt's new writing and lectures were capturing his time and exceeding the journal's limitations of size and purview. The collaboration of friends sharing political and ethical ideals upon which the *Yellow Dwarf* rested could not sustain the slight enterprise in the face of Hazlitt's ambitions and burgeoning literary success. Moreover, its small circulation would hardly allow John Hunt to pay contributors well. And the *Examiner* still flourished, requiring Hunt's attention. While it lasted, however, the *Yellow Dwarf* provided an outlet for the friends' shared, strongly voiced ideas that reflected and in some ways shaped the spirit of their age.

Notes

1. *The Complete Works of William Hazlitt,* ed. P. P. Howe (London, 1932), 7:5. Of 338 pages of essays in this edition, 72 appeared earlier in the *Yellow Dwarf.* For a detailed account of the Hunts' imprisonment and John's book publishing and reputation generally, see Edmund Blunden, *Leigh Hunt: A Biography* (London, 1930), especially pp. 300–301.

2. John Hunt has been omitted from the *Dictionary of National Biography;* the best sketch of his career and its relationship to Hazlitt may be found in *The Complete Works of William Hazlitt,* 7:365 n. 5, from which this quotation derives. John is also mentioned prominently throughout Leigh Hunt's *Autobiography* (London, 1850), and in biographies of Hazlitt by P. P. Howe (New York, 1930), by Herschel Baker (Cambridge, Mass., 1962), and by Ralph M. Wardle (Lincoln, Nebr., 1971).

3. Blunden, p. 146.

4. Much of this information is derived from dictionaries of mythology and folklore generally, and specifically from Nancy Arrowsmith with George Moorse, *A Field Guide to the Little People* (New York, 1977).

5. The *Black Dwarf* reached a circulation of 12,000 in 1819, according to figures cited in Richard D. Altick, *The English Common Reader: A Social History of the Mass Reading Public 1800–1900* (Chicago, 1957), Appendix C.

6. *The Letters of John Keats 1814–1821,* ed. Hyder Edward Rollins (Cambridge, Mass., 1958), 1:228.

7. Hazlitt's authorship has been established convincingly, and his article reprinted, by William H. Marshall in "An Addition to the Hazlitt Canon: Arguments from External and Internal Evidence," *Papers of the Bibliographical Society of America* 55 (1961):347–70.

8. Hazlitt also paid tribute to Wordsworth *as a poet:* in excerpts from Hazlitt's lecture, "On the Lake School of Poetry" (no. 10:79–80), the critic rises above ideological differences in pronouncing Wordsworth the most deep-feeling and deep-thinking poet of his age.

Information Sources

BIBLIOGRAPHY

Altick, Richard D. *The English Common Reader: A Social History of the Mass Reading Public 1800–1900.* Chicago, 1957.

Baker, Herschel. *William Hazlitt.* Cambridge, Mass., 1962.

Blunden, Edmund. *Leigh Hunt: A Biography.* London, 1930.

Hazlitt, William. *The Complete Works of William Hazlitt.* Edited by P. P. Howe. 21 vols. London, 1930–1934.

Howe, P. P. *The Life of William Hazlitt.* New York, 1930.

Hunt, Leigh. *The Autobiography of Leigh Hunt; with Reminiscences of Friends and Contemporaries.* 3 vols. London, 1850.

Marshall, William H. "An Addition to the Hazlitt Canon: Arguments from External and Internal Evidence." *Papers of the Bibliographical Society of America* 55 (1961):347–70.

Rollins, Hyder Edward, ed. *The Letters of John Keats 1814–1821*. Cambridge, Mass., 1958.

INDEXES
> None.

REPRINT EDITIONS
> None. All contributions identified as Hazlitt's have been reprinted. Many were reissued first in his *Political Essays, With Sketches of Public Characters* (London, 1819). These and other contributions (listed above, in the text) have been collected in Howe's edition of *The Complete Works of Hazlitt;* Hazlitt's "Pulpit Oratory 4" was reprinted by William H. Marshall, in the *Papers of the Bibliographical Society of America* 55 (1961):347–70.

LOCATION SOURCES
American
> Complete runs: Columbia University Library; University of Minnesota Library.
> Partial run: Franklin and Marshall College Library.

British
> Complete runs: Bodleian Library; British Museum; Manchester Public Library.
> Partial run: Birmingham Public Library.
> British Library has Hazlitt's own bound, annotated copy of this journal.

Publication History

MAGAZINE TITLE AND TITLE CHANGES
> *The Yellow Dwarf, a weekly miscellany.*

VOLUME AND ISSUE DATA
> Numbers 1–21, 3 January–23 May 1818.

FREQUENCY OF PUBLICATION
> Weekly.

PUBLISHER
> John Hunt, No. 19 Catherine Street, Strand.

EDITOR
> John Hunt.

Mark L. Greenberg

Titles Included in
The Augustan Age and
the Age of Johnson,
1698–1788

Aberdeen Magazine, Literary Chronicle and Review, The, 1788–91
Adventurer, The, 1752–54
Analytical Review, The, 1788–99
Babler, The, 1763–67
Bee, The, 1759
Bristol and Bath Magazine, The, 1782–83
British Champion, The, 1742–43. See *Champion, The*
British Magazine, The, 1746–51
British Magazine, The, 1760–67
Busy Body, The, 1759
Censor, The, 1715–17
Champion (or Evening Advertiser), The, 1739–43
Common Sense: or, the Englishman's Journal, 1737–43
Connoisseur, The, 1754–56
Country Journal; or the Craftsman, The, 1727–50. See *Craftsman, The*
Court and City Magazine, The, 1763. See *Court Magazine, The*
Court, City, and Country Magazine, The, 1764–65. See *Court Magazine, The*
Court Magazine, The, 1761–65
Court Miscellany, The, 1765–71
Covent Garden Journal, The, 1752
Craftsman, The, 1726–50
Critical Review (or Annals of Literature), The, 1756–1817
Critick, The, 1718
Delights for the Ingenious, 1711
Drury Lane Journal, The, 1752. See *Have At You All*
Edinburgh Magazine and Review, The, 1773–76
Edinburgh Magazine, or Literary Amusement, The, 1779–82. See *Weekly Magazine, The*

Parentheses indicate that the additional title appeared only during part of the run of the magazine.

Northern Gazette, Literary Chronicle, and Review, The, 1707. See *Aberdeen Magazine, The*

Novelist's Magazine, The, 1780–89

Olla Podrida, The, 1787–88

Oxford Magazine, 1768–76

Payne's Universal Chronicle, or Weekly Gazette, 1758. See *Idler, The*

Plain Dealer, The, 1724–25

Present State of the Republick of Letters, The, 1728–36

Prompter, The, 1734–36

Rambler, The, 1750–52

Reformer, The, 1748

Review (of the Affairs of France) (of the State of the English Nation), 1704–13

St. James's Magazine (or Literary Chronicle) (or the Literary Transactions of Europe), The, 1762–64

Scots Magazine (Containing a General View etc.) (or General Repository etc.) (and Edinburgh Literary Miscellany), The, 1739–1817

Sentimental Magazine, The, 1773–77

Spectator, The, 1711–15

Student, The, 1750–51

Tatler, The, 1709–11

Templar, and Literary Gazette, The, 1773

Town and Country Magazine, The, 1769–95

True Patriot, The, 1745–46

Universal Chronical, 1758–60. See *Idler, The*

Universal Magazine (of Knowledge and Pleasure) (or Miscellany of Historical etc.), The, 1747–1815

Universal Museum (or Gentlemen's and Ladies' Polite Magazine) (and Complete Magazine of Knowledge and Pleasure), The, 1762–72

Universal Spectator and Weekly Journal, The, 1728–46

Universal Visiter, and Memorialist, The, 1756

Walker's Hibernian Magazine, 1786–1811. See *Hibernian Magazine, The*

Weekly Magazine, or Edinburgh Amusement, The, 1768–84

Weekly Review of the Affairs of France, A, 1704. See *Review*

Westminster Magazine, The, 1773–85

Wit's Magazine, The, 1784–85

World, The, 1753–56

Titles Included in
The Romantic Age,
1789–1836

Album, The, 1822–25
Annals of the Fine Arts, 1816–20
Anti-Jacobin Review (and True Churchmen's Magazine) (and Protestant Advocate), The, 1797–1821
Athenaeum and (London) Literary Chronicle, The, 1828–1921
Augustan Review, The, 1815–16
Beau Monde, Le, 1806–10
Bee, The, 1790–94
Belle Assemblée, La, 1806–37
Blackwood's Edinburgh Magazine, 1817–1980
British and Foreign Review, The, 1835–44
British Critic, The, 1793–1843
British Lady's Magazine, The, 1815–19
British Magazine, The, 1830
British Review and London Critical Journal, The, 1811–25
Cabinet, The, 1807–9
Cabinet Magazine, or Literary Olio, The, 1796–97
Cambrian (and Caledonian) Quarterly Magazine (and Celtic Repertory), The, 1829–33
Chambers's Edinburgh Journal, 1832–53. See *Chambers's Journal*
Chambers's Journal, 1832–1956
Champion (and Sunday Review etc.), The, 1813–22
Companion, The, 1828
Country Literary Chronicle, 1820–24. See *Literary Chronicle and Weekly Review, The*
Court Magazine and Belle Assemblée, The, 1832–37. See *Belle Assemblée, La*
Director, The, 1807
Drakard's Paper, 1813. See *Champion, The*
Dublin Literary Gazette, The, 1830–31
Dublin Review, The, 1836–1969
Dublin University Magazine, The, 1833–77
Eclectic Review, The, 1805–68

Edinburgh Magazine and Literary Miscellany, The, 1817–26
Edinburgh Monthly Magazine, The, 1817. See *Blackwood's Edinburgh Magazine*
Edinburgh Monthly Review, The, 1819–23
Edinburgh Review, The, 1802–1929
Englishman's Magazine, The, 1831
Examiner (and London Review), The, 1808–81
Foreign Quarterly Review, The, 1827–46
Fraser's Literary Chronicle, 1835–36
Fraser's Magazine for Town and Country, 1830–82
Gossip, The, 1821
Honeycomb, 1820
Imperial Magazine, The, 1819–34
Imperial Review, The, 1804–5
Indicator, The, 1819–21
Inquirer, or Literary Miscellany, The, 1814–15
Investigator (or Quarterly Magazine), The, 1820–24
Investigator, The, 1822. See *Champion, The*
John Bull, 1820–92
Journal of the Royal Institution of Great Britain, The, 1830–31. See *Quarterly Journal of Science, Literature, and the Arts, The*
Knight's Quarterly Magazine, 1823–25
Leigh Hunt's (London) Journal, 1834–51
Liberal, The, 1822–23
Literary and Statistical Magazine for Scotland, The, 1817–22
Literary Chronicle and Weekly Review, The, 1819–28
Literary Examiner, The, 1823
Literary Gazette, The, 1817–63
Literary Gossip, The, 1821–22. See *Gossip, The*
Literary Guardian, The, 1831–32
Literary Journal, The, 1803–6
Literary Journal and General Miscellany, The, 1818–19
Literary Magnet, The, 1824–28
Literary Museum, The, 1822–24
Literary Panorama, The, 1806–19
Literary Sketch-Book, The, 1823–24
Literary Speculum, The, 1821–23
Loiterer, The, 1789–90
London and Westminster Review, The, 1836–40. See *Westminster Review, The*
London Magazine, The, 1791. See *New London Magazine, The (AAAJ)*
London Magazine, The, 1820–29
London Museum, The, 1822–23. See *Literary Museum, The*
London Quarterly Review, The, 1834–83. See *Quarterly Review, The*
London Review, The, 1809
London Review, The, 1835–36. See *Westminster Review, The*
McKay's New British Lady's Magazine, 1817–19. See *British Lady's Magazine, The*
Metropolitan Magazine, The, 1831–50
Mirror Monthly Magazine, The, 1847–49. See *Mirror of Literature, Amusement, and Instruction, The*

Titles Included in *The Victorian and Edwardian Age, 1837–1914*

Academy, The, 1869–1915
Academy and Literature, The, 1902, 1910, 1914. See *Academy, The*
Ainsworth's Magazine, 1842–54
All The Year Round, 1859–95
Anglo Saxon Review, The, 1899–90
Arrow, The, 1906–9
Art and Poetry, 1850. See *Germ, The*
Author, The, 1890–
Belgravia, 1866–99
Bentley's Miscellany, 1837–68
Blue Review, The, 1913
Bookman, The, 1891–1934
Bookseller, The, 1858–
British Review and National Observer, The, 1897. See *Scots Observer, The*
Cambridge Review, The, 1879–
Cambridge University Magazine, The, 1839–43
Century Guild Hobby Horse, The, 1884–92. See *Hobby Horse, The*
Chambers's Journal, 1897–1956. See *Chambers's Journal (RA)*
Chambers's Journal of Popular Literature, Science and the Arts, 1854–57. See *Chambers's Journal (RA)*
Chambers's London Journal, 1841–43
Chapbook, The, 1913–14; 1919–25
Christian Teacher, The 1835–44. See *Prospective Review, The*
Contemporary Review, The, 1866–
Cornhill Magazine, The, 1860–1975
Cosmopolis, 1896–98
Court Magazine, 1838–47
Critic, The, 1843–63
Critic: (The London Literary Journal), The, 1850–58. See *Critic, The*
Critic; (A) Weekly Journal of Literature, Art, Science, and the Drama, The, 1858–59. See *Critic, The*

Critic of Books, The, 1848–50. See *Critic, The*
Critic of Literature, Art, Science, and the Drama, The, 1843–44. See *Critic, The*
Dana, 1904–5
Dickensian, The, 1905–
Dome, The, 1897–1900
Douglas Jerrold's Shilling Magazine, 1845–48
English Review, The, 1908–37
Examiner and London Review, The, 1869–70. See *Examiner, The* (1808) (*RA*)
Fortnightly Review, The, 1865–1954
Fun, 1861–1901
Germ, The, 1850
"Golden Hynde," The, 1913–
Good Words, 1860–1911
Granta, 1889–1914
Green Sheaf, 1903–4
Hobby Horse, The, 1886–94
Hood's Magazine, 1844–49
Household Words, 1850–59
Idler, The, 1892–1911
Isis, The, 1892–1914
Lady's World, The, 1886–87. See *Woman's World, The*
Leader, The, 1850–60
Leader and Saturday Analyst, The, 1860. See *Leader, The*
Leigh Hunt's Journal, 1850–51. See *Leigh Hunt's (London) Journal* (*RA*)
Library, 1889–
Literary Guide (and Rationalist Review), 1887–
Literature, 1897–1902
London and Edinburgh Weekly Review, 1865–66. See *Weekly Review*
London Quarterly and Holborn Review, The, 1853–1968
London Review, The, 1850. See *Mirror of Literature . . . , The* (*RA*)
Longman's Magazine, 1882–1905
Macmillan's Magazine, 1859–1907
Mirror Monthly Magazine, The, 1847–49. See *Mirror of Literature . . . , The* (*RA*)
Month, The, 1864–
Monthly Chapbook, The, 1919. See *Chapbook, The*
Monthly Chronicle, The, 1838–41
Monthly Review, The 1900–1907
National Observer, 1890–97. See *Scots Observer, The*
National Review, 1855–64
National Review, 1883–1960
New Age, 1894–1938
New Freewoman, 1913. See *Egoist, The*
New Quarterly Review, 1852–62
New Review, The, 1889–97
New Statesman & Nation, 1913–
Nineteenth Century, The, 1877–1900
North British Review, The, 1844–71
Notes and Queries, 1849–

A Chronology of Social and Literary Events and British Literary Magazines, 1789–1836

BRITISH LITERARY PERIODICALS	YEAR	SOCIAL AND LITERARY EVENTS
	1789	
The *English Review*'s critical assessment of Gibbon's *Decline and Fall* enhances the review's importance.		Blake publishes *Songs of Innocence*, the first true Romantic work.
James Austen (Jane Austen's brother) begins the *Loiterer* while at Oxford.		Bentham writes his *Introduction to Principles of Morals and Legislation*.
	1790	
James Anderson founds the *Bee*, a precursor of nineteenth-century illustrated magazines.		
	1791	
The *Critical Review* joins the *Monthly* in the Whig opposition to Pitt.		Boswell publishes his *Life of Johnson*.
	1793	
Pitt gives Secret Service money to help establish the *British Critic*, a Tory journal to oppose the *Monthly*, *Critical*, *English*, and *Analytical* reviews.		The Reign of Terror begins.

BRITISH LITERARY PERIODICALS	*YEAR*	*SOCIAL AND LITERARY EVENTS*
	(1793)	
The *Analytical* is the first to review Wordsworth's *Descriptive Sketches.*		
	1795	
		Boswell dies.
		John Keats and Thomas Carlyle are born.
	1796	
Coleridge begins the *Watchman* to provide political reports to the Midlands and to advance his Unitarian beliefs.		Britain captures Elba. Spain declares war on Britain.
Richard Phillips (parodied in George Borrow's *Lavengro*) establishes the *Monthly Magazine*, follows the format of the *Gentleman's*, and attracts Lamb, Southey, and Coleridge (pseudonym Nehemiah Higginbotham).		
	1797	
The *Anti-Jacobin Review* represents the repressive, "un-Romantic" position of much of the English population.		
	1798	
Wordsworth and Coleridge's *Lyrical Ballads* appears to praise from the *British Critic*.		
Joseph Johnson is jailed for publishing a seditious pamphlet and forced to give up the *Analytical*.		
	1801	
Archibald Constable ("Napoleon of the British publishing trade") purchases the *Scots Magazine*.		John Henry Newman is born.

BRITISH LITERARY PERIODICALS	YEAR	SOCIAL AND LITERARY EVENTS
	1802	
The *Edinburgh Review* begins publication, with precedent-setting intellectual vigor and independence from booksellers. Instead of merely reviewing specific titles, the *Edinburgh* features review-essays of particular subjects. In the first issue editor Francis Jeffrey begins attacking the Romantics.		The Peace of Amiens is signed by Britain and France.
	1803	
James Mill begins the *Literary Journal* to express the Utilitarianism later espoused in the *Westminster Review*. The Stamp Act forces Leigh Hunt to publish his *Literary Journal* half as frequently.		War is renewed between Britain and France. Bulwer-Lytton is born.
	1804	
Constable merges the *Scots* in the *Edinburgh Review,* and has difficulty attracting important contributors.		Spain declares war on Britain. Benjamin Disraeli is born (–1881).
	1805	
The *Eclectic Review* begins as the major organ for the Dissenters.		Wordsworth writes *The Prelude* (unpublished until 1850).
	1807	
The *Cabinet* is established and focuses on the London theater. George Manners founds the *Satirist,* representing the conservative Tories, to "expose and castigate every species of literary and moral turpitude," including Napoleonic sympathizers and Methodists.		Byron publishes *Hours of Idleness.* Charles and Mary Lamb write *Tales from Shakespeare.* Britain abolishes the slave trade.

BRITISH LITERARY PERIODICALS	*YEAR*	*SOCIAL AND LITERARY EVENTS*
	1808	

Leigh and John Hunt found the *Examiner*, titled in honor of Swift's 1710 journal.

The *Edinburgh Review* denigrates Scott's *Marmion*.

| | 1809 | |

John Murray, with the assistance of Scott, founds the Tory *Quarterly Review* to rival the Whiggish *Edinburgh;* William Gifford is the first editor.

Byron publishes *English Bards and Scotch Reviewers*, attacking particularly Jeffrey (*Edinburgh Review*) and calling on Gifford to scourge the poetasters.

Rudolph Ackermann's *Poetical Magazine* tries to introduce new subjects (ads, law cases) into poetry, but attracts only "greeting-card" poetry until editorial reins are tightened.

Richard Cumberland begins the practice of always identifying contributors in the new *London Review*.

| | 1810 | |

John Hunt founds the *Reflector*, with Leigh Hunt as editor, to reform the theater and politics; the magazine gives Lamb room to experiment with the essays that culminate in the *Elia* volume.

Scott publishes *The Lady of the Lake*.

| | 1811 | |

The *British Review* is founded; in its fourteen-year run Byron is the critical whipping boy for its envangelical and Tory views; his retort in *Don Juan* increases the magazine's prominence.

The Prince of Wales becomes Prince Regent.

William Thackeray is born.

BRITISH LITERARY PERIODICALS	YEAR	SOCIAL AND LITERARY EVENTS
	(1811)	

Scourge appears as a rival of the Tory *Satirist* and as scourge of the *Monthly, Critical, Analytic,* and *British* reviews and the *Examiner.* George Cruikshank executes most of the frontispieces.

1812

The United States declares war on Britain.

Robert Browning, Charles Dickens are born.

1813

The *New Review* purports to list all the books appearing from British presses and all authors treated in review periodicals.

Wellington enters France.

Southey is made Poet Laureate.

Jane Austen publishes *Pride and Prejudice.*

1814

Hazlitt begins contributing to John Scott's *Champion.*

Henry Colburn begins the *New Monthly* as a Tory, anti-Jacobin, anti-Napoleonic "antidote" to the "poison" of Richard Phillips's *Monthly Magazine.*

The Treaty of Ghent ends the British-American War.

Austen publishes *Mansfield Park,* Scott *Waverly,* Wordsworth *The Excursion.*

1816

The Royal Institution founds the *Quarterly Journal of Science, Literature, and Art* largely to disseminate the work of Humphry Davy to the landed gentry.

Austen publishes *Emma,* Coleridge *Christabel* and *Kubla Khan,* and Shelley *Alastor.*

1817

Blackwood's Edinburgh Magazine begins its long run; in October it publishes the "Ancient Chaldee Manuscript" before withdrawing it at Scott's request.

Coleridge publishes the *Biographia Literaria,* Keats *Poems.*

BRITISH LITERARY PERIODICALS	YEAR	SOCIAL AND LITERARY EVENTS
	(1817)	

Colburn begins the *Literary Gazette*, first of the weeklies devoted completely to literature. Catering to simpler tastes of the novel-reading public, its reviews had tremendous influence, but it later became notorious for its puffery of Colburn's and Bentley's titles.

Constable establishes the *Edinburgh Magazine and Literary Miscellany* as a new series of the *Scots*.

The *Scotsman* is begun as a cheap weekly to reach the audience missed by the *Edinburgh Review*.

1818

The *Quarterly Review* publishes John Wilson Croker's censure of *Endymion;* many attribute Keats's decline to the review.

Austen publishes *Northanger Abbey*, Byron begins *Don Juan*, Keats *Endymion*, Scott *The Heart of Midlothian* and *Rob Roy*.

John Hunt begins the *Yellow Dwarf* as an outlet for Hazlitt's essays, calling for a democracy. "Hymn to Pan" (*Endymion*) appears in the issue for 9 May.

1819

Keats's odes "To a Nightingale" and "On a Grecian Urn" appear in *Annals of the Fine Arts*.

George Eliot, John Ruskin, Charles Kingsley are born.

Leigh Hunt begins the *Indicator* to promote Shelley, Keats, and Lamb.

The *Literary Chronicle and Weekly Review* is established with features that other miscellanies missed: "Americana" reprints excerpts from American publications, "Cassanovia" titillates by reporting on adventures of libertines. The editor attacks Hunt and Wordsworth, publishes Byron's *Adonais*.

BRITISH LITERARY PERIODICALS	YEAR	SOCIAL AND LITERARY EVENTS
	(1819)	

The *New Bon Ton* is established; it publishes canto 3 of *Don Juan* but attacks the work in a review.

1820

John Scott edits the *London Magazine,* publishes Lamb's *Elia* essays, Hazlitt's *Table Talk,* De Quincey's *Confessions of an English Opium-Eater.*

George III dies; George IV reigns (–1830).

Keats publishes *Lamia,* Shelley *Prometheus Unbound,* Scott *Ivanhoe.*

The *Retrospective Review* is established to review older works, especially from the seventeenth and eighteenth centuries.

Theodore Hook (Mr. Wagg in *Vanity Fair*) begins *John Bull* and defends George IV's attempts to divorce Caroline.

1821

John Bull attacks Leigh Hunt and De Quincey.

Keats dies.

Shelley publishes *Adonais,* referring to *Quarterly* reviewer John Wilson Croker and *Blackwood's* John Gibson Lockhart as "herded wolves."

Thomas Campbell edits the *New Monthly* and begins to publish Hazlitt, Stendhal, Mary Shelley, Ann Radcliffe, and (for the first time) Elizabeth Barrett Browning.

John Scott is killed in a duel over a quarrel between *London Magazine* and *Blackwood's.*

1822

The *Mirror,* "first long-lived cheap periodical," begins as a miscellany of reprints of popular novels, poems, and various classics.

Matthew Arnold is born; Shelley drowns.

Byron, Shelley, and Hunt collaborate on the *Liberal,* the periodical with the highest literary quality of its time; in its

BRITISH LITERARY PERIODICALS	YEAR	SOCIAL AND LITERARY EVENTS
	(1822)	

four-issue run appeared Byron's *Vision of Judgment,* Shelley's translations from *Faust,* and essays by Hazlitt and Mary Shelley.

John Hunt is prosecuted for publishing Byron's *Vision of Judgment* in the *Liberal*'s first number. The *Liberal* is labeled "evil and impotent," "imbecillic," "obscene," "leprous."

The *Investigator,* concerned with the relation of "sound Literature and pure Religion," declares war on Shelley and the *Liberal.*

Thomas Wallis begins *Nic-Nac,* important today for its history of the English theater.

Blackwood's Edinburgh begins to publish the *Noctes Ambrosianae.*

The retitled *New European* attempts to imitate the coterie atmosphere of *Blackwood's.*

                                      1823

John Hunt proposes the *Literary Examiner* as a companion to the *Examiner* and a continuation of the *Indicator,* but Leigh Hunt writes only three essays for it.

Charles Knight begins his *Quarterly* as a "grown-up" version of the *Etonian* with contributions by Cambridge students Derwent Coleridge, Thomas Macauley, and William Praed.

                                      1824

Jeremy Bentham's protégé John Bowring establishes the *Westminster Re-*   Byron dies.

BRITISH LITERARY PERIODICALS	YEAR	SOCIAL AND LITERARY EVENTS

(1824)

view. John Stuart Mill, unable to edit the review, is its most prolific contributor.

Knight's Quarterly publishes the early work of Bulwer-Lytton and that of De Quincey before contributors' quarrels bring on its demise.

1827

The *Foreign Quarterly Review* is founded as the first serious review given exclusively to foreign literature.

1828

Charles Knight becomes editor of *London Magazine*.

The Duke of Wellington becomes prime minister.

Robert Rintoul revives the *Spectator*, which will support the Parliamentary Reform Bill and the Pre-Raphaelite Brotherhood.

The Catholic Emancipation Act passes.

George Meredith, Dante Gabriel Rossetti are born.

Leigh Hunt begins the *Companion*, almost a continuation of the *Indicator* but containing more theater criticism.

The *Literary Chronicle* merges into the *Athenaeum*, which becomes one of the most successful magazines of the century by including a broad range of topics.

1829

The Cambrian Quarterly capitalizes on the tourist popularity of North Wales to advance Welsh culture.

La Belle Assemblée begins, proclaiming itself as the "only embellished periodical devoted to *Fine Arts and Poetic Literature*," following the demise of *Sharpe's London Magazine*.

BRITISH LITERARY PERIODICALS	YEAR	SOCIAL AND LITERARY EVENTS
	1830	
William Maginn (*Blackwood's* contributor) begins *Fraser's Magazine*, and publishes the work of Carlyle (*Sartor Resartus*), Thackeray, Kingsley.		William IV reigns (–1837).
		Tennyson publishes his *Poems, Chiefly Lyrical;* Moore *The Letters and Journals of Lord Byron.*
Leigh Hunt begins the *Tatler* after the short-lived *Chat of the Week* is closed down for violation of the Stamp Act.		
Arthur Hallam lauds Tennyson's first volume in the *Englishman's.*		
	1831	
Bulwer-Lytton begins a short, politically passionate editorship of the *New Monthly* to advocate passage of the Reform Bill.		Darwin begins his expedition on the H.M.S. *Beagle* (–1836).
Frederick Marryat's *Metropolitan* begins the serial publication of novels as a continuing feature.		
	1832	
Carlyle's memorial essay on Goethe appears in the *Foreign Quarterly Review.*		The Reform Bill enfranchises the upper middle classes.
The *Literary Guardian* becomes one of the first journals to review Lyell's *Principles of Geology.*		Lewis Carroll is born; Scott dies.
Tait's *Edinburgh* begins as an organ of advanced liberalism for the Reform Bill and soon becomes the largest-selling magazine in Scotland.		
	1834	
William Molesworth establishes the *London Review* as an outlet for John Stuart Mill.		Coleridge and Charles Lamb die.
		Robert Peel becomes prime minister (–1835; 1841–46).

BRITISH LITERARY PERIODICALS	YEAR	SOCIAL AND LITERARY EVENTS
	(1834)	
Benthamite Christian Isobel Johnstone becomes literary editor of *Tait's*, after it absorbs Johnstone's *Edinburgh Magazine*, and publishes Leigh Hunt and De Quincey.		
	1836	
Theodore Hook (of *John Bull*) edits the *New Monthly*.		The Stamp Act begins to be phased out (–1861).
The *Westminster Review* and *London Review* merge, with John Stuart Mill as *de facto* editor.		Dickens publishes *Pickwick Papers*.

Index

Lafayette: reviewed in *Foreign Quarterly Review*, 165

Lalippe (Count), 37

Lamartine, Alphonse de, 55, 333

Lamb, Charles: biography in *Imperial Magazine*, 187; contributes to *Annals of the Fine Arts*, 10; to *Champion*, 99, 102; to *Englishman's*, 147–48; to *Examiner*, 151, 153; to *Indicator*, 193; to *London Journal*, 218; to *London Magazine*, 288, 291; to *Monthly Magazine*, 315, 317, n.2; to *New Monthly, Magazine*, 333, 335; to *Quarterly Review*, 361; to *Reflector*, 369, 373–74; reprinted in *Mirror of Literature*, 310; reviewed in *Indicator*, 193; in *Literary Gazette*, 243; in *Literary Panorama*, 275; in *Monthly Magazine*, 314. Works: *Album Verses*, 148; "A Challenge," 99; *Elia*, 288, 291; "Epitaph on a Dog," 193; "Hercules Pacificatus," 147; "The Latin Poems of Vincent Bourne," 148; "Lines on the Celebrated Picture by Leonardo da Vinci," 10; "Lines Suggested by . . . Waltham Cross," 148; "On the Genius . . . of Hogarth," 373; "On the Melancholy of Tailors," 99, 310; "Peter's Net," 148; "Recollections of a Late Royal Academician," 148; "To My Friend the Indicator," 193; *Works*, 102, 275

Lamb, Mary, 68

Landon, Letitia: assists with *Literary Gazette*, 242; contributes to *British Magazine*, 76; to *Literary Magazine*, 264; to *Literary Sketchbook*, 279 n.1; to *New Monthly*, 333, 335; "Lines to . . . Watts," 264; reviewed in *Literary Magnet*, 265

Landor, Walter Savage, 14, 48, 163, 333, 335; *Gebirus*, 14

Landseer, John, 299–301

Lang, Andrew, 23

Lapham, George, 157

Lapham, Gustavus Harding, 157

Lapham, Roderick Harding, 157

Laplace, Pierre Simon, 355

Lardner's Cabinet Cyclopedia, 130

Larkins, S., 171

Lasca, Il. *See* Grazzinia, Antonfrancesco

Lathbury, Daniel, 395

Law, John, 38

Lawrence, Sir Thomas, 8, 10

Lee, Frederick G., 22

Leeds, W. H., 161, 166

LeFanu, J. S., 120, 121

Leigh Hunt's London Journal, 216–20

Leslie, Shane, 115

Lessing, Gotthold, 47; *Nathan the Wise*, 378

Letts, Anthony A., 330 n.10

Letts, John, 329

Letts, John, Jr., 327

Letts, Thomas, 329

Lettson, J. C., 39 n.5

Levellers, 58

Lever, Charles, 113, 116, 170

Lewer, J., 319

Lewer, William, 24

Lewes, George Henry, 48–49, 55, 142, 163–65, 173, 427–28

Lewis, George Cornewall, 140, 160

Lewis, Matthew G., 80, 84, 335

Liberal, 220–28; publishes libelous "Vision of Judgment," 223–24; reviewed in *Literary Chronicle*, 235; in *Literary Speculum*, 281

Liberal Union Club, 140

Lillo, George: *The London Merchant*, 84

Lilly, J., 349

Limbird, John, 239, 261, 308–9

Lind, Jenny, 22

Linsey, Miss, 38

Linwood, William, 127, 133

Liszt, Franz, 22

Litchfield, Harriet, 77

Litchfield, John: "Remarks on Mr. Coleman's Preface to the *Iron Chest*," 77

Literary and Statistical Magazine for Scotland, 228–30

Literary Annual Register, 271

Literary Association of the Friends of Poland, 53

Literary Chronicle and Weekly Review, 230–39

Literary Examiner, 225, 239–41

Literary Gazette, 21, 168, 186, 236, 242–46

Literary Guardian, 246–51

Literary Journal, 251–59

Literary Journal and General Miscellany, 259–61

Literary Magnet, 261–68

Literary Museum, 236, 268–71

Literary Panorama, 271–78

Literary Register, 268

Literary Sketch-Book, 278–79

Literary Souvenir, 264

Literary Speculum, 223, 279–83

Lloyd, Charles, 315

Lockhart, John Gibson: biography in *Fraser's Magazine*, 172; contributes to *Blackwood's*, 46–48, 151; to *Knight's Quarterly*, 210; to *Literary Gazette*, 242–46; edits *Quarterly*

Contributors

JAMES E. BASKER is Acting Allston-Burr Senior Tutor at Eliot House at Harvard College.

N. S. BAUER is Adjunct Associate Professor at the College of New Rochelle.

DARWIN F. BOSTICK, Associate Professor of History at Old Dominion University, studies British periodicals for their treatment of other countries and peoples.

THOMAS F. BOYLE is Assistant Professor of English at Brooklyn College, CUNY. He wrote his dissertation on nineteenth-century periodicals' criticism of fiction.

LARRY L. BRONSON is Assistant Professor of English at Central Michigan State University.

GEORGE ALLAN CATE is Professor of English at the University of Maryland.

K. K. COLLINS, Associate Professor of English at Southern Illinois University at Carbondale, is interested in nineteenth-century periodicals for their treatment of George Eliot and G. H. Lewes.

WINIFRED F. COURTNEY's work, *Young Charles Lamb, 1775–1802*, was published in 1982 by Macmillan (London) and New York University Press.

EILEEN M. CURRAN, Professor of English at Colby College, is associate editor of *The Wellesley Index to Victorian Periodicals*. She has recently held a grant to study women contributors to periodicals before 1850.

KENNETH CURRY, Professor Emeritus of English at the University of Tennessee, Knoxville, is the author of *Sir Walter Scott's Edinburgh Annual Register*.

CORNELIUS P. DARCY is Professor of English at Western Maryland College.

KENNETH W. DAVIS, who teaches at Texas Tech University, wrote his dissertation on *Blackwood's*. An essay on Byroniana in the *Literary Guardian* developed from his research for *British Literary Magazines* and appears in *Papers on Language and Literature*.

CHARLES BROOKS DODSON, Professor of English at the University of North Carolina at Wilmington, is a contributor to the *Directory of Victorian Journalists*.

ROBERT DUNCAN, Professor of English at Southern Illinois University at Edwardsville, wrote his dissertation on the *Literary Gazette*.

BARBARA J. DUNLAP, Associate Professor of English at City College, CUNY, is studying the magazine illustrators of the 1860s and the magazines generated by the Oxford Movement.

W. PAUL ELLEDGE, Professor of English at Vanderbilt University, studied the Romantic movement with Richard Harter Fogle at Tulane University.

HELEN B. ELLIS is Associate Professor of English at the University of Waterloo, Ontario.

TED R. ELLIS III teaches English at East Carolina University and wrote his dissertation on *The Dramatist and the Comic Journal in England, 1830–1870*.

KARSTEN ENGELBERG is a Member of Exeter College, Oxford, and Research Fellow in English at the University of Copenhagen. His doctoral thesis studies Shelley's reputation at mid-century.

RICHARD D. FULTON is Resident Dean for the Council of Graduate Schools, Washington, D.C.

MARK L. GREENBERG, Assistant Professor of Humanities at Drexel University, is a consultant to the "Key Serials Project."

JOHN R. GRIFFIN is Professor of English at the University of Southern Colorado.

PHYLLIS F. HARNICK is a Special Instructor at the University of Rhode Island.

JAY H. HARTMAN is Associate Professor of English at Muhlenberg College.

JOHN O. HAYDEN is Professor of English at the University of California at Davis and author of the standard work, *The Romantic Reviewers 1802–24*.

BILLIE ANDREW INMAN is Professor of English at the University of Arizona.

MISSY DEHN KUBITSCHEK teaches at Eastern New Mexico State University.

DANIEL L. McCUE, JR. is Associate Professor of English at Boston College.

DOUGLAS K. MORRIS, Assistant Professor of English at David Lipscomb College, is interested in the development of editorial fictions in Victorian periodicals.

HELENE E. ROBERTS is Curator of Visual Collections at the Fine Arts Library, Fogg Art Museum, at Harvard University. Her interest in literary periodicals developed from the art criticism they published.

CAROL DE SAINT VICTOR is Director of Women's Studies at the University of Iowa.

LANCE SCHACHTERLE, Professor of English at Worcester Polytechnic Institute, studies the history of serialization and book publication of nineteenth-century fiction.

MARY ANNE SCHOFIELD, Assistant Professor of English at Saint Bonaventure University, has recently published in *ELN* on Wordsworth's work in the Philadelphia *Portfolio*.

AUSTIN SECKERSON is Research Librarian Emeritus at the Radcliffe Infirmary, Oxford.

DOUGLAS H. SHEPARD is Professor of English at State University College at Fredonia, New York.

DICKIE A. SPURGEON is Professor of English at Southern Illinois University at Edwardsville.

NATHANIEL TEICH is Associate Professor of English at the University of Oregon.

J. DON VANN, Professor of English at North Texas State University, is coeditor of *Victorian Periodicals: A Guide to Research* and a member of the advisory board for the *North American Union List of Victorian Serials*.

ROGER P. WALLINS is Associate Professor of English at the University of Idaho.

MARY ANTHONY WEINIG, Professor of English at Rosemont College, is author of the Twayne volume on Coventry Patmore.

MARK A. WEINSTEIN, Professor of English at the University of Nevada, Las Vegas, researches Victorian periodicals for many of his works, including *William Edmondstoune Aytoun and the Spasmodic Controversy* (Yale, 1968).

KEITH WILSON is Associate Professor of English at the University of Ottawa.

About the Editor

ALVIN SULLIVAN is Professor of English at Southern Illinois University, Edwardsville, and Editor of *Papers on Language and Literature*. A specialist in modern British literature and literary criticism, he has written *D. H. Lawrence and The Dial; The Dial—Two Author Indexes;* and articles for *Journal of Modern Literature, Explicator, D. H. Lawrence Review, Modern Fiction Studies,* and *Studies in English Literature.*